Marine Insurance

Bootle
O 8 December 10h00
2 7th D eins at 3:30 lesington

This book expertly introduces and clearly explains all topics covered in marine insurance law courses at undergraduate and postgraduate levels, offering students and those new to the area a comprehensive and accessible overview of this important topic in commercial law.

Beginning by introducing the general principles of the subject, the structure and formation of insurance contracts, *Marine Insurance Law* then looks to individual considerations in detail, including: brokers, losses, risks and perils, sue and labour, reinsurance, and mutual insurance/P&I clubs.

This title has been developed with the needs of courses specifically in mind, and its content has been tailored to include the most important and commonly taught topics in the field. Each chapter contains end of chapter further reading to support student research, ensuring this new textbook provides a reliable and accessible gateway into this important topic in maritime law.

Dr Özlem Gürses is Associate Professor in Maritime Law at Southampton University.

Marine Insurance Law

Özlem Gürses

Routledge
Taylor & Francis Group

LONDON AND NEW YORK

First published 2015
by Routledge
2 Park Square, Milton Park, Abingdon, Oxon, OX14 4RN

and by Routledge
711 Third Avenue, New York, NY 10017

Routledge is an imprint of the Taylor & Francis Group, an informa business

British Library Cataloguing in Publication Data
A catalogue record for this book is available from the British Library

Library of Congress Cataloging-in-Publication Data
 Gürses, Özlem, author.
 Marine insurance law/Özlem Gürses.
 pages cm
 'a GlassHouse Book.'
 Includes index.
 ISBN 978-0-415-72702-0 (hbk) – ISBN 978-0-415-72701-3 (pbk) –
 ISBN 978-1-315-85595-0 (ebk) 1. Marine insurance – Law and legislation – England.
 I. Title.
 KD1845.G87 2015
 346.42'0862 – dc23
 2014035036

ISBN: 978-0-415-72702-0 (hbk)
ISBN: 978-0-415-72701-3 (pbk)
ISBN: 978-1-315-85595-0 (ebk)

Typeset in Joanna
by Florence Production Ltd, Stoodleigh, Devon, UK

Printed and bound in Great Britain by
TJ International Ltd, Padstow, Cornwall

Outline Contents

Detailed Contents

Table of Cases

bold refers to extended discussion or term highlighted in text; n refers to footnote

Table of Statutes and Other Instruments

bold refers to extended discussion or term highlighted in text; n refers to footnote

Preface

English marine insurance law has a history that goes back to the fifteenth century, but the most important early developments occurred in the eighteenth century, with Lord Mansfield's enormous contribution. The 2,000 or so cases decided between the middle of the eighteenth and the end of the nineteenth century were codified by the Marine Insurance Act 1906. That Act did not prove to be definitive. Since then the law has developed constantly, with the interpretation of the Act by the Courts as well as new issues emerging to which the answers are not found in the 1906 Act. In the meantime the SG Policy, perfected in 1779, was replaced in 1982 and since then the Market Reform Contract has been introduced to provide more contract certainty. At the time of preparation of this book, a number of appeals are outstanding on various issues related to marine insurance law, two of the most controversial of those are *Gard Marine & Energy Ltd v China National Chartering Co Ltd* (*The Ocean Victory*) [2014] 1 Lloyd's Rep. 59 and *Versloot Dredging BV v HDI Gerling Industrie Versicherung AG* [2014] EWCA Civ 134. Additionally, based on the Law Commissions' proposals, the Insurance Bill 2014 was introduced into Parliament in July 2014, and this is expected to become law by May 2015. The Bill reforms the duty of good faith in business insurance, warranties and fraudulent claims. The Bill will also allow the implementation of the Third Parties Rights Against Insurers' Act 2010.

This book aims to introduce, in accessible and straightforward style, the principles of English marine insurance law to students.

While writing this book I had the advantage of spending two months at the Max Planck Institute for Comparative and International Private Law, Hamburg. I am grateful to the Institute for the research environment provided during part of my research leave from the University of Southampton. I am most grateful to Professor Robert Merkin who generously read the first draft of each chapter of this book. I am thankful to Robert Veil, Johanna Hjalmarsson, Mateusz Back, Jack Steer, Ayşegül Buğra and Mark Turner for their help and assistance for the completion of this book before the manuscript was delivered to Routledge. All errors and omissions are mine.

Özlem Gürses
Southampton
September 2014

Chapter 1

Introduction to Marine Insurance

Chapter Contents

The word insurance (formerly called assurance) is of Italian origin, and the word policy derives from 'polizza', as promise or undertaking.[1] Lombards were the Italian immigrants who came to England in the thirteenth century to escape from war in the cities of Northern and Central Italy.[2] Lombards were the rich who left their homes, carrying all their valuables with them.[3] With the money and the leadership they brought, Lombards engaged in trade, money lending, and building ships. They became involved in marine insurance in the fifteenth century, lending money to shipowners in the form of bottomry and respondentia. Bottomry is the transaction under which a shipowner borrowed money to carry out a seafaring venture by pledging his vessel as security for the loan.[4] The shipowner was obliged to repay the loan only if the vessel arrived safely. If the vessel was lost, the shipowner was relieved of this obligation.[5] The agreement was a 'bottomry bond' and the word 'respondentia' was used for a similar arrangement under which cargo was given as security.[6]

Insurance on vessels and their cargoes was a response to the expansion of sea trade. In the English jurisdiction the earliest forms of policies were marine, life and fire[7] among which marine insurance was first to emerge.[8] Marine business was conducted by individual merchants.[9] There was no restriction at common law on persons who might offer insurance nor was there any requirement that such persons had the ability to pay claims, which resulted in some big losses not being covered.[10] During the war between several European countries in the early eighteenth century in which England was involved, the South Sea Company took part in funding the conflict and assumed a substantial proportion of the National Debt in return for its shares.[11] As part of the arrangements, the Company was also given exclusive trading rights in the Americas.[12] The success of the South Sea Company led to other attempts to raise capital on speculative, and often fraudulent overseas ventures.[13] Such attempts were called 'bubbles'[14] and the Government passed the Bubble Act of 1720[15] to prohibit companies from being formed and from raising capital other than under the authorisation of an Act of Parliament or Royal Charter. The Bubble Act was also directed at marine insurance, and section 12 prohibited the carrying on of insurance business by corporations, societies and partnerships other than those chartered. Charters were granted only to the Royal Exchange Assurance Corporation and the London Assurance Corporation. For a century those companies had the exclusive right to, and monopoly of, insuring ships and their merchandise as companies, enabling them likewise to undertake the business of fire insurance.[16] Due to the high demand for insurance and the limited capacity of these two companies there was a need for additional resources to provide insurance. There was nothing in the Bubble Act which prevented individuals from offering marine insurance. Thus, such additional contribution was provided by individual underwriters at Lloyd's and mutual associations – protection and indemnity clubs.

---

1   Martin, F., History of Lloyd's and of Marine Insurance in Great Britain, 1876, p 31.
2   Martin, pp 18–19.
3   Martin, pp 18–19.
4   Martin, pp 22–23.
5   Parks, L., The Law and Practice of Marine Insurance and Average, vol 1, London, 1988, p 4.
6   Parks, p 4.
7   Clark, Betting on Lives: The Culture of Life Assurance in England 1695 to 1775 (1999), p 1.
8   Colinvaux's Law of Insurance, 9th edn: 2nd Supplement, 2013, para A1–1.
9   *Strong v Harvey* (1825) 3 Bingham 304.
10   Such as the loss of 92 vessels at the so-called Battle of Lagos when a fleet of English and Dutch warships and merchant vessels was attacked off Smyrna by the French fleet. Underwriters were unable to meet the claims. Colinvaux Supplement, para A1–6.
11   Colinvaux, Supplement, para A1–6.
12   Colinvaux, Supplement, para A1–6.
13   Colinvaux, Supplement, para A1–6.
14   Martin, 87, 89, Colinvaux, Supplement, para A1–6.
15   6 Geo. 1 c 18.
16   Martin, p 95.

Lloyd's of London

Lloyd's was initially a coffee house run by Edward Lloyd who opened the house in 1688 in London.[17] The coffee house was a place to respond to adverts for lost or stolen items or runaway slaves as well as for auctions to selling ships and goods brought by sea.[18] It was also a place where people connected with shipping met and the shipping intelligence received by the Lloyd's coffee house was well known for its reliability.[19] By 1730 Lloyd's was established as the location for marine underwriting by individuals. In 1734 the first edition of Lloyd's List was published;[20] today, Lloyd's List still provides weekly shipping news to London and beyond. In the early period of their existence the two chartered companies had between them about one-tenth of the total marine insurance business done in London, the other nine-tenths being in the hands of private underwriters, mainly those assembling at Lloyd's coffee-house.[21] In 1774 rooms were rented in the Royal Exchange and Lloyd's ended the coffee house era. By 1800 Lloyd's began to dominate shipping insurance on a global scale.[22] It was stated that the monopoly conferred upon the London Assurance Corporation and the Royal Exchange Assurance Corporation acted as protection for the private underwriting interest against the possible competition of a host of marine insurance companies.[23] In 1824 the Bubble Act was repealed insofar as it prevented marine underwriting by corporations, societies or partnerships.[24] Today the risks can be insured by underwriters at Lloyd's or at the London company market. Lloyd's has grown over 325 years to become the world's leading market for specialist insurance. Among the risks that can be insured at Lloyd's are marine, casualty, property and aviation.

Protection and Indemnity Clubs

As stated above, the prohibition of insurance by corporations except the two permitted institutions created the need for individuals to insure marine risks. The individual shipowners established mutual clubs – protection and indemnity associations (P&I Clubs) in which they were both assureds and insurers.[25] A shipowner whose vessel entered into a club is an assured as he is required to pay the premium, which is a 'call' within the context of mutual insurance, to contribute to cover the losses claimed by the members. The same shipowner is also the insurer when he suffers loss and makes a claim, his claim is met by the contributions of the other members by paying their calls. Thus, he receives the premium as an insurer when his claim is to be met by the Club. The word protection refers to the cover for liabilities to personnel and for damage to property, while indemnity covers liabilities to cargo owners under a contract of carriage.[26] Additionally, a number of clubs have formed 'freight, demurrage and defence' (FD&D) divisions which, for an additional optional premium, provide a claims-handling service and insurance of legal costs and fees for those claims not covered

---

17 www.lloyds.com/lloyds/about-us/history/corporate-history/the-early-days

18 Martin, p 62.

19 There were other coffee houses as well as Edward Lloyd's, however, it was said that the success of Mr Lloyd's coffee house was due to his personal activity and intelligence. This was proved in the course of a few years by an event of special interest, the establishment by him of a weekly paper, Lloyd's List, furnishing commercial and shipping news.

20 www.lloyds.com/lloyds/about-us/history/corporate-history/the-early-days

21 Martin, p 101.

22 www.lloyds.com/lloyds/about-us/history/corporate-history/the-early-days

23 Martin, p 103.

24 5 Geo. 4 c 114.

25 *Arthur Average Association for British, Foreign and Colonial Ships, Re* (1874–1875) LR 10 Ch App 542; *Lion Mutual Marine Insurance Association, Limited v Tucker* (1883–1884) LR 12 QBD 176; *Strong v Harvey* (1825) 3 Bingham 304; *Great Britain 100 A 1 Steamship Insurance Association v Wyllie* (1889) 22 QBD 710; *London Marine Insurance Association, Re* (1869) LR 8 Eq 176.

26 Pilley, R., Maritime Law, edited by Baatz, Y., 2014, p 458.

by P&I. By an FD&D cover, Clubs do not indemnify their members in respect of claims, but they bear the costs which are incurred.

Shipowners enter their vessels into Clubs for the purpose of insuring themselves against a wide range of risks not covered by an ordinary policy of marine insurance. For instance P&I insurance covers shipowners' liability for loss of or damage to property carried on board a ship entered.[27] The Clubs may also cover [28] liabilities to passengers, crew or others, for personal injury and death claims; stowaways; crew unemployment indemnity following a casualty; fines; including those for pollution and civil liability for pollution; collisions – one-fourth of damages payable to the colliding vessel;[29] liability for damage to fixed and floating objects and wreck removal. The cover provided by each individual Club is stated in the Club's Rulebook. The Clubs also have bodies of rules governing the relationships between the club and its members and between one member and all the other members. When shipowners enter one of their ships in a P&I Club there comes into being a policy of marine insurance relating to that ship on the terms of the Club's rules.

Section 85(1) of the MIA 1906 defines mutual insurance 'Where two or more persons mutually agree to insure each other against marine losses there is said to be a mutual insurance.' Under section 85(2) 'The provisions of this Act relating to the premium do not apply to mutual insurance, but a guarantee, or such other arrangement as may be agreed upon, may be substituted for the premium.' Mutual insurance associations are permitted to modify the provisions of the MIA 1906, insofar as they may be modified by the agreement of the parties (s.85(3)). Under subsection (4) the provisions of the Act will apply unless they have been expressly or impliedly excluded by the terms of the cover granted by the association, thus the ordinary rules relating to disclosure, warranties, subrogation and the like remain applicable in most cases.[30]

The law of marine insurance

It was stated that there is no record of any trial affecting questions of marine insurance before the end of the sixteenth century.[31] In 1601 Parliament passed an Act establishing an insurance court, however, this court fell into disuse for lack of business as merchants and underwriters preferred the regular courts.[32] During this period the judges were said to be unacquainted with the nature of insurance contracts.[33] A major development in marine insurance occurred in the eighteenth century with the work of Lord Mansfield. During this time insurance was almost entirely marine.[34] In the early development phase of the law of marine insurance the cases were concerned with interpretation of the contemporary policy wording. For instance in *Tiernay v Etherington*[34a] the Court discussed whether the loss of cargo during transhipment was covered by the wording of 'on goods, in Dutch ship, from Malaga to Gibraltar, and at and from thence to England and Holland, both or either; on goods as hereunder agreed, beginning the adventure from the loading, and to continue till the ship and goods be arrived at England, or Holland, and there safely landed'.[35] This was followed by the development of the rules relating to seaworthiness and development of the wording 'free from

---

27 For instance the dispute in *Firma C-Trade SA v Newcastle Protection and Indemnity Association (The Fanti)* [1991] 2 AC 1 concerned a claim by the cargo owner against the shipowner whose vessel was lost together with the cargo of cement on board.
28 See *Empresa Cubana de Fletes v Kissavos Shipping Co SA (The Agathon) (No.2)* [1984] 1 Lloyd's Rep 183.
29 Three-fourths of collision liability may be covered by hull insurers. See Chapter 7.
30 For more information on P&I clubs see Pilley, pp 458–468.
31 Martin, p 121.
32 Parks, pp 7–8.
33 Martin, p 121.
34 *Leon v Casey* [1932] 2 KB 576, 581, Scrutton LJ.
34a [1743] 1 Burr 348.
35 Martin, pp 123–124.

particular average',[36] which aimed to protect underwriters for partial loss claims for commodities particularly susceptible of damage, such as corn, fish, fruit and sugar.[37] However, during this period the policies also began to include clauses 'interest or no interest'. The policies containing these clauses were called 'wager policies' because the assured did not need to prove his interest in the subject matter. It was available to insure ships or cargoes in which the assured had no interest as a means of gaining profit – if the loss occurred the assured would be able to claim the insured value although he did not suffer any loss for lack of insurable interest, if the loss did not occur, all he would lose was the premium.[38] This led to the passing of the Marine Insurance Act 1745,[39] which prohibited policies without interest or 'without further proof of interest than the policy'.

During the time he presided in the Court of the King's Bench from 1756 to 1788, Lord Mansfield's decisions established the foundations of English insurance law.[40] In 1894 the Marine Insurance Bill was introduced to Parliament by Lord Herschell (then Lord Chancellor). It was again introduced in 1895, 1896, 1899 and 1901. It finally was enacted in 1906.[41]

The role of the Institute of London Underwriters should be mentioned here, as referred to below, the SG form was the standard form of wording used when marine policies first emerged. The SG form, however, was not always satisfactory in meeting the requirements of the parties and additional clauses giving greater or different protection were added to the standard form. This had an adverse effect on standardisation as all sorts of differently drafted clauses came to be used for covering the same risk.[42] In 1884 the Institute of London Underwriters (ILU) was formed for the purpose of enabling collective action to be taken in the matter.[43] The ILU prepared standard clauses to be used in marine insurance, this will be discussed below.

The Marine Insurance Act 1906

The principles that govern the relationship between the parties to a contract of marine insurance are found in the common law and in the Marine Insurance Act (MIA) 1906. The object of adopting the 1906 Act was to reproduce as exactly as possible the then existing law, without making any attempt to amend it.[44] Before the 1906 Act was codified, the law of marine insurance rested almost entirely upon common law, only a few isolated points were dealt with by statute.[45] The reported cases were very numerous, as Chalmers noted, being over 2,000 in number.[46] The principles that are derived from those cases decided before 1906 were codified by the Act. For instance, several cases established that there is no seaworthiness warranty[47] in a time policy and section 39(5) of the Act reflects this principle. Inevitably, the sections of the 1906 Act have been subject to

---

36 This means that partial loss is not covered by the policy.
37 Martin, pp 136–137.
38 Insurable Interest is fully explained in Chapter 3.
39 19 George II. Cap. 37.
40 Parks, p 11.
41 6 Edw. 7, chapter 41.
42 Arnould Law of Marine Insurance and Average, 18th edn, 2013, para 2–23.
43 www.ilu.org.uk/history.html. The Institute of London Underwriters (ILU) was set up as the trade association for the company market specialising in marine, aviation and transportation insurance business. At the end of 1998 the ILU merged with LIRMA (the London Insurance and Reinsurance Market Association) which was the trade association acting for non-marine insurance companies. The International Underwriting Association of London (IUA) was set up on 1 January 1999 and all the ILU's then members ceased their membership of the Institute and became members of the IUA.
44 Chalmers/Owen, Marine Insurance, 1901, see Chapter 1.
45 See Chapter 3 and the legislation cited.
46 Chalmers, p vi.
47 See Chapter 5.

interpretations by the Courts since the Act came into force. For instance in *Pan Atlantic Insurance Co Ltd v Pine Top Insurance Co Ltd* the House of Lords clarified the meaning of section 18(3) and added the test of inducement (implied requirement) – which currently does not exist in the MIA 1906 – as a requirement to seek remedy for breach of the duty of good faith. In *Masefield AG v Amlin Corporate Member Ltd*[48] it was clarified that the word 'abandonment' within the meaning of section 60(1) means 'the abandonment of any hope of recovery'. It is therefore crucially important to read the sections of the Act together with the cases discussing the relevant principles.

SG policy

Before it was replaced by the standard Institute clauses, the SG policy was used in forming a contract of marine insurance. The SG form itself appears to derive from forms in use as early as the fifteenth century.[49] It was adopted by Lloyd's in 1779 and when the 1906 Act was adopted the SG form was printed in the First Schedule to the Act as the standard form of policy which may be used, as section 30(1) of the Act provides 'A policy may be in the form in the First Schedule to this Act.' The First Schedule contains a series of rules for its construction.

Further, section 30(2) provides 'Subject to the provisions of this Act, and unless the context of the policy otherwise requires, the terms and expressions mentioned in the First Schedule to this Act shall be construed as having the scope and meaning in that schedule assigned to them.' It was stated in *Kulukundis v Norwich Union Fire Insurance Society*[50] by Scott LJ that most of the law of marine insurance is in essence pure interpretation of the contract contained in the common form of marine policy. However, the SG form became outdated and was not able to meet the requirements of the modern world of trade. Thus, in the early 1980s, following a joint work of the Institute of London Underwriters and Lloyd's Underwriters' Association, standard Institute clauses were recommended which replaced the SG policy in the market. The new clauses were introduced in 1982 and 1983. The Cargo Clauses came into effect in 1982 (dated 1 January 1982), which were revised on 1 January 2009. Clauses for Freight and Hull Insurance respectively followed in 1983 (dated 1 October 1983); modified in 1995. The Hull Clauses were then again revised by the publication of the International Hull Clauses dated 1 November 2003. There are now three sets of Hull Clauses available in the Market: The Institute Hull Clauses (Voyage and Time), dated 1 October 1983; The Institute Hull Clauses (Voyage and Time), dated 1 November 1995; and the International Hull Clauses, dated 1 November 2003. It is up to the parties which set of clauses is to be adopted in any one case. In this book the International Hull Clauses 2003 were included in the analysis of the relevant topics such as marine insurance losses and marine perils.

Contract of marine insurance

As defined by section 1 of the Marine Insurance Act 1906 a contract of marine insurance is 'a contract whereby the insurer undertakes to indemnify the assured, in manner and to the extent thereby agreed, against marine losses, that is to say, the losses incident to marine adventure'. The rules governing formation of a marine insurance contract is explained in this book in Chapter 2. A contract of marine insurance is a contract of indemnity. Some of the principles applicable to

---

48 [2010] 1 Lloyd's Rep 509, para 55.
49 Arnould, para 2–21.
50 [1937] 1 KB 1.

marine insurance primarily derive from this nature. For instance, as analysed in Chapter 3 an assured is required to hold insurable interest in the subject matter insured. Moreover, subrogation is a principle derived from a marine insurance contract being a contract of indemnity, which is referred to in Chapter 13. Section 3(1) of the Act provides that 'Every lawful marine adventure may be the subject of a contract of marine insurance'. It was explained by Chalmers that what is really insured is the pecuniary interest of the assured in or in respect of the property exposed to peril, in other words, the risk or adventure.[51] The Act defines 'marine adventure' as 'Any ship goods or other moveables are exposed to maritime perils' which is referred to as 'insurable property' (s.3(2)(a)). 'The earning or acquisition of any freight, passage money, commission, profit, or other pecuniary benefit, or the security for any advances, loan, or disbursements, is endangered by the exposure of insurable property to maritime perils' (s.3(2)(b)) and 'Any liability to a third party may be incurred by the owner of, or other person interested in or responsible for, insurable property, by reason of maritime perils' (s.3(2)(c)). The terms of subsection (2) are inclusive, not exhaustive.[52] Thus, with the development of technology new risks may emerge which need to be insured by a marine policy.

Section 3 defines 'Maritime perils' as 'the perils consequent on, or incidental to, the navigation of the sea, that is to say, perils of the seas, fire, war perils, pirates, rovers, thieves, captures, seisures, restraints, and detainments of princes and peoples, jettisons, barratry, and any other perils, either of the like kind or which may be designated by the policy.'

The definition of 'sea' was discussed in an Australian case in which the High Court of Australia decided that the 'sea' is not limited to the open ocean. In *Mercantile Mutual Insurance (Australia) Ltd v Gibbs*[53] a marine pleasurecraft policy was issued in relation to the vessel 'Lone Ranger'. The vessel was used by the insurers for commercial purposes which included commercial paraflying to which the cover extended. The insurance included the hull and 'third party liability cover'. A woman was seriously injured when attempting to land while paraflying from the vessel on the estuary of the Swan River in Western Australia, near the conjunction of that river and the Indian Ocean. She sued the assured alleging negligence. It was held that the two sites in which the 'Lone Ranger' operated were estuarine, being waters within the ebb and flow of the tide and they are to be regarded as the 'sea'. Thus, the Marine Insurance Act applied to the dispute.

Despite the definition of marine perils, the Act covers risks arising out of shipbuilding contracts as section 2(2) provides that the provisions of the Act apply where a ship in the course of building, or the launch of a ship, or any adventure analogous to a marine adventure, is covered by a policy in the form of a marine policy. Section 2(2) further states that 'nothing in the Act shall alter or affect any rule of law applicable to any contract of insurance other than a contract of marine insurance as by this Act defined.' Nevertheless, it is noteworthy that in *Clothing Management Technology Ltd v Beazley Solutions Ltd (t/a Beazley Marine UK)*[54] although the policy did not cover a marine peril, the MIA 1906 was applied for the reason that the contract incorporated the Act. The assured's business was showing the sample garments in the UK and then sending the samples to overseas factories with the necessary raw materials to be mass-produced and sent back to the UK. It purchased insurance against loss of clothing and fabric. The policy contained the following clause: Marine Insurance Clause 'Notwithstanding the fact that some or all of the movements covered by this Policy of insurance are not subject to the Marine Insurance Act 1906 it is expressly agreed and declared that all the terms, conditions, warranties and other matters contained with the Marine Insurance Act 1906 shall be applicable hereto.' The Court applied the Act to resolve the dispute between the assured and the insurer regarding the loss of the garments while they were in the factory in Morocco.

---

51 Chalmers, p 5.
52 Chalmers, p 6.
53 [2003] HCA 39.
54 [2012] 1 Lloyd's Rep 571.

Analysing the entire Marine Insurance Act is not within the scope of this book. However, the issues which introduce marine insurance to the reader and are included in this book are as follows: insurable interest (ss.5–9); the duty of good faith (ss.17–20); formation of insurance contracts (ss.21–24), voyage and time policies (s.25); valued, unvalued and floating policies (ss.27–29), warranties (ss.33–41), assignment of policy (s.50–51), the premium (ss.52–54); partial loss (s.56); actual total loss (s.57), constructive total loss (s.60–61); notice of abandonment (s.62–63); measure of indemnity (ss.67–77); sue and labour (s.78); subrogation (s.79) mutual insurance (s.85). Some of the issues mentioned here are analysed in individual chapters and some others are included in this introductory chapter, depending on the scope of the subject. Reinsurance is not defined by the Act, however it is mentioned in section 9(1). Because of the importance of the London market in the global reinsurance industry and the English jurisdiction establishing the rules governing reinsurance contracts, reinsurance is included in this book as the final chapter.

Valued policy

A marine policy may be either valued or unvalued (s.27(1)). It is a valued policy where the policy specifies the agreed value of the subject matter insured, (s.27(2)). It would be convenient for the parties to agree the valuation of the subject matter insured so that the premium will be calculated on the agreed value and when the loss occurs the assured will not need to prove the loss in detail.[55]

Section 27(3) of the MIA 1906 provides that 'Subject to the provisions of this Act, and in the absence of fraud, the value fixed by the policy is, as between the insurer and assured, conclusive of the insurable value of the subject intended to be insured, whether the loss be total or partial.' However, in determining whether there has been a constructive total loss, the value fixed by the policy is not conclusive (s.27(4)). Actual and constructive total losses are analysed in Chapters 8 and 9, respectively.

In practice, nearly all policies upon hull and machinery are now valued policies.[56] Value may be fixed either in a fixed sum or by reference to some other criterion. In *Clothing Management Technology Ltd v Beazley Solutions Ltd (t/a Beazley Marine UK)*[57] the parties fixed the value in the following words: 'Basis of Valuation: Imports/Exports: Invoice Value, plus 0%, plus duty if incurred'. As referred to above CMT's business was showing the sample garments in the UK and then sending the samples to overseas factories with the necessary raw materials to be mass-produced and sent back to the UK. HHJ Mackie QC noted that he was concerned not with value generally but with the expression chosen by the parties in current commercial conditions. Considering the nature of CMT's business the judge found it was to be expected that CMT would have wanted to insure against the loss which they would suffer if the garments or items did not come out of storage at the factory and proceed to customers. This was a valued policy and 'Invoice Value' meant retail price in the sense used by CMT.[58] For CMT the price that customers were going to pay was the value to them of the goods as it was what CMT would lose if they went astray. Insurers were aware of the nature of CMT's business and what CMT was seeking by insurance. HHJ Mackie QC recognised that in this area of commerce, where loss of the goods would generally mean loss of the end contract with customers, the assured would need a value that exceeded the basis for an unvalued policy. The assured would

---

55 *Clothing Management Technology Ltd v Beazley Solutions Ltd (t/a Beazley Marine UK)* [2012] 1 Lloyd's Rep 571, para 70.
56 Arnould, para 2–20.
57 [2012] 1 Lloyd's Rep 571.
58 [2012] 1 Lloyd's Rep 571, para 73.

welcome premiums which reflected that. Thus, it was not a surprise that the parties used 'invoice value' as the agreed value.

In *Berger and Light Diffusers Pty Ltd v Pollock*[59] the open cover was on 'goods and/or merchandise of any description as interests may appear' against all risks whatsoever. It further provided: 'To be valued as declared. In event of loss accident or arrival prior to declaration to be valued at Invoice Value and charges plus 25% . . .'

When the cargo of moulds were shipped the declaration was made and an insurance policy was issued on the following terms: 'goods . . . are and shall be . . . £20,000 on 4 Steel Metal Moulds, unpacked, bound together, Valued at Invoice Value and Charges plus 25%'. Kerr J held that the policy was not valued. The figure of £20,000 was the sum insured, which represented the underwriter's maximum liability. The judge found that if the policy took effect as a valued policy this could only result from the words 'Valued at Invoice Value and Charges plus 25%'. These had been taken from the provision in the open cover which provided that the goods were to be valued on this basis if there had been a loss or if the vessel had arrived prior to declaration under the open cover. The expression 'Invoice Value and charges plus 25%' in the policy required a commercial invoice, that is, one which had come into existence between two parties dealing with each other at arm's length and which therefore reflected the true market value of the goods. However no invoice of this nature was presented to the Court. Unavailability of the invoice as described by Kerr J prevented the policy from being described as a valued policy.

Unvalued policy

As defined by section 28 of the MIA 1906 an unvalued policy is a policy that does not specify the value of the subject matter insured, but, subject to the limit of the sum insured, leaves the insurable value to be subsequently ascertained, in the manner hereinbefore specified. The loss must be proved by evidence of the market value of the subject matter insured.

An unvalued policy may be called an open policy.[60] However, the term open policy may also be used to describe a floating policy as referred to below. Therefore, 'unvalued policy' should be preferred to 'open policy' when describing the policy within the meaning of section 28 of the Act.

Voyage and time policies

Section 25(1) provides that 'Where the contract is to insure the subject-matter "at and from", or from one place to another or others, the policy is called a "voyage policy", and where the contract is to insure the subject-matter for a definite period of time the policy is called a "time policy". A contract for both voyage and time may be included in the same policy.'

The different nature of voyage and time policies was emphasised by the Courts before the 1906 Act adopted in respect of the seaworthiness warranty, which is implied in a voyage policy but not implied in a time policy. Those cases are referred to in Chapter 5.

---

59 [1973] 2 Lloyd's Rep 442.

60 See *Berger and Light Diffusers Pty Ltd v Pollock* [1973] 2 Lloyd's Rep 442, 459. Unvalued policy was called an open policy in Martin's work which was published in 1876. See pp 122–123.

Floating policies and open covers

Both floating and open policies are contracts under which insurers agreed to cover declarations made by the assured to a certain specified amount and within the temporal and geographical limits.[61] In general terms, the assured is required to declare the vessel upon which any particular consignment is to be shipped and the cover is provided for all such property as the merchant expects to have at risk. If the assured's business involves chartering vessels to carry a variety of cargoes from and to ports around the world he might want to negotiate a single arrangement which will cover all that property, rather than negotiating separate insurances for each and every risk.[62]

A floating policy is similar to an open policy, the difference is that the former imposes a maximum sum insured for declarations, so that when declarations reach a given value the cover ceases to apply. An open cover may be subject to a maximum limit per risk but no overall aggregate.[63] Thus the assured can declare any subject matter so long as it is within the scope of the policy. The editors of Arnould stated that floating policies have in practice given way to open covers, although the former may still be found.[64]

An open cover may be seen in three different forms: obligatory, facultative and facultative obligatory. It should be noted that irrespective of the nature of the open cover, insurance will only attach if the risk accepted and declared by the assured falls within the terms of the open cover.[65] Consequently, the risk will not attach if the cargo is not of the correct description, or the vessel does not meet the requirements laid down by the insurers.[66]

Obligatory open cover

Obligatory open covers are similar to floating policies. Under section 29(1) of the MIA 1906 a floating policy is 'a policy which describes the insurance in general terms, and leaves the name of the ship or ships and other particulars to be defined by subsequent declaration'. The subsequent declaration or declarations may be made by endorsement on the policy, or in other customary manner (s.29(2)). Subsection (3) states that unless the policy otherwise provides, the declarations must be made in the order of dispatch or shipment. The subsection further provides 'They must, in the case of goods, comprise all consignments within the terms of the policy, and the value of the goods or other property must be honestly stated, but an omission or erroneous declaration may be rectified even after loss or arrival, provided the omission or declaration was made in good faith.' Thus, a declaration may be made after the shipment but the risk attaches upon shipment. The section reflects the usage applicable before adoption of the MIA 1906. It was expressed by Brett J in *Stephens v Australasian Insurance Co*[67] that '. . . when a policy is effected on goods by ship or ships to be thereafter declared, the policy attaches to the goods as soon as and in the order in which they are shipped; and directly the assured knows of the shipment of the goods he is bound to declare them to the underwriter on the policy, and to declare them in the order in which they are shipped. He is not entitled to declare some of the risks, and remain his own insurer as to others. In case by oversight or otherwise the goods are declared on the policy in an order different from that in which they were shipped, the assured is bound to rectify the declarations and make them correspond with the

---

61 Arnould, para 9–01.
62 *Glencore International AG v Ryan (The Beursgracht) (No.1)* [2002] 1 Lloyd's Rep 574, Arnould, para 9–01.
63 Arnould, para 9–15.
64 Arnould, para 9–01.
65 Arnould, para 9–19.
66 Arnould, para 9–19.
67 (1872) LR 8 CP 18.

order of shipment. The underwriter would require to see the bills of lading, and could insist on the declarations being made to follow the sequence of the bills of lading. The declarations are often thus rectified, and sometimes even after loss.' Section 29 codifies *Ionides v Pacific Fire & Marine Insurance Co*[68] in which a policy of insurance was for specified amounts 'on hides per ship or ships as might be declared'. It was held that by this policy the underwriter insured any goods of the description specified which may be shipped on any vessel answering the description, on the voyages specified in the policy. The object of the declaration was to earmark and identify the particular adventure to which the assured elects to apply the policy. Under this wording the assent of the insurer was not required for this, for he had no option to reject any vessel which the assured may select; nor was it necessary that the declaration should do more than identify the adventure.

Thus, the words 'subsequent declaration' under s.29(1) mean that in a floating policy and an obligatory open cover the underwriters are bound at the moment of shipment.[69] The importance of the declarations being in sequence is that such policies have an aggregate limit. For example, a merchant would take out a policy upon all goods to be shipped during the period of cover up to a stated aggregate value. As all shipments up to the specified limit are automatically insured, the merchant is not able to choose the order in which the risks attach.

In *Glencore International AG v Ryan (The Beursgracht) (No.1)* the policy, although it was an open cover policy, was held to be 'more like a floating policy'.[70] In this case charterer's liability was insured under an 'Open Cover to accept all vessels chartered by the Assured for and during the period of 12 calendar months commencing 1st November 1986 . . . and ending 31st October 1987 . . . Expiry shall not prejudice risks which have attached prior to expiry becoming effective.' It was agreed that the declarations would be made in the form of monthly bordereaux. The charterparty for the risk in question relating to the *Beursgracht* was made on 13 October 1987 for the carriage of an approved cargo, aluminium products, from Santos to Rotterdam. During loading in Brazil on 31 October 1987 there was an accident that caused injuries to a stevedore from which he died four days later. The *Beursgracht* was not included in the declarations made in October and November 1987. The assured settled the claim against them in June 1996 by payment to owners of $75,000 and claimed this sum from the insurers together with £22,541 for the costs of defending and negotiating settlement of the owners' claim. The insurers denied liability for no declaration was made until 23 May 1993, thus, no relevant contract of charterer's liability insurance in relation to the vessel ever came into existence. Because of the language used in the policy with the words 'all vessels chartered' it was held that the assured had no option over the attachment of charters as cover applied to all vessels chartered. The Court found that the making of a declaration was an essential part of the contractual machinery, but nowhere did the wording link the making of declarations to the attachment of risks. The declaration was required for the purposes of premium calculation as the reference to monthly declarations appeared under the heading 'Rates' and the sub-heading 'Voyage charters'. The policy was interpreted by the Court as not having required the assured to declare *Beursgracht* in the next month following the making of the charter; the words simply meant that there would be monthly declarations; and the wording did not say that such declarations had to be made within a month of the assumption of risk under the charter. Charters in relation to such vessels were without exception to attach to the cover. Once the charter fell to be declared within the ambit of the cover, the underwriters were immediately on risk and would have been vested with a claim for premium in debt against the assured in the event that the claimants were somehow unable or unwilling to make a declaration. Because of the nature of the transaction it was almost

68 (1870–71) LR 6 QB 674, 682–683, Blackburn J.
69 *The Beursgracht (No.1)* [2002] 1 Lloyd's Rep 574, Tuckey LJ, para 30.
70 [2002] 1 Lloyd's Rep 574, para 34, Tuckey LJ.

inevitable that the underwriters would not have the risks declared to them in advance, but only in arrears by means of declarations. The objective was to declare the true position under the cover; it did not create any rights and obligations.

It is open to the parties to render declarations as conditions of cover. In *Union Insurance Society of Canton Ltd v George Wills & Co*[71] the contract of marine insurance contained in a floating policy insured all shipments of goods made by the assured between a large number of ports against the usual marine risks. The contract provided 'Declarations of interest to be made to this society's agent at port of shipment where practicable or agent in London or Perth as soon as possible after sailing of vessel to which interest attaches.' The ship *Papanui* sailed from ports Liverpool, Glasgow, Avonmouth and London, leaving London on 21 August 1911; the assured having loaded cargo at each of these ports. The *Papanui* was destroyed by fire on 12 September 1911 as well as all the goods being totally lost. The declaration of interest was not forwarded until 13 September 1911, the day after the loss of the vessel. It was held that the requirement that the assured make a declaration of interest as soon as possible after sailing of the vessel was a warranty. The Court noted that this was an open or floating policy under which the liability of the insurers in the first instance attaches before the sailing of the vessel, and therefore at a time before the declaration of interest is due to be made. However, the Court also considered that the assured undertook to do a particular thing, namely, to make a declaration as soon as possible after the sailing of a vessel which rendered this obligation a subsequent condition which was to be complied with at the time when its performance was due under the contract. The insurer was therefore discharged from liability for the assured's breach of warranty. It was also argued in *The Beursgracht) (No.1)*[72] that the undertaking to make declarations was a warranty. The Court of Appeal recognised that creating a warranty by a declaration clause was open to the parties at the outset of the contract but in the policy discussed the Court found no indication that that was the intention of the parties.

Facultative Obligatory Cover

A 'facultative/obligatory' cover gives the assured a facility to declare risks to the cover at his option, although the underwriter is bound to accept declarations if they fall within the terms of the cover.[73] The making of the declaration attaches the risk to the cover. If the risk declared is within the terms of the cover there is no need for any specific acceptance by the underwriter, but he is not bound until receipt of the declaration.[74] In *Citadel Insurance Co v Atlantic Union Insurance Co SA*[75] the 'Hull open cover' was 'to accept by way of reinsurance any declarations of original risks which might be made' by the brokers to whom the facility was provided. The reinsured had an open option to declare risks falling within the terms of the cover, and the reinsurer was obliged to accept such declarations. Kerr LJ[76] described this type of open cover as a standing offer under which the underwriters agreed to accept any declarations which are made within the terms of the cover. Therefore, so long as a declaration falls within the scope, there is no individual acceptance required from the underwriter as he is already bound by the declaration on account of his standing offer. Each declaration gives rise to a new obligation of the underwriters under the open cover.[77]

---

71 [1916] 1 AC 281.
72 [2002] 1 Lloyd's Rep 574.
73 *The Beursgracht (No.1)* [2002] 1 Lloyd's Rep 574, para 22.
74 *The Beursgracht (No.1)* [2002] 1 Lloyd's Rep 574, para 32.
75 [1982] 2 Lloyd's Rep 543.
76 [1982] 2 Lloyd's Rep 543, 547.
77 [1982] 2 Lloyd's Rep 543, 548.

Assignment

Under English law, a marine policy may be assigned in three different forms: under section 50 of the MIA 1906, section 136 of the Law of Property Act 1925 and in equity.[78]

Assignment under the Marine Insurance Act 1906

At common law, the assignee could not sue in his own name on the policy, but an action could be brought by the assignor as trustee for the assignee.[79] The power of the assignee to sue in his own name was conferred by the Policies of Marine Assurance Act, 1868, s.1, and amended by the MIA 1906. Section 50(1) of the MIA 1906 provides that a marine policy is assignable unless it contains terms expressly prohibiting assignment. The policy may be assigned either before or after loss. A marine policy may be assigned by endorsement thereon or in other customary manner (s.50(3)). The assignee of the policy is entitled to sue thereon in his own name (s.50(2)).

Unless the policy imposes such a condition, the consent of the underwriter is not essential to the validity of an assignment of it.[80] Nor is it required that the insurer should be given notice of assignment.[81] Section 50 is not in mandatory terms, the parties may agree otherwise. In the International Hull Clauses cl.23 provides 'No assignment of or interest in this insurance or in any moneys which may be or become payable under this insurance is to be binding on or recognised by the Underwriters unless a dated notice of such assignment or interest signed by the Assured, and by the assignor in the case of subsequent assignment, is endorsed on the policy and the policy with such endorsement is produced before payment of any claim or return of premium under this insurance.'

The sale of the subject matter insured does not automatically assign the policy of insurance to the purchaser.[82] Section 15 of the MIA 1906 provides that 'Where the assured assigns or otherwise parts with his interest in the subject-matter insured, he does not thereby transfer to the assignee his rights under the contract of insurance, unless there be an express or implied agreement with the assignee to that effect.' Thus, where the subject matter insured is sold, in addition to the contract of sale, it is necessary to assign the policy to the purchaser by the party originally insured, or, at all events, an agreement or understanding to assign it, or to hold it for the benefit of the purchaser. It should be noted that under section 51 of the MIA 1906 'Where the assured has parted with or lost his interest in the subject-matter insured, and has not, before or at the time of so doing, expressly or impliedly agreed to assign the policy, any subsequent assignment of the policy is inoperative: Provided that nothing in this section affects the assignment of a policy after loss.'

The whole interest must be assigned

Section 50(2) of the MIA 1906 provides 'Where a marine policy has been assigned so as to pass the beneficial interest in such policy, the assignee of the policy is entitled to sue thereon in his own name'. The reference in the section to assignment 'so as to pass the beneficial interest in such policy'

---

78 *Raiffeisen Zentralbank Osterreich AG v Five Star General Trading LLC (The Mount I)* [2001] Lloyd's Rep IR 460, para 58 Mance LJ. Mance LJ described this as 'a pot-pourri of three different forms, with variegated terminology'.
79 *Gibson v Winter* (1833) 5 B & Ad 96, *Williams v Atlantic Assurance Co Ltd* [1933] 1 KB 81.
80 Arnould, para 8–36.
81 *The Mount I* [2001] Lloyd's Rep IR 460, para 62, Mance LJ.
82 In *Powles v Innes* (1843) 11 M & W 10, 13 Lord Abinger CB said 'The policy is but a chose in action, and cannot pass merely by the assignment of the ship'.

has been held to require the passing of the whole beneficial interest in the policy.[83] It was held that the principle that the contract is one of indemnity implies that the beneficial interest in the policy cannot be severed from the interest assured while it remains in force.[84] A person cannot be said to have parted with his beneficial interest in ongoing insurance cover, if he remains the person whose interest is insured, even if (for example) he has assigned the entire right to the benefit of any claims which arise in respect of his interest.[85] The assignor remains the insured in such circumstances.

Where the assignor retained at least a limited interest in recoveries that might be made under the policy, the whole beneficial interest is not passed. This was applied in *First National City Bank of Chicago v West of England Shipowners Mutual Protection and Indemnity Association (Luxembourg) (The Evelpidis Era).*[86] In this case E mortgaged his vessel *Evelpidis Era* in return to the loan he obtained from the bank. The loan agreement provided that although insurance might be taken out, otherwise than in the name of the bank, the shipowners should ensure the bank is designated loss payee under a loss payable clause to be annexed to the insurance policies and certificate of entry. Clause 11 of the mortgage deed provided that the vessel was to be kept entered in a P&I association and that the insurances were to be assigned to the mortgagees. The owners' vessel *Evelpidis Era* had entered in the defendant club who gave the bank a letter of undertaking which provided inter alia:

> . . . The vessel's Certificate of Entry will be endorsed with the following clauses: It is noted that . . . Bank . . . are interested as First Mortgagees in the subject matter of this Insurance up to the amount of their mortgage interest. Claims hereunder for all losses shall be paid direct to the Shipowners unless and until the Mortgagees shall have given notice in writing that the Shipowners are in default under the first mortgage on the vessel whereafter such claims shall be payable to the Mortgagees up to the amount of their Mortgage interest . . .

It was held that the whole of the beneficial interest in the policy had not been assigned since the assignment to the mortgagee bank of the benefit of protection and indemnity cover was provided for the Club to continue to pay claims directly to the shipowners or their creditors until receipt of notice to the contrary from the bank.

Similarly, in *Raiffeisen Zentralbank Osterreich AG v Five Star General Trading LLC (The Mount I)*[87] the owner assigned his rights under the insurance to the mortgagee bank. However, the wording of the relevant clauses intended, and did continue, to protect the owner's insurable interests in respect of any losses and liabilities which it incurred as mortgagor or as operator of the vessel. The insurance provided hull and machinery as well as collision and protection and indemnity cover. The hull and machinery cover was assigned but the risks of liability insured by the protection and indemnity and collision cover remained the owner's risks. Thus, section 50 could not apply.

It is important at the outset to distinguish an assignment of the policy from an assignment of sums payable under the policy and claims under the policy. The proceeds of an insurance claim may be assigned and the effect of assignment after loss is to transfer this chose in action to the assignee.[88] *Lloyd v Fleming* is authority that a right to recover unliquidated damages under a policy

83 *Williams v Atlantic Assurance Company Ltd* [1933] 1 KB 81; *The First National Bank of Chicago v The West of England Shipowners Mutual P&I Association (The 'Evelpidis Era')* [1981] 1 Lloyd's Rep 54, 64.
84 *Williams v Atlantic Assurance Co Ltd* [1933] 1 KB 81, Greer LJ.
85 *The Mount I* [2001] Lloyd's Rep IR 460, para 64, Mance LJ.
86 [1981] 1 Lloyd's Rep 54.
87 [2001] Lloyd's Rep IR 460.
88 *E Pellas & Co v Neptune Marine Insurance Co* (1879) 5 CPD 34.

of insurance is assignable, provided that, so far as is practicable, the policy itself is assigned with it.[89] The claims in respect of losses which have already occurred are assignable at law.[90]

Assignment before or after loss

In order to identify when the beneficial interest passes, it is also necessary to distinguish between situations of assignment before and after loss. Before loss, the policy is alive, and the assured cannot be said to have parted with all beneficial interest in it, so long as he retains and does not part with the insurable interest in the subject matter insured (that which the policy is intended to cover).[91] The classic application of s.50 is thus to circumstances where the assured sells the subject matter insured (be it cargo, as happens daily, or a ship) to another person with the benefit of the policy. In the case of an assignment after loss, when the policy and 'all rights under and by virtue of it' are assigned, the assignee becomes 'entitled to the property thereby insured;' for then it is ascertained that the interest in the damages, the chose in action, is the only property which is covered by the policy, consequently the words of the Act are literally complied with by a simple assignment of the benefit of such a claim.[92] This is obviously so, when the subject matter insured has become totally lost so as to exhaust the policy. This may also be so in the case of a partial loss, at least once the policy has expired.[93]

The reason of the distinction is that after the loss the right to indemnity no longer depends on the right of property in the subject matter of the insurance, so far as it still exists, but on the right of property in the thing or the portion of the thing lost.[94] After a loss the policy of insurance and the right of action under it might, like any other chose in action, be transferred in equity, though at common law the action must have been brought in the name of the original contractor, the assignor.[95] There is a very common form of commercial adventure, where goods are sold for a price to cover cost, freight and insurance, payable on receipt of the shipping documents. In such a case the policy and bill of lading are habitually made the subject of sale, whilst the parties are ignorant whether the goods are safe or not. [96] After a loss, different considerations apply.[97]

Limited assignment

A policy may provide broader coverage than the cover assigned by the assignor. In such a case the assignee of the policy can only avail himself of the insurance to the extent that the assignor has agreed to assign his rights to him. In Ionides v Harford[98] a ship was chartered with grain from Galatz to Emden for orders, to discharge in a port of the United Kingdom. The cargo was insured for the voyage from Galatz to Emden, and thence to a port of discharge in the United Kingdom, with leave to call for orders and to naturalise the cargo, to return 20s per cent if the risk ends at the port of naturalisation. The cargo was sold afloat while on the voyage from Galatz to Emden, the price

---

89   Swan v Maritime Insurance Co [1907] 1 KB 116, 123–124.
90   Amalgamated General Finance Co Ltd v CE Golding & Co Ltd [1964] 2 Lloyd's Rep 163, 167, Diplock LJ said obiter 'I do not accept that claims, once the loss has occurred, are unassignable.'
91   The Mount I [2001] Lloyd's Rep IR 460, para 63, Mance LJ.
92   Lloyd v Fleming (1871–1872) LR 7 QB 299, 303.
93   Swan v Maritime Insurance Co Ltd [1907] 1 KB 116 (a case of assignment after a partial loss and after the expiry of a time policy).
94   Lloyd v Fleming (1871–1872) LR 7 QB 299, 302.
95   Lloyd v Fleming (1871–1872) LR 7 QB 299, 303.
96   Lloyd v Fleming (1871–1872) LR 7 QB 299, 303.
97   The Mount I [2001] Lloyd's Rep IR 460, para 66, Mance LJ.
98   (1859) 29 LJ Ex 36.

'including freight and insurance to Emden'. The purchaser received the bill of lading as well as the policy of insurance. It was held that the assignment of the insurance policy was to Emden only, thus, the purchaser could not recover from the underwriter for a loss between Emden and the port of discharge in the United Kingdom.

The insurer's right to defend the claim

Upon assignment, the insurer is entitled to make any defence arising out of the contract which he would have been entitled to make if the action had been brought in the name of the person by or on behalf of whom the policy was effected (s.50(2)). The insurer, thus, can bring a breach of warranty defence against the assignee. In *William Pickersgill & Sons Ltd v London and Provincial Marine & General Insurance Co Ltd*[99] a firm of shipbuilders agreed to build a vessel for certain shipowners. As security for the purchase-money and in pursuance of a covenant to that effect, the owners insured the vessel with certain underwriters and assigned the policy to the builders. Material facts known to the owners but unknown to the builders were not disclosed to the underwriters. In an action on the policy by the builders as assignees of the policy against the underwriters, the latter pleaded the non-disclosure. The court accepted that this is a contractual defence. However, as seen in Chapter 4 whether the duty of good faith defence arises contractually or extra contractually is a controversial matter. However, *Pickersgill* is not overruled and still applicable law.

Reform proposals

As stated above, section 50(3) provides 'A marine policy may be assigned by indorsement thereon or in other customary manner.' The Law Commissions stated in their Consultation Paper dated December 2011 that 'More recently, there has been a move away from paper documents altogether. We were told by a leading cargo insurer that under their contractual terms of insurance the assured includes not only the name stated in the schedule but also "any party to whom insurable interest in the subject matter insured hereunder passes under a contract of sale". This means that the insurance is assigned automatically as soon as insurable interest in the goods passes. All that is required is that the assignor provides the assignee with details of the cover.'[100]

The Law Commissions further noted that marine insurance contracts are no longer assigned by indorsing copies of the full policy. In some cases, the contract may be assigned by indorsing a paper copy of the insurance certificate, but this is now giving way to electronic commerce. Consequently, the Law Commissions proposed that section 50(3) could be amended to say that a marine insurance contract may be assigned in any customary manner or as agreed between the parties to the transfer.[101]

The Law of Property Act 1925

Section 136(1) of the Law of Property Act 1925[102] provides:

> Any absolute assignment by writing under the hand of the assignor (not purporting to be by way of charge only) of any debt or other legal thing in action, of which express notice in writing

---

99 [1912] 3 KB 614.
100 Consultation Paper No. 201, para 16.40.
101 Consultation Paper No. 201, para 16.41 and 17.38.
102 Re-enacting s 25(6) of the Judicature Act 1873.

has been given to the debtor, trustee or other person from whom the assignor would have been entitled to claim such debt or thing in action, is effectual in law (subject to equities having priority over the right of the assignee) to pass and transfer from the date of such notice – (a) the legal right to such debt or thing in action; (b) all legal and other remedies for the same; and (c) the power to give a good discharge for the same without the concurrence of the assignor . . .

The operation of s.136 depends upon there having been an 'absolute assignment' of 'a debt or other legal thing in action' and upon express notice in writing being given to the insurers.[103] Similar to section 50 of the MIA 1906, for an assignment under s.136 of the Law of Property Act, the whole beneficial interest is required to be assigned. Thus, in *The Mount I* neither s.50 of the MIA 1906 nor s.136 was applicable. The owner remained covered as mortgagor and operator of the vessel. Another point to be noted is that under s.136 only a present claim or claims may be assigned.[104] The requirement here is that there is an absolute assignment of the legal thing in action.[105] A legal thing in action may be either the policy as a whole or a right of claim under it.

Assignment in equity

Where the assignment cannot have taken effect under s.50 or s.136, it may take effect in equity, both as between the parties to it and as against the debtor (or here the insurers) in consequence of the notice given to them.[106] Equity recognises and gives effect to any assignment, for value, of a thing in action depending on a future contingency (an 'expectancy').[107] An assignor and assignee are thus bound from the moment of their agreement, while the debtor is (subject to notice) bound as soon as the expectancy develops into an actuality. Once notified to the debtor, equitable assignment will have the effect of obliging the debtor to pay the assignee. Moreover, it will prevent further equities attaching to the debt and protect the assignee against assignments notified subsequently.[108] An equitable assignment may relate either to the whole interest in a thing in action or to a partial interest.[109] Thus, in *The Evelpidis Era* and *The Mount I* the assignments were equitable. The assignee of part of a debt is merely an equitable assignee, and at any rate, unless the equitable assignment is accompanied by a power to give a discharge, it is impossible for the assignee to succeed unless he sues in the name of the assignor[110] but that rule will not be insisted upon where there is no need, in particular if there is no risk of a separate claim by the assignor.[111] The case for joinder will obviously be strongest, if there is an issue between assignor and assignee regarding the existence of an assignment or the equitable assignee has acquired only part of a chose in action. The principle is that equity regards as done that which ought to be done, so a promise to assign takes effect as an assignment as soon as the assignor has received the valuable consideration.[112] Notice of the assignment to the insurers is not required but, as noted above, in the absence of notice to the insurers a subsequent assignee who took his assignment unaware of the earlier assignment may, despite having become aware of that earlier assignment, give notice to the insurers

---

103 *The Mount I* [2001] Lloyd's Rep IR 460, para 62, Mance LJ; *Williams v Atlantic Assurance Co Ltd* [1933] 1 KB 81, Greer LJ.
104 *The Mount I* [2001] Lloyd's Rep IR 460, para 75, Mance LJ.
105 *The Mount I* [2001] Lloyd's Rep IR 460, para 74, Mance LJ.
106 *The Mount I* [2001] Lloyd's Rep IR 460, para 76, Mance LJ.
107 *The Mount I* [2001] Lloyd's Rep IR 460, para 80, Mance LJ.
108 *The Mount I* [2001] Lloyd's Rep IR 460, para 60, Mance LJ.
109 *The Evelpidis Era* [1981] 1 Lloyd's Rep 54.
110 *Williams v Atlantic Assurance Co Ltd* [1933] 1 KB 81, Greer LJ.
111 *Sim Swee Joo Shipping Sdn Bhd v Shirlstar Container Transport Ltd* [1994] CLC 188.
112 *Ashley v Ashley* (1829) 3 Sim. 149; Arnould, para 8–48.

and thereby obtain priority for his own assignment.[113] A promise to assign takes effect as an assignment as soon as the assignor has received the valuable consideration, and if the assignment is of a future claim then the claim is to be treated as having been assigned as soon as it occurs. In *The Mount I* the owner's assignment was supported by ample consideration in the form of the loan advance given by the assignee bank. *The Mount I* was involved in a collision with a vessel that sank as a result of the casualty. It was held that once the collision occurred, any entitlement to indemnity under the policy as against the insurers in respect of the consequences of such collision was in law no longer an expectancy; an insured loss had occurred and there was a present and assignable right to be indemnified against any loss or liability which might result. The previously agreed assignment could in equity operate accordingly and pass to the assignee bank the beneficial interest in relation to any insurance claims. Finally, notice of such assignment was given by or on behalf of the bank to the insurers on 7 October 1997. The insurers were from that moment onwards bound to the assignee, rather than the owner, in relation to any claim under the insurance as and when it fell to be settled. Any equitable assignment is subject to equities, so that the assignee must sue subject to all rights of defence that may be set up against the assignor as a nominal claimant.[114]

Further reading

Arnould, *Law of Marine Insurance and Average*, 18th edn, [2013] Sweet & Maxwell. Chapter 1, The Contract Of Marine Insurance Generally; Chapter 2, Form And Contents Of Marine Policies; Chapter 4, Classes of Marine Insurers; Chapter 9, Floating Policies and Open Cover.

Bennett, *Law of Marine Insurance*, 2nd edn, [2006] Oxford University Press. Chapter 1, Introduction to the Law of Marine Insurance.

Birds et al., *MacGillivray on Insurance Law*, 12th edn, [2014] Sweet & Maxwell. Chapter 1, Nature of Insurance and Insurable Interest.

Clarke, *The Law of Insurance Contracts*, 4th edn, [2014] Informa. Chapter 6, Assignment.

Hazelwood and Semark, *P&I Clubs: Law and Practice*, 4th edn, [2010] Informa. Chapter 1, Introduction and History.

Lord Mance et al. (ed.), *Insurance Disputes*, 3rd edn, [2011] Informa. Chapter 2, The Lloyd's Market by Julian Burling.

Macdonald, 'The marine insurance contract and assignment under the English Marine Insurance Act 1906', *Journal of International Maritime Law* [2003] 9(2): 123–136.

Merkin, *Colinvaux's Law of Insurance*, 9th edn, [2010] Sweet & Maxwell. A. Principles of Insurance Law.

Rose, *Marine Insurance: Law and Practice*, 2nd edn, [2012] Informa. Chapter 1, The Nature of Marine Insurance.

---

113 Arnould, para 8–48.
114 *Gibson v Winter* (1833) 5 B & Ad 96.

Chapter 2

Formation of Insurance Contracts

Chapter Contents

London Company Market

In London, insurance policies may be written in the London Company Market or at Lloyd's. The company market is organised through a market body called the International Underwriting Association (IUA)[1] and involves insurers who are members. The IUA was formed by the merger of two bodies, the Institute of London Underwriters (ILU),[2] which dealt with predominantly marine and aviation risks, and the London Insurance and Reinsurance Market Association (LIRMA),[3] which dealt with non-marine risks. The administrative bureau processing details of the risks written under the auspices of the IUA is the London Processing Centre (LPC).[4] Many of the IUA member companies also have offices and separate underwriting rooms located elsewhere within the City, some being within the Lloyd's building.

The Lloyd's market

As referred to in Chapter 1 the history of Lloyd's goes back to the seventeenth century when London's importance as a trade centre led to an increasing demand for ship and cargo insurance.[5] Today Lloyd's is the world's leading market for specialist insurance.

Lloyd's is a statutory corporation, incorporated by a private Act of Parliament in 1871 by the name of Lloyd's. Lloyd's is not an insurance company; it is a market where its members join together as syndicates to insure risks. Much of Lloyd's business works by subscription, where more than one syndicate takes a share of the same risk. Business is conducted face-to-face between brokers and underwriters in the Underwriting Room in the Boxes where the underwriters have seats and meet the brokers who bring risks to them.

Lloyd's has two distinct parts: the market, which is made up of many independent businesses, and the Corporation of Lloyd's, which is there – broadly speaking – to oversee that market.[6]

Syndicates

Members of Lloyd's organise into syndicates who accept insurance business only through a professional (corporate) managing agent, who employs professional underwriting and other staff for that reason. The managing agent is responsible for the determination of the underwriting policy and strategy of any syndicate it manages, determination of the syndicate's reinsurance programme, management of the syndicate's investments, maintenance of accounting records, and calculation and estimation of reserves. A syndicate, which has no legal personality and is not a partnership, is merely the administrative arrangement through which its members underwrite insurance risk.

Coverholder and binding authority

The Lloyd's Market may place business – especially overseas – under a binding authority given to an overseas broker. A binding authority is an agreement between a managing agent and a coverholder.

---

1   www.iua.co.uk
2   www.ilu.org.uk
3   www.iua.co.uk/IUA_Member/About/IUA_Member/About_the_IUA/About_the_IUA_homepage.aspx?hkey=e86110b6-e04f-4c13-87b9-7ef2e6f71e09
4   www.lcp.uk.com
5   www.lloyds.com/lloyds/about-us/history
6   www.lloyds.com/lloyds/about-us/what-is-lloyds

The binding authority agreement (contract of delegation) is not the contract of insurance. Under this agreement the managing agent delegates its authority, to enter into a contract of insurance to be underwritten by the members of a syndicate managed by it, to the coverholder in accordance with the terms of the agreement. A binding authority agreement can also be used to give a coverholder the authority to issue insurance documents on behalf of Lloyd's syndicates. Insurance documents include certificates of insurance, temporary cover notes and other documents acting as evidence of contracts of insurance. They also set out the coverholder's other responsibilities, such as handling premiums or agreeing claims.

Lineslip

A 'lineslip' is an agreement where a managing agent delegates to another managing agent or authorised insurance company, their authority to enter into contracts of insurance to be underwritten by the members of a syndicate managed by it, in respect of business introduced by a Lloyd's broker named in the agreement. For instance, an insurer who wants to insure marine risks but doesn't necessarily have much experience in this area, may authorise another managing agent who is an expert in the marine market to write marine policies for him.

Formation of insurance contracts

The rules described below apply to insurance contracts irrespective of whether the transaction is one of insurance or reinsurance, or whether the slip is an original slip or an endorsement slip which is circulated during the period of the cover, or whether it is a marine or non-marine risk.[7] It was also accepted that no distinction is to be drawn between insurances at Lloyds and those placed by means of slips in the company market.[8]

Lloyd's brokers bring business into the market on behalf of client-policyholders, and shop around to see which syndicates can cover their specific risk and on what terms. A broker who does not have direct access to the Lloyd's market, particularly overseas producing brokers, will have to appoint a Lloyd's broker to act as his agent.

The London market is a subscription market, meaning that the insurers normally participate in insuring the entire risk by covering given percentages of the risk, to the extent each of them is willing to insure. Thus, the underwriters who accept the broker's offer write 'lines' by way of participation towards the 100 per cent cover which the broker and his client seek from the market.

In 2007 the Market Reform Contract (MRC) was introduced in the London Market. Before the MRC the document which the brokers used to present to the underwriters to offer the risk was called a 'slip'. A slip was a piece of paper, which generally contained very little information about the terms of the insurance contract such as the name of the vessel, the voyage or period for which insurance was required, the valuation (if any) and amount to be insured as well as warranties that were required.

Although the slip used to be used to form a binding agreement, section 22 of the MIA 1906 outlines an additional requirement for insurance contracts. The section states 'Subject to the provisions of any statute, a contract of marine insurance is inadmissible in evidence unless it is embodied in a marine policy in accordance with this Act. The policy may be executed and issued either at the time when the contract is concluded, or afterwards.' The policy then used to be issued,

---

7   See Kerr LJ, *General Reinsurance Corp v Forsakringsaktiebolaget Fennia Patria* [1983] 2 Lloyd's Rep 287, at 290.
8   See Kerr LJ, *General Reinsurance Corp v Forsakringsaktiebolaget Fennia Patria* [1983] 2 Lloyd's Rep 287, at 290.

sometimes much later than the contract was formed by a slip (or there never was an issued policy). This procedure used to be called 'deal now detail later'. Issuance of the policy after the slip was scratched created disputes when there was a discrepancy between the policy and the slip. The English courts heard cases involving a policy and a slip, for instance where the latter includes a warranty by the assured, the policy wording made no mention of it.[9] Moreover, in another case while cover was limited to 48 months in the policy, there was no mention of such a limitation in the slip.[10] There was need for contractual certainty and pursuant to the Financial Service Authority's[11] challenge to the UK insurance industry to end 'deal now detail later' culture, the contract certainty project began in December 2004. In order to ensure that the assured has greater certainty over what he has bought and the Insurer greater certainty over what it has committed to, the Contract Certainty Code of Practice (CCCP) was announced in 2007.[12] Following this the Market Reform Contract (MRC) was introduced to the insurance market. The MRC is essentially a standard form contract for insurers and brokers to use, and which was designed to comply with the CCCP. The MRC offers a clear structure and means that brokers present contracts in a consistent manner. The MRC aims at further clarity to the discussion between brokers and underwriters and enhancement of the efficiency of the placing process.[13] The MRC is a move away from the long-standing culture of slip and policy, and towards a practice based on a single contract document.[14] The MRC was jointly developed by the London Market Association, the International Underwriting Association and the London Market Brokers Committee under the auspices of the London Market Group.

When is a binding insurance contract concluded?

A broker who has a licence to do business at Lloyd's visits the managing agents who write business for syndicates. The broker presents the risk and makes an offer to the managing agent to form a binding agreement. If the agent accepts the offer, he signs the MRC slip and puts its stamp on it. This is called scratching and at the moment the agent scratches the MRC slip a binding agreement between the assured and the members of Lloyd's (underwriter) is formed.[15] An underwriter may not want to subscribe to 100 per cent of the risk; when he scratches the MRC slip the agent also states the percentage that the underwriter is bound by. This percentage is called the relevant underwriter's 'line'. The broker then has to take the slip round the market until he achieves 100 per cent subscription. Thus, it is likely that there will always be more than one underwriter scratching the slip. Section 24(2) of the MIA 1906 provides: 'Where a policy is subscribed by or on behalf of two or more insurers, each subscription, unless the contrary be expressed, constitutes a distinct contract with the assured.' Therefore, each underwriter has their own independent contract with the assured to the extent of the percentage that he agreed to insure. Hobhouse J described this in *General Accident Fire & Life Assurance Corp Ltd v Tanter (The Zephyr)*[16] as 'a mechanism whereby the assured can be put, by means of a single contractual document, in direct and distinct contractual relations with a large number of insurers; what might seem to be a single contract is in fact a bundle of a

---

9   *HIH Casualty & General Insurance Ltd v New Hampshire Insurance Co* [2001] 1 Lloyd's Rep 378, CA [2001] 2 Lloyd's Rep 161.

10 *Youell v Bland Welch & Co Ltd (No.1)* [1990] 2 Lloyd's Rep 423, CA [1992] 2 Lloyd's Rep 127.

11 Now Financial Conduct Authority (FCA).

12 www.londonmarketgroup.co.uk/index.php?option=com_content&view=article&id=210:index&catid=35:contract-certainty-guidance&Itemid=136

13 www.londonmarketgroup.co.uk/index.php/current-resources/placing-documentation/mrc/open-market

14 http://lawcommission.justice.gov.uk/docs/cp201_ICL_post_contract_duties.pdf, Consultation Paper No. 201, para 15.18.

15 *Samuel v Dumas* [1924] AC 431, 478, Lord Sumner.

16 [1984] 1 Lloyd's Rep 58. Appeal was allowed on other grounds than the issues discussed in this chapter. [1985] 2 Lloyd's Rep 529.

large number of distinct contracts on the same terms except as to the amount of each individual insurer's liability'.

The question then may arise as to the status of scratches of the underwriters before the 100 per cent subscription is obtained. If a loss occurs before the 100 per cent subscription is obtained, those who had already agreed to insure the risk might want to argue that they can rescind the contract given that there was not a binding agreement before the 100 per cent subscription was reached. In *Jaglom v Excess Insurance Co Ltd*[17] this issue was addressed by Donaldson J in *obiter*. He expressed the view that each line represents an offer by the underwriter in question on the basis of the slip as it stands, and a binding contract only comes into existence when the slip had been fully subscribed. However, Donaldson J's dictum was rejected by the Court of Appeal in *General Reinsurance Corp v Forsakringsaktiebolaget Fennia Patria*.[18] In *Fennia Patria* it was held that the presentation of a slip by the broker constitutes an offer, and the writing of each line constitutes an acceptance of this offer by the underwriter *pro tanto*.[19] Thus, once the underwriter scratches the MRC, he cannot rescind the contract in between him signing the contract and the broker obtaining 100 per cent subscription.[20] Equally, the assured cannot insist on the insurer cancelling the endorsement which is more insurer-friendly before the 100 per cent subscription for the endorsement is obtained.

A binding agreement is formed when the underwriter scratches an MRC slip unless he makes it clear that he does not intend to be bound by his scratch. The courts have decided that scratching by pencil,[21] underlining the signature[22] or adding 'TBE'[23] (to be entered) next to the signature is not an indication by the underwriter as to withholding his commitment to the risk. The courts emphasised that to qualify the scratching further words were needed on the slip to indicate the intention not to be bound by the contract at that stage. In the three occasions mentioned above, the courts found that the examples were purely administrative and they might have had some meaning internally but they did not mean anything to the assured or any other third parties. For instance, scratching by pencil was found as being nothing more than a reflection of the fact that another document would, for purely administrative reasons, have to be drawn up and signed. 'TBE' in itself connoted only that the underwriter did not have his records readily available to mark up his entry. Underlining the initials with two little lines was found to have been the underwriter's private note for himself or for his partner. This might have had some internal significance for the insurer or his partner but it had no significance whatsoever so far as the other underwriters were concerned. Thus, the underwriter's signature confirming 'it is agreed . . .' was unqualified.

It should be noted that a broker may issue a cover note, which is not a contract of insurance in its own right. If issued, a cover note informs the insurer as to what had been agreed between the broker and the underwriter.

Signing down

While taking the MRC round the market the broker may obtain more than 100 per cent subscription. Oversubscription of a slip (now MRC) has been an accepted practice in the market.[24] Brokers regard

---

17 [1971] 2 Lloyd's Rep 171.
18 [1983] 2 Lloyd's Rep 287.
19 See also Lord Denning, *Eagle Star v Spratt* [1971] 2 Lloyd's Rep 116, at 127; *American Airlines Inc v Hope* [1974] 2 Lloyd's Rep 301.
20 The signing provisions of the MRC in this case where there will be no signing down unless the underwriter specially requests for this at the time he scratches the MRC.
21 *Bonner v Cox* [2005] Lloyd's Rep IR 569. The point did not arise on appeal [2006] 2 Lloyd's Rep 152.
22 *Eagle Star Insurance Co Ltd v Spratt* [1971] 2 Lloyd's Rep 116.
23 *ERC Frankona Reinsurance v American National Insurance Co* [2006] Lloyd's Rep IR 157.
24 *The Zephyr* [1984] 1 Lloyd's Rep 58.

it as an advantage for the reasons that oversubscription enables a broker to show his business to more underwriters and it gives the slip a better appearance as large lines may encourage other large lines.[25] The broker thus may reach 100 per cent sooner. It is recognised on the market that the entitlement of a broker to oversubscribe and sign down an underwriter's line can be vitiated by the underwriter, putting after his written percentage line on the slip, words such as 'to stand'.[26] Such wording is very rare in the marine market but is not uncommon in the aviation market.[27] Before the MRC was introduced to the market it was customary to reduce oversubscribed lines proportionately until the subscription reached 100 per cent.[28] After 2007 it is not only a custom but also provided by a clause in the MRC, 'Signing Provisions', that 'In the event that the written lines hereon exceed 100 per cent of the order, any lines written "to stand" will be allocated in full and all other lines will be signed down in equal proportions so that the aggregate signed lines are equal to 100 per cent of the order without further agreement of any of the insurers.'[29]

Agreements reached via emails

It may be the case that the broker, the assured and the insurer may be based in different jurisdictions as a result of which, instead of sitting in the boxes at Lloyd's to negotiate the contract, the parties may do so via emails. In such a case the moment that a binding agreement is concluded may be determined by applying the rules of contractual construction as discussed in *Allianz Insurance Co Egypt v Aigaion Insurance Co SA.*[30] In this case, the reinsured, Allianz Insurance Company Egypt was based in Egypt, the reinsurers, Aigaion Insurance Co SA, was based in Greece and the broker, Chedid & Associates Ltd, was based in Cyprus, but the transaction was routed through its Beirut office. The email exchanges, which were a matter of construction in this case were as follows: On 27 December 2004, B at Chedid emailed T at Aigaion as follows: 'We are pleased to offer you a share on the above account, details as per attached slips . . .' The slip attached referred to the insurance type as Marine Hull & Machinery, to a MAR (91) form. T replied on 27 January 2005 as follows: 'We are prepared to participate as follow on subject account' and then listed some changes to the terms as offered by B. On 10 March 2005, B responded to T requesting a slight improvement in rate and deductible to secure a firm order. On 15 March 2005, T offered the improvement suggested and upon another exchange T amended the quote and on 30 March 2005, B sent an email 'we are pleased to bind your participation with a share of 30 per cent for 12 months as from 31.03.2005'. On 31 March 2005, T requested B to forward the slip, which B obliged on the same day. On 2 April 2005, T replied 'Cover is bound with effect from 31.03.05 as we had quoted . . .' On 15 April 2005 Aigaion sent its policy documents to Chedid in Beirut. The policy differed in at least two respects from the slip. It contained reference to a class warranty and a 'Payment Terms' clause, which warranted the payment of the premium at the due quarter days.[31] Chedid did not respond to the policy. Allianz made two payments, one in April and another in late June, but they were directed to Chedid's office in Cyprus and were not paid on to Aigaion. On 23 July 2005 one of

---

25   [1984] 1 Lloyd's Rep 58, 68.

26   [1984] 1 Lloyd's Rep 58, 69.

27   *The Zephyr* [1984] 1 Lloyd's Rep 58, 69, Hobhouse J.

28   *The Zephyr* [1984] 1 Lloyd's Rep 58; *General Reinsurance Corp v Forsakringsaktiebolaget Fennia Patria* [1983] 2 Lloyd's Rep 287.

29   Signing provisions add that '(a) in the event that the placement of the order is not completed by the commencement date of the period of insurance then all lines written by that date will be signed in full; (b) the signed lines resulting from the application of the above provisions can be varied, before or after the commencement date of the period of insurance, by the documented agreement of the insured and all insurers whose lines are to be varied. The variation to the contracts will take effect only when all such insurers have agreed, with the resulting variation in signed lines commencing from the date set out in that agreement'.

30   [2009] Lloyd's Rep IR 533.

31   For Warranties see Chapter 5 and for the Premium and Premium Payment Warranties see Chapter 6.

the tugs scheduled to the slip became a constructive total loss. Aigaion rejected the claim by contending that the policy automatically lapsed on 31 May 2005 due to non-payment of premium as per payment warranty. HHJ Chambers QC[32] held that the email of 2 April 2005 was intended to close the deal and the contract was binding from that day. This was approved by the Court of Appeal.[33] Rix LJ[34] took into account of the fact that the parties were in separate countries and could not communicate face to face when initialling or stamping the slip. Rix LJ held that since Aigaion agreed to those terms by its email response, it was as if it had appended its signature to it. Moses LJ[35] added that the reasonable reader would interpret the final exchanges between B and T as concluding a binding agreement.

Requirement of formal policy

Section 22 of the MIA 1906 renders a contract of marine insurance inadmissible as evidence unless it is embodied in a marine policy in accordance with the Act. The section further states that 'the policy may be executed and issued either at the time when the contract is concluded, or afterwards'. A policy is not defined in the MIA 1906 but the details which a policy should include are stated. Accordingly, 'A marine policy must specify the name of the assured, or of some person who effects the insurance on his behalf'[36] and 'A marine policy must be signed by or on behalf of the insurer, provided that in the case of a corporation the corporate seal may be sufficient, but nothing in this section shall be construed as requiring the subscription of a corporation to be under seal.'[37]

It was stated in *Ionides v Pacific Fire and Marine Insurance Co*[38] that the policy was required as evidence of a contract of insurance to prevent tax evasion. The Customs and Inland Revenue Act[39] provided 'no contract or agreement for sea insurance shall be valid unless expressed in a policy' and '*no policy shall be pleaded or given in evidence in any court unless duly stamped*'.[40] The tax did not apply to the contract as such, but to the document, which had to be stamped. Then the Stamp Act 1891 section 93(1) kept the same requirement that 'A contract for sea insurance (other than such insurance as is referred to in the fifty-fifth section of the Merchant Shipping Act Amendment Act, 1862) shall not be valid unless the same is expressed in a policy of sea insurance.' Section 22 of the MIA 1906 is the successor to these provisions.[41] The Finance Act 1959 section 30 used to regulate Stamp duty on policies of insurance. The relevant subsections of section 30 were repealed by the Finance Act 1970.[42] Thus, these legislative developments removed the need for section 22 of the MIA 1906.[43] The Law Commissions thus described section 22 as 'outdated and problematic'[44] and recommended that section 22 should be repealed, together with four linked provisions: section 23, section 24(1), section 89 and Schedule 1.[45] Recently the Law Commission introduced a Bill to reform Insurance Contract Law.[46] However, the Bill does not include a section repealing section 22.

---

32 [2008] 2 Lloyd's Rep 595, para 32.
33 [2009] Lloyd's Rep IR 533.
34 [2009] Lloyd's Rep IR 533, para 33.
35 [2009] Lloyd's Rep IR 533, para 40.
36 Section 23(1).
37 Section 24(1).
38 (1870–71) LR 6 QB 674, 685 Blackburn J, approved by *Court of Exchequer Chamber* (1871–72) LR 7 QB 517.
39 30 Vict. c 23 s 7.
40 Section 9.
41 Consultation Paper No. 201, para 15.2.
42 (c 24), Sch 8 Pt IV.
43 Consultation Paper No. 201, para 15.3.
44 Consultation Paper No. 201, para 14.1.
45 Consultation Paper No. 201, para 15.32.
46 http://lawcommission.justice.gov.uk/publications/insurance-contract-law.htm

Can the MRC be a contract of insurance?

Prior to the MRC, the slip was the complete and final contract between the parties, which fixes the terms of the insurance and the premium. Nevertheless, it was denied that the slip was a policy.[47] In *Ionides v Pacific Fire and Marine Insurance Co* the Courts' concern was mainly the tax evasion and compliance with the requirements of the Stamp Act 1891. Now, after the relevant provisions of the Stamps Act have been repealed and the MRC has been introduced in the market, this question may be reconsidered.

The MRC contains six sections: (1) Risk Details – details of the risk/contract involved, such as insured, type, coverage, conditions, etc.; (2) Information – free text additional information; (3) Security Details – includes (Re)insurers' Liability, Order Hereon, Basis of Written Lines, Basis of Signed Lines, Signing Provisions, insurers' 'stamp' details. These indicate each insurer's share of the risk and their reference(s); (4) Subscription Agreement – this establishes the rules to be followed for processing and administration of post-placement amendments and transactions; (5) Fiscal and Regulatory – fiscal and regulatory issues specific to the insurers involved in the risk; (6) Broker Remuneration and Deductions – information relating to brokerage, fees and deductions from premium.

It therefore becomes a strong argument, that as a matter of law, the MRC meets the requirements listed under section 23 and 24 of the MIA 1906 and as with contracts complying with the CCCP, an MRC may itself constitute a 'marine policy'.[48] Thus, with the repeal of the relevant provisions of the Stamp Act 1891 an assured should be able to make a claim by holding only the MRC, without having a separate policy. By reading the MRC an expert can say with certainty, from a mere perusal of the slip, what perils are insured against and what all the terms and conditions of the insurance are intended to be.[49] The scratch is a sufficient signature within s.24 of the MIA 1906.[50] Moreover, the Law Commission noted that since the abolition of stamp duty on marine policies by the Finance Act 1970, there have been no cases in which a marine insurer has refused to pay a claim because the insured cannot produce a written policy.[51] The Law Commissions added that in consultation, insurers stressed that they would never take such a point.[52]

The leading underwriter clause

It is likely that a particular underwriter might have a reputation in the market as an expert in the kind of cover required and his lead is likely to be followed by other insurers in the market. Therefore, it might make business sense for the broker to first approach the leading underwriter (L/U) and obtain his initial on the slip, which might then persuade the following underwriters that it is an acceptable risk to insure. While scratching the slip the leading underwriter expressly states that he is the leader on the MRC in question, hence the followers can identify the leader. The choice of leader is most important because the leader must command the confidence of the market.[53] In *Aneco*

---

47 *Ionides v Pacific Fire and Marine Insurance Co* (1870–71) LR 6 QB 674, 685, Blackburn J; approved by Court of Exchequer Chamber (1871–72) LR 7 QB 517.

48 Issues Paper 9: The Requirement for a Formal Marine Policy: Should Section 22 Be Repealed, para 3–62. http://lawcommission.justice.gov.uk/docs/ICL9_Requirement_for_Formal_Marine_Policy.pdf

49 Arnould, para 2–10.

50 Arnould, para 2–10.

51 Consultation Paper No. 201, para 15.20.

52 Consultation Paper No. 201, para 15.20.

53 *The Zephyr* [1984] 1 Lloyd's Rep 58, 67 Hobhouse J.

Reinsurance Underwriting Ltd (In Liquidation) v Johnson & Higgins Ltd[54] the leading underwriter Mr K was referred to as 'a prominent figure in the XL market.' When following underwriters come to write the slip they will do so at least in part in reliance on the leader's judgment in agreeing to the terms and rate on the slip.[55] The L/U may, but is not required to, take a larger share than the following underwriters.[56] The assured will have separate insurance agreements with the leader and each of the followers.[57]

General Reinsurance Corp v Forsakringsaktiebolaget Fennia Patria[58] is a case illustrating the formation of an insurance contract, the status of the underwriters' scratching and the independent contracts formed between the assured and each of the underwriters subscribed to the risk. In that case, the reinsurance policy was taken out and after the contract was concluded the reinsured decided to amend it. There were 25 underwriters who followed the leader in this subscription. The leader signed the endorsement which contained the amendment that the reinsured wished to make. Subsequently, the reinsured noticed that without the amendment the reinsurers' exposure would be much larger in relation to a very substantial loss which had just occurred. The reinsured thus insisted that the leader cancelled the endorsement. The dispute went before the court and the issue was whether the reinsured could rescind the endorsement unilaterally. The court decided in favour of the leader that every underwriter's scratching creates a binding agreement at the time of the scratching *pro tanto*. Therefore, in *Fennia Patria* the leading underwriter was bound by the amended reinsurance contract whereas the followers who had not signed the amendment were bound by the original form of the agreement.

Alteration of the insurance contract by the leading underwriter

The obvious commercial purpose of the L/U clause is described as 'simplifying administration and claims settlement'.[59] In *Roadworks (1952) Ltd v Charman*[60] Judge Kershaw QC explained that

> [i]n the London insurance market a risk is often underwritten by several insurers – Lloyd's syndicates, several companies or a combination of both. It is in the interests of both underwriters and brokers that time should not be spent in obtaining the express agreement of every underwriter to every change, even such as a change in the spelling of the name of the insured. Hence, the leading underwriter system has evolved.

A L/U clause may clarify the leader's authority to modify the terms of the insurance contract or to settle the claims by the assured. Consequently, if the L/U is authorised to agree on changes to the contractual terms on behalf of the following market, his consent would be sufficient to bind the following underwriters should the brokers seek any modifications. Where an insurance contract authorises the leader to agree to modify the insurance contract, the scope of such duty should be stated as clearly and as precisely as possible. The L/U's power in this regard brought the discussions as to his legal status, that is, whether he is the agent of the following underwriters. For instance in *Roadworks (1952) Ltd v Charman*[61] the brokers obtained a slip, which was subject to the approval of the

54   [2002] 1 Lloyd's Rep 157, 165.
55   *The Zephyr* [1984] 1 Lloyd's Rep 58, 67 Hobhouse J.
56   *Roar Marine Ltd v Bimeh Iran Insurance Co (The Daylam)* [1998] 1 Lloyd's Rep 423 at 426.
57   *International Lottery Management v Dumas* [2002] Lloyd's Rep IR 237, para 71.
58   [1983] 2 Lloyd's Rep 287.
59   *Roar Marine Ltd v Bimeh Iran Insurance Co (The Daylam)* [1998] 1 Lloyd's Rep 423 at 430; See also *PT Buana Samudra Pratama v Maritime Mutual Insurance Association (NZ) Ltd* [2011] 2 Lloyd's Rep 655.
60   [1994] 2 Lloyd's Rep 99.
61   [1994] 2 Lloyd's Rep 99.

Salvage Association (SA) in respect of its beaching arrangements, and contained a L/U clause. The SA was unable to approve the arrangements. The broker returned to the leader, indicating that it was urgent for cover to be arranged as the barge was about to sail and requested a waiver of the term requiring SA's approval. The leader agreed to make such an amendment. The question was whether the agreement reached between the broker and the leader was binding for the following underwriters. The relevant clause of the policy provided: 'All alterations, additions, deletions, extensions, agreements, rates and changes in conditions to be agreed by the Leading Lloyd's Underwriter and Leading Company Underwriter only. Such agreement to be binding on all Underwriters subscribing hereon.' The matter was to be resolved by the rules of construction and the court held that although the leader believed that he was scratching only for his own syndicate, the effect of the L/U clause was that he had dispensed with the SA subject for D (the following underwriter). The judge said

> a leading underwriter is the agent of the following underwriters. By taking a leading line he knows that there will be following underwriters and he sees the terms of any L/U clause on the slip. He may require the L/U clause to be altered if he is to take a line. The following underwriters see from the slip the identity of the leader or leaders. They see the terms of the L/U clause. By taking a line they not only make a contract with the insured but also make those leader or leaders their agent or agents for the purpose shown in the L/U clause. The leader can ascertain the identity of the following underwriters from the broker at any time and in particular if he is asked for an endorsement. The policy itself, which will identify all the underwriters, is prepared later – perhaps much later – by the Lloyd's Policy Signing Office. That fact is no more than the way in which Lloyd's operates, and does not show or help to show that a leader is not an agent of the following underwriters . . . I therefore have to decide . . . whether the leader as an agent can validly waive a contingent condition. The fact that by doing so he might be in breach of a duty to the following underwriters does not of itself mean that it is not within his power to do so . . . as matters of general contract law: 1. Even a contingent condition can be waived. 2. A principal can authorise his agent to do anything which the principal could have done.

It should be noted that the view that the leading underwriter acts as agent for the following market in his dealings with the assured is not universally accepted. In *Mander v Commercial Union Assurance Co plc*[62] one question raised was whether the L/U's acceptance of risks under an open cover to which numerous other underwriters had subscribed, amounted to an assertion of agency on the part of the leader. Rix J, citing *dicta* to similar effect by Steyn J in *The Tiburon*,[63] suggested that it did not have this effect. Rix J was of the view that the acceptance of a risk by the leader under the open cover was not done as agent of the following market but merely provided the trigger event by which the following market came to be bound by the declaration. Recently, Teare J rejected the agency argument in *San Evans Maritime Inc v Aigaion Insurance Co SA*.[64] The judge said[65] 'Introducing the concept of agency when there is no agreement between Aigaion [the following underwriter] and Catlin [the leader] . . . unnecessarily complicates the operation of the clause.' *San Evans* will be discussed fully in the following paragraphs.

---

62 [1998] Lloyd's Rep IR 93.
63 [1990] 2 Lloyd's Rep 418, at p 422.
64 [2014] EWHC 163 (Comm), appeal is pending.
65 [2014] EWHC 163 (Comm), para 16.

The MRC refers to the General Underwriters Agreement (GUA)[66] with regard to the leader's authority to agree changes on the insurance contract. Therefore, it is arguable that the MRC resolved the matter to a great extent. The MRC contains a 'Subscription Agreement Section' under which the slip leader needs to be identified.[67] Under the heading 'Basis of Agreement' it is required to be identified whether the leading underwriter is entitled to agree all changes to the policy or whether the authority is limited. This section of the MRC may be completed by reference to GUA. Part 1 of GUA contains the list of 'Alterations the Slip Leader may agree on behalf of all Underwriters each for its own proportion.' Part 2 lists 'Alterations the Slip Leader and Agreement Parties may, if unanimous, agree on behalf of all Underwriters each for its own proportion severally and not jointly' and finally Part 3 lists 'Alterations which may be agreed only by all Underwriters each for its own proportion severally and not jointly.' For instance, 'Errors that are clearly typographical errors' is listed under Part 1, hence, the LU's correction of this error will be binding for all the following underwriters. Whereas, 'any waiver of or amendment to any express or implied warranty or any condition precedent to the attachment of the risk' is listed in Part 3 and the broker has to visit each of the subscribing underwriters to obtain their confirmation on such an amendment of the policy.

Settlements reached by the leading underwriter

The leading underwriter may settle the claim with the assured in which case the question of whether the following underwriters are bound by this settlement may arise. With regard to the settlements the MRC contains a clause on 'Basis of Claims' and states 'Claims to be managed in accordance with:

i)   The Lloyd's Claims Scheme (Combined), or as amended or any successor thereto.
ii)   IUA claims agreement practices.
iii) The practices of any company(ies) electing to agree claims in respect of their own participation.'

Insurance contracts may also contain a 'follow settlements'[68] clause. In *San Evans Maritime Inc v Aigaion Insurance Co SA*[69] Teare J said 'The commercial purpose of a follow settlements clause is that from the insurers' point of view it saves time and costs and also makes co-insurance more marketable which is attractive to those seeking insurance. It simplifies claims settlement.' Recently interpretation of the 'follow the leader' clause in terms of the settlement agreement reached by the leader and the assured came before Teare J twice. In *Buana Samudra Pratama v Maritime Mutual Insurance Association (NZ) Ltd*[70] the judge held that the clause covers the quantification of the loss as well as the leader's acceptance that there is no policy defence available, for instance in terms of breach of warranty. In this case the follow the leader clause was in the terms of 'It is agreed to follow Axa HK in respect of all decisions, surveys and settlements regarding claims within the terms of the policy, unless these settlements are to be made on an ex gratia or without prejudice basis.' The insured tug, *Buana Dua*, went aground and was subsequently declared to be a constructive total loss. Axa agreed to pay their 40 per cent share of the claim. The defendant insurer, however, rejected liability by asserting a breach of warranty under the policy. The defendant said that it was not obliged to follow the settlement by the leader in circumstances where there had been a breach of warranty. Teare J focused

66   www.marketreform.co.uk/Documents/RD_Doc. . ./GUA211206.pdf
67   The heading name of Slip Leader, rather than Contract Leader, has been retained in order to maintain consistency with the GUA and other publications.
68   This should not be confused with the 'follow the settlements' clause in reinsurance contracts. For reinsuring clauses see Chapter 15.
69   [2014] EWHC 163 (Comm), para 14.
70   [2011] 2 Lloyd's Rep 655.

on the interpretation of the 'follow the leader' clause that the decision of Axa to settle the claim was a decision or settlement 'regarding claims within the terms of the policy'. The defendant, by virtue of the L/U clause, agreed to follow that decision whether or not there had been a breach of warranty. The judge further noted that the wording referred to all decisions, surveys and settlements, which suggested that it extended to both liability and quantum. Holding otherwise, according to Teare J, would greatly reduce the L/U clause's commercial purpose. In a more recent case, *San Evans Maritime Inc v Aigaion Insurance Co SA*,[71] Teare J once again construed a similar clause with regard to claim for damage to the insured vessel as a result of grounding in Brazil. The 'follow clause' was worded as: 'Agreed to follow London's Catlin and Brit Syndicate in claims excluding ex-gratia payments.' Three Lloyd's syndicates, Catlin, Ark and Brit insured 50 per cent of the interest in the St. Efrem. Twenty per cent of the interest was not insured and 30 per cent of the interest was insured by Aigaion. A claim was made under both policies. The three Lloyd's syndicates settled the claim against them. Clause 7 of the settlement agreement provided as follows:

> The settlement and release pursuant to the terms of this Agreement is made by each Underwriter for their respective participations in the Policy only and none of the Underwriters that are party to this Agreement participate in the capacity of a Leading Underwriter under the Policy and do not bind any other insurer providing hull and machinery cover in respect of the St. Efrem.

The assured claimed from Aigaion US$450,000 being 30 per cent of an 'agreed loss' of US$1.5m. Teare J noted that, under clause 7 of the settlement agreement, Catlin and Brit did not act as an agent of Aigaion. However, this did not change the overall result that Aigaion was bound to the assured to follow the settlement reached by Catlin and Brit. The crucial matter in interpretation was the Follow Clause, which was an agreement between Aigaion and the assured to follow a settlement by Catlin and Brit.[72] The operation of the Follow Clause was not dependent upon Catlin and Brit acting as agent for Aigaion so as to bind Aigaion to the settlement. Moreover, the Follow Clause was not to be understood as authorising Catlin and Brit to act on behalf of Aigaion.[73] Teare J put emphasis on the agreement between the assured and Aigaion that the latter agreed to follow the settlements reached by the leader. The Follow Clause was triggered by the Settlement Agreement to the effect of obliging Aigaion to the assured to follow the settlement reached by Catlin and Brit.

Further reading

Bennett, *Law of Marine Insurance*, 2nd edn, [2006] Oxford University Press. Chapter 2, Formation of Marine Insurance Contracts.

Birds et al., *MacGillivray on Insurance Law*, 12th edn, [2014] Sweet & Maxwell. Chapter 2, Formation of the Contract.

Clarke, *The Law of Insurance Contracts*, 4th edn, [2014] Informa. Chapter 11, Contract Formation.

Merkin, *Colinvaux's Law of Insurance*, 9th edn, [2010] Sweet & Maxwell. Chapter 1, Contract of Insurance.

Merkin et al., *Arnould: Law of Marine Insurance and Average*, 18th edn, [2013] Sweet & Maxwell. Chapter 2, Form and Contents of Marine Policies.

Rose, *Marine Insurance: Law and Practice*, 2nd edn, [2012] Informa. Chapter 6, The Contract.

---

71 [2014] EWHC 163 (Comm).
72 [2014] EWHC 163 (Comm), para 16.
73 [2014] EWHC 163 (Comm), para 21.

Chapter 3

Insurable Interest

Chapter Contents

Introduction

Insurable interest is a complex subject in marine insurance. The complexity is dual: a number of different legislative instruments, as well as the lack of an exact definition or test governing it, cause problems. The matter is sometimes a question of construction in which the courts may find insurable interest because it is commercially convenient or because it is a broad concept. Insurable interest in life insurance and indemnity insurance is regulated and interpreted differently. Since a contract of marine insurance is a contract of indemnity, in this chapter only insurable interest in the context of indemnity insurance will be discussed.

Wagering contracts

In order to prove an interest insurable against a peril, it must be an interest such that the peril would, by its proximate effect, cause damage to the assured.[1] Insurable interest is now a requirement in marine insurance policies, but until the beginning of the eighteenth century a contract of marine insurance could be enforced at common law by the assured notwithstanding the lack of a personal interest in the subject matter of the insurance. For instance a policy containing the words 'interest or no interest', or 'without further proof of interest than the policy' allowed the assured to recover against the underwriters a certain stipulated sum of money, whether he had any interest in the ship/cargo or not.[2] Thus, a policy of insurance was enforceable even if the assured stood neither to lose nor to gain from the success or failure of the adventure or the loss or survival of the insured property. These contracts were, in substance, wagering contracts[3] in which neither party had any interest in the outcome of the future uncertain event, save for that amount which was to be won or lost under the contract.[4] By the Marine Insurance Act 1745[5] for the first time by legislation in England such contracts were rendered null and void in respect of British ships and their cargoes. The purpose behind the requirement that the assured should have an insurable interest before he is permitted to recover under a marine policy was said to be to prevent wagering contracts.[6] Additionally, it has been emphasised that an insurable interest is required for the reason that a marine insurance contract is a contract of indemnity.[7] Editors of Arnould disagree with the former view for the reason that English law recognised contracts of insurance as contracts of indemnity before the 1745 Act.[8] It is submitted that preventing wagering contracts is closely linked with insurance being a contract of indemnity. It is undeniable that insurable interest was needed to prevent gaming and wagering in the eighteenth century.[9] The preamble of the 1745 Act stated: 'It hath

---

1 *Seagrave v The Union Marine Insurance Company* (1865–66) LR 1 CP 305.
2 *Assievedo v Cambridge* (1711) 10 Modern 77; *Murphy v Bell* (1828) 4 Bingham 567, 571, Best CJ. In *Dean v Dicker* (1745) 2 Strange 1250, the insurance was on goods by the *Dursley galley*, interest or no interest, at and from Jamaica to Bristol. In *Goddart v Garrett* (1692) 2 Vernon's Cases in Chancery 269 it was stated that the policy *interested or not interested* was permitted for the encouragement of trade, and not that persons unconcerned in trade, nor interested in the ship, should profit by it.
3 *Sharp v Sphere Drake Insurance (The Moonacre)* [1992] 2 Lloyd's Rep 501.
4 *Sharp v Sphere Drake Insurance (The Moonacre)* [1992] 2 Lloyd's Rep 501, 510, Mr Colman QC.
5 19 Geo. 2 c 37.
6 *Sharp v Sphere Drake Insurance (The Moonacre)* [1992] 2 Lloyd's Rep 501; In *O'Kane v Jones (The Martin P)* Richard Siberry QC said that the concept of insurable interest was introduced as a means of distinguishing 'legitimate' contracts of insurance from gaming and wagering contracts. [2004] 1 Lloyd's Rep 389, 419.
7 *Moran, Galloway & Co v Uzielli* [1905] 2 KB 555, 563. Lord Abinger CB said in *Powles v Innes* (1843) 11 Meeson and Welsby 10, at 13 'contract of insurance . . . is a contract of indemnity only, and nobody can recover in respect of the loss who is not really interested.'
8 N. Leigh-Jones QC, 'The Elements of Insurable Interest in Marine Insurance Law', in The Modern Law of Marine Insurance, vol 2 (2002), pp 136–137; Arnould, para 11–01.
9 See Martin, pp 138–139.

been found by experience, that the making of insurances, interest or no interest, or without further proof of interest than the policy, hath been productive of many pernicious practices, whereby great numbers of ships, with their cargoes, have been fraudulently lost or destroyed.' In *Murphy v Bell*[10] Best CJ stated that by the 1745 Act gambling was not the only thing guarded against,[11] the Act also aimed to prevent illegal traffic, and the means of profiting by the wilful destruction and capture of ships, particularly by privateers, which carried no cargoes, and the crews of which were composed of more persons than it was safe to trust with the secret that the ships were to be wilfully destroyed or purposely exposed to capture.[12] In *Moran, Galloway & Co v Uzielli*[13] Walton J said that 'unless the assured is exposed to a risk of real loss by the perils insured against, the contract is not a contract of indemnity, but is a mere wagering contract, and cannot be enforced'. Thus, it is submitted that insurable interest is a requirement to prevent gaming and wagering contracts as well as a matter arising from a marine insurance contract being a contract of indemnity.

Legislation

As stated above, the first legislation introducing insurable interest as a requirement of marine insurance policy was the Marine Insurance Act 1745 which provided that no assurances should be made on any goods on board any British ships –

> . . . interest or no interest, or with or without further proof of interest than the policy, or by way of gaming or wagering . . . and that every such assurance shall be null and void to all intents and purposes.[14]

So long as a policy contained words to the same effect as those enumerated in the Act, the case fell within the Act although it could be manifest that it was not a gaming insurance.[15] The policy in *Murphy v Bell* was on five tierces coffee, valued at £27 per tierce, and the 'policy was to be deemed sufficient proof of interest'. Best CJ found that the words, that 'policy to be deemed sufficient proof of interest' were of precisely the same import as the words 'without further proof of interest than the policy'. The words, 'should be valued at five tierces of coffee', admitted that five tierces of coffee belonging to the assured were on board, which would dispense with the necessity of proving that any coffee belonging to the assured was on board. As no inquiry was to be made as to whether the assured had any property in the ship insured or not, it was, in effect, an insurance 'interest or no interest', which was rendered null and void by the 1745 Act.[16] Another agreement which was defeated by the 1745 Act was discussed in *Kent v Bird*.[17] The claimant and the defendant made an agreement under which the claimant agreed to pay to the defendant £20 if the vessel arrived at the next port and the defendant agreed to pay £1000 if the vessel made her voyage to China and back to the river Thames. The claimant paid £20 to the defendant at the next port, the vessel then lost her passage. The claimant had some goods on board that were liable to suffer by the loss of the season. While it was still doubtful whether the ship would or would not save her

---

10 (1828) 4 Bingham, p 567.
11 (1828) 4 Bingham, pp 567, 570.
12 (1828) 4 Bingham, pp 567, 570–571.
13 [1905] 2 KB 555, 563.
14 The Life Assurance Act, 1774, applied the same principle to other contracts of insurance except non-marine policies on goods.
15 *Murphy v Bell* (1828) 4 Bingham 567, 570, Best CJ.
16 (1828) 4 Bingham, pp 567, 572.
17 (1777) 2 Cowper, p 583.

passage, the captain had applied to each of the parties, to persuade them to rescind the agreement. The claimant was willing to do so but the defendant refused. Lord Mansfield held that this was a case exactly which was aimed to be prevented by the Marine Insurance Act 1745. If the first of these events happened, the defendant won; but he could not lose unless both happened. This was held to be clearly gaming and wagering, which was not allowed by the Act.

Subsequently, the Marine Insurance Act 1788 required the names of those interested in the insurance to be inserted into the policy, to make it easier to check that they had a valid insurable interest. The Act applied to 'Any Policy or Policies of Assurance upon any Ship or Ships, Vessel or Vessels, or upon any Goods, Merchandizes, Effects, or other Property whatsoever.' Thus, despite its title the Act may not have been confined to marine insurance.

In 1845 the Gaming Act was passed which held that wagers were unenforceable. For general indemnity insurance, therefore, section 18 of the Gaming Act 1845 created an indirect requirement of insurable interest by providing that 'all contracts or agreements, whether by parole or in writing, by way of gaming or wagering, shall be null and void; and no suit shall be brought or maintained in any court of law or equity for recovering any sum of money or valuable thing alleged to be won upon any wager.' Section 18 had the effect of making all contracts of insurance unenforceable where no interest could be demonstrated.[18]

The Marine Insurance Act 1906 (MIA 1906) repealed the Marine Insurance Act 1745 and the Marine Insurance Act 1788 (insofar as it applied to marine policies on goods).[19]

Section 4 of the MIA 1906, entitled 'Avoidance of wagering or gaming contracts', provides:

(1) Every contract of marine insurance by way of gaming or wagering is void.
(2) A contract of marine insurance is deemed to be a gaming or wagering contract –
　　(a) Where the assured has not an insurable interest as defined by this Act, and the contract is entered into with no expectation of acquiring such an interest; or
　　(b) Where the policy is made 'interest or no interest', or 'without further proof of interest than the policy itself', or 'without benefit of salvage to the insurer', or subject to any other like term: provided that, where there is no possibility of salvage, a policy may be effected without benefit of salvage to the insurer.

The Marine Insurance (Gambling Policies) Act 1909 made taking out marine policies without insurable interest a criminal offence, punishable by a fine or imprisonment for up to six months.[20]

The Gambling Act 2005 was adopted to regulate certain types of licensed gambling activities. Gambling contracts that relate to those activities can be enforced at law. For example, it has allowed consumers to take bookmakers to court to be paid out their winnings. The Gambling Act 2005 repealed section 18 of the Gaming Act 1845.[21] In its place, the Act states that 'the fact that a contract relates to gambling shall not prevent its enforcement' (section 335(1)). This provision came into force on 1 September 2007.[22] A wager policy might fall within the definition of betting provided in the Act, which states that betting is making or accepting of a bet on the outcome of an event or process or the likelihood of anything occurring or not occurring. Thus, it is possible to argue that it could no longer be maintained that such a policy is void by reason of gaming legislation.[23]

---

18 Consultation Paper No. 201, http://lawcommission.justice.gov.uk/docs/cp201_ICL_post_contract_duties.pdf, para 11–17.
19 The Act continues to apply to non-marine insurance on 'goods, merchandizes, effects or other property', although it does not appear to have any practical effects. Consultation Paper No. 201, para 11–15.
20 The Law Commissions noted that they have not found any evidence of prosecutions under the Act, which suggests that it has not been used for the purpose for which it was enacted. Consultation Paper No. 201, para 11–25.
21 Gambling Act 2005, s 334(1)(c).
22 SI 2006 No 3272 as amended by SI 2007 No 1157.
23 Arnould, para 11–10.

However, a broader question is whether wager policies remain void under s.4 of the 1906 Act following the entry into force of section 335 of the Gambling Act 2005.[24] That section provides that the fact that a contract relates to gambling shall not prevent its enforcement, without prejudice to any rule of law preventing the enforcement of a contract on the grounds of unlawfulness (other than a rule relating specifically to gambling).

Section 4 of the MIA 1906 has not been repealed by the 2005 Act. On the other hand, section 335(1) will override any rule of law preventing enforcement of a gambling contract where that rule relates specifically to gambling. Section 4(2) of the MIA 1906 deems a policy entered into without insurable interest or the expectation of interest and ppi policies to be gaming or wagering contracts. It is arguable that section 335(1) overrides section 4 of the 1906 Act and permits the enforcement of policies entered into without insurable interest, or on terms including a ppi or similar clause, where such contracts fall within the definition of gambling in the 2005 Act. Section 335(1) however, is expressly without prejudice to any rule of law preventing the enforcement of a contract on grounds of unlawfulness (section 335(2)). On the other hand section 335(2) applies only where the rule is not a rule specifically relating to gambling. It is submitted that section 335(1) of the 2005 Act does not make contracts enforceable that are otherwise void under section 4 of the 1906 Act.[25] Section 4 has not been repealed by the 2005 Act expressly and it is unlikely that it will be deemed to have been impliedly repealed.[26] Section 10 of The Gambling Act 2005 provides that the definition of bet does not include a bet the making or acceptance of which is a regulated activity within the meaning of section 22 of the Financial Services and Markets Act 2000. Marine insurance is a regulated activity. Moreover, the indemnity principle is untouched by the 2005 Act, thus it remains the case that the assured must prove his loss when the peril occurs (section 6(1) MIA 1906).[27] Thus it appears that irrespective of section 335, there is no repeal of the MIA 1906 section 4. It should also be borne in mind that under section 4 a contract is also void for public policy reasons.[28]

Definition of insurable interest

It is difficult to provide a definition which will match all situations.[29] In *Lucena v Craufurd*[30] Lord Eldon and Lawrence J gave two different definitions of which the latter has been cited with approval in a number of cases.[31] Lord Eldon described insurable interest as 'a right in the property, or a right derivable out of some contract about the property, which in either case may be lost upon some contingency affecting the possession or enjoyment of the party.' Thus it appears that the assured must show a legal or equitable interest in the insured property or a right under a contract. This definition is narrow compared to Lawrence J's formulation of insurable interest, that is, 'to be interested in the preservation of a thing is to be so circumstanced with respect to it as to have benefit from its existence, prejudice from its destruction'. Thus, Lawrence J contemplates that an insurable interest in property can exist even if the assured does not have a proprietary or other right

24   See Rose, Marine Insurance: Law and Practice, 2nd edn, para 3.17–3.22.
25   Arnould, para 11–12.
26   Arnould, para 11–12.
27   See Colinvaux, para 4–009.
28   Cheshire v Vaughan [1920] 3 KB 240, 251, Bankes LJ.
29   Feasey v Sun Life Assurance Co of Canada [2003] Lloyd's Rep IR 637, para 66.
30   (1806) 2 B & PNR 269.
31   Moran Galloway & Co v Uzielli [1905] 2 KB 555, 561, Walton J; Wilson v Jones (1866–1867) LR 2 Ex 139, 150–151, Blackburn J.

to that property.[32] It is sufficient to have some relation to, or concern in the subject of the insurance, which relation or concern by the happening of the perils insured against may be so affected as to produce a damage, detriment, or prejudice to the person insuring.[33]

In *Lucena v Craufurd*[34] the assured were commissioners, whose duty was under a statutory commission to take charge of Dutch vessels and cargoes 'which had been or might be thereafter detained in or brought into the ports of the United Kingdom'. Before the commission was issued, certain Dutch vessels and their cargoes had been seized by order of the British Government for the purpose of being brought to the United Kingdom. After the commission was issued, the commissioners insured these ships and their cargoes. The ships with their cargoes were lost before arrival in the United Kingdom, and the commissioners brought an action upon the policy. Under these circumstances Lawrence J expressed his opinion that, as the purpose and object of the commission was only to take care of the Dutch property after its arrival in England, and the commissioners till then had not any power to interfere with it, and could not in their character of commissioners suffer any damage by a loss happening before they had any concern in the ships or goods, they could not be said at the time of the loss to have had any insurable interest. In the words of Lord Eldon: 'That expectation, though founded upon the highest probability, was not interest, and it was equally not interest, whatever might have been the chances in favour of the expectation.'

The modern definition of insurable interest emphasises that the context and the terms of a policy with which the court is concerned will be all important.[35] Waller LJ said in *Feasey v Sun Life Assurance Co of Canada* that the definition of insurable interest in the context of property insurance should not be slavishly followed in different contexts.[36] It is also worth adding that in *Sharp v Sphere Drake Insurance (The Moonacre)*[37] Mr Colman QC sitting as a deputy judge opined that '. . . the essential question . . . to test the existence of an insurable interest has been whether the relationship between the assured and the subject matter of the insurance was sufficiently close to justify his being paid in the event of its loss or damage, having regard to the fact that, if there were no or no sufficiently close relationship, the contract would be a wagering contract.'

Although it does not provide an exhaustive definition,[38] section 5(2) of the MIA 1906 identifies three characteristics which the presence of an insurable interest would normally require:[39]

1 The assured may benefit by the safety or due arrival of insurable property or be prejudiced by its loss or damage or detention or in respect of which he may incur liability.
2 The assured stands in a legal or equitable relation to the adventure or to any insurable property at risk in such adventure.
3 The benefit, prejudice or incurring of liability referred to at (1) must arise in consequence of the legal or equitable relation referred to at (2).

---

32 *Sharp v Sphere Drake Insurance (The Moonacre)* [1992] 2 Lloyd's Rep 501, 511.
33 Similarly, the Law Commissions define insurable interest as 'this means that someone taking out insurance must stand to gain a benefit from the preservation of the subject matter of the insurance or to suffer a disadvantage should it be lost'. Consultation Paper No. 201, para 10.1.
34 (1806) 2 B & PNR 269.
35 *Feasey v Sun Life Assurance Co of Canada* [2003] Lloyd's Rep IR 637, para 66.
36 *Feasey v Sun Life Assurance Co of Canada* [2003] Lloyd's Rep IR 637, para 66.
37 [1992] 2 Lloyd's Rep 501.
38 *O'Kane v Jones (The Martin P)* [2004] 1 Lloyd's Rep 389.
39 *Sharp v Sphere Drake Insurance (The Moonacre)* [1992] 2 Lloyd's Rep 501, 510 Mr Colman QC.

Types of interest

Ownership

Ownership of property carries with it an insurable interest. In a contract of sale existence of a legally binding agreement is required to prove insurable interest. In *Stockdale v Dunlop*[40] it was held that if there is no legally binding agreement upon which the assured agreed to buy goods he has no insurable interest to insure the goods and the profit thereon. Lord Abinger CB stated that if contracts for goods to be purchased in future were allowed to be the subject of insurance, it would be allowing a wager policy to be made.[41]

Contingent interest

Where a seller sells the goods and the title passes to the buyer before payment the seller has a contingent interest in the goods. His interest is contingent upon the buyer rejecting the goods. Under a C&F contract the buyer will have a contingent interest which might accrue to him from the completion of the loading of the cargo on board the vessel and its safe delivery. In *Anderson v Morice*[41a] the buyer insured the cargo of rice, which he purchased from the seller 'at and from Rangoon, to any port in the United Kingdom or Continent, by the *Sunbeam*, on rice, as interest may appear'. While loading at Rangoon, the *Sunbeam* sank together with the greater part of the cargo having been shipped. The rice already shipped was wholly lost but after the sinking the captain signed bills of lading for the cargo shipped, which were endorsed to the buyer who paid for the lost cargo. The buyer was held to have had no insurable interest in the goods that sank. The question was whether the buyer was so situated with respect to the rice in question at the time of its loss that he would, if uninsured, have suffered any loss from the destruction of the rice. The question then followed whether each separate bag was at the risk of the buyer from the time it was put on board the *Sunbeam*, or whether it remained at the risk of the sellers until the whole intended loading was complete. The sale contract was on C&F terms so that the rice was at the risk of the buyer from the time it had been loaded on board the ship, and that therefore he had an insurable interest in it from that time. At the time of the casualty the goods had not been appropriated to the contract so that neither risk nor title had passed yet to the buyer. It was therefore held that while some of the cargo had been loaded, the buyer had no insurable interest and the payment he made was voluntary.

Mortgagor and mortgagee

There may be other persons besides the owner who 'may be prejudiced by its loss' and they also would have an insurable interest. For instance the mortgagee has interest to insure a vessel that is herself the security upon which money has been lent. A mortgagee has, by virtue of his position and his interest in the property, a right to insure for the whole of its value, holding on trust for the owner of the amount attributable to their interest.[42] The mortgagor however is entitled to insure his ship for her full value.

---

40 (1840) 6 Meeson Welsby, p 224.
41 (1840) 6 Meeson Welsby, pp 224, 232.
41a (1876) 1 App Cas 713.
42 *Hepburn v A Tomlinson (Hauliers) Ltd* [1966] AC 451, 478, Lord Pearce.

Profit

Profits may be insured, on the ground that they form an additional part of the value of the goods, in which the party has already an interest.[43] The owner of goods on board a vessel may insure the profits to arise from them. Similarly, a consignee, or a factor in respect of his commission may insure his profit.

Pervasive interest

Pervasive interest may be found in commercial contracts as a matter of commercial convenience.[44] In the case of the construction industry in which several parties undertake performance of contract works on site, for example, a building site, a ship yard or at an oil refinery, it will be convenient if the head contractor takes out a single policy covering all contractors and sub-contractors in respect of loss of or damage to the entire contract works. While the construction contract is being performed, a claim against the sub-contractor may be brought for damage negligently caused to property owned by another party involved in the project. Both the parties who caused the loss and who suffered the loss are insured under a composite policy and it may then be necessary to consider whether in relation to that damaged property the sub-contractor had an insurable interest in the property to claim from the insurer to remedy the loss.[45] It may be argued that the sub-contractor will have an insurable interest in his own goods and equipment during performance of the sub-contract works, but since he has no title to or possessory interest in the other property involved in the project he can have no sufficient interest in such property to constitute an insurable interest. The answer to the argument will be that it is now beyond dispute that an insurable interest in property can exist even if the assured does not have a proprietary or other right to that property.[46] It may also be asserted that the interest of such a contractor is not in the other property but in his potential liability to the owners of such property for loss of or damage to it caused by his breach of contract or duty. It follows that since the insurance in question is an insurance on property and not on liability, there would be no relevant insurable interest. The policy is indeed on property[47] but the courts unanimously rejected such an argument and found insurable interest in favour of a contractor or a sub-contractor. [48] Although the sub-contractors were not given possession of the works as a whole, on any construction site there is ever present the possibility of damage by one tradesman to the property of another and to the construction as a whole.[49] Insurable interest here finds its source in the contractual arrangements, which open the doors of the job site to the

---

43   *Stockdale v Dunlop* (1840) 6 Meeson Welsby, pp 224, 232 Parke B.

44   Commercial convenience has been emphasised in a number of cases as part of the justification of finding insurable interest. See for example, *Hepburn v A Tomlinson (Hauliers) Ltd* [1966] AC 451, 477 and 481 Lord Pearce; *O'Kane v Jones (The Martin P)* [2004] 1 Lloyd's Rep 389, 419 and the construction cases which will be cited below.

45   This issue was discussed in terms of subrogation claims against a co-assured. Irrespective of the discussion in relation to insurable interest, the latest view is that in principle the insurer is entitled to bring a subrogation action against a co-assured. For an in-depth discussion of subrogation in co-insurance, see Chapter 13.

46   Lawrence, J., *Lucena v Carufurd* (1806) 2 B & PNR 269, 301–302; *O'Kane v Jones (The Martin P)* [2004] 1 Lloyd's Rep 389, 421; *National Oilwell (UK) Ltd v Davy Offshore Ltd* [1993] 2 Lloyd's Rep 582, 611.

47   In *Commonwealth Construction Co Ltd v Imperial Oil Ltd* (1977) 69 DLR (3d) 558, the policy covered: 'all materials . . . and all other property of any nature whatsoever owned by the insured or in which the insured may have an interest or responsibility or for which the insured may be liable or assume liability prior to loss or damage . . .' It was held that this is a property insurance, not liability insurance.

48   *Commonwealth Construction Co Ltd v Imperial Oil Ltd* (1977) 69 DLR (3d) 558; *Petrofina (UK) Ltd v Magnaload Ltd* [1984] QB 127, *National Oilwell (UK) Ltd v Davy Offshore Ltd* [1993] 2 Lloyd's Rep 582, *Deepak Fertilisers & Petrochemicals Corp v Davy McKee (London) Ltd* [1999] 1 Lloyd's Rep 387; *Stone Vickers Ltd v Appledore Ferguson Shipbuilders Ltd* [1991] 2 Lloyd's Rep 288. The appeal in *Stone Vickers* was allowed on other grounds, the Court of Appeal therefore did not discuss the insurable interest issue. [1992] 2 Lloyd's Rep 578, 585.

49   *Commonwealth Construction Co Ltd v Imperial Oil Ltd* (1977) 69 DLR (3d) 558.

tradesmen.[50] In *Petrofina v Magnaload* Lloyd J held that it is a matter of convenience to allow the head contractor to take out a single policy covering the whole risk, including all contractors and sub-contractors in respect of loss of or damage to the entire contract works. If each party involved in such arrangements takes out individual policies it would mean extra paperwork or could lead to overlapping claims and cross-claims in the event of an accident.[51] Furthermore, the cost of insuring his liability might, in the case of a small sub-contractor, be uneconomic; the premium might be out of all proportion to the value of the sub-contract. [52] If the sub-contractor had to insure his liability in respect of the entire works, he might as well have to decline the contract.[53]

The authorities referred to a bailee who is able to insure goods for the whole of their value, holding over the amount recovered in excess of his own interest as trustee for others with an interest in the goods, such as the true owner or mortgagee. It is a matter of whether the supplier of a part to be installed into the vessel or contract works under construction might be materially adversely affected by loss of or damage to the vessel or other works by reason of the incidence of any of the perils insured against by the policy in question. The cases referred to in this part established that if the answer to that question is in the affirmative then a sub-contractor should also have sufficient interest in the whole contract works to be included as co-assured under the protection of the head contractor's policy. A sub-contractor ought to be able to recover the whole of the loss insured, holding the excess over his own interest in trust for the others.

In *Stone Vickers Ltd v Appledore Ferguson Shipbuilders Ltd*,[54] for instance, the sub-contractor responsible for constructing and supplying the propeller, tailshaft and ancillary equipment did have such an interest in the whole contract works and accordingly would have been entitled to sue as co-assured under the policy. In *Talbot Underwriting Ltd v Nausch Hogan & Murray Inc (The Jascon 5)*,[55] an offshore pipelay construction barge owned by CPL was sent to S's shipyard in Singapore for repair and refurbishment. Under the contract S was liable to indemnify CPL against all loss or damage to the property, and S was required to insure its liability (clause 13). The insurance in question was a shipbuilders' all risks policy of insurance on the vessel's hull and machinery in respect of the period of the completion work. In the Court of Appeal Moore-Bick LJ recognised that S would have been entitled to retain the proceeds of the policy in order to recover the cost of making good the damage.[56] Its entitlement to receive payment of the contract price, 90 per cent of which was payable on practical completion, depended upon the satisfactory performance of all its obligations and on its ability to hand the vessel over to CPL in the condition required by the contract. All the equipment that had been installed under the contract remained at its risk until that time and it had no choice but to replace, repair or clean it as necessary in order to meet those requirements. Clause 13 gave S an insurable interest in the vessel as a whole (including the hull) and it would have been entitled to recover the cost of making good the damage in order to obtain payment under the contract.

The definition of insurable interest under section 5(2) of the MIA 1906 is also a broad concept and it is sufficient under section 5 for a person interested in a marine adventure to stand in a 'legal or equitable relation to the adventure'.[57] This was confirmed by Mr Siberry QC in *O'Kane v Jones (The Martin P)*,[58] in which *The Martin P* was owned by Nanice Schiffahrts AG (Nanice) and was under the

---

50 In analogy with bailment: *Commonwealth Construction Co Ltd v Imperial Oil Ltd* (1977) 69 DLR (3d) 558.
51 *Petrofina (UK) Ltd v Magnaload Ltd* [1984] QB 127; *National Oilwell (UK) Ltd v Davy Offshore Ltd* [1993] 2 Lloyd's Rep 582.
52 *Petrofina (UK) Ltd v Magnaload Ltd* [1984] QB 127; *National Oilwell (UK) Ltd v Davy Offshore Ltd* [1993] 2 Lloyd's Rep 582.
53 *Petrofina (UK) Ltd v Magnaload Ltd* [1984] QB 127; *National Oilwell (UK) Ltd v Davy Offshore Ltd* [1993] 2 Lloyd's Rep 582.
54 [1991] 2 Lloyd's Rep 288.
55 [2006] 2 Lloyd's Rep 195.
56 [2006] 2 Lloyd's Rep 195, para 56.
57 *Feasey v Sun Life Assurance Co of Canada* [2003] Lloyd's Rep IR 637, para 92, Waller LJ.
58 [2004] 1 Lloyd's Rep 389.

management of ABC Maritime AG (ABC). ABC purchased a Hull and Machinery policy insuring the *Martin P*. The insurance contract stated the assured as: 'ABC Maritime as Managers and/or affiliated and/or associated companies for their respective rights and interests.'

Mr Siberry QC held that ABC had an insurable interest in the vessel which satisfied the requirements of MIA section 5(2). ABC stood in a legal relationship to the vessel deriving from the management agreement. In consequence of this relationship ABC might have benefited by the vessel's safety, it might have been prejudiced by its loss or by damage thereto, and it might have incurred a liability in respect thereof. Although they did not give ABC possession or the right to possession of the vessel, and although the commercial management of the vessel was in other hands, those provisions gave ABC considerable control over the vessel and its operation. The management agreement imposed extensive and ongoing responsibilities upon ABC in relation, among other things, to the maintenance, equipping, repair, survey, classification, crewing, provisioning, operation and navigation of the vessel. Moreover, ABC was entitled to remuneration under the management agreement for the services it provided. Pursuant to clause 8.5, the management agreement automatically terminated if and when the vessel became a total loss: in that event, ABC would be deprived of the opportunity of continuing to earn remuneration thereunder. That was sufficient benefit, and corresponding prejudice, for the purposes of section 5(2).

Shareholder

A shareholder does not have insurable interest in the property owned by the company.[59] This was established in *Macaura v Northern Assurance Company, Ltd*[60] in which the owner of the Killymoon estate sold all the timber on the estate to the Irish Canadian Saw Mills, Ltd. The company paid some of the price by allotting the only shares issued by the company in the name of the owner of the estate. This however did not pay the whole contractual price, therefore the company still owed some for the sale of the timber, which rendered the owner of the estate as the creditor of the company. Except some chattels of small value, the only assets of the Canadian company were the said timber.

The owner of the estate insured the timber in his own name. The greater part of the timber on the estate was destroyed by fire. The action against the insurers was dismissed by the House of Lords for the reason that the assured did not have an interest on the timber as a shareholder of the company. The timber was owned by the company, but practically the whole interest in the company was owned by the assured. He owned almost all the shares in the company, and the company owed him a good deal of money, but the debt was not exposed to fire nor were the shares, and the fact that he was virtually the company's only creditor, while the timber was its only asset, according to Lord Sumner, made no difference. He stood in no 'legal or equitable relation to' the timber at all. He had no concern in the subject matter insured.[61] His relation was to the company, not to its goods, and after the fire he was directly prejudiced by the paucity of the company's assets, not by the fire.[62]

Lord Buckmaster held that the assured is entitled to a share in the profits while the company continues to carry on business and a share in the distribution of the surplus assets when the company is wound up. If he were at liberty to effect an insurance against loss by fire of any item of the company's property, the extent of his insurable interest could only be measured by determining

---

59 *Macaura v Northern Assurance Company, Ltd* [1925] AC 619; *Wilson v Jones* (1866–67) LR 2 Ex 139.
60 [1925] AC 619.
61 [1925] AC 619, 630, Lord Sumner.
62 [1925] AC 619, 630, Lord Sumner. The assured would receive the benefit of any profit and on him would fall the burden of any loss. But Lord Buckmaster held that the principles on which the decision of this case rests must be independent of the extent of the interest held. [1925] AC 619, 625.

the extent to which his share in the ultimate distribution would be diminished by the loss of the asset – a calculation, as Lord Buckmaster found, almost impossible to make. There is no means by which such an interest can be definitely measured and no standard which can be fixed of the loss against which the contract of insurance could be regarded as an indemnity. *Macaura* should be distinguished from *Wilson v Jones*,[63] where the policy was held not upon the cable but upon the shareholder's interest in the adventure of the cable being successfully laid. Both Martin B in the Court of Exchequer and Willes J in the Exchequer Chamber stated that the claimant had no direct interest in the cable as a shareholder in the company.

Valuable benefit

As has been observed up to now the rules about insurable interest might be flexible, in terms of pervasive interest and might also be very rigid as seen in *Macaura*. One of the examples of flexible rules about insurable interest can be observed in *Wilson v Jones*,[64] which is to be distinguished from *Macaura* because of the wording of the policy. In *Wilson v Jones* a joint-stock company sought to establish for profit a telegraph across the Atlantic, and for that purpose to lay down a line of cable for 2000 miles over the bottom of the sea. A shareholder in the Atlantic Telegraph Company purchased a marine policy that provided:

> Lost or not lost, at and from Ireland to Newfoundland, the risk to commence at the lading of the cable on board the *Great Eastern*, and to continue until the cable be laid down in one continuous length between Ireland and Newfoundland, and until 100 words shall have been transmitted from Ireland to Newfoundland, and vice versa . . .

The policy further stated

> . . . it is hereby understood and agreed that the policy, in addition to all perils and casualties herein specified, shall cover every risk and contingency attending the conveyance and successful laying of the cable, from and including its loading on board the *Great Eastern*, until 100 words be transmitted from Ireland to Newfoundland . . .

The adventure failed as the cable was broken in an attempt to haul it in the course of laying it; only one half of the cable was saved. Willes J stated that the assured had no direct interest in the cable. As a shareholder, he had an interest in the profits to be made by the company, but he had none in the property of the company itself. Willes J emphasised the identification of the subject matter insured which in one sense was on the cable; that is, it affects the cable, as an insurance on freight affects the ship. Willes J stated however that, taking into account the language of the policy, the insurance was not on the cable, but on the interest which the assured had in the success of the adventure. Having considered the two following clauses together Willes J held that this was an insurance on the assured's interest in the adventure. (1) 'The said ship, &c., goods and merchandize, &c., for so much as concerns the assured, by agreement between the assured and assurers in this policy are and shall be valued at £200 on the Atlantic cable.'[65] (2) This was followed by the words 'value, say on twenty shares, valued at £10 per share', which indicated that the thing insured was the value of the assured's shares, or rather his interest in the profits to be derived from his shares

---

63 (1866–1867) LR 2 Ex 139.
64 (1866–1867) LR 2 Ex 139.
65 If these words stood alone, they would be obviously an insufficient description of the interest which the plaintiff possessed.

when the cable should have been laid, either on that occasion, or at some future time. The following words were written on the margin: 'It is hereby understood and agreed that this policy, in addition to all perils and casualties herein specified, shall cover every risk and contingency attending the conveyance and successful laying of the cable.'

Macaura was distinguished in *Sharp v Sphere Drake Insurance (The Moonacre)*[66] where the assured was held to have had valuable benefit on the subject matter insured, which was sufficient to prove insurable interest. The assured, Mr Sharp, purchased the *Moonacre* as his personal boat. For tax efficiency purposes the boat was registered in the name of Roarer Investments Ltd. Mr Colman QC, sitting as a deputy judge, noted that it was Mr Sharp's personal boat in every sense and by two powers of attorney Roarer had conferred on Mr Sharp authority to enjoy the use of the vessel exclusively for his own purposes.[67] Mr Sharp insured the *Moonacre* in his own name. The boat sank after a fire caught at her moorings. Mr Colman QC held that the two powers of attorney by which Roarer had conferred on Mr Sharp authority to enjoy the use of the vessel exclusively for his own purposes was a valuable benefit which would be lost if the vessel was lost. As long as the powers of attorney remained he was entitled to use it for his own purposes and to exercise over it such control as he saw fit, so much so that he could even abandon it to the insurers in the event of a constructive total loss. Mr Sharp by reason of the powers of attorney stood in a legal relationship to the vessel in consequence of which he would benefit from the preservation of the vessel and if the vessel were lost or damaged he would suffer loss of a valuable benefit. Mr Colman QC distinguished *The Moonacre* from *Macaura* for the reason that in the latter the assured had neither beneficial rights over or in respect of the timber nor obligations in respect of it.

In line with the abovementioned authorities Waller LJ emphasised in *Feasey v Sun Life Assurance Co of Canada*[68] that the nature of an assured's insurable interest must be discovered from all the surrounding circumstances. The judge noted that there is no hard and fast rule that because the nature of an insurable interest relates to a liability to compensate for loss that insurable interest could only be covered by a liability policy rather than a policy insuring property or life.[69] In *Feasey*, Steamship insured the liabilities of their members for personal injury or death. In about June 1995 in order to cover its liability to its members, rather than entering into a conventional reinsurance, Steamship entered into a Personal Accident and Illness Master Lineslip Policy with Syndicate 957.[70] The syndicate agreed to pay fixed benefits to Steamship in respect of bodily injury and/or illness sustained by a person (an original person) who was engaged in any capacity on board a vessel or offshore rig, entered by a member with Steamship. The basic idea was to provide a fixed level of benefit payable on proof of the fact of death, PTD (Permanent Total Disability) or TTD (Temporary Total Disability) of an Original Person with medical expenses payable in addition. The level of benefits could not and would not track with any precision the amount of the actual liability of the member of Steamship, or Steamship itself, in respect of the death, PTD or TTD relating to the

---

66 [1992] 2 Lloyd's Rep 501.
67 Roarer Investments executed under seal a power of attorney by which it granted to Mr Sharp the power to do and perform various acts and things on behalf of and in the name of the company 'as he shall think proper', including the powers to enter into contracts relating to the chartering and employment of the vessel and for that purpose to make sign and execute all charterparties and other documents which Mr Sharp might think requisite as well as to do all such other acts in or about the management of the vessel as Roarer could do.
68 [2003] Lloyd's Rep IR 637, para 92.
69 [2003] Lloyd's Rep IR 637, para 92.
70 The reason for insuring Steamship in this way was the change that occurred at Lloyd's from January 1995. Accident and Health policies could only be classified as Personal Accident Insurance if payments were on a fixed benefit basis. Liability or contingent cover was treated as long tail business for reserving purposes. Personal Accident cover was treated as short tail and so did not require provision of substantial reserves to be held for long periods.

individual original person. But it was intended that overall Steamship's recovery under the Master Lineslip should track as closely as possible Steamship's overall exposure.

Syndicate 957 reinsured its liability under the Master Lineslip. The reinsurers argued that Steamship had no 'insurable interest' in the lives and wellbeing of the original persons, when entering into the Master Lineslip for the three years from February 1997 and after. Steamship was held to have had insurable interest in the lives and wellbeing of Original Persons as defined by the policy. The policy was not on any view simply a 'life' policy that would pay Steamship on the death of a particular identified individual. It was agreeing to pay fixed sums by reference to bodily injury and/or illness sustained by Original Persons but in relation to losses occurring in respect of member entries. Members were defined as owners and/or other persons interested in any entered vessel to whom the insured had obligations under its rules. The object of the policy was to cover Steamship for the losses it would suffer as the insurer of its members under its rules. The policy did so by reference to fixed sums payable on the occurrence of certain events, those events being within the general ambit of events for which members and thus Steamship would have to pay. Furthermore, Steamship would only be entitled to keep those sums paid as fixed sums where liability as between the member and the Original Person was in fact established. Steamship had a pecuniary interest in covering losses over the three-year period for which it may be liable. The interest existed at the time the policy was taken out as Steamship had a legal obligation which might have led to substantial sums being payable. Such an interest was capable of pecuniary evaluation; at the very least it was possible to say that the overall limit did not exceed the potential liability.

Ordinary creditor

The assured in *Macaura* had no lien or security over the timber and, though it lay on his land by his permission, he had no responsibility to its owner for its safety, nor was it there under any contract that enabled him to hold it for his debt. The assured thus did not have insurable interest on the timber as an ordinary creditor of the company. An *obiter* statement to this effect in *Moran Galloway v Uzielli* was cited with approval by Lord Buckmaster in *Macaura*. In *Moran, Galloway & Co v Uzielli*[71] ship's agents had effected an insurance for a named voyage 'on disbursements against the risk of total and constructive loss of ship only' and brought an action on the policy to recover the balance of advances for which the shipowners were indebted to them. They contended that they had an interest, not merely in freight, but in the ship itself as the practical security for the payment of what was owed to them by the shipowners. They argued that the ship was at all events the principal, if not the only, asset of the shipowners after the freight. The claimant therefore argued that the recovery of the debt owed to them for their advances was in fact dependent on the safe arrival of the ship. In other words, the recovery of the debt was rendered less certain and more difficult by the loss of the ship. Walton J held that the claimants did not have insurable interest insofar as their claim depended upon the fact that they were ordinary unsecured creditors of the shipowners for an ordinary unsecured debt. Insofar as the indebtedness gave rise to a right in rem against the ship itself, they had an insurable interest in the ship sufficient to support a claim on the policy. At the date of the policy and at the date of the loss the claimants had advanced moneys for the necessaries of the *Prince Louis*. The ship was at sea on her voyage to Cardiff. The claimant had a then existing right which would entitle them immediately after the arrival of the ship at Cardiff to arrest her under process; and by so doing, to obtain 'security for prompt and immediate payment'. If the ship were lost, the right to obtain this security on the *Prince Louis* would be gone.

---

71 [1905] 2 KB 555.

Bailee

A bailee is entitled to insure and recover the full value of the goods bailed.[72] A bailee can recover the value of the goods even though he has suffered no personal loss; he will be trustee for the owners. The bailee's possessory interest in the goods is sufficient to enable him to recover the full value of the goods in trover.[73] Bailee is responsible for the goods. Responsibility is here used in a different sense from legal liability.[74] Although a bailee might by contract exclude his legal liability for loss of or damage to the goods in particular circumstances, for example, by fire, he would still be responsible for the goods in a more general sense.[75] Moreover, it is highly convenient to entitle a bailee to insure the full value of the goods.[76] 'Goods in trust' means goods with which the assured was entrusted; not goods held on trust in the strict technical sense – goods with which they were entrusted in the ordinary sense of the word.[77]

In *Hepburn v A Tomlinson (Hauliers) Ltd* a road haulier claimed on an all risks insurance policy taken out by him on tobacco goods and machinery, the property of a third party, in respect of the theft of cigarettes from its lorries. The theft had occurred without any negligence on the part of the haulier. The policy was held on its true construction to be a policy on goods, and not a liability policy. It was held that as bailee the haulier had an insurable interest in the goods up to their full value.[78]

The terms of the bailment agreement are to be taken into account to determine the insurable interest of a bailee. While in *Macaura* the existence of bailment was not enough to give rise to an insurable interest, in *The Moonacre* the terms of the bailment were such that they conferred on the bailee a valuable benefit, and the risk of loss of that benefit could quite properly found an insurable interest in the vessel itself.

Expectation

Where the interest insured is the expectancy of benefit to arise out of the safe arrival of a certain subject of insurance, some legal right in relation to such property must be vested in the assured at the time of loss to enable him to recover.[79] To eliminate the possibility of wager, the mere hope of a future relationship with the property is not sufficient to find an insurable interest.[80] If the assured has an expectation of benefit from some subject which he is not interested in, but only expects to be so interested, this is a mere expectation of an interest, and is thus not an insurable interest.[81] An example of this is the expectation of commissions to arise out of the sale and disposal of a homeward cargo not contracted for at the time of the ship's loss.[82] In *Buchanan v Faber* the benefit to the assured from the preservation of the property arose only from the possibility that the assured would in future make a contract which, if the goods survived, would or could confer benefits on him. In such cases the only relationship between the assured and the property is an expectation or possibility of the future acquisition of a closer relationship giving rise to rights dependent upon

---

72 *Waters v Monarch Fire and Life Assurance Co* (1856) 5 E & B 870.

73 *Waters v Monarch Fire and Life Assurance Co* (1856) 5 E & B 870; *Petrofina (UK) Ltd v Magnaload Ltd* [1984] QB 127, 135.

74 *Petrofina (UK) Ltd v Magnaload Ltd* [1984] QB 127, 135.

75 *Petrofina (UK) Ltd v Magnaload Ltd* [1984] QB 127, 135.

76 *Petrofina (UK) Ltd v Magnaload Ltd* [1984] QB 127, 135, 135–136.

77 *Waters v Monarch Fire and Life Assurance Co* (1856) 5 E & B 870, 880 Lord Campbell CJ.

78 Pervasive interest held in relation to insurance taken out as a requirement of a construction contract is found to exist by analogy with bailment. See the discussion above.

79 Arnould, para 11–36.

80 *Sharp v Sphere Drake Insurance (The Moonacre)* [1992] 2 Lloyd's Rep 501, 511, Mr Colman QC.

81 Arnould, para 11–36.

82 *Buchanan v Faber*, (1899) 4 Com Cas 223; *Stockdale v Dunlop* (1840) 6 Meeson Welsby, p 224.

the preservation of the property.[83] Insurable interest exists once one can establish at the time of loss the existence of rights enjoyed by the assured in respect of the insured property, and that if it is lost or damaged such rights will or may be less beneficial, regardless of the precise nature of the rights or the means by which they have been acquired.[84] There then can be said to exist a risk of loss against which the assured can, consistently with the law against wagering contracts, ask to be indemnified for.

'as interest might appear thereafter.'

Both the subject matter insured and insurable interest are required to be described in the policy. Lord Tenterden CJ expressed in *Crowley v Cohen*[85] the view that the nature of insurable interest may in general be left at large. In *Crowley* the policy provided insurance on 'The said ship, &c. goods and merchandizes, &c. for so much as concerns the assureds, by agreement between the assureds and assurers in this policy, are and shall be twelve thousand pounds on goods as interest may appear hereafter, to pay average on each package or description as if separately insured, warranted free from damage or loss that may arise from wet occasioned by rain, snow or hail . . .' One of the vessels insured departed from London on the 17 January 1829 and on 29 January she sank with the goods on board. It was argued that the policy did not cover the interest of the shipowners, since it purported to protect goods against the usual risks to which the owners of goods are liable, whereas the loss alleged was one arising out of the shipowners' liability as carriers to risks to which carriers are liable. Lord Tenterden CJ stated that here the subject matter is very sufficiently described, and the policy provided that the sum to be received in case of loss was to be for further consideration 'as interest might appear thereafter'. Lord Tenterden found this not an artificial frame. His Lordship noted that it would have been better if it had expressly provided that the object was to indemnify the shipowners as carriers but still, as it stands, the clause was sufficient to describe insurable interest. Patteson J added that it is only necessary, in such a policy as this, to state accurately the subject matter insured, not the particular interest which the assured has in it.

Defeasible interest

Defeasible interest is insurable.[86] If the party in whom interest is averred has parted with his interest after the loss, the underwriter cannot, on that ground, resist his claim on the policy. In *Sparkes v Marshall*[87] B sold to the claimant from 500 to 700 barrels of oats to be shipped by J from Youghall and to be delivered at Portsmouth. Four days afterwards B advised the claimant that J had engaged room in the packet to take about 600 barrels of oats on the claimant's account. On the following day the claimant insured £400 on oats per packet. The oats were shipped; but the packet being bound for Southampton and refusing to touch at Portsmouth, B sold the oats again and delivered the bill of lading to O. In the meantime the packet was lost. It was held that the claimant had a sufficient interest to sue the underwriter on this policy.

---

83   *Sharp v Sphere Drake Insurance (The Moonacre)* [1992] 2 Lloyd's Rep 501, 511, Mr Colman QC.
84   *Sharp v Sphere Drake Insurance (The Moonacre)* [1992] 2 Lloyd's Rep 501, 511, Mr Colman QC.
85   (1832) 3 Barnewall and Adolphus, p 478.
86   Section 7 MIA 1906.
87   (1836) 2 Bingham New Cases 761.

Partial interest

Partial interest in the whole of the cargo loaded on board a ship may be insured. In *Inglis v Stock*[88] D sold to B 200 tons of German sugar 'f.o.b. Hamburg; payment by cash in London in exchange for bill of lading'. B resold to S the same quantity at an increased price, but otherwise upon similar terms. D also sold to S 200 tons upon similar terms. The quantity actually put on board the *City of Dublin* at Hamburg was only 3,900 bags, or 390 tons; no bags were set apart for one contract more than the other. Each bag was marked with its percentage of saccharine matter, and bills of lading with marks corresponding to the bags were sent to D to be retained until payment in accordance with the contracts was made. S was insured under floating policies upon 'any kind of goods and merchandises' between Hamburg and Bristol, and duly declared in respect of this cargo. The ship sailed from Hamburg for Bristol and was lost. After receiving news of the loss D allocated 2,000 bags or 200 tons to B's contract, and 1,900 bags or 190 tons to the other contract. It was contended that a proper division before the loss was required whereas the loss happened before the actual allocation; B's loss was a loss not of 200 tons, but of a 200 tons parcel of 390 tons. The shipment did not have the effect of divesting the prior title of D, or of passing any interest in these sugars to B. Lord Blackburn rejected that this should make any difference. According to his Lordship an undivided interest in a parcel of goods on board a ship may be described as an interest in goods just as much as if it were an interest in every portion of the goods. Lord Blackburn held that in the case of an insurance on goods the assured may show that he had at the time of the loss the whole legal property in the goods which were lost. But this is not the only way in which he can show an insurable interest in goods. The fact that any relation to goods such that if the goods perish on the voyage the person will lose the whole, and if they arrive safe will have all or part of the goods, will give an interest which may be aptly described as goods. D had no interest in favouring one more than the other and were to be paid exactly the same price per bag whether they allocated it to the one or to the other. What damage either B or S could have sustained by the allocation being made in London instead of in Hamburg could not be seen.

Freight

Freight may be defined as the benefit derived by the shipowner from the employment of his ship.[89] A shipowner may prove his insurable interest on the freight by showing that but for the intervention of some of the perils insured against, some freight would have been earned under a contract of carriage.[90] Thus, if there is a charterparty and the ship is lost, he is entitled to recover for the freight.[91] Freight may be payable in advance and where this is so the right of insurance rests with the shipper, as there is no claim against the shipowner for a refund of freight in the event of the vessel being totally lost. Therefore, if part of the freight is advanced and the ship is lost, or the goods are lost, the part so advanced cannot be recovered back by the charterer from the shipowner although it was not due under the terms of the contract without delivery of the goods.[92] Moreover, if the parties agreed that there shall be advance freight which is payable at the commencement of the voyage, the shipowner is entitled to recover the freight from the charterer upon the loss of the ship.[93] The words 'one-third freight, if required, to be advanced, less 3 per cent. for interest

---

88   (1885) 10 App Cas 263.
89   *Flint v Flemyng* (1830) 1 Barnewall and Adolphus 45, 48, Lord Tenterden.
90   *Cepheus Shipping Corp v Guardian Royal Exchange Assurance plc (The Capricorn)* [1995] 1 Lloyd's Rep 622, the shipowner was unable to recover on his loss of hire insurance because the vessel would have been out of the market anyway.
91   *Davidson v Willasey* (1813) 1 Maule and Selwyn, p 313.
92   *Smith, Hill & Co v Pyman, Bell & Co* [1891] 1 QB 742, Lord Esher MR.
93   *Smith, Hill & Co v Pyman, Bell & Co* [1891] 1 QB 742, Lord Esher MR.

and insurance' were interpreted as requiring the shipowner to demand the payment of advance freight before the loss occurred. If the demand was not made by the shipowners at a time when it was enforceable, there is no duty upon the charterers to pay.[94]

Freight is earned for the entirety of the voyage, which makes it necessary to fetch the cargo and carry it to the place of destination.[95] It is a general rule that it commences not only by the vessel sailing with the cargo on board, but also when the owner or hirer, having goods ready to ship, or a contract with another person for freight, has commenced the voyage, or incurred expenses and taken steps towards earning the freight.[96] When a shipowner has got a contract with another person under which he will earn freight, and has taken steps and incurred expense upon the voyage towards earning it, then his interest ceases to be a contingent thing, but becomes an inchoate interest, and is an interest which ought to be paid for by the underwriters if destroyed by one of the perils insured against.[97] In *Barber v Fleming*[98] the vessel was chartered for a voyage from Howland's Island to a port in the United Kingdom, freight to be paid at port of discharge. The ship sailed from Bombay in ballast and was lost on the voyage to Howland's Island. Cockburn CJ[99] stated that 'from the moment that a vessel is chartered to go from port A. to port B., and at port B. to take a cargo and bring home that cargo to England, or to take it to any port, which I will call port C., for freight, the shipowner, having got such a contract, has an interest unquestionably in earning the freight secured to him by the charter; and having such an interest it is manifest that that interest is insurable; and he loses the freight and benefit of his charter just as much by the ship being disabled on her voyage to the port at which the cargo is to be loaded and from which it is to be brought, as he would lose it by the disaster arising from the perils insured against between the port of loading and the port of discharge. It is therefore an appreciable, tangible interest, and I entertain no doubt it is an interest that can be insured'.

Where there is a valued policy on freight, and the ship is lost while taking in her cargo, the assured can only recover for the freight of the goods actually on board, unless a full cargo be then provided for her, or there is a contract either written or a binding promise to supply one. In *Patrick v Eames*[100] under a policy on freight, the ship had sailed from Sierra Leone with the intention of taking in a complete cargo of orchella weed from Cape Verde Islands, and was lost with only 150 bags shipped on board. It did not appear that any more orchella weed was then ready to be loaded, or that any binding contract, whether verbal or otherwise, had been made for supplying it. Lord Ellenborough held that the claimant was entitled to the freight only in respect of the 150 bags actually shipped. Beyond the 150 bags of orchella weed actually on board, the interest of the assured was merely in expectation. This case is different from *Davidson v Willasey*,[101] where a ship was chartered from Liverpool to Jamaica, there to take on board a full cargo for Liverpool at the current rate of freight, to be paid one month after the discharge of her cargo at Liverpool. The freight was insured under a valued policy, the ship was lost by storm while she was at Jamaica, and after taking on board one half of her cargo. Lord Ellenborough emphasised that but for the loss of the vessel the ship would have earned the whole freight. The assured had an inchoate right to the freight at the time when the loss happened. The valuation was made with reference to the freight under the charterparty, the whole of which the plaintiffs have been prevented from earning by one of the perils insured against. The loss therefore was total within the meaning of the policy.

94 *Smith, Hill & Co v Pyman, Bell & Co* [1891] 1 QB 742.
95 *Barber v Fleming*, (1869–70) LR 5 QB 59.
96 (1869–1870) LR 5 QB 59, 71, Blackburn J.
97 (1869–1870) LR 5 QB 59, 71, Blackburn J.
98 (1869–1870) LR 5 QB 59.
99 (1869–1870) LR 5 QB 59, 67.
100 (1813) 3 Campbell, p 441.
101 (1813) 1 Maule and Selwyn, p 313.

Where freight is insured 'at and from'[102] a given port, it is insured as long as the ship is at that port. If the voyage by means of which the chartered freight is to be earned has commenced, there is an inchoate interest in the freight, and the risk attaches, provided the language of the charter, taken with the policy, will warrant that view of the case.

Date for insurable interest

In an indemnity policy the relevant date is the date of loss.[103] The MIA 1906 section 6(1) provides 'The assured must be interested in the subject-matter insured at the time of the loss though he need not be interested when the insurance is effected.'[104] Thus, it is not essential for the assured to have an insurable interest when he effects the insurance but the assured must be interested in the subject matter at the time of the loss.[105] If the assured effects the insurance believing that he will acquire an interest, and acquires it before the loss, he can recover.[106] It must be proved in all cases that the party for whose benefit the policy was made was interested in the subject of insurance at the time of loss.[107] In *Powles v Innes*[108] at the time of affecting the insurance, C, P, and S were each interested in one-third of the vessel. The vessel was lost in January 1839. Before the loss, P, by bill of sale, conveyed his share to S. It was held that there was no right of action that C, P and S could enjoy jointly. Unless there was some understanding that the policy should be kept alive for S's benefit, S, suing on behalf of P, had lost nothing. Lost or not lost clause was originally designed to ensure that claims would not be defeated where the policy was concluded retrospectively, and a loss had already occurred after the agreed inception date, but before the contract was made.[109] In *Sutherland v Pratt*[110] it was held that such a policy is clearly a contract of indemnity against all past, as well as all future, losses sustained by the assured in respect of the interest insured. It operates just in the same way as if the defendant had agreed for a premium that if the goods had at the time of the purchase sustained any damage by perils of the sea, he would make it good, regardless of the plaintiff having already purchased the goods at sea.

Further reading

Arnould, *Law of Marine Insurance and Average*, 18th edn, [2013] Sweet & Maxwell. Chapter 11, Insurable Interest; Chapter 12, Valuation of Insurable Interests.

Bennett, *Law of Marine Insurance*, 2nd edn, [2006] Oxford University Press. Chapter 3, Insurable Interest, Illegality, and Public Policy.

Birds, 'Insurable interest – orthodox and unorthodox approaches', *Journal of Business Law* [2006] Mar, pp 224–231.

Clarke, *The Law of Insurance Contracts*, 4th edn, [2014] Informa. Chapter 4, Insurable Interest in Property.

---

102 See for example, *Foley v The United Fire and Marine Insurance Company of Sydney* (1869–70) LR 5 CP 155 where the freight insured 'At and from Mauritius to rice ports, and at and thence to a port in the United Kingdom.'

103 *Feasey v Sun Life Assurance Co of Canada* [2003] Lloyd's Rep IR 637, para 67.

104 Insurable interest used to be required at the time of effecting the policy as well as at the time of the loss. In *Marsh v Robinson* (1802) 4 Espinasse 98, the policy insuring the Speculation was effected in the names of Elizabeth Marsh and Son. At the time of underwriting the policy, the son was not an owner standing in the registry, and as a result did not have an insurable interest in the Speculation.

105 Keate, Guide to Marine Insurance, 1938, p 12.

106 *Rhind v Wilkinson* (1810) 2 Taunton 237.

107 Arnould, para 11.25.

108 (1843) 11 Meeson and Welsby, p 10.

109 Provided the assured was not aware, and the insurer ignorant, of the loss. See Arnould, para 11–26.

110 (1843) 11 Meeson and Welsby 296.

Dunt, *Marine Cargo Insurance*, [2009] Informa. Chapter 4, Insurable Interest and the Indemnity Principle.

McDonald, 'The insurable interest of international buyers on CIF terms', *Journal of International Maritime Law* [2004] 10(5): 413–421.

Merkin et al., *Colinvaux's Law of Insurance*, 9th edn, [2010] Sweet & Maxwell. Chapter 4, Insurable Interest.

Nicoll, 'Insurable interest: as intended?', *Journal of Business Law* [2008] 5, 432–447.

Rose, *Marine Insurance: Law and Practice*, 2nd edn, [2012] Informa. Chapter 3, Insurable Interest.

Chapter 4

Duty of Utmost Good Faith

Chapter Contents

In English insurance law the duty of good faith is analysed under two separate headings: (1) the duty in consumer insurance[1] and (2) the duty in non-consumer (business) insurance. Marine insurance is business insurance. Therefore, in this chapter the duty of good faith as applies to business insurance is analysed and the differences between the principles applicable to business and consumer insurance will be referred to in footnotes where necessary.

Parties to an insurance contract are under a statutory duty of good faith. The duty can be defined as that 'the party proposing the insurance is bound to communicate to the insurer all matters which will enable him to determine the extent of the risk against which he undertakes to guarantee the assured.'[2] The duty encompasses the disclosure of material facts to the other party to the contract and not to misrepresent material facts. In this respect insurance law differs from contract law since the general principles applicable to contract law do not recognise a duty to disclose material facts known to one contracting party but not to the other.[3]

The nature of the duty of good faith

For an insurer, statements made by the assured regarding the subject matter insured are crucially important. Its importance was emphasised by Lord Mansfield in Carter v Boehm[4] the case which is regarded as the locus classicus[5] of the law of non-disclosure.[6]

In his speech Lord Mansfield stated that:[7]

> Insurance is a contract upon speculation. The special facts, upon which the contingent chance is to be computed, lie most commonly in the knowledge of the insured only; the under-writer trusts to his representation, and proceeds upon confidence that he does not keep back any circumstance in his knowledge, to mislead the under-writer into a belief that the circumstance does not exist, and to induce him to estimate the risque, as if it did not exist. The keeping back such circumstance is a fraud, and therefore the policy is void. Although the suppression should happen through mistake, without any fraudulent intention; yet still the under-writer is deceived, and the policy is void; because the risque run is really different from the risque understood and intended to be run, at the time of the agreement.

Two matters were especially emphasised by Lord Mansfield. First, the duty is imposed because the underwriter relies on the information provided by the assured, which represents the risk.

---

1 The Consumer Insurance (Disclosure and Representation) Act 2012 received Royal Assent on 8 March 2012 and came into force on 6 April 2013.

2 Bates v Hewitt (1866–1867) LR 2 QB 595, at 605, Cockburn, CJ.

3 See Keates v Cadogan (1851) 10 CB 591 'There is no implied duty in the owner of a house which is in a ruinous and unsafe condition, to inform a proposed tenant that it is unfit for habitation; and no action will lie against him for an omission to do so, in the absence of express warranty, or active deceit.' For information about 'A Duty to disclose material facts' see E. McKendrick, Contract Law, 10th edn, chapter 12. See also Walford v Miles [1992] 2 AC 128. However, recently Leggatt J held that the duty of good faith is owed in the context of the performance of the contract: Yam Seng Pte Ltd v International Trade Corp Ltd [2013] 1 Lloyd's Rep 526.

4 (1766) 3 Burrow 1905.

5 See Marc Rich & Co AG v Portman [1996] 1 Lloyd's Rep 430, at 444, Longmore J.

6 It was stated that Lord Mansfield aimed to adopt the duty to be applicable to all contractual areas but in areas outside insurance the law did not develop as Lord Mansfield envisaged. In Pan Atlantic Insurance Co Ltd v Pine Top Insurance Co Ltd [1994] 2 Lloyd's Rep 427, at 448 Lord Mustill noted that '. . .Originally, Lord Mansfield had proceeded in Carter v Boehm, 3 Burr. 1905 on the basis of a general doctrine of good faith applicable to all contracts, and this doctrine was propounded by Park J in his influential early work on insurance, A System of the Law of Marine Insurances, 1st edn (1787); 2nd edn (1790). This general principle did not prevail, but marine insurance continued to be treated as an exceptional case in which non-disclosure and misrepresentation would ordinarily vitiate the contract even though they would not have had that effect at common law.'

7 (1766) 3 Burrow 1905, 1909.

Second, if the representation is not fair, the risk run is different to the risk the insurer has assumed to run. Thus, in case the duty is breached, the contract will need to be remedied.

The scope of the duty of good faith

It should firstly be noted that the principles of the duty of good faith as regulated by section 17–20 of the MIA 1906 are applicable to non-marine as well as marine insurance contracts.[8] Therefore, the cases from both areas will be referred to in explaining the duty in this chapter.

Lord Mansfield stated in *Carter v Boehm* that 'Good faith forbids either party concealing what he privately knows, to draw the other into a bargain, from his ignorance of that fact, and his believing the contrary.'[9] It appears that Lord Mansfield wished the duty to encompass all contractual relationships, nevertheless, since *Carter v Boehm* it has only developed in insurance contract law.[10] The duty was codified by the Marine Insurance Act 1906 s.17 of which provides: 'A contract of marine insurance is a contract based upon the utmost good faith, and, if the utmost good faith be not observed by either party, the contract may be avoided by the other party.'

Section 18 then regulates the duty for non-disclosure, section 19 deals with the agent's duty of disclosure and section 20 regulates the duty for misrepresentation.

The duty thus has two limbs:

1   The duty of disclosure: The assured is bound to make known to the insurers whatever is necessary and essential to enable them to determine the extent of the risk against which they undertake to insure.[11] This is a duty to disclose material facts without necessarily looking for an enquiry by the insurer.[12] The assured's agent, independent of the assured's duty, is obliged to disclose material facts which are known by him and by the assured.[13]
2   Misrepresentation: The assured has a duty to act honestly when answering the questions addressed by the insurer.[14]

A material non-disclosure or misrepresentation will entitle the insurer to seek a remedy irrespective of the assured being innocent, negligent or fraudulent.[15] Section 18(1) provides that

> . . . the assured must disclose to the insurer, before the contract is concluded, every material circumstance which is known to the assured, and the assured is deemed to know every circumstance which, in the ordinary course of business, ought to be known by him.

8   See *Pan Atlantic Insurance Co Ltd v Pine Top Insurance Co Ltd* [1994] 2 Lloyd's Rep 427, at 447, Lord Mustill; *Manifest Shipping Co Ltd v Uni-Polaris Insurance Co Ltd (The Star Sea)* [2001] 1 Lloyd's Rep 389, para 47, Lord Hobhouse; *Assicurazioni Generali SpA v Arab Insurance Group* [2003] Lloyd's Rep IR 131, para 55; *Brotherton v Aseguradora Colseguros SA (No.2)* [2003] Lloyd's Rep IR 746, para 12. *HIH Casualty & General Insurance Ltd v Chase Manhattan Bank* [2003] 2 Lloyd's Rep 61 para 42, Lord Hoffmann; *Highlands Insurance Co v Continental Insurance Co* [1987] 1 Lloyd's Rep 109. At 114.
9   (1766) 3 Burrow 1905, 1910.
10 Lord Mustill stated in *Pan Atlantic* that it was never spelt out how this result has been achieved in insurance. [1994] 2 Lloyd's Rep 427, 448.
11 *Bates v Hewitt* (1866–1867) LR 2 QB 595, at 605, Cockburn, CJ.
12 The duty of disclosure in consumer insurance was abolished by the Consumer Insurance (Disclosure and Representations) Act 2012, s 11.
13 The agent's duty applies in consumer insurance too. Consumer Insurance (Disclosure and Representations) Act 2012, s 9.
14 In consumer insurance the duty is 'to take reasonable care not to make a misrepresentation to the insurer.' Consumer Insurance (Disclosure and Representations) Act 2012, s 2(2).
15 *The Star Sea*, [2001] 1 Lloyd's Rep 389, para 95, Lord Scott; *Bates v Hewitt* (1866–1867) LR 2 QB 595; for an innocent misrepresentation see *St Paul Fire & Marine Insurance Co (UK) Ltd v McDonnell Dowell Constructors Ltd* [1995] 2 Lloyd's Rep 116; *HIH Casualty & General Insurance Ltd v Chase Manhattan Bank* [2003] 2 Lloyd's Rep 61 para 88.

Thus, an innocent non-disclosure will entitle the insurer to seek remedy for breach of the duty of good faith if the assured ought to know the circumstances in the ordinary course of his business. Under section 20 'Every material representation made by the assured or his agent to the insurer during the negotiations for the contract, and before the contract is concluded, must be true.'

Thus, the same principles apply here that an innocent misrepresentation may entitle the insurer to claim breach of the duty of good faith. However, a number of issues regarding misrepresentation should be noted. For instance, a representation may be either a representation as to a matter of fact, or as to a matter of expectation or belief (MIA 1906 s.20(3)). A representation as to a matter of expectation or belief is true if it is made in good faith (MIA 1906 s.20(5)). This principle was relied on by the assured in St Paul Fire & Marine Insurance Co (UK) Ltd v McDonnell Dowell Constructors Ltd.[16] In St Paul Fire the contractors purchased a contractors' all risks insurance on the design and construction of the Parliament building and a four storey administration block in the Marshall Islands. The proposal made to the insurers showed that the projected buildings had piled foundations whereas the true state of affairs, not disclosed to underwriters, was that the contractors intended to design and build shallow spread foundations rather than piled or other deep foundations. There was a misrepresentation, notwithstanding that it was innocently made: there was a clear difference between what was represented and what was correct in fact. The assured argued that if there was a representation then that should be deemed to be true given that that was the contractors' expectation and belief up to the time when the contract was made, and was made in good faith. Evans LJ, however, applied s.20(4). Under the relevant subsection 'a representation as to a matter of fact is true, if it be substantially correct, that is to say, if the difference between what is represented and what is actually correct would not be considered material by a prudent insurer'.

Evans LJ found that the statements about the nature of the foundations was a representation of fact, either as to the nature and description of the project or as to the contractors' present intention as to how the project should be carried out, or both. It was required by s.20(4) of the 1906 Act to be 'substantially correct' but it was not.

Section 20(5) of the MIA 1906 was also relied on in Eagle Star Insurance Co Ltd v Games Video Co (GVC) SA (The Game Boy)[17]. The assured insured the vessel, which he had bought to convert into a floating casino for $1.8m. While she was moored afloat at a shipyard, she sank after an explosion on board. The insurer contended that the vessel's true value was in fact $100,000 and, in any event, significantly less than value of $1.8m. It was common ground between the parties that value is a matter of opinion and that a statement of value can only amount to a misrepresentation if made in bad faith. In The Game Boy the amount said to have been spent to make the vessel seaworthy and to provide minimal facilities for passengers was $225,000 but after analysing the evidence the judge found the figure not realistic for outfitting the vessel so as to enable her to trade as a specialist casino vessel. Moreover, the invoice submitted to prove payment of $101,197 to a shipyard was bogus and was, at all relevant times, known by the assured to be bogus.

The assured's and insurer's experts were heard at the court and both of the expert witnesses agreed that the vessel had a base value of about $100,000, which was in effect a scrap value. They also agreed that, if the vessel was profitably chartered, her value would be increased considerably. The assured submitted evidence to prove the existence of a charterparty and upon hearing the witnesses the judge found that the documents were forged and the witnesses were not credible. Collectively, this created a justifiable suspicion that the charterparty could not have been intended to operate. It followed that the charterparty did not support the contention that the vessel was worth $1,800,000.

16 [1995] 2 Lloyd's Rep 116.
17 [2004] 1 Lloyd's Rep 238.

These facts led to the conclusion that the assured had no genuine belief that the value of the vessel was $1.8m, thus the representation was outside the scope of section 20(5).

Burden of proof

In order to establish a breach of the duty of good faith the insurer has to prove two things:[18]

1 the fact which was not disclosed or misrepresented was material[19]
2 the information withheld would have induced the actual underwriter to act differently, either by refusing to write the risk at all or by writing it only on different terms. The insurer was induced to enter into the contract by virtue of the material non-disclosure or misrepresentation.

While the first test, materiality is a statutory requirement under section 18 and 20 of the MIA 1906, inducement is a requirement which was implied to the Act by the House of Lords in *Pan Atlantic Insurance Co Ltd v Pine Top Insurance Co Ltd*.[20]

The matter which seems to lie at the heart of the duty of good faith is the test of materiality since upon discovery of a fact which was not disclosed or misrepresented, the first step the insurers must satisfy is that the fact was material. If materiality is not established there is no breach of the duty of good faith and therefore the question of inducement no longer falls to be considered.

Materiality

Proof or materiality is, in each case, a question of fact.[21]

In relation to the duty of disclosure section 18(2) provides:

Every circumstance is material, which would influence the judgment of a prudent insurer in fixing the premium, or determining whether he will take the risk.

Section 20(2) defines materiality in the context of misrepresentation:

A representation is material, which would influence the judgment of a prudent insurer in fixing the premium, or determining whether he will take the risk.

The two subsections are worded similarly and therefore they are interpreted in the same way. Materiality does not depend on what the ordinary assured would or would not be expected to disclose to the insurer.[22] Materiality is an 'objective test', that is, the prudent underwriter's opinion is taken into account when determining whether particular fact is material or not. Thus, neither

18 *Pan Atlantic Insurance Co Ltd v Pine Top Insurance Co Ltd* [1994] 2 Lloyd's Rep 427; *Assicurazioni Generali SpA v Arab Insurance Group* [2003] Lloyd's Rep IR 131, para 53.
19 There is no test of materiality in consumer insurance. The standard of care required is that of a reasonable consumer. Consumer Insurance (Disclosure and Representations) Act 2012 s 3(3).
20 [1994] 2 Lloyd's Rep 427. Inducement is a statutory requirement in consumer insurance. Consumer Insurance (Disclosure and Representations) Act 2012, s 4(1)(b).
21 MIA 1906 s 18(4).
22 *Insurance Corp of the Channel Islands v Royal Hotel Ltd* [1998] Lloyd's Rep IR 151, 157 Mance J.

the assured's nor the actual insurer's view is taken into account to assess whether or not the fact in question is material. The insurer may prove materiality by presenting an expert view from the relevant insurance market to the Court.[23]

In terms of the meaning of materiality it is necessary to examine the words '. . . which would influence the judgment of a prudent insurer . . .' which are seen in both sections 18(2) and 20(2). This matter[24] has been discussed in a number of cases and three tests were suggested to define the test of materiality:

1 decisive influence test
2 increased risk test
3 mere influence test.

Decisive influence test

Under this test to prove materiality it must be shown that full and accurate disclosure would have led the prudent insurer either to reject the risk or at least to have accepted it on more onerous terms. The word 'judgment' in 'would influence the judgment of a prudent insurer in fixing the premium or determining whether he will take the risk' equates with 'final decision', as though the wording of these provisions had been 'would induce a prudent underwriter to fix a different premium or to decline the risk'.[25] Consequently, underwriters can prove materiality only if they can satisfy the court by evidence that a prudent insurer, if he had known the fact in question, would have declined the risk altogether or charged a higher premium.[26]

In *Container Transport International Inc v Oceanus Mutual Underwriting Association (Bermuda) Ltd (No.1)*[27] while Lloyd J adopted the decisive influence test, the Court of Appeal disapproved it. The test of materiality once more came before the House of Lords in *Pan Atlantic*. While Lord Lloyd[28] – Lord Templeman agreed – reiterated the view at first instance in CTI,[29] the majority of their Lordships rejected the decisive influence test in favour of the mere influence test.

Increased risk test

This test was adopted by Steyn LJ in the Court of Appeal[30] in *Pan Atlantic*.

The increased risk test relies on Lord Mansfield's judgment in *Carter v Boehm* and especially his Lordship's assessment in adopting the remedy for breach of the duty of good faith that '. . . the

---

23 See for example, *North Star Shipping Ltd v Sphere Drake Insurance plc* [2006] 2 Lloyd's Rep 183; *Sealion Shipping Ltd v Valiant Insurance Co* [2012] Lloyd's Rep IR 141.

24 For this purpose there is no difference between allegations of non-disclosure and misrepresentation. *Container Transport International Inc v Oceanus Mutual Underwriting Association (Bermuda) Ltd (No.1)* [1984] 1 Lloyd's Rep 476, at 490, Kerr LJ.

25 See *Container Transport International Inc v Oceanus Mutual Underwriting Association (Bermuda) Ltd (No.1)* [1982] 2 Lloyd's Rep 178, Lloyd J and Kerr LJ's analysis of Lloyd J's judgment reported at [1984] 1 Lloyd's Rep 476, at 491.

26 *Container Transport International Inc v Oceanus Mutual Underwriting Association (Bermuda) Ltd (No.1)* [1982] 2 Lloyd's Rep 178, at 187, Lloyd J.

27 The assured, CTI, were one of the largest owners and lessors of containers whose business was to lease containers to shipowners and charterers, partly for single voyages or trips, but mainly on a time basis, with some leases extending over many months or even years. CTI's insurance requirements for containers fell into two classes; cover against the total loss of containers, and cover against damage and the costs of repairs. CTI purchased insurance to cover such risks but when the claims were made against the insurers the insurers purported to avoid the policy on the grounds of misrepresentation and non-disclosure contending that (a) CTI had put forward an inaccurate or incomplete and misleading claims record; (b) that they had failed to disclose a refusal by underwriters to renew.

28 His Lordship found this test necessary to mitigate the harshness of the all-or-nothing approach [1994] 2 Lloyd's Rep 427, at 459.

29 [1994] 2 Lloyd's Rep 427, at 458.

30 [1993] 1 Lloyd's Rep 496.

risque run is really different from the risque understood and intended to be run, at the time of the agreement.' The test is whether a prudent underwriter, if he had known the undisclosed facts, would have regarded the risk as increased beyond that which was disclosed on the actual presentation. It is not necessary to prove that the underwriter would have taken a different decision about the acceptance of the risk. The question is whether the prudent insurer would view the undisclosed fact material as probably tending to increase the risk.

The increased risk theory did not find any support by the House of Lords in Pan Atlantic; it was once again rejected in St Paul Fire & Marine Insurance Co (UK) Ltd v McDonnell Dowell Constructors Ltd[31] where Evans LJ stated that where inducement of the actual underwriter has to be proved as well as materiality, there is no reason why material should be limited to factors which are seen as increasing the risk. Evans LJ further added that the increased risk theory cannot be the correct test because (1) the risk may be increased in some respects but decreased in others and the assured need not disclose 'any circumstance which diminishes the risk' s.18(3). The section does not state whether this circumstance is not material within the definition of s.18(2) but the insurer has no right to avoid the policy on the ground that a circumstance of that sort was not disclosed. (2) The duty of disclosure operates both ways because the duty of good faith is reciprocal, so the definition of 'material' is not concerned with the proposer of insurance alone.

Mere influence test

This test is now a settled test in English law to prove materiality.[32] Accordingly, everything is material to which a prudent insurer, if he were in the proposed insurer's place would wish to direct his mind in the course of considering the proposed insurance with a view to deciding whether to take it up and on what terms, including what premium to charge.[33] In Pan Atlantic, Lords Mustill and Goff[34] found the decisive influence test facing insuperable practical difficulties, because the test ignores the fact that it is the duty of the assured to disclose every material circumstance which is known to him, with the result that the question of materiality has to be considered by the assured before he enters into the contract. In their Lordships' view, while it is not unreasonable to expect an assured to be able to identify those circumstances, within his knowledge, which would have an impact on the mind of the insurer when considering whether to accept the risk and, if so, on what terms he should do so, it would be unrealistic to expect him to be able to identify a particular circumstance which would have a decisive effect.

The other reasons for the majority of their Lordships to adopt the mere influence test were:

> The Act did not qualify the word 'influence' 'decisively influence'; or 'conclusively influence'; or 'determine the decision'; or other similar expressions.[35]

> 'Influence the mind' is not the same as 'change the mind'.[36]

31 [1995] 2 Lloyd's Rep 116.
32 Pan Atlantic Insurance Co Ltd v Pine Top Insurance Co Ltd [1994] 2 Lloyd's Rep 427; Bate v Aviva Insurance UK Limited [2013] EWHC 1687 (Comm); North Star Shipping Ltd v Sphere Drake Insurance plc [2006] 2 Lloyd's Rep 183; Lewis v Norwich Union Healthcare Ltd [2010] Lloyd's Rep IR 198.
33 Container Transport International Inc v Oceanus Mutual Underwriting Association (Bermuda) Ltd (No.1) [1984] 1 Lloyd's Rep 476, at 529, Stephenson LJ.
34 [1994] 2 Lloyd's Rep 427, 431 and 441.
35 [1994] 2 Lloyd's Rep 427, at 440, Lord Mustill.
36 [1994] 2 Lloyd's Rep 427, at 440, Lord Mustill.

The expression '. . . influence the judgment of a prudent insurer in . . . determining *whether* he will take the risk' denotes an effect on the thought processes of the insurer in weighing up the risk, quite different from words which might have been used but were not, such as 'influencing the insurer *to take* the risk'.[37]

The mere influence test is now a settled applicable test to determine materiality in the duty of good faith. In *St Paul Fire & Marine Insurance Co (UK) Ltd v McDonnell Dowell Constructors Ltd*,[38] Evans LJ defined the mere influence test as ' "material" like "relevant" denotes a relationship with the subject-matter rather than a prediction of its effect'. In one of the recent examples, *Sealion Shipping Ltd v Valiant Insurance Co*, Blair J[39] stated, 'The term "would influence" is not confined to the case of decisive influence, i.e. where proper disclosure of the non-disclosed or misrepresented fact would result in an actual change of decision (though the position is different where the issue is as to inducement). It is, however, necessary that it *would* influence the thought processes of the underwriter in assessing the risk.'

Inducement

The mere influence test is broad and it might be too harsh on the assured. Moreover, with regard to an actionable misrepresentation, general law of contract requires inducement to be established. In the context of insurance, while the Court of Appeal in CTI expressly rejected the inducement test for the reason that in the MIA 1906 there is no such requirement,[40] the House of Lords in *Pan Atlantic* ruled in favour of the inducement requirement.

Inducement concerns the mind of the actual insurer: his mind was so affected by a material misrepresentation or non-disclosure that the policy was thereby obtained.[41] It is thus 'a causal connection between the misrepresentation or non-disclosure and the making of the contract of insurance'.[42] The question is whether the insurer would have underwritten the risk on precisely the same terms had disclosure been made of all material circumstances.[43]

The answer to the question of whether the inducement test should be implied in the MIA 1906 depends on the determination of the test of materiality applicable to the duty of good faith in insurance. If the test is the decisive influence test, inducement is not needed as a separate requirement because the decisive influence test, as adopted by Lloyd J in CTI, embodies inducement since to prove materiality it is necessary that 'insurers must show that the result would have been affected'.[44] However, the problem with having the inducement test in the decisive influence test is the need to then reconcile two inconsistent elements. While materiality is an objective test, that for inducement is subjective. Proof of inducement by virtue of a prudent underwriter was criticised and disapproved by Parker LJ in CTI. The judge found it inappropriate to impose an objective test of materiality and again an objective test of inducement since the test would put the Court to the task, perhaps years after the event, of endeavouring to ascertain what a prudent underwriter would have done, first in the light of the circumstances actually disclosed by the assured, and secondly, on the hypothesis

---

37   [1994] 2 Lloyd's Rep 427, at 431 and 440, Lord Goff and Lord Mustill, respectively.
38   [1995] 2 Lloyd's Rep 116.
39   [2012] Lloyd's Rep IR 141, para 73.
40   [1984] 1 Lloyd's Rep 476 at 510, Parker LJ.
41   *Zurich General Accident and Liability Insurance Company v Morrison* [1942] 2 KB 53.
42   *Pan Atlantic Insurance Co Ltd v Pine Top Insurance Co Ltd* [1994] 2 Lloyd's Rep 427, at 447, Lord Mustill.
43   *Bate v Aviva Insurance UK Limited* [2013] EWHC 1687 (Comm); *Marc Rich & Co AG v Portman* [1997] 1 Lloyd's Rep 225, at 234.
44   [1982] 2 Lloyd's Rep 178, at 189.

that, in addition to those circumstances, the undisclosed circumstance had been disclosed. In Parker LJ's view such a task was impractical. By looking into the proof of inducement by evidence from a prudent underwriter, Parker LJ found that different prudent underwriters might have different assessments in light of the disclosure or representation of the fact and the Court cannot choose one prudent underwriter rather than another.[45]

In *Pan Atlantic*, however, Lord Goff stated 'the actual inducement test accurately represents the law.'[46] Inducement is proof of actual effect; when the test applicable to determine materiality is the mere influence test, proof of actual effect is not necessarily proof of materiality.[47] In *Pan Atlantic*, by adding the inducement requirement to the proof of materiality, the House of Lords overcame the harshness of the broad mere influence test. Lord Mustill and Lord Goff were in agreement that there is to be implied in the MIA 1906 a qualification that a material misrepresentation will not entitle the underwriter to avoid the policy unless the misrepresentation induced the making of the contract. The word 'induced' is used in the sense in which it is used in the general law of contract. Lord Mustill recognised that sections 17–20 of the MIA 1906 do not mention a connection between the wrongful dealing and the writing of the risk. But for this feature his Lordship doubted whether it would occur to anyone that it would be possible for the underwriter to escape liability even if the matter complained of had no effect on his processes of thought.[48]

The inducement test applies to non-disclosure as well as misrepresentation, as the House of Lords in *Pan Atlantic* confirmed that in practice the line between misrepresentation and non-disclosure is often imperceptible.[49]

Proof of inducement

The test to prove inducement is a 'but for' test. In order to show that a misrepresentation or non-disclosure induced the contract it is necessary to show that, but for the misrepresentation or non-disclosure, the particular underwriter would not have made the contract, either at all or on the terms on which it was in fact made.[50] In other words, the misrepresentation or non-disclosure must be an effective cause of the particular insurer entering into the contract but need not be the sole cause.[51] If inducement is not proved, however material, the misrepresentation or non-disclosure of a fact will not entitle the insurer to seek a remedy for breach of the duty of good faith.

Inducement is a subjective test and focuses on the actual insurer

Being a subjective test inducement requires the actual insurer to prove that he was induced to enter into the contract from his own underwriting practice. If the insurer submits evidence from an insurer other than the actual insurer who wrote the risk it is unlikely that he would persuade the court about inducement.

45 [1984] 1 Lloyd's Rep 476, at 511.

46 [1994] 2 Lloyd's Rep 427, at 431.

47 [1994] 2 Lloyd's Rep 427, at 442, Lord Mustill.

48 [1994] 2 Lloyd's Rep 427, at 447.

49 [1994] 2 Lloyd's Rep 427, at 431 and 452, per Lord Goff and Lord Mustill, respectively.

50 *Assicurazioni Generali SpA v Arab Insurance Group (BSC)* [2003] Lloyd's Rep IR 131, para 80.

51 *Assicurazioni Generali SpA v Arab Insurance Group (BSC)* [2003] Lloyd's Rep IR 131, para 59. At para 218 Ward LJ put the matter in much the same way, emphasising that there had to be some effect on the insurer, but that it did not have to be a decisive effect. *St Paul Fire & Marine Insurance Co (UK) Ltd v McDonnell Dowell Constructors Ltd* [1995] 2 Lloyd's Rep 116. See *Edgington v Fitzmaurice* (1885) 29 Ch D 459 'It is not necessary to show that the misstatement was the sole cause of his acting as he did.'

Lewis v Norwich Union Healthcare Ltd[52] illustrates the subjective nature of the test. In *Lewis* the assured completed a proposal for a Safeguard Income Protection insurance policy. In the proposal form the assured disclosed that he suffered from irritable bowel syndrome and that he had undergone a sphincterotomy. An independent examiner, a GP, confirmed that the assured was an average risk. In July 1999 the assured visited his GP to obtain confirmation for his accountant of the periods when he had been unable to work following his operations. He expressed to this GP that he had pain in his left knee: the GP examined the knee, and detected nothing abnormal. The assured did not disclose this visit to the insurer and the contract was concluded in December 1999 with effect from January 2000. In 2002 the assured gave up work on the grounds of incapacity, namely incontinence and back injury. He submitted a claim to the insurer who then purported to avoid the policy by reason of his failure to disclose the visit to his GP in July 1999. In an action brought by the assured the court found that the fact was material, however the issue focused largely on the proof of inducement. The actual underwriter was DF but she left her job long before the trial. The insurer therefore was not able to bring evidence from DF but asked NH to be heard as actual underwriter. NH's witness statement was not of much help for the insurer given that while on the one hand she said that the knee would have been excluded from cover, in another statement she said it would have 'no cover at all' because of Norwich Union's rules/practice of having a 'two exclusions and out' regime. Having emphasised inducement is a subjective test and focuses on the actual insurer,[53] in the absence of the actual underwriter's evidence, the court was dissatisfied that inducement was proved. It was clear from the evidence that DF acted in a way which was different to how NH would have acted, and in a way which was different to how Norwich Union's own expert stated a prudent underwriter would have acted. For instance, the assured's allergy test results were outstanding for months from June until October and the insurer tried to contact the assured's GP only after the assured asked the insurer to do so. Before the contract was concluded the assured completed a declaration of health in which the assured referred to things other than previously known matters. Despite the newly disclosed issues, DH did not make any enquiries about the 'course of injections' nor did she chase the allergy test results which remained outstanding and which the Senior Underwriter had expressly stated should be obtained in writing. Therefore, none of the evidence submitted to the Court was sufficient to prove inducement.

No inducement if the outcome is the same with full disclosure or true representation

As stated above, proof of inducement requires comparison of two situations: (1) the contract in hand (2) the situation which would have arisen had there been a full disclosure or no misrepresentation. If the outcome is different under the two situations, inducement can be proved but there will be no inducement if the same outcome is achieved in both situations. This was ruled in *Drake Insurance plc v Provident Insurance plc*[54] and was recently applied by Blair J in *Sea Glory Maritime Co, Swedish Management Co SA v AL Sagr National Insurance Co.*[55] The facts of *Drake* are as follows: In February 1995, S approached his brokers, H, for new insurance for his Renault car. S wanted third party, fire and theft cover for himself and in addition for his wife, K, as a named driver. K had suffered an accident just over a year before, January 1994, when a third party had driven into the back of S's car when she was driving it. The accident was not her fault, but under the insurer's system it

52 [2010] Lloyd's Rep IR 198.
53 *Lewis v Norwich Union Healthcare Ltd* [2010] Lloyd's Rep IR 198, para 22.
54 [2004] 1 Lloyd's Rep 268.
55 [2013] EWHC 2116 (Comm).

had to be recorded as a 'fault' accident, despite its circumstances, until the matter had been settled by the third party in the assured's favour. In February 1996, S renewed his insurance with the insurer. Two relevant events had occurred in the previous year. The first was that K's January 1994 accident had been settled by the third party's insurers entirely in S's favour. The second was that in December 1995, S received a speeding ticket, which he paid, thus admitting the conviction, in January 1996. His licence was endorsed with three points. When renewing his cover with the insurer in February 1996, S failed to disclose the conviction. In July 1996, K while driving the car collided with a motor-cyclist, B. The insurer was immediately notified of a claim, first by telephone and then in writing. Upon investigation of the latest accident for which S made a claim the insurer discovered the non-disclosure and the issue before the Court of Appeal was whether the insurer was entitled to avoid the contract for breach of the duty of good faith. The Court of Appeal decided in favour of the assured. Rix LJ and Clarke LJ found that on the true facts at the time of renewal the insurer could not be said to have induced the contract. The conviction together with the 'fault' accident of January 1994 would have increased the premium but without that fault accident, the non-disclosure of the conviction would have made no difference. Their Lordships came to this conclusion on a hypothesis that at the time of renewal the assured failed to inform H in relation to two matters: (1) the speeding conviction in 1995 and (2) the January 1994 accident had been settled satisfactorily. Had he informed H of both those matters, the conviction would have counted as ten points against him, but the information about the settlement of the accident would have meant that that would have been reclassified as a 'no fault' accident and thus would not have counted against him at all. In the circumstances he would still have been entitled to renewal at a normal rate. If the conviction had been mentioned, it would be very likely that the question of the status of the accident had been discussed because it would have been H's duty as S's broker to have raised the issue, and secondly because when the significance of the accident's status was raised in correspondence S addressed it, and kept on doing so. If the conviction had been disclosed, there would have been a discussion of its impact on the premium in light of the status of the earlier accident. Such a discussion would have led to the premium remaining at the normal level and was thus fatal to this part of his case.

Recently, Blair LJ applied this analysis in *Sea Glory Maritime Co, Swedish Management Co SA v AL Sagr National Insurance Co*[56] in which the vessel was detained at Suez in October 2008 before the hull insurance policy was renewed in December 2008. According to the expert evidence this was a material fact, as the expert stated that the port state detentions within 12 months immediately before the renewal would be material for a prudent insurer. The assured was nevertheless successful in this case because the judge found the insurer was not induced to agree the policy by reason of any non-disclosure concerning the vessel's detention history. The judge applied the principle which was approved by Rix and Clarke LJJ in *Drake* stated above that had the claimants disclosed these detentions, when informed that the class surveyor had checked the deficiencies and confirmed that they were rectified, the insurer would have proceeded to renew cover on the same terms. Had the claimants disclosed the PSC detentions, they would have been bound to include the outcome.

Negligent underwriting

If the underwriter was negligent in writing the risk, should his negligence have any impact on the assessment of inducement? In other words, would it be possible to argue that because the underwriter was so negligent in understanding even the nature of the risk he was writing, would it be dangerous to attribute common sense to his judgment as an underwriter in determining inducement? The

---

56 [2013] EWHC 2116 (Comm).

issue was discussed in *Marc Rich & Co AG v Portman*[57] in which the insurer wrote a demurrage cover although all he knew about demurrage was that it meant delay. There were a number of material facts which had not been disclosed to the insurer before the contract was concluded: (1) the route that the carriage was to be performed was a congested route, delays were common at the ports in question during loading and unloading operations, and (2) at the time when the insurance contract was concluded the assured had already experienced considerable demurrage losses. The issue focused on non-disclosure of the assured's loss experience which was held to be material. With regard to proof of inducement the assured's counsel argued that the insurer was too reckless to attribute any common sense to his judgment as an underwriter. The trial judge found that the insurer did not know anything about the ports of Ain Sukhna or about Constantza. The insurer agreed to insure demurrage claims by an endorsement to the policy but he had no idea about the true extent of the charterers' liability, which was initially agreed to be covered, or the scope of cover being sought by the broker in the endorsements. He knew virtually nothing about the sort of liabilities likely to be incurred by charterers of ships; he had never seen a charterparty, could not define demurrage and had no concept of laytime or notices of readiness. The assured reiterated that the insurer knew that he was insuring delay and that he knew nothing about the charterparty, but he knew that before writing extensions to the existing cover it was essential to get the assured's claims experience, and that he should have asked for it.[58] In those circumstances, the assured's counsel contended that no inference could fairly be drawn that if *Marc Rich*'s claims experience had been disclosed to him, the insurer would have read it, understood it or reacted to it. Longmore J had the evidence of the actual insurer as well as another insurer working at the same department. Moreover, expert underwriters stated that the losses were not only serious but were on such a scale as would have rendered the risk uninsurable. Longmore J was thus persuaded that the actual insurer did not think that it was a major risk; it was obvious that *Marc Rich*'s massive loss experience would have completely abrogated that assumption. The insurer, if he had been shown or told that *Marc Rich* had a substantial record or experience of previously incurred demurrage, would either have sought to confirm that that was no part of the cover or, at least, would have decided to discuss the matter with the other underwriter who originally wrote the risk, who would himself have checked that it was nothing to do with the risk. Longmore J found that in either event the risk would not have been written on the terms it was; the Court of Appeal did not interfere with that conclusion. Despite the fact that there were good grounds for supposing that the actual insurer would have been unlikely to pay any attention to information about the causes of delay, if the relevant information was provided, it was still probable that he would have refused to insure the risk given the seriousness of the assured's loss experiences on the route in question.

Misrepresentation by a third party

In addition to the assured's presentation of the risk, if the insurer seeks an expert opinion on the facts upon which the insurer relies and if later it appears that the expert evidence did misrepresent the fact, can the insurer still seek remedy against the assured? In *Small v Atwood*[59] Small agreed to buy Atwood's mine. Small appointed agents to verify Atwood's representations as to Atwood's earning capacity. The agents reported that Atwood's statements were true. After the contract was concluded Small discovered that Atwood exaggerated his earning capacity and sought to rescind the contract but he was unable to do so because he relied on his own agents' statement. Reliance of an expert

---

57   [1997] 1 Lloyd's Rep 225.
58   The waiver argument was rejected by the High Court judge as well as the Court of Appeal, see below.
59   (1836)6 Cl & F 232.

view in an insurance context is seen in *International Lottery Management v Dumas*.[60] It should be noted that in *Dumas* the expert whose statement was not true and was relied on by the insurer was neither the assured's nor the insurer's agent. The facts of the case were briefly as follows: An Israeli businessman attempted to establish a lottery business in Azerbaijan. He prepared a business plan, which was given informal approval by the Ministry of Finance. The assured then registered a subsidiary in accordance with Azerbaijan company law. The assured insured the business against confiscation, expropriation and nationalisation with London insurers. The London insurers were keen to make sure that the licences were granted. The assured presented a document that was mistranslated and confirmed that an authorisation to carry on lottery business was granted whereas in fact the assured obtained a registration and only an informal approval by the Ministry of Finance was given. Before the contract was concluded the insurer sought an independent expert view, which also contained misleading material statements as to the permission granted to the assured and implied that the assured had been granted licences following a proper procedure. After the insurance was placed, the Ministry of Finance informed the assured that the Government had decided to run the lottery as an exclusive state monopoly, despite the encouragement that had up to that date been given to him. HHJ Dean QC held that the assured was not to be held liable for the misrepresentation made by the independent legal expert. He was not the assured's agent. However, this did not relieve the assured from his own duty of good faith given that he was obliged to disclose any material information regarding the matter which the legal expert presented to the insurer because the statement as to whether the licences were granted or not was material. If the principles of contract and insurance law are to be distinguished here it might be explained on the basis that in Contract law there is no duty of disclosure whereas the duty of disclosure is applicable in business insurance contracts.

Presumption of inducement

In some cases, with regard to proof of inducement, a question may arise whether proof of materiality creates a presumption of inducement. In other words, whether proof of materiality shifts the burden of proof from the insurer to the assured, which requires the latter to present evidence displacing the presumption.

There is no such rule that says proof of materiality establishes presumption of inducement so that the burden is on the assured who has to displace the presumption. However, in some cases the courts may apply presumption depending on the facts of the case and what the other underwriters who are involved in the case have established. In *St Paul Fire & Marine Insurance Co (UK) Ltd v McDonnell Dowell Constructors Ltd*[61] the contractors purchased a contractors' all risks insurance. Spread foundation was used in the project although it had been presented to the insurers before the contract was concluded that pile foundations were to be used. Thus, the underwriters purported to avoid the contract for material misrepresentation. Three of the four underwriters who insured the risk brought evidence which persuaded Evans LJ – who gave the only reasoned judgment of the Court of Appeal – that the underwriters, if the true facts had been disclosed, would have either refused the risk or accepted it on different terms. The fourth underwriter, who accepted 20 per cent of the risk, did not give any evidence to this effect and the question was whether he was induced to enter into the contract. Evans LJ found the evidence of the three underwriters was clear: If the underwriters had been told the true state of the ground conditions, they would have called for further information

---

60 [2002] Lloyd's Rep IR 237.
61 [1995] 2 Lloyd's Rep 116.

and in all probability either refused the risk or accepted it on different terms. There was no evidence to displace a presumption that the fourth underwriter like the other three was induced by the non-disclosure or misrepresentation to give cover on the terms on which he did. Consequently, Evans LJ accepted the presumption of inducement in favour of the fourth underwriter.

The Court of Appeal in *Assicurazioni Generali v Arab Insurance Group*[62] affirmed the existence of the presumption which can be rebutted. It was stated by Clarke LJ in *Assicurazioni Generali SpA v Arab Insurance Group (BSC)*[63] that there is no presumption of law that an insurer or reinsurer is induced to enter in the contract by a material non-disclosure or misrepresentation.[64] However, having referred to *St Paul Fire*, Clarke LJ confirmed that there have been cases in which the facts were accepted to be such that it is to be inferred that the particular insurer or reinsurer was so induced even in the absence of evidence from him.[65] Moreover, Longmore J stated in *Marc Rich & Co AG v Portman*[66] 'The presumption will only come into play in those cases in which the underwriter cannot (for good reason) be called to give evidence and there is no reason to suppose that the actual underwriter acted other than prudently in writing the risk. In cases where he is called and the Court genuinely cannot make up its mind on the question of inducement, the insurer's defence of non-disclosure should fail because he will not have been able to show that he had been induced by the non-disclosure to enter into the insurance on the relevant terms. At the end of the day it is for the insurer to prove that the non-disclosure did induce the writing of the risk on the terms in which it was written.'

A further example is *International Management Group (UK) Ltd v Simmonds*,[67] which concerned insurance on an annual cricket tournament between India and Pakistan, known as the Sahara Cup, which was scheduled to take place in the years 1996 to 2000. It was not disclosed to the underwriters that well-placed and well-informed sources within the Cricket boards of India were of the view that the Indian Government would refuse to allow India to play in the 2000 tournament. The Indian Government indeed refused the request, and claims were made against the insurers.

Cooke J was satisfied that each of the underwriters who gave evidence was induced to write the risk in the way he did by the misrepresentations that were made to him or affected by the non-disclosures in assessing it. If any issue of Government approval had been disclosed, whether in answer to questions then or otherwise, the underwriters would either have specifically excluded liability in the event of lack of Government approval or permission, made cover expressly subject to that approval or permission, or declined to write the risk at all until evidence of such approval or permission had been obtained. It is clear that this was a risk which was hard to place. The leaders were reluctant to write the risk in the first place, on the second occasion they were approached they declined to offer a quotation at all. The leading underwriters and indeed the followers who placed subjects on their lines were all clearly dubious about writing the risk and the judge had no difficulty in finding that each was influenced by the nondisclosure and the misrepresentations to accept a risk which they would otherwise have considered in a different light. The issue about the presumption of inducement arose because one of the following underwriters, F from B syndicate, did not appear to give evidence and no statement was taken from him. F had left the employment of the B syndicate and had refused to co-operate unless he was given access to confidential information to which he was not entitled. B was unprepared to provide that information. The judge

---

62 See [2003] Lloyd's Rep IR 131 Clarke LJ and Ward LJ, para 62 and para 219, respectively.

63 [2003] Lloyd's Rep IR 131, para 62.

64 See also *Cape plc v Iron Trades Employers Insurance Association Ltd* [2004] Lloyd's Rep IR 75, at 100 where Rix J stated 'Normally, inducement may be presumed in the sense that it would be for the insured to rebut the *prima facie* presumption that a material disclosure would have influenced the underwriter.'

65 [2003] Lloyd's Rep IR 131, para 62, see also Ward LJ, para 219.

66 [1996] 1 Lloyd's Rep 430, 442.

67 [2004] Lloyd's Rep IR 247.

found it unrealistic to hold against B. It was plain to the judge that B's position as a follower was very much the same as all the other followers.[68] Under the circumstances B was entitled to rely upon a presumption of inducement of the kind referred to in *St. Paul Fire and Marine Insurance Co UK Ltd v McConnell Dowell Constructors Ltd*.[69]

Where a contract is signed by the leading underwriter and the followers, the assured enters into independent contracts with each of the underwriters.[70] Thus, each contract itself will be subject to the duty of good faith. A question may arise in terms of whether a misrepresentation or non-disclosure to the leading underwriter could 'travel' so as to avail following subscribers to the same slip. While there were some negative statements on this matter[71] it was held that the following underwriters rely on the presentation made to the leading underwriter and the non-disclosure or misrepresentation to the leading underwriter is itself a material fact which should be disclosed to the following underwriters.[72] The following underwriters' subscription is upon the basis that the leading underwriter had been given a full and fair presentation so that he was in a position to make a proper evaluation of the risk.[73] If the leading underwriter was given a materially incomplete and misleading presentation which induced his acceptance, each of the followers would be entitled to avoid the cover for failure on the part of the assured to disclose to them the fact of the unfair presentation which was made to the leader.[74] In *International Management Group (UK) Ltd v Simmonds*[75] the facts of which were given above, whilst each of the following underwriters who gave evidence told the judge that he had made his own underwriting decision, it was plain to the judge that they placed considerable reliance upon the leading underwriters on this risk.[76] In *Simmonds* the brokers' evidence was that the risk was not insurable without the two leaders because they would never be able to persuade the following markets to write the risk without such a lead.[77] In these circumstances, the misrepresentations and non-disclosures which prevented a fair presentation of the risks to the leaders represented a material circumstance, which was required to be disclosed to the followers, in order to make a fair presentation to them.[78] Similarly, in *Aneco Reinsurance Underwriting Ltd v Johnson & Higgins Ltd*[79] Cresswell J considered the authorities and decided that the evidence in the case adduced before him did support a finding of fact that the following market accepted the risk on the basis that a full and fair presentation had been made to the leader. He held that the presentation to the leader was not complete and correct. This should have been disclosed to the followers in order to ensure a fair presentation to them but the brokers had failed to do so. The followers were entitled to avoid the policy as well as the leader. In *Dumas*, HHJ Dean QC[80] stated that the applicability of the abovementioned principles does not depend upon any rule of law or proof of a strict custom

---

68 [2004] Lloyd's Rep IR 247, para 148.

69 [2004] Lloyd's Rep IR 247, para 149.

70 *International Lottery Management v Dumas* [2002] Lloyd's Rep IR 237 para 71.

71 *General Accident Fire & Life Assurance Corp Ltd v Tanter (The Zephyr)* [1985] 2 Lloyd's Rep 529 at 539–540, Mustill LJ and *Bank Leumi le Israel BM v British National Insurance Co Ltd* [1988] 1 Lloyd's Rep 71, at 76–78, Saville J expressed forcible doubts on the existence of such a principle as a matter of law, but did comment that where it could be shown that following subscribers to the slip did so on the basis of trusting the skill and judgement of the leader and upon the assumption that he had received full and accurate information about the risk, the 'supposed rule' could perhaps be supported by proof of a custom or usage in the particular market or by an implied representation to the followers that all material circumstances had been accurately provided to the leader.

72 *Aneco Reinsurance Underwriting Ltd v Johnson & Higgins Ltd* [1998] 1 Lloyd's Rep 565.

73 Which was proved upon the facts in *International Lottery Management v Dumas* [2002] Lloyd's Rep IR 237.

74 *International Management Group (UK) Ltd v Simmonds* [2004] Lloyd's Rep IR 247, para 150.

75 [2004] Lloyd's Rep IR 247.

76 [2004] Lloyd's Rep IR 247, para 150.

77 [2004] Lloyd's Rep IR 247, para 150.

78 *International Management Group (UK) Ltd v Simmonds* [2004] Lloyd's Rep IR 247, para 151.

79 [1998] 1 Lloyd's Rep 565, this issue was not discussed on appeal.

80 [2002] Lloyd's Rep IR 237, para 78.

but upon facts establishing the particular way of doing business in the case. HHJ Dean QC found *Aneco* certainly in accordance with market expectation as disclosed in evidence in this case and reflected the practicalities of the way business is conducted in this particular market at Lloyd's.[81]

Material facts

Material facts are analysed under two separate headings:

1   Physical hazard.
2   Moral hazard.

Physical hazard

Physical hazard refers to the risks that are related to the physical characteristics of the subject matter insured. For instance if a yacht is insured the location of where the yacht is moored may be material.[82] In an insurance policy taken out by a charterer against demurrage claims the characteristics of the loading and destination ports (for example, they may be very congested) or the weather conditions in particular seasons at which the voyages will be made may be material.[83]

Port's characteristics

This was discussed in *Marc Rich & Co AG v Portman*[84] in which the assured was a well-known oil and gas commodity trader whose business included buying and selling large quantities of crude oil. For this purpose they chartered vessels to collect oil from loading ports such as Kharg Island in Iran and Constantza in Romania, and deliver it to discharge ports throughout the world. The route from Kharg Island in Iran to Ain Sukhna in Egypt was liable to give rise to problems of demurrage. The popularity of the route often caused congestion at Kharg Island and at Ain Sukhna. The operators at both terminals had stringent terms preventing traders from passing on demurrage liabilities in the event of delay. The assured gave instructions to Dutch brokers to obtain demurrage cover for voyages from Kharg Island to Ain Sukhna with a limit of US$250,000 per vessel for a period of ten days in excess of three. It was not disclosed to the insurer that particular features of the port of Ain Sukhna would be likely to give rise to demurrage claims, for example, bad weather, difficult tides, swell, liability to congestion and other such matters. Neither was it disclosed that the average turnaround time for vessels loading at Kharg Island and discharging at Ain Sukhna within the past six months before the insurance was proposed exceeded six days. Longmore J referred to the particular features of the ports in question as 'adverse port characteristics' and non-disclosure of such facts was material.[85]

---

81   [2002] Lloyd's Rep IR 237, para 78; *International Lottery Management v Dumas* [2002] Lloyd's Rep IR 237, para 78.
82   *Decorum Investments Ltd v Atkin (The Elena G)* [2001] 2 Lloyd's Rep 378 but the fact in this case was held not material because of section 18(3)(a).
83   *Marc Rich & Co AG v Portman* [1997] 1 Lloyd's Rep 225.
84   [1997] 1 Lloyd's Rep 225.
85   However, Longmore J found (this issue was not appealed) that the non-disclosure about the adverse port characteristics was waived by the insurer. See below 'Implied waiver', p. 82 et seq.

Previous loss experiences

If an assured has a substantial loss experience this is a material fact that should be disclosed to the insurer.[86] The insurer is entitled to assume that there has been a fair presentation of the risk. These issues were ruled by Longmore J and approved by the Court of Appeal in Marc Rich the facts of which were stated above. In Marc Rich when the risk was proposed to the insurers the assured's broker was not asked nor did he volunteer anything about the incidence of demurrage liability in respect of vessels previously chartered for the Kharg Island to Ain Sukhna route. On the Kharg Island/Ain Sukhna route Marc Rich had, at the time when the endorsement was entered into, incurred demurrage liabilities of about US$3.9m at the ports in question on more than 50 vessels in the previous ten months before the contract was initialled by the insurer. This fact was, as the Courts agreed, plainly material. The assured argued that the insurer waived his right of full disclosure of the previous loss experience, the issue of which will be discussed below.[87]

If there is a substantial loss experience which was not disclosed the fact that the insurer knows or is presumed to know that a loss experience exists does not make this fact immaterial for the reason that the insurer's actual or presumed knowledge about the existence of loss experience says nothing about the size of the losses.[88] If the losses are modest or insignificant they need not be disclosed[89] and if nothing is disclosed about the loss experience, the insurer is entitled to assume it is insignificant.[90]

The principle that the assured's claim history is not material if it is modest or insignificant was applied in Sealion Shipping Ltd v Valiant Insurance Co.[91] In Sealion the defendant insurer issued to the claimants a loss of hire marine policy on the vessel, for the year commencing 20 May 2008. The daily sum insured was US$70,000, the coverage was limited to 30 days in excess of 14 days any one occurrence and 21 days in respect of machinery claims. The assured made a claim arising from a propulsion motor breakdown which happened on 25 February 2009, after which the vessel was placed off-hire by her charterers. The insurer purported to avoid the policy on the basis of material non-disclosure and/or misrepresentation that the assured stated that 'apart from scheduled dry-dockings and a few hours off hire now and again, the vessel has not experienced any significant off hire period', but in fact the vessel had experienced approximately ten days off-hire in 2004, over two days at the time of the breakdown in September 2004, and a further period of over seven days when repairs were carried out in November 2004. The judge, however, found such loss experience immaterial. Blair J stated that in general, insurers are interested primarily in the potential for claims and, in the circumstances, ten days' loss of hire experienced in 2004 compared to a 21-day excess under the 2008 policy was not material. It was not a particularly long period of off-hire, it occurred nearly four years previous to the placing of the policy with the defendant, it did not result in a claim, and it did not come close to the excess period.

As seen above, whether and to what extent previous loss history is material depends on the type of the policy and the size of the previous claims. One recent example on this matter is Bate v Aviva Insurance UK Limited,[92] which involved a property insurance policy. The representation about the

---

86 Marc Rich & Co AG v Portman [1996] 1 Lloyd's Rep 430, at 443 Longmore J; affirmed by the Court of Appeal [1997] 1 Lloyd's Rep 225.
87 See 'Implied waiver', p. 82 et seq.
88 See Marc Rich & Co AG v Portman [1996] 1 Lloyd's Rep 430, at 443, Longmore J; affirmed by the Court of Appeal [1997] 1 Lloyd's Rep 225.
89 Marc Rich & Co AG v Portman [1996] 1 Lloyd's Rep 430, at 443, Longmore J; affirmed by the Court of Appeal [1997] 1 Lloyd's Rep 225.
90 See Marc Rich & Co AG v Portman [1996] 1 Lloyd's Rep 430, at 443, Longmore J; affirmed by the Court of Appeal [1997] 1 Lloyd's Rep 225.
91 [2012] Lloyd's Rep IR 141. The case was appealed but the materiality issue was not disputed at the Court of Appeal.
92 [2013] EWHC 1687 (Comm).

claims that the assured had made within the last five years was untrue. The assured's answer on the form suggested that there had been a fire caused by a contractor at an address he had left. But the fire occurred on the Estate, his home for twenty years and was caused by his own wholly-owned company. This was a material misrepresentation.

Port State Controls

In *Sea Glory Maritime Co, Swedish Management Co SA v AL Sagr National Insurance Co*,[93] the expert witness stated that a prudent underwriter would only be concerned with detentions in the recent past, which he said was the period 12–18 months before the inception date of a policy. At least on a renewal, it is detentions in the previous twelve months that are relevant. Thus, Blair J rejected the argument that the vessel's five detentions in the four years prior to the date of the Policy were material and should have been disclosed.

Moral hazard

Moral hazard generally concerns the characteristics of the assured. As explained above, a 'material circumstance' is one that would have an effect on the mind of a prudent insurer in estimating the risk and it is not necessary to prove that it should have a decisive effect on his acceptance of the risk or the amount of premium to be paid. Moral hazard refers to the facts which would indicate whether the insurer would like to enter into a business relationship with the assured such as the assured's criminal record or general dishonesty of the assured. One might then argue whether a fact that is not directly related to the risk insured should still be disclosed despite the fact that it may satisfy the mere influence test but has no connection with the risk insured against. In other words, whether the mere influence test should be qualified that only the matters which affect the likelihood and extent of any loss to the insurer under the insurance proposed should be disclosed.[94] An attempt to define materiality to this effect is seen in *The Martin P* where Mr Richard Siberry QC, sitting as a Deputy High Court Judge,[95] stated that the definition of materiality includes not only matters going to the likelihood of a loss to the subject matter by a peril insured but also matters relevant to the likelihood and extent of any subrogation rights. In *North Star Shipping Ltd v Sphere Drake Insurance plc*[96] the assured's counsel argued 'allegations that related to the risk itself were one thing but allegations of dishonesty, which had nothing to do with the risk and nothing to do with either the particular insurance or with insurance at all, were another', to which Waller LJ responded 'I might have been tempted to follow',[97] nevertheless, his Lordship decided for the insurers and found the facts material. Having noted that the law in this area is capable of producing serious injustice, Waller LJ avoided proposing any reform but referred the matter to the Law Commissions.[98] Mance LJ in *Brotherton v Aseguradora Colseguros SA*[99] – as will be mentioned below under 'Allegations of misconduct' – did not find such a qualification satisfactory and said 'The legal test of materiality established by authority and by statute is on the face of it clear. A matter is material if it would influence the mind of a rational underwriter governing himself by the principles and practices on

---

93 [2013] EWHC 2116 (Comm).
94 See *O'Kane v Jones (The Martin P)* [2004] 1 Lloyd's Rep 389, para 222, Mr Richard Siberry QC.
95 [2004] 1 Lloyd's Rep 389, para 222.
96 [2006] 2 Lloyd's Rep 183.
97 [2006] Lloyd's Rep IR 519, para 18.
98 Lord Justice Longmore and Lord Justice Lloyd agreed.
99 [2003] 1 Lloyd's Rep IR 746, para 18.

which underwriters do in practice act or would influence the judgment of a prudent insurer in fixing the premium, or determining whether to take the risk.'[100]

Rumours

Whether rumours are material or not depends on the grounds of the rumours and sources of them. In *North Star Shipping Ltd v Sphere Drake Insurance plc*,[101] Waller LJ expressed his view that allegations of not very serious dishonesty are not material. Nevertheless, in *International Management Group (UK) Ltd v Simmonds*[102] the facts of which were given above, the assured who insured a cricket tournament against cancellation for political risks failed to disclose to the insurers that before the contract was made the assured had been informed that well-placed and well-informed sources within the Cricket boards of India were of the view that the Indian Government would refuse to allow India to play in the 2000 tournament. This fact was found material as having been received from reliable resources rendered the fact more than rumour. In *Simmonds*, Cooke J distinguished immaterial loose rumours, gossip and speculation from material hard intelligence, and held that the information fell into the latter category.

Allegations of misconduct

In *Brotherton v Aseguradora Colseguros SA*[103] the reinsurers purported to avoid the reinsurances of two Columbian reinsureds for non-disclosure of reports in the Columbian media of allegations of misconduct and related investigations involving the original assured's business and officers. The original policies were bankers blanket and professional indemnity insurances covering losses caused by dishonest or fraudulent acts of bank employees. The bank was a state-owned bank, C, the reinsurance was effected from 7 November 1997 and extended in late November 1998 until 31 January 1999. The allegations against the bank officers appeared in media between 28 January 1997 and late November 1997: seven news bulletins and fifteen newspaper articles were published reporting allegations of misconduct and related investigations involving the bank officers. Reinsurers argued that the reports alone, and all the more the reports coupled with the fact of the investigations, were material to be disclosed, firstly as constituting circumstances which might give rise to claims under the reinsurances, and secondly as suggesting moral hazard. The reinsureds argued that there was no basis for the allegations, they were part of a political campaign by the opponents of the then government to smear its supporters and friends in order to discredit the government in the run-up to the 1998 elections. According to the reinsureds, 63 of the 65 criminal investigations of the bank manager had been concluded in his favour; the remaining two were still pending; one of them related to the use of the aeroplane for private purposes and the other related to an alleged infringement of public tendering regulations. Sixteen out of 17 investigations have been closed and only one was live, which was then being challenged before the Colombian courts. Therefore, the reinsureds submitted that materiality, at least in cases of moral hazard, must depend on the known existence of actual moral hazard, rather than the possession of information suggesting the possibility of moral hazard. Mance LJ disagreed. Referring to the mere influence test in *Pan Atlantic*, Mance LJ found it difficult to see any reason why, if the evidence satisfies the court that a prudent underwriter would have regarded information suggesting the possibility of moral hazard as material in the sense

---

100 See also *Insurance Corp of the Channel Islands v Royal Hotel Ltd* [1998] Lloyd's Rep IR 151, 156.
101 [2006] 2 Lloyd's Rep 183, para 19.
102 [2004] Lloyd's Rep IR 247.
103 [2003] 1 Lloyd's Rep IR 746.

identified by Lord Mustill, that should not suffice. This was, according to Mance LJ, the basic legal position.[104]

A question then may follow, if the assured is under investigation for, or has been charged with an offence that he knows that he did not commit, does he still have to disclose the charge to the insurer? The assured argued in *Brotherton* that the only circumstances requiring disclosure are those which actually exist at the time of making the contract, and that allegations or investigations with respect to possible misconduct do not have to be disclosed, if there was in fact no misconduct, even if there was at the time of placement no way of knowing or showing this. Mance LJ, however, disagreed due to the fact that the issues of both materiality and inducement would in all likelihood fall to be judged on the basis that, if there had been disclosure, it would have embraced all aspects of the assured's knowledge. Such disclosure should include the assured's own statement of his innocence, and such independent evidence as he had to support that, by the time of placing. In *Strive Shipping Corp v Hellenic Mutual War Risks Association (Bermuda) Ltd (The Grecia Express)*[105] Colman J stated that non-disclosure of a mere allegation of dishonesty could not justify avoidance if the assured maintained that it was wrong, and would, if allowed, be able to prove this. According to the judge 'it would be open to the assured to disprove his guilt and thereby to disentitle the insurers to avoidance of the policy'.[106] Mance LJ in *Brotherton* disagreed and stated that since what is material depends upon what would influence the judgment of a prudent insurer at the time of the placing, both the known fact of guilt, in the case of an acquittal, and the (known) fact of a conviction, in a case where the assured himself knows that he is innocent, may be capable of being material to a prudent insurer. In the latter case, the assured can disclose not merely the conviction, but all matters supporting his statement that he was wrongly convicted.

The critical question was still, however, whether the validity of reinsurers' purported avoidance for their non-disclosure depends or may depend upon whether the allegations were correct and there was actual misconduct justifying the allegations and investigations. This issue is discussed in detail below under '(Un)conscionable avoidance'.

Pending Criminal/Civil Charges

Pending charges are disclosable whether or not they were well-founded.[107] When accepting a risk underwriters are properly influenced not merely by facts which, with hindsight, can be shown to have actually affected the risk but with facts that raise doubts as to the risk.[108] Pending criminal and civil charges were both discussed in *North Star Shipping Ltd v Sphere Drake Insurance plc*[109] in which the vessel was insured against war risks and then became a constructive total loss after an explosion. There were a number of facts that had not been disclosed and two of them were (1) Four separate pending criminal proceedings against the assured in the Greek courts; the allegation was that the assured persuaded people to part with their money by telling them that it would be invested in copper-bottomed investments whereas the money was used for other purposes and some of it was taken by the assured. The amount said to have been lost is about US$1.35 million. (2) Civil proceedings in Panama against the assured companies claiming damages for fraudulent trading.

---

104 [2003] 1 Lloyd's Rep IR 746, para 21.
105 [2002] 2 Lloyd's Rep 88.
106 [2002] 2 Lloyd's Rep 88, 130.
107 *Inversiones Manria SA v Sphere Drake Insurance Co, Malvern Insurance Co and Niagara Fire Insurance Co (The Dora)* [1989] 1 Lloyd's Rep 69, 94; *March Cabaret Club & Casino Ltd v The London Assurance* [1975] 1 Lloyd's Rep 169.
108 *Inversiones Manria SA v Sphere Drake Insurance Co, Malvern Insurance Co and Niagara Fire Insurance Co (The Dora)* [1989] 1 Lloyd's Rep 69, 93.
109 [2006] 2 Lloyd's Rep 183.

The facts were plainly material. However, the assured's counsel argued that these facts had no relation with the risk insured against in a war risk policy.[110] Therefore, they need not be disclosed before the contract was concluded. He submitted that the court ought somehow to limit the extent to which allegations, which ultimately turned out to be false, should be held to be material to the risk and disclosable. His suggestion was that allegations that related to the risk itself were one thing but allegations of dishonesty, which had nothing to do with the risk and nothing to do with either the particular insurance or with insurance at all, were another. In relation to the Greek criminal proceedings, or the Panamanian civil proceedings, the allegations of dishonesty had nothing to do with the risks being insured and nothing to do with claims under an insurance policy. He argued that *Brotherton* should be distinguished as it was in fact concerned with allegations relating to the risk.

Waller LJ was sympathetic to this submission as he noted that the law in this area is capable of producing serious injustice.[111] If every false allegation of dishonesty must be disclosed in all types of insurance, that may place some assureds in the position of finding it difficult to obtain cover at all, and will certainly expose them to having the rates of premium increased unfairly. The decision in *Drake* may provide an answer in some but very few cases, and in any event as Mance LJ noted *Drake* did seem to provide a remedy for the increased premium that an assured may have had to pay on the basis of a false allegation. Thus, Waller LJ was tempted by the assured's submission but he nevertheless decided that as *Pan Atlantic* accurately recorded, a 'material circumstance' is one that would have an effect on the mind of a prudent insurer in estimating the risk and it is not necessary that it should have a decisive effect on his acceptance of the risk or the amount of premium to be paid.

Waller LJ[112] noted – *obiter* – that spent convictions no longer have to be disclosed but it was unrealistic to contemplate a prudent underwriter giving evidence, that he would not take into account, in assessing the risk or the terms of the insurance, a recent allegation of serious dishonesty the truth or falsity of which has yet to be determined, even if it is quite unconnected with insurance or the risk being insured. Although he highlighted the controversies, Waller LJ refused to explore in any detail what change in the law might mitigate the possible injustice and referred the matter to the Law Commission.[113]

Pending charges against the assured's employees

In *Inversiones Manria SA v Sphere Drake Insurance Co, Malvern Insurance Co and Niagara Fire Insurance Co (The Dora)*[114] it was held that the pending criminal charges against the skipper employed on the assured's yacht was a material fact which should have been disclosed regardless of whether the skipper was innocent or not. The facts of *The Dora* were briefly as follows: A Swiss company, Euro-Exchange, of which B was the chief executive decided to import a number of yachts to Europe from Taiwan. B's plan was to make improvements and additions to the fixtures and fittings of the yachts at an Italian yard and to this end he engaged L. An agreement was made to purchase *Dora* from a Taiwanese shipbuilder and L was instructed to travel to Taiwan to supervise the final stages of construction to which L went together with M as assistant and English interpreter. *Dora* was arranged to be carried to Trieste aboard *Nipponica*. In the meanwhile *Dora* was sold to the assured Panamanian company for $480,000 on condition that the yacht remained in the Mediterranean for a year after delivery.

---

110 This argument was discussed above under 'Moral Hazard' but more detailed discussion will be presented here.
111 [2006] 2 Lloyd's Rep 183, para 17.
112 [2006] 2 Lloyd's Rep 183, para 19.
113 [2006] 2 Lloyd's Rep 183, para 20.
114 [1989] 1 Lloyd's Rep 69.

Nipponica arrived at Trieste with *Dora* on board in June 1983 and L, M and F (the assured's representatives) took delivery of the yacht. On June 26, while *Dora* sailed into Santa Margherita she was boarded by customs officials who found a quantity of yacht fittings in boxes and charged L, M and F with smuggling. L, M and F were later paid a penalty and were released from arrest. In October when she was sailing to Greece a fire broke out in the engine compartment and the yacht sank after an explosion. The insurer contended that they were entitled to avoid the policy on the grounds of non-disclosure and misrepresentation of several facts including that *Dora* and her crew were involved in smuggling charges and the skipper of *Dora*, M, had a criminal record. Phillips J found for the insurer as the facts which were not disclosed were material.

The assured's counsel argued that there was no relevant relationship between those charged with smuggling and the assured. He relied on the facts that (1) When *Dora* and her crew were arrested for smuggling they were acting on behalf of Euro-Exchange. (2) At the time that the insurance was placed L had not yet been engaged to manage *Dora* for the assured company and M had not been appointed as skipper. Phillips J, however, found that both L and M were plainly persons whose moral standards were material to underwriters contemplating the insurance of *Dora*. The judge noted that so far as the Italian authorities were concerned *Dora* was in the possession and control of the assured at the time of her arrest. There was no reason to suppose that L would not continue to use M as the skipper of the vessel, as indeed he intended to do and subsequently did.

In addition to the charge for smuggling a further fact regarding M was that he had pending criminal charges. Despite the assured's counsel's attempt to challenge the contention that M's criminal record need not be disclosed firstly because it was not known to the assured and secondly it was not material, Phillips J found for the insurer. The assured had, according to Phillips J, constructive knowledge of M's criminal record given the fact that the assured should communicate to the insurer every material fact of which the assured in the ordinary course of business ought to have knowledge. In order to discharge the duty the assured should take necessary measures through the ordinary channels of intelligence in use in the mercantile world and acquire all the information as to the subject matter of the insurance.[115] Phillips J took into account that the assured entrusted the management of their vessel to L and, in particular, they entrusted him with the insuring of the yacht. L engaged M as skipper for the voyage to Santa Margherita. Moreover, one of L's most important duties as manager of *Dora* was to appoint a properly qualified skipper of the vessel. The normal course of business required him to check on M's character. He made no such check. Had L made enquiries he would have learned of M's criminal record. Prospective employers are entitled to obtain particulars of these records. M's convictions should have been known to L and to the assured in the ordinary course of business and should have been disclosed to the defendants.

Dishonesty of the assured

A fraudulent attempt to defraud a third party before the insurance contract was concluded is in itself a material fact.[116] In *Insurance Corp of the Channel Islands v Royal Hotel Ltd*[117] M, whose knowledge was attributable to the Royal Hotel, had instructed an accounts clerk with Royal Hotels' parent company, C, to create invoices showing accommodation at the hotel let to C in July, August and September 1991. No such accommodation had in fact been let to C. As was held by the Court, M's purpose and intention in giving the instruction was to manipulate Royal Hotel's occupancy figures so as to create a more favourable picture of its trading performance to present, if it became necessary,

---

115 *Proudfoot v Montefiore* (1867) LR 2 QB 511, at 521, Chief Justice Cockburn.
116 *Insurance Corp of the Channel Islands v Royal Hotel Ltd* [1998] Lloyd's Rep IR 151.
117 [1998] Lloyd's Rep IR 151.

to one or other of Royal Hotel's bankers. A tendency to be dishonest with bankers was a material fact as it would suggest both a risk of distortion of any figures which might be presented in the context of a material damage claim as well as the possibility of other more serious types of dishonesty in relation to the property and claims.[118] Similarly, in *James v CGU Insurance plc*[119] the fact that the assured was in dispute with the Inland Revenue and Customs & Excise over a sum which brought into question the viability of the business was held to be material to disclose in relation to a policy covering the business property and business interruption.

Previous refusals to insure

In the context of marine insurance previous refusals of cover was found not material. In *Glasgow Assurance Corp v Symondson*,[120] Scrutton J stated that the material facts are the subject matter, the ship and the perils to which the ship is exposed, once these facts are disclosed the insurer must form his judgment of the premium or whether to take the risk or not and other's people's judgment of the risk is quite immaterial. Proposal forms may enquire whether the proposer has ever been refused insurance on a previous occasion and any express question as such, doubtlessly, must be answered truthfully.[121] In the non-marine context however, this fact is material. In *Locker & Woolf Ltd v Western Australian Insurance Co Ltd*[122] previous refusal on a motor policy was held to be material to a proposal for fire insurance. This was a material fact because, according to Slesser LJ,[123] if known to the insurers it might lead them to take the view that the proposers were persons with whom it was undesirable to have contractual relations.

Overvaluation

When the assured and insurer agree on the value of the subject matter insured, that is conclusive in terms of the amount of the indemnification that the assured receives if the risk occurs.[124] If the assured declares the value of the subject matter insured higher than the actual value of the vessel the question then may arise whether overvaluation is a material fact which should be disclosed to the insurer. One consideration might be that the nature of the risk is not affected by the amount at which the goods are valued.[125] On the other hand it might be argued that the greater the excess over market value the greater will be the temptation to advance a fraudulent claim.[126] Furthermore, it might be a concern that the excessive valuation may lead not only to suspicion of foul play, but that it has a direct tendency to make the assured less careful in selecting the ship and captain, and to diminish the efforts which in case of disaster he ought to make to diminish the loss as far as possible, and cannot therefore properly be called altogether extraneous to the risks.[127] In *The Dora*,[128] the facts of which were given above under 'Pending charges against the assured's employees', in the policy *Dora*'s value, inclusive of all fixtures and fittings, was represented to be $480,000. This was the real price that the assured paid for her. This exceeded *Dora*'s market value by at least $80,000.

---

118 [1998] Lloyd's Rep IR 151, 158.
119 [2002] Lloyd's Rep IR 206.
120 (1911) 16 Com Cas 109.
121 *Hamilton & Co v Eagle Star & British Dominions Insurance Co Ltd* (1924) 19 Ll L Rep 242.
122 [1936] 1 KB 408.
123 [1936] 1 KB 408, at 414.
124 MIA 1906, s 27(3).
125 See arguments in *Ionides v Pender* (1873–1874) LR 9 QB 531.
126 *North Star Shipping Ltd v Sphere Drake Insurance plc* [2005] 2 Lloyd's Rep 76, para 226, Colman J; *Haigh v De la Cour* (1812) 3 Camp 319.
127 *Ionides v Pender* (1873–1874) LR 9 QB 531, at 538–539.
128 [1989] 1 Lloyd's Rep 69.

Phillips J was persuaded by the expert who stated that underwriters assume and accept that an assured insuring a yacht will put forward the value he subjectively believes the yacht to have. More particularly, the purchaser of a yacht will naturally insure the yacht for the price he pays. One expert said his company's proposal form specifically asks for details of the purchase price. Thus, in the case of a valued policy, where a yacht owner insures for the price he has paid, a discrepancy between the insured value and the open market value was not material.

Valuation of a vessel might include an amount of the ship's net earnings on the voyages for which she has firm freight contracts.[129] Alternatively, valuation of a ship may be fixed in a very rough and ready way, such as cost of building or amount of shipping in the market.[130]

Overvaluation because of good management reasons can also be taken into consideration. The market value might take into account the current condition of the vessel, for instance, if the vessel was time chartered, that might slightly increase the value. Moreover, the owner, in the valuation, might include the previous expenditure on maintenance. Colman J in *North Star Shipping Ltd v Sphere Drake Insurance plc*[131] found it not unreasonable for an assured valuing the vessel at a level reflecting his discounted earlier capital investment as well as the future net revenue to be derived from the time charter. In *North Star* the vessel was insured in the value of US$4m although the market value of the vessel was US$1.35m. With the abovementioned considerations Colman J held that a disparity with market value which was no greater than roughly reflected those components would not normally be treated as material. Upon the facts the judge found up to US$3m would not be outside the range of what was consistent with prudent slip management. This conclusion therefore rendered the additional US$1m cover which went beyond that level, speculative as distinct from reasonably protective.

Waller LJ, in the Court of Appeal,[132] adopted the same test as that of Colman J that the relevant test of materiality is whether the disparity between the insured value and the market value is consistent with prudent ship management. However, unlike Colman J, Waller LJ did not find the £1m in excess of £3m speculative, as the underwriter might prefer to take the extra premium rather than investigate whether the good management reasons establish $4 million as opposed to some lesser figure.[133]

It appears that overvaluation is material if it is so great as to make the risk speculative.[134] In *Eagle Star Insurance Co Ltd v Games Video Co (GVC) SA (The Game Boy)*[135] the Court found overvaluation material due to the significant difference between the vessel's actual value and the value declared for the purpose of insurance. The Court was convinced that the assured could not have honestly believed that the vessel, which was worth $100,000, might be worth $1.8m.

Non-payment of premium

The discussion on non-payment of premium is focused on whether it is itself a material fact or whether it is material only in combination with some other material facts. The considerations supporting the view that non-payment of premium is not material are: (1) s.53(1) together with

---

129 Gow, W., Marine Insurance: A Handbook, 1st edn, London, 1931, p 85.
130 Gow, 85.
131 [2005] 2 Lloyd's Rep 76, para 226.
132 [2006] 2 Lloyd's Rep 183, para 46. Waller LJ did not reach any concluding view in relation to overvaluation given that Colman J's judgment was upheld in relation to the allegations made in the Greek criminal proceedings, and the allegations made in the civil proceedings in Panama.
133 [2006] 2 Lloyd's Rep 183, para 49.
134 *Ionides v Pender* (1873–1874) LR 9 QB 531, at 539.
135 [2004] 1 Lloyd's Rep 238.

policy terms such as the premium warranty, provides the insurer with protection in the event the assured defaults to pay the premium, hence there is no need to refer to s.18(3) of the MIA 1906; (2) it would be unusual to disclose past premium payment records in the absence of any inquiry in relation to it; (3) delay in payment of premiums might be defined by the experts as a common malaise in the marine insurance market; and (4) delays in payment are not necessarily indicative of financial difficulties on the part of the shipowner, and such financial difficulties are not necessarily indicative of actual or prospective poor maintenance.

With these considerations in mind, in The Martin P,[136] Mr Siberry QC held that late payment or failure to pay premium under a previous policy is not in itself material to the risk being insured under a Hull and Machinery policy.

In North Star, Colman J refused to go as far as Mr Siberry QC in The Martin P and did not accept the proposition that non-payment of premium can never be material itself[137] but the judge reserved the position that proof of inducement for non-payment of premium might be a very rare situation. In North Star it was contended that a previous policy was cancelled by hull and machinery underwriters for non-payment of premium and this was a material fact. The Martin P was to be distinguished from North Star due to the fact that in the former the policy contained both a broker's cancellation clause and a premium warranty clause whereas none was seen in the latter. Colman J was of the view that[138] the risk that premium will not be paid on time goes exclusively to the payment of consideration for the underwriter assuming the risk. It is neither a moral hazard nor does it fall within the scope of a matter going to the magnitude of the insured risk. A further consideration in North Star was the cash flow problems that the assured was confronting at the relevant period of time.[139] In Colman J's view, the other material facts in the case including the pending Greek and Panamanian proceedings and the excessive overvaluation of the North Star rendered the previous cancellation of their policy for non-payment of premium an inseparable facet of the assured's financial problems which were material to be disclosed particularly because of their relevance to moral hazard as distinct from the risk of non-payment of premium.[140] In the Court of Appeal, Waller LJ had reservations[141] about Colman J's ruling regarding non-payment of the premium. Waller LJ refused to deal with the other factors which relate to the financial position of the owners but expressed his view that non-payment of premium is either material on its own or not, and since it seems to go to the owner's credit risk, and not to the risk insured, it will not be regarded as material.[142]

(Un)conscionable avoidance

As noted above, in Brotherton v Aseguradora Colseguros SA[143] the critical question was whether the validity of reinsurers' purported avoidance for their non-disclosure may depend upon whether the allegations reflected the true facts and there was actual misconduct justifying the allegations and investigations. In Brotherton the allegations were held to be material and needed to be disclosed despite the fact that the assured knew there was no ground for the allegations and the accused would be able to prove his innocence. The assured in such a case is required to disclose the allegations as well as his belief

136 [2004] 1 Lloyd's Rep 389.
137 [2005] 2 Lloyd's Rep 76, para 234.
138 [2005] 2 Lloyd's Rep 76, para 232.
139 [2005] 2 Lloyd's Rep 76, para 235.
140 [2005] 2 Lloyd's Rep 76, para 236.
141 Waller LJ, as was with the issue on overvaluation, did not reach any concluding view in relation to non-payment of premium given that Colman J's judgment was upheld in relation to the allegations made in the Greek criminal proceedings, and the allegations made in the civil proceedings in Panama.
142 [2006] 2 Lloyd's Rep 183, para 50.
143 [2003] 1 Lloyd's Rep IR 746.

as to his innocence. A further matter was whether the assured is permitted to prove his innocence at a trial to prevent the insurer from avoiding the policy (unconscionability of avoidance). A similar matter was argued in *North Star* because the policy was placed in April 1994, the vessel became constructive total loss on July 1994 and although the charges had been made prior to the placement, the charges were dismissed by the Greek courts in 1995 and 1996 and the hearing dates before Colman J were 11 October 2004 to 3 February 2005. Therefore, the Court of Appeal discussed the correct approach to an allegation of dishonesty, which at the time of placement the assured would maintain was false, and ultimately after placement of the insurance turns out to be false, or an allegation that the insurers do not seek to establish as true.

It is first necessary to refer to *Drake Insurance plc (In Provisional Liquidation) v Provident Insurance plc.*[144] Mr Justice Moore-Bick did not accept that the proof at trial of facts showing that the earlier accident should have been treated as a 'no fault' accident at the time of renewal can prevent the insurer from relying on its avoidance of the policy. The judge expressed his unease at the prospect of an insurer's avoiding the contract for non-disclosure in such circumstances, but he nevertheless found it out of the court's jurisdiction to stop the insurer from avoiding the contract. His reasons were that (1) if grounds exist to justify avoidance, once communicated to the assured it is effective immediately. (2) The insurer does not need to invoke the assistance of the court, nor does the court have jurisdiction to declare that his right to avoid has been lost retrospectively by reason of subsequent events. This is quite distinct from the question whether the right to avoid has arisen in the first place. In *Brotherton*, Mance LJ agreed with Moore-Bick J's ruling in *Drake* for the same reasons stated by the trial judge. Mance LJ[145] also added that since the duty of good faith applies in the formation of the contract, it is simply inept to extend it to the enforcement of the contract in litigation. If grounds exist to justify avoidance the insurer does no more than standing on his own rights in resisting claims on the basis that the contract no longer exists. Mance LJ called the unconscionability argument as 'no more than a way of seeking to avoid by a side-wind the effects in law of the assured's non-disclosure'.[146]

Brotherton was decided by the Court of Appeal on 22 May 2003. Moore Bick J's ruling was appealed in *Drake* and the Court of Appeal's judgment was delivered on 17 December 2003. Rix and Clarke LJJ, at the Court of Appeal in *Drake*, expressed the view that the doctrine of good faith should be capable of limiting the insurer's right to avoid.[147] *North Star* was decided by Colman J on 22 April 2005 and by the Court of Appeal on 7 April 2006. In *North Star* counsel for the assured at trial did not seek to rely on *Drake* to assert that the insurers would be in breach of their duty of good faith in avoiding the policy under such circumstances. In the Court of Appeal, by way of an amendment to the notice of appeal, counsel acting for the assured sought to argue that since by the date of avoidance the owners had been acquitted of all charges in the Greek proceedings, the insurers should not have been entitled to treat the allegations as material at that time; the counsel made clear that his case would be based on a lack of good faith as recognised in *Drake*. The insurer resisted the amendment on the basis that whether or not the point ever had any chance of success, it could not be fair to run the point in the Court of Appeal for the first time since further evidence would have been required in relation to insurers' knowledge as at the time of avoidance. The Court of Appeal did not permit such an amendment as it would take quite exceptional circumstances to contemplate an amendment in the Court of Appeal, which might entail the matter being returned to the judge to hear further evidence, thus the only argument at the Court of Appeal was materiality of criminal convictions and their relevance to this risk insured against which was explained above.

---

144 [2003] Lloyd's Rep IR 781, para 32. The facts of *Drake* were given above.
145 [2003] 1 Lloyd's Rep IR 746, para 48.
146 [2003] 1 Lloyd's Rep IR 746, para 48.
147 See below *Insurers' Duty of Good Faith*.

A further issue discussed in *Brotherton* was, to prevent the insurer from avoiding the policy, whether the assured should be permitted to adduce evidence at trial to prove his innocence. Two points were emphasised by Mance LJ:[148] (1) It is clear that rescission in the general law of contract is by act of the innocent party operating independently of the court. (2) Materiality falls to be considered as at the date of the placing, by reference to the circumstances (which may include no more than intelligence) within an assured's knowledge at that date. Likewise, inducement is assessed on the basis of whether the circumstances withheld would, if known, have caused the insurer to act differently, either by not writing the insurance at all or by only writing it on different terms. Before the contract is concluded, an assured can only disclose what lies within his knowledge, but the assured must at least disclose what is within his knowledge, provided that it is material in the above sense. Moreover, Mance LJ found nothing in *Pan Atlantic* to support a conclusion that avoidance for non-disclosure of otherwise material information should depend upon the correctness of such information, to be ascertained if in issue by trial. Neither, under English law, is rescission subject to any requirement of good faith or conscionability.[149] Holding otherwise would be an unsound introduction to English law. First, it would encourage the assured not to disclose material facts on the possibility that if insurers never found out about the intelligence, the assured would face no problem in recovering for any losses which arose – however directly relevant the intelligence was to the perils insured and to the losses actually occurring. Second, investigating the intelligence would result in expensive litigation, and perhaps force a settlement, in circumstances when insurers would never have been exposed to any of this, had the assured performed its *prima facie* duty to make timely disclosure.

One of the issues discussed by Waller LJ in *North Star* was the significance of a letter obtained from the Serious Fraud Office (SFO) in London. The letter which was dated 30 March 1993 (the insurance was placed in 1994) and written by the Case Controller responsible for a prosecution of B was confirming that the assured was regarded by the office as a victim of a fraud perpetrated by a third party, B. By relying on this letter the assured argued that had there been disclosure at the time of the placement of the insurance of these criminal proceedings, it would have been included in the brokers' presentation to the underwriters. It was asserted that if the underwriters had been shown the SFO letter they would have been reassured sufficiently to accept the risk.

Colman J[150] emphasised that such exculpatory evidence does not diminish the materiality of allegations of fraud in the course of pending proceedings, criminal or civil. Such evidence would go only to inducement in relation to which the question would have to be asked whether the underwriter was induced to write the risk by the failure to disclose information as to the material facts and such exculpatory evidence as would probably have been presented with it. Waller LJ explained that this might only happen in a situation in which it is so clear that there is nothing in the allegation, such as an admission from the person who has made the allegation that he has made a terrible mistake as to identity, that the allegation no longer needs disclosing because it is no longer material.[151] The facts seem to be similar to *Drake* given that the letter did exist before the contract was concluded and the time the charges were made against the assured in Greece; nevertheless, as stated above, in *North Star*, because counsel for the assured did not argue it before Colman J, it was not permitted at the Court of Appeal to rely on *Drake*. If counsel had developed their case by relying on *Drake* before the trial judge, it can be speculated that the judge might follow *Drake*. This argument might be influenced by Colman J's view in *The Grecia Express* on the accepting proof of innocence by

148 [2003] 1 Lloyd's Rep IR 746, para 18.
149 [2003] 1 Lloyd's Rep IR 746, para 34.
150 [2005] 2 Lloyd's Rep 76, para 210.
151 [2006] 2 Lloyd's Rep 183, para 35.

the trial judge to prevent the insurer from avoiding the policy in case of allegations or charges against the assured. Colman J's view in *The Grecia Express* was rejected by the Court of Appeal in *Brotherton* whereas in *Drake*, on the basis of the facts existing before the contract was concluded, it was accepted with regard to proof of inducement. It is still yet to be seen which direction the rulings will go in the future. In *Drake* there were two grounds for Rix LJ's judgment that (1) the insurer did not prove inducement (2) if the ruling on the inducement point was wrong, avoidance in such a case would be in breach of the insurer's duty of good faith. The insurers' duty of good faith, as will be explained below, is a controversial matter given the draconian and in some case inappropriate remedy of avoidance which will not be desirable for the assured who discovers the insurer's breach after the risk occurs. It is submitted that the duty of good faith relied by Rix LJ in *Drake* must be the duty of good faith arising from general principles of openness and fair dealing which does not strictly fall in the scope of section 17. Good faith is a broad subject in the context of the 'general' duty of good faith which presumably is to act in a contractual relationship openly and fairly. The definition of good faith, which sits easily in each case, might not be a very straightforward exercise. Moreover, it would be required to prove the insurer's bad faith. The proof of inducement point, which was raised by Colman J in *North Star* and by the majority in *Drake*, supports the notion that proof of materiality on its own does not entitle the insurer to avoid the contract in the absence of proof of inducement. But it must be remembered that both materiality and inducement have to be assessed on the basis of the facts and situations which did exist before the contract was concluded. Therefore, it sounds in accord with the principles of the duty of good faith as set out by section 17–20 of the MIA 1906, not to permit the assured to prove his innocence at trial after the contract was concluded if the innocence had not yet been proved before the contract was concluded. *Drake* would not help in such a situation. If civil or criminal charges did exist before the contract was concluded it is clearly the case that they are material and they should be disclosed. If the assured knows that he is innocent he still has to disclose the material facts because despite the existence of the charges his innocence is yet officially to be proved. Mance LJ's concerns are well founded in relation to this issue, namely that permitting the assured not to disclose such material facts upon consideration that if there would be a trial between the insurer and himself in the future the assured would be able to prove his innocence, has the danger of introducing a new principle that the assured does not need to disclose criminal charges or allegations for which he was charged with no grounds, so that the assured would be permitted to conceal such material facts before the contract was concluded. He might be hoping that the issue will never be questioned by the insurer in a trial and thus he can escape from his duty of disclosure in this respect regardless of whether he is indeed proven guilty or not. Furthermore, proof of the assured's innocence at trial would impose upon the insurer an obligation to conduct the very kind of investigation that Mance LJ in *Brotherton* held there was no obligation to carry out and which would be unacceptable[152] for all the reasons he gave in that case. It should be remembered that the issue is mitigated by the rule that charges that are not very serious or rumours that do not rely on any resources do not need to be disclosed. It might indeed be the case that the insurer might think there is no smoke without fire but nevertheless, if there are charges they should be disclosed firstly because they are material and secondly they are likely to induce the insurer to enter or not enter into the contract. If the circumstances are similar to *Drake* or *North Star* (with regard to the SFO letter) the lack of inducement argument might well be brought and there seems to be no controversy with the *Drake* ruling on inducement and the principles applicable to the duty of good faith. In such a case *Drake* might help if innocence was proved before the contract was concluded in which case the fact would not have been material any more anyway. The difference between *Brotherton* and *Drake* is that as Rix LJ pointed

---

152 See Arnould, para 15–171.

out,[153] in the former the assured was debarred from adducing evidence of any matters that occurred after the contract of reinsurance had been written, or evidence that was not available to them at that time, with a view to proving that the allegations against the bank officers were without foundation. Whereas in *Drake* the outcome of the January 1994 accident occurred and was known to S prior to contract, even if then unknown to the insurer.

Finally, it is submitted that the insurer's good faith argument has the danger to open endless arguments and discussions as to (1) the definition of good faith, (2) proof of bad faith, and (3) litigation to prove the assured's innocence at the post-contractual stage. Moreover, it would be against the principle that inducement and materiality should be assessed on the basis of the information which did exist before the contract was concluded. If innocence had not yet been proved at that time the insurer might prove inducement which, on the basis of the principles applicable to the duty of good faith, entitles the insurer to avoid the contract.

Disclosure by agent effecting insurance

Section 19 of the Marine Insurance Act 1906 states that a broker is required to disclose all facts known to him and also all facts known to the assured. The effect of s.19 is to impose a duty of utmost good faith upon the broker, independent of the duty imposed upon the assured under s.18 of the 1906 Act.[154]

The broker is under an independent duty to disclose material facts or to state material facts correctly. Breach of this independent duty still renders the policy voidable.

A broker potentially faces personal liability in damages if insurers can prove loss arising from the broker's conduct. Breach of the duty of utmost good faith does not of itself give rise to damages but only to a right of avoidance. However, the broker may face liability in damages where he has fraudulently misstated a material fact, under the common law tort of deceit. Further, s.2(1) of the Misrepresentation Act 1968 may provide a remedy in damages against a broker who has failed to check the truth of his statements. There is thus no remedy in damages for innocent misrepresentation. In addition, there is no remedy in damages for a failure to speak whether the information is withheld fraudulently, negligently or innocently. It should be remembered that a half-truth can be construed as a positive misstatement and thus can give rise to damages for fraud. A broker who disclosed some but not all relevant information can often be regarded as having misrepresented the true position.[155] As the broker is the agent of the assured, any liability in damages which is incurred by the broker may be in the alternative visited on the assured under the principle of vicarious liability with the assured's right of recourse against the broker.

Facts which need not be disclosed

Under section 18(3) of the MIA 1906 there are four circumstances that need not be disclosed. These types of fact are discussed below.

Any circumstance which diminishes the risk

Decorum Investments Ltd v Atkin (The Elena G)[156] concerns insurance of a motor yacht, *Elena G*, purchased by a Russian businessman in 1997. *Elena G* was moored at Sotogrande, a purpose-built resort in

---

153 [2004] 1 Lloyd's Rep 268, para 72–73.
154 *HIH Casualty & General Insurance Ltd v Chase Manhattan Bank* [2003] 2 Lloyd's Rep 61.
155 *HIH Casualty & General Insurance Ltd v Chase Manhattan Bank* [2003] 2 Lloyd's Rep 61.
156 [2001] 2 Lloyd's Rep 378.

Spain, developed around three golf courses, tennis courts, a polo park and a marina. The facilities provided included security arrangements for the benefit of all residents, for instance all roads into the resort were manned or electronic barriers. A private security company provided security guards for patrol with access points and a control tower above the marina as well as extensive CCTV coverage of both the marina and the resort generally.

The yacht became a constructive total loss after a fire broke out on board the vessel in April 1999 whilst she was at Sotogrande. There was in fact no evidence of malicious attack by any third party. The insurer denied liability for non-disclosure of material facts including the threats of physical attack in Russia and in Spain to the assured as well as his family and his assets by Russian political enemies and Russian organised crime. The court found that there was no such threat as argued by the insurers, the assured's motive in establishing armed security protection in Spain was to protect his children from risks of abduction and not to protect his property, such security being typically engaged by Spanish businessmen of his status and financial standing. The yacht was indeed moored in a secured area but this fact, although may have been material, did not fall to be disclosed as the security precautions actually diminished any risk to which the vessel was exposed.

The insurer's argument in terms of materiality of the location of the yacht insured was once again rejected by reason of s.18(3)(a) in another case, The Dora[157] the facts of which were stated above.[158] As will be remembered the yacht was purchased from a shipyard in Taiwan and the plan was to make improvements and additions to the fixtures and fittings of the yachts at an Italian yard. Dora sank after an explosion while sailing to Greece from Italy. The material facts in this case were discussed above, in addition to those there was also a number of facts which diminished the risk which did not have to be disclosed: The insurer argued that at the inception of the risk the fitting out of Dora by the yard in Italy was not completed. Accordingly the stage had not been reached at which the vessel could properly be insured under a policy designed to cover navigation risks that, as alleged by the insurer, should have been disclosed. The judge held that if, on the date that the policy incepted Dora had not come on risk because she was still undergoing alteration, this reduced, rather than increased, the insurer's exposure. Moreover, while she was at the yard in Italy, Dora was probably covered by the yard's builders risk policy in the event of which the insurer had the benefit of participating in double insurance, which again reduced their risk. Furthermore, the risks to which Dora was exposed while at the yard were typical laid up risks under the Institute Yacht Clauses 1977 and lesser in degree than the risks to which the vessel would be exposed when in commission.

Any circumstance that is known or presumed to be known to the insurer

The issue has been discussed especially in relation to the information provided in Lloyd's List, the daily specialist newspaper on shipping-related news, which has been published since the days when Edward Lloyd founded his coffee shop.[159] In Morrison v Universal Marine Insurance Co[160] the broker was instructed to obtain cover on a vessel and her chartered freight. He then received information suggesting that the vessel had stranded, but was doubtful as to its accuracy and procured a line of £500 on chartered freight. The news of the stranding then became known and the action was brought to recover £500 in relation to the only line which had been written. The issue concerned the direction to the jury as to whether the subsequent issue of a policy in terms of the partially completed slip

---

157 [1989] 1 Lloyd's Rep 69.
158 See Pending charges against assured's employees.
159 See www.lloydslist.com
160 (1872–1873) LR 8 Ex 40. The case was appealed but no leave to appeal was given on this ground (1872–1873) LR 8 Ex 197.

constituted an election by the insurers not to rely on the non-disclosure. One of the arguments raised was that the broker did not need to disclose the information from his own knowledge as the information was published in the Lloyd's List, which was (and still is) a daily newspaper containing hundreds of entries relating to shipping in all parts of the world. The insurers were in fact subscribers to this newspaper. Bramwell B's[161] view on this was restrictive. The judge stated that this was an issue about a particular ship rather than being a general matter that must be taken notice of. Thus, to hold the underwriter bound to carry in his head all that is contained in Lloyd's List relating to a ship in which he has no interest would put a difficult and needless burden on the underwriter, whereas, Bramwell B found that to hold the shipowner bound to disclose such information puts no difficulty in the way of the owner. In the modern world such arguments are brought in respect of on-line information centres. In *Sea Glory Maritime Co, Swedish Management Co SA v AL Sagr National Insurance Co*[162] Blair J referred to Bramwell B's abovementioned ruling. In *Sea Glory* the assured argued that the information about the port state controls and detentions was available on-line, and as the expert evidence confirmed, it is market practice for insurers to access such information on renewal. Blair J found that Bramwell B's view reflected the commercial realities of the day and similarly, an underwriter does not have to carry the information in an electronic database in his head either. According to trial judge, on-line information is available to be called up when required, and the evidence of the expert underwriters in the present case is that the usual practice in the market is to do so. Blair J noted that a reasonable underwriter is presumed to know matters which he should have known from the facts in his possession or matters which he had means of learning from the sources available to him but the fact that information is available to an underwriter on-line does not necessarily give rise to a presumption of knowledge.

Blair J in *Sea Glory* discussed whether the assured made a fair presentation of the risk. The question of whether the insurer should be treated as having knowledge of it is something that has to be judged on the particular facts. The assured's argument in terms of the availability of the information on on-line resources was found attractive by Blair J but was not supported by the expert evidence.[163] The editors of the latest edition of Arnould submitted that 'the proposition that there is no presumption of knowledge of facts concerning particular ships merely on the ground that they have been published in Lloyd's List or any other newspaper remains valid'.[164]

Any circumstance as to which information is waived by the insurer

Express waiver

Waiver may be express or implied.[165] Insurers may waive the assured's duty of good faith at the pre-contractual stage by an express clause in the contract to that effect. Such clauses are rare and one example of it can be seen in *HIH Casualty & General Insurance Ltd v Chase Manhattan Bank*[166] the insurance contract provided '. . . the Insured will not have any duty or obligation to make any representation, warranty or disclosure of any nature, express or implied such duty and obligation being expressly

---

161 (1872–1873) LR 8 Ex 40, 54.
162 [2013] EWHC 2116 (Comm).
163 The judge did not base the decision on the finding that the insurers ought to have been aware of it in accordance with section 18(3)(a) of the MIA 1906; in this case the insurer was not induced to enter into the contract by material non-disclosure.
164 Arnould, para 16–194.
165 *Container Transport International Inc v Oceanus Mutual Underwriting Association (Bermuda) Ltd (No.1)* [1984] 1 Lloyd's Rep 476, at 511, Parker LJ.
166 [2003] Lloyd's Rep IR 230.

waived by the insurers ... and shall have no liability of any nature to the insurers for any information provided by any other parties ... and any such information provided by or nondisclosure by other parties ... shall not be a ground or grounds for avoidance of the insurers' obligations under the policy or the cancellation thereof.'[167]

It is worth noting some of the principles expressed by the House of Lords in HIH regarding the express waiver of the assured's duty of good faith. As referred to above, under s.19 of MIA 1906, the brokers are under an independent duty to disclose to the insurer every material circumstance which the assured is bound to disclose (unless it came to his knowledge too late to communicate it to the agent) and that is known to himself. Section 19(a) also provides that the agent to insure is deemed to know every circumstance that in the ordinary course of business ought to be known by, or to have been communicated to, him. The House of Lords held in HIH that any policy wording that sought to absolve the assured from the obligation to make any disclosure was not necessarily to be construed as extending to the broker's duty. Express words would be required to relieve the broker of his independent duty of disclosure.

Another important matter the House of Lords unanimously highlighted was that a truth of statement clause which included the phrase 'any information provided by any other parties' was to be construed covering innocent as well as negligent misrepresentation or non-disclosure. Negligence was a risk which the parties could reasonably have been expected to allocate to one party or the other, so as best to achieve the commercial objectives of the contract.[168] However, on public policy grounds, a contracting party is not permitted to exclude liability for his own fraud.[169]

The controversial matter was whether it was contrary to public policy for the parties to agree that the fraud of a broker could be excluded. The House of Lords did not give a definitive ruling on this issue. Lord Scott was of the view there was no reason of public policy why a party should not exclude his contractual liability for fraudulent misrepresentation by his agent.[170] Public policy would come into play only where the agent's principal knew of or was otherwise complicit in the fraud or where the agent was the alter ego of the principal, as an executive director may be of his company.[171] Lords Hobhouse and Hoffmann seemingly inclined to the opposite view, although found it unnecessary to decide the point. Lord Hobhouse[172] noted that there were two reasons why fraud could not be excluded. One was public policy. The other was the rather different contractual point that if consent to a policy was obtained by fraudulent presentation of the risk, then a clause relieving the assured for liability from the broker's fraud could not itself have been validly consented to by the insurers. If it is the case that liability for the fraud of an agent can as a matter of law be excluded, clear words are required to achieve that result.[173]

The majority view, Lord Scott dissenting, was that even if the fraud of an agent could be excluded, the present wording was not appropriate to extend to fraud, as it was not sufficiently clear.

---

167 In HIH the insured bank released loans to a film producing company to support the production of a number of films. The loan would be repaid through the film revenues, which were assigned to the bank as security for the loan. The bank insured this security, however, the bank was not in a position to know the material facts affecting the risk. The commercial purpose of the insurance was to protect the bank against the risk that the assigned revenue would be insufficient to secure the repayment of the loan. An essential part of the reliability of the security was the insurance contract which would be valueless without the clause waiving the obligation regarding the duty of disclosure and not to make misrepresentation.
168 [2003] Lloyd's Rep IR 230, para 66 and 117.
169 [2003] Lloyd's Rep IR 230, para 16, Lord Bingham.
170 [2003] Lloyd's Rep IR 230, para 122.
171 [2003] Lloyd's Rep IR 230, para 122.
172 [2003] Lloyd's Rep IR 230, para 98.
173 [2003] Lloyd's Rep IR 230, para 16, Lord Bingham.

Implied waiver

The most disputed matter about the pre-contractual waiver arises when an insurer receives a fair presentation of the risk and is on notice of the existence of facts which would raise in the mind of a reasonable insurer a suspicion that there are other circumstances material to the risk but does not make any enquiry about those facts and proceeds to underwrite the risk. Thus, if an insurer does not ask an obvious question to investigate the facts further, despite the signs of existence of further material facts which have not been disclosed by the assured, according to this argument, the insurer should be presumed to have waived the duty of good faith at the pre-contractual stage.

Although it was tried on a number of occasions, the Courts have been rather reluctant to impose such a burden on the insurers. The court has emphasised two points in particular: (1) The duty is imposed on the assured to disclose material facts, the duty is not on the insurer to investigate the material facts, and (2) Before any question of waiver arises it is necessary to enquire whether there was a fair presentation.[174]

It has been observed by the courts[175] that there could be no waiver merely because the insurer was aware of the possibility of the existence of other material circumstances. If this were to be permitted the duty of disclosure would be emasculated to the point of extinction and waiver would become an instrument of fraud. The assured may present a summary of previous experience and so long as this summary is fair the insurer cannot complain that the full details of the experience were not disclosed. But it should be emphasised that the insurer must be entitled to assume that the summary is fair and if he then proceeds to negotiate on the basis of the summary without enquiry as to its accuracy, he waives nothing.[176]

As stated above, in *Marc Rich v Portman* the assured's loss experience was found to be material. The assured nevertheless argued that the insurer waived the duty of disclosure given that the assured's loss experience at the named ports was the natural consequence of the characteristics of the ports, which was not peculiar to the assured but was shared by all other charterers using those ports. Therefore, the assured argued that an underwriter would have been put on notice by the very nature of the contract that the ports had ordinary attributes which would or might have an impact on loading and discharge times at those ports. The presentation in *Marc Rich*, as the assured asserted, was perfectly fair since the insurer knew or ought to have known that the assured had or was likely to have had demurrage claims at the ports in question and, if the insurer wanted to know more, he could have asked but did not do so. Similarly, the assured contended that the insurer knew the particular ports for which coverage was required; if he had wanted to know more about the ports' characteristics, he could again have asked but did not do so.

Longmore J analysed the waiver of disclosure of previous losses and port characteristics separately. With regard to the assured's loss experience the judge rejected the waiver argument and this issue was upheld by the Court of Appeal. While rejecting the waiver argument Longmore J emphasised that the assured proposed coverage for a period of ten days in excess of three, whereas Marc Rich incurred an average demurrage of 8.91 days on the most recent voyages out of Kharg Island. Longmore J found that none of this was disclosed to underwriters despite the fact that the assured knew the relevance of the loss record to the assessment of the terms and rates of insurance. The judge held that the presentation was not fair because the assured decided to keep silent about the loss experience unless he was asked questions. This was the case because the assured had a

---

174 *Marc Rich & Co AG v Portman* [1996] 1 Lloyd's Rep 430, at 444, Longmore J; *Container Transport International Inc v Oceanus Mutual Underwriting Association (Bermuda) Ltd (No.1)* [1984] 1 Lloyd's Rep 476; *Synergy Health (UK) Limited v CGU* [2011] Lloyd's Rep IR 500.
175 *Harrower v Hutchinson,* (1870) LR 5 QB 584 and in *Greenhill v Federal Insurance Co Ltd* (1926) 24 Ll L Rep 383; [1927] 1 KB 65; *Container Transport International Inc v Oceanus Mutual Underwriting Association (Bermuda) Ltd (No.1)* [1984] 1 Lloyd's Rep 476.
176 *Container Transport International Inc v Oceanus Mutual Underwriting Association (Bermuda) Ltd (No.1)* [1984] 1 Lloyd's Rep 476, at 511, Parker LJ.

substantial loss experience and made no mention of this fact to an insurer who must be taken to know that there is or is likely to be a loss experience. The insurer is entitled to assume that there has been a fair presentation of the risk; even if the insurer must be taken to be aware of the existence of a loss experience, he does not know how substantial that loss experience was. A distinction was drawn between a modest or insignificant as opposed to a substantial loss experience.[177] A prudent underwriter will be entitled to assume that if losses exist, they are not such as to be worth mentioning[178] whereas Marc Rich's loss experience fell within the latter category, that is, it was substantial.

There are examples in which the court found for the assured in a waiver argument. For instance in *Marc Rich v Portman*,[179] regarding the port characteristics, Longmore J was ready to accept the waiver argument for the reasons that (1) The ports were named in the endorsements, so that the underwriter did know at what ports demurrage liabilities were going to be incurred. (2) What was disclosed as part of the contract could reasonably lead to further inquiries if the underwriter had been interested. Another example can be given from *Pan Atlantic v Pine Top* in which the broker went to a meeting with the insurer who subsequently agreed to undertake the risk. The broker had two separate documents with him representing the assured's claim record: (1) short record and (2) long record. The short record contained only the record for the years 1980 and 1981. The long record contained the record for the 1977 to 1979 period when the reinsurers were not on risk, as well as the record for the 1980 and 1981 years when they were reinsurers. The record for the 1977 to 1979 period was so bad that it was eventually common ground at the trial that no prudent underwriter would have signed the slip for 1982 on the terms that the reinsurers accepted. Although both records were available at the meeting the broker presented the risk in a way that diverted the insurer's attention from examining the loss records for the underwriting years 1977/1978 and 1979. Therefore, a major issue at the trial was whether there was a fair presentation in respect of the loss record for the 1977/1978 and 1979 underwriting years. The trial judge found it a 'perfectly fair presentation' of the years in question. His finding was upheld in the Court of Appeal and the House of Lords did not disturb that finding.

In *Marc Rich*, at the Court of Appeal, Leggatt LJ distinguished *Pan Atlantic* in that in *Pan Atlantic* a fair presentation for re-rating purposes was available but the underwriter chose not to re-rate. Again that is quite different from the circumstances of *Marc Rich* where the underwriter was being shown a risk for the first time and had no idea that there was a history of losses due to demurrage liability. There could be no waiver merely because the insurer was aware of the possibility of the existence of other material circumstances.[180] The insurer was entitled to assume the fairness of the presentation, he must be on notice of the existence of information before he can be said to waive it.[181]

Longmore J was sitting in the High Court in *Marc Rich v Portman*[182] and a similar waiver argument came before him while he was sitting as a Court of Appeal judge in *WISE Underwriting Agency Ltd v Grupo Nacional Provincial SA*.[183] In *WISE* the London reinsurers reinsured a Mexican insurance company in relation to cargo cover for a Cancun retailer's imports of luxury goods from Miami. The coverage was from Miami to Cancun, from warehouse to any store in Cancun city. A quantity of goods was stolen from a container parked outside the warehouse premises of the assured in Cancun.

Having discovered that the stolen items amounted to a cost value of $817,798, of which some $700,000 related to Rolex watches, the reinsurers, by relying on a policy clause, attempted to give

---

177 See *Sealion Shipping Ltd v Valiant Insurance Co* [2012] Lloyd's Rep IR 141.
178 *Marc Rich & Co AG v Portman* [1996] 1 Lloyd's Rep 430, at 443, Longmore J.
179 *Marc Rich & Co AG v Portman* [1996] 1 Lloyd's Rep 430, at 445, Longmore J.
180 *Harrower v Hutchinson* (1870) LR 5 QB 584 and in *Greenhill v Federal Insurance Co Ltd* [1927] 1 KB 65.
181 *Marc Rich & Co AG v Portman* [1997] 1 Lloyd's Rep 225, 234.
182 [1996] 1 Lloyd's Rep 430.
183 [2004] Lloyd's Rep IR 764.

a notice of cancellation. The reinsurers' argument was that there was a material non-disclosure with regard to the goods being imported. In the Spanish version of the original slip the word *Relojes* was used which, according to the finding of the trial judge, can mean either watches or clocks. In the English version of the original policy the word 'clocks' was used throughout. The reinsurance contract was made on the basis of a slip presentation which was originally in Spanish and was translated into English. The slip contained an Information clause which listed the items and maximum amount insured including 'Clocks: less expensive piece: US$40. Most expensive piece US$18,000 and average cost US$1,500.'

The reinsurers argued that the reinsured ought to have disclosed that the shipments included Rolexes and other high-value branded watches. It was accepted by the trial judge and was not disputed in the Court of Appeal that the fact that the cargo contained Rolex watches was a material fact because watches and in particular brands such as Rolex are regarded by underwriters as attractive targets for thieves. The issue in the Court of Appeal focused on the waiver of disclosure. The assured's counsel stated that it was apparent that the slip had been written by someone whose language was not English, and that for that and other reasons the presentation would give rise to numerous inquiries. Rix LJ was of the view that the presentation was fair[184] and the waiver argument should be accepted. Rix LJ[185] pointed out that there was nothing special or unusual about a Cancun retailer selling watches, what would have been unusual and extraordinary was, in the absence of a suggestion that the retailer was selling antique clocks, to have been selling each year millions of dollars of valuable clocks, at an *average* cost of $1,500 each, rising to $18,000. Jewellery would plainly be capable of including gold or jewelled watches. Rix LJ formulated some sample questions which could have been asked by the reinsurers as a matter of essential common sense such as: 'What are these clocks that are to be carried from Florida to Cancun with such high values and with such regular shipments?' or 'Could 'clocks' be an error in translation for watches, or clocks and watches?' or 'I need to know something more about these clocks: it seems an unusual trade for Cancun.' In any form, as Rix LJ found, it would have led immediately to the disclosure that the clocks were watches, and indeed, given the values involved, high-value branded watches. The judge distinguished *Marc Rich* in which there was nothing at all to put the underwriter on enquiry. Whereas in *WISE*, considering that Cancun is a duty free area where jewellery of up to $50,000 in value is sold, it made no business sense to imagine selling clocks as the main item in terms of values, with average pieces at a cost price of $1,500 and a highest value of $18,000. [186]

The majority of the Court of Appeal however, agreed with the trial judge that in the normal case an underwriter on the London market dealing with a London broker should be able to accept at face value a description of the goods to be insured. The underwriter was entitled to assume that he was being told what the particularly valuable items to be carried were. Contrary to Rix LJ, Longmore LJ was of the view that the method of presentation in *WISE* would put an insurer off enquiry rather than *on* enquiry.[187] Similarly, Gibson LJ[188] found that the fact that 'clocks' of an average value of $1,500, the highest value being $18,000, were being shipped from Miami to Cancun would not itself take the case out of the normal and put the reinsurers on inquiry as to whether the 'clocks' were not clocks but watches.

Asking limited questions

The form and extent of questions put on the proposal form may limit the extent of the duty of disclosure.[189] It was held in *Synergy Health (UK) Limited v CGU*[190] that the test in each case is whether,

---

184 [2004] Lloyd's Rep IR 764, para 66.
185 [2004] Lloyd's Rep IR 764, para 65.
186 [2004] Lloyd's Rep IR 764, para 73.
187 [2004] Lloyd's Rep IR 764, para 114, Longmore LJ.
188 [2004] Lloyd's Rep IR 764, para 132.
189 *Bate v Aviva Insurance UK Limited* [2013] EWHC 1687 (Comm).
190 [2011] Lloyd's Rep IR 500.

on a true construction of the proposal form, a reasonable person would think that the insurer had restricted his right to receive all material information and consented to the omission of the particular information in issue. If an insurer fails to put questions on all material matters, or puts them in an unclear way, he runs the risk of the contention that failure to ask the questions prevents him from relying on non-disclosure afterwards.

In *The Martin P*,[191] which was discussed in detail above under materiality of 'non-payment of premium', by relying on the expert view the judge found that delay in payment of premium is a common malaise in the marine market and disclosure of the premium payment record was unusual. In this case although the waiver issue did not strictly arise to resolve the dispute the judge nevertheless commented on it. Mr Siberry QC stated that determination of waiver depended on a true construction of the proposal form. The test was 'would a reasonable man reading a proposal form be justified in thinking that the insurer had restricted his right to receive all material information and consented to the omission of the particular information in issue?' On the facts the answer was no. The judge pointed out the fact that while it indicated that the insurers were interested in details of the vessel's maintenance programme, the proposal did not contain any questions about the premium payment record, nor did it seek any information about the assured's financial status or indebtedness between the assured and his ship managers or mortgagees.

Any circumstance which it is superfluous to disclose by reason of any express or implied warranty

If a statement made by the assured is a misrepresentation, the insurer has to prove materiality and inducement in order to seek a remedy for breach of the duty of good faith. However, if a statement made by the assured is drafted as an insurance warranty, as discussed in Chapter 5, all the insurer has to prove is the assured is in breach of warranty. The insurer is then automatically discharged from liability[192] without proof of materiality or inducement. Again, as was emphasised in Chapter 5, for breach of warranty, to automatically entitle the insurer to be discharged from liability there is no requirement of proof of a chain of causation between the breach of warranty and the loss. A warranty may be created by virtue of a 'Basis of the Contract Clause'[193] which renders the statements made by the assured in the proposal form the 'basis of the contract'. This type of clause is not common in marine insurance policies, however it is worth noting a case in which a warranty was created by virtue of a clause to this effect, namely *Dawsons Ltd v Bonnin*[194] in which Lord Wrenbury stated that the whole effect of the words 'basis of the contract' is to state that the proposal is to be taken to be the initiation and foundation of the contractual relationship, and the statements contained in the proposal are to be statements on the faith of which the insurers are prepared to contract. According to Lord Wrenbury the statements in the proposal are made material by virtue of the 'basis' clause. Thus, materiality is presumed to have already been proved and the parties are presumed to have agreed not to challenge materiality of such statements later. Drafting a matter as a warranty will therefore give some advantages to the insurer. However, breach of warranty discharges the insurer from future liabilities, thus, the insurer will not be entitled to avoid the policy. In *International Management Group (UK) Ltd v Simmonds*[195] the facts of which were set out above[196]

---

191 [2004] 1 Lloyd's Rep 389.
192 *Bank of Nova Scotia v Hellenic Mutual War Risk Association (Bermuda) Ltd (The Good Luck)* [1991] 2 Lloyd's Rep 191.
193 This type of clause is not permitted in consumer insurance contracts. See Consumer Insurance (Disclosure and Representations) Act 2012, s 6(2).
194 [1922] 2 AC 413.
195 [2004] Lloyd's Rep IR 247.
196 See Presumption of inducement.

the assured insured a cricket tournament against the risk of the cancellation. The tournament was indeed cancelled when the Indian Government refused to give permission for the Indian team to play a series of one-day international matches against Pakistan. There were several issues that were either not disclosed or misrepresented to the insurer before the contract was concluded. In addition to that, the insurance contained a warranty that required strict compliance[197] but was breached. The warranty was worded 'the assured shall ensure that all necessary licences, visas and permits are obtained within sufficient time prior to the insured event'. Clearly, this was not the case since after the insurance was placed the cricket board of India had to write to the Government of India to seek permission to take part in the tournament, which was the subject matter of the insurance. The ruling on warranty rendered the utmost good faith defence irrelevant, but Cooke J nevertheless considered the matter in detail as referred to above.

Warranties were created by virtue of a basis of the contract clause in *International Lottery Management v Dumas*.[198] Despite the fact that the basis of the contract clauses is not common in marine policies it is still worth referring to *Dumas* given that an argument relying on the MIA 1906 s.18(3)(d) was brought by the assured in the case. The assured insured his initiative to establish a lottery business in Azerbaijan against expropriation and confiscation. The assured confirmed that all licences were granted with regard to the lottery business in Azerbaijan but all he had was the company registration and an informal approval by the Ministry of Finance which in fact had no legal value under local law. The statements made by the assured in the proposal form were the basis of the contract that rendered the statement a warranty. The assured argued that because the statement about the licences was a warranty there was no need to disclose the absence of licences due to section 18(3). HHJ Dean QC's analysis on this issue was very brief as the judge held that 'Assuming that an exclusion is to be treated as the same as a warranty, which is arguable as a warranty operates to relieve underwriters independently of causation, the short answer to the point is that the insurer made numerous inquiries concerning the validity of permits and clearly regarded this topic as material'. Nothing turned on this point in the case but the judge's reasoning was nevertheless found 'somewhat curious and flies in the face of the statute.'[199]

Waiver of remedy for breach of the duty of good faith

Waiver by affirmation

Affirmation in the present context means an informed choice to treat the contract as continuing while having the knowledge of the facts giving rise to the right to avoid it.[200] Breach of the duty of good faith entitles the innocent party to avoid the contract.[201] Avoidance does not require any court intervention,[202] it is a self-help remedy which necessitates the party who is avoiding the contract to communicate this with the other contracting party. A person who is entitled to alternative rights inconsistent with one another will need to elect one of the two choices and if he acts in a manner which is consistent only with his having chosen to rely on one of them, the law holds him

---

197 While it was entirely out of BCCI's hands whether or not such permission could be obtained, its duty was an absolute one and did not depend upon fault.

198 [2002] Lloyd's Rep IR 237.

199 Merkin, R., 'Utmost good faith: The placement of the risk', ILM, 2002, vol 14, no 2.

200 *Container Transport International Inc v Oceanus Mutual Underwriting Association (Bermuda) Ltd (No.1)* [1984] 1 Lloyd's Rep 476, at 498, Kerr LJ; *Insurance Corp of the Channel Islands v Royal Hotel Ltd* [1998] Lloyd's Rep IR 151, 161 Mance J.

201 S 17 MIA 1906.

202 See *Brotherton v Aseguradora Colseguros SA (No.2)* [2003] Lloyd's Rep IR 746.

to his choice.[203] In the context of the duty of good faith, the two inconsistent alternative rights are to avoid and not to avoid the insurance contract and if the innocent party chooses the latter, that is called 'waiver by election' or 'electing to affirm' the contract. The party who is electing between the two inconsistent rights should be aware of the facts which give rise in law to these alternative rights.[204] Moreover, the law recognised such an election even though the party making such an election was unaware that this would be the legal entrenchment of what he did.[205] The making of his choice must be communicated unequivocally to the other party before there can be a binding affirmation.[206]

The insurer's election not to avoid the contract may be express or implied, for example, through drawing an inference from the conduct of the innocent party. An objective assessment of the impact of the relevant conduct on a reasonable person in the position of the other party to the contract can determine whether the contract was affirmed or not.[207] For instance, the acceptance of premiums with the knowledge of circumstances entitling the insurer to avoid the policy may estop the insurer from asserting that by reason of those circumstances the policy was avoided.[208] The Courts will also consider whether the insurer returned the premium after discovering the breach of the duty of good faith.[209] *Argo Systems FZE v Liberty Insurance Pte Ltd*[210] concerned the trial of preliminary points about a marine insurance claim arising out of the total loss of a floating casino, *Copa Casino*, in March of 2003. *Copa Casino* had been purchased for scrap and was to be towed as a dead ship from the US Gulf to India. She was insured for the voyage with Liberty. The voyage began on 3 March 2003 but she sank just 13 days later on 16 March in the Caribbean Sea. The insurer refused to pay the claim in his letter dated 18 July 2003 in which he raised a number of points of defence including pre-contractual misrepresentations by the assured. The assured sued Liberty in the United States District Court for the Southern District of Alabama but the action was dismissed in 2006 for want of jurisdiction. On 24 February 2009 the assured sued Liberty in England. In defending this claim Liberty raised non-disclosures and misrepresentations to avoid the policy. The counsel for the assured proffered the following points to prove that the insurer affirmed the contract: Liberty had full knowledge of the facts; despite making assertions of misrepresentation, in their July 2003 letter, Liberty did not give any notice of avoidance but proceeded on the basis only of a denial of coverage. Liberty never offered to return the premium; Liberty cannot be allowed to hold onto the premium in the hope that its policy defences prevail while at the same time reserving the right to seek to avoid. The delay of approximately seven years is so extreme as of itself to be evidence of affirmation. HHJ Mackie QC accepted that Liberty elected to affirm the contract. Liberty refused to pay, relying on its rights under an existing policy. The judge confirmed that seven years was a very long running silence. Although the letter of July 2003 identified the misrepresentation, Liberty neither sought to avoid the policy, nor did it tender the premium. Liberty might not have applied its mind directly to the avoidance issue but the test was objective. As stated above, HHJ Mackie QC found that the absence of an offer to return the premium was of itself not determinative but it was a powerful

203 *Kammins Ballrooms Co Ltd v Zenith Investments (Torquay) Ltd (No.1)* [1971] AC 850 Lord Diplock, 883; *Argo Systems FZE v Liberty Insurance Pte Ltd* [2011] Lloyd's Rep IR 427, para 37.

204 Provided that the party knows sufficient facts to understand that he has that right, it is unnecessary that he should know all aspects or incidents of those facts. What is required for affirmation is knowledge, not any form of constructive knowledge. *Insurance Corp of the Channel Islands v Royal Hotel Ltd* [1998] Lloyd's Rep IR 151, 161 Mance J.

205 *Kammins Ballrooms Co Ltd v Zenith Investments (Torquay) Ltd (No.1)* [1971] AC 850 Lord Diplock, 883.

206 *Insurance Corp of the Channel Islands v Royal Hotel Ltd* [1998] Lloyd's Rep IR 151, 161 Mance J.

207 *Insurance Corp of the Channel Islands v Royal Hotel Ltd* [1998] Lloyd's Rep IR 151, 163 Mance J.

208 *Wing v Harvey* (1853) 1 Sm & G 10.

209 *Argo Systems FZE v Liberty Insurance Pte Ltd* [2011] Lloyd's Rep IR 427, para 40.

210 [2011] Lloyd's Rep IR 427 para 40. The case went to the Court of Appeal but Liberty did not appeal the judge's conclusion on affirmation [2012] Lloyd's Rep IR 67.

factor, particularly in a case where the amount of the premium was high and there would be a reason, other than clerical inefficiency, for insurers to retain it.

Another example of relying on a policy defence where the insurer could have avoided the policy is seen in *WISE Underwriting Agency Ltd v Grupo Nacional Provincial SA*[211] the facts of which were cited above.[212] The assured lost in *WISE* on the pre-contractual waiver argument but won on the waiver by affirmation point. When the loss was notified to him the reinsurer in London in his conversation with the London placing broker, said that he had reviewed the position in relation to the loss and had decided to give 60 days' notice of cancellation. The London placing broker then informed the producing broker in Mexico that: 'Owing to this very recent loss of US$800,000 approx, we have received 60 days notice effective today to cancel this cover.' This notice was passed on to the reinsured in Mexico. Such an attempt to cancel the policy was inconsistent with what the insurer was entitled to do, that is, avoidance of the contract. It was election between two choices which are inconsistent with each other. The insurer, by relying on a policy defence, represented that he still treated the contract as enforceable between the parties whereas avoidance would have put the parties back in the position where they would have been had there been no contract. The majority of the Court of Appeal in *WISE* applied the principle that a notice of cancellation pursuant to the contract can amount to its affirmation, provided it is done at a time when the reinsurer knows of their right to avoid for non-disclosure.[213] Longmore LJ did not find waiver by affirmation but Rix LJ and Gibson LJ were satisfied that there was a waiver. The majority put emphasis on the fact that on a further visit by the London broker to the reinsurer a copy of the abovementioned email was shown to the reinsurer, who took another copy for his own files, from where it came forward in due course as part of the reinsurers' disclosure. The additional evidence was that the broker had been asked by the Mexican brokers to go back to the reinsurer to see if he could get the notice of cancellation withdrawn but that the reinsurer had refused.

In light of the abovementioned authorities the principles of waiver by affirmation may be summarised as follows:[214]

1 Election typically arises where the parties need to know where they stand, whether the contract lives or dies.
2 For there to be an election the representation must communicate a choice of whether or not to exercise a right.
3 An election may be communicated by words or conduct, provided that conduct is clear and unequivocal.
4 There is an election where with knowledge of the relevant facts the electing party has acted in a manner which is consistent only with his having chosen one of the two alternative and inconsistent courses then open to him.[215]
5 Affirmation does not depend on the actual state of mind of the other party, but on the objective manifestation of a choice.
6 The communication of affirmation must demonstrate an informed choice, that is, that the person allegedly foregoing a right was actually aware of that right.

211 [2004] Lloyd's Rep IR 764.
212 See 'Implied waiver', p. 82 et seq.
213 [2004] Lloyd's Rep IR 764. Rix LJ, para 83.
214 See *Argo Systems FZE v Liberty Insurance Pte Ltd* [2011] Lloyd's Rep IR 427 para 37, HHJ Mackie QC.
215 *Motor Oil Hellas (Corinth) Refineries SA v Shipping Corp of India (The Kanchenjunga)* [1990] 1 Lloyd's Rep 391, 398–399 per Lord Goff.

Waiver by estoppel

Breach of the duty of good faith may be waived by promissory estoppel. The requirements to prove waiver by estoppel are discussed in Chapter 5 therefore they will not be repeated here.

Damages for misrepresentation

The Marine Insurance Act 1906 ss.17–20 do not refer to damages and the only remedy stated under section 17 is avoidance of the contract. Awarding damages, where the relevant sections of the Marine Insurance Act 1906 apply, on the ground of liability in tort was finally and authoritatively considered and rejected by the Court of Appeal[216] in *Banque Financiere de la Cite SA v Westgate Insurance Co* which was affirmed by the House of Lords.[217]

In terms of damages for misrepresentation, another possibility to be considered is in contract law damages for negligent and fraudulent misrepresentation, provided under the Misrepresentation Act 1967 section 2(1),[218] and a question may arise as to whether this section may apply in the context of insurance. In *HIH v Chase Manhattan* the House of Lords commented that a claim for damages for misrepresentation based upon s.2(1) of the 1967 Act could be made in the context of a contract of insurance. In *Argo Systems FZE v Liberty Insurance Pte Ltd*[219] HHJ Mackie QC expressed his willingness to follow that approach. A separate question in *Argo* at first instance was whether, assuming such damages are available, they would be awarded in a case where avoidance has been lost. HHJ Mackie QC suggested that this issue demanded a much more detailed debate than was presented before him, and it would be more useful to bring a devoted argument before the Court of Appeal. His view was that in theory an option to claim damages for misrepresentation should not be open to the insurer who lost the right to avoid for the reason that if it is not just for an insurer to be able to avoid the contract, it is not just for it to be able to receive damages. *Argo* was appealed but the issue turned on a discussion of waiver of breach of a warranty which was sufficient for the insurer to win the case so that the Court of Appeal did not discuss the issue of damages for misrepresentation in insurance.

Section 2(2) of the Misrepresentation Act 1967 grants authority to the Courts to award damages in lieu of avoidance of the contract where a misrepresentation made is not fraudulent and if avoidance would be inequitable having regard to the nature of the misrepresentation and the loss that would be caused by it if the contract were upheld as well as the loss that avoidance would cause the other party. The point has not been finally and definitively settled[220] but, although *obiter*, Steyn J *Highlands Insurance Co v Continental Insurance Co.*[221] expressed his unwillingness to apply s.2(2) in the insurance context. In *Highlands*, the reinsured sought an order under s.2(2) of the Misrepresentation Act, 1967, declaring that the reinsurance contract was still existing. Steyn J found that the facts which the reinsured argued to prove inequitable nature of avoidance in the case were not well founded. However, the judge also made it clear that even if he had made findings of fact favourable to the reinsured on the facts argued by the reinsured, he would still have declined to grant relief under s.2(2). The judge emphasised that a remedy as harsh as avoidance applies to the duty of good faith to encourage the parties to act in good faith and it is difficult to conceive of

---

216 [1988] 2 Lloyd's Rep 513.
217 [1990] 2 Lloyd's Rep 377. *Banque Financiere de la Cite SA v Westgate Insurance Co* was applied in *Norwich Union Life Insurance Co Ltd v Qureshi* [2000] Lloyd's Rep IR 1.
218 The section does not apply to non-disclosure therefore the discussion in this paragraph concerns only misrepresentation.
219 [2011] Lloyd's Rep IR 427.
220 See Clarke, Law of Insurance Contracts, para 23–15B.
221 [1987] 1 Lloyd's Rep 109.

circumstances in which it would be equitable within the meaning of s.2(2) to grant relief from such avoidance. Similar to Mance LJ's comment in *Brotherton*, Steyn J here found avoidance by the reinsurers simply through relying on a statutory remedy which they were entitled to exercise. Such policy consideration must militate against granting relief under s.2(2) from an avoidance on the grounds of material misrepresentation in the case of commercial contracts of insurance. Moreover, if s.2(2) were to be regarded as conferring a discretion to grant relief from avoidance on the grounds of material misrepresentation the efficacy of those rules will be eroded.[222]

Duration of the duty of good faith

The duty of good faith as defined by sections 18 to 20 of the MIA 1906 only applies until the contract is made.[223] The duty is pre-contractual, as a consequence, if the assured made a misrepresentation but then corrects the misrepresentation before the insurer enters into the contract, the latter will not be entitled to avoid the contract.[224] Likewise, there is no general duty upon an assured to volunteer information concerning new matters which have come to light after the conclusion of the policy and which affect the risks already accepted.[225] Logic would suggest that such new information might be valuable to the underwriter but it need not be disclosed.[226]

On the other hand, section 17 of the Marine Insurance Act 1906 on its face is not similarly circumscribed[227] and it is accepted that the obligation of good faith as between insurer and assured continues throughout the policy.[228] However, what has not been satisfactorily explained by either the MIA 1906 or by the judiciary is the scope of the duty as well as the proper remedy applicable for its breach.

Scope of the post-contractual duty of good faith

As stated above, the duty of good faith continues throughout the contractual relationship. The duty was said to arise as an implied term[229] or as a rule of law.[230] Caution must be taken in saying that the duty derives from section 17 of the MIA 1906, for the draconian remedy of avoidance is not an adequate remedy for a post-contractual breach of the duty of good faith.[231] Therefore, a clear distinction has to be made between the pre-contractual and the post-contractual duties of good faith.[232] The content and scope of the duties are different at the two different stages.[233]

As to the definition of the post-contractual duty of good faith, in *The Star Sea*, Lord Scott[234] stated that the duty is 'as that of honesty in the presentation of a claim'. Longmore LJ in *K/S Merc-Scandia XXXXII v Lloyd's Underwriters (The Mercandian Continent)*[235] discussed various circumstances under

---

222 [1987] 1 Lloyd's Rep 109, at 118.
223 *Manifest Shipping Co Ltd v Uni-Polaris Insurance Co Ltd (The Star Sea)* [2001] 1 Lloyd's Rep 389, para 48, Lord Hobhouse.
224 *Assicurazioni Generali SpA v Arab Insurance Group (BSC)* [2003] Lloyd's Rep IR 131, para 63.
225 *Commercial Union Assurance Company et al. v The Niger Co Ltd* (1922) 13 Ll L Rep 75.
226 *The Star Sea* [2001] 1 Lloyd's Rep 389, para 54, Lord Hobhouse.
227 *The Star Sea* [2001] 1 Lloyd's Rep 389, para 5, Lord Clyde.
228 *K/S Merc-Scandia XXXXII v Lloyd's Underwriters (The Mercandian Continent)* [2001] 2 Lloyd's Rep 563, para 21. *The Star Sea* [2001] 1 Lloyd's Rep 389.
229 *Black King Shipping Corp v Massie (The Litsion Pride)* [1985] 1 Lloyd's Rep 437.
230 *K/S Merc-Scandia XXXXII v Lloyd's Underwriters (The Mercandian Continent)* [2001] 2 Lloyd's Rep 563.
231 The parties can of course agree that the remedy for post-contractual duty of good faith will be avoidance of the contract in which case avoidance will be a contractual remedy.
232 *The Star Sea* [2001] 1 Lloyd's Rep 389, para 57, Lord Hobhouse.
233 *The Star Sea* [2001] 1 Lloyd's Rep 389, para 48 and 95, Lord Hobhouse and Lord Scott, respectively.
234 [2001] 1 Lloyd's Rep 389, para 102.
235 [2001] Lloyd's Rep IR 802.

which the continuing/post-contractual duty of good faith might be applicable. Accordingly, it might be argued that a duty of good faith arises when the parties seek to vary the contractual risk in which case remedy of avoidance only applies to the variation but not to the original risk. Thus, variations cannot be an example of a post-contractual duty of good faith given that varied contract is a fresh contract that requires a fresh duty of good faith. A similar consideration applies to the renewal of the contract of insurance that requires a fresh duty of good faith before the renewed form of the contract was concluded. Held covered clauses are not different to the two abovementioned examples. A held covered clause under which the insurer holds the assured covered in certain circumstances may be regarded as a variation of the contract given that normally an additional premium has to be assessed. Thus, a fresh duty of good faith will exist before the contract is varied.

Longmore LJ then pointed out two situations in which the continuing duty of good faith may arise: (1) insurer asking for information during the policy,[236] and (2) a liability policy where the insurer exercised their right to take over the assured's defence.[237] In the latter context interests of the assured and the insurers may not be the same but they will be required to act in good faith towards each other. If, for example, the limit of indemnity includes sums awarded by way of damages, interest and costs, insurers may be tempted to run up costs and exceed the policy limit to the detriment of the assured. Longmore LJ found the assured's protection in the duty which the law imposes on the insurer to exercise his power to conduct the defence in good faith.[238]

The Courts have been careful not to extend the pre-contractual duty of good faith as set out in sections 18–20 to the post-contractual stage. In The Star Sea[239] Lord Hobhouse emphasised that it is not right to impose an extensive duty to disclose all facts which the insurer has an interest in knowing and which might affect his conduct at the post-contractual stage in reliance to the pre-contractual duty of good faith. Earlier, in New Hampshire Insurance Co Ltd v MGN Ltd,[240] the insurer contended that they were entitled to disclosure of any new information that had become available in order to determine whether to exercise their right to cancel. The Court of Appeal rejected the argument that there was no continuing duty of disclosure during the currency of any year of insurance by reason of the right to cancel. Staughton LJ stated that the Court 'should hesitate to enlarge the scope for oppression by establishing a duty to disclose throughout the period of a contract of insurance, merely because it contains (as is by no means uncommon) a right to cancellation for the insurer'.[241]

One common issue in both the pre- and post-contractual duty of good faith is that materiality and inducement are required to be established in order to seek a remedy for breach of the respective duties. [242] Nevertheless, while materiality can be defined at the pre-contractual stage it is more elusive[243] post-contractually and no satisfactory answer has been given regarding materiality. In The Mercandian Continent, Aikens J expressed (Longmore LJ agreed) that facts would only be material for these purposes if they had ultimate legal relevance to a defence under the policy.[244]

---

236 The judge noted that if there is no right for the insurer to be given information but he asks for information, no duty of good faith arises as such.

237 The only duty of the insured will be not to materially misrepresent the facts in anything he does say to insurers. If he does make any such misrepresentation, the insurer will have ordinary common law remedies for any loss he has suffered. The Mercandian Continent [2001] 2 Lloyd's Rep 563.

238 It should be noted that there is no right to claim damages if the insurer is delayed to indemnify the assured under the insurance policy. See Sprung v Royal Insurance (UK) Ltd [1999] 1 Lloyd's Rep IR 111.

239 [2001] 1 Lloyd's Rep 389, para 57.

240 [1997] LR 24.

241 [1997] LR 24, 61.

242 The Mercandian Continent) [2001] 2 Lloyd's Rep 563, para 26.

243 The Star Sea [2001] 1 Lloyd's Rep 389, para 54, Lord Hobhouse.

244 Longmore LJ agreed in The Mercandian Continent) [2001] 2 Lloyd's Rep 563, para 39.

There is no dispute as to the existence of the post-contractual duty of good faith but in terms of the period of time to which it applies, The Star Sea held that it is superseded, once the parties become engaged in litigation, by the rules contained in the Civil Procedure Rules.[245] In other words, at the stage of a disputed claim there is no duty upon the assured to make a full disclosure of his own case to the other side in litigation.[246] In The Star Sea it was alleged that the assured was under a continuing duty of good faith to disclose to the insurers any information which might affect their decision to pay or defend the claim. The insurers' contention was rejected. Lord Hobhouse explained that while it was contractual before the litigation, important changes in the parties' relationship come about when the litigation starts,[247] namely their relationship and rights are governed by the rules of procedure.[248]

It is noteworthy that while disclosure of the ship's papers was relied on by Hirst J in The Litsion Pride to hold that making a fraudulent claim is a breach of the continuing duty of good faith, this reasoning was rejected by the House of Lords in The Star Sea which overruled[249] The Litsion Pride in this respect.[250] Lord Hobhouse opined that although there had been statements to the effect that the order of ship papers were justified on the basis of the assured's duty of good faith towards the underwriter, it was far from supporting the continuing application of the duty of good faith.[251] Lord Hobhouse emphasised that the order for ship's papers had been an order made by the common law courts for the disclosure, on affidavit, of all the documentary material which had come into existence in relation to the ship which had suffered the casualty and had any possible relevance to the claim.[252] The duty of good faith applies to both marine and non-marine insurance whereas orders for ship's papers had only been made in marine insurance. The order had been a procedural remedy which could be obtained only from the court.[253] The sanction had been the stay of the action until the order had been complied with and such a failure had never been treated as providing a ground for the insurer to avoid the policy.[254] According to Lord Hobhouse, within the last 40 years, the order became obsolete.[255]

Remedy for breach of the post-contractual duty of good faith

The remedy for breach of the duty of good faith is avoidance but section 17 does not lay down the situations in which avoidance is appropriate.[256] In The Mercandian Continent Longmore LJ denied the suggestion that in every case of non-observance of good faith by the assured the insurer can avoid the contract. The particular problem with avoiding the contract for breach of a post-contractual duty of good faith is that because avoidance puts the parties back to the position they would have been in had the contract not been made, as a restitutionary remedy,[257] the parties have to return their gains under the contract to each other. Therefore, subject to s.84 of the MIA 1906 the insurer has to return the premium and the assured has to return the valid payments that, if there were

---

245 The Star Sea [2001] 1 Lloyd's Rep 389.
246 The Star Sea [2001] 1 Lloyd's Rep 389, para 4, Lord Clyde.
247 The Star Sea [2001] 1 Lloyd's Rep 389, para 74.
248 The Star Sea [2001] 1 Lloyd's Rep 389, para 75, Lord Hobhouse.
249 The Star Sea [2001] 1 Lloyd's Rep 389, para 71. Lord Hobhouse said for Hirst J's judgment in The Litsion Pride 'I consider that it should not any longer be treated as a sound statement of the law.'
250 Making fraudulent claims is accepted as a separate matter to the continuing duty of good faith. See Chapter 12.
251 The Star Sea [2001] 1 Lloyd's Rep 389, para 77, Lord Hobhouse.
252 The Star Sea [2001] 1 Lloyd's Rep 389, para 58, Lord Hobhouse.
253 The Star Sea [2001] 1 Lloyd's Rep 389, para 77, Lord Hobhouse.
254 The Star Sea [2001] 1 Lloyd's Rep 389, para 59, Lord Hobhouse.
255 The Star Sea [2001] 1 Lloyd's Rep 389, para 58.
256 The Mercandian Continent) [2001] 2 Lloyd's Rep 563, para 35, Longmore LJ.
257 The Star Sea [2001] 1 Lloyd's Rep 389, para 51, Lord Hobhouse.

any, had been made before the contract was avoided for the post-contractual breach of the duty of good faith.

If the duty derives from section 17, the only remedy will be avoidance which will be a wholly one-sided, anomalous and disproportionate remedy in favour of the insurer in the post-contract situation.[258] The possibility of claiming damages for breach of duty on the basis of breach of common law duty of care was finally and authoritatively considered and rejected by the Court of Appeal[259] in *Banque Financiere de la Cite SA v Westgate Insurance Co* and was affirmed by the House of Lords.[260] Thus, to mitigate the harsh consequences of having avoidance being the only remedy for breach of the duty of good faith, Longmore LJ held that avoidance is only appropriate in a post-contractual context in situations analogous to circumstances where the insurer has a right to terminate for breach.[261]

Conclusions about the post-contractual duty of good faith

The two examples given by Longmore LJ in *The Mercandian Continent* to illustrate the situations in which the post contractual duty may arise derive from contractual provisions. Lord Scott's[262] definition in *The Star Sea* of the post-contractual duty is 'It is, at least, that of honesty in the presentation of a claim'. Although in the past making a fraudulent claim was analysed under the post-contractual duty of good faith, because of the retrospective effect of avoidance to the valid claims which were already paid by the insurer that view was abolished and now fraudulent claims and post contractual claim are divorced subjects – at least in terms of the remedy applicable to the two distinct matters. This does not deny the fact that making a fraudulent claim might amount to a breach of the post-contractual duty of good faith[263] but what is clear is that the remedy for fraudulent duty of good faith – unless otherwise agreed by the parties is not avoidance of the contract but forfeiture of the entire claim which was affected by the breach.[264]

It is submitted that if the duty arises from contractual obligations, the remedy should be determined by the principles applicable to breach of contract.[265] Longmore LJ did not entirely reject the possibility of avoiding the contract for breach of the post-contractual duty but to mitigate the harsh consequences of avoidance the judge ruled that the insurer should not be able to avoid the contract unless the breach is so serious as to justify termination of the contract.

Presumably Longmore LJ could not deny the existence of the only statutory remedy for breach of the duty of good faith under s.17 of the MIA 1906. However, with respect, Longmore LJ's solution does not seem to render the inadequate remedy of avoidance adequate at the post-contractual stage if there had been valid claims paid by the insurer before the breach of the continuing duty of good faith in the case.

The authorities indicate that the duty seems to arise from general principles of law to act honestly, openly and fairly in contractual relationships between the parties to an insurance contract. A recent cautious example of imposing a post-contractual duty of good faith but not strictly within section 17 is seen from a non-marine case, *Horwood v Land of Leather Ltd*,[266] in which the assured settled the claim on the terms which prejudiced the insurers' subrogation rights. This amounted to breach

---

258 *The Star Sea* [2001] 1 Lloyd's Rep 389, para 51,57, Lord Hobhouse.
259 [1988] 2 Lloyd's Rep 513.
260 [1990] 2 Lloyd's Rep 377.
261 *The Mercandian Continent*) [2001] 2 Lloyd's Rep 563, para 35 Longmore LJ.
262 *The Star Sea* [2001] 1 Lloyd's Rep 389, para 102.
263 See *The Mercandian Continent*) [2001] 2 Lloyd's Rep 563.
264 *Versloot Dredging BV v HDI Gerling Industrie Versicherung AG* [2013] EWHC 1667 (Comm); *Aviva Insurance Ltd v Brown* [2012] Lloyd's Rep IR 211.
265 *The Mercandian Continent*) [2001] 2 Lloyd's Rep 563, para 40, Longmore LJ.
266 [2010] Lloyd's Rep IR 453.

of post-contractual duty of good faith but Teare J did not prescribe avoidance but the assured lost his claim under the policy. It is submitted that if the continuing duty of good faith derives from a contractual obligation, the remedy should be determined in accordance with the principles applicable to contractual remedies. If the duty derives from the general principles of honesty and fairness the situation is vague and may lead to uncertainty in this area, however, as seen above, the judges determine the remedy as justice requires in the circumstances. There is no question about the existence of the duty but the problems mostly focus on the scope of the duty and remedy applicable for its breach. Therefore, the judges' professionalism and skills should be trusted in finding the most adequate and justified remedy for the situation.

Insurers' duty of good faith

In *Carter v Boehm*, Lord Mansfield stated 'Good faith forbids either party by concealing what he privately knows, to draw the other into a bargain, from his ignorance of that fact, and his believing the contrary.' It is neither denied in the modern world that the duty under section 17 is mutual.[267]

The insurer's duty of good faith may be analysed under two separate headings: (1) The duty of good faith under sections 17–20; and (2) The duty of good faith which falls outside the relevant sections but arises as a principle of law because justice and fairness require good faith.

The insurers' duty of disclosure within the meaning of sections 17–18 came before the Courts in *Banque Financiere de la Cite SA v Westgate Insurance Co*[268] in which the insurer knew about the fact that the broker was defrauding the assured but did not warn him about it. B approached the assured bank for a loan of 80 million Swiss Francs to develop a luxury hotel in Spain. The bank wanted the risk of repayment to be insured and B appointed L to place the insurance. The insurance would be assigned to the bank so the beneficiary of the policy would be the bank against default in repayment of the loan. In the process of placing the insurance the broker was fraudulent in that he certified that the banks were insured when in fact the insurance had not been placed at that stage. The banks released the loan despite this fraud and in the end the insurance was placed but with a fraud exception clause. The bank also wanted to be secured by valuable stones and gems, which again, without the knowledge of the bank, were fraudulently overvalued as they were worthless. B and the broker L disappeared after they obtained 80 million Swiss Francs from the bank. Having found out that the valuable stones in fact were worth nothing the bank made a claim under the insurance policy which was bound to be rejected due to the fraud exception clause. The final alternative for the bank was to rely on the breach of the insurer's duty of good faith. It was accepted by the Courts that the pre-contractual duty of good faith is a mutual duty but the remedy provided by the MIA 1906 s.17 is avoidance of the contract. The assured, however, claimed damages for the obvious reason that avoidance in such a case was not an adequate remedy. At first instance Steyn J found for the assured. It is worth noting at this stage the reason which Steyn J relied on in his judgment that:

> (1) Although it is meaningful to accept the principle of mutual duty of good faith, it seems anomalous that there should be no claim for damages for breach of those duties in a case where that is the only effective remedy; (2) If avoidance is the only remedy, the rights of the assured arising from a breach of the obligation of good faith in this case are inadequately protected, that is, the only claim is for a return of the premium; (3) Such a result leads to an

---

267 *The Star Sea* [2001] 1 Lloyd's Rep 389, para 47, Lord Hobhouse.
268 [1990] 2 Lloyd's Rep 377.

imbalance and unfairness in the relationship between the insured and insurer; (4) The assured established a common law duty of care with its requirements.[269]

The Court of Appeal disagreed with Steyn J on the establishment of the common law duty of care point. Slade LJ found no authority whatsoever to support the existence of such a tort and, quite apart from such a lack of authority, there were at least four reasons why Slade LJ found that the court should not create a novel tort of this nature:

(1) The duty of good faith as well as duress and undue influence derived from equity. Duress and undue influence do not recognise damages for their breach, it would not be adequate to separate the duty of good faith and allow the claiming of damages for its breach; (2) Materiality is judged objectively on the basis of the prudent insurer's assessment of the risk and it disregards the assured's opinion about materiality; (3) When drafting section 17 Parliament did not contemplate that a breach of the obligation would give rise to a claim for damages for breach of the duty of good faith; (4) Permitting claims for damages for breach of the duty of good faith would cause harsh results for the assured given that the duty attaches the assured and the insurer with equal force and an assured who had in complete innocence failed to disclose a material fact when making an insurance proposal might find himself subsequently faced with a claim by the insurer for a substantially increased premium by way of damages before any event had occurred which gave rise to a claim.

The House of Lords focused on the causal link between the insurer's breach and the assured's loss and since B's fraud caused the assured's loss there was no need to discuss the insurer's breach of the duty of good faith given that what was not disclosed by the insurer was not material. Lord Bridge noted that an obligation on the insurer to disclose what he knew of L's fraud could only fall within the ambit of the duty as 'material . . . to the recoverability of a claim under the policy' if L's frauds were such as would entitle the insurer to repudiate liability. Having concluded that L's frauds were not in that nature, the insurer's failure to disclose to the banks the dishonesty of L did not amount to the breach of any legal duty.

With respect, it is not easy to accept that Slade LJ's reasons are persuasive in their rejection of the possibility of claiming damages under the circumstances in question. First of all, it is not a settled issue[270] whether the source of the duty of good faith is equity or not, it is possibly common law due to Lord Mansfield's decisions which basically established the duty of good faith as well as many other principles applicable in insurance law.[271] Second, it is difficult to understand why the objective test of materiality is relevant to claim damages for breach of the duty of good faith. Third, the assured would be protected by the principles applicable to non-disclosure, namely, breach of an innocent non-disclosure does not entitle the other party to claim damages. Claiming damages is permitted in contract law for negligent and fraudulent misrepresentation under s.2(1) of the Misrepresentation Act and the issue was touched upon by the House of Lords in HIH v Chase Manhattan. In Pan Atlantic when ruling on the test of materiality and while implying the inducement test in the Marine Insurance Act 1906 the House of Lords analysed the principles applicable to common law misrepresentation. Although there is no parallel duty of disclosure, their Lordships decided not to separate the duty of disclosure from misrepresentation within the scope of the duty of good faith

---

269 Causal connection between the insurers' breach of duty and the assured's losses, reasonable foreseeability of the loss and the losses were not too remote.

270 See Arnould, para 15–17, 15–26.

271 For a discussion on the legal basis of the duty of good faith in insurance see Clarke, Law of Insurance Contracts, para 23–1A, see also 23–15C.

in insurance and they decided that their rulings on materiality and inducement should apply to both non-disclosure and misrepresentation as well as marine and non-marine insurance. It is unfortunate that the possibility of awarding damages was not discussed to great detail at the House of Lords in *Banque Financiere de la Cite SA v Westgate Insurance Co.*

In *Drake*, although this point did not strictly arise to decide the case given that the insurer was held not to have been able to prove inducement to avoid the contract, Rix LJ was prepared to hold that avoiding the contract under those circumstances would amount to breach of the insurer's duty of good faith. In *Drake*, Rix LJ referred to Lord Hobhouse in *The Star Sea* where his Lordship stated that[272] '. . . suitable caution should be exercised in making any extensions to the existing law of non-disclosure and that the courts should be on their guard against the use of the principle of good faith to achieve results which are only questionably capable of being reconciled with the mutual character of the obligation of good faith.' Rix LJ then found that it might be necessary to give wider effect to the doctrine of good faith. Rix LJ also pointed out the necessity to recognise that its impact may demand that ultimately regard must be had to a concept of proportionality implicit in fair dealing. Rix LJ found *Drake* as permitting an opportunity to explore these considerations. The trial judge did not find bad faith on the insurer's side and Rix LJ did not attempt to disturb that finding. However, Rix LJ commented that knowledge or blind-eye knowledge of the fact that the accident was a no fault accident would have made it a matter of bad faith to avoid the policy. If the ruling on inducement was wrong and if the insurer was entitled to avoid the policy, Rix LJ would have questioned if the insurer knew or was shutting its eyes to the fact that the accident was a no fault accident.

Reform of the duty of good faith

The English and Scottish Law Commissions published proposals for the reform of the law of utmost good faith for business insurance in June 2012.[273] In July 2014 the Law Commissions published a Report, *Business Disclosure; Warranties; Insurers' Remedies for Fraudulent Claims; and Late Payment*,[274] containing a final version of its proposals along with a draft Bill. On 17 July 2014 it was announced that an Insurance Bill would be introduced into Parliament, incorporating these proposals. At the time that this chapter is being written the Bill has not been enacted. In this part some of the main reforms that are brought by the Bill will be referred to.

The Bill applies to non-consumer insurance contracts only (cl.2.1). The Bill repeals sections 18, 19 and 20 of the Marine Insurance Act 1906. The assured's duty is to 'make to the insurer a fair presentation of the risk' before a contract of insurance is entered into (cl.3.1). The duty applies to misrepresentations as well as non-disclosure. The duty of fair presentation is complied with if every material representation as to a matter of fact is substantially correct, and every material representation as to a matter of expectation or belief is made in good faith (cl.3.3(c). The duty also encompasses disclosure of every material circumstance that the insured knows or ought to know (cl.3.4(a)). Regarding the insurers' role to inquire further as to the material facts, the Bill states that the assured is required to disclose to the insurer sufficient information to put a prudent insurer on notice that it needs to make further enquiries for the purpose of revealing those material circumstances (cl.3.4(b)). The Bill contains a clause regarding the matters that need not be disclosed (cl.3.5). Accordingly, disclosure is not required if (a) a fact diminishes the risk, (b) the insurer

272 [2001] 1 Lloyd's Rep 389, para 79.
273 http://lawcommission.justice.gov.uk/areas/insurance-contract-law.htm
274 http://lawcommission.justice.gov.uk/consultations/insurance-draft-clauses.htm

knows it, (c) the insurer ought to know it, (d) the insurer is presumed to know it, or (e) it is something as to which the insurer waives information.

Proof of inducement is becoming a statutory requirement under cl.8.1. Remedy for breach of the duty is set out under Schedule 1. A breach for which the insurer has a remedy against the insured is referred to in this Act as a 'qualifying breach'. A qualifying breach is either (a) deliberate or reckless, or (b) neither deliberate nor reckless (cl.8.4). A qualifying breach is deliberate or reckless if the assured (a) knew that it was in breach of the duty of fair presentation, or (b) did not care whether or not it was in breach of that duty (cl.8.5). It is for the insurer to show that a qualifying breach was deliberate or reckless (cl.8.6).

Schedule 1 introduces a proportionate remedy for breach of the duty namely that if a qualifying breach was deliberate or reckless, the insurer (a) may avoid the contract and refuse all claims, and (b) need not return any of the premiums paid. If a qualifying breach was neither deliberate nor reckless, the insurer may avoid the contract if, in the absence of the qualifying breach, the insurer would not have entered into the contract on any terms. The insurer must in that event return the premiums paid. If the insurer would have entered into the contract, but on different terms (other than terms relating to the premium), the contract is to be treated as if it had been entered into on those different terms if the insurer so requires. In addition, if the insurer would have entered into the contract (whether the terms relating to matters other than the premium would have been the same or different), but would have charged a higher premium, the insurer may reduce proportionately the amount to be paid on a claim.

Clause 15 of the Insurance Bill 2014 restricts the use of any contract term that puts the assured in a worse position than provided for by the Bill ('the disadvantageous term') unless the transparency rules in cl 16 are satisfied. Under clause 16 the insurer must take sufficient steps to draw the disadvantageous term to the insured's attention before the contract is entered into or the variation agreed (cl.16.2). The disadvantageous term must be clear and unambiguous as to its effect (cl.16.3).

The Bill is expected to become law by May 2015, and to be brought into force a year or so thereafter.

Further reading

Aikens LJ, 'The post contract duty of good faith in insurance contracts: is there a problem that needs a solution?', *B.I.L.A.J.* [2010] 119, 3–17.
Arnould, *Law of Marine Insurance and Average*, 18th edn, [2013] Sweet & Maxwell. Chapter 15, The Pre-contractual Duty of Utmost Good Faith: General Principles; Chapter 16, Non-disclosure; Chapter 17, Misrepresentation; Chapter 18, The Post-Contractual Duty of Utmost Good Faith and Fraudulent Claims.
Bennett, *Law of Marine Insurance*, 2nd edn, [2006] Oxford University Press. Chapter 4, The Doctrine of Utmost Good Faith.
Birds, 'Good faith in the reform of insurance law', *B.I.L.A.J.* [2004] 111, 2–15.
Birds et al., *MacGillivray on Insurance Law*, 12th edn, [2014] Sweet & Maxwell. Chapter 17, Good Faith and the Duty of Disclosure.
Blackwood, 'The pre-contractual duty of (utmost) good faith: the past and the future', *Lloyd's Maritime and Commercial Law Quarterly* [2013] 3(August), 311–324.
Butcher, 'Good faith in insurance law: a redundant concept?', *Journal of Business Law* [2008] 5, 375–384.
Chetcuti, 'The insurer's post-contractual duty of good faith: search for a balanced regime', *Journal of International Maritime Law* [2010] 16(6): 446–463.
Clarke, *The Law of Insurance Contracts*, 4th edn, [2014] Informa. Chapter 22, Misrepresentation; Chapter 23, Part I Non Disclosure, Part II The Effect of Misrepresentation and Non-Disclosure.
Davey, 'Materiality, non-disclosure and false allegations: following The North Star?', *Lloyd's Maritime and Commercial Law Quarterly* [2006] 4(November), 517–538.

J. Dunt, *Marine Cargo Insurance*, [2009] Informa. Chapter 5, Good Faith, Non-disclosure and Misrepresentation.

Harris, 'Should insurance risk avoidance be reformed and would reform be of a right of equitable rescission or a right sui generis?', *Journal of Business Law* [2013] 1, 23–38.

Hird, 'Utmost good faith – forward to the past', *Journal of Business Law* [2005] March, 257–264.

Longmore, 'Good faith and breach of warranty: are we moving forwards or backwards?', *Lloyd's Maritime and Commercial Law Quarterly* [2004] 2(May), 158–171.

Lewins, 'Going walkabout with Australian insurance law: the Australian experience of reforming utmost good faith', *Journal of Business Law* [2013] 1, 1–22.

MacDonald Eggers, 'Remedies for the failure to observe the utmost good faith', *Lloyd's Maritime and Commercial Law Quarterly* [2003] 2(May), 249–278.

MacDonald Eggers, 'The past and future of English insurance law: good faith and warranties', *UCL J.L. and J.* [2012] 1(2): 211–244.

Lord Mance, 'The 1906 Act, common law and contract clauses – all in harmony?', *Lloyd's Maritime and Commercial Law Quarterly* [2011] 3(August), 346–360.

Merkin, *Colinvaux's Law of Insurance*, 9th edn, [2010] Sweet & Maxwell. Chapter 6, Utmost Good Faith.

Naidoo and Oughton, 'The confused post-formation duty of good faith in insurance law: from refinement to fragmentation to elimination?', *Journal of Business Law* [2005] May, 346–371.

Rainey, 'The Law Commission's proposals for the reform of an insurer's remedies for fraudulent claims made under business insurance contracts', *Lloyd's Maritime and Commercial Law Quarterly* [2013] 3(August), 357–383.

Rawlings and Lowry, 'Insurers, claims and the boundaries of good faith'. *M.L.R.* 2005, 68(1): 82–110.

Rose, 'Informational asymmetry and the myth of good faith: back to basis', *Lloyd's Maritime and Commercial Law Quarterly* [2007] 2(May), 181–224.

Rose, *Marine Insurance: Law and Practice*, 2nd edn, [2012] Informa. Chapter 5, Presentation of the Risk and Good Faith.

Soyer, 'Continuing duty of utmost good faith in insurance contracts: still alive?', *Lloyd's Maritime and Commercial Law Quarterly* [2003] 1(Feb), 39–79.

Soyer, 'Reforming the assured's pre-contractual duty of utmost good faith in insurance contracts for consumers: are the law commissions on the right track?', *Journal of Business Law*, [2008] pp 385–414.

Soyer, 'Reforming pre-contractual information duties in business insurance contracts – one reform too many?', *Journal of Business Law* [2009] 1, 15–43.

Swaby, 'Insurance law: fit for purpose in the twenty-first century?', *Journal of International Maritime Law* [2010] 52(1): 21–39.

Yeo, 'Post-contractual good faith – change in judicial attitude?', *M.L.R.* [2003] 66(3): 425–440.

Chapter 5

Warranties

Chapter Contents

Classification of terms in insurance law differs from classification of terms in contract law. While a warranty is a trivial term in contract law and its breach entitles the innocent party to claim damages only, breach of an insurance warranty may result in draconian consequences. In this chapter creation of warranties and consequences of their breach will be analysed. However, it should be noted that in July 2014 the Law Commissions published a Report, *Business Disclosure; Warranties; Insurers' Remedies for Fraudulent Claims; and Late Payment*, containing a final version of its proposals along with a draft Bill. On 17 July 2014, it was announced that an Insurance Bill would be introduced into Parliament, incorporating these proposals. If the Government Insurance Bill 2014 is enacted in 2015 some of the principles stated in this chapter will have been amended. In this chapter the law as it stands at the date of the publication of this book will be stated and the sections in the Bill aiming to amend the rules applicable to warranties will be referred to briefly.

Definition

Warranties as regulated by the Marine Insurance Act 1906 section 33(1) are promissory warranties by which the assured undertakes that

1   some particular thing shall be done
2   some particular thing shall not be done
3   some condition shall be fulfilled or
4   the assured affirms or negatives the existence of a particular state of facts.

The assured may warrant that the vessel will be classed before the risk attaches by a reputable classification society and the class will be maintained throughout the policy. In insuring his yacht the assured may warrant that the yacht will be fully crewed at all times. If a vessel will be towed from one port to another the assured may warrant that the Salvage Association's Approval will be obtained before the towage begins. In an insurance of a passenger ferry the assured may warrant not to sail the ferry if there is a typhoon warning in the area. In all these examples the assured commits that some particular actions shall be or shall not be done. Breach of such a promise will entitle the insurer to seek a remedy which will be discussed below.

It should be noted that a promissory warranty should be distinguished from the words 'warranted free' which were analysed in the chapters in which the marine insurance losses were covered. While 'warranted free' means the insurers are not to be liable for the things to which the warranty applies,[1] for example, 'warranted free from particular average' means the insurer is not liable for partial losses, a promissory warranty is a promise by the assured that a warranty will be fulfilled.[2]

---

1   *Wayne Tank & Pump Co Ltd v Employers Liability Assurance Corp Ltd* [1973] 2 Lloyd's Rep 237; *Cory v Burr* (1883) 8 App Cas 393 Earl of Selborne LC. In *Cory v Burr* Lord Blackburn said 'There are warranties such as those which were referred to in the ingenious argument that we have last heard, which in effect merely say, We will define the sort of adventure which you shall be engaged in when we are to indemnify you; for example it shall be warranted that the ship shall not sail anywhere except in the Mediterranean, or something of that sort, defining the risk which they are to encounter; and if the ship goes out beyond that distance, then it is like a deviation – she has incurred a different kind of risk from that which the underwriters undertook to bear – it has become altogether a different adventure. That is one description of warranty. But there is another, which has been for a long time used, expressed in the phrase 'warranted free from' particular things. . . . 'warranted free' . . . means that although the general terms of the policy would have covered this, yet considering the special riskiness of the particular matter the underwriters, unless they are paid a premium for consenting to take it in, do not choose to be liable where the particular thing happens which they have stipulated by this warranty that they shall be warranted free from. Now here they are "warranted free from capture and seizure and the consequences of any attempts thereat".'

2   *Bank of Nova Scotia v Hellenic Mutual War Risk Association (Bermuda) Ltd (The Good Luck)* [1992] 1 AC 233, 261–262, Lord Goff.

Creating a warranty

In marine insurance warranties may be express or implied.[3] There is no implied warranty in non-marine insurance.

Express warranty

The MIA 1906 s.35(2) provides that 'An express warranty must be included in, or written upon, the policy, or must be contained in some document incorporated by reference into the policy.' An example of an express warranty can be seen in *Amlin Corporate Member Ltd v Oriental Assurance Corp*[4] where the policy provided 'Notwithstanding anything contained in this policy or clauses attached hereto, it is expressly warranted that the carrying vessel shall not sail or put out of Sheltered Port when there is a typhoon or storm warning at that port nor when her destination or intended route may be within the possible path of the typhoon or storm announced at the port of sailing, port of destination or any intervening point. Violation of this warranty shall render this policy void.'

The vessel sailed despite the typhoon warning and hundreds of passengers together with members of the crew on board died. The assured was clearly in breach of warranty.

Section 35 of the MIA 1906 states that an express warranty may be in any form of words from which the intention to warrant is to be inferred. The clause stated above contains the word 'warranted'. However, the presence or absence of the word 'warranty' or 'warranted' is not conclusive to determine the nature of the contractual term in question.[5] An example of this is seen in *Union Insurance Society of Canton, Limited v Wills*[6] where a floating policy covered all shipments of merchandise of every description commencing to load at first port of loading on or before 28 February 1912, with the exception of full cargoes, at and from certain specified ports. The policy also contained a clause 'Declarations of interest to be made to this society's agent at port of shipment where practicable or agent in London or Perth as soon as possible after sailing of vessel to which interest attaches.'

A vessel loaded with cargo was destroyed by fire and all the assured's goods were totally lost. The insurer denied liability for the reason that the assured had not forwarded a declaration of interest as soon as possible after sailing of the vessel. By construing the contract as a whole, the Privy Council accepted the insurer's argument that the relevant term that requires such declaration was a warranty although the clause was not expressly stated to be a warranty. The Privy Council put emphasis on the object of the promise, which was to protect the interests of the insurer. Their Lordships found that this object had a material bearing on the bargain and that it formed a substantive condition of the contract. Thus, it did contrast with a collateral stipulation for the breach of which damages might be claimed by cross-action or by way of counter-claim.

A similar contractual interpretation is seen in the non-marine context in *HIH Casualty & General Insurance Ltd v New Hampshire Insurance Co.*[7] In *HIH*, the insurer paid over $31m to the investors in films, and sought recovery against the reinsurers concerned. The insurance was a 'pecuniary loss indemnity' insurance. The peril insured was the risk that revenues from the films concerned would fail to reach the sum insured within a certain period. The insurance was designed to enable the investors, whose finance supports the production of the films, to recoup their investment. The slip policy contained

---

3 The MIA 1906 s 33(2).
4 [2013] EWHC 2380 (Comm).
5 [2001] 2 Lloyd's Rep 161, para 101, Rix LJ.
6 [1916] 1 AC 281.
7 [2001] 2 Lloyd's Rep 161.

a clause regarding the number of films to be made. Rix LJ said that the relevant term that 'six film to be made' was a warranty. His Lordship set out the questions to be asked in construing the relevant term that (1) whether it is a term which goes to the root of the transaction; (2) whether it is descriptive of or bears materially on the risk of loss; (3) whether damages would be an unsatisfactory or inadequate remedy. The six film term satisfied all three tests: it was a fundamental term, for even if only one film were omitted, the revenues were likely to be immediately reduced. Rix LJ noted that that will not matter if the revenues already exceed the sum insured, for in that case there can be no loss in any event. However, if revenues fall below the sum insured, the loss of a single film may be the critical difference between a loss or no loss, and will in any event be likely to increase the loss. The term bears materiality on the risk, again, for the same reason. Finally, a cross-claim would be an unsatisfactory and inadequate remedy because it would never be possible to know how much the lost film would have contributed to revenues.

A similar argument was tried by the insurers but rejected by Andrew Smith J in *Project Asia Line Inc v Shone (The Pride of Donegal)*.[8] It was contended that the term 'The insurance provided cover in respect of bunkers and freight "per any vessel . . . classed with major classification society, not exceeding 20 years of age or held covered"' was a warranty. Accordingly, as the insurer asserted, vessels are to be classed at the inception of, and shall remain in class throughout the voyage and this was either a warranty or a condition precedent[9] to the insurers' liability. Andrew Smith J rejected the argument reasoning firstly that no words were identified which call for this interpretation and secondly, the words are prima facie concerned with the scope of the cover; there is no reason to give them any other import.[10] The natural reading of the insurance contract is that the cover extended to vessels as long as they were classified by a major classification society.[11]

Construction of warranties

Express warranties are often subject to the rules of contractual construction. As held in *Investors Compensation Scheme Ltd v West Bromwich Building Society* (No.1)[12] and followed by the Courts consistently,[13] the aim of contractual construction is to determine objectively what the parties intended by inserting the clause which is subject to the interpretation in the contract. The relevant term is construed within the context of the contract and when construing an agreement in order to ascertain the intention of the parties, the court must have regard not simply to the words used but to the commercial purpose which the contract was designed to fulfil.[14]

There are numerous cases illustrating the application of the rules of contractual construction in the context of marine insurance warranties. As seen above, the classification of a term as a warranty may be a matter of construction, and as will be analysed elsewhere in this chapter whether a warranty is continuing in nature, and the scope and meaning of a warranty may again be determined by application of the rules of contractual construction.

The following three cases illustrate the battle between literal reading and reading a warranty within the context of the entire contract. The first case is *Brownsville Holdings Ltd v Adamjee Insurance Co Ltd (The Milasan)*[15] where the 90 foot motor yacht 'MV Milasan' sank by the stern in calm water and

---

8 [2002] 1 Lloyd's Rep 659.
9 For information about conditions precedent see Chapter 15.
10 [2002] 1 Lloyd's Rep 659, para 120.
11 [2002] 1 Lloyd's Rep 659, para 121.
12 [1998] 1 All ER 98.
13 *Chartbrook Ltd v Persimmon Homes Ltd* [2009] 1 AC 1101; *Rainy Sky SA v Kookmin Bank* [2012] 1 Lloyd's Rep 34.
14 *Shell International Petroleum Co Ltd v Gibbs, The Salem* [1981] 2 Lloyd's Rep 316, 327.
15 [2000] 2 Lloyd's Rep 458.

good weather about 25 miles off Cape Spartivento while in the course of a voyage from Piraeus to Puerto Cervo in Sardinia. Between May 1995 and July 1995, she had no professional skipper in charge of her. The Insurers alleged that this put the owners in breach of a warranty in the policy, which was in the following terms: 'warranted professional skippers and crew in charge at all times'. This was held to be a promissory warranty that the assured promised that a state of affairs will exist at the time the policy is concluded and will continue to exist so long as the policy is operative. Another reason indicating that the warranty was of a continuing nature was that the insurers were concerned to ensure that the vessel was properly looked after all the time, both summer and winter, whether cruising or in a marina. Aikens J found that the words 'professional skipper' refer to a person who has some professional experience that qualifies him to be regarded as a 'skipper'. The 'skipper' together with the 'crew' has to be 'in charge' of the vessel 'at all times'. The last phrase was, according to Aikens J, quite clear: there must be a professional skipper and a crew that looks after the vessel the whole time, as opposed to intermittently or at intervals.

The assured was therefore in breach of the warranty during the period when there was no professional skipper on board the yacht to look after or 'be in charge' of her 'all the time' during that period. The yacht had an engineer on board and also a deckhand but Aikens J held that the requirements of the warranty were cumulative. Thus, the lack of a 'professional skipper' during this time put the assured in breach.

A similar warranty fell to be interpreted by Gross J in GE Frankona Reinsurance Limited v CMM Trust No.1400, The 'Newfoundland Explorer'.[16] The assured insured his yacht, under a policy which provided 'Warranted fully crewed at all times'. The yacht was severely damaged by fire at the time she was laid up alongside a berth in the marina at Fort Lauderdale, USA. The fire was caused by the overheating of the generator. No crew members were aboard the vessel at the time of the casualty; the master was at home, some 15 miles and 30 minutes, away. The question was, on the proper construction of the contract of insurance, do the words 'at all times' in the warranty mean 24 hours per day? The judge held that the ordinary meaning of 'crewed' is by the crew performing such duties as are required on board. The natural result is that a vessel is not crewed if the crew is elsewhere. However, Gross J expressed two exceptions to this interpretation under which the crew might leave the yacht and the assured will not be in breach of warranty that (1) emergencies rendering his departure necessary (e.g. a bomb alert) or (2) necessary temporary departures for the purpose of performing crewing duties (e.g. adjusting moorings, working on a fouled propeller, or painting the outside of the hull) or other related activities. For instance in cases where one crew member suffices to comply with the warranty, leaving the yacht in order to purchase food or other supplies for the vessel will not amount to breach of warranty.

Gross J further explained that in terms of crew numbers, whether a vessel is 'fully crewed' or not must depend on what she is doing, whether the vessel will sail for an ocean voyage or be laid up alongside a berth. However, in any case, a vessel will not be crewed, let alone 'fully crewed' if no crew members are on board. Accordingly, Gross J said, 'fully crewed' must mean at least one crew member on board the vessel, whatever she is doing. Consequently, for the vessel to be 'fully crewed at all times' while laid up alongside a berth, there must be at least one crew member on board her 24 hours a day.[17] 'At all times', according to Gross J, means what it says – the whole time, not some of the time.[18]

---

16 [2006] Lloyd's Rep IR 704.
17 [2006] Lloyd's Rep IR 704, para 16.
18 [2006] Lloyd's Rep IR 704, para 16. Gross J noted that he did not base his decision on The Milasan. The warranty was construed in the context of its wording and the particular contract. The judge stated that he took comfort in reaching a conclusion which is consistent with the observations of Aikens J in The Milasan, para 30.

The Milasan and The Newfoundland Explorer were distinguished in Pratt v Aigaion Insurance Co SA (The Resolute).[19] In The Resolute the assured insured his motor fishing trawler on the terms 'Warranted Owner and/or Owner's experienced skipper on board and in charge at all times and one experienced crew member'. There were four crew including the assured. The assured and his crew of three took the vessel out to fish for a day and returned to North Shields where the vessel was stationed alongside the quay. After preparing the vessel for fishing the next day all the crew left the vessel, one to go home, two to visit a pub some 200 yards from the vessel and one to meet a friend at a café. Shortly after the crew left the vessel a fire occurred caused by operation or malfunction of the deep fat fryer or the fridge. Not surprisingly, the insurer relied upon The Milasan and The Newfoundland Explorer.

In the view of Sir Anthony Clarke MR,[20] however, The Milasan did not assist here as it relates to a different clause in a policy which insures a very different type of vessel in different circumstances. Likewise, Gross J's judgment in The Newfoundland Explorer was on a differently worded warranty in its own context.[21] Sir Anthony Clarke MR explained that the natural inference from the wording of the clause is that an experienced skipper was to be on board and that the reason for that is that underwriters wanted protection from risks which a skipper would be needed to guard against.[22] That suggests that the primary purpose of the warranty was to protect the vessel against navigational hazards.[23] The principal time when at least two members of the crew including the skipper would be required was when the vessel was being navigated, including when she was manoeuvring.[24] Consequently, 'at all times' was found by the judge to be an ambiguous phrase for not making clear what the extent of the qualification of the expressions should be. This led to the conclusion that the clause was to be construed contra proferentem, that is, against the insurer.[25] Anthony Clarke MR noted that the clause should have clearly stipulated that the insurer wanted them on board whenever the vessel was left, but it did not.

Present and continuing warranties

Warranties may be drafted in a variety of forms. Present warranties relate to the factual state of affairs existing at the date of the policy, while continuing warranties impose continuing obligations on the assured during the currency of the policy. The distinction between present and future warranties is not always easy to draw, but some guidance can be seen in the following cases. In Agapitos v Agnew (The Aegeon) (No.2)[26] the Aegeon, a roll-on roll-off car ferry which was to undergo conversion to a passenger cruise ship, was insured by Lloyd's and company underwriters under a marine open cover for a period of six months from 9 August 1995. The cover included: 'Warranted London Salvage Association approval of location, fire-fighting and mooring arrangements and all recommendations complied with.' The Aegeon had Salvage Association approval at the inception of the risk, but this expired on 30 August 1995. A new certificate was issued by the Salvage Association

---

19 [2009] 1 Lloyd's Rep 225.
20 [2009] 1 Lloyd's Rep 225, para 17.
21 [2009] 1 Lloyd's Rep 225, para 18.
22 [2009] 1 Lloyd's Rep 225, para 23.
23 [2009] 1 Lloyd's Rep 225, para 23.
24 [2009] 1 Lloyd's Rep 225, para 24.
25 [2009] 1 Lloyd's Rep 225, para 26.
26 [2003] Lloyd's Rep IR 54. Agapitos v Agnew (The Aegeon) (No.1) [2002] Lloyd's Rep IR 573 was discussed in the Fraudulent Claims chapter. In (No.1) the Court of Appeal held that insurers could not rely upon allegedly false statements made in the assured's points of claim as justifying a denial of liability on the basis of a fraudulent claim, as any post-proceedings fraud was a matter for the court and not for the insurers. (No.2) is a sequel case to the earlier ruling of the Court of Appeal. In (No.2) Moore-Bick J discussed the insurer's arguments as the breach of several warranties in the policy.

on 14 December 1995 with effect from that date and to last for six months. Moore-Bick J rejected the assured's assertion that this was a present warranty that was complied with at the inception of the risk, therefore there was no breach of warranty. Moore-Bick J construed the warranty by considering that it is often the case that underwriters who insure a vessel while laid up or undergoing conversion or repairs require as a condition of cover that the Salvage Association approve the vessel's mooring and fire-fighting arrangements. The underwriters expect the owners to comply with any recommendations that the Association may make as to the precautions to be taken to guard against particular hazards. The judge emphasised that The Salvage Association's 'approval certificate' is a formal document that certifies compliance with the warranty imposed by underwriters. Moreover, since any change of location or project has a direct bearing on the vessel's mooring and fire-fighting arrangements, certificates are valid only in respect of the particular location and the particular project to which they refer. Thus, any change of location or project requires a new certificate. Consequently, Moore-Bick J held that while the Salvage Association's approval was given for a limited period, there was no obvious reason why underwriters should impose a warranty of this kind at the date of inception, but be willing to allow the protection it provides to lapse within a matter of a few weeks. The warranty was to be construed as imposing a continuous requirement for Salvage Association approval which was broken by the assured after 30 August.

A similar issue came before Simon J in *Eagle Star Insurance Co Ltd v Games Video Co (GVC) SA (The Game Boy)*[27] the clause which was subject to construction was 'Warranted approval of Lay-up arrangements, Fire Fighting Provisions and all movements by Salvage Association and all their recommendations to be complied with prior to attachment', and was held to be a continuing warranty. The assured bought a vessel with the intention of using it as a floating casino. While the vessel was moored afloat at a shipyard in Greece, an explosive device was detonated at a point approximately 50cms below the waterline on the port side in way of the midships section of the hull. The explosion caused the hull plating to fracture and the resulting damage caused the vessel to list to starboard and to partially sink. The insurer denied liability for breach of warranty through a number of other defences, for example, breach of the duty of good faith. The Insurer's case was that the assured warranted that all the Salvage Association recommendations in SA Certificate EMO 301/98 would be complied with, including the ongoing recommendations. They submit that two of the Ongoing Recommendations were breached. First, contrary to recommendation 13, there was no telephone available at all times. Second, contrary to recommendation 22, there was no security watchman in attendance at the entrance to the vessel at all times.

The judge[28] accepted the insurer's submission. Simon J read the words *prior to attachment* as meaning that the assured warranted prior to attachment that they would comply with the Salvage Association recommendations made at the time of the attachment of the risk. But this did not mean that the assured was required to comply with the recommendation only prior to the attachment of the risk. Bearing in mind the commercial purpose of the clause, Simon J emphasised that the purpose of the clause was to ensure that the assured would comply with and continue to comply with the express terms of the Salvage Association's recommendations throughout the period on risk. It would plainly have been a breach of warranty to remove all the fire-fighting equipment the day after the risk attached.

A recent example of the construction of a warranty was seen in *Sea Glory Maritime Co, Swedish Management Co SA v AL Sagr National Insurance Co*[29] in respect of compliance with the International Safety Management (ISM) Code. Blair J held that a documentary compliance sufficed to fulfil the ISM

---

27 [2004] 1 Lloyd's Rep 238.
28 [2004] 1 Lloyd's Rep 238, para 139.
29 [2014] 1 Lloyd's Rep 14.

warranty of 'Vessels ISM Compliant'. The judge pointed out that it is important to distinguish between compliance with the ISM Code, and compliance with the policy's ISM warranty. With regard to the Safety Management Certificate section 13.7 of the ISM Code 2002 states that, 'Such a Certificate should be accepted as evidence that the ship is complying with the requirements of this Code.' The judge found that whilst it does not state that it is conclusive evidence of compliance, it does recognise that the holding of the certificate has at least evidential effect. A further contractual interpretation issue was the nature of the warranty. With a reference to *The Game Boy*, Blair J held that this was a continuing warranty for the reason that the parties could not have intended that the warranty would continue to be satisfied if the Safety Management Certificate was withdrawn after the inception of cover.

Implied warranties

The MIA 1906 implies warranties in marine insurance contracts. For instance, section 36(1) provides 'Where insurable property, whether ship or goods, is expressly warranted neutral, there is an implied condition that the property shall have a neutral character at the commencement of the risk, and that, so far as the assured can control the matter, its neutral character shall be preserved during the risk.' Moreover, section 39(1) implies a warranty of seaworthiness in a voyage policy and section 41 provides that 'There is an implied warranty that the adventure insured is a lawful one, and that, so far as the assured can control the matter, the adventure shall be carried out in a lawful manner.'

In this chapter, due to its extensive application in the marine insurance industry the warranty of seaworthiness will be analysed.

Warranty of seaworthiness

Voyage policies

Section 39 (1) of the 1906 Act implies a warranty into voyage policies that at the beginning of the voyage the vessel shall be seaworthy for the purpose of the particular adventure insured. Seaworthiness is a relative concept[30] in that whether a vessel is seaworthy or not depends essentially on whether she is fit to meet the perils of the voyage upon which she embarks.[31] The meaning of seaworthiness was discussed in *Steel v State Line Steamship Co*[32] by Lord Cairns stating that '. . . the ship should be in a condition to encounter whatever perils of the sea a ship of that kind, and laden in that way, may be fairly expected to encounter' along the route in question. His Lordship added '. . . the ship shall be reasonably fit for performing the service which she undertakes.' The vessel's state, as to repairs, equipment, and crew, and in all other respects, should, at the time of its sailing on the voyage insured, be fit to encounter the ordinary perils of that particular voyage.[33]

A vessel is not seaworthy if she has insufficient fuel to enable her to proceed on her voyage,[34] or if the voyage requires a certain number of crew and if the shipowner employs less than that

---

30 *Gibson v Small* (1853) 4 HL Cas 353.
31 *Martin Maritime Ltd v Provident Capital Indemnity Fund Ltd (The Lydia Flag)* [1998] 2 Lloyd's Rep 652, 656.
32 (1877) 3 App Cas 72, 77.
33 *Gibson v Small* (1853) 4 HL Cas 353; *Garnat Trading & Shipping (Singapore) Pte Ltd v Baominh Insurance Corp* [2011] 1 Lloyd's Rep 589, approved by the Court of Appeal [2011] 2 Lloyd's Rep 492.
34 *The Pride of Donegal* [2002] 1 Lloyd's Rep 659, para 40.

number,[35] or if the crew is not capable of properly using the fire-fighting equipment on the vessel.[36] Again, if the vessel was defectively designed and therefore not capable of withstanding the ordinary conditions of the voyage, the vessel will be unseaworthy.[37] Further, following the safety measurements implemented by the International Maritime Organisation the vessel must carry necessary documents for the voyage, that is to say those which may be 'required by the law of the vessel's flag or by the laws, regulations or lawful administrative practices of governmental or local authorities at the vessel's port of call.'[38] Moreover, the inclusion of classification clauses in insurance policies is generally seen as a move towards ensuring improved standards of seaworthiness.[39] Thus, the fact that a vessel was in Class at the time of sailing on the voyage is of significant weight when considering whether she was seaworthy, particularly where the vessel has been surveyed and approved by Class shortly before sailing.[40]

The obligation is not merely that the owners should do their best to make the ship fit, but that the ship should actually be fit.[41] Compliance with a warranty of seaworthiness, express or implied, is a condition precedent to the underwriter's liability for a loss.[42] Therefore, the effect of the warranty is that if the vessel is not seaworthy the insurer is not liable for any loss or damage, whether or not that was proximately caused by the unseaworthiness.[43] Once there is a breach of a seaworthiness warranty the insurer can seek a remedy irrespective of whether the breach came about through fault or want of diligence on the part of the assured, or whether unseaworthiness is capable of being avoided.[44]

It should be noted that the warranty attaches at the commencement of the voyage only and there is no implied warranty on the part of the assured for the continuance of the seaworthiness of the vessel, or for the performance of their duty by the master and crew during the whole course of the voyage.[45]

To establish unseaworthiness, it is not necessary to identify the precise defect.[46] *Eridania SpA (formerly Cereol Italia Srl) v Oetker (The Fjord Wind)*[47] established that where a vessel suffers a serious casualty without any outside intervention, the natural inference is that there was something wrong with her which a prudent owner would have rectified if he had known about it.[48] This principle applies irrespective of the defect being one which can subsequently be specifically identified or is one which cannot be specifically identified but whose existence can be inferred from a propensity for failures to occur for unknown reasons and at unpredictable intervals. So long as such a defect actually exists, the risks involved in leaving it unrepaired are sufficiently serious to require remedial action to be taken before the ship proceeds farther.[49] In *The Fjord Wind* Clarke LJ noted that 'seaworthiness is to be judged by reference to the realities of commercial life and does not require absolute

---

35 *De Hahn v Hartley* (1786) 1 Term Rep 343.

36 *The Star Sea* [2001] 1 Lloyd's Rep 389.

37 *JJ Lloyd Instruments v Northern Star Insurance Co (The Miss Jay Jay)* [1985] 1 Lloyd's Rep 264; *Martin Maritime Ltd v Provident Capital Indemnity Fund Ltd (The Lydia Flag)* [1998] 2 Lloyd's Rep 652.

38 *The Pride of Donegal* [2002] 1 Lloyd's Rep 659, para 41; *Sea Glory Maritime Co, Swedish Management Co SA v AL Sagr National Insurance Co* [2013] EWHC 2116 (Comm).

39 *Garnat Trading & Shipping (Singapore) Pte Ltd v Baominh Insurance Corp* [2011] 1 Lloyd's Rep 589.

40 *Garnat Trading & Shipping (Singapore) Pte Ltd v Baominh Insurance Corp* [2011] 1 Lloyd's Rep 589.

41 *Steel v State Line Steamship Co* (1877) 3 App Cas 72, 86, Lord Blackburn.

42 *Christine v Secretan* (1799) 8 TR 192.

43 *The Cendor Mopu* [2011] 1 Lloyd's Rep 560, Lord Saville, para 40; *The Miss Jay Jay* [1985] 1 Lloyd's Rep 264, 270; *The Pride of Donegal* [2002] 1 Lloyd's Rep 659, para 35.

44 Mustill, M. [1988] LMCLQ 310, 345; *Project Asia Line Inc v Shone (The Pride of Donegal)* [2002] 1 Lloyd's Rep 659, para 35.

45 *Sadler v Dixon* (1841) 8 M & W 895, 899; *Busk v Royal Exchange Assurance Co* (1818) 2 B & Ald 73, 83.

46 *The Pride of Donegal* [2002] 1 Lloyd's Rep 659, para 39.

47 [2000] 2 Lloyd's Rep 191.

48 [2000] 2 Lloyd's Rep 191, 198.

49 [2000] 2 Lloyd's Rep 191, 198.

perfection'.[50] In this case the vessel suffered crankpin bearing failures within a few hours of departing down the river Paraná from the loading port, Rosario. Moore-Bick J found and it was approved by the Court of Appeal that the vessel was unseaworthy when she left Rosario. The most telling evidence, which persuaded the judge of this conclusion, was the very fact that there was a failure of the No 6 crankpin bearing within a few hours of the vessel's departure from the loading port.[51] Moore-Bick J added that there was nothing to suggest that the conditions which the vessel encountered in the river were in any respect unusual or that the casualty was the result of any outside intervention.[52] It was not possible to identify the precise cause of the bearing failure but the judge found the inference that there was a defect of some kind in the bearing itself or the lubricating system which rendered the vessel unfit to encounter the ordinary incidents of the voyage.[53]

As stated above, seaworthiness has a relative meaning. The test of seaworthiness is to ask whether a reasonably prudent owner would have required that a particular defect, if he had known of it, be made good before sending the ship to sea.[54] It should be borne in mind that seaworthiness is concerned with the state of the vessel rather than with whether the owners acted prudently or with due diligence.[55] The only relevance of the standard of the reasonably prudent owner is to ask whether, if he had known of the defect, he would have taken steps to rectify it.[56] In *The Fjord Wind* Clarke LJ[57] found that a prudent owner, if he had been aware of the nature of the defect, would have taken steps to correct it rather than risk the consequences. This was held to be the relevant state of knowledge for the finding of unseaworthiness.

Section 39(3) provides that 'Where the policy relates to a voyage which is performed in different stages, during which the ship requires different kinds of or further preparation or equipment, there is an implied warranty that at the commencement of each stage the ship is seaworthy in respect of such preparation or equipment for the purposes of that stage.' As noted above, having insufficient fuel to enable the vessel to proceed on her voyage will render the vessel unseaworthy.[58] However, if the voyage is broken up into distinct stages, e.g. in a long voyage, for the purpose of fuelling, then the vessel must be made seaworthy at the commencement of each stage of the voyage, and the vessel must be supplied with sufficient fuel when starting on each stage.[59] The onus is on the shipowner to prove that he had divided the voyage into stages for, for example, fuelling purposes by reason of the necessity of the case, and that, at the commencement of each stage, the ship had on board a sufficiency of fuel for that stage. This makes for a convenient way of enabling the shipowner to fulfil his warranty by stages instead of once for all at the beginning of the risk.[60]

Time policies

Under a time policy, there is no implied warranty of seaworthiness, either at the inception of the risk or on sailing.[61] However, where the ship is sent to sea in an unseaworthy state with the privity of the assured, the insurer is not liable for any loss attributable to unseaworthiness.

---

50   [2000] 2 Lloyd's Rep 191, 198.
51   [1999] 1 Lloyd's Rep 307, 318.
52   [1999] 1 Lloyd's Rep 307, 318.
53   [1999] 1 Lloyd's Rep 307, 318.
54   *Garnat Trading & Shipping (Singapore) Pte Ltd v Baominh Insurance Corp* [2011] 1 Lloyd's Rep 589.
55   [2000] 2 Lloyd's Rep 191, 199.
56   [2000] 2 Lloyd's Rep 191, 199.
57   [2000] 2 Lloyd's Rep 191, 199.
58   *The Pride of Donegal* [2002] 1 Lloyd's Rep 659, para 40.
59   *Thin v Richards & Co* [1892] 2 QB 141; *The Vortigern* [1899] p 140; *Greenock Steamship Co v Maritime Insurance Co Ltd* [1903] 1 KB 367, Bigham J, appeal was dismissed [1903] 2 KB 657.
60   *Greenock Steamship Co v Maritime Insurance Co Ltd* [1903] 1 KB 367, 373–374, Bigham J.
61   *The MIA 1906 s 39(5), Fawcus v Sarsfield* (1856) 6 El & Bl 192; *Thompson v Hopper* (1858) El Bl & El 1038; *Dudgeon v Pembroke* (1877) 2 App Cas 284.

The reason for non-existence of a seaworthiness warranty in time policies is historical. In *Fawcus v Sarsfield*[62] it was argued by the insurers that on a time policy, if on the day on which the risk is to commence the ship be in a port in any region of the Globe in which there are the means of repairing her and rendering her seaworthy, there is an implied warranty or condition that she shall be repaired and rendered seaworthy before she sails from this port. This was argued to be the case although the assured may not know that she stands in need of repair, and although he may have no funds nor means of raising funds there to repair her. It was held in *Fawcus* that in time policies such a doctrine would be exceedingly inconvenient and would prevent shipowners from having that indemnity and security which time policies have hitherto afforded them. It is inconvenient when the risk begins while the ship is on the high seas: and a similar inconvenience would arise from the implied warranty of seaworthiness, the risk beginning when the ship, in the middle of a long adventure, is in a distant port. In *Gibson v Small*,[63] while rejecting the existence of such a warranty in time policies the Court emphasised the relative meaning of seaworthiness which may not be easily adopted for a time policy. Some of the questions that the court asked in *Gibson v Small* were: how will such a term apply in time policies, that is, policies independent of a voyage contemplated, begun, or to be renewed, which in its terms may embrace only a portion of one voyage, or portions of two voyages, or may include several voyages? Moreover, in that case, what degree of seaworthiness should exist at the commencement of the risk? To what use of the vessel should it relate? The vessel may be within a few days of concluding her homeward voyage from port X and may be about to proceed on a voyage to port Y. The latter voyage may not have been determined upon at the time of effecting the policy. What, in such a case, is to be the measure or test of the seaworthiness to be required at the commencement of the risk?

Thus, when the MIA 1906 was enacted, section 39(5) did not impose a seaworthiness warranty in time policies, however, it provided a remedy for a case in which a shipowner consciously sends his vessel to a voyage in an unseaworthy state. There are three elements that the insurer is required to establish in this defence under section 39(5).[64] First, there must have been unseaworthiness at the time the vessel was sent to sea. Second, the unseaworthiness must have been causative of the relevant loss. Finally, the assured must have been privy to sending the ship to sea in that condition. If one of these three requirements is missing the insurer is liable for the loss. It might be because the loss was caused by the perils of the sea, that is, not attributable to unseaworthiness or it might be because the assured was not privy to the unseaworthiness.[65] If the vessel sinks due to unseaworthiness it may be the case that fortuity is not proved thus the insurer may not be liable. In any case the causation, fortuity and perils of the sea will have to be considered.

Privity

The term seaworthiness was discussed above and causation will be analysed in Chapter 7. It is necessary here to explain the meaning of the word 'privity' which is another requisite for an unseaworthiness defence in a time policy. The following principles were established by the Court of Appeal in *The Eurysthenes*[66] and approved by the House of Lords in *The Star Sea*.[67] 'Privity' means 'with knowledge and consent'. The assured loses his cover if he has consented to or concurred in the ship going to sea when he knew that it was in an unseaworthy condition. In many cases sending

---

62   (1856) 6 El & Bl 192.
63   (1853) 4 HL Cas 353.
64   *The Star Sea* [2001] 1 Lloyd's Rep 389, para 16.
65   See *The Miss Jay Jay* [1985] 1 Lloyd's Rep 264, approved by the Court of Appeal [1987] 1 Lloyd's Rep 32.
66   [1977] QB 49.
67   [2001] 1 Lloyd's Rep 389.

a ship to sea knowing it is unseaworthy will amount to wilful misconduct, but not necessarily so. 'Privity' therefore does not mean that there was any wilful misconduct by the assured, but only that he knew of the act beforehand and concurred in it being done. The assured must have knowledge not only of the facts constituting the unseaworthiness, but also knowledge that those facts rendered the ship unseaworthy, that is, not reasonably fit to encounter the ordinary perils of the sea. Knowledge includes positive knowledge as well as 'turning a blind eye'. Turning a blind eye may be established in the case where the assured deliberately refrains from examining the ship in order not to gain direct knowledge of what he has reason to believe is her unseaworthy state. Blind-eye knowledge requires a conscious reason for blinding the eye. There must be at least a suspicion of a truth about which the assured does not want to know and which he refuses to investigate. Moreover, 'privity' does not mean that the assured himself personally did the act, but only that someone else did it and that he knowingly concurred in it. If it was a wrongful act done by his servant, then he was liable for it if it was done 'by his command or privity', that is, with his express authority or with his knowledge and concurrence. The knowledge must also be the knowledge of the shipowner personally, or of his alter ego, or, in the case of a company, of its head men or whoever may be considered their alter ego. But, if the shipowner satisfies the court that he did not know the facts or did not realise that they rendered the ship unseaworthy, then he ought not to be held privy to it, even though he was negligent in not knowing. In *The Eurysthenes* the Court of Appeal accepted the following as illustrative of the privity of the shipowner assured: If the owner of a ship says to himself: 'I think a reasonably prudent owner would send her to sea with a crew of 12. So I will send her with 12,' he is not privy to unseaworthiness, even though a judge may afterwards say that she ought to have had 14. He may have been negligent in thinking so, but he would not be privy to unseaworthiness. But, if he says to himself: 'I think that a reasonably prudent owner would send her to sea with a crew of 12, but I have only 10 available, so I will send her with 10,' then he is privy to the unseaworthiness, if a judge afterwards says he ought to have had 12. The reason being that he knew that she ought to have had 12 and consciously sent her to sea with 10.

The blind eye knowledge was alleged in *The Star Sea* but it failed on the facts. The insurer failed to prove any suspicion of the master's incompetence in the particular respect which mattered. The *Star Sea* was a dry cargo vessel which belonged to the Kollakis group of companies. On 27 May 1990 the *Star Sea* sailed from Nicaragua bound for Zeebrugge laden with a cargo of bananas, mangoes and coffee. A fire started on the morning of the 29th in the engine-room workshop where the third engineer was using an oxyacetylene torch and it flashed back to the oxygen gas bottles. Attempts to use extinguishers on the fire were defeated by smoke. After about two and a half hours the master decided to use the CO_2 system. The actions then taken were not effective in putting out the fire and it continued to burn although for a while the crew thought it had been extinguished. The vessel had sent out distress calls but the first vessel to arrive departed during the afternoon because the crew thought that the fire was out and that they did not need further assistance. It then became obvious during the early evening that this was not so as the fire spread to the accommodation quarters. During the early hours of the following day a tug arrived and the fire was unsuccessfully fought the next day using the tug's monitors. The fire was extinguished only at Balboa to where the vessel was towed on 1 June but the damage was so extensive that the vessel had become a constructive total loss.

The *Star Sea* was unseaworthy in a number of respects when she set sail from Corinto. The vessel was equipped with a CO_2 fire extinguishing system which, in principle, should have been effective to extinguish the fire, however, the master left to use the system until some two hours after the fire had started. The trial judge found that the failure to use the CO_2 earlier and the failure to use all 4 banks of bottles at once was attributable to the incompetence of the master. Moreover, the engine-room could not be sealed as the funnel dampers were in a defective condition and could not be fully closed. In the Court of Appeal Leggatt LJ said 'an allegation that they ought to have known [is] not an allegation that they suspected or realised but did not make further enquiries'. 'Accordingly, on the evidence, it was simply not open to the judge to make a finding that any of the individuals "suspected" or "believed" that the master was incompetent, lacking the basic knowledge on how to utilise CO_2.' This was approved by the House of Lords.[68] Their Lordships found that unless there is a decision not to check, a finding of negligence to a very high degree did not suffice for a finding of privity. The deliberate decision must be a decision to avoid obtaining confirmation of facts the existence of which the individual has good reason to believe.[69] To allow blind-eye knowledge to be constituted by a decision not to enquire into an untargeted or speculative suspicion would be to allow negligence, albeit gross, to be the basis of a finding of privity. That is not warranted by section 39(5).[70] The master of the *Star Sea*, although recently appointed to the *Star Sea*, had been with the fleet for over 11 years and there was no evidence of any previous incompetence on his part.[71]

If the vessel was unseaworthy in more than one respect and the assured knows about one of the defects but not the other and if the loss was not caused by the defect known by the assured the insurer will be liable. *Thomas v Tyne & Wear Steamship Freight Insurance Association*[72] illustrates this that the *Dunsley* sprung a leak and was lost by a peril insured against while she was on a voyage from Appledore in the Bristol Channel to Birkenhead. The cause of that leak and of the consequent loss of the ship was damage and straining which she had sustained through grounding in the Loire in the previous month, and by reason of that damage she was sailing from Appledore unfit for the voyage, but the shipowner was not aware of that damage and was not privy to sending the ship to sea in an unseaworthy condition so far as that damage was concerned. On the other hand he was privy to sending the ship to sea with an insufficient crew, but that insufficiency of the crew did not cause or contribute to her loss. The insurer was liable for the loss. The principle was stated by Atkin J[73] that 'Where a ship is sent to sea in a state of unseaworthiness in two respects, the assured being privy to the one and not privy to the other, the insurer is only protected if the loss was attributable to the particular unseaworthiness to which the assured was privy.'

Time policies – contractual warranties

An express term in a time policy may be included to the effect of imposing a seaworthiness warranty on the assured. However, such a warranty may need to be considered together with other clauses of the contract. In *Martin Maritime Ltd v Provident Capital Indemnity Fund Ltd (The Lydia Flag)*[74] the vessel was insured by a policy which covered loss of or damage to the subject matter insured caused by negligence of repairers provided such loss or damage has not resulted from want of due diligence by the assured (cl.6.2.4). It was warranted that 'at the inception of this policy the vessel . . . shall be in a seaworthy condition and thereafter during the valid period of this policy the insured shall exercise due diligence to keep the vessel seaworthy . . .' (cl.11). The *Lydia Flag* lost her rudder at Abidjan and sustained damage. The vessel was negligently repaired and therefore it was unseaworthy at the commencement of the voyage. The insurer was nevertheless held to be liable for the loss. The interpretation adopted by Moore-Bick J was that warranty No. 11 is worded in absolute but wholly general terms. Clause 6 on the other hand, deals with certain identified perils which are specifically covered by the policy. Clause 6 was to be read as providing, where appropriate, exceptions upon the general terms of the warranty contained in warranty No. 11. The judge held that cover was not lost insofar as the vessel may be unseaworthy at the inception of the policy as a result of

68 [2001] 1 Lloyd's Rep 389, Lord Scott, para 115.
69 [2001] 1 Lloyd's Rep 389, Lord Scott, para 116.
70 [2001] 1 Lloyd's Rep 389, Lord Scott, para 116.
71 [2001] 1 Lloyd's Rep 389, Lord Scott, para 117.
72 [1917] 1 KB 938.
73 [1917] 1 KB 938, 941.
74 [1998] 2 Lloyd's Rep 652.

latent defect or negligence, as in this case, of repairers, provided of course that unseaworthiness has not resulted from want of due diligence on the part of the owners or managers.[75]

There is no warranty that goods are seaworthy

The MIA 1906 section 40(1) provides that 'in a policy on goods or other moveables there is no implied warranty that the goods or moveables are seaworthy'. Under the 1906 Act therefore, the fact that the goods are not reasonably fit in all respects to encounter the ordinary perils of the seas of the adventure insured, does not automatically deprive the assured of cover.[76] A clear example of this is seen in *The Cendor Mopu* which will be discussed extensively in Chapter 7. Although the mobile offshore drilling unit was not capable to withstand the ordinary conditions of the voyage, the insurer was held to be liable for the loss of its three legs as there is no warranty that the goods are to be seaworthy and the Supreme Court was satisfied that the loss was caused by perils of the sea.

Remedy

The remedy is set out in section 33(3) of the MIA 1906, that is, if a warranty is not complied with, subject to any express provision in the policy, the insurer is discharged from liability as from the date of the breach of warranty. The automatic discharge from liability was said to reflect the fact that the rationale of warranties in insurance law is that the insurer only accepts the risk provided that the warranty is fulfilled.[77] Automatic discharge has prospective effect, therefore, section 33(3) makes it clear that the discharge takes place without prejudice to any liability incurred by him before that date. It was held by the House of Lords in *The Good Luck*[78] that discharge of the insurer from liability is automatic, that is to say, it is not dependent upon any decision by the insurer to this effect.[79] *The Good Luck* was insured against war risks. The owner warranted not to permit the ship to enter a war zone without prior notification to the insurers. *The Good Luck* entered into a prohibited zone in the Arabian Gulf where she was hit by Iraqi missiles and became a constructive total loss. The House of Lords approved Hobhouse J's ruling that the insurer ceased to insure the *Good Luck* once she entered into a prohibited area.

The breach does not bring the contract to an end.[80] It is possible that there may be obligations of the assured under the contract which will survive the discharge of the insurer from liability, for example a continuing liability to pay a premium.[81]

The parties may agree on an alternative remedy for the breach. For instance in *Amlin Corporate Member Ltd v Oriental Assurance Corp*[82] the assured warranted that the vessel shall not sail or put out of Sheltered Port when there is a typhoon or storm warning at that port. The warranty further stated 'Violation of this warranty shall render this policy void'.

The insurer is discharged from liability at the date of the breach, however, the parties may agree otherwise by their contract of insurance. The International Hull Clauses 2003, clause 13

---

75 [1998] 2 Lloyd's Rep 652, 656.
76 *The Cendor Mopu* [2011] 1 Lloyd's Rep 560, para 42, Lord Saville.
77 [1992] 1 AC 233, 263, Lord Goff.
78 [1992] 1 AC 233, 262.
79 *Agapitos v Agnew (The Aegeon)* (No.2) [2003] Lloyd's Rep IR 54, para 28. The insurer may waive the breach, which will be discussed below.
80 [1992] 1 AC 233, 263.
81 [1992] 1 AC 233, 263. The issue will be discussed in *JA Chapman & Co Ltd (In Liquidation) v Kadirga Denizcilik ve Ticaret AS* [1998] Lloyd's Rep IR 377, which will be referred to in Chapter 6.
82 [2013] EWHC 2380 (Comm).

imposes some obligations on the assured regarding classification of the vessel and the ISM certificate. Unless the Underwriters agree to the contrary in writing, in case of breach of clause 13.1, the insurance terminates automatically at the time of the breach (cl.13.2). However, clause 13.2.1 adds that if the vessel is at sea at such date, the termination of the insurance is deferred until the vessel's arrival at her next port.

Strict compliance

It is for the insurer to establish the pleaded breach of the warranty.[83] All the insurer has to prove is that the policy contained a warranty which has been breached by the assured. At the date of the breach the insurer is automatically discharged from liability. However, section 34(1) states that under some circumstances a warranty may be excused. Accordingly, 'Non-compliance with a warranty is excused when, by reason of a change of circumstances, the warranty ceases to be applicable to the circumstances of the contract, or when compliance with the warranty is rendered unlawful by any subsequent law.'

Unless the requirements of section 34(1) are satisfied, a warranty must be strictly complied with, whether it be material to the risk or not.[84] For instance, where there is a warranty to sail on the 1st of August, and the ship did not sail till the 2nd, the warranty would not be complied with.[85] Moreover, the insurer is discharged from liability irrespective of the chain of causation between the breach and the warranty. Imagine a fish farm that is insured by the assured under a policy that imposes on the assured a duty to employ a guard who will watch the fish farm for 24 hours. If this obligation is drafted as a warranty and if the assured never employs a person who will keep an eye on the fish farm for 24 hours (or if he employs someone who then leaves the job and who is not replaced), the assured will be in breach of warranty. Upon damage to or loss of the fish farm, the assured will not be entitled to claim against the insurer for the reason of breach of warranty, irrespective of the cause of the loss or the damage. If the fish farm, for example, is destroyed by a severe storm, with regard to the insurer's liability, it makes no difference whether the guard would have been able to stop the storm or not, in other words, whether the breach of warranty caused the loss or not. Irrespective of the chain of causation, the insurer is discharged from liability. All the insurer has to establish is that the relevant obligation was drafted as a warranty and the assured breached it.[86] In *State Trading Corporation of India Ltd v M Golodetz Ltd*[87] Kerr LJ said 'the consequence of the breach is that the cover ceases to be applicable' unless the insurer waives the breach. This demonstrates that by being in breach of his warranty, an assured takes himself outside the cover which he has agreed with his insurer.[88] This is because a warranty is part of the statement of the cover provided by the insurance.[89] The insurance ceases to bind even though any subsequent loss had nothing to do with the breach of warranty[90] for the reason that the insurer had only agreed to cover the risk provided the warranty was performed.[91]

---

83 *Garnat Trading & Shipping (Singapore) Pte Ltd v Baominh Insurance Corp* [2011] 1 Lloyd's Rep 589, approved by the Court of Appeal [2011] 2 Lloyd's Rep 492; *Amlin Corporate Member Ltd v Oriental Assurance Corp* [2013] EWHC 2380 (Comm).
84 *De Hahn v Hartley* (1786) 1 Term Rep 343, 345; *Union Insurance Society of Canton, Limited v Wills* [1916] 1 AC 281, 286.
85 *De Hahn v Hartley* (1786) 1 Term Rep 343, 345.
86 *Forsikringsaktieselskapet Vesta v Butcher* [1989] 1 Lloyd's Rep 331. This case will be discussed in Chapter 15. The facts of this case are used here to illustrate the principle. The reader should remember that in *Vesta*, the original insurance and reinsurance warranty was governed by Norwegian law where the chain of causation between the breach of the loss is required.
87 [1989] 2 Lloyd's Rep 277, 287.
88 *HIH Casualty & General Insurance Ltd v New Hampshire Insurance Co* [2001] 2 Lloyd's Rep 161, 124, Rix LJ.
89 *HIH Casualty & General Insurance Ltd v New Hampshire Insurance Co* [2001] 2 Lloyd's Rep 161, 124, Rix LJ.
90 *HIH Casualty & General Insurance Ltd v New Hampshire Insurance Co* [2001] 2 Lloyd's Rep 161, 124, Rix LJ.
91 *HIH Casualty & General Insurance Ltd v New Hampshire Insurance Co* [2001] 2 Lloyd's Rep 161, 124, Rix LJ.

It is worth noting here that as referred to above, in HIH v New Hampshire one of the questions in determining the true nature of the 'six films to be made' clause was whether the clause bore materially to the risk. On the other hand, when a warranty is breached, the insurer is discharged from liability automatically irrespective of a material bearing of the breach to the risk. Thus, one might question the materiality element in the HIH v New Hampshire ruling. It should be remembered that in HIH the issue was defining the nature of the relevant obligation imposed by the contract and in the absence of the word warranty it was necessary to use the materiality test to determine the objective intention of the parties. In The Good Luck, Lord Goff emphasised that the remedy of automatic discharge is a result of the fact that the rationale of warranties in insurance law is that the insurer only accepts the risk provided that the warranty is fulfilled.[92] It is submitted that the express use of the word 'warranty' suffices to indicate the parties' intention that the insurer insured the risk under the condition of compliance with the warranty. Such intention does not become clear where the word warranty does not appear in the clause and the court may apply the rules of construction in light of the tests set by the HIH case.

Another aspect of strict compliance is that once a warranty is broken, the assured cannot avail himself of the defence that the breach has been remedied, and the warranty complied with, before loss (s.34(2)). This subsection codifies De Hahn v Hartley[93] where the vessel sailed with 46 people while the assured warranted to sail with 50. During the voyage he employed six more people, the vessel was lost shortly after he complied with the warranty. However, his claim against the insurer was unsuccessful as once there was a breach the insurer was not liable and remedying the breach later did not change this result. Similarly, in Quebec Marine Insurance Company v The Commercial Bank of Canada[94] the insured vessel was not seaworthy for her voyage when she sailed as the boiler had a defect in it. During the voyage the boiler became unmanageable and the defect was remedied. The vessel resumed her voyage but she met bad weather and was lost. The underwriters were not liable. Lord Penzance commented in response to the argument that when the breach was remedied before the loss the insurer should be liable 'It is impossible not to see that such a doctrine would tend, if carried to its legitimate consequences, to fritter away the value of this warranty altogether.'[95]

Waiver

Although a breach of warranty, once committed, cannot subsequently be remedied by the assured, it is open to underwriters to waive it and thereby, in effect, reinstate.[96] Under section 34(3) when the insurer waives a breach of a promissory warranty, the effect is that, to the extent of the waiver, the insurer cannot rely upon the breach as having discharged him from liability.[97]

A right may be waived either by express words or by conduct inconsistent with the exercising of the right; and even where there is no actual waiver, the person having the right may so conduct himself that it becomes inequitable for him to enforce that right.[98]

---

92   [1992] 1 AC 233, 263, Lord Goff.
93   (1786) 1 Term Rep 343.
94   (1869–71) LR 3 PC 234.
95   (1869–71) LR 3 PC 234, 244.
96   Agapitos v Agnew (The Aegeon) (No.2) [2003] Lloyd's Rep IR 54, para 70.
97   The Good Luck [1992] 1 AC 233, 263, Lord Goff.
98   Samuel v Dumas, [1924] AC 431, 442, Viscount Cave.

Express waiver

An insurer may, by an express clause of the contract, waive a defence which would otherwise be available by law. The wording of such an exclusion must be express, pertinent, and apposite.[99] For express waiver of the seaworthiness warranty the seaworthiness admitted clauses used to be included in the policies. An example of this clause can be seen in *Parfitt v Thompson*[100] that 'the said company further agreed that the said ship or vessel, the "Hutchinson" above-named, should be considered, and was thereby allowed to be, seaworthy in her hull, tackle, and materials for the said voyage, the insured thereby declaring, that, to the best of their belief, and according to their knowledge and information, the said ship was then, to wit, at the time of making the said insurance, in all respects seaworthy for the said voyage'. The effect of a seaworthiness admitted clause was 'a dispensation of the usual warranty of seaworthiness'.[101] Consequently, it enabled the assured to recover, in appropriate circumstances, for a deemed loss by perils of the seas, which the underwriter (having admitted the vessel's seaworthiness) would be unable to challenge.[102] Although the clause appeared in the 1963[103] cargo clauses, it was replaced by the 1982 cargo clauses, which were then revised in 2009. The 2009 Cargo Clauses now contain an unqualified waiver of the implied warranties. The 2009 Institute Cargo Clauses (A,B,C) cl.5 provides that the insurance will not cover loss damage or expense arising from unseaworthiness of the vessel if the assured is privy to unseaworthiness at the time the cargo is loaded (cl.5.1.1). Moreover, the insurer will not be liable for the loss caused by unfitness of container or conveyance for the sea carriage where loading was carried out by the assured or their employees and they are privy to such unfitness at the time of the loading. Clause 5.1.1 does not apply where the insurance contract has been assigned to a third party who purchased the subject matter insured in good faith. Under clause 5.3 the insurers waive any breach of the implied warranties of seaworthiness of the ship and fitness of the ship to carry the subject matter insured to its destination.

It may be a matter of construction if a breach of warranty is waived by an express term of the contract. The following clause was discussed in *HIH v New Hampshire* to determine whether breach of warranty was included in the waiver. Clause 8's title was '*Disclosure and/or Waiver of Rights*' and clause 8.1 provided 'To the fullest extent permissible by applicable law, the Insurer hereby agrees that it will not seek to or be entitled to avoid or rescind this Policy or reject any claim hereunder or be entitled to seek any remedy or redress on the grounds of invalidity or unenforceability of any of its arrangements . . . or non-disclosure or misrepresentation by any person or any other similar grounds.' The Court of Appeal agreed with David Steel J who held that the clause did not include breaches of warranty.[104] The judge opined that the phrases 'invalidity or enforceability of any arrangements' and 'non-disclosure or misrepresentation' are both extra contractual:[105] the former is dealing with arrangements collateral to the insurance contract and the latter is dealing with pre-contractual negotiations. Breaches of warranty, however, are breaches of the contract of insurance itself. Therefore, it did not fall 'similar grounds' within cl.8.1.[106]

---

99 *Sleigh v Tyser* [1900] 2 QB 333, 337–338.

100 (1844) 13 M & W 392.

101 *Parfitt v Thompson* (1844) 13 M & W 392, 395, Pollock CB

102 *Parfitt v Thompson* (1844) 13 M & W 392, 395, Pollock CB; Arnould, para 20–41.

103 The Institute Cargo Clauses 1963 cl 8 used to contain a seaworthiness admitted clause in the following words 'The seaworthiness of the vessel as between the Assured and Underwriters is hereby admitted. In the event of loss the Assured's right of recovery hereunder shall not be prejudiced by the fact that the loss may have been attributable to the wrongful act of the ship-owners or their servants, committed without the privity of the Assured.'

104 [2001] 2 Lloyd's Rep 161, para 118.

105 [2001] 2 Lloyd's Rep 161, para 118.

106 [2001] 2 Lloyd's Rep 161, para 118.

Implied waiver

Waiver may bear different meanings: it may refer to a forbearance from exercising a right or to an abandonment of a right.[107] The latter may arise by virtue of a party making an election between two alternative and inconsistent courses of action open to him. The principle of election applies when a state of affairs comes into existence in which one party becomes entitled to exercise a right, and has to choose whether to exercise the right or not.[108] As analysed in Chapter 4 breach of the duty of good faith opens to the insurer two alternative and inconsistent courses of action: to avoid or not to avoid the contract. His election has generally to be an informed choice, made with knowledge of the facts giving rise to the right.[109] Once an election is made, however, it is final and binding.[110]

Waiver by election does not apply in breach of warranty for the obvious reason that breach of warranty results in the insurer's automatic discharge from liability.[111] No other positive action is needed to make that discharge of liability effective.[112] Hence the insurer is not required to elect between the two alternative and inconsistent courses of action. In section 34(3) of the MIA 1906 the words '*a breach of warranty may be waived by the insurer*' refer to that type of 'waiver' which is concerned with the forebearance from exercising a legal right.[113] Thus for waiver of breach of warranty, the assured must rely on the doctrine of waiver by estoppel.[114] Equitable estoppel occurs where a person, having legal rights against another, unequivocally represents by words or conduct that he does not intend to enforce those legal rights. If in such circumstances the other party acts, or refrains from acting, in reliance upon that representation, with the effect that it would be inequitable for the representor thereafter to enforce his legal rights inconsistently with his representation, he will to that extent be precluded from doing so.[115] A similarity between an election and promissory estoppel is that each requires an unequivocal representation of the relevant party's rights. However, an election is different from equitable estoppel in that the latter requires a reliance of the representee on the unequivocal representation by the representor that he will not insist upon his legal rights against the representee, and such reliance will render it inequitable for the representor to go back upon his representation. His representation is therefore in the nature of a promise which, though unsupported by consideration, can have legal consequences; hence it is sometimes referred to as promissory estoppel. An election, however, is not dependent upon reliance on it by the other party. Moreover, while no question arises of any particular knowledge on the part of the representor, and the estoppel may be suspensory only, an election is final once made and it is a prerequisite of election that the party making the election must be aware of the facts which have given rise to the existence of his new right.[116] In estoppel it is not the representor's knowledge which is important but how their conduct appeared to the representee.[117]

---

107 *Motor Oil Hellas (Corinth) Refineries SA v Shipping Corp of India (The Kanchenjunga)* [1990] 1 Lloyd's Rep 391, 397, Lord Goff.

108 *The Kanchenjunga* [1990] 1 Lloyd's Rep 391, 399, Lord Goff.

109 *The Kanchenjunga* [1990] 1 Lloyd's Rep 391, 399, Lord Goff.

110 Moreover it does not require consideration to support it, and so it is to be distinguished from an express or implied agreement, such as a variation of the relevant contract, which traditionally requires consideration to render it binding in English law. *The Kanchenjunga* [1990] 1 Lloyd's Rep 391, 399, Lord Goff.

111 [2001] 2 Lloyd's Rep 161, 121–122; *Kirkaldy & Sons Ltd v Walker* [1999] Lloyd's Rep IR 410, 422.

112 *Argo Systems FZE v Liberty Insurance Pte Ltd* [2012] 1 Lloyd's Rep 129 Aikens LJ, para 38.

113 *Argo Systems FZE v Liberty Insurance Pte Ltd* [2012] 1 Lloyd's Rep 129 Aikens LJ, para 38.

114 *Kirkaldy & Sons Ltd v Walker* [1999] Lloyd's Rep IR 410, 422.

115 *Hughes v Metropolitan Railway Co* (1877) 2 App Cas 439.

116 *The Kanchenjunga* [1990] 1 Lloyd's Rep 391, 399, Lord Goff.

117 *HIH Casualty & General Insurance Ltd v Axa Corporate Solutions (formerly Axa Reassurance SA)* [2003] Lloyd's Rep IR 1, para 24.

In *Weir v Aberdeen*[118] the insured vessel was unseaworthy at the commencement of the voyage as she had a greater cargo than she could safely carry. The defect was discovered and part of the cargo was discharged. After the breach was remedied, the vessel suffered damage for reasons that were not attributable to unseaworthiness. Insurers were held liable in this case for the reason that at the outset of the voyage, although they had known about unseaworthiness, they still insured the vessel thus they waived the breach. They were aware of the fact that the vessel was overladen and had to discharge part of the cargo.

A waiver argument was once again successful in *Samuel v Dumas*[119] where the marine policy contained a warranty that 'the amount insured for account of assured' on (inter alia) freight (ppi) 'should not exceed a certain limit'. The same insurer agreed to effect an insurance against loss of freight by war risks only in a sum exceeding the amount allowed by the warranty. During the currency of the marine policy the vessel was lost, the assured's claim against the insurer failed for the court found that the ship was scuttled. One of the issues discussed was whether the insurer waived the breach of warranty as the same insurer issued the two policies mentioned. Viscount Cave and Lord Parmoor (Viscount Finlay and Lord Sumner dissenting) held that the insurer, by being a party to the issue of the policy on the freight against war risks, was precluded by waiver or acquiescence from treating the marine policy as void for breach of the warranty.

The unequivocal representation required to establish promissory estoppel depends to a great extent on the nature and circumstances of the communications passing between the parties.[120] In this respect silence and 'standing by', that is, doing nothing are equivocal actions so that in the absence of special circumstances,[121] silence and inaction are, when objectively considered cannot, by themselves, constitute an unequivocal representation as to whether a person will or will not rely on a particular legal right in the future.[122]

In *The Milasan*,[123] in addition to the points referred to elsewhere in this chapter, the assured contended that the insurers waived compliance with the warranty by accepting the second instalment of the premium for the policy in November 1995 despite their knowledge that there had been no professional skipper on board from 1 May to 1 July 1995. Having reiterated the principle that waiver by estoppel requires proof of a clear and unequivocal representation by the representor and reliance by the person to whom the representation was made, the Court rejected the argument as there was no plea of an express representation in the communications between the assured and the insurer relating to the claim. Moreover, the assured did not present any evidence with respect to reliance on the insurer's demand for the second instalment of the premium as a representation that they were waiving compliance with the warranty.

Waiver of breach of a warranty was once again unsuccessfully argued in *Argo Systems FZE v Liberty Insurance Pte Ltd*[124] where a floating casino was insured for a voyage under tow from Alabama, United States to India. The policy contained a number of warranties, including one that stated: '*warranted no release, waivers or "hold harmless" given to Tug and Towers*' (the hold harmless warranty). The floating casino was lost during the voyage and the assured's claim was declined by the insurer which led the assured to bring an action against the insurer in Alabama. This action was rejected for lack of personal

---

118 (1819) 2 B & Ald 320.

119 [1924] AC 431.

120 *Agapitos v Agnew (The Aegeon) (No.2)* [2003] Lloyd's Rep IR 54.

121 The only exception to this rule is where the law imposes a duty to speak or act. *HIH Casualty & General Insurance Ltd v Axa Corporate Solutions (formerly Axa Reassurance SA)* [2003] Lloyd's Rep IR 1, para 26.

122 *HIH Casualty & General Insurance Ltd v Axa Corporate Solutions (formerly Axa Reassurance SA)* [2003] Lloyd's Rep IR 1, para 26; *Argo Systems FZE v Liberty Insurance Pte Ltd* [2012] 1 Lloyd's Rep 129 Aikens LJ, para 46, in reference to Robert Goff LJ in *Allied Marine Transport Ltd v Vale Do Rio Doce Navigado SA ('The Leonidas D')* [1985] 1 WLR 925 at 937E.

123 [2000] 2 Lloyd's Rep 458.

124 [2012] 1 Lloyd's Rep 129.

jurisdiction over the insurer. Then the assured sued the insurer in England. The insurer, while rejecting the claim when it was initially made in 2003 as soon as the casualty occurred stated

> [the insurer therefore] reserves the right to alter its position in light of discovery of previously undisclosed information which would materially alter the facts and circumstances known. Should the assured wish to provide any additional information concerning this claim, we will review it. The foregoing is without prejudice to all the remaining terms and conditions of the policy, along with any other defenses that may be discovered after further investigation.

Neither in this letter nor during the proceedings in Alabama did the insurer raise breach of the hold harmless warranty. In the action brought in England in 2009, the insurer included breach of the hold harmless warranty in the points of defence. The assured asserted that the insurer was estopped from being able to rely on that breach as no allegation of a breach of the hold harmless warranty had been made at any stage in the US proceedings. The Court of Appeal rejected this argument as there was no unequivocal representation by the insurers in terms of forebearance of their right for breach of warranty. In their letter to the assured in 2003 the insurers expressly said '*The foregoing is without prejudice to all the remaining terms and conditions of the policy*' which, according to Aikens LJ, is a clear indication that the insurers were reserving the right to rely on any of those remaining terms and conditions of the policy in the future if advised to do so.

'Held covered' clauses

A held covered clause entitles the assured, as soon as he discovers that the warranty has been broken, to require the underwriter to hold him covered.[125] In other words, by virtue of a held covered clause the underwriter is kept on risk, notwithstanding that, in the absence of the clause, he would be discharged from liability or the risk would fall outside the policy.[126] As appears, the clause is used to mitigate the harsh consequences of a breach of a warranty.[127] It provides protection for the assured, generally, in return for additional premium and notice of the relevant situation, where the insurer has otherwise a contractual defence against the assured. The early examples of the held covered clauses are seen in the cases decided in the late nineteenth century. For instance in *Simon v Sedgwick*[128] the insurer agreed to provide cover for 'Deviation and/or change of voyage and/or transhipment, not included in this policy, to be held covered at a premium to be arranged.' A similar wording is seen in *Greenock Steamship Co v Maritime Insurance Co Ltd*[129] that 'Held covered in case of any breach of warranty, deviation and/or any unprovided incidental risk or change of voyage, at a premium to be hereafter arranged.' The assured was held covered in *Hyderabad (Deccan) Company v Willoughby*[130] where the insured cargo was a parcel of gold bullion, which was to be carried from India to London. The policy described the risk as 'including all risks of every description from the mines by escort to railway station at Raichur (forty miles) thence by rail (400 miles) to Bombay thence to London and until delivered at its destination at assay office and/or bank in London'. There was stamped in the margin of the policy the following words: 'It is agreed to hold assured covered in event of deviation or change of voyage at a premium to be hereafter arranged.' Three bars of

---

125 *Greenock Steamship Co v Maritime Insurance Co Ltd* [1903] 1 KB 367, 374 Bigham J.
126 *Liberian Insurance Agency Inc v Mosse* [1977] 2 Lloyd's Rep 560, 567.
127 Mustill, M [1988] LMCLQ 310, 345.
128 [1893] 1 QB 303.
129 [1903] 1 KB 367, appeal was dismissed [1903] 2 KB 657.
130 [1899] 2 QB 530.

gold were sent from the mines to Raichur in the charge of one of the assured's officials. On arrival it was found that one of the bars of gold had been stolen. The voyage had to be deviated at the assured's offices at Secunderabad due to some administrative issues and some outstanding paperwork. If there had been no deviation clause in the policy the insurer would have ceased to be liable the moment the intention to deviate was put into practice. It was held that the deviation was unjustifiable; but it was a deviation in the course of the voyage; the intention to forward the box to London was never abandoned and the assured was entitled to recover for the stolen piece of gold.

By the held covered clause the underwriter does not agree to hold the assured covered on terms which differ from those of the policy, other than as to premium.[131] Accordingly, if the original cover was on all risks terms, the clause will not affect this. As the clauses read, the underwriter is entitled to extra premium as is reasonably proportionate to the extra risk.[132] It follows that the clause can only be intended to operate if the omission, erroneous description or change of voyage is of such a nature that a new premium for a policy on identical terms can be arranged.[133] It was held that the clause only applies if the assured, on the basis of an accurate declaration of all the facts affecting the risk but excluding knowledge of what was to happen in the event, could have obtained a quotation in the market at a premium which could properly be described as 'a reasonable commercial rate'.[134] Furthermore, some upper limit to the new premium is to be considered. It was held that the clause cannot contemplate a situation in which the only premium which could be arranged was 100 per cent of the sum insured.[135] In *Liberian Insurance Agency Inc v Mosse* the assured was held not to be entitled to rely on the held covered clause. In this case a cargo of enamelware was insured for carriage from Hong Kong to Monrovia under the Institute Cargo Clauses (All Risks) which contained a held covered clause in the following words 'Held covered at a premium to be arranged in case of change of voyage or of any omission or error in the description of the interest vessel or voyage.' The goods were described as 'Enamelware (cups and plates) in wooden cases.' In fact, large quantities were neither cups nor plates. When they arrived, some of the goods were found to be damaged. Donaldson J considered that the consignment was an end of production one and contained a variety of qualities including a high proportion of seconds and a significant proportion of the cargo was packed in cartons. Under these circumstances the judge found that no underwriter would have quoted a reasonable commercial rate of premium on 'all risks' terms unless he was protected by an f.p.a. (free of particular average) warranty.

If the assured is to take advantage of the held covered clause he must give notice to the underwriters seeking cover in accordance with the clause within a reasonable time of learning of the change of voyage or of the omission or error in the description.[136] The determination of 'reasonable time' will depend upon all the circumstances. For instance if the assured learns the true facts when the insured property is in the grip of a peril, which is likely to cause loss or damage, a reasonable time will be very short indeed.[137]

The assured may still take advantage of the held covered clause even though he gave the required notice after the loss has occurred. If the assured found out about the breach only after the loss has occurred and if there is nothing practicable to be done on the receipt of the notice under the circumstances of the case the insurer will be liable.[138] Naturally, the additional premium could not

---

131 *Liberian Insurance Agency Inc v Mosse* [1977] 2 Lloyd's Rep 560, 567.
132 *Greenock Steamship Co v Maritime Insurance Co Ltd* [1903] 1 KB 367, 374 Bigham J; *Hewitt v London General Insurance Co Ltd* (1925) 23 Ll L Rep 243, 246.
133 *Liberian Insurance Agency Inc v Mosse* [1977] 2 Lloyd's Rep 560, 568.
134 *Liberian Insurance Agency Inc v Mosse* [1977] 2 Lloyd's Rep 560, 568.
135 *Liberian Insurance Agency Inc v Mosse* [1977] 2 Lloyd's Rep 560, 568.
136 *Liberian Insurance Agency Inc v Mosse* [1977] 2 Lloyd's Rep 560, 566.
137 *Liberian Insurance Agency Inc v Mosse* [1977] 2 Lloyd's Rep 560, 566.
138 *Greenock Steamship Co v Maritime Insurance Co Ltd* [1903] 1 KB 367; *Mentz, Decker & Co v Maritime Insurance Co* [1910] 1 KB 132.

be arranged as soon as the breach occurred. The rule in such a case is that the premium is to be calculated as it would have been calculated by the parties, if they had known of the deviation at the time that it happened.[139] In *Hewitt v London General Insurance Co Ltd*[140] the clause provided 'In the event of the voyage being changed or of any deviation from the terms of this policy the same to be held covered at premium to be arranged hereafter.' A cargo of nitrate was to be carried from Tocopilla to France via the Panama Canal. The ship sailed from Tocopilla on 21 January 1919, with orders to proceed to Texas, unless otherwise instructed at Colon. At Colon she received orders to go to New Orleans where she arrived on 22 February 1919. She stayed there two months loading further cargo and doing repairs and then started for La Pallice. She was lost at New Orleans by collision on 27 April 1919. The reinsured did not in fact know it until after the loss had happened; and then he found it out only because the loss was posted at Lloyd's and advertised in the ordinary way. Once the loss had occurred no practical benefit would have accrued to the reinsurers from being told any sooner than they were in fact told of the deviation or subsequent loss, and they knew it as soon as the knowledge was of any good to them at all. Nothing could be suggested when the judge asked what could the reinsurers have done if there had been notice as soon as the risk occurred.

In *Hewitt v London General Insurance Co Ltd* Branson J applied the principle stated above that if the notice was given after the loss has occurred, the parties must assume the breach was known to them at the time it happened and ascertain what it would then have been reasonable to charge.[141] On the facts of the case Branson J concluded that the assured had to pay no additional premium. The evidence showed that the deviation to New Orleans was not a serious one. It prolonged the voyage by some 500 miles. The voyage was 5,000 miles, making the extension no more than 10 per cent of the total. Moreover, this was a reinsurance contract which was disputed and under the original insurance the insurer did not charge an extra premium in respect of the deviation because it was considered that the deviation did not cause any material addition to the risk.

The International Hull Clauses 2003 clause 10 includes navigation provisions such as 'the assured shall not enter into any contract with pilots or for customary towage which limits or exempts the liability of the pilots and/or tugs and/or towboats and/or their owners except where the Assured or their agents accept or are compelled to accept such contracts in accordance with established local law or practice'.[142] Clause 11 provides that the insurer will not be liable for the loss which occurs during the breach of clause 10. However, it is open to the assured to give notice to the insurer immediately after receipt of notification of such breach and any amended terms of cover and any additional premium required by them are agreed.

Finally, it should be noted that the assured cannot take advantage of the clause if he has not acted in utmost good faith.[143] The controversies regarding the post-contractual duty of good faith were discussed in Chapter 4. Here it is only to be noted that the remedy for breach of the duty of good faith in the case of a claim under the held covered clause should not entitle the insurer to avoid the entire contract *ab initio* but a contractual remedy should be sought. It will be likely that the assured will not be entitled to seek to be held covered if he does not act in good faith in making the claim.

139 *Greenock Steamship Co v Maritime Insurance Co Ltd* [1903] 1 KB 367; *Mentz, Decker & Co v Maritime Insurance Co* [1910] 1 KB 132.
140 (1925) 23 Ll L Rep 243.
141 *Hewitt v London General Insurance Co Ltd* (1925) 23 Ll L Rep 243, 246.
142 Clause 10.3.
143 *Liberian Insurance Agency Inc v Mosse* [1977] 2 Lloyd's Rep 560, 568.

The basis of the contract clauses

It is mostly seen in the non-marine context that presentations made by the assured may be converted into warranties by virtue of the basis of the contract clause. The effect of the clause is that if a statement made by the assured is false the insurer is discharged from liability irrespective of the chain of causation between the loss and the statement. For instance, in *Dawsons v Bonnin*[144] the policy which insured a motor lorry against damage by fire and third party risks recited that the proposal should be the basis of the contract and be held as incorporated in the policy. In the proposal form the address at which the vehicle will usually be garaged was stated as the assured's ordinary place of business in Glasgow. This was not true, as the lorry was usually garaged at a farm in the outskirts of Glasgow. The lorry was destroyed by fire in the garage. The insurer was not liable for the loss. The House of Lords explained that when answers, including that in question, are declared to be the basis of the contract this can only mean that their truth is made a condition, exact fulfilment of which is rendered by stipulation as essential to its enforceability.[145] Basis meant 'the foundation of a thing; that on which a thing stands or lies'; thus, if the statements of fact are untrue or the promissory statements are not carried out, the risk does not attach.[146]

The basis of the contract clause was abolished in consumer insurance by section 6(2) of the Consumer Insurance (Disclosure and Representations) Act 2012. The Government Insurance Bill 2014, which will be referred to in detail below also aims to abolish the basis clauses in business insurance.

Difference from conditions

Insurance conditions are interpreted differently to insurance warranties and contract law conditions. The creation of conditions and the remedy for their breach are analysed in Chapter 15.[147]

Reform proposal and the draft Bill

In July 2014 the Law Commissions presented a draft Bill to Government proposing reform of several areas in insurance law including warranties. The Bill does not attempt to reform the definition of warranties or the rules governing creation of warranties but it focuses on the basis of the contract clauses and remedies for breach of warranties.

Clause 9 provides that a representation made by the assured in connection with a proposed non-consumer insurance contract, or variation to a non-consumer insurance contract is not capable of being converted into a warranty by means of any provision of the non-consumer insurance contract or of any other contract. Clause 10 contains detailed provisions regarding breach of warranties. Accordingly, any rule of law that a breach of a warranty (express or implied) in a contract of insurance results in the discharge of the insurer's liability under the contract is abolished (cl.10(1)). Clause 10(2) permits the assured to remedy the breach and reinstate the insurance cover. However, the clause notes that the insurer will not be liable in respect of any loss occurring, or attributable to something happening, after a warranty (express or implied) in the contract has been

---

144 [1922] 2 AC 413.
145 [1922] 2 AC 413, 425 Viscount Haldane.
146 [1922] 2 AC 413, 432 Viscount Cave.
147 Conditions are placed in Chapter 15 for the reason that in order to explain the claims provisions in reinsurance it is necessary to fully analyse insurance conditions.

breached but before the breach has been remedied. However, clause 10(2) does not apply in the case of the warranty ceasing to be applicable because of a change of circumstances or compliance with the warranty is rendered unlawful by any subsequent legal enactment, or the insurer waives the breach of warranty.

The insurers are not liable for any loss occurring after the warranty has been broken but before it has been remedied unless the loss is the result of a peril occurring prior to the breach of warranty but giving rise to loss thereafter. It is to be noted that there is no causation test but merely a factual issue as to whether the breach was continuing at the date of the loss.

Contracting out of cl.9 on the conversion of representations into warranties is also prohibited (cl.15.1). As regards other warranties, contracting out by means of a disadvantageous term is not permissible unless the requirements of utmost good faith have been satisfied in relation to the term and the insurer has taken sufficient steps to draw the term to the assured's attention before the contract is entered into (cl.15.2).

Further reading

Aikens, 'The Law Commissions' proposed reforms of the law of "Warranties" in Marine and Commercial Insurance: will the cure be better than the disease?', Chapter 6 in Soyer (ed.), *Reforming Marine and Commercial Insurance Law* [2008] Informa.

Bennett, 'Good luck with warranties', *Journal of Business Law* [1991] November, pp 592–598.

Bennett, *The Law of Marine Insurance*, 2nd edn, [2006] Oxford University Press. Chapter 18 contains promissory warranties and held covered clauses and part of Chapter 19 contains warranty of seaworthiness in voyage policies.

Bennett, 'Reflections on values: the Law Commissions' proposals with respect to remedies for breach of promissory warranty and pre-formation non-disclosure and misrepresentation in commercial insurance', Chapter 8 in Soyer (ed.), *Reforming Marine and Commercial Insurance Law*, [2008] Informa.

Clarke, 'Insurance warranties: the absolute end?', *Lloyd's Maritime and Commercial Law Quarterly* [2007] 4, 474–493 (not only on marine warranties but generally on insurance warranties).

Davey, 'Remedying the remedies: the shifting shape of Insurance Contract Law', *Lloyd's Maritime and Commercial Law Quarterly* [2013] 4, 476–495.

Davey, 'The reform of insurance warranties: a behavioural economics perspective', *Journal of Business Law* [2013] 1, 118–139.

Gilman et al., *Arnould: Law of Marine Insurance and Average*, 18th edn, [2013] Sweet & Maxwell. Chapter 19, Express Warranties; Chapter 20, Implied Warranties – Seaworthiness; Chapter 21, Illegality of the Risk.

Hodges, 'The quest for seaworthiness: a study of US and English Law of Marine Insurance', Chapter 6 in Thomas (ed.), *Modern Law of Marine Insurance* [2002] Volume 2, London: LLP.

Lewins, 'Australia proposes marine insurance reform', *Journal of Business Law* [2002] May, pp 292–303.

Longmore, 'Good faith and breach of warranty: are we moving forwards or backwards?', *Lloyd's Maritime and Commercial Law Quarterly* [2004] 2, 158–171.

Lord Mance, 'The 1906 Act, common law and contract clauses: all in harmony?', *Lloyd's Maritime and Commercial Law Quarterly* [2011] 3, 346–360.

Merkin, *Colinvaux's Law of Insurance*, 9th edn, [2010] Sweet & Maxwell, Chapter 7.

Nicoll, 'HIH litigation', *Law Quarterly Review* [2003] 119(October), 572–582.

Rose, *Marine Insurance: Law and Practice*, 2nd edn, [2012] Informa. Chapter 9.

Soyer, 'Identifying express warranties and distinguishing them from the other terms of a marine insurance contract', *International Journal of Insurance Law* [1999] 4, 322–334.

Soyer, 'Defences available to a marine insurer', *Lloyd's Maritime and Commercial Law Quarterly* [2002] 2, 199–213.

Soyer, 'Marine warranties: old rules for the new millennium?', Chapter 5 in Thomas (ed.), *Modern Law of Marine Insurance* [2002] Volume 2, London: LLP.

Soyer, *Warranties in Marine Insurance*, 2nd edn, [2006] Cavendish Publishing.
Soyer, 'Reforming insurance warranties: are we finally moving forward?', published as Chapter 7 in Soyer (ed.), *Reforming Marine and Commercial Insurance Law* [2008] Informa.
Soyer, 'Beginning of a new era for insurance warranties?', *Lloyd's Maritime and Commercial Law Quarterly* [2013] 3, 384–400.
Wilhelmsen, 'Harmonisation of marine insurance clauses: duty of disclosure, duty of good faith, alteration of risk and warranties', *Journal of International Commercial Law* [2003] 2(1), 13–36 (discusses warranties in continental and common law jurisdictions).

Chapter 6

The Premium

Chapter Contents

The premiums are paid to the insurer in consideration for the policy coverage provided. Lawrence J defined insurance in *Lucena v Craufurd*[1] as 'a contract by which the one party in consideration of a price paid to him adequate to the risk, becomes security to the other that he shall not suffer loss, damage, or prejudice by the happening of the perils specified to certain things which may be exposed to them'.

In marine insurance, as seen below, brokers are personally liable for the payment of premiums. Thus, in principle, the insurer looks to the broker for payment of the premium and the broker has a cause of action in his own right against the assured for non-payment of the premium. The principles governing payment of the premium in marine insurance are set out below.

The custom[2]

According to the ordinary course of trade between the assured, the broker, and the underwriter, the assured does not in the first instance pay the premium to the broker, nor does the latter pay it to the underwriter.[3] By the usage in marine insurance, the premium, as between the underwriter and the assured, is considered to have been paid at the time of the subscription:[4] the underwriter acknowledges his receipt of it; and if he does not actually receive it, he accepts the broker as his debtor, and substitutes him for this purpose in the place of the assured.[5] In *Power v Butcher*[6] Parker J and Bayley J explained that by the course of dealing, the broker has an account with the underwriter in which the broker gives the underwriter credit for the premium when the policy is effected.[7] In most instances the assured is unknown to the underwriter; the underwriter gives credit to the broker alone as there is an account between him and the broker.[8] The assured is thus (fictionally) considered as having paid the premium to the underwriter and the underwriter having lent it to the broker and therefore becoming his creditor.[9] Consequently, the underwriter is precluded from suing the assured himself for unpaid premiums that was credited in the account between the underwriter and the broker. The judges noted that the broker is presumed to be an agent of both the assured and the underwriter in relation to payment of the premium – he is a principal to receive the money from the assured, and to pay it to the underwriters.[10] By issuing the policy the

---

1 (1806) 2 Bosanquet and Puller (New Reports) 269, 301.
2 As will be seen in the following paragraphs the broker is personally liable for the premium according to the usage which relies on an account between the insurer and the broker that the premium is presumed to have been paid by the assured and lent back to the broker; therefore the broker is liable personally for payment of premiums. This is commonly referred to as either fiction or usage. The Law Commissions distinguish custom and fiction; while the former refers to the broker being personally liable for payment of premium, the fiction is that the premium was lent back to the broker. See the Broker's Liability for Premiums (Section 53) Issues paper 8, July 2010 http://lawcommission.justice.gov.uk/docs/ICL8_Brokers_Liability_for_Premiums.pdf. Chitty LJ said in *Universo Insurance Co of Milan v Merchants Marine Insurance Co Ltd* [1897] 2 QB 93, at 101 that whether it is a fiction or not a fiction it 'is law too firmly established to justify us in disregarding it' p 101.
3 *Power v Butcher* (1829) 10 B & C 329.
4 *Jenkins v Power* (1817) 6 Maule and Selwyn 282, 287–288 Lord Ellenborough CJ; *Universo Insurance Co of Milan v Merchants Marine Insurance Co Ltd* [1897] 2 QB 93.
5 *Shee v Clarkson* (1810) 12 East 507, 508–509.
6 (1829) 10 B & C 329.
7 (1829) 10 B & C 329, 347, Parker J. *Edgar v Fowler* (1803) 3 East 222.
8 *Universo Insurance Co of Milan v Merchants Marine Insurance Co Ltd* [1897] 2 QB 93, 100, Chitty LJ.
9 *Xenos v Wickham* (1862) 13 CB NS 381, especially see the submission of Lush QC at pp 386–387.
10 *Shee v Clarkson* (1810) 12 East 507, 510, Lord Ellenborough CJ. Professor Merkin is of the opinion that the fiction can be explained by the broker's dual agency, and not merely him acting as an agent for the assured. 'The Duties of Marine Insurance Brokers' in The Modern Law of Marine Insurance, R Thomas (ed.), (LLP 1996) Ch 9, 283; See discussions on the statutes of the broker in regard to accepting the payment from the assured E Gloster, Who Pays the Piper – Who Calls the Tune? Recent Issues Arising in the Context of s 53 of the Marine Insurance Act 1906, [2007] LMCLQ 302; The Broker's Liability for Premiums (Section 53) Issues paper 8, July 2010 http://lawcommission.justice.gov.uk/docs/ICL8_Brokers_Liability_for_Premiums.pdf, para 2.9.

underwriter acknowledges the receipt of the premium, thus he would have no claim upon the assured for the premium.[11] The giving of credit in account by the broker to the underwriter, and the underwriter having acknowledged the receipt of the premium through the terms of the policy, is equivalent to actual payment.[12]

The account referred to in the usage was explained in more detail in *Great Western Insurance Co v Cunliffe*:[13]

> ... On the credit system ... the broker is debited with the premium, and credited with 5 per cent for brokerage in his account with the underwriter, upon the insurance being effected. The account is continued up to the 31st of December in each year, and in this account the underwriter is debited with the losses which have arisen upon the risks protected by insurances; and if upon the balance of the account the amount of the premiums, less brokerage, exceeds the amount of the losses, so that the underwriter has money to receive, the underwriter allows to the broker a reduction of 12 per cent upon the balance which the broker pays to the underwriter. On the other hand, if the losses exceed the premiums, less brokerage, the broker does not receive any allowance upon the amount of the premiums which he pays in account. This deduction or allowance of 12 per cent is called discount.[14]

In *Universo Insurance Co of Milan v Merchants Marine Insurance Co Ltd*[15] the usage was described as the universal understanding in the business of marine insurance in England as that is the manner in which the contract is to be carried out. In *Universo* the insurers brought an action against the assured to recover the premium due under an insurance contract with the assured. The insurers' case was rejected. Lord Esher stated that by his action against the assured the insurers attempted to challenge a course of business which had existed for a hundred years or more without any possible ground. The customary course of business Lord Esher referred to was that the underwriter does not look to the assured for payment of the premium, but to the broker who effected the policy between the two. In other words, having agreed with the assured the payment of the premium, the underwriter agrees to take the credit of the broker instead of the assured. Lord Esher noted that it is not a contradiction of the terms of the policy, but a mode of carrying them out. The policy says that the assured is to pay the premium, but the mode in which the payment is to be made is according to the customary way of doing business in the English insurance industry. Chitty LJ[16] said that the fiction was raised for the purpose of justice, which was 'to give effect to the true understanding of mercantile men, and to sustain the universal course of business between business men'. It was also noted that this custom has never been departed from and still exists.[17] Shortly after *Universo* was decided, the usage was codified by section 53 of the Marine Insurance Act 1906. Section 53(1) provides:

> Unless otherwise agreed, where a marine policy is effected on behalf of the assured by a broker, the broker is directly responsible to the insurer for the premium, and the insurer is directly responsible to the assured for the amount which may be payable in respect of losses, or in respect of returnable premium.

---

11   (1829) 10 B & C 329, 339–340, Bayley J.
12   (1829) 10 B & C 329, 347, Parke J.
13   (1873–74) LR 9 ch App 525, 529–530.
14   See also *Baring v Stanton* (1876) 3 ch D 502, 505.
15   [1897] 2 QB 93.
16   [1897] 2 QB 93, 101.
17   [1897] 2 QB 93, 97, A.L. Smith LJ.

The custom applies to marine policies obtained in the Lloyd's as well as in the London company market[18] but it was held not to exist in the context of non-marine insurance.[19] As will be mentioned throughout this chapter the Law Commissions have discussed the application of section 53 in their Issues Papers 8 and 9, and in December 2011 in the Consultation Paper No. 201 they proposed that 'Section 53(1) should be re-enacted in a way that does not preserve the common law underpinnings. The policyholder should be liable to pay premium to the insurer, and should pay the broker as agent. Any liability assumed by the broker should be in addition to the policyholder's liability, not a substitute.'[20]

Effect of receipt on policy

Section 54 of the MIA 1906 provides that 'Where a marine policy effected on behalf of the assured by a broker acknowledges the receipt of the premium, such acknowledgement is, in the absence of fraud, conclusive as between the insurer and the assured, but not as between the insurer and broker.' The Law Commissions discussed in the Issues Paper 8 whether section 54 refers to the fiction that the premium was lent back to the broker or the custom that the broker is personally liable for payment of the premium. The Law Commissions found section 54 controversial for the reason that if the section codified the fiction, section 53(1) rendered section 54 entirely superfluous.[21] According to the Law Commissions, this is the case because section 54 clearly states that the insurer's acknowledgment is binding only against the assured but not the broker. The policyholder under section 53(1) is presumed to have paid the premium regardless of any acknowledgment of the policy regarding the payment. Thus, section 54 seems to be redundant.[22] The Law Commissions also stated that while the fiction presumes that the insurer is deemed to have received the premium as against all parties, including the broker, the broker remains liable to pay the premium, but on different grounds, the insurer lent the premium back to it. The Law Commissions expressed that 'The fact that section 54 provides that an acknowledgment in the policy is not conclusive as between the broker and the insurer is therefore contrary to the "fiction of lending"'.[23]

It is submitted that sections 53 and 54 codified the fiction and they both confirm the fiction-custom which renders the broker personally liable for the payment of premium. Prior to the adoption of the 1906 Act, Chitty LJ observed in *Universo* that '. . . in a Lloyd's policy the underwriter confesses that the premium has been paid to him by the assured, although in fact it has not been so paid. A Lloyd's policy is not under seal; consequently the underwriter is not estopped by the policy itself from shewing that the payment which he has acknowledged has not in fact been made. In an ordinary case of contract not connected with marine insurance, and apart from the custom, an acknowledgment of the receipt of money forming the consideration for the promise would go strongly to shew that the person in whose favour the receipt is given is liable to pay the consideration which has not in fact been paid. But on a Lloyd's policy the custom steps in and negatives any such liability on the part of the assured, and it prevails to the extent of relieving him from all liability to pay the premium.'[24] Bayley J[25] stated in *Power v Butcher* that the insurer acknowledges

---

18 *Universo Insurance Co of Milan v Merchants Marine Insurance Co Ltd* [1897] 2 QB 93, 100, Chitty LJ.
19 *Wilson v Avec Audio-Visual Equipment* [1974] 1 Lloyd's Rep 81, 82–83 Edmund Davies, LJ; *Pacific & General Insurance Co Ltd v Hazell* [1997] LR 65.
20 http://lawcommission.justice.gov.uk/docs/cp201_ICL_post_contract_duties.pdf, para 19–18.
21 http://lawcommission.justice.gov.uk/docs/ICL8_Brokers_Liability_for_Premiums.pdf, para 3–28.
22 http://lawcommission.justice.gov.uk/docs/ICL8_Brokers_Liability_for_Premiums.pdf, para 3–30.
23 http://lawcommission.justice.gov.uk/docs/ICL8_Brokers_Liability_for_Premiums.pdf, para 3–31.
24 [1897] 2 QB 93, 100.
25 (1829) 10 B & C 329, 340.

the receipt of the premium in the ordinary case of a policy by simple contract. The judge went on to say that

> In such a case the action would be maintainable at the suit of the broker, on the principle that he was entitled to call upon the assured for the payment of those premiums which he had become liable to pay to the underwriters, and which they had acknowledged the receipt of. The assured has had the benefit of the policies; and if the underwriters were liable upon the risk, they were warranted in calling upon the broker to pay the premiums. In point of justice, the assured ought to pay the broker, or in the event which has happened, of his failure, his assignees. In an ordinary case the assurers would have no claim upon the assured for the premium, because by the policy they acknowledge the receipt of it.[26]

The fiction and therefore its codification and implications of the acknowledgment of the receipt of the premium are clear and sections 53 and 54 reflect that. Section 53 is by no means devoid of controversies, as will be explained below. On the other hand, section 54 does not seem to be as problematic as presented by the Law Commissions. In Consultation Paper 201 the Law Commissions stated that section 54 does not have any purpose in modern insurance law and therefore it should be repealed.[27] Section 54 may however operate alongside section 53(1).

Producing brokers – placing brokers

The relationship between producing and placing brokers and the assured is explained in Chapter 14 of this work. Section 53(1) does not deal expressly with the rights and liabilities as between the broker and the assured. It is a general rule that the broker has a cause of action in his own right against the assured in respect of unpaid premiums.[28] The placing broker, being immediately concerned in effecting the policy, is liable to pay the premium so that the underwriter can turn to the placing broker for premium. In the absence of any contract between the placing broker and the assured, the placing broker has a right to seek indemnity from the producing broker but not from the assured, who is liable to indemnify only the producing broker. If the assured becomes insolvent so that the producing broker is unable to obtain payment from him, the producing broker is not relieved from his obligation to indemnify the placing broker.[29] If there is a return premium owed to the assured by the underwriters, and this is paid to the placing broker, then the placing broker is entitled to set off that return premium against sums owed by the producing broker to him in premium.[30]

The amount of premium

The policies normally expressly state the amount of premium owed to the underwriter. However, in case the policy does not expressly provide for the amount to be paid, section 31 of the Marine Insurance Act states that:

---

26 (1829) 10 B & C 329.
27 http://lawcommission.justice.gov.uk/docs/cp201_ICL_post_contract_duties.pdf, para 20.38.
28 *JA Chapman & Co Ltd (In Liquidation) v Kadirga Denizcilik ve Ticaret AS* [1998] Lloyd's Rep IR 377.
29 Arnould, para 6–08.
30 *Velos Group Ltd v Harbour Insurance Services* [1997] 2 Lloyd's Rep 461.

1   Where an insurance is effected at a premium to be arranged, and no arrangement is made, a reasonable premium is payable.

2   Where an insurance is effected on the terms that an additional premium is to be arranged in a given event, and that event happens but no arrangement is made, then a reasonable additional premium is payable.

An agreement to agree an essential term or terms is not a binding agreement. If the parties agree that the premium will be arranged at a later date, this does not prevent a binding agreement between the parties. That will indicate that they agreed on the payment of premium and that the amount will be arranged. Section 31(1) provides a default rule in case the parties do not arrange for the amount of the premium. A case where the court discussed a similar matter, at which the issue was whether the agreement was binding or not, is *Willis Management (Isle of Man) Ltd v Cable & Wireless plc*.[31] In that case the parties agreed that a fair share which would be discussed and determined by the parties in good faith will be paid by Willis. The Court of Appeal found that this was not an agreement to agree an essential term and thus it was a binding agreement between the parties. Willis had acted as Pender's (the insurer's) underwriting manager. Mr F was employed by Willis, Pender brought an action against Mr F for conspiracy, procuring breaches of contract and liability to account as a constructive trustee on the basis of dishonest assistance in their breaches of trust. There were email exchanges between Willis and Pender in which Willis proposed that it would accept legal responsibility for Mr F's conduct and would not dispute the facts. However, there would need to be a mechanism (such as arbitration) agreed between Pender and Willis for quantifying the extent of Willis' contribution. Willis stated in emails that it would not accept responsibility for the whole loss but 'for a share . . . which we are agreeing to discuss' under a standstill agreement which gave time 'as long as such discussions proceeding in good faith and haven't broken down'. The dispute turned on the issue of whether there was a binding agreement. The Court of Appeal held that there was such a binding agreement; the evidence clearly showed that it was for the parties to discuss and agree the way in which the Willis share would be determined. The parties contemplated arbitration or mediation to determine Willis' share, but only in the context of an agreed statement of the principles to be applied. There is no suggestion that they intended the court to determine these matters, let alone that they intended it to carry out this task without the benefit of the parties' agreed statement of principles. The court cannot make for the parties an agreement that they have not made for themselves. In this case what the parties agreed was to negotiate a fair share on principles to be discussed and agreed. They expressly contemplated that such principles would include a clause for arbitration or mediation, in case an ultimate agreement on a fair share was not possible.

Premium's due date

In the absence of an express term in the policy, the premium is payable by the broker and then by the assured to the broker when the contract is made.[32] If the policy contains a clause in terms of the date at which the premium will be due,[33] the due date will be a matter of construction of the relevant clause. For example, in *Heath Lambert Ltd v Sociedad de Corretaje de Seguros*,[34] on the true construction

---

31   [2005] 2 Lloyd's Rep 597.
32   *Heath Lambert Ltd v Sociedad de Corretaje de Seguros* [2004] Lloyd's Rep IR 905, para 24.
33   *Heath Lambert Ltd v Sociedad de Corretaje de Seguros* [2004] Lloyd's Rep IR 905, para 14, 20.
34   [2004] Lloyd's Rep IR 905.

of the premium payment warranty, the Court of Appeal found that the premium was not payable when the contract was made but later. In *Heath Lambert* the relevant warranty was in the following terms: 'Warranted premium payable on cash basis to London Underwriters within 90 days of attachment.'

In construing the clause to determine the due date to pay the premium the Court of Appeal put emphasis on the word 'payable' which, according to Clarke LJ, naturally refers to the moment when the duty to pay arises. Thus the premium was not payable when the contract was made but 'on cash basis to London Underwriters within 90 days of attachment'.[35] Clarke LJ stated that the premium cannot be both payable when (1) the contract was made and (2) 'within 90 days of attachment'.[36] The use of the word 'payable' means that the obligation to pay the premium was only to pay before the expiry of 90 days from attachment.[37] The effect of section 53(1) of the 1906 Act, unless otherwise agreed, is that this obligation is the one assumed by the broker and not the assured. It follows that the broker could not be in breach of its obligation to pay the premium until the 90 days expired.[38] In *Heath Lambert*, Clarke LJ referred to *JA Chapman & Co Ltd (In Liquidation) v Kadirga Denizcilik ve Ticaret AS*[39] in which each instalment of premium was to be 'paid to underwriters within 75 days of due date' and the due dates were separately set out.[40] Clarke LJ distinguished a warranty as to when premium is in fact be 'paid' from a warranty as to when premium is 'payable'. Thus, a warranty as to when premium will be paid suggests that the premium was payable earlier, whereas a warranty as to when it is payable indicates when the obligation to pay arises.[41]

Another point the Court of Appeal highlighted in *Heath Lambert* is the usage of the words 'in cash' in the premium payment warranty. In the absence of a clause requiring payment in cash, the obligation of the broker to pay the premium to the underwriter would be discharged in the ordinary way, i.e. in account between them.[42] This clause makes it clear that the premium is payable in cash, not in any other way. Purported payment otherwise than in cash would not satisfy the requirements of the clause.[43] The broker owed a duty to the underwriters to pay the premium in cash within 90 days of attachment of the risk. Failure to pay would put the assured in breach of warranty. The Court of Appeal held that once the broker paid the premium for the assured, the latter becomes liable to indemnify the broker on receiving notice of payment. If there is a brokers' cancellation

---

35 [2004] Lloyd's Rep IR 905, para 25.
36 [2004] Lloyd's Rep IR 905, para 26.
37 [2004] Lloyd's Rep IR 905, para 26.
38 [2004] Lloyd's Rep IR 905, para 26.
39 [1998] Lloyd's Rep IR 377.
40 International Hull Clauses cl 35 provides a clause which is similar to the clause in *Chapman v Kadirga* that:
    35.   Premium payment
    35.1 The assured undertakes that the premium shall be paid
    35.1.1 in full to the Underwriters within 45 days (or such other period as may be agreed) of inception of this insurance; or
    35.1.2 where payment by instalment premiums has been
        a) the first instalment premium shall be paid within 45 days (or such other period as may be agreed) of inception of this insurance; and
        b) the second and subsequent instalments shall be paid by the date they are due.
    35.2 If the premium (or the first instalment premium) has not been so paid to the Underwriters by the 46th day (or the day after such period as may have been agreed) from the inception of this insurance, (and, in respect of the second and subsequent instalment premiums, by the date they are due), the Underwriters shall have the right to cancel this insurance by notifying the Assured via the broker in writing.
    35.3 The Underwriters shall give not less than 15 days' prior notice of cancellation to the Assured via the broker. If the premium or instalment premium due is paid in full to the Underwriters before the notice period expires, notice of cancellation shall automatically be revoked. If not, this insurance shall automatically terminate at the end of the notice period.
41 [2004] Lloyd's Rep IR 905, para 27.
42 [2004] Lloyd's Rep IR 905, para 28.
43 [2004] Lloyd's Rep IR 905, para 28.

clause in the policy, non-payment of the premium by the assured to the broker could activate the brokers' cancellation clause.[44]

The due date is crucial to calculate the limitation period for an action for payment of premium. In *Heath Lambert* the reinsurance was placed in January 1996 and was endorsed at various times until and including 2 July 1996. The claim form was issued on 23 July 2002. If Heath Lambert's cause of action had accrued on 2 July, its claim would have been time barred. If the premium was payable within 90 days after 2 July 1996, the claim would not have been time barred. As it was held that the clause gave 90 days' credit to the broker in respect of the payment of premium, no premium was due immediately but was payable within 90 days of inception and in cash, failing which there was a breach of warranty.[45] Clarke LJ held that there was no indication in the clause that the credit was granted to the broker alone and not also to the assured for the repayment of the premium. The premium would not remain payable if it was deemed to have been paid.[46] Thus, at least some of the claim which arose after 2 July was held not to have been time barred.

The custom can be excluded

A marine policy may exclude the custom as section 53 permits the parties to do so with the wording 'unless otherwise agreed'. The question as to whether the parties ousted the fiction by their contract is a matter of construction. Clear words are required to prove that the parties 'agreed otherwise'. If there is doubt or if the relevant clause is found ambiguous the court may decide that the custom was not excluded.

In *Universo Insurance Co of Milan v Merchants Marine Insurance Co Ltd*[47] the policy which was effected through brokers stated that:

> Whereas it hath been proposed to the Universo Insurance Company by the Merchants Marine Insurance Company, Limited . . . to make with the said company the insurance hereinafter mentioned and described, Now this policy witnesseth that, in consideration of the said person or persons effecting this policy promising to pay to the said company the sum of £37 as a premium of and after the rate of 7 per cent for such insurance, the said company takes upon itself the burthen of such insurance to the amount of £500.

The broker argued that by this clause the assured had undertaken personal responsibility for payment of the premium therefore his action against the assured should be maintained. The Court however rejected the broker's argument; it was held that this statement in the policy means that the assured's promise to pay the premium to the broker was a promise to pay in the customary manner. Thus, the fiction was not ousted by the assured's undertaking.

Premium payment warranty

On the one hand, the fiction confirms that the premium between the assured and the insurer had already been paid due to the relationship between the insurer and the broker under which the insurer gives credit to the broker. If the premium has already been paid it may be argued that when

---

44 [2004] Lloyd's Rep IR 905, para 36. For broker's cancellation clause see p. 134.
45 [2004] Lloyd's Rep IR 905, para 30.
46 [2004] Lloyd's Rep IR 905, para 31.
47 [1897] 2 QB 93.

the assured warrants to pay the premium such a warranty can never be broken.[48] Thus, the presence of a premium payment warranty is arguably inconsistent with the operation of the general rule and is thus an indication of an agreement ousting the general rule. In *JA Chapman & Co Ltd (In Liquidation) v Kadirga Denizcilik ve Ticaret AS*,[49] in which the broker paid the assured for non-payment of the premium, the assured argued that the fiction was ousted due to the existence of the premium payment warranty. The Court of Appeal decided that a premium payment warranty on its own is not sufficient to prove that the parties ousted the fiction. The policy has to be read as a whole to see whether the parties intended not to apply the fiction, and reading the policy as a whole, Sir Brian Neill found that the other clauses, including the broker's cancellation clause, clearly suggest that the ordinary rule is to be applied. It was argued that the fiction cannot survive when the policy provides a warranty breach of which would discharge the insurer from liability automatically. The Court of Appeal, however, held that the warranty and the fiction can be read together so that if the underwriters did not receive the premium on the due date then there would be a breach of warranty with the usual consequence that would flow from that. The payment by the assured was to be made to the brokers, and they were to be responsible for paying the underwriters. The Court held that the fiction operates in respect of the assured's liability to the broker and the broker's liability to the insurer alike.

A differently worded premium payment warranty was discussed in *Heath Lambert Ltd v Sociedad de Corretaje de Seguros*[50] in which the Court of Appeal did not express a view as to whether a warranty can or cannot be broken. Clarke LJ stated in his judgment that 'No-one suggested that the warranty did not have effect as a warranty because of the fiction.'[51] The judge however added that the premium payment warranty which provided that the premium was payable in cash displaced the fiction that the broker is deemed to have paid the premium when due. Clarke LJ combined the premium payment clause and section 53 of the 1906 Act and held that the premium was payable in cash by the broker to the underwriters within 90 days of the attachment and that the assured was liable to the broker on the same basis. This interpretation left no room for a fiction that the broker paid the underwriters in cash when it did not.[52]

A contrary view was expressed by Rix J in *Prentis Donegan & Partners Ltd v Leeds & Leeds Co Inc*[53] where an 'Automatic Termination' clause provided:

> This Policy shall automatically terminate (no notice to the Assured(s) being required) and all liability of Underwriters herein shall end at noon of the tenth day following non-payment of any of the last three instalments on the due date thereof, unless such payments are made within such ten day period.

Rix J was of the view that the automatic termination clause cannot operate for the reason that the assured's obligations in respect of the premium would always have been timeously discharged.[54]

After the Court of Appeal's decisions in *Heath Lambert* and *Chapman* it is arguable that –contrary to Rix J's view in *Prentis* – there is no hard and fast rule that a warranty may never be broken. The operation of such a warranty is a matter of construction of the entire policy. The most recent view on this issue has been expressed by HHJ Chambers QC in *Allianz Insurance Co Egypt v Aigaion Insurance Co SA*.[55] He stated, *obiter*, that 'I cannot imagine that an intelligent member of the Lloyd's marine

---

48 *Prentis Donegan & Partners Ltd v Leeds & Leeds Co Inc* [1998] 2 Lloyd's Rep 326.
49 [1998] Lloyd's Rep IR 377.
50 [2004] Lloyd's Rep IR 905.
51 [2004] Lloyd's Rep IR 905, para 23.
52 [2004] Lloyd's Rep IR 905, para 32.
53 [1998] 2 Lloyd's Rep 326.
54 [1998] 2 Lloyd's Rep 326, 335.
55 [2008] 2 Lloyd's Rep 595, para 67.

insurance market looking at the Act in 1906 could have been expected to read the fiction into the section with the consequence that, not only could an insurer obtain the premium from the broker but, without more, no policy could ever be treated as invalid for non-payment of the premium because the assured was always to be treated as having paid it.'

Adjusted premium clauses

The amount of premium is normally fixed in the policy at the outset. Some policies may contain a clause which requires additional payment of premium by the assured to provide coverage in some defined circumstances. For instance in *Sharp v Sphere Drake Insurance (The Moonacre)*[56] the insurance contract excluded coverage in case the yacht, the subject matter insured, was used as a houseboat unless this was notified to the insurer and additional premium was arranged for such coverage. A similar clause was used in *Black King Shipping Corp v Massie (The Litsion Pride)*[57] for the coverage in the case of the vessel insured entering a war zone. In such a case it is arguable that the custom does not apply given that the premium has not been calculated yet; the broker cannot be presumed to have paid the premium, the amount of which has not been determined yet.[58] In *The Litsion Pride*, the vessel was insured against war risks. The policy incorporated the War Risk Trading Warranties, which provided inter alia that:

> This coverage shall extend worldwide, but in the event of a vessel . . . insured hereunder sailing for . . . or being within the Territorial Waters of any of the Countries or places described in the Current Exclusions . . . additional premium shall be paid at the discretion of Insurers . . .

It was argued, and Hirst J accepted the argument,[59] that an additional premium could never fictionally be deemed to have been paid by the policyholder or lent back by the insurer. As a result it was held that section 53(1) could in principle never apply to adjusted premium clauses.

With respect it is submitted that this matter should be considered together with the justifications for the fiction which is the account between the assured and the insurer adjusted at the end of a 12 month period on 31 December in each year, as well as broker's dual agency. Therefore, in order to presume that the premium has already been paid by the broker, the exact determination of the premium is not necessarily needed given that the broker's debt and the insurer's debt will in any event be adjusted at the end of the accounting year.[60]

Consequences of non-payment of premium

It has been seen that although the premium is deemed to have been paid, the parties can agree otherwise and a clause in the policy with regard to the assured's obligation to pay the premium is a matter of construction in each individual case. When the custom does not apply and therefore the premium is not deemed to have been paid, it will be necessary to discuss the consequences of non-payment of the premium.

Payment of the premium is not a condition precedent to the attachment of the risk or to the insurer's liability. Therefore, unless the policy expressly provides otherwise, in principle, the risk

---

56 [1992] 2 Lloyd's Rep 501.
57 [1985] 1 Lloyd's Rep 437.
58 See Gloster, 310.
59 [1985] 1 Lloyd's Rep 437, 510–512.
60 Gloster, 311.

attaches despite non-payment of the premium and the insurer may be liable for the loss suffered by the assured even though the obligation to pay the premium has not been discharged yet.[61] An insurer who does not wish to be bound by the contract or does not want the risk to attach before the assured performs his premium payment obligation should provide so expressly in the contract.

Moreover, a failure to pay premium would not usually of itself amount to a repudiation of the contract.[62] A term in the policy regarding the payment of premium, unless otherwise stipulated in the contract, is an innominate term,[63] which means that the insurer can terminate the contract for non-payment only if such a breach is so serious as to go to the root of the contract.[64] In *Fenton Insurance Co Ltd v Gothaer Versicherungsbank*[64a] Potter J stated that:

> In cases concerned with insurance, where accounts are rendered and paid through the medium of brokers and/or underwriting agents and delays in payment are not infrequent, it seems to me that one could rarely, if ever, infer a repudiatory intention under a treaty of this kind by reason of non-payment of balances simpliciter (by way of distinction from a failure persisted in despite receipt of demands and/or protests).

In *Pacific & General Insurance Co Ltd v Hazell*, Moore-Bick J confirmed that a failure to pay premium would not usually of itself amount to a repudiation of the contract.

Thus, unless the policy clearly provides otherwise, 'time is not of the essence' for the purpose of payment of premium.[65] There may be an administrative error or oversight or mistake on either the assured's or insurer's part in terms of payment of the premium, which does not necessarily indicate that the assured intends to repudiate the contract. If the insurer desires to terminate the contract in case the assured defaults in payment of premium the contract must provide expressly that time for payment of the premium is to be 'of the essence'. In such a case if the assured does not pay the premium in time the insurer can terminate the contract. If the contract does not provide that payment of the premium is of the essence, the insurer may render it of the essence by giving notice to the assured requiring the payment of the minimum and deposit premium within a stated time at the end of which, if the assured still does not pay, the insurer is entitled to terminate the contract.[66]

Broker's cancellation clause

A broker's cancellation clause entitles the broker to cancel the policy in the event of non-payment of premium. The reason for such a term vesting rights in a broker is that he is personally liable to the underwriters for premium under section 53 of the Marine Insurance Act 1906.[67] In *Heath Lambert Ltd v Sociedad de Corretaje de Seguros*[68] the Brokers' Cancellation Clause included the following:

> Notwithstanding anything contained in this Policy to the contrary, Blackwell Green Limited, in addition to their lien on the policy, shall be entitled to cancel this Policy in the event of any

---

61 *Figre Ltd v Mander* [1999] Lloyd's Rep IR 193.
62 *Figre Ltd v Mander* [1999] Lloyd's Rep IR 193.
63 *Figre Ltd v Mander* [1999] Lloyd's Rep IR 193.
64 *Hongkong Fir Shipping Co Ltd v Kawasaki Kisen Kaisha Ltd (The Hongkong Fir)* [1961] 2 Lloyd's Rep 478.
64a [1991] 1 Lloyd's Rep 172.
65 *Figre Ltd v Mander* [1999] Lloyd's Rep IR 193.
66 *Figre Ltd v Mander* [1999] Lloyd's Rep IR 193.
67 *Velos Group Ltd v Harbour Insurance Services Ltd* [1997] 2 Lloyd's Rep 461, 464.
68 [2004] Lloyd's Rep IR 905.

premium not having been paid to them when due and the Underwriters hereby agree to cancel this Policy on presentation at the request of Blackwell Green Limited and to return any premium payable thereon in excess of a pro rata premium up to the date of the cancellation.

Clarke LJ held that the terms of the broker's cancellation clause showed that Heath Lambert was a party to the terms of the policy, at least for some purposes.[69]

Moreover, in *Chapman v Kadirga*, the Court of Appeal put emphasis on the construction of the contract as a whole to determine whether or not the parties 'agreed otherwise' to the effect that the fiction was replaced with the premium payment warranty. The cancellation clause was one of the elements of the policy which persuaded the court that the parties intended to apply the fiction to the relationship between the insurer, broker and the assured for the reason that they expressly stated that the broker would be entitled to cancel the premium in case the assured does not pay the premium to the broker.

Brokers' lien

A marine insurance broker is personally liable for payment of the premium and he is entitled to a commission in return for the service to his client. Moreover, as seen in Chapter 14, an assured who desires to make a claim under the policy instructs his broker to contact the insurer to make such a claim. Section 53(2) of the Marine Insurance Act 1906 provides that:

Unless otherwise agreed, the broker has, as against the assured, a lien upon the policy for the amount of the premium and his charges in respect of effecting the policy; and, where he has dealt with the person who employs him as a principal, he has also a lien on the policy in respect of any balance on any insurance account which may be due to him from such person, unless when the debt was incurred he had reason to believe that such person was only an agent.

'Lien on the policy' is a type of security embodied in the right to retain the possession of physical property until a debt has been discharged.[70] The assured owns the policy but his right under the policy is subject to the broker's right of lien.[71] In *Fisher v Smith*[72] it was stated that 'the bargain was that the policy should remain with the person who had made it and paid for it, and that he should hold it until his debt should be discharged'. Phillips LJ explained this principle in *Eide UK Ltd v Lowndes Lambert Group Ltd*: 'a broker who has a lien over the policy has a commensurate right to retain claims proceeds collected under the policy in so far as necessary to satisfy the debt secured by the lien'.[73] It is a general principle of the law of agency that no one can create a lien beyond his own interest.[74] In other words, a lien is limited to the amount of the broker's claim for the premium or other charges.[75]

Section 53(2) confers two separate liens on a broker.[76]

69 [2004] Lloyd's Rep IR 905, para 15.
70 *Eide UK Ltd v Lowndes Lambert Group Ltd* [1998] 1 Lloyd's Rep 389, 397.
71 *Castling v Aubert* (1802) 2 East 325.
72 (1878) 4 App Cas 1, 11, Lord O'Hagan.
73 *Eide UK Ltd v Lowndes Lambert Group Ltd* [1998] 1 Lloyd's Rep 389, 397; *Heath Lambert Ltd v Sociedad de Corretaje de Seguros* [2006] Lloyd's Rep IR 797 para 26, HHJ MacKie QC.
74 *Eide UK Ltd v Lowndes Lambert Group Ltd* [1998] 1 Lloyd's Rep 389, 40.
75 *Heath Lambert Ltd v Sociedad de Corretaje de Seguros* [2006] Lloyd's Rep IR 797; *Levy v Barnard* (1818) 8 Taunton 149.
76 *Fisher v Smith* (1878) 4 App Cas 1, Arnould, para 6–25.

1   A lien against the assured, upon the policy, for the amount of the premium and his charges in respect of effecting the policy (the specific lien).[77]

2   A lien against the person who employs him as a principal, on the policy, in respect of any balance on any insurance account which may be due to him from this, unless when the debt was incurred he had reason to believe that such person was only an agent (the general lien).

The broker thus has a lien against the assured for whose benefit the policies were effected, as well as against any intermediaries who might have intervened between the assured and himself.[78]

'Lien on the policy' – possessory lien

The lien of an insurance agent, as of every other agent, depends at common law on the continuance of possession;[79] the lien of the broker revives where the policy comes again into his possession.[80]

Under section 22 of the Marine Insurance Act 1906 '. . . a contract of marine insurance is inadmissible in evidence unless it is embodied in a marine policy . . .' It may be argued that holding the policy in hand the broker has a strong security 'lien on the policy' given that the assured will not be able to make a claim under the insurance contract. However, in *Swan v Maritime Insurance Co*[81], Channell J rejected the insurer's argument that the claimant cannot sue upon the policy which the claimant did not have possession of. Channell J noted that 'The policy may be lost, but the action can be maintained just the same if the plaintiff can prove it. The production of the policy at the trial, if it is in dispute, is necessary, but it can be produced by subpoenaing the person who has it, and the non-production is merely a ground for suspecting that somebody else has an interest in it. And it would be a complete answer to the underwriters' objection to pay on the ground of non-production that they were not under a liability to anyone else.'[82] In *Eide UK Ltd v Lowndes Lambert Group Ltd*[83] Phillips LJ found that *Swan*, coupled with the subsequent abolition of the stamping requirement,[84] has had the effect of reducing the value of the possessory lien on the policy. In *Amalgamated General Finance Co Ltd v CE Golding & Co Ltd*[85] the assured shipowner insured his two vessels with the insurers through the defendant brokers. The brokers paid the premium and the assured and the brokers made an agreement in respect of the payment of the premium by the assured. The assured then fell into financial difficulties and sought help from the claimant finance company. The assured subsequently assigned his rights under the insurance contract to the claimant. The broker claimed his lien on the amount recovered from the insurers for the premium had not been paid by the assured. The claimant sued the broker over that amount given that the assured assigned his rights under the policy for the money owed to the claimant. Diplock J[86] noted that the broker could not have prevented the assignment of the claims against the underwriters but he could exercise his lien on the policy for the unpaid premiums and put difficulties in the way of the assured, if they sought to collect the claims direct from the underwriters. Phillips LJ, however, in *Eide*, expressed his suspicion

---

77   The Law Commissions defined specific and general liens as follows: A general lien extends to any debt (within the relationship between the parties involved) which A owes. A specific lien extends only to debts which relate to the contract under which B holds the property. http://lawcommission.justice.gov.uk/docs/cp201_ICL_post_contract_duties.pdf para 20.02.

78   *Fisher v Smith* (1878) 4 App Cas 1, 5.

79   *Levy v Barnard* (1818) 8 Taunton 149; Arnould, para 6–31.

80   *Levy v Barnard* (1818) 8 Taunton 149.

81   [1907] 1 KB 116, 122–123.

82   *Swan v Maritime Insurance Co* [1907] 1 KB 116, 122–123.

83   [1998] 1 Lloyd's Rep 389.

84   A marine policy used to be required to be stamped. This requirement was abolished by The Finance Act 1959.

85   [1964] 2 Lloyd's Rep 163.

86   [1964] 2 Lloyd's Rep 163, 170.

about Diplock J's view on this. Phillips LJ said: 'At all events I suspect that the observation of Diplock J. in *Amalgamated General Finance Co Ltd v GE Golding & Co Ltd* . . . that a broker can put difficulties in the way of a claimant who tries to circumvent a broker's lien by recovering without production of the policy remains true.'[87] It should also be noted that in *Hunter v Leathley*[88] the broker who effected the policy was called as a witness for the assured in an action against the insurer, and was required to produce the policy. The broker objected, claiming to have a lien on it for premiums advanced by him. He nevertheless had been served with a subpoena, ordering him to bring the policy into court. He was held to be bound to produce the policy but inasmuch as he would not thereby be deprived of his lien. The important point therefore here is to take measures to protect the broker's lien when the assured is permitted to claim under the policy without producing the policy. As Phillips LJ noted, production of the policy may be a contractual requirement in which case such reduction in value of the possessory lien might be prevented. Alternatively, if the broker is obliged to produce the policy to prove the assured's claim under it the broker might insist to reserve his right of lien under section 53 of MIA 1906.

As discussed in Chapter 2, the Law Commissions proposed in Issues Paper 9 that section 22 of MIA 1906 is obsolete and should be repealed.[89] The best approach is therefore to have a contractual provision which makes it a condition precedent to the insurer's liability to produce the policy before making a claim.

Specific lien

A broker who has a lien over a policy of marine insurance is normally entitled, when he collects under the policy, to apply the proceeds collected in discharge of the debt that was protected by the lien. In *Eide*, Phillips LJ stated that the precise basis of this right does not appear clearly from the authorities, but it should have become established as a matter of mercantile usage, for it is a natural adjunct of the lien on the policy.[90] It is a part of the duty of a broker who remained in possession of the policy to collect the insurance proceeds and in the words of Phillips LJ, 'that duty would have been anomalous indeed if the act of collecting under the policy had destroyed the security afforded by the lien'.[91] In *Man v Shiffner and Ellis*[92] Lord Ellenborough CJ stated that 'as the plaintiff could only have recovered the policy out of the hands of the [agents] by satisfying their lien, so the same lien attached on the proceeds of that policy recovered from the underwriters'.[93]

Thus, if either market practice or contractual agreement places the broker in a position to insist on collecting under a policy, the broker will enjoy a degree of security.[94] Recently this principle was confirmed by HHJ MacKie QC in *Heath Lambert Ltd v Sociedad de Corretaje de Seguros*.[95] The facts of *Heath Lambert* were given above. The action continued after the Court of Appeal held that a significant part of the claim was time-barred and that the amount owing to Heath Lambert (HL, the London placing broker) was US$261,632.81. Subsequently, Scort (Venezuelan broker) ceased to be represented, Banesco (Venezuelan reinsured) continued to defend the action, and counterclaimed for US$325,000 collected by HL from the underwriters in respect of a particular average claim.

---

87 [1998] 1 Lloyd's Rep 389, 398.
88 (1830) 10 B & C 858.
89 http://lawcommission.justice.gov.uk/docs/ICL9_Requirement_for_Formal_Marine_Policy.pdf
90 *Eide UK Ltd v Lowndes Lambert Group Ltd* [1998] 1 Lloyd's Rep 389, 400.
91 *Eide UK Ltd v Lowndes Lambert Group Ltd* [1998] 1 Lloyd's Rep 389, 400.
92 (1802) 2 East 523.
93 (1802) 2 East 523, 529–530.
94 *Eide UK Ltd v Lowndes Lambert Group Ltd* [1998] 1 Lloyd's Rep 389.
95 [2006] Lloyd's Rep IR 797.

HL asserted the right to set off against this sum the amount that it was owed in respect of premiums, leaving (after interest and charges) a balance to be handed over to Banesco of US$11,911.34. The counsel for Banesco argued that as HL was authorised to collect and to account directly to Banesco, not to Scort, it would be wrong and inconsistent with its collection authority for HL to treat the loss proceeds as otherwise due to Scort, and attracting a lien, when HL is obliged to account to Banesco. HL collected the loss proceeds as agent for Banesco and as a result it had no lien in respect of the claim for premium against Scort. HHJ MacKie QC referred to the origins of the common law lien as explained by Diplock J in *Tappenden v Artus*[96] that a common law lien which arose independently of the law of contract, although not enforceable by action, affords a defence to an action for recovery of the goods by a person who, but for the lien, would be entitled to immediate possession. HHJ MacKie QC found the position the same with a statutory lien and with the proceeds of the policy as much as with the physical policy document.[97] The judge noted that in *Eide* – as noted above – it was expressed that the precise basis of this lien may be unclear but HHJ MacKie QC stated that the right is not. Accordingly, there was no doubt that HL had a lien over the proceeds of the policy both as against Banesco and any other intermediary, whether or not Banesco were under a direct obligation to pay the premium. That lien may be maintained until the premium is paid or the claim is in some other way satisfied. HHJ MacKie QC added that the lien asserted by HL should be upheld for these reasons as well as being consistent with that set out in *Eide* and with justice. It would be obviously unfair for HL to be required to hand over the proceeds of the claim under a policy without being reimbursed for unpaid premiums.

It is, of course, always possible for a broker to agree that he will not assert any claim over proceeds collected for an assured.

General lien

Section 53(2) provides '. . . where he has dealt with the person who employs him as a principal, he has also a lien on the policy in respect of any balance on any insurance account which may be due to him from such person, unless when the debt was incurred he had reason to believe that such person was only an agent.'

If the broker has been immediately instructed by the assured he has a lien on the policy not only for the premium and commission due on the particular transaction, but also for the amount of the general balance of his insurance account.[98] As described in Chapter 14, a broker may be employed by another agent and in such a case, if he knows that his employer is an agent, he has no lien on the policy in respect of his general balance against his immediate employer. The only question is whether he knew or had reason to believe that the person by whom he was employed was only an agent; and the party who seeks to deprive him of his lien must make out the affirmative.[99]

Mann v Forrester[100] illustrates the abovementioned rules. The claimant merchant ordered some cargo from White and Lubbern (WL) who sent the cargo and employed the defendant broker to effect a policy on the cargo. The defendants effected the policy accordingly, and debited WL with the premiums. The policy was allowed to remain in the defendants' hands, and before they had notice of the claimant's interest, they had received £650 from the underwriters, and they received £200 afterwards. When they had the notice, they were creditors of WL for the amount of £167.

---

96 [1964] 2 QB 185, 194–195.
97 [2006] Lloyd's Rep IR 797, 800.
98 Arnould, para 6–27.
99 *Westwood v Bell* (1815) 4 Campbell 349, 353.
100 (1814) 4 Campbell 60.

This sum they deducted from the £200 subsequently received, and the balance of £33 they paid over to WL's assignees.

The claimant merchant could not recover any part of the money received by the defendants before the notice; but it was insisted that he was entitled to the full sum of £200 received afterwards. Lord Ellenborough held that the broker, having had no notice that this policy was not for WL, had a lien upon it for their general balance. They must be supposed to have made advances on the credit of the policy, which was allowed to remain in their hands. Therefore, they had a right to satisfy their general balance from the money received under the policy, whether before or after the notice communicated to them of the claimant's interest. But after that notice, the excess beyond the satisfaction of their balance was considered to be money had and received by them for the claimant's use. Therefore, the claimant was entitled to a verdict for £33. This principle was approved in *Cahill v Dawson*[101] where a merchant in Spain instructed his agent D in Liverpool to insure a cargo of fruit. The agent in Liverpool instructed a London broker, L, to procure the insurance in question. L then employed N to place the risk with an insurer. N effected the policy, and, a loss having occurred, received the money from the underwriters, but refused to hand it over to the broker in Liverpool, insisting on a lien as against L in respect of premiums due to him under other policies. The first issue to be resolved was whether the agent in Liverpool was in breach of his duty by appointing an agent in London instead of placing the risk in Liverpool. The court nevertheless stated his view that if N had known that the agent in Liverpool was in fact an agent he could have acquired no right to retain the proceeds of the policy for a claim against L, because he would have known that L was acting merely as agent for D. Thus, the 1906 Act now provides that a lien against a person who employed the agent depends on the status of the employer and the knowledge of the sub-agent regarding such status. The importance of the lien on the policy is, thus, that it enables the broker to maintain a set-off in respect of a receipt of claims proceeds notwithstanding that he has acquired knowledge of the existence of a previously undisclosed assured prior to the receipt, provided that he had no such knowledge when the lien on the policy arose. If the broker retains possession of the policy, discovery of the existence of a previously undisclosed principal will not defeat the accrued security of the lien on the policy, or the commensurate right to set off where a collection is made under the policy. If, however, the broker parts with possession of the policy and then discovers the existence of the undisclosed principal, he will have no continuing security, even if he recovers possession of the policy.[102]

In *Eide UK Ltd v Lowndes Lambert Group Ltd*, Phillips LJ held that section 53(2) does not apply to composite insurance. In *Eide* the vessel *Sun Tender* was mortgaged to the Bank Colne Standby Ltd. The *Sun Tender* was demise chartered and the charterparty required the charterer to insure the vessel to protect the interests of the owner, charterer and mortgagees of the vessel. Colne instructed the brokers to procure two hull and machinery policies. The policies described the insured as: 'Colne Standby Ltd and/or subsidiary and/or associated companies and/or where required by contract all other companies and/or persons concerned in contracts attaching to this insurance, shall be deemed to be jointly and/or additionally insured for their respective rights and interests.'

The owners assigned their interests in the policies to the bank. The *Sun Tender* sustained damage to her starboard main engine and was redelivered by Colne Standby to the owners in her damaged condition on or about 12 June 1993. Before redelivery of the *Sun Tender* and termination of the charterparty, Colne Standby incurred disbursements of £19,871.07 in respect of 'part permanent repairs'. Following the vessel's redelivery, the owners arranged and paid for the further repairs which cost £303,560.07.

---

101 (1857) 3 CB NS 106.
102 See *Near East Relief v King, Chasseur & Co Ltd* [1930] 2 KB 40, 44.

The brokers collected from the underwriters the sum of £300,931 by way of claims proceeds, acting pursuant to letters of authorisation signed on behalf of Colne Standby and the bank. The sum paid by the underwriters represented the owners' repair costs of £303,560 and Colne Standby's repair costs of £19,871, totalling £323,431, less a deductible of £22,000. The brokers were entitled to deduct a 1 per cent collecting commission, leaving a balance of £297,921. The bank's share of this sum was £279,629.42. The brokers paid the entirety of the claims proceeds into a mixed bank account.

At the time that these proceeds were received Colne Standby owed to the brokers a balance of £728,109.82 on an insurance account. This sum was wholly made up of debts in relation to insurances other than the policies.

The issue was thus whether section 53(2) gave the brokers a right to retain the claims proceeds in part satisfaction of Colne Standby's liabilities under their insurance account.

Phillips LJ held that Section 53(2) does not apply to composite insurance.[103] The judge held that the latter part of the subsection suggests that the draftsmen were addressing only the simple position of one employer and one assured. 'Where he has dealt with the person who employs him as a principal' is not appropriate language to describe dealings between a broker and an employer who places insurance both on his own behalf and on behalf of other interests.

The Law Commissions discussed broker's lien in their Issues Paper 8 in 2010 and expressed the view that section 53(2) is satisfactory and does not need to be reformed. In Issues Paper 9 the Law Commissions stated that section 53(2) should be amended or replaced, so as to clarify the law in this area. Due to the link between the two sections, sections 22 and 53(2) must be considered together, so that any reform of the former does not adversely affect the operation of the latter.[104] In Consultation Paper 201 the Law Commissions proposed that where the broker has paid the premium on behalf of the assured, it should be entitled to exercise any right the insurer has to recover the debt from the policyholder. Since it has been proposed that section 22 should be repealed, with the end of formal policies, the broker's lien over the policy becomes practically defunct. Therefore, the Law Commissions proposed that section 53(2) ought to be repealed and replaced with a form of security for the broker which does not depend on the existence of a policy document. This cannot be a lien in the technical sense, as lien requires a tangible object.[105] The broker would have a specific statutory right to set off any premium or commission against the proceeds on that policy.[106]

Return of premium

Section 53(1) of MIA 1906 provides that '. . . the insurer is directly responsible to the assured for the amount which may be payable in respect of losses, or in respect of returnable premium.' Thus, the insurer is directly responsible to the assured for the return of the premium.[107]

Total failure of consideration

Section 84 of MIA 1906 provides detailed provisions regarding return of premium. The contract of insurance is a contract of indemnity under which the insurer receives a premium for running

---

103 Eide UK Ltd v Lowndes Lambert Group Ltd [1998] 1 Lloyd's Rep 389, 401.
104 http://lawcommission.justice.gov.uk/docs/ICL9_Requirement_for_Formal_Marine_Policy.pdf, para 5.35.
105 http://lawcommission.justice.gov.uk/docs/cp201_ICL_post_contract_duties.pdf, para 20.27.
106 http://lawcommission.justice.gov.uk/docs/cp201_ICL_post_contract_duties.pdf, para 20.28.
107 See also s 82(a) MIA 1906.

the risk of indemnifying the assured. If the risk has never begun after the contract is concluded, the premium shall be returned for total failure of consideration for the insurer to keep the premium.[108] Section 84(1) provides 'Where the consideration for the payment of the premium totally fails, and there has been no fraud or illegality on the part of the assured or his agents, the premium is thereupon returnable to the assured.'

Where the policy is void or is avoided by the insurer, the premium is returnable in the absence of fraud or illegality on the part of the assured (section 84(3)(a)). Where the assured has no insurable interest throughout the currency of the risk, the premium is returnable, provided that this rule does not apply to a policy effected by way of gaming or wagering (s.84(3)(c)).

The Consumer Insurance (Disclosure and Representations) Act 2012 reformed the duty of good faith in consumer insurance and the Act brought proportionate remedies for breach of the duty of good faith. Additionally, it is provided by the 2012 Act that section 84 of the Marine Insurance Act 1906 is to be read subject to the provisions of the schedule in relation to contracts of marine insurance which are consumer insurance contracts.[109] The insurer may avoid the contract if a qualifying misrepresentation was deliberate or reckless. In such a case the insurer need not return any of the premiums paid, except to the extent (if any) that it would be unfair to the consumer to retain them.[110] If a qualifying misrepresentation is careless, the insurer may avoid the contract on the condition that the insurer would not have entered into the consumer insurance contract on any terms. The insurer must return the premiums paid in this case.[111] The Draft Insurance Contracts Bill, which aims to reform the duty of good faith in business insurance, provides identical provisions for business insurance.[112]

The premium is indivisible

As soon as the risk has commenced, the obligation to pay the entire premium at once arises. There shall be no apportionment or return of premium afterwards irrespective of the period of time between the commencement of the risk and the event which occurred under which the assured claims the return of premium. It was held that when the risk has begun, there never shall be a return, although the ship may be captured within 24 hours from the inception of the risk.[113] In *Tyrie v Fletcher*[114] the ship *Isabella* was insured at and from London to any port or place, where or whatsoever, for twelve months, from 19 August 1776, to 19 August 1777, both days inclusive. The ship sailed from the port of London, and was taken by an American privateer, about two months afterwards. The premium was held to be indivisible, it was calculated for the coverage for the twelve months and as soon as the risk had begun it was due to be paid at once. Lord Mansfield held that the contract entered into was one entire contract from 19 August 1776 to 19 August 1777. The parties 'might have insured from two months to two months' and made a division but by insuring the vessel for twelve months under the policy they made no division of time at all. The assured, according to Lord Mansfield, declared that 'if you the underwriter will insure me for twelve months, I will give you an entire sum; but I will not have any apportionment'.

The question of whether or not the premium is divisible is a matter of construction of the contract. In *Loraine v Thomlinson*[115] the policy insuring the ship *Chollerford* was to provide cover from

---

108 *Tyrie v Fletcher* (1777) 2 Cowper 666, 669; *Loraine v Thomlinson* (1781) 2 Douglas 585, 588, Lord Mansfield.
109 Schedule 1, Part 4, section 17.
110 Schedule 1, Part 1, section 2.
111 Schedule 1, part 1, section 5.
112 www.publications.parliament.uk/pa/bills/lbill/2014-2015/0039/15039.pdf
113 *Tyrie v Fletcher* (1777) 2 Cowper 666, 669; *Loraine v Thomlinson* (1781) 2 Douglas 585, 588, Lord Mansfield.
114 (1777) 2 Cowper 666.
115 (1781) 2 Douglas 585.

13 March, 1779 until 13 March 1780. Although the policy stated that 'Premium received 16th March, 1779', the premium was not paid as it was the custom in Newcastle not to pay the premium at the time of making the insurance, but at various times after the policies have been effected, and, sometimes, not till twelve months after. The ship was lost in a storm, within the first two of the 12 months for which the insurance was made, and the defendant tendered to the plaintiff £3 as the premium for the two months. Lord Mansfield held that the entire premium, £18, should have been paid. It was an insurance for 12 months, for one gross sum of £18 which was to be paid down at once.[116]

The modern authorities confirmed that the premium, unless otherwise agreed by the parties, is indivisible. The parties may agree that the premium will be payable in instalments but in such a case, in principle, the premium is still indivisible and if the insurer is discharged from liability for breach of warranty the obligation to pay the premium does not come to an end automatically. To have that effect the contract should expressly provide that the assured will not pay the premium after the insurer is discharged from liability or if the entire premium has been paid, the premium will be returned pro-rata. In *JA Chapman & Co Ltd (In Liquidation) v Kadirga Denizcilik ve Ticaret AS*,[117] it was discussed whether the assured was still obliged to pay the premium after the insurer was discharged from liability as a result of a breach of warranty. The trial judge held that the premium was apportionable to successive periods of insurance, so that, a breach having occurred in respect of one period, instalments in respect of subsequent periods did not become payable. The policy provided that

> If the premium is to be paid by instalments the instalments have to be paid as follows:
> One fourth to be paid as a first instalment due and payable when insurance attaches.
> One fourth due and payable at three months from inception.
> One fourth due and payable at six months from inception.
> One fourth due and payable at nine months from inception.

Chadwick LJ[118] held that the trial judge failed to appreciate that, although the payment of premiums clause provided for there to be four instalment payments, there remained only one single premium. The wording 'if the premium is to be paid by instalments' made it clear that there was one single premium, namely the entire risk accepted by insurers under the policy – and the manner in which the premium was to be paid – by instalments at three monthly intervals. The fact that the successive instalments were due and payable on dates which occurred at three monthly intervals during the term of the policy did not lead to the conclusion that the premium, which comprised the aggregate of those instalments, was itself divisible between successive three-month periods.[119] Notwithstanding that the insurers were released from liability by the breach, there remained a liability on the assured to pay the instalments that had not become due at the date of the breach.

The risk may be divisible

The risk in some policies may be distinct and divisible in its nature. The contract may not be entire, rather there may be two or more parts in the contract. For instance, in *Stevenson v Snow*[120] there were two distinct voyages: from London to Portsmouth and from Portsmouth to Halifax. The insurance

---

116 (1781) 2 Douglas 585, 587.
117 [1998] Lloyd's Rep IR 377.
118 [1998] Lloyd's Rep IR 377, 389.
119 [1998] Lloyd's Rep IR 377, 389.
120 (1761) 3 Burrow 1237.

depended on the contingency of the ship sailing with convoy from Portsmouth. In *Bond v Nutt*[121] first a loss of the ship in port and then any loss in her passage home were insured provided that she sailed on a certain day. This necessarily divided the risk, and made two voyages. There were thus two risks: 'at Jamaica' and 'from Jamaica'. The latter risk depended on the contingency of the ship having sailed on or before the first of August: that was a condition precedent to the insurance on the voyage from Jamaica to London.

In the two abovementioned cases the losses insured against were distinct: there were two distinct points of time, effectively two voyages, which were clearly in the contemplation of the parties. In *Bond v Nutt* the premium for the second part of the insurance risk was held to be returnable for the reason that the ship had not sailed on 1 August and the risk had never begun.[122]

Section 84(2) of the MIA 1906 provides: 'Where the consideration for the payment of the premium is apportionable and there is a total failure of any apportionable part of the consideration, a proportionate part of the premium is, under the like conditions, thereupon returnable to the assured.'

'At and from'

Whether the risk is one entire risk is a matter of construction. If the policy insures the subject matter insured 'at and from' ports specified in the policy the risk attaches while the vessel is at the port.[123] In *Moses v Pratt*[124] the policy insured the vessel *Argus* and freight at and from port or ports in Cuba to port or ports in St. Domingo, and from thence to any port or ports in the United Kingdom. The *Argus* was chartered by the assured shipowner for a voyage from Liverpool to Cuba and St Domingo and back. The *Argus* proceeded to Cuba and St Domingo, where no cargo was provided for her. It was insisted that they were in any event entitled to the return of premium on the freight, no goods having ever been loaded, the policy did not attach. Lord Ellenborough held that had the ship been lost while waiting to take in a cargo, the underwriters would have been liable for the whole sum insured upon the freight. The charterparty created an interest on which the policy had attached, and there had been an inception of the risk, although no goods were actually put on board. Therefore there was no entitlement to the return of premium. Similarly, in *Bermon v Woodbridge*[125] the ship *Le Pactole* and her cargo was insured 'at and from Honfleur, to the coast of Angola, during her stay and trade there, at and from thence to her port or ports of discharge in St Domingo, and at and from St. Domingo back to Honfleur.' The ship sailed to Angola, and, then, after staying some time there, to the West Indies. On her way from Angola, she put in at Cayenne on the coast of America, and from Cayenne went to Martinico, confessedly out of the course to St Domingo.

Lord Mansfield set the question as 'whether the policy contains one entire risk on one voyage, or whether it is to be split into six different risks? For, by splitting the words, and taking "at" and "from" separately, it will make six; viz. 1. At Honfleur; 2. From Honfleur to Angola; 3. At Angola, &c'. Once the risk has begun it cannot be severed, therefore the premium cannot be apportioned. In *Bermon* Lord Mansfield held that it was one entire voyage as the assured and the insurers considered the premium as an entire sum for the whole, without division. Lord Mansfield found that in *Stevenson v Snow*[126] and *Bond v Nutt* there were contingencies specified in the policy. If they did not happen the insurance would cease. In *Bermon*, however, as his Lordship found, the policy did not provide any such contingency.

---

121 (1777) 2 Cowper 601.
122 *Stevenson v Snow* (1761) 3 Burrow 1237.
123 *Annen v Woodman* (1810) 3 Taunton 299.
124 (1815) 4 Campbell 297.
125 (1781) 2 Douglas 781.
126 (1761) 3 Burrow 1237.

It is also open to the parties to stipulate that the premium is non-returnable.[127] Alternatively, the policy can provide for a pro-rata return of premium. Section 83 of MIA 1906 provides that:

> Where the policy contains a stipulation for the return of the premium, or a proportionate part thereof, on the happening of a certain event, and that event happens, the premium, or, as the case may be, the proportionate part thereof, is thereupon returnable to the assured.

International Hull Clauses 2003, cl.35.4, provides 'In the event of cancellation under this Clause 35, the premium is due to the Underwriters on a pro rata basis for the period that the Underwriters are on risk but the full premium shall be payable to the Underwriters in the event of loss, damage, liability or expense arising out of or resulting from an accident or occurrence prior to the date of termination which gives rise to a recoverable claim under this insurance.'

The War and Strikes Clauses, cl.6, provide for a pro-rata net return of premium in the event of cancellation by notice or automatic termination of the insurance. The Institute Time Clauses (Freight) also provide, in cll.15 and 16, that where cover has terminated automatically by reason of either a change in the vessel's class or a change in the ownership or flag of the vessel, a pro-rata return of premium is to be made.

Gross premium to be returned

The assured pays the premium to the broker who then deducts commission agreed with the insurers and transmits the net premium to them.[128] If the premium is to be returned in full because it has never been earned, a question may arise whether the insurers are required to return the gross premium or whether the assured is entitled only to the net premium from the insurers and has to look to the broker instead for repayment of the brokerage which itself has by definition not been earned. As mentioned in Chapter 14, the broker is paid by the insurers and not by the assured even though the broker is otherwise the assured's agent, and this rule indicates that gross premium is repayable by the insurers.[129]

Account adjustment between the broker and the insurer

The broker may be authorised to settle the claim on behalf of the assured with the underwriter. As the broker and the insurer have an account under which they adjust the payments of premium and losses with regard to the policies subscribed through brokers, they may settle the claim, releasing the broker from payment of premium for other policies placed by the broker. As a result the underwriter may set off the amount payable by him upon the policy against the balance due to him from the broker for premiums on other policies effected by him. Such a settlement may not necessarily have implications on the assured's claim against the broker who was authorised to receive the policy money from the insurer. The assured will claim the entire amount from the broker – for the amount the broker was employed to receive. However, if the broker becomes insolvent before paying the policy amount to the assured, when the assured claims the amount from the insurer, the question may then arise if the settlement between the broker and the insurer is binding

---

127 Arnould, para 6–56.
128 Arnould, para 6–36.
129 Arnould, para 6–36.

on the assured. The answer depends on the authority given by the assured to the broker. *Prima facie*, the authority to receive money would be to receive payment in cash.[130] If the assured had known the usage before the authority was given to the broker and if the assured is deemed to have given consent to such an adjustment, he will be bound by the adjustment made between the broker and the insurer. However, if the custom was not known by the assured and as a result the assured had not consented to such an adjustment he will not be bound by it.[131] In *Scott v Irving*[132] a cargo of cotton was shipped on board the *Union* at Gibraltar, to be carried to Havannah. An account had, for several years before, been kept between the insurer and M, the broker, in the usual way in which accounts between underwriters and brokers are kept in conducting insurance business at Lloyd's, and M was debited in this account for the premiums on the said policy. The *Union* duly proceeded on her voyage, and on 27 September 1824 was wrecked, and the cargo totally lost. The assured instructed M to obtain a settlement of the loss. M soon afterwards became bankrupt; and until the time of his failure the policy remained in his hands. The assured then demanded payment from the insurer who claimed to have paid the loss to the broker according to the usage that an account is kept between broker and underwriter to the end of the year, 31 December, when they strike a balance, averages, deductions, and returns being placed to the credit of the broker; but losses, if they exceed the amount due from the broker at the time when they are known, are settled before the end of the year; and on that settlement, the amount due from the broker for premiums up to the date of the knowledge of the loss, is set against the loss. Lord Tenterden CJ held that the general rule is that the broker is the debtor of the underwriter for the premiums, and the underwriter the debtor of the assured for the loss. If the usage relied upon in this case were allowed to prevail, it would have the effect of making the broker, and not the underwriter, the debtor to the assured for the loss. Such a usage, as Lord Tenterden confirmed, can be binding only on those who are acquainted with it, and have consented to be bound by it. The assured therefore may be bound by the usage only if he knew of it and assented to it. The authority given by the assured to the broker was a general authority to receive payment in money. If the underwriter paid in cash to the broker and if the broker became insolvent before he passed the money to the assured this actual payment cannot be reclaimed from the insurer – the insurer already paid it to the assured's agent. On the other hand, it was held in *Scott v Irving* that the amount that was settled between the broker and the insurer under the account the broker had can be recovered from the insurer for the reason that the principles that govern this kind of issue are that M was the agent of the assured to receive payment from the underwriter in cash, or that which was equivalent to payment in cash. The general authority will not enable the broker to set off a private debt of his own, namely, the sum due to the underwriter for premiums, against the debt of the underwriter to the assured. *Scott v Irving* was applied in *Sweeting v Pearce*.[133] Here the assured shipowner employed W, an insurance broker, to effect a policy upon a ship at Lloyd's, and, after the happening of a loss, gave W the ship's papers, for the purpose of enabling him to adjust the loss with the underwriters. The broker settled the loss with the underwriter in accordance with a usage prevailing at Lloyd's.[134] Since the insurance broker was

---

130 *Sweeting v Pearce* (1861) 9 Common Bench Reports (New Series) 534, 536.
131 *Matveieff & Co v Crossfield* (1903) 8 Com Cas 120, 51 WR 365.
132 (1830) 1 Barnewall and Adolphus 605.
133 (1861) 9 CB NS 534; *Stewart v Aberdein* (1838) 4 Meeson and Welsby 211.
134 The insurer underwrote the policy for £50. The *Caroline* was lost and the assured shipowner brought to the office of W the papers relating to the loss in order to have it adjusted, and to receive payment from the underwriters. The loss was adjusted at £96, and the sum payable by the insurer amounting to somewhat less than £50 was placed to his debit by W in their books, in an account current between them. The insurer placed the like sum to the credit of W in his books, and afterwards, but before the end of the year, gave them fresh credit for premiums to an amount exceeding £50. This account was settled at the end of the year, and the balance was in favour of the insurer and this continued until W stopped payments. A credit-note in the usual form was sent to the plaintiff W.

employed to collect and receive the money due on the policy, he ought to have received it in money. Setting it off in account between himself and the underwriter was not a discharge by the underwriter of the assured's claim. The custom was not known by the assured. It would be unreasonable to hold the assured bound by the custom for the reason that that would be substituting the broker (who was insolvent in this case) as a new debtor for assured in the place of the underwriter.[135] Moreover, Bramwell B emphasised that the legal presumption of authority given to a person who is to receive satisfaction for another for a money demand is that he is to receive it by payment of money only;[136] hence W were to receive satisfaction by payment of money. The judge stated 'The custom set up is, that the persons who are by legal presumption to receive in money, and in money only, are not to receive in money.'[137] The custom therefore was held to be in contradiction to the authority given to the agents by their principal.[138] Thus, when the assured says to the broker 'receive payment of the loss' that means 'receive it in money, and not otherwise.'[139]

In *Stolos Compania S.A. v Ajax Insurance Co Ltd (The 'Admiral C')*[140] the principles decided in the abovementioned cases were restated. The broker, CDL, placed insurance of *The Admiral C* against perils of the sea. The risk occurred during the currency of the policy. The insurance contract provided: 'All claims hereunder to be collected through CDL.' CDL, however, got into financial difficulties and were in liquidation by the time the claim was to be made against the insurer; thus the assured instructed other brokers to collect on their behalf. The insurer argued that under the policy the claim can be collected only through CDL and that the course of dealing between CDL and the insurer involved a mutual set-off of sums due to CDL in respect of claims and sums due to the insurer by way of premiums. The insurer argued that on balance there was a large sum due to the insurer and accordingly the insurer had a good defence to the assured's claim. Moreover, the insurer argued that according to the custom, as between the insurance brokers and policy holders all dealings were on an 'in-account' basis; that is to say, subject to set-off as described above.

The additional matter in this case was that CDL were authorised to collect payments and it was argued that the assured impliedly consented to CDL and the insurer settling the claim with the effect of operating the custom. The Court of Appeal found this argument unsustainable. In line with the previous authority on this matter, the court confirmed that in its natural and ordinary meaning the word 'collected' meant 'collected in cash'.[141] The words were incapable of meaning 'brought into account between brokers and insurers in the manner customary in the market'.[142]

Sir David Cairns[143] approved Goff J's view that the word 'collect' connotes an actual handing over of the money, and that it is inconsistent with the argument that the claim can be satisfied by set-off between underwriters and brokers. If the insurer is correct, it would mean that the assured was bound to use even insolvent brokers and to accept payment on account between brokers and underwriters. This was a debt owed to the assured and not to the brokers. The provisions imply an authority to the brokers to collect claims. The wording was inserted simply for the benefit of the brokers, in common for instance with the 'cancelment notice clause' immediately preceding it, which was clearly intended for the benefit of the brokers by providing that they were to have the right to cancel in the event of non-payment of premium.

---

135 (1861) 9 CB NS 534, 540, Crompton J.
136 (1861) 9 CB NS 534, 540, 541, Bramwell B.
137 (1861) 9 CB NS 534, 540.
138 (1861) 9 CB NS 534, 540, 541, Bramwell B.
139 (1861) 9 CB NS 534, 541, Bramwell B.
140 [1981] 1 Lloyd's Rep 9.
141 [1981] 1 Lloyd's Rep 9, 10 Sir David Cairns.
142 [1981] 1 Lloyd's Rep 9, 10 Sir David Cairns.
143 [1981] 1 Lloyd's Rep 9, 10.

Further reading

Bennett, *The Law of Marine Insurance*, 2nd edn, [2006] Oxford University Press. Chapter 6.

Flaux, 'Brokers' liability for premium: section 53 of the Marine Insurance Act revisited', *British Insurance Law Association Journal* [1998] 97, 34–42.

Gilman et al., *Arnould: Law of Marine Insurance and Average*, 18th edn, [2013] Sweet & Maxwell. Chapter 6.

Gloster, 'Who pays the piper – who calls the tune? Recent issues arising in the context of s.53 of the Marine Insurance Act 1906', *Lloyd's Maritime and Commercial Law Quarterly* [2007] 3(August), 302–314.

Merkin, *Colinvaux's Law of Insurance*, 9th edn, [2010] Sweet & Maxwell, Chapter 8.

Rose, *Marine Insurance: Law and Practice*, 2nd edn, [2012] Informa. Chapter 8.

Tettenborn, 'Section 53 of the Marine Insurance Act 1906: An Exercise in Streamlining?', *Lloyd's Maritime and Commercial Law Quarterly* [2013] 3(August), 401–408.

Thomas, 'Brokers, marine insurance premiums and the London market: the case for reform', *Journal of International Maritime Law* [2012] 18(2): 107–108.

Chapter 7

Causation and Marine Perils

Chapter Contents

An insurer is liable for the loss which is caused by an insured peril. In marine insurance policies the proximate, not the remote, causes are to be regarded.[1] Thus, whether or not a loss is covered by a marine policy depends on ascertaining its proximate cause.[2] Section 55(1) of the Marine Insurance Act 1906 provides 'Subject to the provisions of this Act, and unless the policy otherwise provides, the insurer is liable for any loss proximately caused by a peril insured against, but, subject as aforesaid, he is not liable for any loss which is not proximately caused by a peril insured against.'[3] Section 55(2) provides exclusions to the cover from a contract of marine insurance and the policy may provide further exclusions. Therefore when there is an issue regarding the policy cover it is necessary to determine the proximate cause of the loss. If the relevant cause is one of those covered by the policy of insurance the insurer may be liable for the loss.

The Marine Insurance Act 1906 does not define the method to determine the proximate cause of a loss. Before *Leyland Shipping Co Ltd v Norwich Union Fire Insurance Society Ltd*[4] the proximate cause had been the immediate cause, that is, the cause which was latest in point of time.[5] *Leyland Shipping* changed the law and it is now a settled rule of law that the relevant cause is not closest in time to the loss, but is proximate in efficiency.[6]

True meaning of causa proxima (proximate cause)

It was established in *Leyland Shipping Co Ltd v Norwich Union Fire Insurance Society Ltd*[7] that the cause which is truly proximate is that which is proximate in efficiency. Lord Shaw regarded treating proxima causa as the cause which is nearest in time as out of the question.[8] His Lordship added 'Causation is not a chain, but a net. At each point influences, forces, events, precedent and simultaneous, meet, and the radiation from each point extends infinitely. At the point where these various influences meet it is for the judgment as upon a matter of fact to declare which of the causes thus joined at the point of effect was the proximate and which was the remote cause.'[9] That efficiency may have been preserved although other causes may in the meantime have sprung up which have not yet destroyed it, or truly impaired it, and it may still therefore remain the real efficient cause to which the event can be ascribed.[10]

In *Leyland Shipping*, the *Ikaria* was insured by a policy which was 'Warranted free of capture seizure and detention and the consequences thereof or of any attempt threat piracy excepted, and also from all consequences of hostilities or warlike operations whether before or after declaration of war.' On 30 January 1915, during her voyage from South America to Havre, she stopped near Havre for the purpose of taking up a pilot but then she was struck by a torpedo fired by a German submarine. Two large holes were made in the vessel, and No. 1 hold filled with water. The crew brought her into the outer harbour of Havre. She was moored alongside the Quai d'Escale, where she was always afloat and would have been saved if she had been allowed to remain there. A gale sprang up on the 31st, causing the vessel to range and bump against the quay. The port authorities

---

1   *Leyland Shipping Co Ltd v Norwich Union Fire Insurance Society Ltd* [1918] AC 350, 365.

2   *Global Process Systems Inc v Syarikat Takaful Malaysia Bhd (The Cendor Mopu)* [2011] Lloyd's Rep IR 302, para 18.

3   The provisions discussed in this chapter are general principles. As the section states 'unless the policy otherwise provides', the wording of the policy may lead to a different result.

4   [1918] AC 350.

5   *Ionides v Universal Marine Insurance Co* (1863) 14 CB NS 259; *Pink v Fleming* (1890) 25 QBD 396.

6   *The Cendor Mopu* [2011] Lloyd's Rep IR 302, para 19; *Leyland Shipping Co Ltd v Norwich Union Fire Insurance Society Ltd* [1918] AC 350.

7   [1918] AC 350.

8   [1918] AC 350, 369.

9   [1918] AC 350, 369.

10 [1918] AC 350, Lord Shaw, 369.

ordered that she should leave the quay as they were concerned that she might sink, blocking the quay which was needed for the war. The vessel was anchored with her head towards the Batardeau. There was a good deal of wind and sea and she became a total loss on 2 February.

The main question was the proximate cause of the total loss of the Ikaria. If the cause was the torpedo the insurer would not be liable because of the exclusion clause but if the cause was not the torpedo it would be the gale, and the insurer would be liable.

The House of Lords decided that the loss was caused by the torpedo. The vessel was at all times in the grip of the casualty. Lord Shaw stated that the true efficient cause never loses its hold.[11] After the torpedo struck her she was a doomed ship, unless she could get into a real place of safety. She nearly got to a place of safety, but never quite did so. What happened was in the circumstances the natural sequence following the injury by the torpedo. She was down by the head, and therefore struck the ground. Their Lordships held that the combined action of striking the ground and rising and falling with the tide, together with the swelling of the cargo, which had been wetted, strained her and broke her up, so that she eventually became a total wreck.

The question whether a cause was a proximate cause was to be answered by applying the common sense of a business or seafaring man.[12] This can be illustrated by referring to Whiting v New Zealand Insurance Co Ltd.[13] In Whiting the subject matter of the insurance was some ladies' hats made in Formosa and shipped from Japan. The hats were made of wood and other fibres, manufactured first into paper, then spun into yarn, then coated with a liquid cellulose compound, then woven at Formosa and afterwards sent back to Japan and then shipped. A large quantity of these hats was consigned to the assured by a firm of shippers in Kobe in the autumn of 1929. The larger proportion of the hats arrived in sound condition by a number of ships; but a part of one shipment and the whole of another arrived mouldy. The question was one of fact, assessing how and why these hats became mouldy in these two instances. The insurers argued that the cause was something internal, some peculiarity in the way the hats were manufactured, which was accentuated in these particular parcels. Roche J rejected this argument reasoning that there were too many sound shipments not only in that autumn but over more than a twenty-year period of time during which the hats had remained in good condition. Thus the judge eliminated the possibility that something wrong with the manufacture or something inherent in the goods themselves potentially caused the loss. No accidents were reported during the voyage and the goods were well packed. The judge was persuaded that the hats must have been subject to surface water when they were on the quay before they were carried onto the ship or in the lighter. The judge found that there was surface water on the quay which affected these cases, with moisture seeping from the cases into the goods themselves. The wet conditions made for a particularly moist atmosphere which demonstrably conducive to the growth of mould. Moisture of this sort originated in most of the cases from fresh water. Standing in pools of water on the quay is a peril which is insured against. Accordingly, the insurers were held liable for damage occasioned by that cause.

Concurrent causes

There may be more than one possible cause to be considered in terms of determining the proximate cause of the loss and in such a case it will be necessary to determine the dominant cause of the

---

11 [1918] AC 350, 371, Lord Shaw.

12 Leyland Shipping Co Ltd v Norwich Union Fire Insurance Society Ltd [1918] AC 350, 363, Lord Dunedin; Noten v Harding [1990] 2 Lloyd's Rep 283; Venetico Marine SA v International General Insurance Co Ltd [2014] Lloyd's Rep IR 243, para 279.

13 (1932) 44 Ll L Rep 179.

loss.[14] This is also important because exclusions only operate when the excepted peril is a proximate cause. This was the case in *Leyland Shipping* in which the question was whether it was the torpedo or the gale that caused the loss. Lord Shaw stated that 'Where various factors or causes are concurrent, and one has to be selected, the matter is determined as one of fact, and the choice falls upon the one to which may be variously ascribed the qualities of reality, predominance, efficiency.'[15]

In *Wayne Tank and Pump Co Ltd v Employers Liability Assurance Corporation Ltd*[16] the issue was similar to *Leyland Shipping* that the court had to determine the dominant cause from the two possible alternative causes. Wayne Tank and Pump Co Ltd (Waynes) installed new equipment into a mill that was owned by Harbutt's Plasticine Ltd (Harbutts). Waynes were found liable for the loss Harbutts suffered as a result of a fire that was caused by Waynes' negligence in installing the equipment. Waynes claimed from its public liability insurer who relied on a policy exception that 'The company will not indemnify the insured in respect of liability consequent upon . . . (5) death injury or damage caused by the nature or conditions of any goods or the containers thereof sold or supplied by or on behalf of the insured.' There were two separate causes discussed for the loss in question. One cause was the conduct of the assured in supplying the useless and dangerous material called durapipe coupled with a useless thermostat. The installation was completely unsuitable for the purpose. It was an extreme danger, because, when heated up, the durapipe would sag, the wax would escape, and, the whole thing would go up in flames. The second cause was the conduct of a servant of the assured in switching on the heating tape and leaving it unattended throughout the night and at a time when the installation had not been tested.

The dangerous nature of the installation, the first cause, was plainly within the exception clause. Taking that cause alone, the insurance company would be exempt, by reason of the exception clause. The second cause, namely, the conduct of the man in switching on the heating tank and leaving it unattended all night, was not within the exception clause. Taking that cause alone, the insurance company would be liable under the general words and would not be exempted by the exceptions. It was necessary for the court to decide which of the two causes was the effective or dominant cause. Applying the rule of causa proxima established in *Leyland Shipping* the court found that the first cause, the dangerous nature of the installation was the dominant cause so the insurers were not liable.

Lord Denning further commented on a situation where there was not one dominant cause, but two causes which were equal or nearly equal in their efficiency in bringing about the damage, one of which renders the insurers liable and the other exempts them from liability, and affirmed the insurers' right to rely on the exception clause. In explaining this rule Lord Denning referred to *Board of Trade v Hain Steamship Co Ltd*[17] where Viscount Sumner said that where there is one loss which is the product of two causes, joint and simultaneous – and loss due to one of the causes is exempt being 'warranted free' – then the underwriters are not liable. The reason is that if the underwriters were held liable for loss, they would not be free of it. Since they excluded their liability for a particular matter, exempting them from liability altogether will be the way of giving effect to the insurer's stipulation.

In *Leyland Shipping* and *Wayne Tank* the court determined which of the two causes was dominant. However, as Lord Denning mentioned in *Wayne Tank*, in some cases it may not be possible to determine which of the two perils, each of which independently of each other were capable of

---

14 *Wayne Tank & Pump Co Ltd v Employers Liability Assurance Corp Ltd* [1974] QB 57; *Leyland Shipping Co Ltd v Norwich Union Fire Insurance Society Ltd* [1918] AC 350, 363, Lord Dunedin.

15 *Leyland Shipping Co Ltd v Norwich Union Fire Insurance Society Ltd* [1918] AC 350, 370, Lord Shaw.

16 [1974] QB 57.

17 [1929] AC 534.

causing the loss, was the dominant cause. The difficulty arises because each peril was equal or nearly equal in their efficiency in bringing about the damage. It is necessary in this case to analyse each cause independently to see if each is insured or excluded peril under the policy. The rule is that if there are two perils that caused the loss, one is insured and the other is excepted, the exception applies.[18] On the other hand if one of the causes is an insured and the other is uninsured, but not expressly excluded, the insured peril prevails.[19]

Wayne Tank was applied in *Midland Mainline Ltd v Eagle Star Insurance Co Ltd*[20] where a broken rail caused a rail disaster. The broken rail was in turn caused by gauge corner cracking (GCC), a type of rolling contact fatigue. Immediately after the derailment Railtrack, the owner and operator of the UK mainland railway network, imposed a number of emergency speed restrictions (ESRs) on parts of the network where GCCs were known to exist. The ESRs disrupted the timetables of train operating companies. Five train operating companies commenced proceedings against the subscribers to insurances covering business interruption losses. The policy that Eagle Star subscribed to contained a 'denial of access' extension under which cover was granted in the event of the assured being prevented from or hindered in the use of any part of the rail network. The extension was stated to be 'subject to all the terms and conditions and provisions of the Policy'. The policy itself contained a wear and tear exclusion, which excluded liability for loss arising from: inherent vice, latent defect, gradual deterioration, wear and tear, frost, change in water table level, its own faulty or defective design or materials. It was held that it was the wear and tear that caused the ESR to be imposed and, although the ESR was the immediate cause of the loss the wear and tear was the proximate cause of the loss. It was further stated that if they were both proximate causes the insurers could still have relied upon the exception.

Burden of proof

The burden of proving, on a balance of probabilities, that the ship was lost by perils insured against, is on the assured.[21] In an old case, *Green v Brown*,[22] upon its own facts, the Court accepted the presumption that the vessel must have been lost by perils of the sea. The ship *Charming Peggy* was insured in 1739, for a voyage from North Carolina to London. All the evidence given was that she sailed out of port on her intended voyage, and had never since been heard of. Witnesses testified at court that in such a case, especially where everybody on board was presumed to have drowned, the presumption was that she foundered at sea. It was held that it would be unreasonable to expect certain evidence of such a loss. The Court was not left in doubt in *Green v Brown* most probably because all the crew were presumed to have drowned. It is always open to a court, even after the kind of a prolonged inquiry with a mass of expert evidence, to conclude that the proximate cause of the ship's loss, even on a balance of probabilities, remains in doubt, so that the assured has failed to discharge the burden of proof which lay upon him.[23] In *La Compañia Martiartu v The Corporation of the Royal Exchange Assurance*[24] the vessel sank in deep water in fine weather with a smooth sea and little or no wind blowing. The crew abandoned the ship three hours before she sank, and were found in their boats by a fishing fleet and taken on board. The trial judge came to the conclusion that the steamer was lost through seawater entering the ship as the result of a collision, and accordingly he

---

18   *The Miss Jay Jay* [1987] 1 Lloyd's Rep 32, Lawton LJ.
19   *The Miss Jay Jay* [1987] 1 Lloyd's Rep 32, Lawton LJ.
20   [2004] 2 Lloyd's Rep 604.
21   *Rhesa Shipping Co SA v Edmunds (The Popi M)* [1985] 2 Lloyd's Rep 1.
22   (1743) 2 Strange 1199.
23   *The Popi M* [1985] 2 Lloyd's Rep 1, 3, Lord Brandon.
24   [1923] 1 KB 650.

gave judgment for the assured. In the Court of Appeal the question arose whether, if each party in turn failed to convince the Court of their respective contentions, there was any presumption in favour of the respondents that the ship was lost by a peril of the sea. Having noted the existence of a presumption as accepted in *Green v Brown*, Scrutton LJ stated that if there is evidence on each side as to the cause of the admission of seawater, which leaves the Court in doubt whether the effective cause is within or without the policy, the assured fails to discharge the burden of proof for he has not proved a loss by perils insured against. In *La Compañía Martiartu* the matter was left in doubt as to whether the ship was scuttled or lost by perils of the sea and on the balance of probabilities the assured failed to prove his case. The view that where the Court is left in doubt the assured has not been able to prove his case was applied in *Rhesa Shipping Co SA v Edmunds (The Popi M)*[25] in which, similar to *La Compañía Martiartu*, the vessel the *Popi M* sank in calm weather in the Mediterranean Sea off the coast of Algeria in deep water when laden with a cargo of bagged sugar. The question was whether, on the balance of probabilities, the vessel was lost by perils of the sea. The shipowner argued that if a seaworthy vessel sinks in calm waters it should be presumed that it was lost by perils of the sea. Bingham J[26] made no finding regarding the state of the vessel as the evidence left his Lordship in doubt whether the vessel was seaworthy. The ship was an old one built in 1952. By 1976 she had become seriously run down. She had been repaired but the ship as a whole, and her shell plating in particular, were still in a generally dilapidated condition. During the voyage prior to her sinking the ship experienced good weather and light seas. The assured argued that the *Popi M* could not have collided with a submerged rock because the ship was navigating in a much-used sea lane, and the relevant charts showed deep water all round without any rocks. The collision with a floating object was not a possibility either, given that such an object would have been washed clear of the ship's side by the bow wave which the ship, proceeding at her full speed, would have been creating.

The elimination of these two possibilities left the shipowners with only one remaining possibility, namely, a collision with a submerged submarine, travelling in the same direction as the ship and at about the same speed.[27] Although this was again an improbable cause, the judge nevertheless accepted the latter submission by applying the Sherlock Holmes' exception that '. . . when You have eliminated the impossible, whatever remains, however improbable, must be the truth.' The Court of Appeal[28] dismissed the insurer's appeal but the House of Lords reversed the judgment. Lord Brandon[29] observed that this was not a case of a ship being lost with all her crew in circumstances where the immediate cause of the entry into her of sufficient water to make her sink is unexplained. Lord Brandon stated that if the occurrence of an event is extremely improbable, a finding that it is nevertheless more likely to have occurred than not, does not accord with common sense.[30] This is especially so when it is open to the judge to say simply that the evidence leaves him in doubt whether the event occurred or not, and that the party on whom the burden of proving that the event occurred lies has therefore failed to discharge such a burden.[31] According to Lord Brandon, it was open to the trial judge to consider the third alternative, namely, that the evidence left him in doubt as to the cause of the aperture in the ship's hull, and that, in these circumstances, the assured had failed to discharge the burden of proof which was on them.[32]

---

25 [1985] 2 Lloyd's Rep 1.
26 [1983] 2 Lloyd's Rep 235, 245.
27 In this connection an unarmed torpedo was mentioned, but very sensibly not treated as a serious possibility.
28 [1984] 2 Lloyd's Rep 555.
29 [1985] 2 Lloyd's Rep 1, 4.
30 [1985] 2 Lloyd's Rep 1, 6.
31 [1985] 2 Lloyd's Rep 1, 6.
32 [1985] 2 Lloyd's Rep 1, 6. The *Popi M* was applied – in the non-marine context – in *Milton Keynes BC v Nulty* [2013] Lloyd's Rep IR 243.

It is now a settled principle that with regard to determination of the proximate cause of a marine loss, referring to the Sherlock Holmes' exception in The Sign of Four would be an erroneous approach.[33] This has recently been confirmed by Popplewell J in *Ace European Group Ltd v Chartis Insurance UK Ltd*,[34] which was approved by the Court of Appeal.[35] In the words of Popplewell J[36] the settled rule is that where the assured and insurer each put forward a rival explanation for the cause of a loss, the judge may either decide that one or the other explanation is the probable cause on the balance of probabilities. If the judge is left in doubt, such that even if he rejects the insurer's explanation, he cannot say that the assured's explanation is more probable than any alternative (uninsured) explanation. In other words, it is impermissible for a judge to conclude in the case of a series of improbable causes that the least improbable or least unlikely is nonetheless the cause of the event.[37]

In *Ace European Group Ltd v Chartis Insurance UK Ltd* the issue was related to the carriage of some economiser blocks for use in two boilers, which generated the heat to drive steam turbines to be used at the assured's waste recycling plant at Colnbrook near Slough. They were carried by road and sea from Romania. Six months after being on the site fatigue crack damage to the tubes was discovered. It was common ground that the fatigue cracking was caused by resonant vibration. The question was 'when did the resonant vibration causing the fatigue cracking occur?' The assured had two policies: a marine policy which covered damage in transit; and an Erection All Risks (EAR) policy which covered damage on site. The marine insurers asserted that the damage had been caused by wind on site, whereas the EAR insurers contended that the loss was the result of vibration on the voyage. Popplewell J referred to Thomas LJ in *Ide v ATB Sales Ltd*[38] that '. . . as a matter of principle, if there were only three possible causes of an event, then it was permissible for a judge to approach the matter by analysing each of those causes. If he ranked those causes in terms of probability and concluded that one was more probable than the others, then, provided that those were the only three possible causes, he was entitled to conclude that the one he considered most probable, was the probable cause of the event, provided it was not improbable.' Popplewell J eliminated, in the evidence, the possibility of wind excitation on site as the proximate cause of the loss. This therefore left the judge with the alternative hypothesis of vibration during transit in order to determine whether it is more likely than not to have occurred. On the balance of probabilities Popplewell J found that it was the proximate cause.[39] The judge reiterated that if the conclusion was that the vibrating was not a probable cause, either because the evidence was so unsatisfactory, or because such a conclusion was so improbable, it cannot as a matter of common sense be described as more likely than not to have occurred. Thus it cannot be treated as a proximate cause of the damage.[40]

Insured perils

The Marine Insurance Act 1906 section 55(1) which is titled 'Included and Excluded Losses' provides 'Subject to the provisions of this Act, and unless the policy otherwise provides, the insurer is liable for any loss proximately caused by a peril insured against, but, subject as aforesaid, he is not

---

33 [2012] 2 Lloyd's Rep 117, para 77; *Ide v ATB Sales Ltd* [2008] PIQR P13.
34 [2013] Lloyd's Rep IR 485.
35 [2013] Lloyd's Rep IR 485.
36 [2012] 2 Lloyd's Rep 117, para 79.
37 [2012] 2 Lloyd's Rep 117, para 79; *Ide v ATB Sales Ltd* [2008] PIQR P13, para 4, Thomas LJ.
38 [2008] P.I.Q.R. P13, para 6.
39 [2012] 2 Lloyd's Rep 117, para 79, para 132. The Court of Appeal held that it was open to Popplewell J to reach the conclusion the judge did and it was indeed more likely than not that the damage occurred during the transportation to Colnbrook. [2013] Lloyd's Rep IR 485, para 35.
40 [2012] 2 Lloyd's Rep 117, para 79, para 83.

liable for any loss which is not proximately caused by a peril insured against.' As will be seen below, the standard clauses incorporated in marine policies may list the risks covered by the policy. In this chapter first the risks included in the MIA 1906 will be analysed and then the chapter will refer to the standard hull and cargo insurance clauses.

Perils of the sea

It might be considered that, reading literally, perils of the sea might cover everything that happens at sea.[41] However, both the authorities[42] and the statutory definition of 'perils of the sea' indicate that this is not the case. Perils of the sea is defined by para 7 of the schedule to the Marine Insurance Act 1906 as referring

> only to fortuitous accidents or casualties of the seas. It does not include the ordinary action of the winds and waves.

Peril is defined as fortuity; in other words, not something which is bound to happen.[43] Defined by its antithesis, the word 'fortuitous' carries the connotation that the cause of the loss should not have been intentional or inevitable.[44] There must be some casualty, something which could not be foreseen as one of the necessary incidents of the adventure.[45] The reason for such a definition is that the purpose of the policy is to secure an indemnity against accidents which may happen, not against events which must happen.[46] For instance natural and inevitable action of the winds and waves, which results in what may be described as wear and tear is not covered by perils of the sea.[47] Moreover, it has been established that the term 'perils of the sea' does not cover every accident or casualty which may happen to the subject matter of the insurance on the sea.[48] It is true that some sea or weather conditions or accidents of navigation that produce a result which but for these conditions would not have occurred is required to establish a peril of the sea.[49] If a vessel strikes upon a sunken rock in fair weather and sinks, this will be covered by perils of the sea. A loss by foundering, owing to a vessel coming into collision with another vessel falls within the same category. It was clarified by The Cendor Mopu that it is not the state of the sea itself that must be fortuitous but rather the occurrence of some accident or casualty due to the conditions of the sea.[50]

It must be a peril 'of' the sea[51] which does not necessarily cover everything which occurred 'on' the sea.[52] The distinction between perils 'of' and 'on' the sea was made in Thames and Mersey Marine Insurance Co Ltd v Hamilton Fraser & Co,[53] in which a pump on board the Inchmaree was insured by a policy of marine insurance. A part of the pump was burst because a valve, which should have let the water into the boiler, was stopped up while the pump was being worked by a donkey-engine.

---

41 William Gow, Marine Insurance A Handbook, 1931, p 96.

42 See below footnote.

43 Versloot Dredging BV v HDI Gerling Industrie Versicherung AG [2013] 2 Lloyd's Rep 131, para 31.

44 Versloot Dredging BV v HDI Gerling Industrie Versicherung AG [2013] 2 Lloyd's Rep 131, para 32.

45 The Xantho (1887) 12 App Cas 503, 509.

46 The Xantho (1887) 12 App Cas 503, 509.

47 MIA s 55(2)(c).

48 La Compañia Martiartu v The Corporation of the Royal Exchange Assurance [1923] 1 KB 650.

49 Grant Smith & Co v Seattle Construction & Dry Dock Co [1920] AC 162, 171, Lord Buckmaster; The Miss Jay Jay [1985] 1 Lloyd's Rep 264.

50 The Cendor Mopu, [2011] Lloyd's Rep IR 302, para 103, Lord Clarke.

51 Thomas Wilson Sons & Co v Owners of Cargo of the Xantho (The Xantho) (1887) 12 App Cas 503, 509.

52 Cullen v Butler (1816) 5 M & S 461; Versloot Dredging BV v HDI Gerling Industrie Versicherung AG [2013] 2 Lloyd's Rep 131, para 34.

53 (1887) 12 App Cas 484.

The House of Lords held that the damage to the donkey-engine was not through its being in a ship or at sea. The same thing would have happened had the boilers and engines been on land, if the same mismanagement had taken place.[54] The sea, waves and winds had nothing to do with it. Consequently, it is not sufficient to make the peril one 'of the seas' merely on the basis that it happens whilst preparing for a voyage, or whilst the vessel is at sea, or even that it involves seawater.[55]

The difference between perils of the sea and perils on the sea has recently been discussed by Popplewell J in *Versloot Dredging BV v HDI Gerling Industrie Versicherung AG*.[56] In *Versloot* the insurers argued that the entry of seawater was caused by crew negligence which could happen on the land as well as on the sea, therefore it was not pure peril of the sea. As noted below, negligence of a ship's crew is an insured peril. Popplewell J stated that the entry of seawater itself is a peril of the sea. The fortuity which gives rise to the ingress need not independently be 'of the seas'.[57] The causative fortuity and the ingress of seawater are both part of the accident or casualty and must be looked at together.[58] Popplewell J referred to *Hamilton v Pandorf*[59] in which a cargo of rice was damaged during transit from Akyab to Bremen by seawater, which found its way into the hold of the vessel through a hole gnawed by a rat, in a leaden pipe connected to the bathroom of the vessel. The House of Lords held that the cargo was damaged by perils of the sea. It is true that rats making a hole was not a peril of the sea[60] or if the assured claimed for the damage done to the pipe the underwriters would not be liable for the reason that the loss was caused due to a risk not peculiar to the sea, but incidental to the keeping of that class of goods, whether on shore or on board of a voyaging ship.[61] Here, however, the cause of the loss was the seawater which entered through a hole which was opened by a rat.

Ordinary action of the wind and waves

The definition of perils of the sea excludes ordinary action of the wind and waves. Reading literally, one might consider if only violent or extraordinary wind and waves are regarded as perils of the sea. In *Mountain v Whittle*[62] the phrase 'ordinary action of the winds and waves' was defined as referring to the degree of bad weather faced by the vessel. In *Mountain v Whittle* the assured let her houseboat, the *Dorothy*, to a firm of contractors who had undertaken to raise a sunken vessel, and who required accommodation for the men engaged in this task. When the workmen left, the *Dorothy* was towed to a dockyard for necessary repairs. The tug actually employed was of disproportionate size and power. During the towage, due to the size and strength of the tug, the breast wave was larger than usual and it caused the sinking of the *Dorothy*. The *Dorothy* was not seaworthy but the policy was a time policy so there was no warranty of seaworthiness. It was, however, necessary for the assured to establish that the loss was due to a peril of the sea. The House of Lords decided that the nature of this wave constituted a 'sea peril'. The incidence and dimensions of the wave in question amounted to a fortuitous casualty of the sea and was not accounted for merely by the ordinary action of winds or waves. It was held that there must be some special circumstance such as heavy waves causing

---

54   (1887) 12 App Cas 484, 492–493, Lord Bramwell.
55   *Versloot Dredging BV v HDI Gerling Industrie Versicherung AG* [2013] 2 Lloyd's Rep 131, para 34.
56   [2013] 2 Lloyd's Rep 131. The case was appealed but there was no appeal against the ruling about the perils of the sea. [2014] EWCA Civ 1349.
57   [2013] 2 Lloyd's Rep 131, para 45.
58   [2013] 2 Lloyd's Rep 131, para 45.
59   (1887) 12 App Cas 518.
60   (1887) 12 App Cas 518, 527, Lord Bramwell.
61   (1887) 12 App Cas 518, 525, Lord Watson.
62   [1921] AC 615.

the entrance of the seawater to make it a peril of the sea. The *Dorothy* was exposed to a wash of an extraordinary character through the great size and power of the tug to which she was lashed.

However, long before *Mountain v Whittle* was decided, in *The Xantho*, Lord Herschell found the interpretation that only the losses which were occasioned by extraordinary violence of the winds or waves were results of perils of the sea too narrow a construction of the words.[63] His Lordship stated that it is beyond question, that if a vessel strikes upon a sunken rock in fair weather and sinks, this is a loss by perils of the sea. A similar issue came before the courts in *The Miss Jay Jay*,[64] in which case the yacht was defectively designed, and damaged during a voyage at which she did not encounter extraordinary weather conditions. Mustill J stated that the principal object of the definition is to rule out losses resulting from wear and tear and the definition of perils of the sea as reflected in s55(2)(c) of the 1906 Act, which excludes from cover ordinary wear and tear.[65] Mustill J added that the word 'ordinary' attaches to 'action', not to 'wind and waves'.[66] Therefore, a loss may occur by perils of the sea although the weather conditions were not abnormal. This interpretation was approved by the Supreme Court in *The Cendor Mopu*. Lord Mance found unattractive a solution which depends upon identifying gradations of adverse weather conditions.[67] His Lordship held that a fortuitous external accident or casualty, whether identified or inferred, is necessary, but it need not be associated with extraordinary weather.[68]

Consequently, if the action of the wind or sea is the immediate cause of the loss, a claim lies under the policy notwithstanding that the conditions were within the range which could reasonably have been anticipated.[69] It was submitted that this point may become a little clearer if the word 'consequences' is substituted in place of the more ambiguous term 'action'.[70]

Entry of seawater

A loss caused by the entrance of seawater is not necessarily a loss by perils of the sea.[71] Whether entry of seawater is a peril of the sea depends on the reason for its entry. The unintentional admission of seawater into a ship, whereby the ship sinks, is a peril of the sea.[72] As seen above ingress of seawater caused by crew negligence is a fortuitous accident which normally constitutes a peril of the sea.[73] If the water got into the vessel because of the defective character of the seams there might be no loss by peril of the sea – the loss would have been by the defective condition of the vessel if the unseaworthiness is a debility of a kind which prevents the ingress being fortuitous because it is inevitable in any sea conditions.[74] In *Seashore Marine SA v Phoenix Assurance plc (The Vergina) (No.2)*[75] the vessel was salved and the assured claimed the salvage liabilities from the insurers. It was held that if the vessel had not been salved, then she would have capsized and been lost. Aikens J found

63   *Canada Rice Mills Ltd v Union Marine & General Insurance Co Ltd* (1940) 67 Ll L Rep 549, 557.
64   [1985] 1 Lloyd's Rep 264.
65   [1985] 1 Lloyd's Rep 264, 271.
66   [1985] 1 Lloyd's Rep 264, 271.
67   [2011] Lloyd's Rep IR 302, para 79.
68   [2011] Lloyd's Rep IR 302, para 71.
69   [2011] Lloyd's Rep IR 302, para 39, Lord Saville.
70   Merkin, R., 'Marine insurance: perils of the seas, inherent vice and causation', Ins LM 2011, March, 1–5.
71   *Mountain v Whittle* [1921] AC 615, Viscount Finlay, 623; *Versloot Dredging BV v HDI Gerling Industrie Versicherung AG* [2013] 2 Lloyd's Rep, para 35.
72   *Cohen Sons & Co v National Benefit Assurance Co Ltd* (1924) 18 Ll L Rep 199, 202, Bailhace J.
73   *Versloot Dredging BV v HDI Gerling Industrie Versicherung AG* [2013] 2 Lloyd's Rep, para 36.
74   *Mountain v Whittle* [1921] AC 615, Viscount Finlay, 623; *The Mis Jay Jay* [1985] 1 Lloyd's Rep 264; *Versloot Dredging BV v HDI Gerling Industrie Versicherung AG* [2013] 2 Lloyd's Rep, para 37.
75   [2001] 2 Lloyd's Rep 698.

that there would have been two 'proximate' causes of that loss of the vessel, (i) the increase in the vessel's list caused by the negligent acts of the Chief Engineer in operating the switches on the ballast control console; and (ii) the fortuitous incursion of seawater into the No 3 hold via an open scupper valve after the vessel had achieved a starboard list. Aikens J concluded that the entry of seawater via an open scupper valve was a fortuitous accident because it resulted from a state of affairs that was accidental, unintended and not inevitable.[76] It thus appears that the fortuity may lie in what causes the hole, or what causes the seawater to reach or enter the hole, or a combination of both.[77] The passage of water through a hole in the vessel will be a peril of the sea if the occasion for the water to enter the vessel is a fortuitous external accident, notwithstanding that water would enter the vessel through the hole in any state of wind, sea or weather. If there is such a fortuity, the entry of the seawater is not the ordinary action of the wind and waves because the sea has had an extraordinary effect on the vessel.[78]

Perils of the sea and unseaworthiness

As analysed fully in Chapter 5 in a policy on goods there is no implied warranty that the goods are seaworthy.[79] In a voyage policy there is an implied warranty that the ship is seaworthy at the commencement of the voyage.[80] Breach of this warranty will discharge the insurer from liability irrespective of the chain of causation between the breach of warranty and the loss, therefore there will be no issue of proximate cause of the loss. In a time policy there is no warranty of seaworthiness at the commencement of the voyage, however, if the vessel is sent to the sea in an unseaworthy state with the knowledge of the shipowner, the insurer will not be liable for the loss which is attributable to the unseaworthiness.[81] Thus, in a time policy the proximate cause will be a matter for the assured who claims under the policy to prove. A question arose in a number of cases whether a vessel which was not strong enough to resist the perils of the sea can be properly said to be lost by perils of the sea. This is a question of law, not one of fact as stated by Lord Penzance in *Dudgeon v Pembroke*.[82] In *Dudgeon* the vessel was unseaworthy and it was clear that she went ashore by the force of the winds and waves, and finally broke up and went to pieces. Lord Penzance said 'If a loss proximately caused by the sea, but more remotely and substantially brought about by the condition of the ship, is a loss for which the underwriters are not liable, then, quite independently of the warranty of seaworthiness, which applies only to the commencement of the risk . . ., the underwriters would be at liberty, in every case of a voyage policy to raise and litigate the question whether, at the time the loss happened, the vessel was, by reason of any insufficiency at the time of last leaving a port where it might have been repaired, unable to meet the perils of the sea, and was lost by reason of that inability.'

Dudgeon v Pembroke was applied in *Frangos v Sun Insurance Office Ltd*[83] and a similar issue came before the courts once again, in *JJ Lloyd Instruments v Northern Star Insurance Co (The Miss Jay Jay)*[84] in which the motor yacht *Miss Jay Jay* suffered damage while on a passage from Deauville to Hamble. Neither the

76 [2001] 2 Lloyd's Rep 698, 712.
77 *Versloot Dredging BV v HDI Gerling Industrie Versicherung AG* [2013] 2 Lloyd's Rep 131, para 33.
78 *Versloot Dredging BV v HDI Gerling Industrie Versicherung AG* [2013] 2 Lloyd's Rep 131, para 33.
79 MIA 1906 s 40(1).
80 MIA 1906 s 39(1).
81 MIA 1906 s 39(5); *Fawcus v Sarsfield*, (1856) 6 E & B 192; *Thompson v Hopper*, (1858) EB & E 1038; *Dudgeon v Pembroke* (1877) 2 App Cas 284.
82 (1877) 2 App Cas 284.
83 (1934) 49 Ll L Rep 354.
84 [1985] 1 Lloyd's Rep 264. The Court of Appeal dismissed the appeal [1987] 1 Lloyd's Rep 32.

wind nor the waves were exceptional. The yacht was defectively designed, thus was unseaworthy but the defects in design were latent so that it was not to the assured's knowledge that the boat was or might have been unseaworthy. The sea conditions were markedly worse than average, but not so bad as to be exceptional. A boat of *Miss Jay Jay*'s size and configuration would, if properly designed and built, have made the passage from Deauville to Hamble in the conditions actually encountered without suffering damage. Referring to *Frangos* and *Dudgeon*, Mustill J stated in *The Miss Jay Jay* that a chain of causation running – (i) initial unseaworthiness; (ii) adverse weather; (iii) loss of watertight integrity of the vessel; (iv) damage to the subject matter insured – is treated as a loss by perils of the sea, not by unseaworthiness. The weather was not exceptional, but this was immaterial.[85] The immediate cause was the action of adverse weather conditions on an ill-designed and ill-made hull.

Exceptions

Under section 55(2)(c) of the Marine Insurance Act 1906, unless the policy otherwise provides, the insurer is not liable for ordinary wear and tear, ordinary leakage and breakage, inherent vice or nature of the subject matter insured, or for any loss proximately caused by rats or vermin, or for any injury to machinery not proximately caused by maritime perils.

It is for the insurers to prove that the loss was proximately caused by one of the exceptions stated in section 55(2)(2).[86]

Inherent vice — *only if covered*

The definition of inherent vice was given in *Soya GmbH Mainz Kommanditgesellschaft v White*.[87] In that case a cargo of soya beans was insured against risks of heating, sweating and spontaneous combustion. The goods arrived in a heated and deteriorated condition. The insurers denied liability on the grounds that the proximate cause of the damage was inherent vice or nature of the subject matter insured, for which they were not liable under s.55(2)(c) of MIA 1906; and that the cover only extended to heating, sweating or spontaneous combustion brought about by some external cause. The House of Lords decided that as a matter of construction the policy did 'otherwise provide' within the meaning of the opening words of section 55(2)(c) so that the perils of heating, sweating and spontaneous combustion arising from inherent vice or nature of the subject matter insured were covered. Lord Diplock defined inherent vice as referring to:

> . . . a peril by which a loss is proximately caused; it is not descriptive of the loss itself. It means the risk of deterioration of the goods shipped as a result of their natural behaviour in the ordinary course of the contemplated voyage without the intervention of any fortuitous external accident or casualty.

The inherent vice exception was argued but rejected by the Privy Council in *Canada Rice Mills Ltd v Union Marine & General Insurance Co Ltd*.[88] Some 50,600 bags of rice were shipped on the *Segundo*.

---

85   [1985] 1 Lloyd's Rep 264, 272.
86   *The Cendor Mopu*, [2011] Lloyd's Rep IR 302, para 20, Lord Saville.
87   [1983] 1 Lloyd's Rep 122.
88   (1940) 67 Ll L Rep 549.

The cargo throughout was well stowed with adequate air spaces. Upon arrival at its destination it was found that all the rice had heated. There was no complaint as to the sufficiency of the ventilation system. The evidence also established that the rice was in good and sound condition when shipped. The insurers asserted that the damaged condition of the rice was due not to perils insured against but to the inherent vice of the goods when shipped. Rice is a commodity which may become heated if not fully ventilated while being carried in the ship's hold. It has a considerable moisture content, and has a capacity for absorbing further moisture which needs to be carried off by ventilation. Improper ventilation leads to a process of fermentation and damages the grain. The appellants' case was that the damage was due to interference with the ventilation consequent on bad weather during the voyage, which caused the closing of the cowl ventilators which were necessarily kept open to maintain thorough ventilation. The ventilators have to be closed when water would get to the cargo if they were not closed. As a result of this a process of fermentation was thus started, and this continued for the rest of the voyage even though the ventilators were not again closed. At the trial, which took place in the Supreme Court of British Columbia the jury found that the shipment was damaged by heat caused by the closing of the cowl ventilators and hatches from time to time during the voyage. It was held that the loss was caused by perils of the sea, as the ventilators were closed due to weather and to prevent the entry of the seawater.

In *Noten v Harding*[89] it was held that the cargo was damaged by inherent vice, in other words, the cargo damaged itself. In this case leather gloves were damaged by moisture which condensed on the inside of the top of the containers and then fell onto the gloves packed inside them. As Bingham LJ described it, leather is hydroscopic, that means that it will absorb moisture. As the temperature of air drops it becomes less able to contain moisture. When placed in a humid atmosphere it will over a period absorb moisture until it equilibrates with the ambient humidity. Shipments were made during the monsoon season in Calcutta where the gloves were manufactured. They absorbed moisture from the humid atmosphere of Calcutta, the absorption continued so long as they remained in that atmosphere or until they equilibrated with it. Once the gloves had been stuffed in the container they rapidly equilibrated with the atmosphere in the container, either absorbing a little moisture from it or discharging a little moisture into it. Upon arrival at Rotterdam, the container was discharged into a temperature markedly colder than the temperature of the mass of gloves stowed in the container. The outside of the container cooled. The temperature at the top of the container was below the dew point, so that moisture condensed on the inside of the top of the container and fell in droplets onto the cartons of gloves below. The Court of Appeal held that the goods deteriorated as a result of their natural behaviour in the ordinary course of the contemplated voyage, without the intervention of any fortuitous external accident or casualty.[90] The damage was caused because the goods were shipped wet.[91] There was nothing in the facts to suggest any untoward or unusual event of any kind.[92] It was not unusually humid or hot in Calcutta at the time of shipment nor particularly cold in Rotterdam. There was nothing to suggest that the position of the containers in the stow was unusual, nor was there any combination of fortuitous events. The gloves damaged themselves, thus the insurer was not liable.

For an illustration of inherent vice it is also worth mentioning *The Knight of St Michael*[93] the facts of which are given below under the 'fire' peril. In this case the claim against the insurer was for the loss of freight. The judge *obiter* noted that if the action had been by the cargo owners against

---

89 [1990] 2 Lloyd's Rep 283.
90 [1990] 2 Lloyd's Rep 283, 288.
91 [1990] 2 Lloyd's Rep 283, 288.
92 [1990] 2 Lloyd's Rep 283, 289.
93 [1898] P 30.

their underwriters for the loss of the coal, the claim would have been defended on the ground that the loss was due to the inherent vice of the coal.[94]

Inability of the subject matter insured to withstand the ordinary conditions of the voyage

When the subject matter insured is not capable of withstanding the ordinary conditions of voyage and if, in turn, it is lost the question will arise, should this be analysed as 'inherent vice' or 'perils of the sea'? It was held in *Mayban General Assurance Bhd v Alstom Power Plants Ltd*[95] that the insurer will not be liable in this case. In *Mayban*, a large electrical transformer was found damaged when it arrived at its destination after being carried on board the vessel *Eliane Trader*. The assured claimed the cost of repair from the insurers who argued that the damage had resulted from the transformer's inability to withstand the ordinary incidents of carriage by sea from the United Kingdom to Malaysia during the winter months. Moore-Bick J accepted the insurer's argument that the damage was caused by the prolonged working of the joints brought about by the motion of the vessel in which the transformer was being carried. The judge held that goods tendered for shipment must be capable of withstanding the forces that they can ordinarily be expected to encounter in the course of the voyage, which may vary depending on the route and the time of year. If, however, the conditions encountered by the vessel were no more severe than could reasonably have been expected, the conclusion must be that the real cause of the loss was the inherent inability of the goods to withstand the ordinary incidents of the voyage. Moore-Bick J's view of the case seems to be predicated on a requirement that the cargo is seaworthy. The judge stated that '. . . goods tendered for shipment must be capable of withstanding the forces that they can ordinarily be expected to encounter . . .' However, the MIA 1906 s.40(1) provides that 'In a policy on goods or other moveables there is no implied warranty that the goods or moveables are seaworthy'.

Mayban was overruled by the House of Lords in *Global Process Systems Inc v Syarikat Takaful Malaysia Bhd (The Cendor Mopu)*.[96] The *Cendor Mopu* was purchased by the assured for conversion into a mobile offshore production unit for use in the Cendor Field off the cost of East Malaysia. The assured insured her for carriage from Texas to Malaysia on the barge *Boabarge 8*. The insurance policy incorporated the Institute Cargo Clauses (A) of 1 January 1982. Clause 4.4 excluded 'loss, damage or expense caused by inherent vice or nature of the subject matter insured' from the cover provided by the policy. The legs were massive tubular structures, each weighed 404 tons. The rig was carried on the barge with its legs in place above the jackhouse, so that the legs extended some 300 feet into the air. The voyage began on 23 August 2005. On the evening of 4 November 2005, the starboard leg broke off at the 30-foot level and fell into the sea. The following evening the forward leg broke off at the same level, and some 30 minutes later the port leg broke off at the 18-foot level; both legs also fell into the sea. It was the loss of the three legs that was the subject matter of the claim under the policy.

It was common ground that what the barge experienced was within the range of weather that could reasonably have been contemplated for the voyage. The loss resulted from metal fatigue in the three legs which is a progressive cracking mechanism resulting from repeated or fluctuating stresses each at a level lower than that required to cause fracture of an uncracked component. Generally, there are three stages to the fatigue failure of any component, namely initial cracking, propagation of the cracking and finally complete fracture. The initial cracking occurs in regions of

---

94 [1898] pp 30, 33.
95 [2004] 2 Lloyd's Rep 609.
96 [2011] 1 Lloyd's Rep 560.

stress-raising features, such as corners or notches, where stresses are concentrated. In *The Cendor Mopu* the corners of the pinholes were stress-raising features. The initial fatigue cracks occurred there and then propagated until they reached a point where they were subjected to what was described as a 'leg breaking' stress that completely fractured the weakened leg. Once the first leg had failed, the stresses on the remaining legs increased. Lord Mance stated that it was known from the outset that the legs of the rig were at risk of fatigue cracks during the voyage. It was a condition of the policy that the appointed surveyors approved the arrangements for the tow. These surveyors issued a Certificate of Approval in which they required that the legs be inspected again once the barge reached Cape Town (roughly the halfway point) for crack initiation so that remedial work could be undertaken should it be found necessary. The rig was examined at Saldanha Bay where some repairs were made in order to reduce the stress concentrations around the pinholes. The legs were nevertheless lost during the voyage. It seems arguable that similar to *Mayban*, in *The Cendor Mopu*, the cracking was the simple product of the exhaustion of the fatigue life of the legs on passage under the influence of the ordinary action of the wind and waves, and did not therefore involve any fortuitous external accident or casualty. The Supreme Court however found that *Mayban* was wrongly decided and held that the loss was caused by perils of the sea, not by inherent inability of the legs to withstand the conditions of the voyage. In relation to the inherent vice argument Lord Mance said that in *Noten v Harding*[97] the damage was not covered because the conditions under which it occurred were entirely ordinary atmospheric conditions, the gloves essentially damaged themselves under such conditions through their own moisture content.[98] Lord Mance held that the sudden breakage of the first leg, followed by that of the other two legs, is much more readily understood as involving a marine accident or casualty.[99] It was neither expected nor contemplated. It only occurred under the influence of a leg-breaking wave of a direction and strength catching the first leg at just the right moment, leading to increased stress on and the collapse of the other two legs in turn.[100]

Lord Mance further took into consideration that it was an express condition of the insurance that the rig was surveyed before it sailed on the voyage from Galveston. It was well recognised that stresses would be imposed on the legs by virtue of the motion of the waves. The surveyor advised and the parties appreciated both the need to put into a South African port for inspection and the likelihood that some cracking would be found and some repairs would have to be undertaken. In the event, the rig suffered the further loss of all three legs, not just because cracking appears to have developed further or sooner than expected, but ultimately because the first, and then each leg was caught, in just the 'right' way, by a leg-breaking wave. Lord Mance was of the view that to hold that the insurance did not cover such a loss, if it materialised, would seem to deprive it of much of its utility.

Lord Clarke referred to the definition of inherent vice as provided by Lord Diplock in *Soya v White*. Accordingly, if there was 'intervention of any fortuitous external accident or casualty' the law treats the loss as caused by that fortuitous external accident or casualty and not by inherent vice. Lord Clarke stated that in referring to 'any fortuitous accident or casualty', Lord Diplock must have had in mind the definition of perils of the sea in Schedule 1 to the Act which refers 'only to fortuitous accidents or casualties of the seas'.[101] Lord Clarke found that Lord Diplock was defining 'inherent vice' in opposition to perils of the sea, thereby avoiding any overlap between the insured

---

97 [1990] 2 Lloyd's Rep 283.
98 [2011] Lloyd's Rep IR 302, para 64.
99 [2011] Lloyd's Rep IR 302, para 65.
100 [2011] Lloyd's Rep IR 302, para 65.
101 [2011] Lloyd's Rep IR 302, para 111.

risk and the excluded risk. Thus where a proximate cause of the loss was perils of the sea, there was no room for the conclusion that the loss was caused by inherent vice. This was applied in *Ace European Group Ltd v Chartis Insurance UK Ltd*, in which Popplewell J reiterated that where it is established that a proximate cause of the loss is a fortuity occurring during the period of cover, there is no room for inherent vice to be treated as another proximate cause of the loss.[102] In this case the damage which occurred during transportation was proximately caused by resonant vibration which was an external fortuitous accident or casualty. There is therefore no room as a matter of law for inherent vice to be an additional proximate cause.[103]

Concurrent causes were referred to in this chapter. In *The Cendor Mopu* there were two candidates for the 'proximate cause': (1) perils of the sea, in the form of the stresses put upon the rig by the height and direction of the waves encountered by the barge; and (2) inherent vice or nature of the subject matter insured. The House of Lords decided that the loss was caused by perils of the sea, inherent vice was not the cause of the loss which then made it unnecessary to decide the issue under the rules that apply to concurrent causes. Lord Clarke found that section 55(2)(c) is not an exception but an amplification of the proximate cause rule and thus an example of a circumstance of a loss not proximately caused by a peril insured against. Lord Mance[104] expressed no concluded view as to the application of the rules on concurrent causes in marine insurance. His Lordship stated that clause 4.4 on the face of it simply makes clear the continuing relevance in the context of all risks cover of the limitation on cover against perils of the sea provided by section 55(2)(c). His Lordship distinguished *The Miss Jay Jay* and *Midland Mainline Ltd v Eagle Star Insurance Co Ltd* since in those cases there were true exceptions that removed cover against an insured risk in a specific type of situation giving rise to such risk. In *The Cendor Mopu*, however, the hypothesis was '. . . two concurrent risks arising independently but combining to cause a loss'. His Lordship stated that it may be that the same principle applies (as the Court of Appeal's dicta in *The Miss Jay Jay* suggests), but he did not form any concluded views.

Ordinary wear and tear

Similar to inherent vice, in the case of ordinary wear and tear the loss occurs without any fortuitous external accident or casualty. It is inevitable for a ship which is used for carriage by sea to experience a certain degree of decay and diminution in value, which is commonly referred to as wear and tear. Ordinary wear and tear and ordinary leakage and breakage would cover loss or damage resulting from the normal vicissitudes of use in the case of a vessel, or of handling and carriage in the case of cargo.[105] Mustill J[106] in *The Miss Jay Jay* defined fortuity in reference to *The Xantho* that '. . . the purpose of the policy is to secure an indemnity against accidents which may happen, not against events which must happen.'[107] Ordinary wear tear and inherent vice falling within the category of 'which must happen' is not covered under the Marine Insurance Act 1906.[108]

102 [2012] 2 Lloyd's Rep 117, para 138.
103 [2012] 2 Lloyd's Rep 117, para 139. The finding about inherent vice was not appealed at the Court of Appeal [2013] Lloyd's Rep IR 485.
104 [2011] Lloyd's Rep IR 302, para 88.
105 [2011] Lloyd's Rep IR 302, para 81, Lord Mance.
106 [1985] 1 Lloyd's Rep 264, 272.
107 [1985] 1 Lloyd's Rep 264, 272.
108 See ICC 2009 (A,B,C) cl.4.2.

Negligence and misconduct of the assured or his employees or agents

The MIA 1906 section 55(2)(a) provides 'The insurer is not liable for any loss attributable to the wilful misconduct of the assured, but, unless the policy otherwise provides, he is liable for any loss proximately caused by a peril insured against, even though the loss would not have happened but for the misconduct or negligence of the master or crew.' That is, the insurer will be liable for the loss which was caused by the perils of the sea but would not have occurred but for the negligence of the assured or his servants or agents.[109] Where it is clear that the loss is immediately occasioned by a peril of the sea, the cause of the loss is still perils of the sea, despite being brought about by negligent navigation.[110] Recently in the Commercial Court Andrew Smith J approved this in *Venetico Marine SA v International General Insurance Co Ltd*[111] where the third officer was seriously negligent in that he did not do anything to prevent the vessel drifting on the current before she grounded or was about to ground. The judge found that it could not be accepted that the causal impact of his negligent omission was so potent in terms of efficiency as to displace as the proximate causes of the damage the events that he did not prevent.

As stated above with regard to entry of seawater, provided the immediate cause of the ingress is fortuitous, then prima facie the loss will be by perils of the sea. This is none the less so if the cause of the ingress is crew negligence.[112] However, wilful misconduct of the assured will provide a defence for the insurer. As section 55(2)(a) states, only the misconduct of the assured excuses the insurer from liability but not that of the servants' or agents'. Collins LJ stated in *Trinder Anderson & Co v Thames and Mersey Marine Insurance Co*[113] that 'The wilful default of the owner inducing the loss will debar him from suing on the policy in respect of it on two grounds, either of which would suffice to defeat his right: first, because no one can take advantage of his own wrong, using the word in its true sense which does not embrace mere negligence . . .; secondly, because the wilful act takes from the catastrophe the accidental character which is essential to constitute a peril of the sea.' Collins LJ emphasised[114] that 'the idea of something fortuitous and unexpected is involved in both the words "peril" or "accident". Nothing short, therefore, of dolus in its proper sense will defeat the right of the assured to recover in respect of a loss of which but for such dolus the proximate cause would be a peril of the sea'.[115]

Where two persons interested in the same property or adventure are jointly insured by one policy, the misconduct of one of the assureds is not sufficient to defend the claim for the other assured unless the insurance is joint, that is, the interests of the assureds are inseparably connected so that a loss or gain necessarily affects them both.[116] In the case of a composite insurance purchased for the benefit of a mortgagee and the owner of a vessel the interests are separable, thus, a defence applicable to the owner is not sufficient to contaminate the policy for the mortgagee.[117]

Misconduct may prevent the casualty from being fortuitous, so that a loss of a type which would, if it were fortuitous, be recoverable, cannot be recovered by the assured.[118] In *Samuel*

109 *Trinder Anderson & Co v Thames and Mersey Marine Insurance Co* [1898] 2 QB 114.

110 *Trinder Anderson & Co v Thames and Mersey Marine Insurance Co* [1898] 2 QB 114, 123, A.L. Smith LJ.

111 [2014] Lloyd's Rep IR 243, para 285.

112 *Versloot Dredging BV v HDI Gerling Industrie Versicherung AG* [2013] 2 Lloyd's Rep 131, para 36; *Seashore Marine SA v Phoenix Assurance plc (The Vergina) (No.2)* [2001] 2 Lloyd's Rep 698; *Venetico Marine SA v International General Insurance Co Ltd* [2014] Lloyd's Rep IR 243.

113 [1898] 2 QB 114, 127–128.

114 Referring to Lord Halsbury in *Hamilton v Pandorf* 12 App Cas 518, at p 524.

115 [1898] 2 QB 114, 127–128.

116 *Samuel v Dumas* [1924] AC 431.

117 *Samuel v Dumas* [1924] AC 431.

118 Arnould, para 22–07.

v *Dumas*[119] it was held that when a ship is scuttled the proximate cause of loss is the misconduct of those responsible, and not any peril of the sea. Viscount Cave said that 'There appears to me to be something absurd in saying that, when a ship is scuttled by her crew, her loss is not caused by the act of scuttling, but by the incursion of water which results from it. No doubt both are part of the chain of events which result in the loss of the ship, but the scuttling is the real and operative cause – the nearest antecedent which can be called a cause; and the subsequent events – the entry of the seawater, the slow filling of the hold and bilges, the failure of the pumps and the break-up of the vessel – are as much parts of the effect as is the final disappearance of the ship below the waves . . . On the whole I think that the scuttling of the *Grigorios* was the proximate cause of her loss.' Viscount Finlay[120] held that the scuttling of this vessel occurred on the seas, but it was not due to any peril of the sea. It was not fortuitous, but deliberate, and had nothing of the element of accident or casualty about it. The entrance of the seawater cannot for this purpose be separated from the act which caused it. A peril of the sea must be fortuitous, while here the seawater was let in deliberately.[121]

Delay

Losses caused by delay are excluded by section 55(2)(b) of the MIA 1906. The cases decided before the MIA 1906 indicate that delay was an excluded peril for two reasons: (1) traditionally delay was never covered by insurance policies; and (2) where there is a delay, in case of loss of perishable cargo, the cause of the loss was the nature of the cargo not the perils of the sea. In *Tatham v Hodgson*[122] the ship while carrying slaves from Africa to America was met by tempestuous weather and through the mere perils and dangers of the sea was greatly delayed in her voyage. The slaves died for shortage of food occasioned by the delay: instead of the ordinary voyage, which is from six to nine weeks, the voyage was not completed until after six months and eight days. The relevant legislation,[123] prohibited the owners recovering on account of the mortality of slaves by natural death. It was held that this was not a loss by the perils of the sea, but a mortality by natural death, thus the assured was not entitled for a recovery from the insurers. Holding otherwise, according to Grose J,[124] would have been opening a door to the very mischiefs that the Legislature intended to guard against; it would encourage the captains of slave ships to take an insufficient quantity of food for the sustenance of their slaves. Lawrence J[125] noted that if the slaves had died of fevers or other illness occasioned by the length of the voyage, the assured certainly could not have recovered. Here the length of the voyage occasioned the illness of which the slaves died.

    Tatham v Hodgson was applied in *Lawrence v Aberdein*[126] in which some cargo of animals was insured by the policy 'warranted free of mortality and jettison'. During the voyage some of the animals died from the violent pitching and rolling of the ship, occasioned by the storm and consequent agitation of the sea. Bayley J[127] held that the assured would have been entitled to recover, either in case of the total destruction of the animals, or for any less injury, provided it was occasioned by

119 [1924] AC 431, 446–447.
120 [1924] AC 431, 454.
121 [1924] AC 431, 454.
122 (1796) 6 Term Reports 656.
123 34 Geo. 3, c 80, s 10.
124 (1796) 6 Term Reports 656, 659.
125 (1796) 6 Term Reports 656, 659.
126 (1821) 5 Barnewall and Alderson 107.
127 (1821) 5 Barnewall and Alderson 107, 112.

any of the perils insured against. The words, 'warranted free from mortality', are introduced into this policy by the underwriter for his benefit. The word 'mortality' applies generally to that description of death which is not occasioned by violent means. Holroyd J[128] held that as the injury, which immediately preceded and caused the death of the animals, proceeded directly from the violence of the storm, the loss is to be considered a loss by the perils of the sea. In *Pink v Fleming*[129] the cargo of oranges and lemons were damaged because of delay as well as bad handling when they were discharged at a port where the ship was to be repaired after a collision. At the time this case was decided the proximate cause rule was 'the last cause [in] time' and the insurer was not liable for the reason that not the collision but the delay caused the loss that the cargo owner suffered. Bowen LJ[130] emphasised that it was not the collision or any peril of the sea but the perishable character of the articles combined with the handling in the one case and the delay in the other. In *Pink*, the Court applied *Taylor v Dunbar*[131] in which the claimant, a wholesale butcher in London, insured a cargo of dead pigs and beef shipped at Hamburg bound for London. The dead pigs were in no way affected or injured by the sea or by the storm or tempest: but it was discovered that the dead pigs, owing to the length of time to which the voyage was protracted and delayed by the weather, had become putrid; and they were necessarily thrown overboard at sea. Montague Smith J[132] stated that in *Taylor*, similar to that in the present case, the loss had arisen in consequence of the putrefaction of the meat from the voyage having been unusually protracted. That is a loss which does not fall within any of the perils enumerated in this policy. Retardation or delay was not insured by the policy and the meat was not affected by the sea or by the storm. The case was found to resemble *Tatham v Hodgson*. In distinguishing the case from *Lawrence v Aberdein*, Montague Smith J. said:[133]

> If we were to hold that a loss by delay, caused by bad weather or the prudence of the captain in anchoring to avoid it, was a loss by perils of the sea, we should be opening a door to claims for losses which never were intended to be covered by insurance, not only in the case of perishable goods, but in the case of goods of all other descriptions. By the common understanding both of assured and assurers, delay in the voyage has never been considered as covered by a policy like this.

Delay is also excluded by the Institute Cargo Clauses (A) (B) and (C) cl.4.5.

Insured perils under standard hull and cargo clauses

The Inchmaree Clause

The Inchmaree Clause is one of insurance against perils, though not necessarily perils of the sea.[134] In *Thames and Mersey Marine Insurance Co v Hamilton, Fraser & Co* the donkey-pump was destroyed by a valve being closed when the pump was being worked, and that valve was closed either through the negligence of the engineers of the vessel, or through a latent defect. Replacing the pump cost £72, which the assured claimed from the insurer. It was held that the closing of the valve was not

---

128 (1821) 5 Barnewall and Alderson 107, 114.
129 (1890) 25 QBD 396.
130 (1890) 25 QBD 396, 399.
131 (1868–69) LR 4 CP 206.
132 (1868–69) LR 4 CP 206, 209.
133 (1868–69) LR 4 CP 206, 211.
134 *Hutchins Bros v Royal Exchange Insurance Corp* [1911] 2 KB 398, 410, Fletcher Moulton LJ.

recoverable as it was not caused by a peril of the sea. The Inchmaree Clause was then introduced to give the protection denied by this decision.[135] It covers the negligence of servants, the explosion and bursting of boilers, the breakage of shafts, which is rather damage in itself than a peril causing damage, and loss or damage through latent defects.

Under the International Hull Clauses 2003 the Inchmaree clause is worded as follows:

> 2.2. This insurance covers loss of or damage to the subject matter insured caused by
>
> 2.2.1 bursting of boilers or breakage of shafts but does not cover any of the costs of repairing or replacing the boiler which bursts or the shaft which breaks
>
> 2.2.2 any latent defect in the machinery or hull but does not cover any of the costs of correcting the latent defect
>
> 2.2.3 negligence of Master, Officers, Crew or Pilots
>
> 2.2.4 negligence of repairers or charterers provided such repairers or charterers are not an Assured under this insurance
>
> 2.2.5 barratry of Master, Officers or Crew
>
> provided that such loss or damage has not resulted from want of due diligence by the Assured, Owners or Managers.

Bursting of boilers or breakage of shafts

Breakage of shafts covers only damage to hull or machinery caused by it.[136] For instance, if, by reason of the breakage of the shaft, the machine is torn to pieces, such loss will be covered by the Inchmaree clause. On the other hand, the breakage of the shaft itself is not covered for the reason that such loss is not loss of or damage to machinery caused by the breakage of the shaft.

Latent defect in the machinery or hull

A latent defect is a defect which could not be discovered on such an examination as a reasonably careful skilled man would make.[137] The Inchmaree clause intends to make the insurer liable for the loss which was caused by the latent defect during the currency of the policy. Thus, in any claim under the Inchmaree clause, the assured has to prove some change in the physical state of the vessel. If a latent defect has existed at the commencement of the policy period and all that has happened is that the assured has discovered the existence of that latent defect then there has been no loss 'through a latent defect';[138] in such a case the vessel is in the same condition as it was at the commencement of the period.

In *Oceanic SS Co v Faber*, Walton J construed the Inchmaree clause in the following words:

> . . . the effect and sense of this clause is not that the underwriters guarantee that the machinery of the vessel is free from latent defects, or undertake, if such defects are discovered during the currency of a policy, to make such defects good . . . The underwriters agree to indemnify the owner against any loss of or damage to the hull or machinery through any latent defect, so that a claim does not fall within the clause unless there is loss of or damage to hull or

---

135 *Oceanic SS Co v Faber* (1906) 11 Com Cas 179 approved by CA (1907) 13 Com Cas 28; *Hutchins Bros v Royal Exchange Insurance Corp* [1911] 2 KB 398, 403–404; Scrutton J.

136 *Oceanic SS Co v Faber*; *Hutchins Bros v Royal Exchange Insurance Corp* [1911] 2 KB 398.

137 *Charles Brown & Co Ltd v Nitrate Producers Steamship Co Ltd* (1937) 58 Ll L Rep 188; *Prudent Tankers SA v Dominion Insurance Co* (*The Caribbean Sea*) [1980] 1 Lloyd's Rep 338, 347–348.

138 *Oceanic SS Co v Faber*; *Hutchins Bros v Royal Exchange Insurance Corp* [1911] 2 KB 398.

machinery or some part of the hull or machinery, and there is no claim unless that damage has been caused through a latent defect ... Therefore there must be a latent defect causing loss of or damage to the hull or machinery, and causing that loss of or damage to the hull or machinery, during the currency of the policy under which the claim is made.

In *Oceanic SS Co v Faber* during the currency of the policy, a fracture was discovered in the shaft when the vessel was docked at San Francisco. The shipowners were obliged to replace the shaft by a new one the cost of which they claimed from the underwriters. Walton J found that the fracture was caused by imperfect welding made in 1891. The flaw arising from the imperfect welding had not made itself visible on the surface until 1902 in the form of a crack. The loss or damage here was the fracture, the crack. The crack was the development of the flaw that was a manifestation of the latent defect. Such development of a latent defect, in the view of Walton J, was not 'damage to the machinery through a latent defect'. In other words, it was not a damage caused by the latent defect, but it was the latent defect itself.

Walton J's speech in *Ocean* was applied in *Hutchins Bros v Royal Exchange Insurance Corp*[139] in which case in casting the stern frame of the vessel a defect was caused, which made the stern frame an inappropriate stern frame to put into any vessel. That defect had been concealed by the makers of the stern frame with some metal and steel wash; and such was the condition of the vessel when the policy was executed. During the currency of the policy, the defect was discovered while the ship was undergoing repairs. The owner claimed the cost of replacing a stern frame because of a crack or fissure. This was also held to be a latent defect itself. Fletcher Moulton LJ[140] said:

> To hold that the clause covers it would be to make the underwriters not insurers, but guarantors, and to turn the clause into a warranty that the hull and machinery are free from latent defects, and, consequently, to make all such defects repairable at the expense of the underwriters.

Damage to hull or machinery caused through a latent defect in the machinery is something different from damage involved in a latent defect in the machinery itself.[141] In *Scindia Steamships (London) Ltd v London Assurance*[142] the shaft was subjected to an ordinary operation of repair, which any shaft of proper strength and construction would be able to sustain without any difficulty. However, owing to what was described as a 'smooth flaw extending downwards from the top as the shaft then lay' deep into the metal, involving about one-half of the material, the other half of the shaft remained and was broken. The only damage beyond the damage to the propeller (which was paid by the underwriter) was the actual damage which happened to the shaft itself, that is, the breakage of the shaft. Branson J noted that there was no proof that the latent defect developed during the currency of the policy. The latent defect existed before the risk attached under the policy in question, it went on developing, and the shaft was broken not by anything in the shape of a peril, but to an ordinary operation of ship repairing. Thus, the underwriters were not liable for the cost of repair or replacement of the defective shaft itself.

In *Hutchins Bros v Royal Exchange Insurance Corp*[143] Scrutton J listed what is recoverable under this part of the Inchmaree Clause. Accordingly,

---

139 [1911] 2 KB 398.
140 [1911] 2 KB 398, 411.
141 *Scindia Steamships (London) Ltd v London Assurance* [1937] 1 KB 639, 651.
142 [1937] 1 KB 639.
143 [1911] 2 KB 398, 406.

1   Actual total loss of a part of the hull or machinery, through a latent defect coming into existence and causing the loss during the period of the policy.[144]
2   Constructive total loss under the same circumstances, as where, though the part of the hull survives, it is by reason of the latent defect of no value and cannot be profitably repaired.
3   Damage to other parts of the hull happening during the currency of the policy, through a latent defect, even if the latter came into existence before the period of the policy. The pre-existing latent defect which becomes visible during the policy itself is not damage, indemnity for which is recoverable.

A claim made under the Inchmaree clause was accepted in *CJ Wills & Sons v World Marine Insurance Co Ltd (The Mermaid)*.[145] The *Mermaid* was a dredger, which had two chains for hoisting up her dredging ladder, each some 500 feet long with over 1,000 links were supplied in 1890 and 1892 respectively. In 1909 a link broke when the ladder was being hoisted. The dredger was in motion, the end of the ladder dropped to the bottom of the water, it stuck, and the ladder was turned over. It fell on the dredger deck and caused extensive damage. The broken link was found hanging on the chain and a defect was found in the weld. If the weld had been sound and without defect the link, though worn, would have been of ample strength to stand the strain. This was a latent defect which caused damage to hull and machinery.

Exceptions

Where the defect is attributable to ordinary wear and tear, there can be no recovery under the Inchmaree clause.[146] Goff J stated in *The Caribbean Sea*[147] that if defects develop as a result of a defective design in the ship as she trades, e.g. if such defects develop and have the result that a fracture occurs and the ship sinks, such a loss is not caused by ordinary wear and tear, and so is not excluded by s.55(2)(c) of the Act. A ship may be properly and carefully maintained and yet a defect may not be discovered although a more meticulous examination would have revealed its existence.[148]

If the loss was caused through inherent vice the exception will override the Inchmaree clause which otherwise covers loss of or damage to the subject matter insured through latent defects. The *Scindia* case supports this conclusion.[149] This is in line with the principles explained in The *Cendor Mopu* that if the loss is caused by inherent vice there is no room for the operation of perils of the sea.[150]

Additional cover for loss of or damage to the hull or machinery

The Court of Appeal's judgment in *Promet Engineering (Singapore) Pte Ltd v Sturge (The Nukila)*[151] prompted some modifications of the Inchmaree clause when IHC 2003 was drafted. The *Nukila* was a mobile self-elevating accommodation and work platform with three legs which ended in a spudcan, effectively a large steel box strengthened with internal bulkheads and brackets. The circumferential welds attaching the top plates of the spudcans to the legs were not properly profiled. From 1983

---

144 This was the kind of latent defect alleged in the *Inchmaree* case.
145 13 March 1911. The case is reported in a note at [1980] 1 Lloyd's Rep 350.
146 *Prudent Tankers SA v Dominion Insurance Co (The Caribbean Sea)* [1980] 1 Lloyd's Rep 338, 347.
147 [1980] 1 Lloyd's Rep 338, 347.
148 [1980] 1 Lloyd's Rep 338, 347.
149 See pp 647–648 and Arnould, para 23–59.
150 *The Cendor Mopu* [2011] Lloyd's Rep IR 302.
151 [1997] 2 Lloyd's Rep 146.

to February 1987 the Nukila operated without any untoward incident. But in February 1987, whilst a routine inspection of the legs and spudcans was being carried out by divers, they observed serious cracks in the top-plates of all three of the spudcans. Closer examination revealed that the metal of the legs themselves also contained serious cracks as did some of the internal bulkheads of the spudcans. The condition revealed was dangerous and threatened the whole safety of the Nukila. Repairs were carried out and the owners sought to recover from the defendant underwriters. Hobhouse LJ emphasised that where marine structures are badly designed that may lead to a concentration of stress which will then over a period of time cause the condition of metal fatigue to arise. The fatigue crack will continue to grow until the metal shears or some other failure of the structure occurs. The presence of a fatigue crack will weaken the structure and therefore tend to cause other fractures or failures of the structure. Hobhouse LJ found that at the commencement of the period of cover there was a latent defect in the welds joining the underside of the top-plate of each spudcan to the external surface of the leg tube. The cracking occurred as a result of the ordinary working of the platform at sea and the presence of the latent defects in the welds. Those features during the period of cover caused extensive fractures in the full thickness of the tube extending in places both above and below the defective weld, extensive fractures in the metal of the top-plating and bulkheads of the spudcans and other fractures at other locations. According to Hobhouse LJ this was on any ordinary use of language damage to the subject matter insured, the hull, of the Nukila caused by the condition of the Nukila at the commencement of the period, that is, by the latent defects. As Hobhouse LJ noted, the facts of the Nukila are different to Scindia in which no loss by a peril insured against had been proved. In Scindia the shaft was already in a condition which required it to be condemned and its value was already no more than its scrap value. Moreover, in the cases referred to above in which the latent defect became clear no loss was proved to have occurred during the currency of the policy, what occurred was only that the latent defect became visible. The amount recovered included the cost of repairing the defect itself and not simply the cost of making good the additional damage caused by the defect.

The wording of the IHC 2003 now provides that the insurer and the assured should share the cost of repairing the defect itself. The IHC 2003 clause 2.3 provides: 'Where there is a claim recoverable under Clause 2.2.1, this insurance shall also cover one half of the costs common to the repair of the burst boiler or the broken shaft and to the repair of the loss or damage caused thereby.'

Clause 2.4 of the IHC 2003 provides similar cover for the correction of the latent defect and to the repair of the loss or damage caused thereby.

Under the IHC 2003 the assured may claim full indemnity for the cost of repairing or replacing any boiler or shaft or the cost of correcting a latent defect. In Part 2 of the IHC Clause 41 (Additional Perils) is worded as follows:

41.1 If the Underwriters have expressly agreed in writing, this insurance covers
    41.1.1 the costs of repairing or replacing any boiler which bursts or shaft which breaks, where such bursting or breakage has caused loss of or damage to the subject matter insured covered by Clause 2.2.1, and that half of the costs common to the repair of the burst boiler or the broken shaft and to the repair of the loss or damage caused thereby which is not covered by Clause 2.3
    41.1.2 the costs of correcting a latent defect where such latent defect has caused loss of or damage to the subject matter insured covered by Clause 2.2.2, and that half of the costs common to the correction of the latent defect and to the repair of the loss or damage caused thereby which is not covered by Clause 2.4
    41.1.3 loss of or damage to the vessel caused by any accident or by negligence, incompetence or error or judgment of any person whatsoever

Provided that such loss or damage has not resulted from want of due diligence by the Assured, Owners or Managers.[152]

Unseaworthiness and coverage for latent defect

Causation and seaworthiness has been discussed above. A question may arise that is, which of the warranty of seaworthiness or the Inchmaree clause will take precedence when the two types of clause are inserted in a marine policy insuring the hull and machinery of a vessel? As fully analysed in Chapter 5 in a voyage policy, under s.39(1) of the MIA 1906, there is an implied warranty of seaworthiness at the commencement of the voyage. Breach of a warranty automatically discharges the insurer from liability. Thus, where a shipowner is in breach of the implied seaworthiness warranty under s.39(1), the risk never attaches and in case the ship is lost on a voyage, the insurer will not be liable for the loss irrespective of its cause. Section 39(5) does not imply a similar warranty in a time policy, however, the insurer will not be liable for the loss which is attributable to the unseaworthiness of the vessel if the vessel was sent on a voyage in an unseaworthy state with the knowledge of the assured. Therefore, in a time policy, risk may attach despite the unseaworthy state of the vessel and if there are claims which were caused by perils of the sea the insurer will be liable for the loss, and if a loss is caused by unseaworthiness the insurer may or may not be liable depending on proof of the assured being aware of the unseaworthiness. In the *Lydia Flag*, Moore Bick J construed a contractual seaworthiness warranty in a time policy that was inserted in the policy by the parties. The vessel lost its rudder in 1996. The loss of the rudder was caused as a result of negligence of some kind on the part of ship repairers who dismantled the rudder and reassembled it for the purposes of examining the tail shaft when the vessel was dry-docked in Piraeus in December, 1995. The policy contained a number of warranties of which No. 11 provided 'Warranted that at the inception of this policy the vessel named herein shall be in seaworthy condition and thereafter during the valid period of this policy the insured shall exercise due diligence to keep the vessel seaworthy and in all respects fit, tight and properly manned, equipped and supplied.' The policy also contained the Inchmaree Clause, which covered negligence of repairers. The question was one of construction of how warranty 11 was to be read in conjunction with the Inchmaree Clause. Moore Bick J said 'One would be surprised to find that having taken insurance of this kind and the vessel being unseaworthy by reason of a latent defect at the inception of the policy the owners would be completely without cover if the vessel was lost as a result, for example, of a collision with another vessel for which no fault could be attached to the owners of the vessel simply because there was a latent defect which had not in any way contributed to the casualty. That leads me to wonder whether a sensible construction can be placed on this policy which would not deprive the owners of cover under circumstances of that kind but would still give some meaning to all the clauses of the policy.' The judge then emphasised that under this policy certain points are specifically covered and one of the risks specifically covered was the presence of a latent defect. Accepting the owner's counsel's argument the judge also noted that Warranty No. 11 was worded in absolute but wholly general terms. The Inchmaree clause, on the other hand, deals with certain identified perils which are specifically covered by the policy. The construction that Moore Bick J approved was to read the Inchmaree clause as providing, where appropriate, exceptions upon the general terms of the warranty contained in Warranty No. 11.

It is seen that Moore Bick J's judgment relies on construction of the policy terms. The case does not lay down any generally applicable principle either to time or voyage policies. The editors

---

152 Under Clause 41.1.3 master, officers, crew or pilots shall not be considered owners within the meaning of Clause 41.1 should they hold shares in the vessel.

of Arnould[153] state that a similar approach to construction would be appropriate in relation to the implied warranty in a voyage policy.

The facts of The *Lydia Flag* are not easy, given that the parties included a seaworthiness warranty in a time policy, the warranty included a due diligence provision and the policy covered negligence of repairers which led to the latent defect and therefore unseaworthiness. Unseaworthiness in time and voyage policies should be distinguished carefully. In a time policy whether unseaworthiness is an excepted peril or not depends on the assured's knowledge of the unseaworthy state of the vessel as well as the question of whether the loss was attributable to the unseaworthiness. If the loss is not attributable to the unseaworthiness – assuming that the cause was an insured peril – the insurer will be liable. A vessel's unseaworthy state, in a time policy, does not on its own suffice to discharge the insurer from liability. However, if the loss was caused by the unseaworthiness, and if the assured is privy to such unseaworthiness the insurer will not be liable. In other words, in a time policy, if a latent defect caused unseaworthiness, and if the assured is complicit in the unseaworthiness, and if the loss was attributable to it, the insurer will not be liable. However, if the assured's privity cannot be established, or the loss is not deemed attributable to the unseaworthiness, as held in The *Miss Jay Jay*, the insurer will be liable. Moore-Bick J's judgment above seems to be in line with this analysis although the policy contained an unseaworthiness warranty which contains a due diligence provision. It seems unlikely that this analysis will be applicable to voyage policies where warranties are subject to much harsher principles. In a voyage policy if the vessel was unseaworthy because of a latent defect the risk never attaches therefore it is not possible to hold the insurer liable unless the insurer waives the breach of warranty.

Due diligence

In the proviso to the Inchmaree clauses, 'want of due diligence' is a lack of reasonable care.[154] Negligence constitutes a covered peril in its own right, but it is limited to the negligence of specified persons – the master, officers, crew, pilots, repairers and charterers are identified in the Inchmaree clause. But the negligence of the assured itself is not covered.[155] Thus, insurer's non-liability may be proved by proof of negligence of the assured who is not listed under the Inchmaree clause. The Underwriters bear the burden of proving the two requisite elements, namely that the assured was negligent and that such negligence was causative of the loss.

The Collision Liability Clause

Clause 6.1. of IHC 2003 provides:

> The Underwriters agree to indemnify the Assured for three fourths of any sum or sums paid by the Assured to any other person or persons by reason of the Assured becoming legally liable by way of damages for
> 6.1.1. loss of or damage to any other vessel or property thereon
> 6.1.2. delay to or loss of use of any such other vessel or property thereon

---

153 Arnould, para 23–58.

154 *Sealion Shipping Ltd v Valiant Insurance Co.* Blair J followed Nova Scotia Court of Appeal in *Secunda Marine Services Ltd v Liberty Mutual Insurance Co* 2006 NSCA 82 holding that the standard is one of negligence [2012] 1 Lloyd's Rep 252, para 101–102; *Versloot Dredging BV v HDI Gerling Industrie Versicherung AG* [2013] 2 Lloyd's Rep 131, para 70.

155 *Sealion Shipping Ltd v Valiant Insurance Co* [2012] 1 Lloyd's Rep 252, para 101. The case was appealed but the due diligence point was not argued on appeal. [2013] 1 Lloyd's Rep 108.

6.1.3   general average of, salvage of, or salvage under contract of, any such other vessel or
        property thereon,

where such payment by the Assured is in consequence of the insured vessel coming into collision
with any other vessel.

Some liabilities are excluded by Clause 6.4. For instance removal or disposal of obstructions, wrecks, cargoes or any other things whatsoever (6.4.1) and the cargo or other property on, or the engagements of, the insured vessel (6.4.3), loss of life, personal injury of illness (6.4.4) are not covered by IHC.[156]

Legally liable to pay as damages

Damages for which the assured may be liable and may claim from the insurers under the collision liability clause encompasses contractual as well as tortious liability. It was held in *Hall Bros Steamship Co Ltd v Young*[157] that the clause does not extend to every pecuniary liability arising in respect of the collision but only to such liabilities as arise by way of damages.[158] 'Damages' are sums which fall to be paid by reason of some breach of duty or obligation, whether that duty or obligation is imposed by contract, by the general law, or legislation.[159] In *Hall Bros*, the *Trident* was insured under the Institute Time Clauses which contained a similar clause to that stated above. While proceeding with a cargo of cereals from the River Plate to Dunkirk, the *Trident* arrived off Dunkirk and stopped to take up a pilot. The pilot boat *Vétéran*, which belonged to the Pilotage Administration of Dunkirk, was drawing alongside the vessel when her steering gear broke down and she came into collision with the vessel. The vessel and the pilot boat were both damaged. It was admitted that the *Trident* was in no way to blame. French law had a provision that damage sustained by the pilot boat in the course of pilotage operations was chargeable to the ship, unless the pilot had been guilty of gross negligence ('faute lourde'). The shipowner paid for the pilot boat's damages and then claimed three-quarters of that sum from the underwriters under the collision liability clause.

The insurer was found not to be liable for the loss in question for the reason that the payments 'by way of damages' to which it refers are payments which the obligation to make arises from a fault of some kind on the part of the ship insured.[160] The obligation which arises is an obligation to make good the damage suffered by the pilot vessel in the circumstances stated. It has nothing to do with any duty on the vessel itself, but it is a provision under which the vessel is compelled to bear a particular charge irrespective of any question of duty imposed upon it. *Hall Bros* was applied in *Bedfordshire Police Authority v Constable*[161] in which case the question was whether a police authority's obligation, under the provisions of the Riot (Damages) Act 1886, to compensate property owners for damage to their property caused by riots, is covered by the public liability section of an insurance policy. The relevant section promises to indemnify the assured authority in respect of sums which the authority 'may become legally liable to pay as damages for accidental damage to property arising out of the business' of the authority.

Longmore LJ[162] focused on the reason for the 1886 Act placing the burden of paying compensation to the victims of riot damage on the police authority, which is that the police are

---

156 For the full list of exclusions see Clause 6.4 IHC. The excluded risks under clause 6.4 may be insured by P&I clubs.
157 [1939] 1 KB 748.
158 [1939] 1 KB 748, 756, Sir Wilfrid Greene MR.
159 [1939] 1 KB 748, 756, Sir Wilfrid Greene MR.
160 [1939] 1 KB 748, 759, Sir Wilfrid Greene MR.
161 [2009] Lloyd's Rep IR 607.
162 [2009] Lloyd's Rep IR 607, para 26.

responsible for law and order and that they are (notionally) in breach of that responsibility. It follows that once the police are in breach of such responsibility the compensation payable is a sum which the police authority is 'liable to pay as damages'.

Collision with any other vessel

Clause 6.1. requires a collision with any other vessel. In *McCowan v Baine, The Niobe*,[163] it was held that it would be a narrow interpretation of its wording if it is read as 'a ship cannot be said to "come into collision with any other ship" except by direct contact, causing damage, between the two hulls (including under the term hull all parts of a ship's structure).' While the *Niobe* was being towed to Cardiff her tug came into collision with and sank another vessel, whose owners recovered damages both from the *Niobe* and the tug. In an action by the owners of the *Niobe* upon the policy against one of the underwriters for payment of his proportion of the sum paid by such owners on account of the collision, the underwriter pleaded that under the policy he was only liable for damage arising from the collision with the *Niobe*. The majority of the House of Lords held that the collision of the tug with the damaged vessel must be taken to have been a collision of the *Niobe* with another vessel within the meaning of the policy, and that the underwriters were liable. The rule was extended to cases in which the injury was caused by the impact, not only of the hull of the ship insured, but of her boats or steam launch, even if those accessories were not (as in this case) insured as being, in effect, parts of the ship.[164] Where a ship in tow has control over the navigation of the tug, the two vessels – each physically attached to the other for a common operation, that of the voyage of the ship in tow, for which the tug supplies the power to sail – were for many purposes one vessel.[165] In *The Niobe* the decision of the House of Lords rested upon the interpretation that the tug was part of the apparatus of the tow.[166] It was accordingly held that the tow was to blame although there had not been in fact any contact between her and the other vessel. In *Bennett Steamship Co Ltd v Hull Mutual Steamship Protecting Society Ltd*,[167] Lord Reading refused to extend *The Niobe* to a case in which a vessel ran into the nets attached to and extending from a fishing vessel which was about a mile distant from the steamship; there was no contact between the hulls of the two vessels.

Cross liability

Clause 6.2. of IHC provides:

> The indemnity provided by this Clause 6 shall be in addition to the indemnity provided by the other terms and conditions of this insurance and shall be subject to the following provisions:
> 6.2.1 where the insured vessel is in collision with another vessel and both vessels are to blame then, unless the liability of one or both vessels becomes limited by law, the indemnity under this Clause 6 shall be calculated on the principle of cross-liabilities as if the respective Owners had been compelled to pay to each other such proportion of each other's damages as may have been properly allowed in ascertaining the balance or sum payable by or to the Assured in consequence of the collision
> 6.2.2 in no case shall the total liability of the Underwriters under Clauses 6.1 and 6.2 exceed their proportionate part of three fourths of the insured value of the insured vessel in respect of any one collision.

---

163 [1891] AC 401, 404.
164 [1891] AC 401, 404.
165 [1891] AC 401, 404.
166 *Bennett Steamship Co Ltd v Hull Mutual Steamship Protecting Society Ltd* [1914] 3 KB 57, 60 Lord Reading.
167 [1914] 3 KB 57, 60.

Thus, it appears that liability between the shipowners and their respective underwriters, unless the liability of one or both vessels becomes limited by law, is determined on a different principle from that governing the liabilities of the shipowners *inter se*.

Assuming that a collision occurs between two vessels, A and B, and both vessels have the same fault and A suffers £1,000 of loss and B's loss is £4,000, A will be liable for half of B's loss and B will be liable for half of A's loss. A will claim from the hull underwriters £1,000 plus three-fourths of his liability to B. In other words, in addition to £1,000, A will claim three-fourths of £2,000. A's insurer will have subrogation rights against B for half of the loss A suffered, i.e., £500. B will claim from his insurer £4,000 and three-fourths of £500 and B's underwriter will have subrogation rights against A for £2,000.

Fire and explosion

Fire involves combustion or ignition.[168] Mere heating, which has not arrived at the stage of incandescence or ignition is not fire.[169] Nevertheless, *The Knight of St Michael*[170] demonstrates that this is not an absolute rule but in some exceptional cases the loss may still be covered as a fire peril under the policy although there was not an ignition as it was prevented by the assured. In this case, 3,206 tons of coal was shipped at Newcastle, New South Wales to be carried to Valparaiso. The freight was payable on delivery. The owner insured the freight under a policy in the then usual form, which covered 'fire' as well as '. . . of all other perils, losses, and misfortunes.' The vessel sailed for Valparaiso on 1 February. On 2 February it was discovered that part of the cargo was hot, and that the heat was increasing rapidly. The master, for the general safety of the ship, freight and cargo, determined to put into the port of Sydney. The vessel arrived at Sydney on 4 February. Following surveys held on the cargo 1,706 tons of coal were discharged and sold. The vessel finally delivered the remaining 1,500 tons of coal at Valparaiso. No freight was paid in respect of the coal sold at Sydney, and the owner claimed his loss from the underwriters. It was necessary for the safety of the whole voyage for the vessel to discharge the cargo in the port of Sydney. Having noted such necessity, Gorell Barnes J held that it was reasonably certain that if she had continued on her direct voyage the temperature of the coal would have continued to rise until spontaneous combustion ensued, and that had she so continued the ship and cargo would in all probability have been destroyed by fire. The question was, under these circumstances, was the loss of freight caused by perils insured against? Fire was an insured peril but it did not actually break out. It was, however, reasonably certain that it would have broken out, and the condition of the ship and cargo was such that there was an actual existing state of peril of fire, and not merely a fear of fire. Gorell Barnes J found no difference between these facts and where the fire actually broken out. In the alternative, the judge held that if this cannot, strictly speaking, be termed a loss by fire, it was a loss *ejusdem generis*, and covered by the general words 'all other losses and misfortunes, &c.' The current Institute Freight clauses do not contain the general words. However, considering the circumstances of *The Knight of St Michael*, the loss occasioned where action is taken to avert an imminent outbreak of fire, is covered by the policy as it is still regarded as loss by fire.[171]

As referred to above, crew negligence is not excluded therefore, if the fire is as a result of the negligence of the crew, that is covered by the policy. Arson by a third party is covered by the risk

---

168 Arnould, para 23–29.
169 *Tempus Shipping Co Ltd v Louis Dreyfus & Co* [1930] 1 KB 699, 708, Wright J.
170 [1898] p 30.
171 Arnould, para 23–29.

of fire. In *Schiffshypothekenbank Zu Luebeck AG v Norman Philip Compton (The Alexion Hope)*[172] Lloyd LJ stated[173] 'In principle, I find it difficult to draw a distinction between setting something on fire and the fire itself, as the proximate cause of the loss which follows. Different considerations may well be held to apply in the case of perils of the sea, since perils of the sea are defined by r. 7 of the Rules of Construction annexed to the Marine Insurance Act as referring only "to fortuitous accidents or casualties of the seas". There is no such limitation in the case of fire.' Lloyd LJ emphasised that s.55(2)(a) uses the phrase 'The insurer is not liable for any loss attributable to the wilful misconduct of the assured', not 'or any third party.'

The word 'explosion' implies some sudden violent and noisy event resulting from a chemical or similar reaction, so that the rupture of the outer casing of a boiler by a piece of its metal blower which had broken off internally was not an explosion, even if it appeared to be one to observers.[174]

Piracy

Piracy is a forcible robbery at sea.[175] The MIA 1906 Schedule 1 rule 8 provides 'The term "pirates" includes passengers who mutiny and rioters who attack the ship from the shore.' In the context of insurance business piracy may take place in an open sea or territorial waters.[176] In *Athens Maritime Enterprises Corp v Hellenic Mutual War Risks Association (Bermuda) (The Andreas Lemos)*[177] Staughton J said 'I see no reason to limit piracy to acts outside territorial waters.'[178] The motive of an act of robbery is also taken into account to determine whether it is a piratical act, that is, if a robbery at sea is motivated by public and political objectives this will not be piracy.[179] In *Bolivia v Indemnity Mutual Marine Assurance Co Ltd*[180] goods which belonged to the Bolivian Government, and were intended for Bolivian troops, were insured upon a voyage from a place at the mouth of the Amazon to Bolivia. The insurance covered 'pirates' and 'all other perils'. During the course of the voyage the vessel was stopped by an armed vessel called the *Solimoes*. Those on board the *Solimoes*, who were acting on behalf of the republic which wanted to re-establish itself, seized and carried away the whole of the goods insured. Pickford J[181] analysed the business meaning of the word 'piracy', that its essence consists in the pursuit of private, in contrast to public, ends. The judge stated that primarily the pirate is a man who satisfies his personal greed or his personal vengeance through robbery or murder. Pickford J distinguished this from a man who acts with a public object whose moral attitude is different, and the acts themselves will be kept within well-marked bounds. Thus, a pirate in the business sense is a man who is plundering indiscriminately for his own ends, and not a man who is simply operating against the property of a particular State for a public end. Such an act may be illegal and even criminal and may be described as piracy by international law, but it is not, within the meaning of a policy of insurance.[182]

Thus, it appears that there are two different analyses of piracy: piracy within the business sense that an insurer agrees to insure and piracy in public law, that is, in international law (*jure gentium*).

---

172 [1988] 1 Lloyd's Rep 311.
173 [1988] 1 Lloyd's Rep 311, 316.
174 *Commonwealth Smelting Ltd v Guardian Royal Exchange Ltd* [1986] 1 Lloyd's Rep 121.
175 *Republic of Bolivia v Indemnity Mutual Marine Assurance Co Ltd* [1909] 1 KB 785, Kennedy LJ.
176 *Athens Maritime Enterprises Corp v Hellenic Mutual War Risks Association (Bermuda) (The Andreas Lemos)* [1983] QB 647, 655.
177 [1983] QB 647.
178 [1983] QB 647, 658.
179 *Republic of Bolivia v Indemnity Mutual Marine Assurance Co Ltd* [1909] 1 KB 785.
180 [1909] 1 KB 785.
181 Approved by the Court of Appeal [1909] 1 KB 785.
182 See also *Rickards v Forestal Land Timber & Railways Co Ltd (The Minden)* [1942] AC 50, 80, Lord Wright.

In the business sense the meaning of piracy is determined in the particular contract upon which the action is brought.[183] In *Re Piracy Jure Gentium*[184] it was held that actual robbery is not an essential element in the crime of piracy *jure gentium*, and that a frustrated attempt to commit piratical robbery is equally piracy *jure gentium*. Staughton J discussed further elements of piracy in *The Andreas Lemos*.[185] The judge held that in accordance with the commercial sense of the matter theft without force or a threat of force is not piracy under a policy of marine insurance. The judge explained that by the word 'piracy' an insurer insures the loss caused to shipowners because their employees are overpowered by force, or terrified into submission. Staughton J found the very notion of piracy inconsistent with clandestine theft. Thus, 'piracy' does not cover the loss caused to shipowners when their nightwatchman is asleep, and thieves steal clandestinely. The judge added that 'It is not necessary that the thieves must raise the pirate flag and fire a shot across the victim's bows before they can be called pirates. But piracy is not committed by stealth.' Moreover, the judge held that where the act of appropriation of the insured property is completed before any force is used or threatened, this does not constitute piracy. If an act of stealing does not fall within the definition of piracy as occurred in *Bolivia* it might be analysed under violent theft.

Masefield AG v Amlin Corporate Member Ltd[186] is mentioned elsewhere in this book.[187] In this case the vessel *Bunga Melati Dua* was captured by pirates together with cargoes of biodiesel on board. The vessel and cargo was recovered about 11 weeks after the vessel was captured. Piracy was an insured peril but the loss claimed by the assured was economic loss and the facts did not satisfy the requirements of either actual or constructive total loss, thus the insurer won the dispute.

Thieves

The term 'thieves' does not cover clandestine theft or a theft committed by any one of the ship's company, whether crew or passengers (MIA Schedule 1, rule 9). The theft must be by one or more outsiders. The word 'violent' refers only to the manner of the theft; it is not, therefore, necessary that any individual has been harmed or threatened with harm. That was decided in *La Fabriques de Produits Chimiques v Large*,[188] in which it was held to be sufficient that crowbars had been used to force entry. The effect of this decision is to equate 'violent theft' with that which is not 'clandestine'.

Barratry of master, officers or crew

Barratry means an act of the master or mariners of a ship in fraud of his duty to his owners.[189] Rule 11 of the MIA 1906 Schedule 1 describes barratry as 'every wrongful act wilfully committed by the master or crew to the prejudice of the owner, or, as the case may be, the charterer'. It is a necessary ingredient of the definition that the wilful act should have been committed 'to the prejudice of the owner'.[190] The onus is on the insurer to prove that the requirements of barratry were met

---

183 *Republic of Bolivia v Indemnity Mutual Marine Assurance Co Ltd* [1909] 1 KB 785, Kennedy LJ.

184 [1934] AC 586.

185 [1983] QB 647.

186 [2011] Lloyd's Rep IR 338.

187 See the chapters on Sue and Labour, Actual Total Loss, Constructive Total Loss.

188 [1923] 1 KB 203.

189 *Bottomley v Bovill* (1826) 5 B & C 210, 212.

190 *Continental Illinois National Bank & Trust Co of Chicago v Alliance Assurance Co Ltd (The Captain Panagos DP)* [1989] 1 Lloyd's Rep 33, 40, Neill LJ.

on the facts.[191] Where the master, intentionally and successfully, let water into the ship for the purpose of sinking her, it would be a barratry unless it was done with the privity of the owner. In *Vallejo v Wheeler*[192] the vessel was chartered for a voyage from London to Seville, she was to stop at some port in the west of Cornwall, to take in provisions. After she sailed from London the master deviated to Guernsey, which was out of the course of the voyage. The captain went there for his own convenience, to take in brandy and wine on his own account, after which he intended to proceed to Cornwall. The ship sprung a leak after she left Guernsey, she was refitted at Dartmouth. On her way to Cornwall from there she received further damage, and at her arrival was totally incapable of proceeding on the voyage, and the goods were much damaged. It was held that 'knavery of the masters or mariners' fell within the definition of barratry. Where it is a deviation with the consent of the owner of the vessel, and the master is not acting for his own private interest, it is nothing but a deviation with the consent of the owner, and the underwriter is excused. This was however a case of a barratry as the master acted for his own benefit, and without the consent, or privity, or any intended good to his owner. Barratry is not confined to the running away with the ship, but comprehends every species of fraud, knavery or criminal conduct in the master by which the owners or freighters are injured.[193] Thus, it also appears that where the owner consents to the criminal or fraudulent act of the master, that is not a barratry.[194]

Barratry is distinguished from scuttling for which there must be connivance of the owners to the barratrous acts of the crew.[195] Proof of privity of the assured to the barratrous act of the crew is on the insurer. In *The Elias Issaias*[196] the Court of Appeal rejected the argument that proof of scuttling creates presumption that the insurer was privy to the deliberate sinking of the vessel.

Improper treatment of the vessel by the captain will not constitute barratry. This may damage the vessel but it is not a barratry unless it is proved that the master acted against his own judgment.[197] In *Todd v Ritchie*, the ship was damaged as a result of the captain's act in that when she sprung a leak, before any survey had taken place, he broke up her ceiling and end bows with crowbars. There was no evidence of any criminal intent on the part of the captain, his object was apparently to ensure her condemnation. Lord Ellenborough said that 'in order to constitute barratry, which is a crime, the captain must be proved to have acted against his better judgment; as the case stands, there is a whole ocean between you and barratry'.[198] A mere mistake by the captain as to the meaning of the instructions, or a misapprehension of the best mode of acting under the instructions, and carrying them out, would not amount to barratry.[199]

Cargo risks

Under the 2009 Institute Cargo Clauses there are three classes of cover: A (all risks), B (restricted risks) and C (more restricted risks). The insuring clause aside, all three sets of clauses are identical.

---

191 *The Elias Issaias* (1923) 15 Ll L Rep 186, 191, Atkin LJ.
192 (1774) 1 Cowp. 143.
193 *Vallejo v Wheeler* (1774) 1 Cowp. 143, 155–156.
194 *Pipon v Cope* (1808) 1 Camp. 434; *Hobbs v Hannam* (1811) 3 Campbell 93.
195 *The Elias Issaias* (1923) 15 Ll L Rep 186.
196 (1923) 15 Ll L Rep 186.
197 *Todd v Ritchie* 171 ER 459.
198 171 ER 459, 460.
199 *Bottomley v Bovill* (1826) 5 B & C 210, 212.

The ICC (A) Cover

Meaning of 'all risks'

When goods are insured under ICC (A) Clauses, they are insured against 'all risks' subject to the exclusions listed in the standard clauses. When there is a claim under the policy the assured has to prove that the loss comes within the terms of his policies. Where all risks are covered by the policy and not merely risks of a specified class or classes, the assured discharges the burden of proof when he has given evidence reasonably showing that the loss was due to a casualty.[200] He is not bound to go further and prove exactly how his loss was caused.[201]

In an all risks policy, 'all' does not literally mean 'all', and there are limits to the cover.[202] The policy cannot be held to cover all damage however caused.[203] Where the policy is an all risks policy the nature of insurance does not change the fact that insurance is still against uncertainty, thus it does not cover something which is bound to happen, for example, ordinary wear and tear or the loss which happens as a result of the assured's own misconduct.[204] This, however, does not mean that anything which could be shown not to be a certainty or not to be inherent vice must necessarily be one of the things coming within the policy.[205] In other words, if the loss was caused by an excepted peril, the insurer will not be liable for the loss in question. It was held in *Berk v Style*[206] that 'all risks of loss and/or damage from whatsoever cause arising irrespective of percentage' does not cover loss caused by inherent vice. In *Berk*, a cargo of kieselguhr was carried from North Africa to London. On arrival in London it was discovered that large numbers of the bags in which the kieselguhr was packaged were torn and broken, and that a quantity of the kieselguhr was loose. The claimant incurred considerable expense in rebagging and relanding the goods which he then claimed from the insurers. Sellers J held that 'from whatsoever cause arising', cannot be held to cover all damage however caused, for such damage as was inevitable from ordinary wear and tear and inevitable depreciation was not within the policies. The cargo was packed in paper bags and the bags were defective on shipment and inadequate to endure the normal wear and tear of handling and carriage. The special expenditure incurred in rebagging while in the lighter was due to the inherent vice of the bags. Thus, it had been almost certain at the time of shipment that the type of expense claimed from the insurers would be incurred. Accordingly this was not recoverable from the insurers for the reason that insurance is not against certainty.

The interpretation of all risks referred to above was once again approved in *London and Provincial Leather Processes Ltd v Hudson*.[207] In this case the policy was 'against all and every risk whatsoever, however arising. All claims to be paid irrespective of percentage. Including confiscation and/or prohibition of re-export, other than a loss arising out of war or process'. The assured were manufacturers of leather goods who bought raw skins in North Africa, shipped them direct to a German firm in Berlin to be processed and subsequently to be shipped to the United Kingdom. The German firm sub-contracted part of the work which they had to do for the assured to another firm, M. M were claiming a lien on these skins belonging to the assured, because they did not get payment from the German firm. Goddard LJ found that M converted the assured's goods which, according to

---

200 British & Foreign Marine Insurance Co Ltd v Gaunt [1921] 2 AC 41, Lord Sumner.
201 British & Foreign Marine Insurance Co Ltd v Gaunt [1921] 2 AC 41, Lord Birkenhead LC.
202 British & Foreign Marine Insurance Co Ltd v Gaunt [1921] 2 AC 41, Lord Sumner.
203 British & Foreign Marine Insurance Co Ltd v Gaunt [1921] 2 AC 41. ICC (A) Clause 4.
204 British & Foreign Marine Insurance Co Ltd v Gaunt [1921] 2 AC 41, Lord Sumner.
205 London and Provincial Leather Processes Ltd v Hudson [1939] 2 KB 724, 732.
206 [1956] 1 QB 180.
207 [1939] 2 KB 724.

Goddard LJ's interpretation, was covered under an all risks policy. The assured was deprived of the possession of the goods which was not much different to a case where the goods were stolen.

Inherent vice was covered expressly in *Overseas Commodities Ltd v Style*[208] by the following clause 'Being against all risks of whatsoever nature and/or kind. Average irrespective of percentage. Including blowing of tins, Including inherent vice and hidden defect'. Similarly, an express cover is seen in *Soya GmbH Mainz KG v White*[209] where the policy provided 'This insurance is to cover against the risks of heat, sweat and spontaneous combustion only . . .' A bulk cargo of soya beans was shipped from Indonesia to Belgium and the Netherlands. It is a natural characteristic of soya beans when shipped in bulk that if the moisture content of the hulk exceeds 14 per cent, micro-biological action, the nature and causes of which are unknown, will inevitably cause the soya beans to deteriorate during the course of a normal voyage from Indonesia to Northern Europe. The range of moisture content between 14 and 12 per cent is the 'grey area'. The soya beans had a moisture content of between 13 and 12 per cent, that is, within the grey area. Micro-biological action did in fact take place upon the voyage as a result of which the beans were discharged in a heated and deteriorated state. No incident was shown to have occurred upon the voyage whereby the moisture content present in the bulk on shipment had been increased from any external source. Lord Diplock defined inherent vice as 'the risk of deterioration of the goods shipped as a result of their natural behaviour in the ordinary course of the contemplated voyage without the intervention of any fortuitous external accident or casualty'.

ICC (A) Clause 1 defines the risk insured as 'This insurance covers all risks of loss of or damage to the subject matter insured except as excluded by the provisions of Clauses 4,5,6 and 7 below.' Some of the exclusions listed in the Clauses referred to are loss damage or expense attributable to wilful misconduct of the assured (cl.4.1), ordinary leakage, ordinary loss in weight or volume, or ordinary wear and tear of the subject matter insured (cl.4.2) loss damage or expense caused by inherent vice or nature of the subject matter insured (cl.4.4) loss damage or expense caused by delay, even though the delay is caused by a risk insured against (4.5). These exceptions were analysed above.

ICC (B) and (C) – restricted risks

Risks covered by ICC (B) and (C) are as follows:

ICC (B) CLAUSES: RISKS COVERED

1   This insurance covers, except as excluded by the provisions of clauses 4, 5, 6 and 7 below
    1.1   loss of or damage to the subject matter insured reasonably attributable to
        1.1.1   fire or explosion
        1.1.2   vessel or craft being stranded grounded sunk or capsized
        1.1.3   overturning or derailment of land conveyance
        1.1.4   collision or contact of vessel craft or conveyance with any external object other than water.
        1.1.5   discharge of cargo at a port of distress
        1.1.6   earthquake volcanic eruption or lightning
    1.2   loss of or damage to the subject matter insured caused by
        1.2.1   general average sacrifice

---

208 [1958] 1 Lloyd's Rep 546.
209 [1983] 1 Lloyd's Rep 122.

1.2.2   jettison or washing overboard

1.2.3   entry of sea lake or river water into vessel craft hold conveyance container or place of storage

1.3   total loss of any package lost overboard or dropped whilst loading on to, or unloading from, vessel or craft.

(C) CLAUSES: RISKS COVERED

1   This insurance covers, except as excluded by the provisions of clauses 4, 5, 6 and 7 below

1.1   loss of or damage to the subject matter insured reasonably attributable to

1.1.1   fire or explosion

1.1.2   vessel or craft being stranded grounded sunk or capsized

1.1.3   overturning or derailment of land conveyance

1.1.4   collision or contact of vessel craft or conveyance with any external object other than water

1.1.5   discharge of cargo at a port of distress

1.2   loss of or damage to the subject matter caused by

1.2.1   general average sacrifice

The most common risks listed in the B and C clauses were analysed above and will not be repeated here. It should be noted that as different to (A) clauses, piracy is not an insurable risk under (B) and (C) clauses. In the (B) clauses it is seen that cl.1 uses the words 'attributable to' in the first part and in the second part of the clause the words 'caused by' are used. It should be noted that these two phrases express the same meaning. In *The Cendor Mopu* Lord Mance noted that, in the context of MIA 1906, s.39(5), the phrase 'attributable to' arguably means the same as 'caused by'. Lord Mance was of the view that the phrase was used in recognition of the fact that, at the time the legislation was drafted, the proximate cause was thought to be the very last in a chain of events, so that the phrase was devised to recognise that there might be an earlier operative event which could not as a matter of law at the time be recognised as the proximate cause.

Both to blame

In order to explain the 'Both to Blame Collision Clause' under the Cargo Clauses, it is first necessary to refer to the same type of clause in contracts of carriage.

A typical clause of this kind in a contract of carriage is as follows:[210]

If the Vessel comes into collision with another ship as a result of the negligence of the other ship and any act, neglect or default of the Master, mariner, pilot or the servants of the Owner in the navigation or in the management of the Vessel, the owners of the cargo carried hereunder shall indemnify the Owner against all loss or liability to the other or non-carrying ship or her owners in so far as such loss or liability represents loss of, or damage to, or any claim whatsoever of the owners of said cargo, paid or payable by the other or recovered by the other or non-carrying ship or her owners as part of their claim against the carrying ship or Owner. The foregoing provisions shall also apply where the owners, operators or those in charge of any ships or objects other than, or in addition to, the colliding ships or object are at fault in respect of a collision or contact.

---

210 Clause 20(b)(iv) Asbatankvoy charterparty.

ICC (A)(B)(C) Clauses all contain a 'Both to Blame Collison Clause' in the following words 'This insurance indemnifies the Assured, in respect of any risk insured herein, against liability incurred under any Both to Blame Collision Clause in the contract of carriage. In the event of any claim by carriers under the said Clause, the Assured agree to notify the Insurers who shall have the right, at their own cost and expense, to defend the Assured against such claim.'

Reading these two clauses together, the Both to Blame Collision clause in a cargo insurance policy operates as follows: where the cargo is lost or damaged in a collision for which both vessels are to blame and the Carrier is not liable to the cargo owner for damage to cargo by the collision under the terms of the contract of carriage, the owner of the non-carrying vessel may still be obliged to pay for the loss of the cargo and the damage to the carrying vessel. However, the owner of the non-carrying vessel may also claim the amount paid to the cargo owner from the carrying vessel reflecting the Carrier's degree of blame for the collision. Thus, while the carrying vessel is not liable to the cargo owner under the contract of carriage, he has to contribute to the loss of the cargo owner in respect of the proportion of his fault in the accident. But, under the 'Both to Blame Collision Clause' in the contract of carriage, the Carrier can claim this from the cargo owner.

The purpose of the 'Both to Blame Collision Clause' in a cargo insurance policy is to ensure that the cargo owner will recover full indemnity from the insurer despite the Both to Blame Collision Clause in the contract of carriage. The cargo owner receives full indemnity from the insurer, however when the insurer subrogates into the rights of the assured against the non-carrying vessel, the non-carrying vessel would deduct from his liability an amount proportionate to the amount that the carrying vessel had to pay which would be paid by the cargo owner to the carrying vessel under the both to blame collison clause.

Further reading

Bennett, *The Law of Marine Insurance*, 2nd edn, [2006] Oxford University Press. Chapter 9, Principles of Causation; Chapter 10, Marine Risks; Chapter 11, The Inchmaree Clause; Chapter 12, Collision and Contact Losses; Chapter 15, Excluded Losses.

Bennett, 'Fortuity in the law of Marine Insurance', *Lloyd's Maritime and Commercial Law Quarterly* [2007] 3(August), 315–361.

Dunt and Welbourne, 'Insuring cargoes in the new millenium: the Institute Cargo Clauses', Chapter 6 in Thomas (ed.), *The Modern Law of Marine Insurance*, Volume 3 [2009] Informa.

Gauci, 'Piracy and its legal problems: with specific reference to the English Law of Marine Insurance', *Journal of Maritime Law and Commerce* [2010] 41(4), October, 541–560.

Gilman et al., *Arnould: Law of Marine Insurance and Average*, 18th edn, [2013] Sweet & Maxwell. Chapter 22, Losses Covered by the Policy: General Principles; Chapter 23, Marine Risks.

Hill, 'Wilful misconduct', Chapter 7 in Thomas (ed.), *Modern Law of Marine Insurance*, Volume 2 [2002] London: LLP.

Hjalmarsson and Lavelle, 'Thirty years of inherent vice from *Soya v White* to *The Cendor Mopu* and beyond', Chapter 10 in Clarke (ed.), *Maritime Law Evolving* [2013] Hart Publishing.

Hopkins, 'Latent defects and the "Inchmaree" clause revisited', *International Journal of Shipping Law* [1997] 4, 220–221.

Lord, 'Approximate causes and perils of the seas', *British Insurance Law Association Journal* [2013] 126.

Lowry and Rawlings, 'Proximate causation in insurance law', *Modern Law Review* [2005] 68, 310–319.

Muchlinski, 'Proof of scuttling', *Lloyd's Maritime and Commercial Law Quarterly* [1989] 1(February), 25–27.

O'Shea, 'Marine insurance: weather damage to cargo – casualty – inherent vice', *Journal of International Maritime Law* [2004] 10(5): 400–402 (examines *Mayban v Alstom*).

Parks, 'Marine Insurance: The Inchmaree Clause', *Journal of Maritime Law and Commerce* [1979] 10(2) January, 249–270.

Passman, 'Interpreting sea piracy clauses in marine insurance contracts', *Journal of Maritime Law and Commerce* [2009] 40(1) January, 59–88.

Rose, *Marine Insurance: Law and Practice*, 2nd edn, [2012] Informa. Chapter 13, Insured Risks; Chapter 14, Marine Risks; Chapter 15, Inchmaree Risks; Chapter 16, Liabilities; Chapter 18, Exclusions; Chapter 19, Causation.

Soady, 'Critical analysis of piracy, hijacking, ransom payments, and whether modern London insurance market clauses provide sufficient protection for parties involved in piracy for ransom', *Journal of Maritime Law and Commerce* [2013] 44(1) January, 1–28.

Song, 'Is negligence a cause of loss in marine insurance?', *British Insurance Law Association Journal* [2014] 127, 57–70.

Soyer, 'Defences available to a marine insurer', *Lloyd's Maritime and Commercial Law Quarterly* [2002] (2), 199–213.

Soyer, 'Coverage against unlawful acts in contemporary marine policies', Chapter 7 in Thomas (ed.) *The Modern Law of Marine Insurance*, Volume 3, [2009] London: Informa.

Todd, 'Piracy for ransom: insurance issues', *Journal of International Maritime Law* [2009] 15(4): 307–321.

Tsichlis, 'Causation issues in barratry cases', *Journal of Maritime Law and Commerce* [2004] 35(2) April, 255–282.

Wan and Wan, 'Causa proxima non remota spectatur: the doctrine of causation in the law of marine insurance', *Journal of Maritime Law and Commerce* [2003] 34(3) July, 479–496.

Wennekers, 'Issues of modern piracy in marine insurance law: a comparative study of English and German law', *Journal of International Maritime Law* [2012] 18(5): 372–397.

Chapter 8

Actual Total Loss

Chapter Contents

Forms of loss in marine insurance

A loss may be total or partial. While the only total loss acknowledged in the non-marine context is an actual total loss,[1] in marine insurance a total loss may be an actual total loss (ATL) or a constructive total loss (CTL). Both are equally total losses,[2] that is, the assured is entitled to claim for a loss of the whole subject matter insured.[3] The definition of actual total loss is found in section 57 of the Marine Insurance Act 1906. Constructive total loss can itself come in several forms and section 60 defines a constructive total loss. Partial loss is referred to in section 56 as any loss other than a total loss.

A policy may cover 'total loss only' which is also expressed as 'free from average'. In such a case, unless a stipulation to the contrary appears in the policy, both actual and constructive total loss is included in the 'total loss only' cover.[4]

Actual total loss

As regards actual total loss the emphasis has been placed on the insurer's undertaking which is to cover the assured's loss in case the subject matter insured does not arrive at the port of destination. Lord Abinger in *Roux v Salvador*[5] defined actual total loss, 'The underwriter engages, that the object of the assurance shall arrive in safety at its destined termination. If, in the progress of the voyage, it becomes totally destroyed or annihilated, or if it be placed, by reason of the perils against which he insures, in such a position, that it is wholly out of the power of the assured or of the underwriter to procure its arrival, he is bound by the very letter of his contract to pay the sum insured.' David Steel J stated in *Masefield AG v Amlin Corporate Member Ltd*[6] that ATL occurs where property is beyond recovery. In some of the cases it is seen that actual total loss was referred to as absolute total loss.[7] Constructive total loss will be fully analysed in Chapter 9. Here it suffices to mention that while a notice of abandonment is required to establish a CTL, no notice of abandonment need be given in the case of an ATL[8] – this is because there is nothing to abandon.[9] The doctrine of CTL in marine insurance law has meant that the test for an ATL has been applied with the utmost rigour:[10] as an assured has always had the option of claiming for a CTL.[11]

Three forms of actual total loss are contemplated by MIA 1906, s.57:

1   Where the subject matter insured is destroyed.
2   Where the subject matter insured is so damaged as to cease to be a thing of the kind insured.
3   Where the assured is irretrievably deprived of the insured subject matter.

---

1   Thus outside marine insurance, the doctrine of actual total loss may be found to be more flexible. For instance a motor-car may be treated as a total loss when it is not worth repairing. See *Masefield AG v Amlin Corporate Member Ltd* [2011] 1 Lloyd's Rep 630 Rix LJ, para 16. The phrase 'constructive total loss' belongs to the language of marine insurance, and can have no meaning as applied to a ship except in connection with marine insurance. See *Court Line Ltd v King, The* (1944) 78 Ll L Rep 390, 398, Lord Justice Du Parcq.
2   *Kastor Navigation Co Ltd v AGF MAT (The Kastor Too)* [2004] 2 Lloyd's Rep 119; Rix LJ, para 8.
3   *Kaltenbach v Mackenzie* (1878) 3 CPD 467.
4   Templeman, F. Marine Insurance: Its Principles and Practice, Macdonald and Evans, 1918, 57.
5   (1836) 3 Bing. NC 266, 286.
6   [2010] 1 Lloyd's Rep 509, para 41.
7   *Roux v Salvador* (1836) 3 Bing. NC 266.
8   MIA 1906, s 57(2).
9   *Mullett v Shedden* (1811) 13 East 304; *Rankin v Potter* (1873) LR 6 HL 83.
10 *Clothing Management Technology Ltd v Beazley Solutions Ltd (t/a Beazley Marine UK)* [2012] 1 Lloyd's Rep 571, para 25.
11 *Masefield AG v Amlin Corporate Member Ltd* [2011] 1 Lloyd's Rep 630 Rix LJ, para 16.

Where the subject matter insured is destroyed

There has not been a great deal of controversy in the context of destruction of the subject matter insured. A total loss, in one sense, means where goods go to the bottom of the sea, or where the goods are burnt or utterly destroyed.[12]

It will be a partial loss if the goods are imperishable and under the assured's control and the assured still has the opportunity of sending them to their destination. Thus, although the ship may be damaged or become a total loss the cargo may be saved and if the cargo could be transhipped on another vessel and sent to the port of destination with any reasonable prospect of arriving there in *specie,* however damaged, there cannot be a total loss if the assured fails to tranship the goods.[13] In such a case the loss is partial even though the assured sells the goods where they have been landed, instead of taking measures to transmit them to their original destination. In *Anderson v Wallis*[14] the insurance was on the cargo of copper, iron, and nails. On her voyage from London to Quebec the ship encountered heavy gales and was obliged to make for the nearest port, Kinsale. She was capable of repair, the repairs were accordingly set about, but she could not be repaired in time to prosecute her voyage that season. At the port of repair there was not any ship to be procured to forward the cargo. The cargo was sold as a damaged cargo and notice of abandonment was given. The copper was not damaged at all and the iron and nails were not damaged to any considerable extent. The repair of the vessel would have delayed the voyage but it did not become impossible to deliver the cargo to the port of destination in its original condition. The Court held that the only description of loss was a temporary suspension of the voyage, which did not amount to a total loss. The question is whether the voyage was lost. *Manning v Newnham*[15] was distinguished from *Anderson v Wallis*. In *Manning*, the ship had to sail to the nearest port as she was taking in water while she was loaded with a cargo of sugar. It was impossible to repair her so she was sold together with the cargo as there was no ship at the port large enough to bring the cargo to the destination. Lord Mansfield held that if the voyage, in consequence of a peril within the policy, was lost or was not worth pursuing, that was a total loss. While the voyage was lost in *Manning* it was not the case in *Anderson*.

If the cargo is saved but never arrives at its destination to the consignee there is a total loss. In *Bondrett v Hentigg*[16] the ship had been wrecked but some of her cargo was saved and got to shore. It fell however into the hands of the natives of the Isle of France, who destroyed part and plundered the rest. It was a total loss of the goods which was saved from the wreck. The goods got on shore but they never came again into the hands of the owners.

When goods are insured free from average and when part of the goods insured is lost the question may arise as to whether that is a total loss of part of the cargo or whether that is a partial loss of the cargo insured. The answer depends on the wording of the policy. The MIA 1906 s.76(1) provides that 'Where the subject-matter insured is warranted free from particular average, the assured cannot recover for a loss of part, other than a loss incurred by a general average sacrifice, unless the contract contained in the policy be apportionable; but, if the contract be apportionable, the assured may recover for a total loss of any apportionable part.'

Where perishable goods are insured for a lump sum and in bulk, of all same description, then the total loss of part of the bulk is a particular average loss and gives no claim under a policy which is free of particular average.[17] If £75 worth of wheat is lost from a cargo of wheat valued at £1,600,

---

12 *Stringer v English and Scottish Marine Insurance Company* (1869–70) LR 5 QB 599, Martin B.
13 *Glennie v The London Assurance Company* (1814) 2 M & S 371. Depending on the expenses to tranship, the goods may be a constructive total loss which will be discussed below.
14 (1813) 2 M & S 240.
15 (1782) 3 Douglas 130.
16 (1816) Holt 149.
17 *Ralli v Janson* (1856) 6 Ellis and Blackburn 422.

which was loaded on board a vessel, and if the insurance was upon the bulk there cannot be any total loss of a portion of the cargo only.[18] In *Ralli v Janson*,[19] 2,688 bags of linseed were insured from Calcutta to London, 1,160 of which were brought to England, the rest were lost during sea voyage. The assured claimed a total loss upon each of the bags lost. The insurance was 'warranted free from average, unless general, or the ship be stranded'. It was argued that the fact that the cargo was shipped in bags made a difference, each bag was a distinct object capable of separate insurance and valuation and that there was a total loss of each of those portions of the lost cargo.

The Court rejected this argument. It was held that the warranty applies in terms to all seed loaded on board the vessel, without restriction to seed loaded in bulk or in any particular manner. The Court clarified that if the terms of the policy had provided, for instance by separate valuation, that it was intended to distinguish one portion of the seed from another, and made a separate insurance upon each portion as well as a joint one upon all, it would have been arguable that this was a total loss of the bags lost. This was done in *La Fabrique de Produits Chimiques Société Anonyme v Large*[20] in which three distinct parcels of perishable goods – namely, 1 case containing vanillin valued at £462, 1 case containing vanillin valued at £363, 1 case containing caffeine valued at £275 – were insured against certain perils in a lump sum value of £1,100. The policy was warranted free from particular average and covered risks from warehouse to warehouse. The two cases of vanillin were stolen from a transporting warehouse in London. The Court held that the loss of the two packages of vanillin was not a particular average loss of the whole of the goods insured, but was a total loss of these particular goods. The goods insured were of different species, and also that they were separately valued. The whole sum valuation of £1,100 was merely the addition of the separate values of the three cases.

If there are express words in the policy which make each package a separate insurance, the loss of one package is a total loss of that particular package. In *Duff v Mackenzie*,[21] the goods on board the ship 'The Lion' were described as 'master's effects' (the nautical instruments, the chronometer, the clothes, books, furniture) and were insured for a voyage from Sicily to the United Kingdom. The insurance was 'free from all average'. Some of the goods insured were totally lost by the perils insured against, but others were saved. The assured's claim in terms of total loss of each article was accepted on the total loss basis. It was held that the articles which constitute the 'master's effects' had no natural or artificial connection with each other, but were essentially different in their nature and kind, in their value, in the use to be made of them, and the mode in which they would be disposed on board. Even where the goods insured are all of the same species, if they are contained in cases or packages which are themselves separately valued, the loss of one of those packages is a total loss of that package and not a particular average loss of the whole.

Where the subject matter insured is so damaged as to cease to be a thing of the kind insured

In terms of loss of a ship, Willis J said in *Barker v Janson*[22] that 'If a ship is so injured that it cannot sail without repairs, and cannot be taken to a port at which the necessary repairs can be executed, there is an actual total loss, for that has ceased to be a ship which never can be used for the purposes of a ship.'

---

18 *Hills v The London Assurance Corporation* (1839) 5 Meeson and Welsby 569.
19 (1856) 6 Ellis and Blackburn 422.
20 [1923] 1 KB 203.
21 (1857) 3 Common Bench Reports (New Series) 16.
22 (1867–68) LR 3 CP 303, 305.

In respect of total loss of cargo it may be the case that the goods may be damaged during sea voyage and it may become impossible to deliver them to the port of destination in their original form or in a saleable condition. In *Roux v Salvador*,[23] a cargo of 1000 salted hides, of the value of £1,117, was declared under an insurance policy which was free of average unless the ship should be stranded. The goods were shipped on board the *Roxalane* who encountered bad weather and sprung a leak in the course of her voyage from Valparaiso for Bordeaux. The *Roxalene* was put into Rio de Janeiro for repair. It was discovered that the cargo was washed and wetted by the seawater, which had entered into the vessel, and also by the effect of the dampness produced in the hold by the leak. As a consequence, partial fermentation ensued, the progress of which could not be stopped by any means practicable in Rio de Janeiro. The jury found that by the process of fermentation and putrefaction, which had commenced, a total destruction of them before their arrival at the port of destination became as inevitable as if they had been cast into the sea or consumed by fire. It thus became impossible to carry the hides in a saleable state to the port of destination. If it had been attempted to take them to Bordeaux, they would altogether have lost the character of hides before they arrived there. The 1,000 hides were then sold by public auction, for the gross sum of £273. It was held that the cargo became a total loss. The principles that Lord Abinger set out in this case which apply in ATL are (1) the existence of the goods, or any part of them, *in specie*, is neither a conclusive, nor, in many cases, a material circumstance to determine ATL. (2) Even though goods (which are imperishable) are damaged but not utterly destroyed it may still be regarded as a total loss if it is certain that in case of shipment on to another or the same vessel the species itself would disappear before their arrival at the port of destination losing all their original character. (3) In such a case the loss is total because the assured has no means of recovering his goods, whether his inability arises from their annihilation or from any other insuperable obstacle.

Roux v Salvador was applied in *Saunders v Baring*[24] in which, on her voyage from Cardiff to Yokohama, the vessel carrying the cargo of coal experienced very severe weather and it became necessary to jettison some part of the cargo. The nearest port of refuge was Hong Kong where the cargo was unshipped and found so damaged that there would be great danger of spontaneous combustion if it were taken to Yokohama. The cargo was sold. Blackburn J held that the cargo became a total loss as it was so damaged by perils of the sea that sale of the cargo became necessary.

Despite the fact that the goods may be delivered to the consignee, if they are unmerchantable, and incapable of being used for the purposes for which goods of their species are ordinarily used, they are not considered to have arrived *in specie*. In *Asfar v Blundell*[25] the vessel sank in the Thames loaded with a cargo of dates. The dates remained for three tides under water, and when recovered were found to be saturated with Thames water and sewage. It had suffered from fermentation and putrefaction so as to be unfit for human food. They were, however, sold and exported for purposes of distillation, and were never unrecognisable as dates. Lord Esher stated that the test is whether, as a matter of business, the nature of the thing has been altered. His Lordship noted that when the subject matter insured is damaged this does not necessarily mean that its nature was altered too. For instance, a cargo of wheat or rice may be damaged, but may still remain the things dealt with as wheat or rice in business. If it is so changed in its nature by the perils of the sea as to become an unmerchantable thing, which no buyer would buy and no honest seller would sell, then there is a total loss. The dates had been so deteriorated that they had become something that was not merchantable as dates. Similarly, in *Berger and Light Diffusers Pty Ltd v Pollock*[26] the claim was for damage

---

23 (1836) 3 Bingham New Cases 266.
24 (1876) 3 Asp MLC 132.
25 [1896] 1 QB 123.
26 [1973] 2 Lloyd's Rep 442.

by rust sustained by four large steel injection moulds during a voyage from Melbourne to London on the steamship *Paparoa*. The moulds were a total loss as the result of the damage sustained during the voyage because the rust destroyed the limited value which they had before the voyage and left them incapable of being used as moulds, with no more value than scrap metal. The moulds had no value in their damaged state. Plainly they had lost their commercial identity and value as moulds for purposes of manufacturing the product for which they were designed or any other use other than scrap.

The analysis of whether the property has ceased to be a thing of the kind insured involves consideration of the particular characteristics of the insured property, before the casualty was sustained. In *Fraser Shipping Ltd v Colton*[27] the *Shakir III*, a semi-submersible heavy lift carrier, had been decommissioned and was being towed, as a dead ship, for break up in a Chinese port. On her voyage to China tug and tow parted, and the *Shakir III* stranded on the Chinese island of Wuzhu Zhou. Although the *Shakir III* was grounded and incapable of proceeding without salvage and a degree of repair, its essential components were not so damaged or dissipated. She retained her original appearance and character as a single vessel, she was a dead ship, she was still capable of being towed away for scrap. Potter LJ[28] stated 'In those circumstances, and bearing in mind that the vessel was a dead ship under tow and heading for break-up, it does not seem to me that, by reason of its grounding and/or the damage it had sustained, it had lost its essential identity or ceased to be a thing of the kind insured.'

Many of the abovementioned authorities were referred to in a recent case in which Andrew Smith J had to decide, among other issues, whether the vessel was an ATL. In *Venetico Marine SA v International General Insurance Co Ltd*[29] the vessel grounded and the assured argued that she became an ATL because she had ceased to be 'an operational vessel, and had become a dead ship, in that she could not be operated or restored to an operational condition' as a result of which she had 'ceased to be a thing of the kind assured'. Andrew Smith J[30] rejected the argument for the reason that in the two and a half weeks after the grounding the vessel carried out commercial operations such as proceeding to Dahej and discharging her cargo. The vessel would be an ATL if it were physically or legally impossible to carry out repairs that would restore her as an operating vessel.[31]

The assured further argued that the vessel could not be moved to a place such as Mumbai for underwater inspection and temporary repairs, before going to a graving dock for permanent repairs. The crucial question according to Andrew Smith J was whether the vessel was in such a state that she would necessarily sink or otherwise fail to reach Mumbai.[32] The assured's argument was that she could not be towed there safely which, as Andrew Smith J described, introduced 'an ingredient into the test of what is an ATL that is not considered in the authorities and might be thought not readily reconciled with the rigorous test for an ATL of impossibility'.[33] The judge recognised that there might be circumstances in which the dangers to life or other risks associated with repairs are so great, and the chances of successful salvage are so small, that it would be unrealistic to contemplate repairs but he did not need to engage with these questions.[34] The question was whether uninsured but otherwise prudent owners would, if properly informed, have taken the risk involved in having the vessel repaired.[35]

---

27 *Fraser Shipping Ltd v Colton* [1997] 1 Lloyd's Rep 586.
28 [1997] 1 Lloyd's Rep 586, 591.
29 [2014] 1 Lloyd's Rep 349.
30 [2014] 1 Lloyd's Rep 349, para 398.
31 [2014] 1 Lloyd's Rep 349, para 399.
32 [2014] 1 Lloyd's Rep 349, 403.
33 [2014] 1 Lloyd's Rep 349, 403.
34 [2014] 1 Lloyd's Rep 349, 403.
35 On the facts the ATL claimed on this basis too.

Where the assured is irretrievably deprived of the insured subject matter

Meaning of irretrievable deprivation

'Irretrievable deprivation' *prima facie* depends upon whether, by reason of the vessel's (or goods') situation, it was wholly out of the power of the assured or the underwriters to procure its arrival.[36] For a deprivation to be regarded as irretrievable regaining the possession of the subject matter insured has to be impossible. A claim for actual total loss failed in *George Cohen Sons & Co v Standard Marine Insurance Co Ltd*[37] in which an obsolete warship grounded off the Dutch coast. It was not contended that the ship was destroyed. It was not and could not be contended that she was so damaged as to cease to be a thing of the kind insured, but it was suggested that the assured was irretrievably deprived thereof, and that accordingly she was an actual total loss. The vessel could be got off, it would be a matter of great elaboration and difficulty, and high expenditure might have to be incurred, but it could be done so far as the physical feat was concerned.

One of the situations at which impossibility of recovery was established in the old cases was sale of the subject matter insured under a decree of a Court of competent jurisdiction in consequence of a peril insured against. In such a case the owner loses the property of the subject matter insured by an adverse valid and legal transfer of his right of property and it was regarded as being as much a total loss as if it had been totally annihilated.[38] In *Stringer v English and Scottish Marine Insurance Company*[39] the ship and cargo were seized by an American cruiser and taken to New Orleans, where a suit was instituted by the captors against the ship and cargo for the purpose of having them adjudged a lawful prize. The owners at that time elected to treat the seizure as a partial loss. The Prize Court gave judgment against the captors, and ordered restitution but the captors appealed. The owners, who then for the first time knew that an appeal had been preferred, gave notice of abandonment, which the underwriters refused to accept. Subsequently, the owner informed the underwriters that the Prize Commissioner had offered to the Court to sell the ship and cargo. The sale of the goods could have been prevented by depositing the full value of the goods, or giving bail for them in the Prize Court, which was subject to great and sudden currency fluctuations. Neither the assured nor the insurer offered to pay the bail and the ship and cargo were sold by order of the Court.

The assured's claim for a total loss was accepted and one of the reasons that the assured succeeded in his claim was that no reasonable assured would have paid the bail under those circumstances, especially considering the currency fluctuations and the conditions of the goods which had deteriorated. It was held that when the sale took place, the property in the goods was taken out of the owner, so that it became impossible for him to take the goods under his original ownership to the port of discharge. The consequence was that there was a total deprivation of the ownership of the goods in the assured for the purpose of the adventure, and that he was, therefore, entitled to the whole value of his goods under the valued policy.

It might be considered that, similar to *George Cohen*, recovery was possible in *Stringer* by either depositing the whole value of the cargo or giving a bail in the court. *Stringer* is a case which is not easy to comprehend. It was discussed in *Masefield v Amlin* in which Rix LJ[40] said '. . . what created the ATL in *Stringer* was the sale itself, which forever dispossessed the plaintiff in that case of his cargo. The issue there was not whether there was a total loss or not, but what had caused it:

---

36 *Fraser Shipping Ltd v Colton* [1997] 1 Lloyd's Rep 586.
37 (1925) 21 Ll L Rep 30.
38 *Cossman v West* (1888) LR 13 App Cas 160; *Mullett v Shedden* (1811) 13 East 304.
39 (1869–70) LR 5 QB 599.
40 [2011] 1 Lloyd's Rep 630, para 40.

the capture, or the owner's own breach of duty in looking after his cargo . . . If in *Stringer* the bail had been given, however unreasonable the price of it was, there would have been no sale and (subject to the decision of the Supreme Court on the prize issue) no total loss.' Indeed Kelly CB[41] stated in *Stringer* 'the decree for sale, and the sale itself having taken place under circumstances in which there was no default on the part of the owner of the goods, we have to consider whether that sale justified the plaintiffs in then treating the case as one of total loss . . . the decree for the sale of the goods and the sale of the goods under that decree, which for ever took out of the possession of the owner the goods themselves, and took away from him the power of ever repossessing himself of the goods in specie, entitled the plaintiffs to treat the case as one of total loss. This loss of the goods arose, though not directly, out of the original capture (which was of itself, if it had been so treated, a total loss), through a series of consequences, viz. the institution, the different steps, and the continuance of the suit until the decree was pronounced; and the sale under the decree was – if I may use the expression – a completion of the total loss.'

In line with recovery being impossible, irretrievable deprivation requires that the arrival of the subject matter insured at its port of destination must wholly be out of the power of the assured or the insurers. This was held by Potter LJ in *Fraser Shipping Ltd v Colton*[42] in which, whilst under tow, the vessel was stranded on a Chinese island. The vessel was insured against ATL only. It was clear that the costs of salvage would be prohibitive. Potter LJ sitting in the Commercial Court held that it should be looked at whether the vessel could have been physically salved or not. The undisputed evidence in this respect was to the effect that it was feasible to salvage the vessel subject to accessibility and cost.

Capture and seizure

The question of whether deprivation was irretrievable or not has mostly been discussed in relation to capture of vessels by pirates or warships.

Capture alone is not regarded as an actual total loss[43] but capture followed by condemnation was stated to be no doubt an actual total loss[44] since the vessel had in fact been condemned; the war was supposed to last indefinitely, and, therefore, there was no chance within any reasonable time of the ship being restored.

It is a matter of fact if capture is an actual total loss[45] and it should be borne in mind that acts of pirates 'do not in themselves necessarily occasion any loss'[46] as the intention of pirates can be various.[47] Pirates may 'steal' the vessel and may use her for trading or for further piratical acts. They may simply retain possession of the vessel and her crew to extract a ransom, which they know from past experience will be paid. For the purposes of establishing irretrievable deprivation the assured must establish that the recovery is impossible.[48] Piratical seizure, in the absence of a policy of ransom, may amount to an ATL, where the pirates escape with their prize for their own use and there is no prospect whatever of finding or recovering vessel or cargo.[49] Therefore a possibility of

---

41 (1869–1870) LR 5 QB 599, 603–604.
42 [1997] 1 Lloyd's Rep 586.
43 *Marstrand Fishing Co Ltd v Beer* (1936) 56 Ll L Rep 163; *Masefield AG v Amlin Corporate Member Ltd*, Rix LJ, [2011] 1 Lloyd's Rep 630, para 56.
44 *Marstrand Fishing Co Ltd v Beer* (1936) 56 Ll L Rep 163; *Mullett v Shedden* (1811) 13 East 304.
45 [2011] 1 Lloyd's Rep 630, Rix LJ, para 56.
46 *Cory v Burr* (1883) 8 App Cas 393.
47 See *Masefield AG v Amlin Corporate Member Ltd* [2010] 1 Lloyd's Rep 509, para 49.
48 David Steel J, [2010] 1 Lloyd's Rep 509, para 35.
49 [2011] 1 Lloyd's Rep 630, Rix LJ, para 56.

recovery, irrespective of the effort or money that has to be spent, will prevent the vessel from being an actual total loss. The test of irretrievable deprivation is clearly far more severe than the test of unlikelihood of recovery of possession. In *Panamanian Oriental Steamship Corporation v Wright*[50] the vessel was seized at Saigon in March, 1966, after unmanifested goods had been discovered by customs officials. She was confiscated by order of a Special Court and had not been recovered. In due course the owners received legal advice that release could only be achieved by payment of bribes to various officials. Mocatta J stated that although the order of confiscation divested the assured of the legal ownership of the vessel as is the case after condemnation of a ship by a Prize Court, the assured was not irretrievably deprived of their vessel.

Similar to *Stringer*, in *Andersen v Marten*[51] the issue was one of causation. The *Romulus* was insured for twelve months from 12 January 1905, in a policy for total loss only 'Warranted free from capture, seizure and detention, and the consequences of hostilities, piracy and barratry excepted.' The *Romulus* was carrying coal to Vladivostock, a naval port and base of naval operations in the war then raging between Russia and Japan. While attempting to avoid Japanese cruisers the *Romulus* was so injured by ice that the master made for Hakodate, a Japanese port, for refuge. She was then captured by a Japanese cruiser for carrying contraband. The Japanese officer ordered the master to proceed to Yokosuka but the vessel took on much water, altered her course and went aground. Ultimately she became a total loss as she lay. The question was one of causation, whether there was a total loss by capture, seizure, detention, or the consequences of hostilities. It was held that the vessel became a total loss by capture. There was on that day a total loss which, as things were then seen, might afterwards be reduced if in the end the vessel was released.

Capture by pirates was discussed in *Masefield AG v Amlin Corporate Member Ltd*[52] in which the cargo owners claimed a total loss despite the fact that the cargo was released together with the vessel following a capture and payment of ransom, and cargo was not physically damaged, although the assured suffered economic loss due to late delivery at Rotterdam. The *Bunga Melati Dua* was seized by Somali pirates in the Gulf of Aden on 19 August 2008. At the time of the seizure she was carrying biodiesel from Malaysia to Rotterdam. Negotiations for the payment of a ransom for the release of the vessel, her crew and cargoes were almost immediately commenced by the vessel's owners, MISC. The cargo owner was not party to those negotiations. On 18 September the cargo owner served a notice of abandonment which was rejected by its insurer. The value of the vessel and her cargo amounted to $80m.

No attempt was made to recover the vessel or cargo by military intervention. Nor were there any diplomatic or other such attempts to obtain their release but the vessel, her crew and cargoes were released on 29 September, less than six weeks after her capture, on payment of a ransom of US$2m by MISC. The voyage to Rotterdam was completed on 26 October 2008. The *Bunga Melati Dua* reached Rotterdam on 26 October 2008. The cargo had not deteriorated during the delay, but it had missed its market in the meantime. The market for biofuel is seasonal, and effectively closes after the end of September. The insured's two parcels therefore had to be stored until the following year, when it was sold at a price substantially less than its insured value. The insured gave credit for the recovery made on re-sale, less expenses, and claimed the balance in the sum of $7,608,845.30. The insured value had been $13,326,481.75 (including freight). Piracy was an

---

50 *Panamanian Oriental Steamship Corporation v Wright* [1970] 2 Lloyd's Rep 365, the appeal was allowed by the Court of Appeal on the exclusion clause, the Court of Appeal did not make any comments about irretrievable deprivation [1971] 1 Lloyd's Rep 487.
51 [1908] AC 334.
52 [2011] 1 Lloyd's Rep 630.

insured risk.[53] At first instance the cargo owner alleged that the cargo became ATL and CTL. With regard to the claims for ATL, David Steel J found the actual fact of recovery within a short period not directly material or decisive but 'may assist in showing what the probabilities really were, if they had been reasonably forecasted'.[54] This was the case for the reasons that both the contemporaneous correspondence and the information in the public domain showed that all interested persons were fully aware that the cargoes were likely to be recovered. Other vessels seized by Somali pirates had been promptly released following negotiations over a relatively short period and it took 11 days for the vessel and cargo to be released after notice of abandonment was given. David Steel J said 'an assured is not irretrievably deprived of property if it is legally and physically possible to recover it (and even if such recovery can only be achieved by disproportionate effort and expense)'.[55] In the Court of Appeal the cargo owner claimed only a CTL which will be discussed in Chapter 9.

As stated above, in *Stringer*, recovery was not beyond the assured's or the insurer's control and the court still held that the cargo was a total loss. In *Masefield v Amlin*, Rix LJ distinguished *Stringer* for the reason that in the latter what created the ATL was the sale itself, which forever dispossessed the plaintiff in that case of his cargo. As described by Rix LJ in *Masefield*, the issue in *Stringer* was not whether there was a total loss or not, but what had caused it. In *Masefield*, payment of a ransom always rendered the recovery of the cargo possible. If in *Stringer* the bail had been given, however unreasonable the price of it was, there would have been no sale and (subject to the decision of the Supreme Court on the prize issue) no total loss. Moreover, in *Masefield*, the cargo owners had lost only possession and not dominion over (or property in) their goods.[56] It was not an irretrievable deprivation, it was a typical 'wait and see' situation.[57]

Two cases should be noted here: *Cologan v London Assurance Company*[58] and *Dean v Hornby*[59] in which it was held that capture operates as a total loss, unless it be redeemed by subsequent events to the assured's free control.[60] In *Cologan* while a cargo of wheat, fish and staves were on board to be carried to Teneriffe, the *Friendship* was captured by an American privateer. She was then recaptured by another warship and was sent to Bermuda. On her passage to Bermuda she took water in her hold and 471 staves were overboard. Some of the wheat had to be destroyed for not being suitable for public health, some was damaged and the rest of the cargo was warehoused. The fish was sold to a profit. The vessel was permitted to sail to Madeira, not to Teneriffe due to embargo. Teneriffe was the destination whereas after the recapture the vessel was sent to Bermuda where she was placed under an embargo. She was released from the embargo upon condition of altering her destination to Madeira. The object of the policy was, as the Court stated, to insure the risk against the failure, by reason of any of the perils mentioned in the policy, of the cargo reaching the port of destination.[61] The voyage in this case however was defeated.[62] Therefore, it was held that there had been no restitution of any part of cargo as the ship and cargo never were effectually redeemed

---

53   The policy was an all risks policy with a war exclusion clause which read as follows: '6. In no case shall this insurance cover loss, damage or expense caused by . . . 6.2 capture, seizure, arrest restraint or detainment (piracy excepted), and the consequences thereof or any attempt thereat.'

54   [2010] 1 Lloyd's Rep 509, David Steel J, para 29. David Steel J referred to *Bank Line, Limited v Arthur Capel and Company* [1919] AC 435 per Lord Sumner at p 454.

55   [2010] 1 Lloyd's Rep 509, para 31.

56   David Steel J, [2010] 1 Lloyd's Rep 509, para 45.

57   Rix LJ, [2011] 1 Lloyd's Rep 630, para 56.

58   (1816) 5 Maule and Selwyn 447.

59   (1854) 3 Ellis and Blackburn 180.

60   (1816) 5 Maule and Selwyn 447, 456 Abbott J.

61   (1816) 5 Maule and Selwyn 447, 455–456, Bayley J.

62   (1816) 5 Maule and Selwyn 447, 454, Lord Ellenborough CJ.

from capture. The goods were not entirely annihilated but there was a total loss because capture and recapture and being forwarded to Madeira rendered the goods of no use whatever.

In *Dean v Hornby*[63] the *Eliza Cornish* was insured on a time policy against perils including 'pirates'. She was captured by pirates while she was in the Straits of Magellan but then she was recaptured by the *Virago*, an English warship. A prize master took command and sailed her to Valparaiso. On learning of these facts in April 1852, her owners gave notice of abandonment to the underwriters, apparently under the impression that the vessel had been condemned as a prize at Valparaiso, but that was not in fact the case. She sailed for Liverpool with the remainder of her cargo still under the command of a prize master. On this voyage she met with bad weather, and as a result the surveyors recommended that she was unfit for repairs and she should be sold. However the buyer of the *Eliza Cornish* repaired her for a trifling sum and she then arrived in England where her old owner, the assured, and his underwriter, by agreement took proceedings (in early 1853) to regain possession of her, without prejudice to their rights *inter se*. The admiralty court awarded possession to her old owner, she was sold, and her price deposited to await the outcome of the issue between those parties, which appears to have been whether the owner assured was entitled to be paid for a total loss. Lord Campbell CJ stated that when she was taken by pirates a total loss occurred. After that, she was never restored to the owners; nor had they had an opportunity of regaining possession. They had lost possession because of events over which they had no control, and therefore were entitled to the indemnity for which they had paid. Lord Campbell CJ said that if once there has been a total loss by capture, that is construed to be a permanent total loss unless something afterwards occurs by which the assured either has the possession restored, or has the means of obtaining such restoration. His Lordship added that mere right to obtain the vessel is nothing: if that were enough to prevent a total loss, there never would in this case have been a total loss at all, for pirates are the enemies of mankind, and have no right to the possession. The question therefore is, had the owners ever, after the capture, the possession or the means of obtaining possession?

A total loss may be converted into a partial loss if the subject matter insured is restored to the assured's possession.[64] In *Dean v Hornby*, it was held, there never was a restoration, nor the means of regaining possession as what was done after the capture by the pirates was the act of the re-captor, the vessel remained out of the control of the assured, the re-captor brought her to another port where she was sold and she was then brought to England. The possession was taken away by the claimants and never restored to them. The assured, therefore, never had an opportunity of taking possession and consequently there never ceased to be a total loss. [65] This was different to *Masefield v Amlin* as in *Masefield* there was a reasonable hope if not likelihood of recovery.[66] David Steel J[67] found the impact and effect of a capture is very fact sensitive. The judge noted that where a vessel is seized as a prize and condemned in a prize court, property is transferred and on any view the former owner is irretrievably deprived of the vessel. On the other hand mere seizure by pirates without more has no impact on the proprietary interests in a vessel. David Steel J emphasised that what had been transferred in *Masefield* was possession and not title and the question was whether recovery of

---

63   (1854) 3 Ellis and Blackburn 180.

64   *Dean v Hornby* (1854) 3 Ellis and Blackburn 180, 192, Wightman J.

65   The Court did not clarify if it was a CTL or ATL but since the court mentioned notice of abandonment it can be presumed that the vessel became a CTL. In *Masefield AG v Amlin Corporate Member Ltd* [2011] 1 Lloyd's Rep 630, para 32, Rix LJ stated that there is no positive sign that the court was being asked to consider ATL as distinct from CTL. The emphasis on the giving of notice of abandonment in the judgments of Lord Campbell and Coleridge J makes sense only on the basis that a CTL was in mind. The focus of the argument was plainly not between an ATL and a CTL, but between a total loss and a partial loss. David Steel J expressed a similar view at para 40.

66   David Steel J, [2010] 1 Lloyd's Rep 509, para 35.

67   [2010] 1 Lloyd's Rep 509, para 39.

possession was legally or physically impossible. Rix LJ[68] added that in *Dean v Hornby* the recapture by the Crown was for the purposes of the Crown, not the owner. As the judgments state, the owner never thereafter regained possession or the means of possession.

Dean v Hornby was distinguished in *Thornely v Hebson*[69] in which, similar to *Masefield*, the owners, before they brought the action, had the means of obtaining possession. In *Thornely v Hebson* the *William* was insured for £1,200. After leaving Hull she struck on a sandbank, and put into Dover to be repaired. She sailed from Dover on 19 December, 1816, and proceeded on her voyage. After the vessel left Dover she was damaged as a result of having encountered a heavy gale, she leaked so much that the crew left the vessel as they were no longer able to navigate her. Notwithstanding the state of the *William*, eight men from the *Hyder Ali* volunteered to go on board the *William* in the hope of bringing her into port. The *Hyder Ali* arrived at New York with the late crew of the *William* on 4 March, and then (the ultimate fate of the *William* being unknown) an abandonment was made to the underwriters of the vessel which the defendant insurers refused to accept, as intelligence had arrived in England that the men from the *Hyder Ali* had succeeded in bringing the *William* into Newport, a port in Rhode Island. The *William* arrived at Newport on 10 March 1817. The vessel was sold under the decree of the Admiralty Court at Rhode Island, which the assured might have prevented by raising money and paying the salvage. The assured relied on two circumstances in order to constitute this a total loss: the first was the desertion of the ship by the crew, and the second was the sale at Rhode Island. It was held that there was no total loss. Abbott CJ stated that it was the duty of the assured to raise the money to pay the salvage. Bayley J held that the desertion of the crew did not amount to a total loss. Here the vessel was taken possession of by persons acting not adversely but for the joint benefit of themselves and the owners. Thus, the owners were never dispossessed of the vessel. Then, as to the second point, the sale, in order to constitute a total loss, must have been found to have been necessary, and wholly without the fault of the owners. Here, the vessel originally worth £1,200 was sold for £315. If the owners had exerted themselves, and were unable to raise money, in order to release the ship and put her into a proper state of repair, the sale might have been necessary, but there was no proof of such exertion. The Court noted that the sale would not amount to a total loss, so as to entitle the assured to recover, if it was in their power to have prevented it. The custody of the vessel was in the salvors until the salvage was paid; but the owners still had legal possession. Consequently, it was held that the sale was not necessary, and that the claimant was not entitled to recover.

A question may arise in terms of the legality of paying a ransom which was discussed in *Masefield v Amlin*. David Steel J was unpersuaded that paying ransom is against public policy.[70] The judge recognised the fact that so far as harm is concerned it is true that ransom payments incentivise piratical seizure, the more so if there is insurance cover. On the other hand if the crews of the vessels are to be taken out of harm's way, the only option is to pay the ransom. Diplomatic or military intervention cannot usually be relied upon and failure to pay may put other crews in jeopardy. Rix LJ pointed out that there is no legislation against the payment of ransoms, which is therefore not illegal. The repeal of limited legislation in the past (the Ransom Act 1782, which only outlawed the payment of ransom in respect of British ships taken by the King's enemies or persons committing hostilities against the King's subjects, and which was repealed by section 1 of the Naval Prize Acts Repeal Act 1864) only serves to emphasise this fact. Pirates have been spoken of as the enemies of mankind. On the other hand, there is no universal morality against the payment

---

68   [2011] 1 Lloyd's Rep 630, para 33.
69   (1819) 2 Barnewall and Alderson 513.
70   [2010] 1 Lloyd's Rep 509, para 60.

of ransom, the act not of the aggressor but of the victim of piratical threats, performed in order to save property and the liberty or life of hostages.

Actual total loss of freight

An insurance on freight is an undertaking that the owner of the ship shall not be prevented by any of the perils insured against from having a right to recover freight from the persons who have bound themselves to pay it.[71] Actual total loss of freight may occur whenever the occurrence of the event, on which the earning of freight depends, is rendered absolutely impossible, or in any practical sense utterly hopeless, by means of the perils insured against.[72] Determination of total loss of freight depends on the conditions under which freight might be earned by the assured. It is necessary to determine in the first place whether or not as between charterer and shipowner the right to receive the freight has been lost by perils of the sea.[73] In *Carras v London & Scottish Assurance Corp Ltd (The Yero Carras)*[74] the vessel did not become a CTL as the cost of repair was less than the insured value of the vessel. The freight was held to become an ATL for the reason that the charterparty was cancelled as the vessel did not load the cargo before the cancellation date. The freight was lost because the charterparty under which it was to be earned was destroyed by the perils of the sea.

Under the charterparty the freight may be earned only on the condition of the arrival of the goods on a particular ship at the port of destination. When such arrival is rendered impossible or hopeless, for example, by her foundering at sea, this ought, in principle, to be an actual total loss on freight, quite irrespective of all questions as to the state of the cargo.[75] It may be the case that freight is earned only if the cargo arrives at the port of destination in an undamaged condition. In such a case if the vessel is lost during voyage the freight will be lost too if the cargo is not transferred and carried to the destination by another vessel. Alternatively, the earning of the freight insured may be made to depend on the delivery of the goods according to the terms of the bill of lading. In such a case as the earning of the freight does not depend on the arrival of a particular ship, the cargo may be transhipped in case the vessel is damaged and cannot proceed with the voyage.[76] The expenses incurred to transfer the goods on a substituted ship may be regarded as sue and labour expenses. However, it should be noted that neither the Institute Time Clauses Freight 1995 nor the Institute Voyage Clauses Freight provide a clause rendering sue and labour expenses recoverable.

The loss may be partial if, under the charterparty terms, the owner has a right to receive freight for so much of the voyage as was at an end. For the insurance purposes the freight might not be apportioned when the terms of the policy exclude any demand for a part of the voyage. If the voyage is indivisible, apportionment will not be possible either.

Brett J explained in *Rankin v Potter* that there is no loss on freight by reason of partial damage to the ship or of partial damage to cargo. There is a partial loss of freight under a general policy on freight, if there be a general average loss caused by a peril insured against giving rise to a general average contribution; or under certain circumstances if there be a total loss of part of a cargo; or if in case of total loss of the ship the cargo be sent on in a substituted ship; or if in case of a total

71 *Atty v Lindo* (1805) 1 B & PNR 236, 241 Sir J Mansfield Ch J.
72 Arnould, para 28–28.
73 *Atty v Lindo* (1805) 1 B & PNR 236; *Carras v London & Scottish Assurance Corp Ltd (The Yero Carras)* (1935) 53 Ll L Rep 131 Greene LJ.
74 (1935) 53 Ll L Rep 131.
75 Arnould, para 28–28.
76 *Shipton v Thornton* (1838) 9 Adolphus and Ellis 314 where the owner was held to have been entitled to claim the contractual freight although the freight he had to pay upon transhipment was lower than the contractual freight.

loss of the cargo the ship earns some freight in respect of other goods carried on the voyage insured. In *Rankin v Potter* the vessel was damaged and it appeared the cost of repair would exceed the value of the vessel after repair. In such a case the freight was totally lost.

In *Carras v London and Scottish Assurance Corporation, Limited*[77] the vessel was abandoned to the underwriters following a stranding. The insurer settled the claim and the vessel was surrendered to the salvors in discharge of their claim, was sold by them and was repaired in 1932. Freight was insured subject to the Institute Voyage Clauses – Freight. Clause 4 reads as follows: 'In the event of the total loss, whether absolute or constructive, of the vessel, the amount underwritten by this policy shall be paid in full, whether the vessel be fully or only partly loaded or in ballast, chartered or unchartered.' It was held that the freight was lost because the charterparty under which it was to be earned was destroyed by the perils of the sea. The earning of freight under a charterparty of a specific vessel depends on the continued existence of that vessel as a cargo carrying vessel, at least in a case like this where no cargo is on board and the vessel is on her way to the port where she should be tendered to the charterers. If, therefore, in such a case the ship is lost or destroyed, the performance of the charterparty and the earning of the freight is prevented and if that is due to perils of the sea the shipowner is relieved from liability in damages to the charterers by the usual exception of perils of the sea in the charterparty. But apart from the loss or destruction of the vessel, the freight may be lost and the shipowner may be relieved as against the charterers if the vessel is so damaged and disabled as to be incapable of being repaired save at an expense exceeding her value when repaired.

It should be noted that the Institute Voyage Clauses Freight clause 13 and Institute Time Clauses Freight clause 15 set out rules about total loss of freight. The two clauses are identical that: (1) In the event of the total loss (actual or constructive) of the vessel named herein the amount insured shall be paid in full, whether the vessel be fully or partly loaded or in ballast, chartered or unchartered. (2) In ascertaining whether the vessel is a constructive total loss, the insured value in the insurances on hull and machinery shall be taken as the repaired value and nothing in respect of the damage or break-up value of the vessel or wreck shall be taken into account. (3) Should the vessel be a constructive total loss but the claim on the insurance on hull and machinery be settled as a claim for partial loss, no payment shall be due under Clause 13 (or 15).

Time when actual total loss must be constituted

Total loss occurs when the subject matter insured is destroyed or annihilated or when it ceases to be a thing of the kind insured. In such cases timing will not be an issue. Irretrievable deprivation may be questioned in some cases where a vessel is captured, after a claim against the underwriters for payment of a total loss, but before the claim is settled there is a recapture. In such a case there are two *obiter* views expressed that the loss ceases to be a total loss.[78] The test for irretrievable deprivation is whether, by reason of the vessel's (or goods') situation, it was wholly out of the power of the assured or the underwriters to procure its arrival.[79] Moreover, for a deprivation to be regarded as irretrievable regaining the possession of the subject matter insured has to be impossible. If these tests are satisfied objectively and after the assured and the insurer settled the claim if the subject matter insured is recovered, this should not change the nature of the settlement since, at the time of the settlement, deprivation was objectively believed to be irretrievable. As discussed in

---

77   [1936] 1 KB 291.
78   *Goldsmid v Gillies* (1813) 4 Taunt. 803, 805–806; *Tunno v Edwards* (1810) 12 East 488, 490.
79   *Fraser Shipping Ltd v Colton* [1997] 1 Lloyd's Rep 586.

Dean v Hornby and *Masefield v Amlin*, depending on the facts, a capture may create an ATL and a subsequent recapture may convert the loss to a partial loss. Therefore it is arguable that both at the time of the fact occurred and at the time of the settlement or writ ATL should exist.

This is subject to proof of mutual mistake made by both of the parties before the settlement was entered.

Further reading

Bennett, *The Law of Marine Insurance*, 2nd edn, [2006] Oxford University Press. Chapter 21.

Gilman et al., *Arnould: Law of Marine Insurance and Average*, 18th edn, Sweet & Maxwell 2013. Chapter 28.

Khurram, 'Total loss and abandonment in the law of Marine Insurance', *Journal of Maritime Law and Commerce* [1994] 25(1) January, 95–118.

Rose, *Marine Insurance: Law and Practice*, 2nd edn, [2012] Informa. Chapter 21 and 23.

Soyer, 'Piratical capture actual total loss?', *Journal of International Maritime Law* [2011] 17(2): 80–82.

Chapter 9

Constructive Total Loss

Chapter Contents

Definition

A constructive total loss (CTL) is a concept peculiar to marine insurance.[1] It is an intermediate form of loss between partial and actual total loss.[2] The editors of Arnould describe ATL as a total loss in law and in fact and CTL is a total loss in law but not in fact.[3] If the requirements for a CTL are met the assured may claim for a total loss of the vessel although the vessel say, was not destroyed. On the other hand, the assured is not obliged to claim for a CTL, he may choose to claim for a partial loss.[4]

Under section 60(1) of the MIA 1906 there is a constructive total loss where

a) the subject matter insured is reasonably abandoned on account of its actual total loss appearing to be unavoidable, or

b) because it could not be preserved from actual total loss without an expenditure which would exceed its value when the expenditure had been incurred.

Section 60(2) supplements[5] subsection (1) by providing:

in particular, there is a constructive total loss –

i) Where the assured is deprived of the possession of his ship or goods by a peril insured against, and

  a) it is unlikely that he can recover the ship or goods as the case may be, or

  b) the cost of recovering the ship or goods, as the case may be, would exceed their value when recovered; or

ii) In the case of damage to a ship, where she is so damaged by a peril insured against, that the cost of repairing the damage would exceed the value of the ship when repaired.

Section 60(2)(ii) further provides 'In estimating the cost of repairs, no deduction is to be made in respect of general average contributions to those repairs payable by other interests, but account is to be taken of the expense of future salvage operations and of any future general average contributions to which the ship would be liable if repaired'; or

iii) In the case of damage to goods, where the cost of repairing the damage and forwarding the goods to their destination would exceed their value on arrival.

The subject matter insured is reasonably abandoned on account of its actual total loss appearing to be unavoidable (s.60(1))

The word 'abandonment' within the meaning of s.60(1) of the MIA 1906 is not a notice of abandonment in the sense of Sections 61, 62 and 63 of the MIA 1906, but 'the abandonment

---

1 *Rickards v Forestal Land Timber & Railways Co Ltd (The Minden)* [1942] AC 50, 83, Lord Wright; *Court Line v King, The* (1944) 78 Ll L Rep 390, 400, Stable LJ; *Moore v Evans* [1918] AC 185; *Kastor Navigation Co Ltd v AGF MAT (The Kastor Too)* [2004] 2 Lloyd's Rep 119, para 8.

2 Outside marine insurance, the only total loss which is acknowledged is an actual total loss. *Kastor Navigation Co Ltd v AGF MAT (The Kastor Too)* [2004] 2 Lloyd's Rep 119, para 8.

3 As will be explained below, to convert CTL into a total loss in fact a notice of abandonment is needed. Arnould, para 29-01.

4 *Da Costa v Newnham* (1788) 2 Term Rep 407. The MIA 1906 s 61 provides: 'Where there is a constructive total loss the assured may either treat the loss as a partial loss, or abandon the subject-matter insured to the insurer and treat the loss as if it were an actual total loss.'

5 S 60(2) does not merely illustrate s 60(1) but supplements it: *Robertson v Nomikos* [1939] AC 371, Lord Porter; *Rickards v Forestal Land Co Ltd* [1942] AC 50 per Lord Wright at p 84. *The Bamburi* [1982] 1 Lloyd's Rep 312.

of any hope of recovery'.[6] When the ship is spoken of as 'abandoned on account of its actual total loss appearing to be unavoidable', the word is used in nearly the same sense as when according to the law of salvage the ship is left by master and crew in such a way as to make it a 'derelict', which confers on salvors a certain but not complete exclusiveness of possession, and a higher measure of compensation for salvage services.[7] But to render the ship a 'derelict', it must have been left (a) with that intention (b) with no intention of returning to her; and (c) with no hope of recovering her.[8] The forecast of the probability of actual total loss would, at any rate a century ago, nearly always have to be made by the master on the spot; and even in these days of easy and quick wireless communication, the decision would very often devolve on the master.[9]

In *Masefield AG v Amlin Corporate Member Ltd*[10] – the facts of which were given in the actual total loss chapter – the vessel and its cargo were not abandoned in the relevant sense.[11] On the contrary, the shipowners and the cargo owners had every intention of recovering their property.[12] There was no reasonable basis for regarding an ATL as unavoidable.[13] The fact that the pirates were holding the ship to ransom to which the owners succumbed does not alter this analysis.[14]

Where the subject matter insured is reasonably abandoned because it could not be preserved from actual total loss without an expenditure which would exceed its value when the expenditure had been incurred (s.60(1))

This is an economic test.[15] Lord Abinger stated in *Roux v Salvador*[16] that in the case of, for instance, perils of the sea rendering the ship unnavigable without any reasonable hope of repair or by which the goods are partly lost, or so damaged, that they are not worth the expense of bringing them, or what remains of them, to their destination, the test to determine CTL is 'if a prudent man not insured, would decline any further expense in prosecuting an adventure, the termination of which will probably never be successfully accomplished'.[17] The test was recently approved by Andrew Smith J in *Venetico Marine SA v International General Insurance Co Ltd.*[18]

Deprivation of possession of ship or goods (s.60(2)(i)(a)

Recovery is unlikely

Under this heading an assured does not have to prove an ATL if he is able to show that he is deprived of possession of ship or cargo by a peril insured against and recovery is 'unlikely'.[19] What is required

6 *Masefield AG v Amlin Corporate Member Ltd* [2010] 1 Lloyd's Rep 509, David Steel J, para 55.
7 *Court Line v King, The* (1944) 78 Ll L Rep 390.
8 *Court Line v King, The* (1944) 78 Ll L Rep 390.
9 *Court Line v King, The* (1944) 78 Ll L Rep 390.
10 [2011] 1 Lloyd's Rep 630.
11 *Masefield AG v Amlin Corporate Member Ltd* [2010] 1 Lloyd's Rep 509, David Steel J, para 55.
12 [2010] 1 Lloyd's Rep 509, para 56.
13 [2010] 1 Lloyd's Rep 509, para 57.
14 [2010] 1 Lloyd's Rep 509, para 58.
15 *Court Line v King, The* (1944) 78 Ll L Rep 390.
16 (1836) 3 Bingham New Cases 266.
17 (1836) 3 Bingham New Cases 266, 286.
18 [2014] 1 Lloyd's Rep 349, para 438.
19 *Masefield AG v Amlin Corporate Member Ltd* [2011] 1 Lloyd's Rep 630 Rix LJ, para 15.

to be established is the loss of 'free use and disposal' of the ship or goods.[20] Although the Act is in general a codification of prior common law, the common law test in the case of CTL dispossession had been where recovery was 'uncertain', not 'unlikely'. So in this respect, the Act changed the law.[21]

The test is objective. It depends on the judgment of the reasonable man, not of the assured himself.[22] The judgment is to be exercised on the true facts existing at the relevant time, not merely on the facts as known or appearing to the assured.[23]

The words 'within a reasonable time' are implicit in subsection 2(i)(a).[24] In *Polurrian Steamship Company, Limited v Young*,[25] the *Polurrian* sailed from Newport on 9 October 1912, with a cargo of coals. On 25 October she was captured by the Greek navy and her cargo was removed and used for coaling the Greek fleet. On 26 October notice of abandonment in writing was given to the insurers. The ship was detained by the Greek Government until 8 December 1912, when they released her. Warrington J stated that the test of 'unlikelihood of recovery' has now been substituted for 'uncertainty of recovery'. The assured was held to have to establish fully (1) that at the date of the commencement of this action they were deprived of the possession of the *Polurrian*; and (2) that it was not merely quite uncertain whether they would recover her within a reasonable time, but that the balance of probability was that they could not do so. In *Panamanian Oriental Steamship Corp v Wright* (The *Anita*)[26] it was established that the recovery of the vessel within reasonable time was unlikely. In The *Anita* the vessel was seized at Saigon in March, 1966, after unmanifested goods had been discovered by customs officials. She was confiscated by order of a Special Court and had not been recovered until August 1968. The assured gave a notice of abandonment in May 1966 and this was held to be a constructive total loss of the vessel.

The assured was successful in his claim under this heading in *Bayview Motors Ltd v Mitsui Marine & Fire Insurance Co Ltd*[27] where the insurance claim was for the loss of motor vehicles that had been shipped from Japan to the Dominican Republic for onward carriage to the Turks and Caicos Islands. The vehicles arrived at Santo Domingo on 11 August 1997. Neither the bill of lading nor the cargo manifest mentioned the fact that they were intended for shipment on to the Turks and Caicos. Under the Dominican Customs Regulations onward transmission was permissible only where a statement to that effect had been made at the port of origin and consent had been given by the Dominican customs authorities. Although the claimants completed the necessary documents to comply with the local customs regulations the cars were not released. They were placed by the Dominican customs authorities in a fenced parking lot within the area of the port of Santa Domingo. At some point the vehicles were removed from the parking lot by the customs authorities, and the claimants were informed by the Port Authority in November 1997 that the vehicles had 'gone'; they had been taken by 'Customs' about a month earlier. The assured's claim for a CTL was approved

20 The Bamburi [1982] 1 Lloyd's Rep 312; Royal Boskalis Westminster NV v Mountain [1997] LR 523, 535, Rix J. The case was appealed but Rix J's finding on the CTL argument was not appealed. [1999] QB 674. The Detainment Clause in the Institute War and Strikes Clauses Hulls – Time 1983 provides:
    In the event that the Vessel shall have been the subject of capture seizure arrest restraint detainment confiscation or expropriation, and the Assured shall thereby have lost the free use and disposal of the Vessel for a continuous period of 12 months then for the purpose of ascertaining whether the Vessel is a constructive total loss the Assured shall be deemed to have been deprived of the possession of the Vessel without any likelihood of recovery.
21 Masefield AG v Amlin Corporate Member Ltd [2011] 1 Lloyd's Rep 630 Rix LJ, para 15.
22 Royal Boskalis Westminster NV v Mountain [1997] LRLR 523, 534, Rix J.
23 Royal Boskalis Westminster NV v Mountain [1997] LRLR 523, 534, Rix J.
24 Polurrian Steamship Co Ltd v Young, [1915] 1 KB 922 at p 937, Societe Belge SA v London & Lancashire Insurance Co (1938) 60 Ll L Rep 225 at p 234, Irvin v Hine, [1950] 1 KB 555 at p 569. The Bamburi [1982] 1 Lloyd's Rep 312.
25 [1915] 1 KB 922.
26 [1970] 2 Lloyd's Rep 365.
27 [2002] 1 Lloyd's Rep 652 (The Court of Appeal dismissed the appeal [2003] 1 Lloyd's Rep 131).

by the Court, the vehicles had not disappeared but had fallen into the hands of those who, in the real world, would not be returning them.

Bayview was affirmed in a recent case of *Clothing Management Technology Ltd v Beazley Solutions Ltd (t/a Beazley Marine UK)*.[28] In this case a British clothing manufacturer, CMT, manufactured clothing at a factory in Morocco. After working for a few years without a problem, in 2008 the owners of the Moroccan manufacturing company disappeared, leaving its workers unpaid. The workers occupied the factory and refused to finish the garments. CMT made a claim on its insurance for £180,527.60, being the price which CMT would have charged its customers for the garments to be manufactured from the clothing fabrics and trimmings not recovered from the factory in Morocco. Before the workers occupied the factory CMT made payments to the workers but negotiations broke down in early November 2008, at which point CMT understood that the workers would be stripping the factory of all its machinery and fabric. HHJ Mackie QC held that the garments became a constructive total loss. It became unlikely in early November 2008 that CMT could recover possession of the goods within a reasonable time to meet its commitments to customers. This was the case due to the nature of the products in question: fashion garments, which have a relatively short commercial life. Similar to *Bayview*, the Court accepted that the garments were not going to come out of the factory within a reasonable time, and they had a limited life as finished goods capable of being sold at or approaching invoice value. This was not physical impossibility but it was mercantile impossibility.

One might consider whether the outcome in *Masefield v Amlin* would have been different if the arguments along the same lines as those successful in *Beazley* had been brought forward. It was clear in *Masefield* that the cargo would lose its market (similar to the fashion garments in *Beazley*) therefore recovery of the goods (which would sell and make profit) within reasonable time was unlikely. However *Masefield* still seems different to *Beazley* for the reason that in the former recovery of cargo was not unlikely, it was a wait and see situation. Whereas in *Beazley* it was clear that the local courts would likely be sympathetic to the workers and the legal battle to recover the garments could last for years.

The cost of repairing the damage would exceed the value of the ship when repaired (s.60(2)(i)(b))

Under this heading the determinative issue is not whether the subject matter insured was destroyed or annihilated, but the cost of repair. In other words, repairing the ship may be physically possible but in matters of business it may be impracticable due to the cost of repair, which exceeds the value of the ship once repaired.[29]

Insured value

Section 60(2)(ii) of the MIA 1906 states 'In the case of damage to a ship, where she is so damaged by a peril insured against that the cost of repairing the damage would exceed the value of the ship when repaired'. However, as seen below, the relevant value, by virtue of the Institute Clauses, will be the insured value, not the actual value when repaired.

---

28 [2012] 1 Lloyd's Rep 571. The policy in *Beazley* did not insure a marine risk. Nevertheless since the policy incorporated it, the Marine Insurance Act 1906 was applied to resolve the dispute between the insurer and the assured.

29 *Moss v Smith*, (1850) 9 CB 94, 103; *Holdsworth v Wise* (1828) 7 Barnewall and Cresswell 794.

The relevant standard is what it would cost to make the vessel as good as she was before the casualty.[30] The question is, how would the claimants reasonably have gone about repairing the damage, judging them by the standards of owners who were uninsured and behaving prudently?[31] Under a valued policy, the test has been formulated in terms of repairing the vessel to the same condition, as nearly as possible, as at the time when the valuation was agreed.[32] Although the common law held that in a valued policy whether the subject matter of insurance be ship or goods, the valuation is the amount fixed by agreement at which in case of loss the indemnity is to be calculated,[33] the MIA 1906 s.27(4) provides 'Unless the policy otherwise provides, the value fixed by the policy is not conclusive for the purpose of determining whether there has been a constructive total loss'. On the other hand, cl.21 of the International Hull Clauses (01/11/03) provides:

21.1 In ascertaining whether the vessel is a constructive total loss, 80% of the insured value of the vessel shall be taken as the repaired value and nothing in respect of the damaged or break-up value of the vessel or wreck shall be taken into account.

21.2 No claim for constructive total loss of the vessel based upon the cost of recovery and/or repair to the vessel shall be recoverable hereunder unless such cost would exceed 80% of the insured value of the vessel.

In making this determination, only the cost relating to a single accident or sequence of damages arising from the same accident shall be taken into account.'

Some of the cost of repairs may be ultimately recoverable by the owners of the interest insured from the owners of other interests in general average. Section 60(2)(ii) states that such a recovery is irrelevant to any question of constructive total loss. If, for instance, the cost of repairing a ship will be £4m and her repaired value will be £3.5m, this is a case of constructive total loss, notwithstanding the fact that half the cost of the repairs may be eventually recoverable from the owners of the cargo.

On the other hand, contributions by third parties to the cost of salvage must be deducted when deciding whether the vessel is a constructive total loss.[34] In *Kemp v Halliday*[35] a ship sank with heavy cargo on board. The most convenient mode of saving ship or cargo or both was by raising the ship together with the cargo. It was held that in considering whether the ship became a CTL the contribution by the cargo owner to the cost of raising the ship and cargo would be taken into account.

---

30 *Pitman v Universal Marine Insurance Company* (1882) 9 QBD 192, 195, Lindley J.
31 *Roux v Salvador* (1836) 3 Bing. NC 266, 286, Lord Abinger; *Venetico Marine SA v International General Insurance Co Ltd* [2014] 1 Lloyd's Rep 349, para 438, 466.
32 Arnould, para 29–36.
33 *Shawe v Felton* (1801) 2 East 109; *Woodside v Globe Marine Insurance Co Ltd* [1896] 1 QB 105; *Burnand v Rodocanachi Sons & Co* (1882) 7 App Cas 333, 335 Lord Selborne.
34 S 60(2)(ii).
35 (1865–66) LR 1 QB 520.

Constructive total loss of goods

The MIA 1906 s.60(2)(i) states that there is a CTL of goods where the assured is deprived of the possession of his ship or goods by a peril insured against, and

a) it is unlikely that he can recover the ship or goods, as the case may be, or
b) the cost of recovering the ship or goods, as the case may be, would exceed their value when recovered.

In the case of damage to goods, there is a CTL where the cost of repairing the damage and forwarding the goods to their destination would exceed their value on arrival (s.60(2)(iii)).

Clause 13 of the Institute Cargo Clauses provides that: 'No claim for constructive total loss shall be recoverable hereunder unless the goods are reasonably abandoned either on account of their actual total loss appearing to be unavoidable or because the cost of recovering, reconditioning and forwarding the goods to the destination to which they are insured would exceed their value on arrival.'

Loss of voyage

Loss of voyage may be relevant for CTL of cargo. In *British and Foreign Marine Insurance v Sanday*[36] it was held that where goods are insured at or from one port to another port the insurance is not confined to an indemnity to be paid in case the goods are damaged or destroyed, but extends to an indemnity to be paid in case the goods do not reach their destination. This may be variously described as an insurance of the venture, or an insurance of the voyage, or an insurance of the market, as distinguished from an insurance of the goods simply and solely. The MIA 1906 does not list this case as CTL, however s.91(2) enacts that the rules of the common law, including the law merchant, save insofar as they are inconsistent with the express provisions of the Act, shall continue to apply to contracts of marine insurance.

In *Sanday*, two British vessels laden with merchandise belonging to British merchants for sale in Germany were on a voyage from Argentina to Hamburg when war broke out between the United Kingdom and Germany and the further prosecution of the voyage became illegal. The cargo owners had insured the goods on both vessels, the perils insured against included restraints of princes. Shortly after the outbreak of the war the vessels were directed to proceed to British ports, which they did. The cargo owners warehoused their goods and gave notice of abandonment to their underwriters, claiming on a constructive total loss. The House of Lords accepted the claim. Their Lordships found it well settled that when goods are insured at and from the port of loading to the port of destination, there is a loss if the adventure is frustrated by a peril insured. Insurance was not merely against the actual merchandise being injured, but also an insurance of its safe arrival. The goods were insured for their safe arrival at Hamburg, and the destruction of that adventure was directly caused by His Majesty's declaration. Lord Atkinson said '. . . if the loss of the voyage, the loss of the chance of arriving at the port of destination, and the consequent loss of the market appear to be unavoidable, there would be a constructive total loss of the subject-matter.'

For a CTL of a vessel Lord Wright expressed a contrary view in *Rickards v Forestal Land Timber & Railways Co Ltd (The Minden)*.[37] His Lordships said 'The primary subject of the insurance is the goods

---

36 [1916] 1 AC 650.
37 [1942] AC 50, 90.

as physical things, but there is superimposed an interest in the safe arrival of the goods. This is very old law. Lord Mansfield insisted on applying the same rule to an insurance on the ship, but his view was rejected and it was said that the loss of the voyage has nothing to do with the loss of the ship. The ship is a vehicle employed in general trading, not wedded to any particular adventure.'

Thus, there appears to be a difference between loss of adventure in insurance of cargo and insurance of goods. In *Rickards*, Lord Wright accepted that a policy on goods is covering a composite interest, the physical things or chattels, and also the expected benefit from their arrival.[38]

Date at which CTL to be assessed

The Marine Insurance Act is silent on the question of what is the point of time to be taken in ascertaining whether there was a constructive total loss. By the English common law the relevant time is at the date of the notice of abandonment and the date of issue of the writ.[39] In practice if a notice of abandonment is not accepted by underwriters, they agree that a writ be deemed to be issued.[40] The assured's rights finally crystallise on the issuance of the writ, that is, at the commencement of the action.[41] If the abandoned property is recovered before issue of writ, the assured cannot claim for a total loss,[42] whereas if there then existed a right to maintain a claim for a constructive total loss by capture, that right would not be affected by a subsequent recovery or restoration of the insured vessel.[43]

The cause of action arises on the date of the casualty, so the limitation period starts from that date.[44] However, this does not mean that there is a vested right to sue for a total loss immediately upon the casualty. Lord Mansfield said in *Hamilton v Mendes*[45] that the notion of a 'vested right in the plaintiff, to sue as for a total loss before the recaptor', is fictitious only for the reason that the assured is not obliged to abandon but he has an election. No right can vest as for a total loss, until he has made that election. He cannot elect before intelligence about the loss and if there is no loss despite the capture he cannot elect at all because he has no right to abandon, when the thing is safe.

Notice of abandonment

A claim for a constructive total loss has to be notified to the insurers in the form of a 'notice of abandonment'.[46] Notice of abandonment is different to the word abandonment as used in s.60(1) of the MIA 1906, which is abandoning the vessel to her fate without any hope of recovery.[47] Abandonment may also be used to describe the cession to underwriters by the assured of their property and interest in the ship.[48] Sometimes 'notice of abandonment' and 'abandonment' are used interchangeably. [49]

---

38 [1942] AC 50, 90– 91.
39 *Royal Boskalis Westminster NV v Mountain* [1997] LRLR 523, 534, Rix J; *Polurrian Steamship Company, Limited v Young* [1915] 1 KB 922; *Ruys v Royal Exchange Assurance Corp* [1897] 2 QB 135.
40 *Royal Boskalis Westminster NV v Mountain* [1997] LRLR 523, 534, Rix J.
41 *Royal Boskalis Westminster NV v Mountain* [1997] LRLR 523, 534, Rix J.
42 *Royal Boskalis Westminster NV v Mountain* [1997] LRLR 523, 534, Rix J.
43 *Polurrian Steamship Company, Limited v Young* [1915] 1 KB 922; *Ruys v Royal Exchange Assurance Corp* [1897] 2 QB 135.
44 *Bank of America National Trust and Savings Association v Chrismas (The Kyriaki)* [1993] 1 Lloyd's Rep 137.
45 (1761) 2 Burrow 1198, 1211.
46 Section 62(1) MIA 1906.
47 *Masefield AG v Amlin Corporate Member Ltd* [2010] 1 Lloyd's Rep 509, para 55 David Steel J.
48 *The WD Fairway*, [2009] 2 Lloyd's Rep 191, para 25.
49 *The WD Fairway*, [2009] 2 Lloyd's Rep 191, para 25.

Constructive total loss is distinct from the right to claim for a CTL, the latter being dependent upon a notice of abandonment.[50] Constructive total loss occurs before and independent of a notice of abandonment, however, it is the precondition to treat the loss as a CTL to tender a notice of abandonment.[51] If no notice of abandonment is given – unless the notice is excused by section 62 – the loss is treated as a partial loss.[52] Therefore, a notice of abandonment is a notification of an election between two alternative quanta of damage (partial loss or CTL).[53] The assured is never bound to give a notice of abandonment; he can always repair if he chooses, and refrain from insisting on a total loss.[54]

The doctrine is to a certain extent technical[55] in that although the assured has in reality suffered a constructive total loss and although he is upon general principles entitled to recover, he nevertheless will fail unless he has given a notice of abandonment. In *Knight v Faith*[56] the insured ship was stranded, got off, and brought into the harbour of Sta. Cruz in September. She remained there with her crew on board for a month, and, during that time, was pumped, and her cargo was discharged into other vessels. She was found to be so damaged by the accident that the necessary repairs could not be done at Sta. Cruz, as there was no dockyard, workmen or materials there; nor could she be taken to any port where she could prudently have been repaired. Thus, the master had to sell her but no notice of abandonment was given. The ship was not an ATL given that she retained her character as a ship after the stranding. This could have been a CTL but in the absence of notice of abandonment the assured could only claim for a partial loss.

The notice of abandonment is an offer[57] made by the shipowner to the underwriter to vest the property in the ship in the underwriter, so that he may deal with it as his own.[58] It shall communicate unequivocally, and in plain terms, that the assured offers to abandon to the underwriters all his interest in the thing insured.[59] The object of notice, which is entirely different from abandonment, is that he may tell the underwriters at once that he elected to treat the loss as a total loss.[60] Then the insurer may either reject or accept the notice of abandonment. The doctrine of notice of abandonment was introduced to enable the insurers to repair the ship if they should deem such a proceeding to their advantage as well as securing all the advantages to which, if liable for a total loss, they would be entitled as owners of the ship from the time when the damage was sustained to which the loss is ascribed.[61] Thus, it appears that notice of abandonment is required in favour of the underwriters, so as to prevent the assured from obtaining by fraud more than a full indemnity.[62] The abandonment excludes any presumption which might have arisen from the silence of the assured, that they still meant to adhere to the adventure as their own.[63]

50 *Robertson v Nomikos* [1939] AC 371.
51 *Robertson v Nomikos* [1939] AC 371, Lord Wright.
52 The MIA 1906 s 62(1).
53 *Bank of America National Trust and Savings Association v Chrismas (The Kyriaki)* [1993] 1 Lloyd's Rep 137, 151.
54 *Pitman v Universal Marine Insurance Co* (1882) 9 QBD 192, 196 Lindley, J.
55 *Castellain v Preston* (1883) 11 QBD 380, 387, Brett LJ.
56 (1850) 15 Queen's Bench Reports 649.
57 It is important how the notice is drafted. The assured's letter to the underwriter may be interpreted as an invitation to treat rather than an offer in which case no notice of abandonment is given. *Kusel v Atkin* [1997] CLC 554.
58 *Western Assurance Co of Toronto v Poole* [1903] 1 KB 376, 383, Bigham J.
59 Arnould, para 30–13.
60 *Kaltenbach v Mackenzie* (1878) 3 CPD 467, 480, Cotton LJ.
61 *Knight v Faith* (1850) 15 Queen's Bench Reports 649, 659.
62 *Castellain v Preston* (1883) 11 QBD 380, 387, Brett LJ.
63 *Cologan v London Assurance Company* (1816) 5 Maule and Selwyn 447, Abbott J.

Form of notice and acceptance of abandonment

The MIA 1906 s.62(2) provides that 'Notice of abandonment may be given in writing, or by word of mouth, or partly in writing and partly by word of mouth, and may be given in any terms which indicate the intention of the assured to abandon his insured interest in the subject matter insured unconditionally to the insurer.'[64]

The acceptance of an abandonment may be either express or implied from the conduct of the insurer. The mere silence of the insurer after notice is not an acceptance.[65] Where notice of abandonment is properly given, the rights of the assured are not prejudiced by the fact that the insurer refuses to accept the abandonment.[66]

Timing of notice of abandonment

Notice of abandonment must be given with reasonable diligence after the receipt of reliable information of the loss, but where the information is of a doubtful character the assured is entitled to a reasonable time to make inquiry.[67] Brett LJ held in *Kaltenbach v Mackenzie*[68] that it is not at the moment of the first hearing of the loss that notice of abandonment must be given, but that the assured must have a reasonable time to ascertain the nature of the loss with which he is made acquainted. If he hears merely that his ship is damaged, that may not be enough to enable him to decide whether he ought to abandon or not; he must have certain and accurate information as to the nature of the damage.[69] If he gets information upon which any reasonable man must conclude that there is very imminent danger of her being lost, the moment he gets that information he must immediately give notice of abandonment.[70]

The notice of abandonment was regarded too late in *Anderson v Royal Exchange Assurance Company*[71] in which the *Fanny* sailed with the wheat insured on board and ran ashore. The hull of the ship was for four weeks entirely under water at high water, and until the cargo was taken out she could not be raised or removed. The whole of the cargo was damaged. The wheat was taken out of the ship and kiln dried. The assured gave a notice of abandonment after some part of the remainder of the cargo of wheat was sold to feed hogs, and the residue thereof was thrown into the sea as unfit for use. The abandonment was held to be out of time. The court found that the assured took the chance of endeavouring to make the best of the accident for himself, and then gave the notice when he found that he could not recover his loss with his efforts.

Circumstances at which notice of abandonment is not needed

Notice of abandonment is unnecessary where, at the time when the assured receives information of the loss, there would be no possibility of any benefit to the insurer if notice were given to him.[72] Notice of abandonment may be waived by the insurer[73] and a notice is not necessary where an insurer has re-insured his risk.[74]

---

64 The MIA s 62(2).
65 The MIA s 62(5).
66 The MIA s 62(4).
67 The MIA s 62(3).
68 (1878) 3 CPD 467, 472.
69 (1878) 3 CPD 467, 472.
70 (1878) 3 CPD 467, 474.
71 (1805) 7 East 38.
72 The MIA 1906 s 62(7).
73 The MIA 1906 s 62(8).
74 The MIA 1906 s 62(9).

If the insurer pays for a CTL despite the fact that no notice of abandonment has been given the insurer may be deemed to have waived the requirement of a notice. Notice may be unnecessary where for instance an assured only learns of the constructive total loss after the vessel has also become an actual total loss.[75] Notice of abandonment was held to be not necessary in *Kastor Navigation Co Ltd v AGF MAT (The Kastor Too)*[75a]. In this case a fire began in the engine room of the vessel *Kastor Too* on 9 March 2000 at about 14:20. Fifteen hours later at between 05:00 and 06:00 on 10 March she sank in deep water. It was held that the vessel became a CTL by fire and there was simply no opportunity to give notice of abandonment before the vessel had become an actual total loss by reason of entering the seawater. Section 62(7) was also applied in *Clothing Management Technology Ltd v Beazley Solutions Ltd (t/a Beazley Marine UK)*[76] the facts of which were referred to above. In *Beazley* there was no realistic possibility of the insurers being able to exercise effective control over salvage. Insurers knew what was going on and could have intervened, with consent, which the assured would readily have given, should they have wished to do so. There was no possibility of benefit to the insurers if notice had been given to them. Similarly, in *Bayview Motors Ltd v Mitsui Marine & Fire Insurance Co Ltd*[77] notice of abandonment was unnecessary for the reason that the vehicles had been by then distributed and used, and pursuing legal action against the local Customs authorities would prove a lengthy and fruitless exercise since their assets were non-attachable, as per local law.

Acceptance of abandonment

Notice of abandonment is rarely accepted.[78] Where notice of abandonment is accepted the abandonment is irrevocable. The acceptance of the notice conclusively admits liability for the loss and the sufficiency of the notice.[79] If the assured gives notice and the underwriters accept the abandonment, or if the assured recovers as for a total loss, the property insured thereby becomes the property of the underwriters.[80] But if he elects to do this, as the thing insured, or a portion of it still exists, and is vested in him, the very principle of the indemnity requires that he should make a cession of all his right to the recovery of it, and that too, within a reasonable time after he receives the intelligence of the accident, that the underwriter may be entitled to all the benefit of what may still be of any value; and that he may, if he pleases, take measures, at his own cost, for realising or increasing that value.[81] In all these cases not only the thing assured or part of it is supposed to exist in *specie*, but there is a possibility, however remote, of its arriving at its destination, or at least of its value being in some way affected by the measures that may be adopted for the recovery or preservation of it.[82]

Abandonment, within the context of abandoning the property of the subject matter insured to the insurer, is not peculiar to policies of marine insurance; it is part of every contract of indemnity.[83] 'Abandon' means 'give up for lost', and that the owners are renouncing all their rights

75 *The Kastor Too* [2004] 2 Lloyd's Rep 119, para 9, Rix LJ.
75a [2004] 2 Lloyd's Rep 119.
76 [2012] 1 Lloyd's Rep 571.
77 [2002] 1 Lloyd's Rep 652.
78 *The WD Fairway*, [2009] 2 Lloyd's Rep 191, para 42. Tomlinson J said that it is rarely if ever accepted because underwriters believe that by acceptance of a notice of abandonment they will assume the burden of ownership.
79 S 62(6).
80 *Robertson v Nomikos* [1939] AC 371, Lord Porter.
81 *Roux v Salvador*, (1836) 3 Bingham New Cases 266, 286, Lord Abinger.
82 *Roux v Salvador*, (1836) 3 Bingham New Cases 266, 286, 287, Lord Abinger.
83 *Kaltenbach v Mackenzie* (1878) 3 CPD 467, Brett LJ; *Rankin v Potter* (1873) LR 6 HL 83 Lord Blackburn.

in the ship except the right to recover insurance.[84] A valid abandonment in s.63 necessarily means an abandonment by the assured to the insurer and passes the property to him.[85] In s.61 the word 'abandonment' seems to import an act on the part of the assured, but in truth it amounts usually to nothing more than his making up his mind to give notice of abandonment to the insurer under section 62(1), at the risk of losing his right of election under section 61.[86] As referred to above, this is different to the abandonment as is contemplated by s.60(1), where the act is done in consequence of an actual total loss appearing unavoidable.[87]

Upon acceptance of notice of abandonment the ownership of the ship passes to the insurer and the insurer is entitled to everything which that ship can earn.[88] The insurer is not entitled to anything that has been earned by the use of that ship before she was his ship. If freight is payable upon arrival of the goods, the insurer, as owner, is entitled by the delivery of the cargo at the port of destination to the freight for the use of the ship during the whole voyage. The insurer is not entitled to the freight which was prepaid, paid before the time when she became his ship. That freight is not earned by him by the use of the ship, it is earned by the man who got it, and who was paid it at the time it was paid when he was the owner of the ship.[89]

Upon acceptance of notice of abandonment the insurer admits his liability to pay for a CTL and admits that the offer to cede given by the assured is validly made.[90] Upon acceptance of notice of abandonment he would acquire an equitable lien. An equitable lien would arise before payment for a CTL in circumstances where insurers have conclusively admitted liability for the CTL and irrevocably elected to take over the interest of the assured in the wreck.[91] On payment for a CTL he would on the conventional analysis acquire equitable ownership in the appropriate proportion. Once payment is made, the insurer obtains full legal title under s.79(1).[92]

It is open to the underwriters not to take over the interest of the assured.[93] Payment for a CTL coupled with an express election to take over the interest of the assured in the vessel will be effective to transfer to insurers the assured's legal or at least equitable title to the vessel.[94] It was stated that insurers have it within their power to create in their favour proprietary rights in the vessel either by acceptance of notice of abandonment or, if it is different, by irrevocable election to take over, on the promised payment for a CTL, the interest of the assured in the wreck.[95] So long as the assured continues to press for payment for a CTL after underwriters have declined notice of abandonment, the assured impliedly repeat their offer to cede their interest to underwriters and it is open to underwriters to accept that offer.[96] If there was a subsequent payment for constructive total loss without any acceptance of the notice of abandonment then the insurers retained their right to opt to exercise proprietary rights over the subject matter under s.79(1).

In *Dornoch Ltd v Westminster International BV, The WD Fairway*, the insurers had rejected the notice of abandonment but paid for a constructive total loss, and thereafter some had elected to take over

84   *Court Line v King, The* (1944) 78 Ll L Rep 390.
85   *Court Line v King, The* (1944) 78 Ll L Rep 390.
86   *Court Line v King, The* (1944) 78 Ll L Rep 390.
87   That abandonment, for example, by the master and crew leaving the ship with the intention of never returning, etc., may lead up to and justify a subsequent abandonment to the insurer, but the two are wholly different acts, and distinct in kind. *Court Line v King, The* (1944) 78 Ll L Rep 390.
88   *The Red Sea* [1896] p 20.
89   *The Red Sea* [1896] p 20.
90   *The WD Fairway* [2009] 2 Lloyd's Rep 191, para 35.
91   *The WD Fairway* [2009] 2 Lloyd's Rep 191, para 48.
92   *The WD Fairway* [2009] 2 Lloyd's Rep 191, para 79.
93   *The WD Fairway* [2009] 2 Lloyd's Rep 191, para 27.
94   *The WD Fairway* [2009] 2 Lloyd's Rep 191, para 41.
95   *The WD Fairway* [2009] 2 Lloyd's Rep 191, para 42.
96   *The WD Fairway* [2009] 2 Lloyd's Rep 191, para 44.

the vessel while others had not. The vessel was sold, and at that point the remaining insurers purported to exercise their right to take over the vessel. Those insurers who had exercised their statutory rights were individually entitled to a share in a vessel represented by their proportion of the paid loss and were not bound by the sale because at the time of the sale the assured had no title to pass to the purchaser.[97] By contrast, those insurers who had not exercised their rights to take over the vessel (who had not elected) before the purported sale had neither a legal nor an equitable interest in the vessel so that the purchaser acquired rights in the vessel which could not be displaced by the subsequent sale. If an abandonment has been accepted, the insurer is entitled to elect to take over the insured subject matter and all rights attaching thereto, in accordance with s.63, and the insurer thereby obtains an equitable lien over the subject matter.

Constructive total loss of freight

It is not easy to consider a case in which freight might become a CTL that requires the assured to give a notice of abandonment. An actual total loss of ship will occasion an actual total loss of freight, unless when the ship is lost, and the whole or a part of such cargo is saved, and might be sent on in a substituted ship so as to earn freight.[98] An actual total loss of the whole cargo will occasion an actual total loss of freight, unless such loss should so happen as to leave the ship capable, as to time, place, and condition, of earning an equal or some amount of freight by carrying other cargo on the voyage insured.[99] If the vessel becomes a CTL and the assured abandons the vessel to the insurer the freight is lost too but this will be an ATL of the freight after such abandonment, he has no longer the means of earning the freight, or the possibility of ever receiving it if earned, such freight going to the underwriters on ship.[100]

This does not mean that there can never be a CTL of freight. Brett J in *Rankin v Potter* identified that where the ship is damaged but cargo which was on board has been saved under circumstances which leave it doubtful whether such cargo might or might not be forwarded in a substituted ship, or if the original cargo should be lost and the ship may or may not probably earn some freight by carrying other goods on the voyage insured, it may be that in order to make certain his right to recover as for a total loss on the policy on freight, the assured should give notice of abandonment of the chance of earning such substituted freight.

A constructive total loss of a vessel and a total loss of freight are two distinct matters that a vessel may be captured and recaptured so that recovery of the vessel before the claim form is issued may prevent the assured from recovering for CTL but this does not affect the loss of the freight under the charterparty for instance if the cancellation date has been missed. In *Roura & Forgas v Townend*[101] the claimant sold a quantity of jute to Spanish buyers under contracts, an essential term of which was that the jute should be shipped before the end of January, 1918. The claimant chartered a vessel to perform the contract and insured the profit of the charterparty for £30,000. The cancelling date in the charter was 31 December 1917. The chartered vessel was captured on 10 November but was recaptured in 27 February 1918. There was a constructive total loss of the *Igotz Mendi* by her capture, and before the ship was restored to the owners such capture resulted in a total loss to the plaintiffs of their rights and profit under the charter. In short, the event agreed upon as necessary to give a right to indemnity had happened, and had irrevocably caused the loss of the subject matter

97 *The WD Fairway* [2009] 2 Lloyd's Rep 191, para 64.
98 *Rankin v Potter* (1873) LR 6 HL 83, Brett J.
99 *Rankin v Potter* (1873) LR 6 HL 83, Brett J.
100 *Benson v Chapman* (1843) 6 Manning and Granger 792.
101 [1919] 1 KB 189.

of the insurance. In these circumstances, the restoration of the vessel itself to its owners did nothing to extinguish or minimise the claimant's loss. *Roura* was applied in *Robertson v Nomikos*,[102] where the owner of the *Petrakis Nomikos* insured the hull and machinery of the vessel for £28,000 and the freight in the sum of £4,110. The latter insurance was subject to the Institute Time Clauses – Freight, which provided (inter alia) as follows: '5. In the event of the total loss, whether absolute or constructive of the steamer, the amount underwritten by this policy shall be paid in full, whether the steamer be fully or only partly loaded or in ballast, chartered or unchartered.' The vessel was chartered to carry a full cargo of crude oil from Venezuela to the United Kingdom. While undergoing some repairs at Rotterdam, a violent explosion occurred on board followed by a fire. The cost of repair was £37,400; owing to the increase in tonnage values, when repaired, the vessel's value would be £45,000. The shipowner made a claim for partial loss on the hull and machinery policies and the underwriters paid £27,000. The charterparty was never performed, and the shipowner had not received any part of the freight payable thereunder. Thus, the shipowner claimed the full value of the insured freight from the insurers who rejected the claim reasoning that clause 5 only applies if the shipowner has elected to treat the loss under his hull policies as a constructive total loss by giving a notice of abandonment. Lord Wright rejected the insurers' arguments. His Lordship noted that the hull policies and the freight policy are distinct contracts and are only to be read together insofar as one incorporates the other. Clause 5 cannot be construed by considering what action the shipowner took on his hull policies.

Successive total losses

The doctrine of merger of unrepaired partial loss with a subsequent total loss (see section 77(2) of the Act) may apply where 'by a peril insured against there is a constructive total loss and no notice of abandonment is given, then if in the ordinary course of an unbroken sequence of events following upon the peril insured against the constructive total loss becomes an actual total loss – as, for instance, if there is a capture followed by confiscation'.[103]

Thus, if the first loss although being a CTL was treated as a partial loss, subsequent total loss will entitle the assured to claim under the merger rule. The subsequent total loss is required to occur within the currency of the policy and be caused by the perils of the sea.[104] If the two losses entitle the assured to claim for total losses no merger takes place between the losses. This was illustrated by *The Kastor Too* in which the first loss was a CTL but the assured did not give a notice of abandonment. As referred to above, the facts established that there was 15 hours between the fire and the vessel sinking upon taking seawater, that is, between the CTL and ATL of the vessel. The notice of abandonment was held not to have been necessary as there would have been no benefit for the underwriters even if it had been tendered before the vessel became an ATL. The merger was argued by the insurers because if the first loss, CTL, had merged into an ATL, the latter having been caused by an uninsured peril as no fortuity was established with regard to the entering of seawater, the insurer would not have been liable. The trial judge found that there were two separate casualties. Had the vessel not sunk, she would have been a constructive total loss by reason of fire. There were two losses, and there was no merger of the first with the second. Therefore, in the absence of merger, it could not be said that the owners had suffered no loss by fire, for the loss was complete before the actual loss by sinking. The owners had never treated the constructive

102 [1939] AC 371.
103 *Fooks v Smith* [1924] 2 KB 508.
104 Arnould, para 29–11.

total loss by fire as a partial loss and had not elected to do so by reason of originally claiming only for an actual total loss. In either case the claim was for a total loss and involved the owners ultimately abandoning the vessel to insurers against payment.

Further reading

Bennett, *The Law of Marine Insurance*, 2nd edn, [2006] Oxford University Press. Chapter 21, Losses; Chapter 22, Claims and Claims Handling.

Gilman et al., *Arnould: Law of Marine Insurance and Average*, 18th edn, [2013] Sweet & Maxwell. Chapter 29, Constructive Total Loss; Chapter 30, Abandonment.

Khurram, 'Total loss and abandonment in the law of Marine Insurance', *Journal of Maritime Law and Commerce* [1994] 25(1) January, 95–118.

Rose, *Marine Insurance: Law and Practice*, 2nd edn, [2012] Informa. Chapters 23 and 24.

Sinclair, 'The *Kastor Too* (10 March 2004): the interaction between actual total losses and constructive total losses', *Insurance & Reinsurance Law Briefing* [2004] 91,May, 1–4.

Soyer, 'Marine insurance: fire – perils of the sea – constructive total loss', *Journal of International Maritime Law* [2004] 10(5): 398–400.

Soyer, 'Claiming under a cargo policy for piracy', *Journal of International Maritime Law* [2010] 16(2): 94–97.

Weale, 'Frustration and constructive total loss', *Lloyd's Maritime and Commercial Law Quarterly* [2013] 2, May, 260–270.

Chapter 10

Partial Loss (Particular Average)

Chapter Contents

A policy of marine insurance does not guarantee that the subject matter insured will arrive safe and sound at the destination; it aims to indemnify the assured against the results of certain perils. Partial loss (particular average) is defined by s.64(1) of the Marine Insurance Act 1906 which states, 'A particular average loss is a partial loss of the subject-matter insured, caused by a peril insured against, and which is not a general average loss.' For instance if severe weather damages the hull of the vessel, which can be repaired, or if because of the severe weather seawater gets into the hold and one fourth of a cargo of sugar dissolves and as a result the shipowner loses one fourth of the freight payable under the contract of carriage, there will be partial losses suffered by the vessel, by the cargo and a partial loss of freight, respectively.

Measure of indemnity

Measure of indemnity is dealt with by sections 67–78 of MIA 1906. Section 67(1) provides that the sum which the assured can recover in respect of a loss on a policy by which he is insured, in the case of an unvalued policy to the full extent of the insurable value, or, in the case of a valued policy to the full extent of the value fixed by the policy is called the measure of indemnity.

Section 16 of the MIA 1906 lays down the manner in which the insurable value of the subject matter must be ascertained, subject to any express provision or valuation in the policy.

Section 67 has to be read in conjunction with section 16 of the Act.

Section 16 provides: Measure of insurable value.

Subject to any express provision or valuation in the policy, the insurable value of the subject matter insured must be ascertained as follows:

1   In insurance on ship, the insurable value is the value, at the commencement of the risk, of the ship, including her outfit, provisions and stores for the officers and crew, money advanced for seamen's wages, and other disbursements (if any) incurred to make the ship fit for the voyage or adventure contemplated by the policy, plus the charges of insurance upon the whole; the insurable value, in the case of a steamship, includes also the machinery, boilers, and coals and engine stores if owned by the assured, and, in the case of a ship engaged in a special trade, the ordinary fittings requisite for that trade;

2   In insurance on freight, whether paid in advance or otherwise, the insurable value is the gross amount of the freight at the risk of the assured, plus the charges of insurance;

3   In insurance on goods or merchandise, the insurable value is the prime cost of the property insured, plus the expenses of and incidental to shipping and the charges of insurance upon the whole;

4   In insurance on any other subject matter, the insurable value is the amount at the risk of the assured when the policy attaches, plus the charges of insurance.

The object is to provide an indemnity placing the assured in the same position he was in at the beginning of the risk, thus insurable value is, in total and partial losses, to be ascertained at the commencement of the risk.[1] In *Aitchison v Lohre*, Brett LJ stated 'the ship must be repaired, or estimates may be procured for repairing her, so as to make her as nearly as possible equal to what she was before the damage caused to her by the perils insured against, and in either case at such reasonable cost as the shipowner can by reasonable effort procure'.[2]

---

1   *Pitman v Universal Marine Insurance Company* (1882) 9 QBD 192; *British & Foreign Insurance Co Ltd v Wilson Shipping Co Ltd* (1920) 4 Ll L Rep 371; Arnould, para 27–02.

2   *Aitchison v Lohre* (1878) 3 QBD 558, 564.

Partial loss of goods

The rules as to the 'measure of indemnity' for a particular average loss on goods are thus summarised in s.71 of the MIA 1906 as follows:

> Partial loss of goods, merchandise, &c.
>
> Where there is a partial loss of goods, merchandise, or other moveables, the measure of indemnity, subject to any express provision in the policy, is as follows:
>
> 1 Where part of the goods, merchandise or other moveables insured by a valued policy is totally lost, the measure of indemnity is such proportion of the sum fixed by the policy as the insurable value of the part lost bears to the insurable value of the whole, ascertained as in the case of an unvalued policy;
>
> 2 Where part of the goods, merchandise, or other moveables insured by an unvalued policy is totally lost, the measure of indemnity is the insurable value of the part lost, ascertained as in the case of total loss;
>
> 3 Where the whole or any part of the goods or merchandise insured has been delivered damaged at its destination, the measure of indemnity is such proportion of the sum fixed by the policy in the case of a valued policy, or of the insurable value in the case of an unvalued policy, as the difference between the gross sound and damaged values at the place of arrival bears to the gross sound value;
>
> 4 'Gross value' means the wholesale price, or, if there be no such price, the estimated value, with, in either case, freight, landing charges, and duty paid beforehand; provided that, in the case of goods or merchandise customarily sold in bond, the bonded price is deemed to be the gross value. 'Gross proceeds' means the actual price obtained at a sale where all charges on sale are paid by the sellers.

Accordingly, when an integral part of the goods insured is totally lost, the underwriters will have to pay the same proportion of the insurable or agreed value which the goods lost bear to the whole goods of the same description covered by the insurance; in other words, the exact amount lost must be paid for at its value, whether insurable or agreed.[3]

Under section 16(3), the sole basis upon which a particular average loss on goods fully insured can be adjusted is, as regards the underwriter, either their prime cost on board or their value in the policy. The underwriter on goods does not engage to put the assured in the same condition he would have been in had his goods arrived safely at the port of destination, but solely to put him (with regard to such goods) in the situation he was in at the beginning of the risk.[4] Brett LJ said in *Pitman v Universal Marine Insurance Co*,[5] 'The question then is, what is the loss against which the underwriter agrees to indemnify? . . . In the case of an insurance on marketable goods it is known to both that the object of the assured in conveying such goods from one place to another is that they may be sold at a profit. In order that such a result may ensue they should arrive and arrive undamaged. If they do not arrive at all, the assured is put in the same position as he was at the beginning of the adventure if he is paid the price at which he originally bought the goods. If the goods are damaged, he is put into that position by being paid a percentage of such price.'

---

3 Arnould, para 27–10.
4 Arnould, para 27–05 .
5 (1882) 9 QBD 192, 212.

The proportion of loss is calculated by comparing the selling price of the sound goods with the damaged part of the same goods at the port of delivery.[6] The difference between these two subjects of comparison affords the proportion of loss in any given case, that is, it gives the aliquot part of the original value, which may be considered as destroyed by the perils insured against.[7] This then gives the amount of indemnity to be paid to the assured (for example, if the one-half, the one-fourth, or one-eighth of the loss to be made good in terms of money).[8] The underwriter who shall pay by this rule, will pay such proportion or aliquot part of the value in the policy, as corresponds with the diminution in value occasioned by the damage.[9]

The loss must in this case, as in the case alluded to, be calculated upon the gross proceeds of the goods insured.[10] In *Hurry v Royal Exchange Assurance Company*,[11] the invoice price of hemp, including the premiums of insurance, and all insurable interest at the time, was £5,997. Had it not met with damage, the gross produce would have been £7,799; but being damaged, the gross produce was only £6,000, making a difference of £1,799. The net produce, after deducting the charges for freight, duties, and other expenses, would have been £5,809; but in consequence of the damage, the gross produce was only £5,999 and the net produce only £3,942. It was held that the loss ought to be computed by charging upon the invoice price such a proportion of the difference between the sound and damaged prices at the port of delivery as the invoice value bears to such sound price, viz. that as the sound price of £7,799 had sustained a loss of £1,799, the invoice price of £5,997 will sustain a loss of £1,384.

Partial loss of the ship

Brett LJ stated in *Pitman v Universal Marine Insurance Company*[12] that if the ship is damaged the loss to the owner is in being prevented from using the ship as a means of earning freight. The assured desires to cover the cost of repairs because the business inconvenience to the shipowner can only be met by repairing the ship so as to make her as good a carrier as she was before.[13]

Section 69 states the measure of indemnity for partial loss of the ship. Accordingly,

1   Where the ship has been repaired, the assured is entitled to the reasonable cost of the repairs, less the customary deductions, but not exceeding the sum insured in respect of any one casualty.
2   Where the ship has been only partially repaired, the assured is entitled to the reasonable cost of such repairs, computed as above, and also to be indemnified for the reasonable depreciation, if any, arising from the unrepaired damage, provided that the aggregate amount shall not exceed the cost of repairing the whole damage, computed as above.
3   Where the ship has not been repaired, and has not been sold in her damaged state during the risk, the assured is entitled to be indemnified for the reasonable depreciation arising from the unrepaired damage, but not exceeding the reasonable cost of repairing such damage, computed as above.'

---

6   *Usher v Noble* (1810) 12 East 639.
7   *Usher v Noble* (1810) 12 East 639.
8   *Usher v Noble* (1810) 12 East 639.
9   *Johnson v Sheddon* (1802) 2 East 581.
10 *Hurry v Royal Exchange Assurance Company* (1802) 3 Bosanquet and Puller 308.
11 (1802) 3 Bosanquet and Puller 308.
12 (1882) 9 QBD 192, 212–213.
13 (1882) 9 QBD 192, 212–213.

As seen above, the measure of indemnity is expressed by reference to three distinct factual situations by the three subsections: (1) where the ship has been repaired; (2) where the ship has been partially repaired; and (3) where the ship has not been repaired. The common element in each of the three situations is the limitation that the measure of indemnity is not to exceed the sum insured. That is expressly provided by subsection (1) and the provision is then applied by reference in both subsections (2) and (3) by the words 'computed as above'.[14]

Section 69 states the law subject to any express provision of the policy. In other words, it sets out the common law and recognises that the parties can, by the terms of the policy, agree to modify or exclude the measure of indemnity which would otherwise apply under the commercial law.

Prima facie the measure of indemnity under subsection (3) is the depreciation arising from the unrepaired damage.[15] The time for assessing the measure of indemnity for unrepaired damage is when the risk under the policy in question expires.[16] In *The Medina Princess*, Roskill J[17] held 'The underwriters' liability for unrepaired damage cannot be determined until the policy expires, whether that expiry is by effluxion of time in the case of a time policy, or by the completion of or abandonment of the voyage in the case of a voyage policy or by sale in the case of either type of policy or otherwise.'[18]

Reasonable cost of repair

Section 69(3) requires the measure of indemnity to be quantified on the basis of what it would have cost to repair if the repairs had been carried out.[19] Reasonable cost of repair, in the words of Roskill J, is 'What would have to be expended to put the ship right.'[20] The cost of towage is recoverable under the policy as part of the partial loss claim.[21] Crew's wages during repairs as part of the cost of repairs is not recoverable.[22] The cost of discharging the cargo, which has become putrid by reason of a sea peril and is rightly refused by the consignee at the port of discharge, is not recoverable from the hull and machinery insurer.[23]

Reasonable fees for classification surveyors and other surveyors were properly allowable as part of the cost of repairs[24] and drydocking dues are recoverable.[25] Clause 18 of the International Hull Clauses provides:

> Other than in general average, the Underwriters shall not be liable for wages and maintenance of the Master, Officers and Crew or any member thereof, except when incurred solely for the necessary removal of the vessel from one port to another for the repair of damage covered by the Underwriters, or for trial trips for such repairs, and then only for such wages and maintenance as are incurred whilst the vessel is underway.

---

14   *Kusel v Atkin (The Catariba)* [1997] 2 Lloyd's Rep 749.
15   *Helmville Ltd v Yorkshire Insurance Co Ltd (The Medina Princess)* [1965] 1 Lloyd's Rep 361, 515.
16   *Kusel v Atkin (The Catariba)* [1997] 2 Lloyd's Rep 749, 756.
17   [1965] 1 Lloyd's Rep 361, 516.
18   [1965] 1 Lloyd's Rep 361, 517.
19   [1965] 1 Lloyd's Rep 361, 521.
20   *The Medina Princess* [1965] 1 Lloyd's Rep 361, 520.
21   [1965] 1 Lloyd's Rep 361, 521.
22   [1965] 1 Lloyd's Rep 361, 523.
23   *Field v Burr* [1899] 1 QB 579.
24   [1965] 1 Lloyd's Rep 361, 523.
25   [1965] 1 Lloyd's Rep 361, 523.

For wooden ships it was customary that the cost of repairs was subject to a deduction of one-third new for old where the vessel was not at the time of the injury a new one.[26] The amount, therefore, of the partial loss arising in respect of the expense of repairing a damaged wooden ship, is the reasonable cost of so repairing her as to make her as nearly as possible equal to what she was before the damage caused to her by the perils insured against, less one-third new for old; that is to say, less one-third of the expense of the labour and materials used in making the repairs. This mode is applicable irrespective of the greatness of the difference between the value of the vessel before she was damaged and after she was repaired. In other words, whether the ship is, by the repairs which are necessary to make her equal to what she was before the damage, made only a little or very largely of greater value than she was before the damage.[27] That was the rule where a ship was repaired, and delivered over to the owner again for his benefit; in such cases it was right that such an allowance should be made, upon the ground which has been stated, that the owner was put in a better position than he was before, by having new work for old.[28] The one-third deduction rule is inapplicable to iron ships, and the practice is to provide for them by special clauses of 'No thirds to be deducted except as regards hemp rigging and ropes, sails, and wooden deck'.[29] Clause 18 of the International Hull Clauses 2003 provides 'Claims recoverable under this insurance shall be payable without deduction on the basis of new for old.'

Unrepaired vessels

In Pitman in his dissenting judgment Brett LJ held that if the assured does not repair but leaves the ship unrepaired until the end of the risk, assuming no subsequent total loss intervened, he is to be compensated as if he had repaired. In this case he will be entitled only to the cost of the repairs he might have made by estimate instead of by actual expenditure.[30] However, s.69(3) provides that 'Where the ship has not been repaired, and has not been sold in her damaged state during the risk, the assured is entitled to be indemnified for the reasonable depreciation arising from the unrepaired damage'. Thus, the measure of indemnity in respect of an unrepaired partial loss is based upon the reasonable depreciation of the vessel. The Marine Insurance Act 1906 does not state how the depreciation is going to be assessed. Lindley J[31] held in Pitman that the depreciation in value of the ship as a result of the damage was to be calculated by comparing the value of the sound ship at the port of distress with her value there when damaged, and that the resultant proportion should be applied to the ship's real value at the inception of the risk, in the case of an unvalued policy, or to her agreed value in the case of a valued policy.[32] While the proportionate amount of depreciation is found on the basis of the sound value of the vessel immediately before the casualty, the depreciation that the insurer will be liable for must clearly be calculated by reference to the insured value in a valued policy.[33]

---

26 *Aitchison v Lohre* (1879) 4 App Cas 755, at 762 Lord Blackburn; Cotton LJ.

27 Brett LJ, *Aitchison v Lohre* (1878) 3 QBD 558, 564.

28 *Da Costa v Newnham* (1788) 2 Term Rep 407; *Fenwick v Robinson* (1828) 3 Car. & p 323.

29 Chalmers and Archibald, The Marine Insurance Act, 1906, 3rd edn, Butterworth, 1922, p 124.

30 (1882) 9 QBD 192, 208–209.

31 (1882) 9 QBD 192, 201.

32 See *Irvin v Hine*, [1950] 1 KB 555, 572; *Lidgett v Secretan* (1870–71) LR 6 CP 616, 626 where Willes J stated the assureds '. . . are to get the amount of the diminution in value of the vessel at the end of the . . . risk, the difference between her then value and what she would have been worth but for the damage she had sustained.'

33 S 27 MIA 1906, *Elcock v Thomson* [1949] 2 KB 755, *Pitman v Universal Marine Insurance Co* (1882) 9 QBD 192, *Steamship 'Balmoral' Co Ltd v Marten* [1902] AC 511 at pp 521–522. *Irvin v Hine* [1950] 1 KB 555.

In *Elcock v Thomson*,[34] despite being a non-marine case the Court applied section 69(3). A mansion was insured against fire, valued at £106,850. The mansion was damaged by fire. Its actual value before the fire was £18,000, and its actual value after the fire was £12,600. The depreciation in value was £5,400 in £18,000, in other words, a depreciation of 3 in 10. The cost of reinstatement would have been some £40,000, but the mansion was not in fact reinstated. Morris J held that indemnification for reasonable depreciation must take into account any agreed valuation. The judge was of the view that when parties have agreed upon a valuation then, in the absence of fraud or of circumstances invalidating their agreement, they have made an arrangement by which for better or for worse they are bound.[35] The loss recoverable from the insurer was three-tenths of the agreed value of £106,850 = £32,055.

In *Compania Maritima Astra SA v Archdale (The Armar)*,[36] while on a voyage from New Orleans to Japan with a cargo of rice, the *Armar* went aground off the coast of Cuba. After four days of salvage operations the *Armar* was refloated. She arrived at a shipyard in Savannah, her cargo was discharged and the vessel was drydocked for the purpose of ascertaining the extent of her damage. The vessel had been insured against total loss for $1.2m. The sound replacement value of the ship was $675,000. The Court held that section 69(3) applied. Rabin J, sitting at the New York Supreme Court, stated that while the Act is otherwise a model of brevity and lucidity, and elsewhere sets forth an explicit formula for the partial loss of cargo (Section 71), the intended formula to define 'reasonable depreciation' in the case of valued hull insurance is not clear. The judge referred to *Elcock v Thomson*, where the formula of recovery used was a percentage of the insured value equal to the percentage of actual depreciation. In *The Armar* this formula was applied as follows: the value of the vessel in her present condition was $218,000. Her sound value undamaged was $675,000. The difference was $457,000. An equal percentage of the insured value would be $812,400, which would be the maximum that the assured could recover for repairs. The cost of repairs was $736,315, which was within the bounds of the limitation imposed by the formula and thus recoverable.

Partial loss of the freight

Section 70 of the MIA 1906 provides 'Subject to any express provision in the policy, where there is a partial loss of freight, the measure of indemnity is such proportion of the sum fixed by the policy in the case of a valued policy, or of the insurable value in the case of an unvalued policy, as the proportion of freight lost by the assured bears to the whole freight at the risk of the assured under the policy.'

There is a partial loss of freight under a general policy on freight, if there is a general average loss caused by a peril insured against giving rise to a general average contribution; or under certain circumstances if there is a total loss of part of a cargo; or if in case of total loss of the ship the cargo is sent on in a substituted ship; or if in case of a total loss of the cargo the ship earns some freight in respect of other goods carried on the voyage insured.[37]

---

34   [1949] 2 KB 755.
35   S 27 MIA 1906; *City Tailors Ltd v Evans* (1921) 9 Ll L Rep 394; *Elcock v Thomson* [1949] 2 KB 755.
36   [1954] 2 Lloyd's Law Rep 95.
37   *Rankin v Potter* (1873) LR 6 HL 83, 98–99 Brett J.

Successive losses

Section 77 of the Marine Insurance Act 1906 provides that the insurer is liable for successive losses, even though the total amount of such losses may exceed the sum insured (s.77(1)). Under the same policy, if a partial loss, which has not been repaired or otherwise made good, is followed by a total loss, the assured can only recover in respect of the total loss (s.77(2)).

Although no one partial loss could give rise to a right of indemnity in excess of the insured value, the aggregate of more than one such partial loss could do so.[38] If a ship is damaged and repaired and becomes a total loss subsequently, the assured may recover for both the cost of repair and the total loss of the vessel. In *Le Cheminant v Pearson* the ship sailed and was damaged by perils of the sea, and sue and labour expenses were incurred to save the ship. Following this the ship was captured and became a total loss. The action was brought to recover the sue and labour expenses as well as the total loss of the ship. It was held that in addition to the total loss of the ship the assured can recover the expenses for sue and labour 'without making any distinction whether it was recoverable as an average loss from damage repaired, or within the words of the permission to "sue, labour, and travail, &c."'[39] This rule applies when the subject matter insured was actually repaired.

If no repairs have been made, as stated above, under s.77(2), no previous partial loss can be recovered in addition to the total loss of the subject matter insured. Willes J explained in *Lidgett v Secretan*:[40]

> A partial loss is not paid for if there is a total loss of the vessel during the period covered by the policy; because, when the underwriter pays the total loss, he actually discharges all partial losses occurring during the voyage – except such as fall within the suing and labouring clause, which are apart from the sum insured.

In *Livie v Janson*[41] during the currency of the insurance the ship was damaged by ice driving the ship ashore. The master and crew endeavoured without success to get the ship off and the next morning she was discovered and seized by the American authorities. The question was, does the total loss by subsequent seizure and condemnation denude the assured of the right to recover in respect to the previous partial loss by sea-damage? The court held that it does: the substantive loss was the total loss of the vessel which was attributable to the seizure only.

Livie v Janson was applied in *British & Foreign Insurance Co Ltd v Wilson Shipping Co Ltd*[42] in which case during the currency of the policy the vessel sustained damage by marine risks, but, to the extent of £1,770, this damage was not repaired. On a subsequent voyage, but during the currency of the policy, the vessel became a total loss by war perils. The question was whether under a policy of marine insurance the assured can recover in respect of damage sustained by the ship insured during the currency of the policy when the ship is totally lost before the damage is in fact repaired. The issue is to be considered under two different headings separately. First, where the total loss is caused by a peril insured against by the policy in question and therefore the insurer is liable and second, where the loss is not covered by the policy and thus the insurer is not liable. The first case is governed by s.77(2) of the MIA 1906. The second case is not dealt with by the Act. In *Livie v Janson*, Lord Ellenborough stated 'We may lay it down as a rule, that where the property deteriorated is

---

38 *Kusel v Atkin (The Catariba)* [1997] 2 Lloyd's Rep 749, 758.
39 *Le Cheminant v Pearson* (1812) 4 Taunt. 367.
40 (1870–71) LR 6 CP 616.
41 (1810) 12 East 648.
42 [1921] 1 AC 188.

afterwards totally lost to the assured, and the previous deterioration becomes ultimately a matter of perfect indifference to his interests, he cannot make it the ground of a claim upon the underwriters. The object of a policy is indemnity to the assured; and he can have no claim to indemnity where there is ultimately no damage to him from any peril insured against. If the property, whether damaged or undamaged, would have been equally taken away from him, and the whole loss would have fallen upon him had the property been ever so entire, how can he be said to have been injured by its having been antecedently damaged?' In *British & Foreign Insurance Co Ltd v Wilson Shipping Co Ltd*,[43] Lord Birkenhead[44] said that Lord Ellenborough is

> clearly right. If not, the assured whose vessel becomes a total loss during a voyage in the course of which she meets a succession of gales, each of which causes damage, would, in a case to which s. 77, sub-s. 2, of the Act of 1906 does not apply, be in a position to claim under his policies for each of these losses in succession, although none of them is or could be repaired, and he could at the same time recover the value of the ship as a total loss if she is wrecked during the currency of the policies. Such a result would, of course, be contrary to the principles upon which marine insurance has always been conducted. The owner would not in such a case merely be indemnified against loss, but he would receive a profit.

In *British v Wilson*, Lord Birkenhead adopted the reasoning of Bailhace J at first instance that:

> Whether an underwriter is or is not liable for unrepaired damage cannot be ascertained until the expiration of the policy. If before the expiration of the policy there is a total loss he is not liable to pay for the earlier unrepaired damage sustained during the currency of the same policy, and it makes no difference whether the total loss falls upon him or is due to an excepted peril against which the owner is insured or uninsured. The true doctrine is that the smaller merges in the larger and the rule is not limited to the ground upon which it was based by Lord Ellenborough – namely, that there was no continuing prejudice. . . . The question in every case must be, did the total loss happen before the underwriter's liability for the unrepaired damage accrued? If yes, he is not liable; if no, he is liable. It would be strange if an underwriter's liability . . . should vary with the terms of some contract not needing to be disclosed to him, which the owner has made with some stranger to the contract of insurance.[45]

Consequently, the rule laid down by the decisions is that when a vessel, insured against perils of the sea, is damaged by one of the risks covered by the policy and before that damage is repaired she is lost, during the currency of the policy, by a risk which is not covered by the policy, then the insurer is not liable for such unrepaired damage.[46]

Successive unrepaired partial losses

Successive unrepaired partial losses are not mentioned under section 77. The issue however came before the court in *Kusel v Atkin (The Catariba)*[47] where it was held that the rule stated under section 77(2) applies to this case too. In other words, successive partial losses, unrepaired at the date of

---

43 [1921] 1 AC 188.
44 [1921] 1 AC 188, 194.
45 [1921] 1 AC 188, 198–199.
46 [1921] 1 AC 188, 199, Lord Birkenhead.
47 [1997] 2 Lloyd's Rep 749.

termination of cover, must, by analogy, be treated as having caused the assured only such actual pecuniary loss as is measured by reference to the cumulative depreciation of the vessel's value at the time of termination of cover. In *Kusel v Atkin (The Catariba),*[48] the vessel ran aground off the British Virgin Islands on 10 August 1995 (the first casualty). The vessel was towed to Sopers Hole where she was beached. On 6 September the island was struck by Hurricane Luis, which damaged the vessel severely (the second casualty). At the time when the hurricane struck the damage sustained in the course of the first casualty had not been repaired. The cost of repairing the damage attributable to either the first or the second casualty did not exceed the insured value of the vessel but the cumulative cost of repairing both the damage attributable to the first and to the second casualties did exceed the insured value of the vessel. It was held that section 77(1) has to be read consistently with section 69(3) so that the former does not override the latter so as to remove the limit of recovery by reference to the insured value. Subsection (1) relates to successive losses in respect of which the total measure of indemnity specified by the Act could exceed the insured value. That would be the case where successive partial losses were sustained and *repaired before* the termination of cover, as provided for under s.69(1). Although no one partial loss could give rise to a right of indemnity in excess of the insured value, the aggregate of more than one such partial loss could do so. It is to that eventuality that s.77(1) is directed. In other words, the subsection can consistently with s.69(3) only refer to successive *repaired* losses. When there are successive unrepaired losses, by the express terms of s.69(3), the measure of indemnity may in turn be capped by whichever is the lower of the reasonable cost of repairing the damage and the insured value of the vessel.

Further reading

Bennett, *The Law of Marine Insurance*, 2nd edn, [2006] Oxford University Press. Chapter 21.
Gilman et al., *Arnould: Law of Marine Insurance and Average*, 18th edn, [2013] Sweet & Maxwell. Chapter 27.
Rose, *Marine Insurance: Law and Practice*, 2nd edn, [2012] Informa. Chapter 22.

---

48 [1997] 2 Lloyd's Rep 749.

Chapter 11

Sue and Labour Expenses

Chapter Contents

Mitigation of loss

Principles of contract law

In contract law a claimant who makes a claim for damages is under a duty to mitigate his loss. This is, however, not a duty in the sense that he can be sued if he fails to do so, because the effect of a failure to mitigate is that the claimant cannot recover damages in respect of the portion of his loss that is attributable to his own conduct or lack thereof.

There are two aspects of the mitigation doctrine:

- the claimant must not unreasonably increase the loss suffered as a result of the breach
- the claimant must take reasonable steps to minimise his loss. The claimant need only take reasonable steps and the law does not make onerous demands of a claimant in this respect.

An illustration of the duty is seen in *Payzu v Saunders*[1] in which it was held that the claimant was not entitled to the difference between the contract price and the market price of the silk, which was rising at the time, on the ground that their rejection of the defendant's offer to supply the silk in cash terms constituted a failure to mitigate their loss.[2]

In terms of taking reasonable steps to minimise the loss, what is reasonable will depend on the facts of the individual case and the circumstances of the claimant. The claimant's circumstances were taken into account in *Wroth v Tyler*[3] where the claimants' failure to mitigate was not unreasonable given that he lacked the financial resources to make a substitute purchase.

Insurance Law

In an insurance contract what the insurer undertakes is to indemnify the loss that the assured suffers upon the occurrence of the risk insured against. It is said that what the insurer pays under an insurance contract is 'damages'.[4] The question then may arise whether an assured is under the duty to mitigate damages which he may be entitled to claim if the peril insured against occurs. This question is answered differently under marine and non-marine insurance.

Before discussing the existence of the duty it should be noted that the duty comes into play in insurance in terms of claiming the expenditure incurred by the assured to prevent or minimise the insured loss from the insurer. Therefore, in contrast to contract law principles, in the insurance context, what is discussed is not whether the assured will lose the amount which is attributable to his failure to prevent or minimise the loss, but whether the assured can claim expenses incurred for that purpose.

---

1 [1918–19] All ER Rep 219.
2 In this case, under the initial agreement the buyer would pay for the goods in instalments. However, the buyer delayed in making payments and the seller (wrongly) assumed that the buyer repudiated the agreement. When the buyer made demand for contractual delivery the seller offered to deliver the goods only if the buyer pays cash upon delivery. The buyer refused the offer and bought the same type of goods from another supplier but for a more expensive price. The buyer then sued the seller for wrongful repudiation of the contract and claimed damages for the price difference. The Court held that the buyer could have mitigated his loss but he did not, therefore the buyer was not entitled to recover his loss which was attributable to his failure.
3 [1973] 1 All ER 897.
4 *Sprung v Royal Insurance (UK) Ltd* [1999] 1 Lloyd's Rep IR 111.

The existence of the duty to mitigate in insurance

In contract law, the existence of the duty to mitigate does not depend upon an express clause in the contract to this effect but the law recognises the duty in appropriate cases. In marine insurance the relevant issue is analysed under the 'sue and labour' expenses and the policies commonly include a clause to this effect.[5] Moreover, section 78(4) of the MIA 1906 states: 'It is the duty of the assured and his agents, in all cases, to take such measures as may be reasonable for the purpose of averting or minimising a loss.'

This section does not apply to non-marine insurance; therefore, in the non-marine context, it is strictly necessary to include a clause which entitles the assured to claim such expenditure. The English courts have rejected the argument that[6] 'Every contract of insurance carries an implied term that the insured will make reasonable efforts to prevent or minimise loss which may fall to the insurer. If such prevention or mitigation involves the insured in expenditure, it is an implied term of the insurance policy that the insured is entitled to be indemnified in respect of that expenditure.' This principle was recently confirmed by Flaux J[7] who stated:

> . . . as a matter of English law, in non-marine liability insurance, there is no concept of "sue and labour", so that, if the insured acts to defend a claim and thereby avoids the insurer being under any liability, there is no entitlement to an indemnity against the costs and expenses incurred in defending successfully the liability which would otherwise have arisen under the insurance, in the absence of some express provision to that effect.

Whether or not the duty is implied in marine insurance has not been expressly discussed as the marine insurance policies normally include a sue and labour clause. Whether the duty is implied in the non-marine context, however, came before the English courts because it is not commonplace for a non-marine policy to include a clause to that effect.

Sue and labour clauses – marine insurance

The wording of the sue and labour clause in the standard (Lloyd's SG)[8] form of English marine policy is as follows:

> In case of any loss or misfortune, it should be lawful to the assured, their factors, servants, and assigns, to sue, labour, and travel for, in, and about the defence, safeguard, and recovery of the said goods and merchandises and ship, &c., or any part thereof, without prejudice to that insurance, to the charges whereof the assurers should contribute each one according to the rate and quantity of his sum assured.

---

5   For instance, Institute Cargo Clauses (A,B,C) Clause 16 is titled: 'MINIMISING LOSSES Duty of Assured' and it provides: 'It is the duty of the Assured and their employees and agents in respect of loss recoverable hereunder;16.1 to take such measures as may be reasonable for the purpose of averting or minimising such loss; and 16.2 to ensure that all rights against carriers, bailees or other third parties are properly preserved and exercised and the Insurers will, in addition to any loss recoverable hereunder, reimburse the Assured for any charges properly and reasonably incurred in pursuance of these duties.'

6   *Yorkshire Water v Sun Alliance & London Insurance* [1997] CLC 213.

7   *AstraZeneca Insurance Co Ltd v XL Insurance (Bermuda) Ltd* [2013] EWHC 349 (Comm), para 137.

8   The reported cases, which are remarkably few in number, nearly all arose in the context of the old clause in the SG form. The 'usual form' in this paper therefore refers to the wording in the SG form.

The object of the sue and labour clause is to encourage the assured to take reasonable steps to prevent or minimise the risk insured against. Therefore, by virtue of the sue and labour clause the insurers bind themselves to pay in proportion any expense incurred. Such an expense should be (1) reasonably incurred, (2) the effort should be that of the assured's or their agents and (3) the purpose of the expenditure should be to preserve the thing from loss.[9] Having properly sued and laboured in accordance with authority given by the clause, the assured is entitled to look to the underwriter to reimburse him the expenses so incurred. The assured's right to claim the expenses does not depend on whether he was successful to prevent the loss or not.[10]

Expenses which are put forward as those of sue and labour (under a usual form of sue and labour clause) should meet the following requirements:[11]

- so far as causation is concerned, they have to be generated in some way by the incidence of a peril insured against;
- so far as their purpose is concerned, they have to be incurred for the purpose of averting or minimising a loss which would otherwise be covered by the terms of the policy; and
- so far as their character is concerned, they must have been reasonably incurred in or about the defence, safeguarding or recovery of the subject matter insured and must also be unusual or extraordinary or the result of unusual or extraordinary labour.

These elements will be analysed one by one in the following paragraphs.

I. Causation: To what extent is it necessary to show the probability of loss?

The question is whether it must be proved that the loss is one which would have occurred during the currency of the policy. In other words how immediate the risk of loss has to be.[12]

In *Aitchison v Lohre*,[13] at the Court of Appeal Lord Justice Brett said:

> . . . if by perils insured against the subject-matter of insurance is brought into such danger that without unusual or extraordinary labour or expense a loss will very probably fall on the underwriters, and if the assured or his agents or servants exert unusual or extraordinary labour, or if the assured is made liable to unusual or extraordinary expense in or for efforts to avert a loss, which, if it occurs, will fall on the underwriters, then each underwriter will, whether in the result there is a total or a partial loss, or no loss at all, not as part of the sum insured, but as a contribution independent of and even in addition to the whole sum insured, pay a sum bearing the same proportion to the cost or expense incurred as the sum they would have had to pay if the probable loss had occurred, or to the loss, which because the efforts have failed has occurred, as that loss bears to the sum insured.

In the House of Lords, their Lordships focused on another matter – whether salvage expenses could be recovered under the sue and labour clause – therefore they did not discuss if the loss should have been very probable or not. The issue, however, was discussed to a great extent in

---

9   *Aitchison v Lohre* (1879) 4 App Cas 755.
10 *Kuwait Airways Corp & Anor v Kuwait Insurance Co SAK* [1999] CLC 934, Lord Hobhouse, 948.
11 Rix J in *Royal Boskalis Westminster v Mountain* [1997] LRLR 523, 606.
12 *Integrated Container Service v British Traders Insurance Co* [1984] 1 Lloyd's Rep 154, Dillion LJ, 161.
13 (1878) 3 QBD 558, 566.

Integrated Container Service v British Traders Insurance Co.[14] Here ICS leased more than 1,000 containers to Oyama Shipping Co Ltd whose business was in the Far East moving cargo to and from Japan, Taiwan and the Philippines. In 1975, Oyama were found to be insolvent while it had on hire 1,016 containers the value of which was between 2,000 and 3,000 dollars each. ICS began a rescue operation which cost them almost US$134,000 by which they traced and recovered all but two of their containers. ICS then claimed US$53,777.28 by virtue of a sue and labour clause contained in an All Risks policy to which the insurers subscribed in the proportion of 41.15 per cent.[15] The sue and labour clause provided:

> . . . in case of any Loss or Misfortune, it shall be lawful to the Assured, their Factors, Servants and Assigns, to sue, labour, and travel for, in and about the Defence, Safeguard and Recovery of the said Goods and Merchandises, or any part thereof, without Prejudice to this Assurance; to the Charges whereof the Assurers will contribute, each Company rateably, according to the amount of their respective subscriptions hereto.

With regard to the question of whether or not the expenses incurred to prevent a type of loss which would have been covered by the insurance the Court of Appeal commented that because the policy provided all risks cover, so long as the assured established the existence of a threat of loss or damage, no matter if that threat resulted from the insolvency of the lessee, they were entitled to recover monies laid out to avert a loss which might result from a variety of reasons. In relation to the nature of the expenses the court was persuaded that the assured took extraordinary means to recover their containers. The next issue therefore was to consider to what extent it was necessary to show the probability of loss; whether it must be proved that the loss was one which would have occurred during the currency of the policy.

Eveleigh LJ stated that there was nothing in the clause or statute which required the assured to show that a loss would 'very probably' have occurred. The judge added (referring to *Aitchison v Lohre*):

> There have been very few cases on the effect of the sue and labour clause. I do not think that Lord Justice Brett was choosing words which were intended to be given almost statutory force and to lay down the elements which have to be proved before the assured can recover under the clause. He was dealing with a case where a loss would very probably have occurred and where underwriters would very probably have had to bear it. He was not concerned with the question whether the loss was probable or very probable.

Eveleigh LJ focused on what a 'reasonable assured' would have done in such circumstances. The judge stated that the words of section 78 of the MIA 1906 'to take such measures as may be reasonable for the purpose of averting or minimising a loss' imposed a duty to act in circumstances where a reasonable man intent upon preserving his property, as opposed to claiming upon insurers, would act. It should therefore not be possible for insurers to be able to contend that, upon an ultimate investigation and analysis of the facts, a loss, while possible or even probable, was not 'very probable'. Eveleigh LJ found it wholly unreasonable to penalise an assured upon the basis that, while he has shown that a reasonable man would have done as he did, yet in light of all that

---

14   [1984] 1 Lloyd's Rep 154.
15   The claim included the payments made in respect of customs and storage charges in order to secure the release of containers; the cost of transhipment to an Oyama depot; the cost of removal from the Oyama depots to that of ICS; the travelling expenses of those engaged in the rescue work and legal fees for advice obtained from Japanese lawyers.

has transpired, the loss would not have been probable. Therefore the true test applicable in this case was whether or not in all the circumstances the assured had acted reasonably to avert a loss when there was a risk that insurers might have to bear it.

In addition to the observations made by Eveleigh LJ, in *Integrated Container*, Dillon LJ was of the view that the words in the sue and labour clause 'in case of any Loss or Misfortune' included a threatened loss or misfortune, and not merely a loss or misfortune which has actually occurred. The insolvency of Oyama was not a risk insured against under the policy, since it did not in itself involve any loss or misfortune to, or indeed have any effect on the subject matter of the insurance, that is, the containers. It did however have the result that ICS became entitled, as against Oyama, to resume possession of all the containers under the terms of the lease to Oyama. The position when ICS intervened was that the containers were held in warehouses by port authorities or agents for Oyama or other warehouse keepers who claimed liens on the containers for charges unpaid by Oyama. There were odd containers that were at sea, but they were eventually to be returned to one or other of those locations. None of the containers was in immediate danger of being disposed of or physically damaged, but it would inevitably follow that, if ICS did not exert themselves, they would never get the containers back at all. Either the containers would be sold towards satisfaction of unpaid charges by port authorities or warehousemen, or they would be eventually annexed by third parties as articles apparently abandoned by the true owners: in either case, Dillon LJ found, the containers would then be lost to ICS.

In *Royal Boskalis Westminster v Mountain*[16] the insurers once again submitted that the peril must actually be in operation at the time of the sue and labour expenditure. In *Integrated Containers* it was held that 'in case of any Loss or Misfortune' included a threatened loss or misfortune. In *Royal Boskalis*, Rix J put emphasis on the lack of authority which had required that some actual loss must already have been suffered for the sue and labour clause to operate. It was sufficient if some misfortune had occurred and this was not the same thing as saying that some peril insured against had actually taken effect. Rix J further stated that section 78 does not say that a peril must have begun to operate for the sue and labour right or duty to come into effect, nor does it attempt to define the circumstances under which that right or duty arises save as may be inferred from such language as occurs in subsections (3) and (4) and in particular the repeated phrase 'for the purpose of averting or diminishing a [any] loss'. Thus, Rix J concluded that the matter was one of general principle. The judge emphasised the essence of the right and duty, which was that the insurer should be saved from loss by encouraging and requiring an assured to act reasonably for the purpose of averting or diminishing loss covered by the policy. As a result, it was reasonable to infer that both right and duty were intended to operate not only where a peril had actually begun to operate, but also where it threatened to do so. According to Rix J, where the peril has begun to operate, or even where it is obviously imminent, there is a clear case for the right and duty to sue and labour.

In *Royal Boskalis* a Dutch company who owned a dredging fleet with ancillary dredging equipment was contracted to a dredging project at Umm Qasr in Iraq with an arm of the Iraq Ministry of Transport and Communications, the General Establishment of Iraqi Ports (GEIP). The fleet was insured against war risks. The dredging contract provided for Iraqi law and Paris arbitration under ICC rules. The project was scheduled to be completed at the end of September, 1990. While the dredging work was still being performed Iraq invaded Kuwait on 2 August 1990. Although other contractors abandoned work being done in Iraq after the invasion, the assured claimant did try and complete the dredging contract. The invasion and international sanctions against Iraq delayed the progress of the work so that the project was not in the event completed until 30 October 1990. In the meantime on 16 September 1990, the Iraqi Revolutionary Command Council resolved to promulgate

---

16 [1997] LRLR 523.

Law No. 57. This took effect on 24 September 1990 but the law purported to have retrospective effect to 6 August 1990, the date when UN sanctions were imposed on Iraq. Article 7 of Law No. 57 said that all assets of the companies of those countries which had enacted sanction legislation against Iraq 'shall be seized'. Subsequently there were negotiations between the assured and the Iraqi government about the basis on which the dredging fleet would be demobilised and released. The parties signed a finalisation agreement in December 1990. The Iraqis' price for permitting demobilisation of the dredging fleet and its personnel was (1) the abandonment of all claims that the joint venture might have under the dredging contract (which the joint venture claimed was about Dfl. 84 m.) and (2) the payment into accounts of the Central Bank of Jordan held in Swiss and Austrian banks of Dfl. 24,250,000, the ultimate balance of a deposit which had been held at the Amsterdam-Rotterdam Bank in Holland under a letter of credit opened by GEIP as security for payments to be made by GEIP to the joint venture under the dredging contract. Following the finalisation agreement the dredging fleet and personnel were able to leave Iraq safely. The assured then claimed from the insurers under the sue and labour clause in the policy. The argument was that the value of the claims for extra payment under the dredging contract, which the assured had waived or relinquished under the finalisation agreement, should be described as sue and labour expenses. With regard to the first requirement stated above and discussed under the current heading, Rix J found that at least potentially there was in operation a peril insured against. This was the case because Law 57 did constitute a restraint or detainment of princes (albeit not one that caused the vessels' detention) and that its practical, even if not legal, effect was an interference in the free use and disposal of the vessels. However, Rix J found that because the primary and decisive purpose of the expenses incurred in performance of the project was the performance and completion of the project, that type of the expenses did not fall under the sue and labour clause. The alternative claim of the assured with regard to the waiver of claims against GEIP will be discussed in detail under a separate heading in the following paragraphs.

II. Purpose: to avert or minimise a loss which would otherwise be covered by the terms of the policy

The expenses incurred by the assured have to be incurred to prevent or minimise the loss which would have otherwise been covered by the policy. Thus it is important to determine the cover provided by the insurance. For instance if the policy is for total loss only and if the expenditure incurred was to prevent a partial loss of the subject matter insured, the insurer is not liable for the expenses incurred by the assured.[17] Two cases illustrate the point. In *Great Indian Peninsula Railway Company v Saunders*,[18] the insurance was on goods 'warranted free from particular average'. The ship was damaged during the voyage and was taken into an intermediate port under circumstances that constituted its constructive total loss. The cargo was not lost, it was landed and delivered to its owners, and the owners took the cargo to its destination in an undamaged state. The cargo owners paid £825 more for the new voyage and sought to recover this from the insurers under 'the labour and travel clause', which empowered the assured to sue, labour, and travel to save the thing assured from impending loss. The court emphasised that the expenses that can be recovered under the suing, labouring and travelling clause were expenses incurred to prevent impending loss within the meaning of the policy. Here, however, the expenses claimed did not fall within this category: the goods were given up to its owners in perfect safety and these expenses were not incurred to prevent a total loss. *Great Indian v Saunders* was applied in *Booth v Gair*[19] in which a cargo of 118 boxes

---

17 For types of losses see Chapters 8 to 10.
18 (1862) 2 Best and Smith 266.
19 (1863) 15 CB NS 291.

of bacon was shipped on board the ship *Plantagenet* at New York to sail for Liverpool. The cargo was insured by a policy which contained a sue and labour clause in its then usual form. The policy was also warranted 'free from average, unless general, or the ship be sunk, stranded, or burnt'. The *Plantagenet* met with heavy gales and for the preservation of the ship and cargo she bore away to Bermuda as a port of refuge. The ship was so badly damaged that she could only be repaired at Bermuda at an expense exceeding her value when repaired. Surveys were then held upon the cargo, parts of it, including a portion of the bacon the subject of this case, were found to be too damaged for re-shipment, and were sold on the advice of the surveyors, and the remainder (including the remainder of the bacon the subject of this case) was transhipped on board two vessels, the *Magnet* and the *Surprise*, for Liverpool.

The assured claimed from the insurer the difference between the amount of the freight by the *Plantagenet* and the sum total of the freight of the *Magnet* and the *Surprise*, and the shipping and transhipment charges of the cargo. The Court applied *Great Indian v Saunders* and noted that if the assured intended to confine the warranty to partial loss from damage to the cargo, and to have the liability of the underwriter for expenses of transhipment, the policy could have expressed that intention but it did not in this case.

The cases of *Great Indian v Saunders* and of *Booth v Gair* were distinguished in *Kidston v Empire Marine Insurance Company*[20] in which the court awarded the cost of transhipment under sue and labour expenses. In *Kidston* the subject matter of insurance was the chartered freight of a ship for £2,000, the freight being valued at £5,000, for a voyage from Chincha Islands to the United Kingdom. The policy contained the usual suing and labouring clause and a warranty against particular average. During the voyage the ship was so extensively damaged in a storm that it put into the port of Rio, where it became a total wreck. The goods were landed and forwarded in another ship to their destination, at an expense less than the chartered freight, and on their arrival the chartered freight was paid. The assured was successful in his claim for a proportionate part of the expense incurred in forwarding the goods by the second ship. The court held that upon the ship becoming a wreck at Rio, and the goods having been landed there, inasmuch as no freight pro rata *itineris* could be claimed, a total loss of freight had arisen. The expenses incurred in forwarding the goods to England by another ship were charges within the suing and labouring clause because they were incurred for the benefit of the underwriters to protect them against a claim for total loss of freight, to which they would have been liable but for the incurring of these charges. The Court distinguished *Kidston* from *Great Indian* and *Booth v Gair* for the reason that the latter were cases of insurance upon goods, to which the pro rata doctrine had no application, and where, the whole or a great portion of the goods still existing in *specie*, it was impossible to hold that a total loss had arisen.

Another issue related to the scope of the insurance cover was seen in *Xenos v Fox*[21] where the *Smyrna* came into collision with the *Mars* as a result of which the *Mars* sank. The owners of the *Mars* sued the *Smyrna* and her owners for the recovery of damages for the loss of the *Mars* but the Court dismissed the action and left each party to bear their own costs.

The owners of the *Smyrna* incurred considerable costs in these proceedings and claimed these expenses from the insurer under the suing and labouring clause. The Court however decided that the sue and labour clause had no application whatever to the facts of this case because that clause applied to a loss or misfortune happening to the thing insured.[22] A similar discussion is seen in

---

20 (1866–1867) LR 2 CP 357.

21 (1868–1869) LR 4 CP 665.

22 The Court also put emphasis on the running-down clause which was a distinct contract, under which the underwriters engaged to pay a proportion of any damages which may be awarded against the assured in a suit for a collision which may be defended with their previous consent in writing. If damages had been recovered by the owners of the *Mars* against the claimant, that would have brought the case within the clause.

Cunard Steamship Company, Limited v Marten[23] where the policy was effected to protect the shipowner against 'liability of any kind to owners of mules and/or cargo up to £20,000, owing to the omission of the negligence clause in contract and/or charterparty and/or bill of lading'. The policy contained the ordinary suing and labouring clause in the following terms:

> And in case of any loss or misfortune it shall be lawful to the assured, their factors, servants, and assigns, to sue, labour, and travel for, in, and about the defence, safeguard, and recovery of the said goods and merchandises and ship, &c., or any part thereof, without prejudice to this insurance; to the charges whereof we, the assurers, will contribute each one according to the rate and quantity of his sum herein assured.

The ship sailed from New Orleans but she was stranded owing to the negligence of the shipowner's servants. It was held that the subject matter of the policy was not mules but the shipowner's liability to the cargo owners owing to the omission of the negligence clause in contract and/or charterparty and/or bill of lading. The sue and labour clause on the other hand referred to 'the said goods and merchandises and ship'. Thus it was held that the sue and labour clause was intended to apply only to an insurance on 'goods, merchandises, and ship' and did not cover the shipowner's liability to the cargo owner for the loss caused by his servants' negligence.

It should be noted that collision defence and attack costs are expressly excluded from the scope of the Duty of Assured Clause in the current Hull Clauses. In this respect, the scope of the Clause is the same as that of the traditional clause in the SG form.

III. Character: they must have been reasonably incurred in or about the defence, safeguarding or recovery of the subject matter insured and must also be unusual or extraordinary or the result of unusual or extraordinary labour

Several cases discussed this third element of the sue and labour clause on various issues such as the meaning of expenses and charges which should be incurred, the reasonableness of incurring the expenses, and the unusual and extraordinary nature of the expenses. As a starting point *Lee v Southern Insurance Company*[24] can be mentioned under which the case discussed whether the expenses were incurred reasonably. In this case the cargo which was valued at £600 was insured for the voyage from Cammeroons to Liverpool. The vessel sailed with a cargo of palm oil and in the course of her voyage she encountered bad weather off the coast of Ireland; and, after having sustained considerable damage, she was stranded on the Welsh Coast, near Pwllheli, and drifted onto the beach. The cargo was discharged upon the surveyors' recommendation and was forwarded by rail to Liverpool. The total expense of forwarding the cargo by rail to Liverpool was £212. When the assured claimed this extra cost from the insurers under the sue and labour clause the Court found that the vessel was in such a condition that she might have been repaired and have pursued her voyage and the cargo could have been stored in a warehouse and then could have been reshipped onto the vessel once it was repaired; the total cost of warehousing and reshipping the cargo would have been about £70. The expenses that were incurred as a result of the course that was adopted by the assured therefore were not properly incurred.[25]

---

23 [1903] 2 KB 511.

24 (1869–70) LR 5 CP 397.

25 The insurers were required to reimburse the assured for the expenses incurred but only up to the reasonable amount of £70.

With regard to the meaning of the word 'incurred' the courts discussed whether a 'waiver' of the valid claims to prevent or minimise further losses covered by the insurance can be claimed under the sue and labour clause. In *Royal Boskalis*, the facts of which were given above, it was common ground that the finalisation agreement and hence the waiver of claims was entered into to preserve the insured property from loss from an insured peril, that is, continued seizure and detention, that the peril was operative and imminent and that the loss, had it occurred, would have been of a type recoverable under the policy. The dispute between the parties turned on the meaning of 'charges', and especially whether the ransom price, which took the form of a waiver of claims, can amount to charges or expenses. Rix J stated that the meaning will depend on the context. He said 'In my judgment there is no difference in principle between a sum paid out by way of ransom and a valid claim waived by way of ransom. It is common ground that a ransom paid to recover assured property may be properly the subject of a sue and labour claim. I do not see why a waived claim may not, upon appropriate facts, be just as much regarded as a ransom.' In the Court of Appeal Stuart Smith LJ agreed that expense involves the payment or disbursement of money or money's worth.

The effect of illegality

The effect of illegality is clearly seen in the case of *Royal Boskalis* in which while Rix J found that some of the expenses incurred to prevent or minimise the insured loss were recoverable under the sue and labour clause, the Court of Appeal held that since the finalisation agreement containing the waiver could not be enforced because the agreement had been obtained by duress or illegality, it would have had no effect on the assured's claims and they had suffered no loss.

Rix J found that whether the waiver of claims was unenforceable and ineffective was legally irrelevant when considering whether the claimants had sustained any and if so how much loss. The judge based his conclusion on the proposition that the existence of a remedy to make good the loss did not preclude the existence of the loss. However, the Court of Appeal adopted a different approach. They held that since insurance is designed to provide an indemnity against real loss, not notional loss, in this case quantification of that loss required a realistic comparison between the assured's position before the agreement was signed and after it had been signed. Before the agreement the assured had claims for additional payment under the dredging contract and they had the advantage of D.fl. 24,250,000 deposited in the bank as security for payment of their claims and the assured could only enforce them by going to arbitration. The assured could advance the selfsame claims before the arbitrators; but they would or could be met by an additional defence, the waiver. On the other hand G.E.I.P. could not rely on the waiver. Thus, Stuart Smith LJ found (Phil and Phillips LJJ agreed) that if the waiver would not be enforced by the arbitrators, then the claims were unaffected by it, and there was no loss. The assured's claim under the sue and labour clause could only be established insofar as they could show that Paris arbitrators would give effect to the waiver.

Ransom

Ransom, if it is not illegal, is recoverable under the sue and labour clause.[26] In England the Ransom Act 1782 which provided that 'all contracts and agreements which shall be entered into . . . by any person or persons for ransom of any . . . ship or vessel . . . shall be absolutely void in law, and of

---

26 See *Royal Boskalis Westminster v Mountain* [1997] LRLR 523.

no effect whatsoever' was repealed.[27] Therefore it is possible to argue that since payment of ransom is not illegal as there is no legislation against the payment of ransom, so long as the requirements set out by a sue and labour clause are met, the amount paid as ransom should be recovered from the insurers. Stuart-Smith and Phillips LJJ in *Royal Boskalis*, although *obiter* confirmed that ransom, if not illegal, can be claimed under the sue and labour clause. In *Masefield AG v Amlin Corporate Member Ltd*, Phil LJ[28] noted that the comment in *Royal Boskalis* was only *obiter* and the judge left it open for consideration that although payment in face of such a threat may be reasonable within the meaning of section 78(4) of the 1906 Act, knowledge that such payment is recoverable from insurers may have the effect of encouraging such threats. Rix LJ, however,[29] referred to the different opinions about paying ransom and said:

> There is thus something of an unexpressed complicity: between the pirates, who threaten the liberty but by and large not the lives of crews and maintain their ransom demands at levels which industry can tolerate; the world of commerce, which has introduced precautions but advocates the freedom to meet the realities of the situation by the use of ransom payments; and the world of government, which stops short of deploring the payment of ransom but stands aloof, participates in protective naval operations but on the whole is unwilling positively to combat the pirates with force. [. . .] In these morally muddied waters, there is no universally recognised principle of morality, no clearly identified public policy, no substantially incontestable public interest, which could lead the courts, as matters stand at present, to state that the payment of ransom should be regarded as a matter which stands beyond the pale, without any legitimate recognition. There are only elements of conflicting public interests, which push and pull in different directions, and have yet to be resolved in any legal enactments or international consensus as to a solution. [. . .]

Finally, Rix LJ noted in *Masefield v Amlin* that 'the fact that there may be no duty to make a ransom payment, does not mean that there is any obligation not to make such a payment'.[30]

In conclusion, it appears that paying ransom is not illegal and an assured will have to pay ransom to save the subject matter insured and therefore to prevent or minimise the risk insured, in principle, this can be recovered under the sue and labour expenses. Rix LJ noted in *Masefield* that the conflicting public interests with regard to paying ransom push and pull in different directions but when analysing the elements stated by Rix LJ it appears that the tendency is to allow the assured to recover the payment of ransoms from the insurers if such payment prevented or minimised the risk insured.

A further issue to be discussed with regard to the payment of ransom is the quantification of such payment. The quantification issue is discussed in the following heading.

The *quantum meruit* principle

In *Aitchison v Lohre*[31] Earl Cairns LC said: '. . . if any expenses were to be recoverable under the suing and labouring clause, they must be expenses assessed upon the *quantum meruit* principle.' In *Royal Boskalis Westminster v Mountain*, the insurer argued that the amount which was waived by the assured

---

27   See the Supreme Court Act 1981, section 152(4) and Schedule 7.
28   [2011] 1 Lloyd's Rep 630, para 64.
29   [2011] 1 Lloyd's Rep 630, para 71.
30   [2011] 1 Lloyd's Rep 630, para 75.
31   (1879) 4 App Cas 755 at 766–767.

to the Iraqi Government is not recoverable. The insurers accepted that paying a ransom is an expenditure but waiving claims is not; waived claims have to be quantified, unless they can be quantified, they cannot be claimed as sue and labour expenses. Both Rix J and Court of Appeal rejected this argument. Rix J[32] emphasised that 'properly incurred' meant reasonably and necessarily incurred as a result of unusual or extraordinary labour or expenditure, therefore difficulties of quantification should not affect the matter of whether the assessment is made on a quantum meruit basis or on a figure of out of pocket expenditure. At the Court of Appeal, Stuart Smith LJ[33] stated that what Aitchison v Lohre ruled was that a salvor acting pursuant to maritime law and not under contract with the shipowner was not the agent of the assured. Earl Cairns LC referred to salvage expenses which are not assessed upon the quantum meruit principle. Salvage award is given irrespective of the proportion to the actual expense incurred and the actual service rendered. The largeness of the sum is based upon the consideration that if the effort to save the ship (however laborious in itself, and dangerous in its circumstances) had not been successful, nothing whatever would have been paid. Stuart Smith LJ[34] noted that the object of the sue and labour clause was to encourage the assured to take reasonable steps to prevent or minimise the risk insured against but not to provide an additional remedy for the recovery of indemnity for a loss which was, by maritime law, a consequence of the peril. According to Stuart Smith LJ, Lord Cairns LC's abovementioned statement could only be obiter and if it was not obiter, it was not correct. If the observations of Lord Cairns LC are correct, a ransom, which cannot possibly be valued on a quantum meruit principle, and is paid by the shipowner, not to his agent for his exertions in saving the ship but to a stranger who is detaining it, cannot be recovered under the sue and labour clause.[35]

Phil LJ[36] stated that in Aitchison v Lohre the claim did not fail simply because the salvors were not paid on an ordinary quantum meruit basis but on a salvage basis which reflected the risk of 'no cure no pay'. Furthermore, the salvors were not contractually engaged to perform the services at all; they rendered them as volunteers, not as agents engaged by the master under contract. Phil LJ thus held that the fact that a payment cannot be valued as a quantum meruit does not prevent a claim under the sue and labour clause. This conclusion was also linked with the waiver of claims, which was again discussed in Royal Boskalis, and Phil LJ was of the same view that the expense is incurred by way of waiving a claim rather than that making a payment does not prevent a claim under the sue and labour clause.

Apportionment

The apportionment principle was explained by Walton J in Cunard Steamship Company Ltd v Marten,[37] as follows:

> . . . the underwriters are to bear their share of any suing and labouring expenses, . . . only in the proportion of the amount underwritten to the whole value of the property or interest insured. If the assured has insured himself or goods to the extent of one-half only of the value of his property or interest in the goods insured, he, in respect of each and every item of suing and labouring expense, recovers one-half and bears one-half himself.

---

32 [1997] LRLR 523, 561.
33 [1997] LRLR 523, 613.
34 [1997] LRLR 523, 613.
35 [1997] LRLR 523, 613.
36 [1997] LRLR 523, 633.
37 [1902] 2 KB 624.

Thus if half the goods must be treated as uninsured, then the sue and labour expenditure must be apportioned between the goods insured and uninsured. The apportionment principle was applied in *Royal Boskalis* by Rix J as follows: in the early days after the invasion the assured would have been able to extricate all their personnel unofficially from Iraq, for instance by taking the overland route to Jordan, at the cost of leaving all its equipment behind. But the assured decided that it would work on to complete the project. The price paid by the assured in the form of the waiver of its claims was paid for the purpose of freeing not only the fleet but also the European personnel; there was 'one package' with a 'dual purpose'. It was clearly impossible to put a financial value on the safety of the personnel but the judge found it appropriate to apportion expenses by taking an equal value to the interests preserved by that inextricable dual purpose. Consequently, the assured was entitled to recover only 50 per cent of the ultimately ascertained value of the waiver claims. As stated above the Court of Appeal found the finalisation agreement unenforceable for duress and illegality and therefore the sue and labour expenses were not recoverable but nevertheless Phillips LJ expressed some *obiter* observations with regard to this matter. The judge found it impossible to carry out an arithmetical apportionment between property and lives at risk. Since preservation of life cannot be equated with preservation of property, Phillips LJ stated that Rix J should have held the assured entitled to recover the full cost of entering into the finalisation agreement rather than only half that cost. Phillips LJ's view was recently applied in *Atlasnavios-Navegacao, LDA v Navigators Insurance Company Ltd*[37a] in which Flaux J refused to apportion the sue and labour expenses which were incurred for the dual purpose of securing the release of the vessel and also defending the crew members.

It should be noted that apportionment of the sue and labour expenses is available in marine insurance where the subject matter is underinsured: where ship or cargo is under-insured, sue and labour expenses will only be recoverable in the same proportion that insured value bears to actual value.[38] In marine liability and non-marine liability insurance it has been held that there is no room to apply the apportionment principle. Recently the Court of Appeal discussed the issue in *Standard Life Assurance Ltd v ACE European Group*[39], which will be mentioned below.

Supplementary or not

The sue and labour expenses can be recovered in addition to the policy limit, in other words, it is a supplementary claim.[40] Although the sue and labour clause is often seen in its usual form which is established by the standard wording applicable to the type of insurance in question, the parties may modify the standard clauses. In *Kuwait Airways Corp & Anor v Kuwait Insurance Co SAK*[41] the clause was in the following wording:

> Sue, labour and costs and expenses and salvage charges and expenses incurred by on or on behalf of the assured in or about the defence, safety, preservation and recovery of the insured property and also [extraordinary general average sacrifice and expenditure] and costs and expenses arising out of all search and rescue operations. Provided always that these costs and expenses shall be included in computing the losses hereinbefore provided for, notwithstanding that the company may have paid for a total loss.

Lord Hobhouse held that the wording was capable of having only one meaning, that the limits on the liability of the underwriters were to apply not only to the primary indemnity but also so as

---

37a [2014] EWHC 4133 (Comm).
38 *Royal Boskalis Westminster v Mountain* [1997] LRLR 523, 647 Phillips LJ.
39 [2012] EWCA Civ 1713.
40 MIA 1906, Section 78(1).
41 [1999] CLC 934.

to include any sue and labour expenses incurred. The 'losses hereinbefore provided for' must mean the losses in respect of the primary obligation to indemnify. The ordinary rule continues to apply that payment for a total loss does not exclude the right to recover sue and labour expenses. But this proviso requires that any sue and labour expenses be included with the primary losses for which cover is provided in the contract. It follows that, where there is a limit on the indemnity, that limit must be applied to the aggregate of the primary loss and the sue and labour expenses.

The sue and labour expenses are paid as a supplementary cover under the IHC 2003 Clause 9.5 however the maximum limit that the insurer pays for the sue and labour expenses is equal to the insured amount.

Consequences of breach of section 78(4)

Section 78(4) provides 'It is the duty of the assured and his agents, in all cases, to take such measures as may be reasonable for the purpose of averting or minimising a loss.' The relevant question here is whether breach of section 78(4) gives a defence to the insurer either in the form of rejecting the claim made by the assured or in the form of a set off depending on the degree of the assured's negligence in complying with section 78(4). The issue has been discussed by the English courts and the views are varied although the tendency is that section 78(4) does not entitle the insurer to an independent remedy for breach of a contractual duty. In *Netherlands v Youell*[42] Phillips LJ noted that there had been no recorded case where underwriters have successfully invoked a breach of the duty referred to in s.78(4). In this case the Dutch Royal Navy was insured under marine policies against builders risks in relation to two submarines which were being built for them by a Dutch shipyard, RDM. The navy claimed under those policies in respect of debonding and cracking of the paintwork applied by RDM to the submarines. The insurers argued that s.78(4) gave them a defence to the assured's claim on the ground, among others, that RDM, as the navy's agents, failed to take such measures as were reasonable to avert or minimise the loss in respect of which the claim was made. The answer to the insurer's argument is closely linked to section 55(2)(a) which states that 'The insurer is not liable for any loss attributable to the wilful misconduct of the assured, but, unless the policy otherwise provides, he is liable for any loss proximately caused by a peril insured against, even though the loss would not have happened but for the misconduct or negligence of the master or crew.' If the question therefore is to be redrafted it will be as follows: is section 78(4) to be interpreted in a way that if the assured or assured's agent is negligent in taking reasonable steps to avert or minimise the loss insured by the policy, such negligence will oust the cover under section 55(2)(a)?

In *British and Foreign Marine Insurance Co v Gaunt*[43] the issue was whether underwriters of an 'all risks' policy on cargo were liable for water damage to that cargo. The insurers argued that the loss was caused by the omission of the assured or his servants to take precautions to protect the goods from the wet and therefore the assured was not entitled to recover. The underwriters submitted that section 78(4) was not necessarily limited to suing and labouring, it lays down a general rule consistently with s.55(2)(a). The Court rejected the insurers' argument and held that section 78(4) which referred to suing and labouring cannot be read as meaning that if the agents of the assured are not reasonably careful throughout the transit he cannot recover for anything to which their want of care contributes. In *Netherlands v Youell*,[44] Phillips LJ further commented that it was established

---

42   [1998] CLC 44.
43   [1921] 2 AC 41.
44   [1998] CLC 44.

by section 55(2)(a) that where such negligence or misconduct caused or permitted a peril insured against to impact on the property insured, the negligence or misconduct on the part of the assured's agent would not be a bar to a claim. Section 78(4) raises a different question to that, namely whether negligence or misconduct on the part of an agent of the assured assumes greater consequence when it occurs in the context of dealing with the consequences of an insured peril after it has struck. This interpretation invites a further question that if the assured was negligent in taking reasonable steps to avert or minimise the risk insured against and if such negligence breaks the chain of causation between the initial proximate cause and occurrence of the loss, will the assured lose his right to recovery under the policy?

Therefore the conclusion is that section 78(4) does not impose a conventional contractual duty which displaces, after a casualty has occurred, the general principle embodied in s.55(2)(a). Phillips LJ held that breach of section 78(4) provides a defence only in a rare case of where breach of that duty is so significant as to be held to displace the prior insured peril as the proximate cause of the loss. As fully analysed in Chapter 7 if the breach of s.78(4) is as a result of the negligence of master, officers and crew, that negligence is normally covered by the policy and again the likelihood of breach of section 78(4) giving rise to a defence for an insurer decreases, if not disappears.

Astrovlanis Compania Naviera SA v Linard (The Gold Sky)[45] Mocatta J expressed some *obiter* observation on this issue. The judge found that 'the assured and his agents' in s.78 (4) did not include the master or other members of the crew. Holding otherwise would negative much of the cover given by s.55(2)(a). Section 78(4), according to Mocatta J, was not intended to cut down the effect of s.55(2)(a). What is understood from Mocatta J's judgment is that the word 'agents' is capable of a wide range of different meanings depending upon the context and circumstances in which it is used. In the context of section 78(4), in order to negative the effect of s.55(2)(a) the agent must be authorised to take the reasonable step in question and if he refuses to take such reasonable steps then such breach would deprive the assured of claiming under the policy either entirely or by way of set off. The judge justified this opinion by stating that the master of a ship is primarily the servant of her owner; his authority as master is strictly limited and in general he only has wide powers as an agent to bind his principal and employer in cases where he has to act as agent of necessity. In the absence of instructions from his owners to take such reasonable steps, the master of a vessel must not be taken to be included within the words 'the assured and his agents' in section 78(4), so that a failure by the master to take such measures as may be reasonable will militate against his owners' claim against insurers. Mocatta J said that the words 'his agents' should be read as inapplicable to the master or crew, unless expressly instructed by the assured in relation to what to do or not to do in respect of suing and labouring. Phillips LJ, however, in *Netherlands v Youell*, expressly disagreed with the analysis of the nature and effect of s.78(4) reached by Mocatta J in *The Gold Sky*.

As stated above in footnote 5, cl.16 of the ICC Clauses imposes a duty on the assured, their employees and agents in respect of loss recoverable under the relevant cargo clauses (1) to take such measures as may be reasonable for the purpose of averting or minimising such loss, and (2) to ensure that all rights against carriers, bailees or other third parties are properly preserved and exercised. Insurers agree to reimburse the Assured for any charges properly and reasonably incurred in pursuance of these duties. In *Noble Resources and Unirise Development v George Albert Greenwood (The Vasso)*[46] the insurers' argument as to cl.16 constituting a warranty failed. Hobhouse J took into consideration that (1) cl.16 is a contractual provision which substantially corresponds to s.78 of the Marine Insurance Act, 1906. (2) Neither cl.16 nor s.78 has any role in defining the scope of the primary

---

45   [1972] 2 Lloyd's Rep 187.
46   [1993] 2 Lloyd's Rep 309.

cover. (3) Both cl.16 and s.78 provide expressly the duty of the assured to minimise or avoid a loss and the assured to be indemnified against the expenses that he so incurs. Thus, Hobhouse J defined the duty provided by them as collateral which arises once an insured peril has begun to take effect and confers collaterally an additional indemnity in connection with the performance of that duty.

The conclusion is that the breach of the duty will meet a contractual remedy. It may cause loss to the insurer in which case the insurer will have a claim for damages against the assured in respect of such breach of duty insofar as the insurer has been caused loss. Where the assured's failure to comply with the duty causes the insurer to lose a subrogation right against a third party, the insurer's loss will be equivalent to the value of the loss of that right. This may be equivalent to the full amount of the assured's claim.

It is worth noting that in *Netherlands v Youell*,[47] Phillips LJ noted that there has not been a case since 1906 where an assured has been found guilty of failing to sue and labour. The same finding was approved by Rix LJ in *Masefield AG v Amlin Corporate Member Ltd*.[48]

Apprehension of loss

It is worth setting out the difference between an actual loss caused by an insured peril, sue and labour expenses which were incurred to prevent or minimise the insured loss and finally, apprehension of loss. The principles of causation were fully discussed in Chapter 7 and losses in marine insurance were analysed in Chapters 8–10. Accordingly, the actual loss of or damage to the subject matter insured, caused by an insured peril, is covered by the policy of insurance.[49] Consequently, where there is no loss or damage as defined in the policy which was caused by perils insured against, the insurer will not be liable for a loss that the assured might have suffered as a result of an apprehension of a peril. In *Cator v Great Western Insurance Company of New York*[50] a vessel that was loaded with a cargo of tea met with bad weather in the course of her voyage and some (449) packages of tea were damaged by seawater. The remainder of the tea, 1,262 packages, arrived in a perfectly sound and good condition. The court found that when tea is sold, it is usually sold in the order of the consecutive numbers marked on the packages; and, if the numbers be broken by some being omitted, or if some of the chests are marked as damaged, suspicions are raised that the remaining packages may be affected. As a result, those other packages, though perfectly sound and uninjured, do not receive so high a price as they would have done had none of the packages been damaged. In this case the damage to 449 packages prejudiced the sale of the 1,262 sound chests. The assured sought to recover the difference in price that arose as a result of such prejudice. It was held that the underwriters insure against damage to the goods by the perils insured against; but they do not insure against damage by prejudice or suspicion. The courts recognised that such prejudice or suspicion might be reasonable and be general in business, however, it was not what the insured agreed to insure against. According to the court, holding the insurers liable in this case would create indirect, collateral and consequential liabilities from suspicion and prejudice, which it would be almost impossible for the underwriters to estimate in fixing a premium proportionate to the risk.

---

47 [1998] CLC 44, 54.
48 [2011] 1 Lloyd's Rep 630, para 76.
49 Business interruption losses may be included in the policy by an express provision to that effect.
50 (1872–1873) LR 8 CP 552.

In *Hadkinson v Robinson*,[51] a cargo of pilchards had been shipped on board the ship *Pascaro*, at and from Mounts Bay or any port in Cornwall to Naples. Whilst the ship was proceeding on her said voyage the port of Naples was closed to British ships and against all merchandises the property of any such subjects carried in such ships. The ship then sailed to another port where the cargo was sold at a considerable loss. The assured's claim was rejected by the court. The court found that the policy included capture and detention of princes, and any loss which necessarily arises from such acts is a loss within the policy. The assured's claim arose from the ship not proceeding to that port to which she was destined. In circumstances where underwriters have insured against capture and restraint of princes, and the captain, learning that if he enters the port of destination the vessel will be lost by confiscation, and therefore avoids that port, whereby the object of the voyage is defeated, this does not amount to a peril operating to the total destruction of the thing insured.

The type of losses that the assureds claimed in the abovementioned cases might have been claimed as sue and labour expenses if the requirements of claiming such expenses were met, however, sue and labour was not argued in either of the cases referred to above. The focus was on apprehension of an insured peril and the question was if the loss was occasioned by a risk within the policy.[52]

Duty to mitigate in non-marine insurance

There is no statutory provision regulating the duty as such under non-marine insurance. Therefore, whether or not the assured is under the duty to mitigate the loss, or in case the assured has taken reasonable steps to avert or minimise the loss insured by the policy, whether he is entitled to recovery of the expenditure incurred for that purpose is answered in reference to the policy wording.

In the non-marine context the courts have rejected the principle that the assured is under any common law duty to mitigate loss.[53] In *City Tailors v Evans*[54] the assured purchased a 'Profits Insurance' for his business at the Old Street. The profits were valued at £100 per working day, and insurers undertook to pay that sum for each working day that work may be wholly stopped owing to fire, up to 325 working days. A fire occurred as a result of which the premises at Old Street were almost entirely destroyed and work was partially stopped there for the full period covered by the policy. The assured was able to secure temporary premises where they continued the manufacturing business, which owing to the fire they could not continue at Old Street. Disputes arose between the parties as to the amount the insurer should indemnify. With regard to interpretation of condition 3 which required the assured to use due diligence in doing all things reasonably practicable to minimise any interruption of, or interference with, the business and to avoid or diminish the loss, Bankes LJ stated 'I do not think that the Condition can be read as imposing an obligation upon the assured in the event of a fire to continue their business in fresh premises in order to reduce the underwriters' loss; on the other hand, there is room for contending that if the assured do continue their business in fresh premises they ought not as against the underwriters, and under a contract which is in its nature a contract of indemnity, to be allowed to retain both the profits of the business in the new premises and the valued loss of profits of the business in the old premises, and that a term should be implied in the contract that the former should be taken into account in diminution of the loss.'

The matter was discussed in the context of liability insurance in *Yorkshire Water v Sun Alliance & London Insurance*.[55] The assured in this case was the owner and operator of a waste tip ('the Deighton

---

51 (1803) 3 Bosanquet and Puller 388.
52 *Hadkinson v Robinson* (1803) 3 Bosanquet and Puller 388.
53 See *All Leisure Holidays Ltd v Europaische Reiseversicherung AG* [2012] Lloyd's Rep IR 193.
54 (1921) 9 Ll L Rep 394.
55 [1997] CLC 213.

tip'), on the banks of the River Colne. The waste tip was used for sewage sludge. In 1992 an embankment of the Deighton tip failed and a vast quantity of sewage sludge was deposited in the River Colne and into the Deighton works. Commercial properties situated nearby were affected and proceedings were started. The assured then spent over £4m carrying out urgent flood alleviation works on its own property to avert further damage to the property of others and to prevent or reduce the possibility of further claims. The assured sought to recover that expenditure from its public liability insurers. The policy did not provide an express clause imposing a duty on the insurer to cover costs incurred by the assured to prevent or minimise the loss insured by the policy. Neither was the assured's claim for such costs covered by the insuring clause that provided cover for '. . . all sums which the Insured shall become legally liable to pay as damages or compensation . . . in respect of loss or damage to property.' However, an alternative argument brought by the assured was that 'Every contract of insurance carries an implied term that the insured will make reasonable efforts to prevent or minimise loss which may fall to the insurer. If such prevention or mitigation involves the insured in expenditure, it is an implied term of the insurance policy that the insured is entitled to be indemnified in respect of that expenditure.'

The Court of Appeal rejected the implied term argument for the following reasons: (1) In the case of expenses incurred by the assured to prevent liability to third parties it is impossible to quantify such damage, since *ex hypothesi* it has not occurred. Accordingly the expense of the alleviation works may greatly exceed any possible or likely damage to third parties and the limit of indemnity is wholly inappropriate in such circumstances. This is different than property insurance under which recovery is limited to the value of the property insured; any expense incurred in its preservation is therefore subject to the same limit. (2) A reasonable assured and a reasonable insurer would have agreed to such a term during negotiation of the policies if the incidence of liability for the flood alleviation works had been raised. (3) In the law of contract there exists a corollary principle that losses that are reasonably avoidable are not recoverable ('the duty to mitigate'); this applies to insurance law and therefore there is no basis for implying such a term by operation of law. The term suggested by the assured was not to be implied for business efficacy reasons either. The policy works perfectly without such a term. If such a term were implied it would create a new area of indemnity in addition to those expressed by the policy and for which the assured has not paid any additional premium for the loss he seeks to include. (4) So far as liability to third parties is concerned the principles of marine insurance are not significantly different from non-marine. It would be very difficult to contend that in marine liability policies there is an implied term such as the assured contended for in this case; consequently, there exists no reason why it should be implied in a non-marine policy. (5) The proposed term would be virtually unworkable. In a claim as argued in this case, it would not be possible to decide what expenditure of the assured was reasonable. If the only potential liability was the £300,000, could it be said that £4m worth of alleviation works was reasonable? (6) An implied term as argued by the assured would be inconsistent with the express wording of the contract, which provided 'The assured at his own expense shall take reasonable precautions to prevent any Occurrence or to cease any activity which may give rise to liability under this Policy and to maintain all buildings furnishings ways works machinery plant and vehicles in sound condition.'

Thus it is now a settled principle of law that in marine or non-marine liability insurance[56] it is not appropriate to imply a term which suggests that the insurer should indemnify the costs incurred

---

56 As seen in *Yorkshire Water*, the court also stated that it was difficult to argue that the duty to sue and labour is implied if not contractually agreed. Considering that the duty is statutorily imposed, although in principle not providing a remedy to the underwriter for its breach, and all standard policy wordings include a provision on suing and labouring the aim of which is to encourage the assured to take reasonable steps to avert or minimise the loss and the underwriter undertakes to cover such expenditure incurred by the assured.

by the assured to prevent or minimise the loss insured by the policy. A prudent insurer and assured are expected to include a clause to that effect in their policies if they wish to. Where it is provided by the insurance contract that the insurer will meet the sue and labour/or mitigation expenses, and if the assured incurs such expenses to prevent or minimise both insured and uninsured risks, the question may arise whether the expenses should be apportioned so that the insurers will be liable only for the proportion that was incurred aiming at the insured risks. The matter was recently discussed by the Court of Appeal in *Standard Life Assurance Ltd v ACE European Group*,[57] where the Court of Appeal reiterated that the 'apportionment' principle is applicable to marine property insurance where the subject matter saved is under-insured. In *Standard Life* the assured faced claims from customers dissatisfied with the return on their investments from the assured's investment fund, and sought to make good the losses by paying substantial sums into the investment fund (Cash Injection). The key issue was whether the Cash Injection fell within the definition of mitigation costs. It was argued by insurers that the assured had a dual purpose in making such payments, namely, the prevention of claims (insured) and the preservation of its reputation (uninsured) and hence there should be an apportionment of the Cash Injection between 'the insured and uninsured interests at risk and sought to be preserved by the Cash Injection'. The insurers' argument was rejected by Eder J whose judgment was approved by the Court of Appeal. Eder J stated that although the reality was that the expenditure was directed to two objectives, nevertheless it was neither sound in principle nor desirable to penalise the assured by reducing the amount that would otherwise have been recoverable. Moreover, the fact that the word 'solely' or 'exclusively' does not appear in the clause[58] persuaded Eder J that the language of the clause did not require the mitigation costs to be incurred solely or exclusively in taking action to avoid or to reduce third party claims of the stipulated type. The judge found further support from the principle that where there are two proximate causes of loss, one an insured peril and one outside the scope of the policy, the insured will be able to recover provided the latter is not expressly excluded.[59]

In the Court of Appeal, Tomlinson LJ, delivering the leading judgment, found that there could be no apportionment in the context of liability insurance, for two reasons: it could not be said that the assured was underinsured simply because his aggregate liabilities exceeded the sum insured, so that in principle there was no room for the principle of average; and in any event a mathematical allocation of suing and labouring costs was impossible.[60] Consequently, it has become clear in English law that such apportionment, principles of which derived from the nineteenth century marine cases, may suit well in marine property insurance but it is rather ill-fitting in non-marine and marine liability policies.

Further reading

Bennett, *The Law of Marine Insurance*, 2nd edn, [2006] Oxford University Press. Chapter 24.
Clarke, 'Wisdom after the event: the duty to mitigate insured loss', *Lloyd's Maritime and Commercial Law Quarterly* [2003] 4(November), 525–543.
Cohen, 'Particular charges in carriage of goods by sea and marine cargo insurance', *Lloyd's Maritime and Commercial Law Quarterly* [2004] 4(November), 453–459.

---

57 [2012] EWCA Civ 1713.

58 The relevant clause provided 'Mitigation Costs shall mean any payment of loss, costs or expenses reasonably and necessarily incurred by the Assured in taking action to avoid a third party claim or to reduce a third party claim (or to avoid or reduce a third party claim which may arise from a fact, circumstance or event) of a type which would have been covered under this policy (notwithstanding any Deductible amount).'

59 *JJ Lloyd Instruments v Northern Star Insurance Co (The Miss Jay Jay)* [1987] 1 Lloyd's Rep 32.

60 See also *Royal Boskalis Westminster NV v Mountain* [1997] LRLR 523.

Gauci, 'Obligation to sue and labour in the law of marine insurance – time to amend the statutory provisions?' Part 1, *International Journal of Shipping Law* [2000] 1(March), 2–10.

Gauci, 'Obligation to sue and labour in the law of marine insurance – time to amend the statutory provisions?', Part 2, *International Journal of Shipping Law* [2000] 2(June), 87–94.

Gilman et al., *Arnould: Law of Marine Insurance and Average*, 18th edn, [2013] Sweet & Maxwell. Chapter 25.

Macdonald Eggers, 'Sue and labour and beyond: the assured's duty of mitigation', *Lloyd's Maritime and Commercial Law Quarterly* [1998] 2(May), 228–244.

Rose, 'Aversion and minimisation of loss under English marine insurance law', *Journal of Maritime Law and Commerce* [1988] 19(4) October, 517–550.

Rose, 'Failure to sue and labour', *Journal of Business Law* [1990] May, 190–202.

Rose, *Marine Insurance: Law and Practice*, 2nd edn, [2012] Informa. Chapter 20.

Chapter 12

Fraudulent Claims

Chapter Contents

The rule relating to fraudulent insurance claims is a special common law rule.[1] Even when the policy is silent about the remedy for fraudulent claims the rule still applies.[2] This conclusion was derived from *Britton v The Royal Insurance Co*, where Willes J said that the rules applicable to fraudulent claims are 'in accordance with legal principle and sound policy'.[3]

The history of the common law rule applicable to such claims goes back to the nineteenth century when it was the common practice to insert in fire policies conditions that they would be void in the event of a fraudulent claim.[4] The rule in this area therefore has been developed over centuries and several issues have been discussed by the courts to help identify the scope of the common law rule applicable to fraudulent claims. The definition of fraud, the state of mind of the assured, materiality, the extension of the rules to the use of fraudulent means and devices by the assured, the juridical basis of the rule and the link between the duty of good faith and fraudulent claims have to be examined to understand under what circumstances the special common law rule in this area becomes applicable. The most controversial matter among these is the extension of the rule to the use of fraudulent means and devices. Part 4 of the Government Insurance Bill 2014, referred to elsewhere in this book, includes clauses on fraudulent claims. Such clauses will be mentioned at the end of this chapter. It is worth mentioning here that the Bill does not bring any reform proposal regarding the use of fraudulent means and devices.

It should be noted that the special common law rule on fraudulent claims only applies between the making of the claim and the start of litigation.[5]

What is a fraudulent claim?

Fraud is not mere lying. Generally, it is seeking to obtain an advantage, usually monetary, or to put someone else at a disadvantage by lies and deceit.[6] In the context of insurance it would be sufficient to come within the definition of fraud if it is clear that the deceit had been used to secure easier or quicker payment of the money than would have been obtained if the truth had been told.[7]

Fraudulent insurance claims have been observed in various forms. First example may be given where the assured makes a claim although he has not suffered a fortuity giving rise to loss. Scuttling of a vessel will fall within this class. In this case a deliberate sinking of a vessel will not be a peril covered by the policy for there is no fortuity but that the assured's misconduct caused his loss. The proximate cause rules will likely provide a defence for the insurer but additionally, this will be classified as a fraudulent claim because the perils of the sea claim is fraudulent. This is a dishonest presentation of a claim on a totally different factual basis from the truth. The second class of fraudulent claims is where the assured claims, knowing that he has suffered no loss, or only a lesser loss than that which he claims[8] or is reckless as to whether this is the case.[9] *Galloway v Guardian Royal Exchange*

---

1   *AXA General Insurance Ltd v Gottlieb* [2005] Lloyd's Rep IR 369, para 31, Lord Mance.

2   *Versloot Dredging BV v HDI Gerling Industrie Versicherung AG* [2013] 2 Lloyd's Rep 131, para 145 (Popplewell's judgment in *Versloot* was approved by the Court of Appeal: [2014] EWCA Civ 1349); *Agapitos v Agnew (The Aegeon) (No.1)* [2002] Lloyd's Rep IR 573, para 2; *The Star Sea*, Lord Hobhouse, para 62.

3   (1866) 4 F & F 905, 909; *Galloway v Guardian Royal Exchange (UK) Ltd* [1999] Lloyd's Rep IR 209, 211 Lord Woolf MR; *Orakpo v Barclays Insurance Services Co Ltd* [1995] LR 443.

4   *Galloway v Guardian Royal Exchange (UK) Ltd* [1999] Lloyd's Rep IR 209, Lord Woolf MR; see *Goulstone v Royal Insurance Co* (1858) 1 F & F 276; *Levy v Baillie* (1831) 7 Bing. 349.

5   *The Game Boy* [2004] 1 Lloyd's Rep 238; *Versloot*, [2013] 2 Lloyd's Rep 131, para 176.

6   Roche J while directing the jury in *Wisenthal v World Auxiliary Insurance Corp Ltd* (1930) 38 Ll L Rep 54, 62. The Fraud Act 2006 s1 also provides definition of various different types of fraud.

7   *Wisenthal v World Auxiliary Insurance Corp Ltd* (1930) 38 Ll L Rep 54, 62.

8   *Agapitos v Agnew (The Aegeon) (No.1)* [2002] Lloyd's Rep IR 573, para 30.

9   *Agapitos v Agnew (The Aegeon) (No.1)* [2002] Lloyd's Rep IR 573, para 30.

(UK) Ltd[10] fits in this definition in which the assured suffered loss as a result of a burglary which took place at his premises. In addition to the contents that he genuinely lost, he claimed £2,000 for loss of a computer, which in fact did not take place. This was a fraudulent statement as he submitted a claim for the loss he did not suffer. The second part of the definition, exaggeration of the claim, may be illustrated by *Joseph Fielding Properties (Blackpool) Ltd v Aviva Insurance Ltd*[11] in which the assured exaggerated his genuine loss of £6,700 to the amount of £9,870. The claim was fraudulent. Moreover, in *Orakpo v Barclays Insurance Services Co Ltd*[12] the part of the claim based on loss of rent was indeed grossly exaggerated. It assumed that all 13 bedrooms would have been fully occupied for the ensuing two years and nine months after the first casualty, notwithstanding that there were only three occupants when that casualty occurred. The assured lost the entire benefit with regard to his claim.

The third group of fraudulent claims was defined as a claim which is honestly believed in when initially presented, but the assured subsequently realises that it is exaggerated, but continues to maintain it.[13] This may be classified under the second category stated above.[14] The difference between the second and third class is that in the former the assured knew at the outset that he did not suffer loss as much as he claimed from the insurer, in the latter he became aware of the exaggeration at a later stage in his claim.

The fraudulent claims rule has been constantly developed by the courts and the fourth class was added by an *obiter* analysis of Mance LJ in *Agapitos v Agnew (The Aegeon) (No.1)*[15] to the use of fraudulent means and devices. In this class of fraudulent claims the assured believes that he has suffered the loss claimed, but seeks to improve or embellish the facts surrounding the claim, by some lie.[16] Fraudulent means and devices invalidate the claim because the claim is presented on a false factual basis with the assured's prospects of success and desire to improve the claim.[17] The object of a lie is to deceive, which may never be discovered. The case thus may be fought on a false premise, or the lie may lead to a favourable settlement before trial.[18]

The fifth class of fraudulent claims is that where there is a known defence to the claim which the assured deliberately suppresses. Mance LJ in *Agapitos v Agnew (The Aegeon) (No.1)*[19] was of the view that 'fraud in relation to a defence' would fall within the fraudulent claim rule. This class will cover all types of defence, including a breach of warranty or duty of good faith.[20] This group may be

---

10   [1999] Lloyd's Rep IR 209.

11   [2011] Lloyd's Rep IR 238.

12   [1995] LR 443.

13   *Agapitos v Agnew (The Aegeon) (No.1)* [2002] Lloyd's Rep IR 573, para 15. Mance LJ added:
'It would be strange if an insured who thought at the time of his initial claim that he had lost property in a theft, but then discovered it in a drawer, could happily maintain both the genuine and the now knowingly false part of his claim, without risk of application of the rule.'

14   Bugra/Merkin, '"Fraud" and fraudulent claims', BILA Journal, 125, October 2012, 3–23, at 7.

15   In *Agapitos v Agnew (The Aegeon) (No.1)* [2002] Lloyd's Rep IR 573 the passenger ferry *Aegeon* was insured against hull and machinery port risks under a slip policy the conditions of which included 'Wtd no hot work'. An endorsement initialled later provided that 'Refurbishment/maintenance works have recommenced and Hot Works on decks is due to commence soon.' It further provided 'Wtd LSA certificate and all recs. complied with prior commencement of hot work.' The Aegeon was lost following a fire that occurred during hot works. The insurer argued that the assured was in breach of warranty that the assured had failed to obtain the warranted certificate either prior to the commencement of hot works. After the proceedings were commenced the assured disclosed sworn statements by two workmen as to the commencement date of the hot works. The insurer argued that during the conduct of the proceedings the assured put forward a knowingly false case about when the hot works began. The fraudulent claims rule does not apply after legal proceedings commenced, which was the case in *Agapitos*, therefore Mance LJ's comments regarding fraudulent means and devices were *obiter*.

16   *Agapitos v Agnew (The Aegeon) (No.1)* [2002] Lloyd's Rep IR 573, para 30.

17   *Agapitos v Agnew (The Aegeon) (No.1)* [2002] Lloyd's Rep IR 573, para 37.

18   *Agapitos v Agnew (The Aegeon) (No.1)* [2002] Lloyd's Rep IR 573, para 37.

19   [2002] Lloyd's Rep IR 573, para 18.

20   [2002] Lloyd's Rep IR 573, para 18.

analysed under class four above, if, for instance, there is a breach of warranty and if the assured presents fake documents attempting to prove that there was no breach.

Dishonesty

In all the abovementioned examples it is clearly the case that the assured was acting dishonestly. Dishonesty within the context of fraud was described by Lord Herschell in *Derry v Peek*[21] that '. . . fraud is proved when it is shewn that a false representation has been made (1) knowingly, or (2) without belief in its truth, or (3) recklessly, careless whether it be true or false.' His Lordship further explained that the third case in his definition expresses the case where one who makes a statement under such circumstances can have no real belief in the truth of what he states. An honest belief in its truth prevents a false statement being fraudulent. If, however, any of the three limbs of the *Derry v Peek* test are fulfilled, the statement will have been made without an honest belief in its truth.[22]

The burden of proving dishonesty is on the insurer and the assured's state of mind is a question of fact for the trial judge to determine.[23] The standard of proof is the balance of probabilities.[24] Dishonesty requires knowledge by the defendant that his statement would be regarded as dishonest by honest people. Lord Hutton stated in *Twinsectra Ltd v Yardley* that 'dishonesty requires knowledge by the defendant that what he was doing would be regarded as dishonest by honest people, although he should not escape a finding of dishonesty because he sets his own standards of honesty and does not regard as dishonest what he knows would offend the normally accepted standards of honest conduct'.[25] Proof of negligence even gross negligence will not be sufficient to prove fraud,[26] however, recklessness will render a claim fraudulent. Recklessness as to the truth of a statement means not caring whether it be true or false.[27] In this context 'not caring' does not mean not taking care; it means indifference to the truth which was described by Popplewell J as 'the moral obloquy of which consists in a wilful disregard of the importance of truth'.[28]

If fraud be proved, the motive of the person guilty of it is immaterial.[29] A person who acts fraudulently cannot say by way of defence that he thought he was justified in acting fraudulently because, for example, he had been treated badly by the other party.[30]

Materiality and inducement

Proof of dishonesty on its own does not sufficiently establish a fraudulent claim. Additionally, proof of materiality is required but materiality in this context is not the same as the materiality test which applies to the duty of good faith. In order for the fraudulent claims rule to apply, where a claim

---

21 (1889) 14 App Cas 337, 374.

22 [2013] 2 Lloyd's Rep 131, para 153.

23 *Versloot Dredging BV v HDI Gerling Industrie Versicherung AG* [2014] EWCA Civ 1349, para 58.

24 [2013] 2 Lloyd's Rep 131, para 153.

25 *Twinsectra Ltd v Yardley* [2002] 2 AC 164, para 36. *Twinsectra* is not an insurance case, however, the courts referred to the case while discussing dishonesty in the context of fraudulent insurance claims. See *Versloot* [2013] 2 Lloyd's Rep 131, para 153; *Aviva Insurance Ltd v Brown* [2012] Lloyd's Rep IR 211, para 101.

26 [2013] 2 Lloyd's Rep 131, para 155.

27 [2013] 2 Lloyd's Rep 131, para 155.

28 [2013] 2 Lloyd's Rep 131, para 154–155.

29 *Derry v Peek*, Lord Herschell (1889) 14 App Cas 337, 374.

30 *Aviva Insurance Ltd v Brown* [2012] Lloyd's Rep IR 211, para 68.

for a loss known to be non-existent or exaggerated, the part of the claim which is non-existent or exaggerated should not itself be immaterial or unsubstantial.[31]

The question will then follow with regard to the quantum which determines the 'substantial' nature of the fraud. In other words some standards should be set in relation to how much of the claim being fraudulent is substantial enough to be regarded as fraudulent? In *Galloway v Guardian Royal Exchange (UK) Ltd*[32] the genuine claim amounted to £16,133.94 and the assured made a fraudulent claim for £2,000. The Court of Appeal held that this was a substantially false claim. Lord Woolf MR was of the view that[33] in determining whether or not the fraud is material the whole of the claim is to be looked at. His Lordship added 'But if you have a claim (which admittedly there is for a much more substantial sum than the part which is fraudulent) where the part which is fraudulent is nonetheless in relation to £2,000 (which amounts to about 10 percent of the whole) that is an amount which is substantial and therefore an amount which taints the whole.'[34] Millett LJ agreed that the fraud was substantial. However, in ascertaining the substantial nature of the fraud his Lordship found the size of the genuine claim irrelevant. Millett LJ expressly rejected the proposition that whether the claim was 'fraudulent to a substantial degree' is to be tested by reference to the proportion of the entire claim which is represented by the fraudulent claim.[35] That would, according to his Lordship, lead to the absurd conclusion that the greater the genuine loss, the larger the fraudulent claim which may be made at the same time without penalty. Millett LJ emphasised that the assured took advantage of the happening of an insured event to make a dishonest claim. Hence, the fraudulent claim should be considered as if it were the only claim and, taken in isolation it should be considered whether the making of that claim by the assured is sufficiently serious to justify the remedy sought for the insurer.[36]

Millett LJ's observations in Galloway were applied in *Joseph Fielding Properties (Blackpool) Ltd v Aviva Insurance Ltd*[37] in respect of the claim for damage to the assured's property which was exaggerated: while the amount paid to a third party to fix the property was £6,700, the assured presented an invoice of £9,870. HHJ Waksman QC[38] held that the fraud was substantial – the claim was worth at least around £2,500 less than the sum claimed of £9,870 looking at the figures alone. Similarly, in *Direct Line Insurance v Khan*,[39] the claim for the damage to property and its contents as a result of a fire was £61,342, and a fraudulent claim for rental of alternative accommodation was for £8,257. Applying *Galloway*, the rental claim was found 'sufficiently substantial' to taint the whole claim and make it irrecoverable.

The observations of Millett LJ were referred to in *Versloot* where Popplewell J stated that if the approach of Millett LJ in *Galloway* be right, a fraudulent element of £2,000 (and quite possibly considerably less) is sufficiently substantial to vitiate a marine insurance claim of £3m or more.[40]

---

31 *Versloot* [2013] 2 Lloyd's Rep 131, para 156; *Agapitos v Agnew (The Aegeon) (No.1)* [2002] Lloyd's Rep IR 573, para 33; [1999] Lloyd's Rep IR 209, 213. In *Goulstone v Royal Insurance Co*, the question of materiality was expressed to be whether the claim was 'wilfully false in any substantial respect' (1858) 1 F & F 276.

32 [1999] Lloyd's Rep IR 209.

33 [1999] Lloyd's Rep IR 209, 213.

34 [1999] Lloyd's Rep IR 209, 213, 214.

35 [1999] Lloyd's Rep IR 209, 214.

36 [1999] Lloyd's Rep IR 209, 214. Millett LJ used the words '. . .whether, taken in isolation, the making of that claim by the insured is sufficiently serious to justify stigmatising it as a breach of his duty of good faith so as to avoid the policy.' The fraudulent claims rule, as it currently stands, is divorced from the duty of good faith and the remedy for such claims is not avoidance of the policy. Therefore, rather than 'avoidance' a more general term 'remedy' is used in the above text.

37 [2011] Lloyd's Rep IR 238.

38 [2011] Lloyd's Rep IR 238, para 89.

39 [2002] Lloyd's Rep IR 364.

40 *Versloot* [2013] 2 Lloyd's Rep 131, para 157; similarly see Christopher Clarke LJ at the Court of Appeal [2014] EWCA Civ 1349, para 109.

In the context of the use of fraudulent means and devices, materiality was defined as 'the relationship which the fraudulent means or device must bear to the valid claim'.[41] In *Agapitos v Agnew (The Aegeon) (No.1)*,[42] Mance LJ tentatively suggested[43] that '. . . the courts should only apply the fraudulent claim rule to the use of fraudulent devices or means which would, if believed, have tended, objectively but prior to any final determination at trial of the parties' rights, to yield a not insignificant improvement in the insured's prospects – whether they be prospects of obtaining a settlement, or a better settlement, or of winning at trial.' Materiality in fraudulent means and devices will be illustrated below.

Once materiality is proved either in the case of a claim where the assured suffered no loss, or less than claimed, or in the case of fraudulent means and devices used to improve a valid claim, proof of inducement is not required to seek remedy for the assured's fraud.[44] Proof of dishonesty and materiality will be sufficient for the insurer to defend the claim.

Remedy for making fraudulent claims

Link with the duty of good faith

When the assured makes a fraudulent claim the insurer is not liable for the claim. But the basis of non-liability had not been clear due to the fact that the juridical basis for the rule has caused some difficulty.[45] Hoffmann LJ[46] held in *Orakpo v Barclays Insurance Services Co Ltd*,[47] that in the absence of any express terms, such a term would be implied into the policy as it would be reasonable to regard as forming part of a contract of insurance. On the other hand some judges supported that the obligations of good faith continue long after the policy has been entered into and are still relevant when it comes to considering claims.[48] This has been said to be a necessary and beneficial discipline in order to ensure that insurers are not exposed to wilfully exaggerated claims.[49] In *Britton v The Royal Insurance Company*[50] in explaining the remedy for fraudulent claims, Willes J stated 'The contract of insurance is one of perfect good faith on both sides, and it is most important that such good faith should be maintained.' Support to this view was seen in Galloway and it was held in *Black King Shipping Corp v Massie (The Litsion Pride)*[51] that submitting a fraudulent claim is a breach of the duty of good faith. In *The Litsion Pride* the shipowner had intended to trade to the Persian Gulf. However, in order to save war risks premium due under the relevant 'held covered' provision, he entered the Gulf without informing the insurers. After the vessel was hit by a missile, the owners concocted and back-dated a letter to the brokers, purporting to advise the intended voyage. Hirst J held that the falsely dated letter was a fraud directly connected to the claim and a breach of the section 17 duty of utmost good faith. However, this aspect of *The Litsion Pride* was overruled by The Star Sea.

---

41 *Versloot* [2013] 2 Lloyd's Rep 131, para 149.
42 [2002] Lloyd's Rep IR 573.
43 [2002] Lloyd's Rep IR 573, para 38.
44 *Agapitos v Agnew (The Aegeon) (No.1)* [2002] Lloyd's Rep IR 573, para 36–37; *Versloot*, [2013] 2 Lloyd's Rep 131, para 166.
45 *Versloot* [2013] 2 Lloyd's Rep 131, para 147.
46 [1995] LRLR 443, 451.
47 [1995] LRLR 443.
48 *Britton, Galloway v Guardian Royal Exchange (UK) Ltd* [1999] Lloyd's Rep IR 209, Lord Woolf MR.
49 *K/S Merc-Scandia XXXXII v Lloyd's Underwriters (The Mercandian Continent)* [2001] 2 Lloyd's Rep 563; *Britton v Royal Insurance Co* (1866) 4 F & F 905 , 906 per Willes J and *Orakpo v Barclays Insurance Services Co Ltd* [1995] LR 443 per Hoffmann LJ.
50 (1866) 4 F & F 905, 910.
51 [1985] 1 Lloyd's Rep 437.

The problem emphasised by their Lordships was the remedy for breach of section 17, which is avoidance of the policy *ab initio*. That would mean that if the assured makes a genuine claim under his policy which was paid by the insurer and during the currency of the same policy if another claim is made but by, say, using fraudulent means and devices, the insurer would be entitled to avoid the policy. Because avoidance will be treating the contract as if it never existed, the assured would have to return the valid claim paid by the insurer, pre-dated the fraudulent claim. In *The Star Sea*, Lord Hobhouse stated that *Orakpo v Barclays Insurance Services Co Ltd*[52] cannot be regarded as authority for the proposition that the making of a fraudulent claim would entitle the insurer to avoid the contract ab initio.[53] In *K/S Merc-Scandia XXXXII v Lloyd's Underwriters (The Mercandian Continent)*[54] Longmore LJ's preferred view was that both the obligation not to make a fraudulent claim and the inability to recover if a fraudulent claim is, in fact, made stem from a rule of law rather than any implied term.[55] Longmore LJ left the door open to apply the duty of good faith in such a case as he said 'This rule of law may itself stem from the good faith obligation that exists between underwriters and their assured and thus be a compelling example of the post-contract application of section 17 of the Marine Insurance Act.' Longmore LJ however added that this issue is not clear given that the judgments on which the rule of law is founded do not use the language of avoidance (as does section 17) but the phrase 'all benefit under the policy' or 'all claim' on the policy. The judge noted that it is always open to the parties to provide expressly the consequences of making a fraudulent claim.

There is no doubt that the parties should act in good faith at a post-contractual stage. However, as fully discussed in Chapter 4, the proper remedy for breach of the post-contractual duty of good faith is not clear in English law. Longmore LJ suggested in *The Mercandian Continent* that for breach of the post-contractual duty of good faith, the insurer should be entitled to avoid the policy only if the circumstances are serious enough to justify termination of the policy at the same time. However, Longmore LJ's analysis does not close the door to the possibility of avoiding the policy for the post-contractual duty of good faith in case of which the assured would lose valid claims paid before the post-contractual duty of good faith breach occurred. All the views expressed above reveal that linking the fraudulent claims with the duty of good faith set out by section 17 of the MIA 1906 have many uncertainties. It is submitted that the latest view is that the post-contractual duty of good faith exists, it manifests itself in different forms in each case, and the judges apply remedy which they may find appropriate in the case.[56] The Government Insurance Bill 2014 does not suggest any reform or clarification in terms of breach of the post-contractual duty of good faith. While the position in the area of good faith remains in dispute, remedy for fraudulent claims, as it currently stands, has been settled such that it is divorced from the post-contractual duty of good faith, and a contractual remedy of forfeiture of claim applies to the fraudulent claims rule.

Forfeiture of the claim

In the absence of a specific remedy determined by the parties at the outset of the contract, it was decided in the early development of the rule on fraudulent claims that the entire claim is forfeited if the assured makes a fraudulent claim.[57] Willes J said in *Britton v The Royal Insurance Company* that 'It would be most dangerous to permit parties to practise such frauds, and then, notwithstanding their

---

52   [1995] LR 443.

53   *The Star Sea* [2001] 1 Lloyd's Rep 389, para 66, Lord Hobhouse.

54   [2001] 2 Lloyd's Rep 563.

55   *The Star Sea* [2001] 1 Lloyd's Rep 389, para 46, Lord Hobhouse.

56   See Chapter 4.

57   *Britton v The Royal Insurance Company* (1866) 4 F & F 905.

falsehood and fraud, to recover the real value of the goods consumed.'[58] The law forfeits not only that which is known to be untrue, but also any genuine part of the claim.[59] Therefore, upon a fraudulent claim, the assured will recover nothing, even if his claim is in part good.[60] Lord Hobhouse said in *The Star Sea*[61] that 'Just as the law will not allow an insured to commit a crime and then use it as a basis for recovering an indemnity . . ., so it will not allow an insured who has made a fraudulent claim to recover. The logic is simple. The fraudulent insured must not be allowed to think: if the fraud is successful, then I will gain; if it is unsuccessful, I will lose nothing.' As discussed above, there were also series of cases and statements linking the post-contractual duty of good faith with fraudulent claims. However, the recent views confirmed that remedy for making a fraudulent claim is not avoidance of the contract *ab initio*.[62] In *Agapitos v Agnew (The Aegeon) (No.1)*,[63] Mance LJ favoured the view that the common law principle governing fraudulent claims has a separate origin and existence to any principle that exists under or by analogy with s.17 of the Marine Insurance Act 1906. Having reiterated this view in *AXA General Insurance Ltd v Gottlieb*, his Lordship expressed that there is no basis or reason for giving the common law rule relating to fraudulent claims a retrospective effect on prior, separate claims which have already been settled under the same policy before any fraud occurs.[64] Mance LJ held that the remedy for fraudulent insurance claims is to forfeit the whole of the claim to which the fraud relates.[65] As the fraud invalidates the entire claim, if the insurer has made any interim payments regarding the same claim before the fraud was discovered, such payments are recoverable from the assured.[66] The interim payments are affected by the fraud because if the whole claim is forfeit, then the fact that sums have been advanced towards it is of itself no answer to their recovery.[67] The sums previously paid on that claim will have been paid on a consideration which has now wholly failed.[68] Thus, it becomes visible that the assured is penalised by making a fraudulent claim.[69] Moreover, once the assured attempted to deceive, that is irremediable so that a correction or retraction would be ineffective.[70]

In *Versloot* the Court of Appeal found the rule justifiable despite the harsh results that its application may lead to. The Court of Appeal approved that there is no proportionality limitation on the right of the underwriters to treat the claim as forfeited. It was held that the principle did not contravene the Human Rights Act 1998. Although an amount payable under an insurance policy was a possession and the assured had been deprived of the possession, the principle satisfied the requirement that it pursued a legitimate aim by means reasonably proportionate to the aim sought to be realised. The fraudulent claims doctrine had a legitimate public policy aim, to deter fraud in the making of claims and to frustrate any expectation that, if the fraud failed, the fraudster would not lose out.

It should be noted that there is no suggestion in the authorities that fraud has an automatic terminating effect.[71] The insurer may be entitled to terminate the contract when there is a fraudulent

---

58 (1866) 4 F & F 905, 909.

59 *Agapitos v Agnew (The Aegeon) (No.1)* [2002] Lloyd's Rep IR 573, para 19; *Orakpo v Barclays Insurance Services Co Ltd* [1995] LR 443; [2013] 2 Lloyd's Rep 131, para 145.

60 *The Star Sea* [2001] 1 Lloyd's Rep 389, para 62; *Galloway v Guardian Royal Exchange (UK) Ltd* [1999] Lloyd's Rep IR 209, Lord Woolf MR.

61 [2001] 1 Lloyd's Rep 389, para 62.

62 *Galloway v Guardian Royal Exchange (UK) Ltd* [1999] Lloyd's Rep IR 209, Lord Woolf MR.

63 [2002] Lloyd's Rep IR 573, para 45.

64 [2005] Lloyd's Rep IR 369, para 22.

65 [2005] Lloyd's Rep IR 369, para 32.

66 [2005] Lloyd's Rep IR 369, para 32.

67 *AXA General Insurance Ltd v Gottlieb* [2005] Lloyd's Rep IR 369, para 27.

68 *AXA General Insurance Ltd v Gottlieb* [2005] Lloyd's Rep IR 369, para 27.

69 *Versloot Dredging BV v HDI Gerling Industrie Versicherung AG* [2013] 2 Lloyd's Rep 131, para 166, 169.

70 *Stemson v AMP General Insurance (NZ) Ltd* [2006] Lloyd's Rep IR 852, para 34; *Versloot Dredging BV v HDI Gerling Industrie Versicherung AG* [2013] 2 Lloyd's Rep 131, para 166.

71 Bugra/Merkin, 4.

claim since the fraud is fundamentally inconsistent with the bargain and the continuation of the contractual relationship between the insurer and the assured.[72]

It is thus now settled that remedy for fraudulent claims is forfeiture of the claim. However, this rule may be amended by the parties who may agree what type of remedy will be imposed for making a fraudulent claim. An express clause may provide that 'the policy is avoidable' or 'the insurer does not pay for any claim which is fraudulently made and the insurer may be given right to terminate the contract upon discovery of a fraudulent claim'.[73] Non-marine policies generally contain a fraudulent claim clause. For instance in *Joseph Fielding Properties (Blackpool) Ltd v Aviva Insurance Ltd*[74] Condition 7 of the general policy conditions applicable to the subject policy read as follows:

> *Fraud*
>
> We will at our option avoid the policy from the inception of this insurance or from the date of the claim or alleged claim or avoid the claim
>
> a) if a claim made by you or anyone acting on your behalf to obtain a policy benefit is fraudulent or intentionally exaggerated, whether ultimately material or not, or
>
> b) a false declaration or statement is made or fraudulent device put forward in support of a claim.

In *Aviva Insurance Ltd v Brown*[75] the insurer had inserted the following clause into the contract: 'We will not pay any claim which is in any respect fraudulent.'

More on fraudulent means and devices

The extension of the fraudulent claims rule to the use of fraudulent means and devices has been applied in a number of cases.[76] This means that the remedy[77] for making a fraudulent claim, which has been established well by the common law courts since the nineteenth century, applies equally to the genuine claims which were attempted to be supported by fraudulent means and device. For instance in *Sharon's Bakery (Europe) Ltd v AXA Insurance UK plc*,[78] the assured lost some of the machinery in the bakery he was running in London. The fire was accidental and there was a genuine claim, however, the assured, having not holding an invoice for the purchase of the machinery lost, issued a fake invoice to prove the title and the amount of the loss that he suffered. The rule applied in *Eagle Star Insurance Co Ltd v Games Video Co (GVC) SA (The Game Boy)*[79] where the assured insured the vessel he had purchased; his intention was to operate her as a floating casino. The vessel's actual value was $100,000–150,000 whereas the assured valued the vessel at the outset of the contract as $1.8m. The insurer purported to avoid the contract for material misrepresentation but the assured argued that he had reasonable grounds to believe that the value was $1.8m. To support his claim the assured

---

72 *The Star Sea* [2001] 1 Lloyd's Rep 389, para 66 Lord Hobhouse.
73 *Britton v The Royal Insurance Company* (1866) 4 F & F 905.
74 [2011] Lloyd's Rep IR 238.
75 [2012] Lloyd's Rep IR 211.
76 *Eagle Star Insurance Co Ltd v Games Video Co (GVC) SA (The Game Boy)* [2004] 1 Lloyd's Rep 238, *Aviva Insurance Ltd v Brown* [2012] Lloyd's Rep IR 211; [2013] 2 Lloyd's Rep 131. This extension was recognised by the Supreme Court in *Summers v Fairclough Homes Ltd* [2013] Lloyd's Rep IR 159, para 29; it also applied by the Privy Council in *Stemson v AMP General Insurance (NZ) Ltd* [2006] Lloyd's Rep IR 852, para 35–36.
77 The remedy is forfeiture of the whole claim. This will be analysed below.
78 [2012] Lloyd's Rep IR 164.
79 [2004] 1 Lloyd's Rep 238.

submitted documents such as a charterparty, invoices showing made to a shipyard for maintenance to render the ship seaworthy. The judge found that the assured had used fraudulent devices to support the claim since the signatures on some of the documents were forged and the invoices were fake.

It is worth mentioning that in the two recent occasions, while having found themselves bound by the extension of the rule to fraudulent means and devices, the judges expressed their regret for their decisions due to the harshness of the consequences reached in the cases in question. The first of these cases is *Aviva Insurance Ltd v Brown*[80] wherein the assured insured his house against risks including subsidence and the costs incurred in rebuilding the house along with the cost of temporary accommodation if the house became uninhabitable due to subsidence. He made a claim under the policy for subsidence in 1989. A further claim was made in 1996. After some considerable delay, Aviva admitted the claim but the repair works were not carried out until 2008. Aviva paid the cost of repairs of £176,951.68. As part of the claim, Aviva also paid an amount in respect of alternative accommodation in the sum of £58,500. During negotiations regarding alternative accommodation the assured sent a letter to the loss adjusters appointed by the insurer with regard to a property No.38 which said 'Please find enclosed details of a house that I consider will be suitable as alternative accommodation. I have spoken to the agents who have been in touch with the owner. Could you please obtain permission from the insurers that I can proceed to rent this house and that they will pay the deposit and rent.' In the end this arrangement did not take place, the assured moved into another property for alternative accommodation. Eder J was persuaded that the assured acted fraudulently in putting forward No.38; in fact he owned the property and in his letter, he, in effect, represented that the owner was someone other than the assured himself. Eder J held that this was not 'insubstantial', 'insignificant' or 'immaterial'.[81] As a consequence, the assured's entire claim was forfeited which entitled the insurer to recover its payment for alternative accommodation as well as the amount paid for the cost of repairs of the assured's home as both were part of the same claim arising out of the subsidence at the assured's home. Eder J recognised the harshness of this result but added that this was the inevitable result of the facts and the well-established policy of the law.[82]

More recently, in *Versloot Dredging BV v HDI Gerling Industrie Versicherung AG*,[83] the owners of DC *Mervestone* suffered an ingress of water which flooded the engine room, and incapacitated the vessel. The vessel's main engine was damaged beyond repair. The claim by the owners under the policy is for the resultant loss in the sum of £3,241,310.60. The underwriters contended the claim was forfeit because the owners employed fraudulent devices in support of the claim when presenting it to underwriters in 2010 and 2011. It was alleged that K for the managers deliberately or recklessly gave a false narrative of the casualty in a letter to the underwriter's solicitors. Arguably, he did that because he had been advised of the due diligence proviso and understood a need to distance the owners themselves from any fault in relation to the casualty, and was therefore keen to explain the quantity of water reaching the engine room by a narrative which involved the bilge alarms working but being ignored by the crew. Popplewell J found and the Court of Appeal approved[84] that the false statement was directly related to the claim and intended to promote the claim. It met the limited objective element of the test of materiality that, if believed, it would have tended at that stage to yield a not insignificant improvement in the owner's prospects of getting the claim paid.[85]

---

80 [2012] Lloyd's Rep IR 211.
81 [2012] Lloyd's Rep IR 211, para 96.
82 [2012] Lloyd's Rep IR 211, para 122.
83 [2014] EWCA Civ 1349.
84 [2014] EWCA Civ 1349, para 62.
85 Materiality is analysed below.

Popplewell J expressed his unwillingness to apply Mance LJ's test in *Agapitos v Agnew* and proposed an alternative materiality test which is 'the policy of the law should be to require at least a sufficiently close connection between the fraudulent device and the valid claim to make it just and proportionate that the valid claim should be forfeit'.[86] Nevertheless, feeling obliged to do so, Popplewell J applied the materiality test as adopted in *Agapitos v Agnew*.[87] The shipowner's appeal was dismissed. At the Court of Appeal Christopher Clarke LJ found *Agapitos v Agnew*, although not binding, still 'authoritative'.[88]

The controversy seems to derive from the fact that the claim is a genuine claim, when fraudulent means and devices are used to promote a claim, the assured does not claim any more than what he suffered. Applying the fraudulent claims rule to the use of fraudulent means and devices therefore may create very harsh consequences since the assured loses his entitlement for a genuine claim under the policy. This extension nevertheless may be found justifiable for the reason that in the case of the assured submitting a fake invoice to prove the claim, it is difficult for the insurer to be reassured as to the genuine amount of the loss. Then, it is possible to counter argue that upon discovery of fraudulent means and devices, a market rate for the subject matter insured might help ascertain the amount of the assured's loss. As referred to above the fraudulent claims rule was justified by Lord Hoffmann in *The Star Sea*[89] in the following words 'The fraudulent insured must not be allowed to think: if the fraud is successful, then I will gain; if it is unsuccessful, I will lose nothing.' Lord Hoffmann's concerns may well explain the logic behind the fraudulent claims rule but it does not equally apply to fraudulent means and devices because in the latter context, if he was permitted to recover despite the fraud, the assured would still recover the loss that he genuinely suffered, no more or no less than that as would have been observed in *Aviva* and *Versloot* above.

Proposals for reform

The law on fraudulent claims is currently subject to reform. The Law Commission found that the law was considered unclear and in need of consolidation.[90] As referred elsewhere in this book, the Insurance Bill 2014 was introduced in parliament which included recommendation regarding fraudulent claims. The proposals are at present said to be likely to come into force in 2016. Section 11 of the Government Insurance Bill 2014 is in the following words:

Remedies for fraudulent claims

1   If the insured makes a fraudulent claim under a contract of insurance –
    a)   the insurer is not liable to pay the claim,
    b)   the insurer may recover from the insured any sums paid by the insurer to the insured in respect of the claim, and
    c)   in addition, the insurer may by notice to the insured treat the contract as having been terminated with effect from the time of the fraudulent act.

---

86   [2013] 2 Lloyd's Rep 131, para 177.
87   [2013] 2 Lloyd's Rep 131, para 181; [2013] 2 Lloyd's Rep 131, para 146. It is worth noting that Popplewell J (Mr Popplewell) was the counsel of the insurers in *The Aegeon* whose arguments were accepted by Mance LJ.
88   [2014] EWCA Civ 1349, para 107.
89   [2001] 1 Lloyd's Rep 389, para 62.
90   The Law Commissions fully analysed Fraudulent Claims in Consultation Paper No. 201: http://lawcommission.justice.gov.uk/docs/cp201_ICL_post_contract_duties.pdf.

2   If the insurer does treat the contract as having been terminated –

    a)   it may refuse all liability to the insured under the contract in respect of a relevant event occurring after the time of the fraudulent act, and

    b)   it need not return any of the premiums paid under the contract.

3   Treating a contract as having been terminated under this section does not affect the rights and obligations of the parties to the contract with respect to a relevant event occurring before the time of the fraudulent act.

4   In subsections (2)(a) and (3), 'relevant event' refers to whatever gives rise to the insurer's liability under the contract (and includes, for example, the occurrence of a loss, the making of a claim, or the notification of a potential claim, depending on how the contract is written).

In their report the Law Commissions emphasised the need for certainty in remedy for fraudulent claims.[91] Thus, the reform proposal contains only sections regarding remedies and clause 12 refers to the effect of a fraudulent claim where there is more than one assured.

It has been presented in this chapter that there are a number of anomalies regarding the fraudulent claims rule the most of which are:

1   A low threshold of the materiality test
2   Extension of the rule to fraudulent means and devices

The issues which have been settled by the case law are

1   Definition of fraud
2   The juridical basis of the rule which is not the duty of good faith as this view was rejected by the House of Lords in The Star Sea and at least twice more by the Court of Appeal in The Aegeon and AXA v Gottlieb
3   The assured's motive in making a fraudulent claim is irrelevant, the judge has no discretion to adjust the claim but once fraud is proved to forfeit the whole claim
4   The fraudulent claims rule should be analysed contractually and if the assured's fraudulent conduct goes to the root of the contract the insurer should be entitled to terminate the contract.

As seen, the Government Insurance Bill 2014 gives statutory certainty to the remedy for fraudulent claims that have been settled by the case law. Under clause 11 the insurer will not be liable for the claim that is invalidated by the assured's fraud. It has become clearer with clause 11 that the insurer may terminate the contract upon the assured making a fraudulent claim. The valid claims which took place and paid before the fraud occurred are not affected by the fraudulent claim that was made after such claims arose and were paid. The interim payments that the insurer made regarding the claim tainted by the fraud are recoverable from the assured. It is unfortunate that the Bill does not refer to the use of fraudulent means and devices or the materiality or inducement tests in proof of fraudulent claims.

Recently, the Court of Appeal's decision in Versloot established more firmly the application of the fraudulent claims rule to the use of fraudulent means and devices. Christopher Clarke LJ – who gave the leading judgment – expressed that a fraudulent device is a sub-species of a fraudulent claim. [92] According to his Lordship, it is consistent to apply the fraudulent claims rule to the fraudulent means and devices as well as fraudulent claims.[93] Moreover, the learned judge expressed that the

---

91   http://lawcommission.justice.gov.uk/docs/lc353_insurance-contract-law.pdf
92   [2014] EWCA Civ 1349, para 108.
93   [2014] EWCA Civ 1349, para 108.

foundation of the rule is the obligation of the utmost good faith – an incident of the special relationship between insured and insurer. The effect of the rule is that if the assured lies to his insurer in respect of anything significant in the presentation of the claim he will not recover anything from the insurer.[94] Although the judge recognised the harshness of the result of a fraudulent devices rule, he nevertheless found its application justifiable.[95] According to Christopher Clarke LJ, the objective of using fraudulent devices is the desire to bolster a claim that appears to have potential weaknesses. The assured's motivation in using fraudulent devices might be to avoid or cut short lines of inquiry or investigation that might prevent or postpone the payment of it. The risk to the insurer is, as his Lordship pointed out, that the device may achieve its purpose, so that the insurer fails to explore the claim properly and pays out in respect of a claim where he may have a defence. Therefore, it will never be known if the result would have been the same if fraudulent devices had not been used.

Further reading

Arnould, *Law of Marine Insurance and Average*, 18th edn, [2013] Sweet & Maxwell. Chapter 18, The Post-Contractual Duty of Utmost Good Faith and Fraudulent Claims.

Birds et al., *MacGillivray on Insurance Law*, 12th edn, [2014] Sweet & Maxwell. Chapter 16, Misrepresentation.

Bugra and Merkin, '"Fraud" and fraudulent claims', *BILA Journal* [2012] 125(October) 3–23.

Davey, 'Unpicking the fraudulent claims jurisdiction in insurance contract law: sympathy for the devil?', *Lloyd's Maritime and Commercial Law Quarterly* [2006] 2(May), 223–241.

Hjalmarsson, 'The law on fraudulent insurance claims', *Journal of Business Law* [2013] 1, 103–117.

Hjalmarsson, 'The standard of proof in civil cases: the insurance fraud perspective', *International Journal of Evidence and Proof* [2013] 17(1): 47–73.

Soyer, *Marine Insurance Fraud* [2014] Informa.

Tarr, 'Fraudulent insurance claims: recent legal developments', *Journal of Business Law* [2008] 2, 139–157.

Thomas, 'Fraudulent insurance claims: definition, consequences and limitations', *Lloyd's Maritime and Commercial Law Quarterly* [2006] 4(Nov), 485–516.

---

94 [2014] EWCA Civ 1349, para 109.
95 [2014] EWCA Civ 1349, para 112.

Chapter 13

Subrogation

Definition

A person who has taken out a marine insurance policy may also have a claim against a third party if loss has been caused by him. In such a case the assured will have two remedies, one from the insurer and one from the third party. If the assured makes his first claim against the third party the latter cannot argue that the assured first must claim from the insurer. Moreover, in assessing damages recoverable from the third party the proceeds of insurance are to be disregarded.[1] If the assured first directs his claim to the insurer, the insurer cannot refuse to indemnify the assured since the assured may have distinct rights against some other person.[2] In such a case the assured may obtain a double recovery. He may first recover his loss from the insurer whose payment will not discharge the third party from his liability to the assured. If otherwise were permitted, that is, if the insurer's payment discharged the third party from his liability, the third party would be permitted to take advantage of an insurance contract under which he did not pay any premium. However, a further issue which has to be emphasised is that the principle which governs the compensation of the assured's loss states that a marine insurance contract is a contract of indemnity that the assured, under an insurance contract, is entitled to receive the amount representing his loss but no more than that.[3] Thus, it appears that the principle of indemnity does not allow the assured to obtain a double recovery.[4] Therefore, equity established that upon payment of the policy amount to the assured, the insurer subrogates into the assured's rights against the third party.[5] Subrogation places the insurer in the position of the assured with regard to the latter's claim against the third party.[6] The double recovery is then prevented and the third party is not relieved from his wrongdoing by the insurer's payment.

In the Marine Insurance Act 1906, subrogation is regulated by section 79 in the following words:

1   Where the insurer pays for a total loss, either of the whole, or in the case of goods of any apportionable part, of the subject-matter insured, he thereupon becomes entitled to take over the interest of the assured in whatever may remain of the subject-matter so paid for, and he is thereby subrogated to all the rights and remedies of the assured in and in respect of that subject-matter as from the time of the casualty causing the loss.

2   Subject to the foregoing provisions, where the insurer pays for a partial loss, he acquires no title to the subject-matter insured, or such part of it as may remain, but he is thereupon subrogated to all rights and remedies of the assured in and in respect of the subject-matter insured as from the time of the casualty causing the loss, in so far as the assured has been indemnified, according to this Act, by such payment for the loss.'

---

1   *Yates v Whyte* (1838) 4 Bingham New Cases 272.
2   *Dickenson v Jardine* (1867–68) LR 3 CP 639. If the assured recovers from the third party before being indemnified by the insurer the amount recovered from the third party is taken into consideration in assessing the amount to be paid by the insurer. Lord Blackburn, *Simpson v Thomson* (1877) 3 App Cas 279, 293.
3   *Yates v Whyte* (1838) 4 Bingham New Cases 272. Sue and labour expenses may be recovered in addition to the insured amount, see *Castellain v Preston* (1883) 11 QBD 380, 386 and 392, Brett LJ. See Chapter 11 for Sue and Labour expenses.
4   *Dickenson v Jardine* (1867–68) LR 3 CP 639.
5   Subrogation does not apply to insurance contracts which are not contracts of indemnity such as life insurance and sickness policies. *Meacock v Bryant & Co* (1942) 74 Ll L Rep 53, 56–57 Atkinson J.
6   *Castellain v Preston* (1883) 11 QBD 380, at 388 Brett LJ; *Darrell v Tibbitts* (1880) 5 QBD 560, 563 Brett LJ; *Mason v Sainsbury* (1782) 3 Douglas 61, 65, Buller J; *Yates v Whyte* (1838) 4 Bingham New Cases 272, 285, Bosanquet J *Randal v Cockran* (1748) 1 Vesey Senior 98; *White v Dobinson* (1844) 14 Sim. 273, 274. These cases established that the insurer and assured are regarded as being one person; as a result the insurer is to be put into the assured's position because 'the person originally sustaining the loss was the owner; but after satisfaction made to him, the insurer'.

It has been submitted that section 79 of MIA 1906 is not a model of clarity[7] but two issues should be noted here. First, subsection 1 regulates 'abandonment' which is a different principle to subrogation. Abandonment is fully analysed in Chapter 9, but will briefly be discussed in this chapter in relation to distinguishing abandonment from subrogation. Second, even though it appears in the Marine Insurance Act 1906, section 79 has been said to express more general principles.[8] Thus it has been seen that the courts have referred to marine and non-marine cases without distinguishing the principles in the two different types of insurance.[9] The issues regulated by section 79 will be mentioned in the following paragraphs where such matters arise.

The effect of subrogation

Two different issues have to be separated with regard to subrogation. First, as noted above, the assured may recover from the third party, who cannot argue that his debt has been extinguished by the insurer's payment to the assured.[10] In such a case, that is, where the assured recovers in diminution of an insured loss, the insurer may vest in rights in respect of the proceeds of the assured's recovery to take advantage of any benefit which accrues to the assured which diminishes the loss.[11] Second, once the insurer indemnifies the assured the latter's rights against the third party may be vested in the insurer. The insurer is entitled to take over all of the rights of the assured, whether in contract or tort, legal or equitable, against the person responsible for the loss.[12]

Insurer's rights in respect of the proceeds of the assured's recovery

It was mentioned above that the assured's rights against the third party survive despite indemnification by the insurer.[13] The right to sue and recover from the wrongdoer belongs to the assured. Therefore, indemnification by the insurer is not a bar to the assured recovering from the third party. However, the principle of indemnity does not allow the assured to have a double recovery. Therefore, any recovery by the assured after indemnification by the insurer will be for the benefit of the insurer.[14] Some of the early authorities on subrogation held that the assured may obtain such benefit from the third party as trustee for the insurer.[15] However, this was disapproved by the House of Lords in *Napier and Ettrick v RF Kershaw Ltd (No.1)*.[16] In *Napier* their Lordships held that

---

7　Merkin, Steele 'Insurance and The Law of Obligations', OUP, 2013, 106.

8　*Caledonia North Sea Ltd v British Telecommunications* [2002] 1 Lloyd's Rep 553, 559 Lord Bingham.

9　See, for example, *Lord Napier and Ettrick v RF Kershaw Ltd (No.1)* [1993] 1 Lloyd's Rep 197.

10　*Darrell v Tibbitts* (1880) 5 QBD 560, 565 Cotton LJ; *North British & Mercantile Insurance Co v London Liverpool & Globe Insurance Co* (1877) 5 Ch D 569, Mellish LJ, at 584–585.

11　*Burnand v Rodocanachi* (1882) 7 App Cas 333, 339.

12　*Castellain v Preston* (1883) 11 QBD 380, 388.

13　If that was not the case, the insurer would never have a right of subrogation.

14　*Yates v Whyte* (1838) 4 Bingham New Cases 272.

15　*Blaauwpot v Da Costa* (1758) 1 Eden 130; *Randal v Cockran* (1748) 1 Vesey Senior 98.

16　[1993] 1 Lloyd's Rep 197. See Lord Browne-Wilkinson in *Napier and Ettrick v RF Kershaw Ltd (No.1)* in which his Lordship found the imposition of a trust and thus to impose fiduciary liabilities on the assured neither commercially desirable nor necessary to protect the insurers' interests. According to his Lordship the contract of insurance contains an implied term that the assured will pay to the insurer out of the moneys received in reduction of the loss the amount to which the insurer is entitled by way of subrogation. That contractual obligation is specifically enforceable in equity against the defined fund. This specifically enforceable right gives rise to an immediate proprietary interest in the moneys recovered from the third party. This proprietary interest is adequately satisfied in the circumstances of subrogation under an insurance contract by granting the insurers a lien over the moneys recovered by the assured from the third party. This lien will be enforceable against the fund so long as it is traceable and has not been acquired by a bona fide purchaser for value without notice.

in order to protect the rights of the insurer under the doctrine of subrogation, equity considers that the damages payable by the wrongdoer to the insured person are subject to an equitable lien or charge in favour of the insurer. The reason for imposing such a charge by equity was described as that once the insurer has paid under the policy, it has an interest in the right of action against the wrongdoer and an interest in the establishment, quantification, recovery and distribution of the damages awarded against the wrongdoer. Despite having been indemnified by the insurer if the assured still recovers for a loss from a wrongdoer, according to their Lordships, the assured is guilty of unconscionable conduct if he does not procure and direct that the sum due to the insurer shall by way of subrogation be paid out of the damages.[17] The insurer can give notice to the wrongdoer of his equitable charge. When the wrongdoer is ordered or agrees to pay the amount in question and has notice of the rights of the insurer to subrogation, the wrongdoer can either pay the damages into court or decline to pay without the consent of both the insured person and the insurer. The insurer will then be entitled to injunctions restraining the third party from paying and the assured from receiving any part of the damages recovered from the third party.[18] The result is that the insurer is a secured creditor for its subrogation entitlements in the event of the assured's insolvency before or after the sum due to him has been paid by the third party.[19]

Insurer's rights in respect of the assured's rights against the third party

The principle of the insurer's payment does not extinguish the third party's debt to the assured, thus, recovery upon a contract with the insurer is no bar to a claim for damages against the wrongdoer was mentioned above.[20] If there were no recovery available from the third party for the reason that the insurer indemnified the assured's loss, the third party would take all the benefit of a policy of insurance without paying the premium.[21] The third party's liability would only be extinguished by an action brought in the name of the person indemnified (subrogation) or in the name of the indemnifier suing as assignee of the rights of the person indemnified (assignment).[22] A number of issues have to be noted here. Firstly, the insurer, as he is placed in the assured's position, cannot acquire any better right than the assured possesses.[23] This means that the third party, in an action against him by the insurer after subrogation, can submit the points of defence that would be available to him in an action against him by the assured. If, for instance, the assured's claim has become time-barred, the third party can raise such defence against the insurer. Another example is that where the underlying contract between the assured and the third party contains an arbitration clause the insurer is bound by the term providing to arbitrate rather than litigate the dispute.[24] Moreover, insurers cannot be substituted as claimants in an action commenced in the name of the assured after it had been dissolved.[25] When the company is dissolved the assured ceases to exist so that there will be no company in whose name any action may be started.[26] This highlights one of the practical differences between assignment and subrogation. Given that subrogation involves an action brought in the name of the assured, if the assured no longer exists as a company such a claim is no longer possible. However with an action commenced by an insurer via assignment, the insurer

---

17 [1993] 1 Lloyd's Rep 197, 205, Lord Templeman.
18 The House of Lords here approved an old authority on the matter: *White v Dobinson* (1844) 14 Sim. 273.
19 Colinvaux, para 11–020.
20 *Mason v Sainsbury* (1782) 3 Douglas 61; *Yates v Whyte* (1838) 4 Bingham New Cases 272; *Caledonia North Sea Ltd v British Telecommunications* [2002] 1 Lloyd's Rep 553, 571, Lord Hoffmann.
21 *Yates v Whyte* (1838) 4 Bingham New Cases 272; *Parry v Cleaver* [1969] 1 Lloyd's Rep 183.
22 *Esso Petroleum Co Ltd v Hall Russell & Co Ltd (The Esso Bernicia)* [1989] 1 Lloyd's Rep 8, 21, Lord Jauncey.
23 *Schiffahrtsgesellschaft Detlev von Appen GmbH v Voest Alpine Intertrading GmbH (The Jay Bola)* [1997] 2 Lloyd's Rep 279; Arnould, para 3–15.
24 *Schiffahrtsgesellschaft Detlev von Appen GmbH v Voest Alpine Intertrading GmbH (The Jay Bola)* [1997] 2 Lloyd's Rep 279.
25 *MH Smith Ltd (Plant Hire) v DL Mainwaring* [1986] 2 Lloyd's Rep 244.
26 *MH Smith Ltd (Plant Hire) v DL Mainwaring* [1986] 2 Lloyd's Rep 244, 245 Lord Justice O'Connor.

would be entitled to sue in his own name if the assignment had been given before the company was dissolved.

In *Napier and Ettrick v RF Kershaw Ltd* (No.1), while the House of Lords held that the insurer has an equitable charge over the recoveries from the third party, their Lordships did not express any concluded view as to whether the equitable lien or charge attaches also to the rights of action vested in the assured to recover from a third party. In *Morley v Moore*[27] – long before *Napier* was decided – the assured's insurer instructed him not to institute an action against the tortfeasor in respect of a loss for which a full indemnity had been received from the insurer. The assured proceeded nevertheless and he was held to have right to do so. After *Napier* was decided, in *Re Ballast plc, St Paul Travellers Insurance Co Ltd v Dargan*,[28] Lawrence Collins J denied the existence of any form of equitable lien over the cause of action (as opposed to the proceeds of any claim). *Re Ballast* thus indicates that *Morley v Moore* remains good law, a point specifically made by Lawrence Collins J in *Re Ballast plc*.

Elements of subrogation

(1) The insurer must pay

The insurer's right to subrogation cannot be enforced prior to payment by the insurer.[29] This principle was argued to have been ousted in *Rathbone Brothers plc v Novae Corporate Underwriting*[30] in which the policy provided 'the insurer shall be subrogated . . . before or after any payment under this policy'. Burton J however did not find the wording clear enough to oust the principle.[30a]

This highlights another difference between assignment and subrogation, in that the former does not require the insurer to pay before being assigned the assured's right to sue the third party.

(2) A subrogation action is required to pursue the claim in the name of the assured[31]

This is the case due to the fact that the benefit of the assured's personal right is transferred to the insurer in subrogation.[32] The insurer's action brought in his own name was rejected in *London Assurance Company v Sainsbury*[33] where Lord Mansfield[34] said 'If the insurer could sue in his own name, no release by the insured would bar, nor would a verdict by him be a bar. It is impossible that the insured should transfer, and yet retain his right of action . . . as against the person sued the right of action cannot be transferred, nor the defence varied.'

The law allows an insurer to take from its assured an assignment of the assured's rights against a third party in respect of an insured loss.[35] Here subrogation can again be distinguished from assignment, as an assignment by an assured to his underwriter of the assured's rights against the contract breaker or tortfeasor is enforceable by the underwriter in the underwriter's own name.[36]

---

27 [1936] 2 KB 359.

28 [2007] Lloyd's Rep IR 742.

29 *Castellain v Preston*, (1883) 11 QBD 380, 389.

30 [2013] EWHC 3457 (Comm).

30a The point did not arise on appeal as the Court of Appeal decided that the insurer had no right of subrogation. Nevertheless, Elias LJ expressed his agreement with Burton J on this point [2014] EWCA Civ 1464, para 109.

31 *Simpson v Thomson* (1877) 3 App Cas 279; *Mason v Sainsbury* (1782) 3 Douglas 61; *Yates v Whyte* (1838) 4 Bingham New Cases 272; *Esso Petroleum Co Ltd v Hall Russell & Co Ltd (The Esso Bernicia)* [1989] 1 Lloyd's Rep 8.

32 *Simpson v Thomson* (1877) 3 App Cas 279, 293.

33 (1783) 3 Doug. KB 244.

34 (1783) 3 Doug. KB 244, at 253–254.

35 *Compania Colombiana de Seguros v Pacific Steam Navigation Co* [1965] 1 QB 101.

36 *Compania Colombiana de Seguros v Pacific Steam Navigation Co (The Colombiana)* [1963] 2 Lloyd's Rep 479; *Esso Petroleum Co Ltd v Hall Russell & Co Ltd (The Esso Bernicia)* [1989] 1 Lloyd's Rep 8; *King v Victoria Insurance Co, Ltd* [1896] AC 250.

(3) The insurer can recover only up to the amount he paid to the assured

In subrogation, the insurer cannot recover any more than the amount paid to the assured, irrespective of the assured's gain, for example as a result of currency fluctuations.[37]

In *Yorkshire Insurance Co Ltd v Nisbet Shipping Co Ltd*[38] the assured insured his vessel under a valued policy at £72,000. Upon total loss of the vessel in 1945 the insurer paid the shipowner £72,000. In 1946 the assured then, with consent of insurer, instituted proceedings in Canada against Canadian Government for damages for loss of the vessel. An amount of 336,039.52 Canadian dollars was paid to the shipowner in Canada in 1958. As a result of devaluation of sterling in 1949, the equal of 336,039.52 Canadian dollars amounted to £126,971 when converted into sterling in London. The insurer claimed the full amount received by the assured from the Canadian Government. It was held that the insurer's rights under section 79(1) were limited to recovering any sum that he had overpaid to the extent of the amount the insurer paid to the assured. Subsequently, as the amount received from the third party by the assured exceeded the sum paid by the insurer, the insurer could not recover from the assured the amount of such excess, and therefore, the insurer was entitled to £72,000, and no more.

It should be noted that in the case of a recovery from the third party which includes interest the insurer and the assured would share the interest proportionately taking into account the date of any payment by the insurer to the assured.[39]

The juridical basis of subrogation

The early decisions that established the doctrine of subrogation clearly noted that subrogation is a principle of equity.[40] The relationship between the assured and the third party is not altered upon payment of the insurer; the third party is still liable for his wrongdoing and upon payment to the assured the insurer steps into the assured's shoes and becomes the injured party against the third party. It is also seen, albeit rarely, that in the early decisions on subrogation, the common law origin of subrogation also had found some support. For instance in *Darrell v Tibbitts*[41] Thesiger LJ said that a subrogation action may be supported upon one of two grounds: (1) The common law principle that the insurer indemnifies the assured as the latter suffered loss, if the assured is indemnified by the third party the ground for the payment by the insurer disappears, thus the money paid by the insurer should be returned; (2) As a kind of action in equity that having indemnified the assured under the insurance contract against the loss sustained by him the insurer has a right to be subrogated into the place of the assured in respect of the assured's rights against the third party. Then in *Yorkshire Insurance Co Ltd v Nisbet Shipping Co Ltd*,[42] Diplock J stated that the doctrine derives from an implied term of the contract. According to the learned judge, terms should be implied in marine insurance contracts to give business efficacy to an agreement whereby the assured in the case of a loss against which the policy has been made shall be fully indemnified, and never

---

37   There will be no such limit on recovery by the assignee.
38   [1961] 1 Lloyd's Rep 479.
39   Colinvaux, para 11–017.
40   *Randal v Cockran* (1748) 1 Vesey Senior 98; *Yates v Whyte* (1838) 4 Bingham New Cases 272; *Quebec Fire Assurance Company v St. Louis* (1851) VII Moore, PC 286; *Castellain v Preston* (1883) 11 QBD 380; *Burnand v Rodocanachi* (1882) 7 App Cas 333, Lord Blackburn, 339.
41   (1880) 5 QBD 560.
42   [1961] 1 Lloyd's Rep 479, 483.

more than fully indemnified.[43] In *Napier and Ettrick v RF Kershaw Ltd (No.1)*,[44] however, the House of Lords rejected Diplock J's view that subrogation concerns solely the mutual rights and obligations of the parties under the contract. Lord Goff emphasised that the history of subrogation demonstrated that it had been developed as an equitable principle[45] and it was unusual to express the principle of subrogation as arising from an implied term in the contract. In agreement with Lord Goff, Lord Templeman stated that the references in the early cases on subrogation to the equitable obligations of an insured person towards an insurer entitled to subrogation are discernible and immutable.[46]

Subrogation here can again be distinguished from assignment. The former occurs spontaneously upon payment and the assured does not have to grant a subrogation right to the insurer as equity finds it appropriate that the insurer steps into the assured's shoes once the requirements are met. Assignment on the other hand requires the assignor assigning his rights to the assignee by an agreement.

Insurer's subrogation rights

The insurer pays in full under the policy, but that payment does not fully indemnify the assured against his actual loss

Whether the insurer is entitled to his subrogation right depends on the nature of the policy. If the policy is a valued policy the value determined by the parties is conclusive, therefore the assured is not allowed to argue that the loss he suffered is greater than the loss indemnified by the insurer.[47] The insurer will then be entitled to his subrogation right.

If the policy is unvalued it is still arguable that from the wording of section 79(2), upon payment the insurer subrogates into the assured's rights.[48] In *Commercial Union Assurance Co v Lister*[49] it was held that the assured will have control of the proceedings against the third party until he receives the full indemnity. In such a case the assured's obligations come into play which demand that when in control of the proceedings the assured must not act in a way so as to prejudice the insurer's subrogation rights.

A claim on a policy is settled for less than its full value

The terms of the settlement agreement are important at this stage as the settlement agreement may confirm that it was a full and final settlement in which case the assured might not be able to argue that he did not receive full indemnity. The insurer then subrogates into the rights of the assured up to the amount paid by the insurer.

---

43 See also *Morris v Ford Motor Co* [1973] 2 Lloyd's Rep 27.
44 [1993] 1 Lloyd's Rep 197.
45 [1993] 1 Lloyd's Rep 197, 207.
46 [1993] 1 Lloyd's Rep 197, 205.
47 *Burnand v Rodocanachi Sons & Co* (1882) 7 App Cas 333, Lord Selborne LC, 335.
48 Arnould, para 31–13.
49 (1873–1874) LR 9 Ch App 483.

Limitations to subrogation

Subrogation may be excluded or modified by the terms of the policy.[50] As mentioned above in *Rathbone Brothers plc v Novae Corporate Underwriting*[51] the words 'the insurer shall be subrogated . . . before or after any payment under this policy' were held not to alter the requirements of subrogation in terms of the necessity of payment before the insurer subrogates into the assured's rights. An insurer may waive his subrogation rights by an express waiver clause included in the policy. For instance in *National Oilwell (UK) Ltd v Davy Offshore Ltd*[52] the insurer waived rights of subrogation against co-assureds under the policy as well as against 'any employee, agent or contractor of the Principal Assureds or any individual, agent, firm affiliate or corporation for whom the Principal Assureds may be acting or with whom the Principal Assureds may have agreed prior to any loss to waive subrogation'.[53]

The assured is the party that has suffered loss but is also the party responsible for that loss

The insurer can only exercise his right of subrogation in the name of the assured. If the assured is the party who also caused the loss by his own wrongdoing the insurer cannot exercise his rights of subrogation as the assured cannot sue himself. A collision between sisterships is a clear example of this. In *Simpson v Thomson*,[54] B was the sole owner of two vessels, the *Dunluce Castle* and the *Fitzmaurice*, which came into collision at sea. The collision was due entirely to the negligence of those in charge of the *Fitzmaurice*, and the result of it was that the *Dunluce Castle* and her cargo were wholly lost. B, as owner of the ship in fault, instituted a suit for the purpose of limiting his liability to those who had suffered as a result of the collision to a sum equalling the value of the ship in fault, calculated at £8 per ton, and paid into a bank under order of the Court, that sum to be distributed by the Court among those entitled to it. The underwriters who had insured the *Dunluce Castle* paid B £6,000 for a total loss under a valued policy. For this sum they had claimed to rank with the other claimants upon the fund in Court, and the question was whether they were entitled to do so. There were several claimants on the fund, in particular the owners of the cargo that was on board the *Dunluce Castle* at the time she was injured, and the underwriters on that vessel. The fund was insufficient for payment of all the claims in full, and the owners of the cargo were held to be entitled to object to the right of the underwriters of the *Dunluce Castle* to claim from the fund. The Court held that no claim ought to be allowed against the fund in respect of any right derived from the shipowner who established the fund and can only be enforced in his name. Thus, the *Dunluce Castle*'s insurers' claim from the fund was not answerable in damages.

The nature of recovery by the assured from the third party

The absolute meaning of the word 'subrogation' was stated to be that the insurer must be placed in the position of the assured.[55] In other words, insurer's subrogation rights are not limited to the right of the insurer in cases where the contract in respect of which benefit had been received related

---

50 *Talbot Underwriting Ltd v Nausch Hogan & Murray Inc (The Jascon 5)* [2006] Lloyd's Rep IR 531.
51 [2013] EWHC 3457 (Comm).
52 [1993] 2 Lloyd's Rep 582.
53 See International Hull Clauses 2003 cl.28 and 40.8.
54 (1877) 3 App Cas 279.
55 *Castellain v Preston* (1883) 11 QBD 380, 388 Brett LJ.

to the same loss or damage as that against which the contract of indemnity was created by the policy.[56] Such broad nature of subrogation was expressed by Brett LJ[57] as follows:

> ... the underwriter is entitled to the advantage of "every right of the assured", whether such right consists in contract, fulfilled or unfulfilled, or in remedy for tort capable of being insisted on or already insisted on, or in any other right, whether by way of condition or otherwise, legal or equitable, which can be, or has been exercised or has accrued, and whether such right could or could not be enforced by the insurer in the name of the assured by the exercise or acquiring of which right or condition the loss against which the assured is insured, can be, or has been diminished.

In *Castellain v Preston*[58] the assured agreed to sell a house to a third party purchaser. Between exchange and completion, the house was destroyed by fire. The assured was not only indemnified by his insurer for the costs of making good the fire damage but also obtained the full purchase price from the purchaser on the basis that the risk had passed to the purchaser under the contract. The contract of sale had nothing to do with destruction by fire but the insurer was held to be entitled to recover from the assured a sum equivalent to that which they had paid. Clearly such a principle is in line with the rule that the assured is not entitled to recover more than the loss that he suffered. In order to determine the insurer's subrogation right upon recovery from or a claim against a third party the true test is, can the right to be insisted on be deemed to be one the enforcement of which will diminish the loss?[59] If there is money or any other benefit received which ought to be taken into account in diminishing the loss or in ascertaining what the real loss is against which the contract of indemnity is given, such an amount is taken into account to calculate what the real loss is. The benefit may not be a contract or right of suit which arises and has its birth from the accident insured against but what is taken into account is whether it diminishes the loss insured. In *Assicurazioni Generali de Trieste v Empress Assurance Corporation Ltd*[60] the insurer issued an open cover with the condition that the assured was not entitled to declare vessels that belonged to M. The insurer then reinsured 50 per cent of his interest up to £1,000. The reinsured made a payment to the assured with respect to loss of vessels that belonged to M. This occurred without the knowledge of the reinsured and when the reinsured contested some other claims by the assured it appeared that the assured had previously misrepresented a claim regarding the vessels belonging to M, which was indemnified by the reinsured and the reinsurers. The assured had been held liable for damages that the reinsured suffered as a result of the assured's misrepresentation. The reinsured refused to pass that recovery to the reinsurers and upon an action by the latter, Pickford J applied *Castellain v Preston*. The claim was to recover the amount of damage that the reinsured had suffered by reason of having to pay the loss, and the recovery from the assured was received by reason of the enforcement of a right which diminished such loss. The reinsured claimed to deduct the expenses incurred to obtain recovery from the third party. Pickford J allowed the reinsured to deduct expenses reasonably and properly incurred in enforcing their claim to that sum against the assured from the amount to be paid to the reinsurer.

---

56 *Castellain v Preston* (1883) 11 QBD 380, 394 Cotton LJ.
57 *Castellain v Preston* (1883) 11 QBD 380, 388.
58 (1883) 11 QBD 380.
59 *Castellain v Preston* (1883) 11 QBD 380, 404 Bowen LJ.
60 [1907] 2 KB 814.

Gifts (voluntary payments)

The question of whether the insurer can claim a subrogation right over a recovery by the assured which was given as a gift to him by the third party can be analysed in line with the principle stated in the above paragraph. The question that should be posed is, 'Was the gift given for the benefit of the insurers as well as for the benefit of the assured'? If the gift was given in order to diminish the loss against which the insurers were bound to indemnify the assured, the payment is for the insurer's benefit as well as the assured.[61] Thus the insurers will be entitled to the benefit. On the other hand the gift will stay with the assured if it was given for his benefit only.[62] In Burnand v Rodocanachi Sons & Co[63] the cargo that was insured against war risks on a valued policy was destroyed by capture and destruction by a Confederate cruiser. The cargo owner was indemnified by the insurer on an actual total loss basis. The valued amount was less than the actual value of the cargo. The United States, out of a compensation fund created after the loss and distributed under an Act of Congress passed subsequently to the loss, paid to the assured the difference between their real total loss and the sum received from the underwriters. It was held that the underwriters were not entitled to recover the compensation from the cargo owners as the Government of the United States did not pay it with the intention of reducing the loss.

It thus appears that[64] the focus should be on the real character of the transaction. When the intention of giving a gift is to benefit the assured only, enabling the insurer to claim from such a gift would be diverting the gift from its objective.[65] It was also expressed that the insurer's right of subrogation is confined to that which is a right or incident belonging to the assured, as an incident of the property at the time when the loss takes place,[66] whereas at that time a gift cannot be said to have been appertaining to the assured as owner of the property; it is not known at the date of the loss if a voluntary payment is going to be made in the future.

It is a question of fact in each case whether a gift has or has not been paid in diminution of the loss and the answer depends upon the intention of the donor.[67] In Colonia Versicherung AG v Amoco Oil Co (The Wind Star),[68] the insurer, Colonia Versicherung AG, insured a cargo of naphtha, shipped from the refinery of Amoco in Texas to ICI Chemicals & Polymers Ltd in the United Kingdom. The cargo was found to have been contaminated at arrival in the UK. The contamination occurred in Amoco's shorelines after leaving the shoretanks but prior to shipment on board Wind Star in Texas due to Amoco's negligence. ICI and Amoco settled the claim for about US$8m. In return to paying ICI's damages Amoco was granted an unconditional release from any and all claims by ICI as well as an assignment of all ICI's rights under the insurance policy. When Amoco made a claim against the insurer the insurer claimed to deduct the amount settled with ICI. Potter J rejected Amoco's argument that the settlement amount had to be disregarded for the reason that the payment was to be regarded as equivalent to a 'gift'. The judge distinguished Burnand reasoning that the intention underlying the payment was to be ascertained from construction of the Act of Congress. The plain intention of the Act was to compensate for uninsured losses and the Act was not one in respect of which the payee enjoyed any right of action for enforcement. 'It was only a gift to which the

---

61 Burnand v Rodocanachi Sons & Co (1882) 7 App Cas 333, 340 Lord Blackburn.
62 Merrett v Capitol Indemnity Corp [1991] 1 Lloyd's Rep 169.
63 (1882) 7 App Cas 333.
64 (1883) 11 QBD 380, Bowen LJ, 404–405.
65 Cotton LJ, Castellain v Preston (1883) 11 QBD 380, at 395; see the discussion in Assicurazioni Generali de Trieste v Empress Assurance Corp Ltd [1907] 2 KB 814.
66 Cotton LJ, Castellain v Preston (1883) 11 QBD 380, at 395.
67 Colonia Versicherung AG v Amoco Oil Co (The Wind Star) [1995] 1 Lloyd's Rep 570; Merrett v Capitol Indemnity Corp [1991] 1 Lloyd's Rep 169.
68 [1995] 1 Lloyd's Rep 570.

assured had no right at any time until it was placed in their hands'.[69] The appeal was dismissed.[70] In agreement with Potter J at first instance, Hirst LJ at the Court of Appeal referred to the wording of the assignment to determine the intention of the payment to ICI. Accordingly, by payment and assignment, the parties intended to

> ... resolve any disputes that exist or may arise between them as a result of the transactions . . . and this desire is fulfilled by cl. 1.2 under which ICI release and discharge Amoco from ... all claims liabilities obligations and causes of action whatsoever contingent or not contingent, known or unknown, which it now has, had or may have arising out of the transaction ...

This was a true commercial settlement of any possible claims by Amoco against ICI irrespective of any liability by the former against the latter. Moreover, the assignment was expressly qualified by the words 'except to the extent of the insurance underwriter's subrogation rights'. Hirst LJ construed the words in their wide sense, so as to include Colonia's rights as against ICI to treat Amoco's payment as diminishing (in fact in this instance extinguishing) ICI's loss.

Obligations of the assured and the insurer

Permission to use his name by the insurer

The assured has his right against the third party irrespective of full or partial indemnity from the insurer.[71] If the assured did not retain his right to recovery from the third party, the insurer would have nothing to subrogate into. As stated above the insurer must bring the subrogation action (unless there is an assignment of the assured's rights to the insurer) in the name of the assured. The assured is therefore required to permit the insurer to use his name in the action against the third party. The insurer, on payment, may request the assured to sign a letter of subrogation, authorising the insurer to proceed in the name of the assured against any wrongdoer who has caused the relevant damage to the assured. If the assured refuses to permit the insurer to use his name in a claim against the third party the insurer can bring proceedings to compel him to do so.[72] In such a case insurers bring an action against both the assured and the third party, in which (1) they claim an order that the assured shall authorise him to proceed against the third party in the name of the assured, and (2) they seek to proceed (so authorised) against the third party.[73]

Acting in good faith (not to prejudice the insurers' subrogation rights)

An assured may compromise any claim he has against a third party in respect of his insured losses.[74] By such a compromise if the assured prejudices the insurer's subrogation rights the insurer will be entitled to seek a remedy from the assured. The remedy depends on the timing of the compromise of the claim in question. If the assured, for instance, enters into an agreement with a third party which prejudices the insurer's subrogation rights before the insurance contract is concluded, the

---

69   *Castellain v Preston* (1883) 11 QBD 380, 389, Brett LJ.
70   [1997] 1 Lloyd's Rep 261.
71   *Commercial Union Assurance Co v Lister* (1873–74) LR 9 Ch App 483.
72   *Esso Petroleum Co Ltd v Hall Russell & Co Ltd (The Esso Bernicia)* [1989] 1 Lloyd's Rep 8; *King v Victoria Insurance Co, Ltd* [1896] AC 250.
73   *Esso Petroleum Co Ltd v Hall Russell & Co Ltd (The Esso Bernicia)* [1989] 1 Lloyd's Rep 8.
74   *Re Ballast plc v Dargan* [2007] Lloyd's Rep IR 742, 756.

existence of such an agreement is likely to be regarded as a material fact which needs to be disclosed to the insurer.[75] As fully discussed in Chapter 4 of this work, breach of duty of disclosure in business insurance entitles the insurer to avoid the insurance contract. The Court of Appeal discussed the matter in *Tate & Sons v Hyslop*[76] in which the assured made an agreement with lightermen under which the latter were to be liable only for negligence and were not to face the more onerous duties owed by common carriers. The Court of Appeal accepted that as a result of such an arrangement the underwriters would not have the same valuable recourse over against the lightermen as they otherwise would have had but for such an arrangement. The Court highlighted that in the case in which the lightermen carried the goods without his full liability attaching, they would charge a larger premium than they would in the case where there was such full liability. Consequently, the arrangement which minimised the lightermen's liability to the assured, and therefore the insurer's right of subrogation, was found as a material fact which should have been disclosed to the insurer. It should be noted that the Court of Appeal did not analyse the matter as a general principle of whether prejudicing the insurer's subrogation right before the contract is concluded is always a material fact that should be disclosed. In this case it was clear that the cargo insurer operated a dual premium structure under which a higher premium was charged where lightermen were liable only in negligence. When a similar dispute arises the insurer doubtless has to prove that the arrangements existed between the assured and the insurer before the insurance contract was made a material fact and non-disclosure of such a material fact induced the insurer to enter into the contract. Non-disclosure of it before the insurance contract is concluded will entitle the insurer to avoid the contract for breach of the duty of good faith.

Once the insurance contract is made, the assured's obligation not to prejudice the insurers' subrogation right becomes contractual. It is implied into an insurance contract that in exercising his rights of action against third parties the assured will act in good faith for the benefit of himself as well as for the benefit of the insurer.[77] Breach of this implied term will entitle the insurer to claim damages suffered as a result of such breach by the assured.[78] This would be either not indemnifying the assured or if the payment had already been made by the insurer to claim the amount paid back by way of damages for prejudice of the insurer's subrogation rights. It is important to determine the time at which the insurer's subrogation rights arise. Two stages might be considered here: (1) The insurer's subrogation rights arise once the contract is concluded;[79] It is inherent in the insurance contract that the insurer has a contingent right of subrogation, which attaches and vests in them at the moment when the policy is effected by the insurer; (2) It arises upon payment after the loss occurs. If the second view is correct, an agreement between the assured and the third party, which has an effect of prejudicing the insurer's (future) subrogation right, will not give any remedy to the insurer as the insurer's right has not arisen, therefore nothing has been prejudiced at that stage. However, if subrogation is a contingent right in the sense that the state of affairs postulated may never arise, once the contingency has arisen, the right vested as a contingency has become an effective right and the assured's abovementioned agreement will thereby be in breach of an implied term of the contract which prejudiced the insurer's subrogation right. As also analysed below under 'increased risk policy' it is submitted that the latter is the approach that should be adopted for a fair and just solution for the parties to an insurance contract.

A recent example of this is seen in *Horwood v Land of Leather Ltd*[80] in which Land of Leather suffered loss as a result of selling some leather products by Linkwise, which caused skin allergies to the

---

75 *Societe Anonyme d'Intermediaries Luxembourgeois (SAIL) v Farex Gie* [1995] LR 116.
76 (1885) 15 QBD 368.
77 *Napier and Ettrick v RF Kershaw Ltd (No.1)* [1993] 1 Lloyd's Rep 197, 204, Lord Templeman.
78 *West of England Fire Insurance Co v Isaacs* [1897] 1 QB 226.
79 *Boag v Standard Marine Insurance Co Ltd* [1937] 2 KB 113, 123. *Boag* is fully discussed below under 'Increased value policy'.
80 [2010] Lloyd's Rep IR 453.

people who purchased them. Land of Leather had to return the stocks and had to deal with adverse media coverage. Land of Leather and Linkwise entered into a settlement agreement that contained the following:

> Land of Leather Holdings PLC & Linkwise Furniture Co Ltd agree that in return for a credit note from Linkwise of US$900,000 payable in six instalments of US$150,000 Land of Leather will undertake to buy US$20,000,000 of products from Linkwise in 2008.
>
> Land of Leather also confirm they will make no further claim on Linkwise in respect of alleged allergic reactions to their products though no proof exists that the cause was Linkwise products.

The claims by customers against Land of Leather were claims in respect of which Land of Leather was insured under a products liability policy. The insurer clearly had an interest in claiming an indemnity from any person whose conduct caused Land of Leather to be liable in respect of such claims. According to the policy terms it was a condition precedent that the assured shall not, except at his own cost take any steps to compromise or settle any claim or admit liability without specific instructions in writing from the Insurer. The assured was clearly in breach of this clause which provided the remedy that the insurer sought. Teare J nevertheless considered the assured's prejudice of the insurer's subrogation rights. Accordingly, the judge accepted that a term was implied in the policy that required the assured to act reasonably and in good faith and with due regard to insurer's interests and rights of subrogation under the policy. In the words of Teare J,[81] 'the implied term arises because the insurer has a right to be subrogated to the rights of the insured when he indemnifies him pursuant to the policy of insurance. If the insured acts without regard to that contingent right he may harm the value of that right to the insurer. The most obvious harm occurs where the insured settles a claim he may have against a third party for an indemnity and so deprives the insurer of its benefit in whole or in part. But in principle, harm may be caused to the insurer's rights of subrogation where the claim against the third party is not lost or reduced in value by settlement. For example, the documents necessary to establish such claim may be destroyed. I therefore consider that the implied duty must be one which obliges the insured to act in good faith and reasonably with regard to the interests of the insurer'.

Standard clauses incorporated in marine policies may impose express obligation on the assured to preserve the insurer's subrogation rights against third parties. For instance the Institute Cargo Clauses (A) 1963 cl.9 provided 'It is the duty of the Assured and their Agents, in all cases, to take such measures as may be reasonable for the purpose of averting or minimising a loss and to ensure that all rights against carriers, bailees or other third parties are properly preserved and exercised.' In such a case the question may arise as to the insurer's liability for the expenses incurred by the assured to preserve the insurer's interest. This was discussed in *Netherlands Insurance Co Est 1845 Ltd v Karl Ljungberg & Co AB (The Mammoth Pine)*[82] in which a consignment of plywood was insured for a voyage from Singapore to Denmark. The policy incorporated a sue and labour clause as well as the Institute Cargo Clauses (A) 1963 cl.9. When the goods were discharged in Denmark in March, 1980, some of the goods were found to be missing and others to be damaged. Any claim against the carriers would become time barred in March, 1981. The assured made his claim against the insurers under the policy in January 1981, and liability was denied by them shortly afterwards. As he was contractually obliged to do so, the assured sued the carrier in Japan in order to preserve the time bar. His action in Singapore against the insurer for the loss of the cargo was compromised.

---

81   [2010] Lloyd's Rep IR 453.
82   [1986] 2 Lloyd's Rep 19.

However, the insurer refused to pay the expenses that the assured incurred to sue the carrier in Japan to preserve the insurer's rights under the insurance contract. The insurer argued that the bailee clause in the policy imposed upon the assured the obligation to preserve the claim against the carriers for the benefit of the insurers but at the assured's expense.

As the Privy Council held, it was the obligation of the assured under the bailee clause to commence the Japanese proceedings in order to ensure that all rights against the carriers were properly preserved. Clearly, costs may be incurred in performing such an obligation by commencing litigation to preserve a time bar and also in pursuing litigation so commenced in order to prevent it from lapsing or being otherwise prejudiced by delay. There was no express term in the contract imposing an obligation on the insurer to indemnify the assured against any expenditure thereby incurred. Thus, the Privy Council discussed whether business efficacy required implying a term into the policy with the effect of entitling the assured to claim such expenses from the insurer. The first part of cl.9 obligated the assured to sue and labour, namely that the assured was required to take reasonable steps to prevent and minimise the insured loss.[83] The assured is entitled to claim expenses incurred for such steps and such a claim is supplementary to the amount insured by the policy. In order to answer the question that arose in *The Mammoth Pine*, the Privy Council tried to reconcile the sue and labour clause with the assured's duty to preserve the insurer's rights; while the former entitled the assured to claim the expenses by law, there is no such general principle applicable to the latter and the contract did not expressly provide that such expenses can be claimed.

The Privy Council doubted that the terms of the sue and labour clause in the standard form had much impact upon the construction of the bailee clause included in the Institute Cargo Clauses. Their Lordships did not accept a general proposition that the mere fact that an obligation is imposed upon one party to a contract for the benefit of the other, that it carried with it an implied term that the latter shall reimburse the former for his costs incurred in performance of the obligation. However, the Privy Council noted that the relevant obligation was indeed for the benefit of the insurers and it was a material factor which should be taken into account. Thus their Lordships concluded that a term was implied in the contract, in order to give business efficacy to it, that expenses incurred by an assured in performing his obligations under the second limb of the bailee clause shall be recoverable by him from the insurers insofar as they relate to the preservation or exercise of rights in respect of loss or damage for which the insurers were liable under the policy.

It is submitted that sue and labour and a term imposing an obligation on the assured to preserve the insurer's subrogation right represent two distinct principles. The expenses which may be covered under a sue and labour clause are those incurred to prevent or minimise the insured loss, that is mainly the loss that will cause harm to the assured which then might lead the assured to claim under the insurance contract. It may be necessary to take such steps before or after the loss occurs as the case may be, depending on the facts of each case. Moreover, in order to establish a sue and labour claim it is necessary to prove that the assured has incurred such expenses whilst an imminent danger to the subject matter insured was present. However, no such danger is required in respect of performance of the assured's duty not to prejudice the insurer's subrogation rights. An action of the assured performed at a time when no danger in terms of the insured loss is in question may prejudice the insurer's rights. For instance the assured and the third party may reach an agreement to the effect of limiting the third party's liability to the assured. Such an agreement will prejudice the insurer's subrogation rights if it is made before the insured loss occurs but after the insurance contract was concluded, and if the cover provided by the policy is higher than the limitation agreed between the assured and the third party. In such a case no issue of sue and labour will arise. The agreement between the assured and the third party will limit what the assured and therefore the

---

83 The sue and labour clauses are fully analysed in Chapter 11 of this work.

insurer after subrogation can claim against the third party but it will have no bearing on the occurrence of the loss insured under the policy or the amount of the actual loss that the assured may suffer upon the occurrence of the insured risk. The incentive in enabling the assured to claim sue and labour expenses is to encourage the assured to take steps to prevent or minimise the loss which may then reduce the insurer's exposure under the insurance contract. In this respect the assured's action in The Mammoth Pine which aimed to preserve the time bar might have had the double effect of (1) reducing the insurer's exposure under the insurance contract because the assured may recover some from the third party and (2) preserving the insurer's subrogation rights. However, the first objective, again, is distinct from sue and labour because the loss has already occurred and can be assessed, the action against the third party in Japan will not reduce or increase the actual loss suffered.[84] The action in Japan was for the benefit of the insurer as well as the assured. The reason for holding the insurer liable pro rata for expenses incurred was not because the action in Japan amounted to a sue and labour expense but because of the double benefit that was gained by the insurer as well as the assured. Thus it was just and fair to ask the insurer to contribute to such an expense. Moreover, if that action was sue and labour, the assured might be able to claim the whole expense, not merely the proportion representing his protected interest. Sue and Labour and a duty to preserve the insurer's subrogation rights may be regulated under the same clause as seen in International Cargo Clauses (A, B and C) 2009 clause 16. In such a case the courts analyse the duty to sue and labour and preserve the insurer's rights (bailee clause) separately.[85]

International Hull Clauses cl.49 provides that insurers shall pay the reasonable costs incurred by the assured to preserve the insurer's subrogation rights in the same proportion as the insured losses bear to the total of the insured and uninsured losses. The Institute Cargo Clauses 2009 (A, B and C) cl.16.2 provides it as the duty of the assured 'to ensure that all rights against carriers, bailees or other third parties are properly preserved and exercised and the Insurers will, in addition to any loss recoverable hereunder, reimburse the Assured for any charges properly and reasonably incurred in pursuance of these duties'. Breach of cl.16 gives rise to a cross-claim for damages which in appropriate circumstances may amount to a full defence to a claim under the policy.[86]

A further question might be whether the assured's inactivity, in the absence of an express contractual obligation requiring him to take steps to preserve the insurer's rights, entitles the insurer to seek remedy against the assured. It was submitted that, as found in IHC cl.9, such inactivity might be breach of an implied term to the effect that the assured should take reasonable steps to preserve the insurer's rights.[87] Horwood v Land of Leather might be brought to support such an argument to further allege that the assured might be in breach of the duty of good faith by staying inactive while being aware of the necessity of the steps that should be taken to preserve the insurer's subrogation rights.[88] Two further issues will arise here – if the assured's inactivity is a breach of contract or breach of duty of good faith, what will the remedy be for such a breach or breaches? Second, the expenses that the assured will incur to preserve the insurer's right will be an issue if he rejects to reimburse the assured with regard to such expenses. The remedy is most likely to be that the assured will lose his right of indemnification to the extent that his inaction prejudiced the

---

84 It may only affect the amount of interest to be paid depending on the time of payment by the third party.

85 See Noble Resources v Greenwood (The Vasso) [1993] 2 Lloyd's Rep 309.

86 Noble Resources v Greenwood (The Vasso) [1993] 2 Lloyd's Rep 309. In The Vasso Hobhouse J rejected the submission that cl.16.2 is a warranty.

87 Colinvaux, para 11–009.

88 See Clarke, para 31–6A where the author submits that the assured has no duty to commence an action against the third party in the absence of an express clause imposing such an obligation. Clarke suggests that the insurer's protection should be found in the express terms of the contract. For instance if the insurance contract obligates the assured to notify a loss within a period of time shorter than the limitation period of a claim against the third party that should provide protection for the insurer, not an implied term obligation for the assured to commence a suit. See also Rose, para 27–33.

insurer's subrogation rights. Remedy for breach of post-contractual duty of good faith is fully analysed in Chapter 4 where it is seen that there is no unified applicable remedy for breach of the post-contractual duty of good faith but the judges may rely on the duty to find a just solution to the dispute in question. It is arguable that such a just solution might be awarding damages for the insurer to the extent that his subrogation rights are prejudiced. With regard to the second matter, as seen above, in *Netherlands Insurance Co Est 1845 Ltd v Karl Ljungberg & Co AB (The Mammoth Pine)*,[89] the insurer was held to cover the expenses recoverable insofar as they related to the preservation or exercise of rights in respect of loss or damage for which the insurers were liable under the policy. In *The Mammoth Pine* the insurance contract expressly obligated the assured to take such steps that would protect the insurer's interest. In the absence of such an express provision it will be difficult to prove both that the assured has an implied term requiring him to take steps to protect the insurer's subrogation rights and the insurer will indemnify the assured for the expenses incurred. The safest approach to protect the insurers' interest will be to expressly indicate these issues under the policy.

The insurer's duty not to prejudice the rights of the assured

An insurance contract contains an implied term that the insurer will not exercise rights of subrogation to the prejudice of the assured.[90] The insurer's breach of such an implied term, however, will not deprive the insurer of his subrogation rights.[91] Subrogation confers proprietary interest (in the form of a lien) in favour of the insurer over sums received by the assured from third parties; such an interest cannot be undermined by inequitable conduct by the insurer.[92] HHJ Thornton QC held in *England v Guardian Insurance Ltd*,[93] that if the assured suffers loss as a result of the insurer's conduct the assured can still rely on his rights under the policy of insurance. It will be open to the assured to seek to set-off as damages any loss which the insurer's conduct has caused them, since that conduct would constitute a breach of that implied term.

Subrogation action against co-assured

As stated above, a subrogation action has to be brought in the name of the assured which necessitates the limitation that a subrogation action cannot be brought against the assured if it is they who are liable for the loss, as the assured cannot sue himself. While the position is very clear when the assured and the wrongdoer is the same person,[94] it has become very controversial in English law whether an insurer is entitled to bring a subrogation action against a co-assured in a composite insurance policy where one of the co-assureds is the wrongdoer.

It is here necessary to point out the distinction between joint and composite policies.[95] In joint insurance the interests of the assured persons in the subject matter of the insurance are joint, meaning that all the joint assureds are exposed to the same risks and suffer a joint loss by an insured peril. A typical example is insurance of their house by husband and wife. In composite insurance several assureds may insure their own interests which are not necessarily the same. The insurance is known

---

89 [1986] 2 Lloyd's Rep 19.
90 *England v Guardian Insurance Ltd* [2000] Lloyd's Rep IR 404, para 52.
91 *England v Guardian Insurance Ltd* [2000] Lloyd's Rep IR 404, para 52.
92 *England v Guardian Insurance Ltd* [2000] Lloyd's Rep IR 404, para 52.
93 [2000] Lloyd's Rep IR 404, para 52.
94 *Simpson v Thomson* (1877) 3 App Cas 279.
95 See *Arab Bank plc v Zurich Insurance Co* [1999] 1 Lloyd's Rep 262; *General Accident Fire and Life Assurance Corp Ltd v Midland Bank Ltd* (1940) 67 Ll L Rep 218.

as composite insurance where a number of persons who are individually interested in the subject matter of a marine adventure take out insurance for the benefit of all in which each has a right to sue in respect of his own interest.[96] For instance, a shipowner and a demise charterer may insure the vessel in a composite policy in which the assured's property right and the demise charterer's interest in using the vessel might be taken into consideration. Alternatively, while the shipowner may insure his interest in ownership in a hull insurance; the demise charterer, under the same policy, may insure his liability to the shipowner in case the vessel's hull is damaged by the charterer's negligence. The starting point should be the principle that the assured cannot sue himself. A co-assured is certainly an insured person under the insurance contract. But does he fall outside the insurance contract or is he regarded as a third party when the injured party who has a claim against the assured is the other co-assured?

The cases that discussed the matter first questioned if there was a rule of law preventing the insurer from bringing a subrogation action against a co-assured in relation to the claim that was insured under a composite insurance policy. In The Yasin[97] Lloyd J was of the view that the reason for the insurer being prevented from bringing a subrogation action against the co-assured was not due to a fundamental principle to this effect, but was rather as a result of ordinary rules about circuity. In other words, where one of the co-assureds claims under the policy the insurer may indemnify if the insurance contract covers the loss but then the insurer may subrogate into the indemnified co-assured's rights against the other co-assured who then in return is entitled to claim under the insurance contract. However, if the subject matter insured is a property which belongs to one of the co-assureds, A, and if the other co-assured, B's claim against the insurer is for his liability to A, as the insurance contract covered the loss of or damage to property but not the liability of B, there would be no obstacle for the insurer to bring a subrogation action against B as the circuity principle will not help B.

Apart from some disputes which arose from a policy taken out for the benefit of landlords and tenants, the issue mentioned here has mostly been discussed in insurance in relation to construction contracts including contracts to build ships, power plants and oil platforms. The common nature of such contracts is that normally the employer who owns the construction – the subject matter of insurance – enters into contracts with contractors who may then sub-contract the project. The construction contract is likely to contain a clause that requires either the employer or the contractor to purchase an insurance contract covering the parties involved in the agreement. The premium for such an insurance is sometimes paid by the contractor and sometimes by the employer, depending on the underlying contract between them which is independent to the insurance contract. Again, it has been seen in many occasions that the work or the extensions of the work might get damaged as a result of a fire which was caused by the contractors' (or sub-contractors') negligence. It is a generally accepted principle that, save deliberate conduct of the assured, if a fire is an insured peril, the damage caused by fire is covered irrespective of the negligence of the assured.[98] After indemnifying the co-assured who suffered loss the insurer will inevitably look into his subrogation rights against the wrongdoer who will most likely to be a co-assured under the same policy. Can the insurer succeed in his claim against the co-assured? More precisely, the question should be, is the insurer entitled to bring a subrogation action against a co-assured? The question has been discussed in a number of cases. In Petrofina (UK) Ltd v Magnaload Ltd,[99] Lloyd J decided in favour of the co-assured in a similar matter. The reason for such holding was the principle of circuity.

---

96 Eide UK Ltd v Lowndes Lambert Group Ltd [1998] 1 Lloyd's Rep 389, 400, Phillips LJ.

97 [1979] 2 Lloyd's Rep 45, at 55.

98 Mark Rowlands Ltd v Berni Inns Ltd [1985] 2 Lloyd's Rep 437; Scottish & Newcastle plc v GD Construction (St Albans) Ltd [2003] Lloyd's Rep IR 809.

99 [1983] 2 Lloyd's Rep 91.

In *Petrofina* the main contractors for the construction of an extension at an oil refinery took out a contractors' all risks insurance policy indemnifying the assured against loss and damage to the property in question. The definition of the persons insured included the employer, the main contractor and the sub-contractors, and the defendants were one of the sub-contractors on the site. Due to alleged negligence on the part of the defendants, a gantry became displaced and fell so as to cause considerable damage to the work in progress. The employer claimed against the insurers under the policy, who duly paid the claim. The insurers then brought an action in the name of the employer against the defendants, claiming damages for negligence. The preliminary issue was whether the insurers had the necessary right of subrogation to sue in the name of the employer. It was held that since the defendants were co-assured with the employer, and since the main contractor had been entitled to effect the insurance upon the whole of the property in the name or on behalf of all the assured, including the defendants, the insurers had no right of subrogation to bring the action in the name of the employer. Lloyd J rejected the argument that each assured was only insured in respect of his own property, or property for which he is responsible, as each of the named assured, including all the sub-contractors, were insured in respect of the whole of the contract works[100] including property belonging to any other of the assured, or for which any other of the assured were responsible. Another case in which the insurer's subrogation action was rejected is *Mark Rowlands Ltd v Berni Inns Ltd*[101]. In this case fire destroyed the entire building that belonged to the claimant. The fire was caused by negligence of the tenant. The quantum of the claim included the cost of reinstating the whole building with the monies that the landlord received from their insurers. The underlying contract required the tenant to pay an 'insurance rent' through which the tenant paid 25 per cent of the annual premiums. Although the policy was in the name of the landlord the court was of the view that the mutual intention of the parties should be to insure for the benefit of the tenant as well as the landlord. *Petrofina* was distinguishable on its facts as the defendants were co-assured with the claimants under the same policy whereas in *Mark Rowlands*, the insurance was on the name of the landlord only.

The circuity doctrine did not find much support. The problem with circuity is that while a co-assured may suffer loss for damage to his property, the other co-assured who caused the loss will be sued for his negligence, in other words, his liability to the co-assured. If the insurance contract insures the property but not liability of the co-assured, circuity will not stop the insurer from bringing his subrogation action. An alternative justification to the circuity doctrine is that a term is implied in the underlying contract that once the parties agree to take out a composite policy they agree not to claim against each other. Therefore, when there is a loss the insurer will be the party to whom the claim should be addressed. Since the underlying contract contains such an implied undertaking, the insurer will have no claim against the co-assured to subrogate into. For instance in *Hopewell Project Management Ltd v Ewbank Preece Ltd*,[102] Mr Recorder Jackson QC *obiter* commented that on the assumption that the defendants were co-assureds,[103] the subrogation action by the insurer would have been rejected given that 'it would be nonsensical if those parties who were jointly insured under the CAR policy could make claims against one another in respect of damage to the

---

100 For a detailed discussion of insurance interest in co-insurance, see Chapter 3 'Insurable Interest'.
101 [1985] 2 Lloyd's Rep 437.
102 [1998] 1 Lloyd's Rep 448. In *Hopewell* the claimant agreed to build a power station at Navotas which was a fishing complex to the north of Central Manila. The defendant provided certain engineering services. The claimant purchased gas turbines, to be used in its power station, which were shipped to the Philippines. The installation of the gas turbines in the power station was carried out by the defendants whose negligence caused damage to the gas turbines. In an action against the defendants for a claim approximately for US$6m the judge found the relationship between the claimant and the defendant as one of client and consulting engineer which would be unusual to be classified as that of a 'contractor' or 'sub-contractor'. Thus the defendants did not fall within the definition of assured.
103 [1998] 1 Lloyd's Rep 448, 458.

contract works. Such a result could not possibly have been intended by those parties.' The judge had little doubt that they would have said so to an officious bystander. Lord Hope in *Cooperative Retail Services Ltd v Taylor Young Partnership Ltd*[104] again obiter, expressed his agreement with Mr Recorder Jackson QC on this matter. In *CRS* the point did not arise for determination for the reason that the underlying contract between the co-assureds rendered the contractor not liable to the employer for the loss in question. Thus, the employer had no claim against the contractor under the contract, which would therefore not give any right of action to the insurer. Nevertheless, both Lord Bingham and Hope referred to the principle in question and they commented against subrogation action against the co-assured. Lord Bingham defined it as an obvious absurdity[105] bringing an action against the co-assured whom will be indemnified by the insurer for his liability under the underlying contract with the employer. Although his Lordship stated that the rationale of this rule may be a matter of some controversy Lord Bingham found the rule itself beyond doubt.[106] Having agreed with Mr Recorder Jackson QC's aforementioned statement, Lord Hope[107] stated that had it been necessary to decide, the co-assureds would have been able to resist the claim against them for the reasons stated in *Hopewell*.

At this stage, it is worth mentioning three other cases which either applied or distinguished CRS. In *Surrey Heath Borough Council v Lovell Construction Ltd*,[108] the contract provided for the contractor to obtain a joint names policy to cover specified perils but also required the contractor to indemnify the employer for damage to the works caused by the contractor's negligence. It was argued that there is an overriding principle, derived from insurance law, that where a policy of insurance is effected for the benefit of two persons jointly, neither can sue the other in respect of any matter within the policy even if there is apparently a collateral contractual term between them entitling the one to sue. Dillon LJ however found this submission too wide[109] and left the matter to construction of the insurance and construction contracts. It was held that the obligation on the contractor to provide an indemnity applied even if the loss was one which was required to be insured under the joint names policy.

Surrey Heath was distinguished in CRS for the reason that in the former the court was concerned with a contract which did not expressly exclude the works from the property in relation to which the contractor provided the employer with an indemnity if it was damaged through his negligence. In *CRS*, however, the contractual arrangements meant that if a fire occurred, they should look to the joint insurance policy to provide the fund for the cost of restoring and repairing the fire damage (and for paying any consequential professional fees) and that they would bear other losses themselves (or cover them by their own separate insurance) rather than indulge in litigation with each other.

Slightly different facts came before the court in *Scottish & Newcastle plc v GD Construction (St Albans) Ltd*,[110] which involved a dispute in which the employer failed to take out an insurance policy which was required to contain an express subrogation waiver by the insurer against the co-assureds. The policy was expected to cover any damage to the existing structure caused by a number of specified perils, including fire. A fire damaged the work. The preliminary issue was whether liability for damage to identified property which results from a negligently caused fire was excluded as it was required to be insured by the employer against specified perils, including fire. The contractor was liable to the employer against any expense, liability, loss, claim or proceedings in respect of any

104 [2002] Lloyd's Rep IR 555.
105 [2002] Lloyd's Rep IR 555, para 7.
106 [2002] Lloyd's Rep IR 555, para 7.
107 [2002] Lloyd's Rep IR 555, para 65.
108 (1990) 6 Const. LJ 179.
109 (1990) 6 Const. LJ 179, 120.
110 [2003] Lloyd's Rep IR 809.

loss, injury or damage whatsoever to any property real or personal insofar as such loss, injury or damage arises out of or in the course of or by reason of the carrying out of the works. *Scottish & Newcastle* was slightly different to *CRS* because in *CRS* the insurance contract did not have a clause by which the insurer expressly waived his subrogation rights, whereas in *Scottish & Newcastle* the policy was required to state that. The court, however, still found in *Scottish & Newcastle* that the principle applicable in *CRS* and in *Scottish & Newcastle* is the same: it makes no sense for the contract to be construed to permit loss or damage caused by the specified perils to be recoverable by one of the parties in cases where the peril occurs as a result of the negligence of the other party or those for whom he is responsible.[111] Longmore LJ found an express link in *CRS* and in *Scottish & Newcastle* between the liability imposed on the contractor, the specific aspect of such liability which is excluded and the existence of insurance (intended to benefit both contractor and employer) in respect of that excluded liability. Thus *CRS* was applied and *Barking and Dagenham LBC v Stamford Asphalt Co Ltd*[112] was distinguished. In *Barking*, the employer promised to take out insurance in the joint names of employer and contractor against loss or damage to the existing structures (together with the contents owned by him . . .) and to the works. The employer was entitled to an indemnity for loss caused by the contractor's negligence. Fire damaged the works and the employer failed to take out the joint names insurance, and the contractor argued that its indemnity should be reduced by the amount that would have been recoverable under the insurance had it been effected. The defence failed because the provision for joint names insurance was intended to cover only those losses that were not caused by the negligence of the contractor.

In *Scottish & Newcastle*, Aikens J refused to apply the construction in *Barking* for the reasons that the wording of the relevant clauses in the two cases were different.

It is submitted that the matter can be analysed by referring to *Mason v Sainsbury* where Lord Mansfield formulated the question in subrogation as 'Who is first liable?' This question was directed not to any issue of chronology but to establishing where the primary responsibility lay to make good the loss.[113] If the party who is liable first is the insurer, there will be no action against the third party wrongdoer since the insurer's payment will extinguish the liability in question. If the party who is first liable is the third party, the insurer's payment does not alter the third party's position against the assured.[114] In a typical case of subrogation, where no co-assured is involved, the answer is straightforward and the person who is first liable is the third party. In the context of co-insurance, before raising the question of who is first liable it should be discussed whether a co-assured is an insured party or a third party in the triangle of insurer – the other co-assureds – and himself. It might be argued that a co-assured who is liable for the other co-assured's loss is not a third party under the insurance contract given that, contractually, he is a party to the insurance arrangement. By the underlying contract which required a purchase of a composite insurance policy, the parties are deemed to have impliedly agreed that in relation to the loss insured, they will not bring a claim against each other. Consequently, the party who is liable first in such a case is the insurer. Upon the insurer's payment the liability for the insured loss will be extinguished and there will be no right against a co-assured to subrogate into. The insurer may not argue that this all happened without his knowledge; clearly the insurer will know that the policy is of composite type and one co-assured may cause the loss to another due to the contractual relationship between the co-assureds. It therefore goes without saying that there exists an implied term in the underlying contract that the parties will not claim against each other in relation to the loss insured by the insurance policy. In *Simpson v Thomson* it was stated that in the case of co-insurance the insurance was

---

111 [2003] Lloyd's Rep IR 809, para 59.
112 [1997] CLC 929.
113 *Caledonia North Sea Ltd v British Telecommunications* [2002] 1 Lloyd's Rep 553, 559.
114 This issue was also emphasised in *North British and Mercantile Insurance Co v London, Liverpool, and Globe Insurance Co* (1877) 5 Ch D 569.

for the benefit of all the co-assureds and the underwriters cannot complain that they have had to meet the risk against which they insured. In *National Oilwell (UK) Ltd v Davy Offshore Ltd*,[115] Colman J referred to *Simpson v Thomson* and said that there would be no available right of subrogation, if the owner of the guilty ship had been a co-assured under the policy on the innocent ship for the same perils. As stated by Colman J, a co-assured is as much the assured in respect of the relevant perils as if he were the same person as the owner of the subject matter insured. A subrogation action against a co-assured would in effect involve the insurer seeking to reimburse a loss caused by a peril against which he had insured for the benefit of the very party against whom he now sought to exercise rights of subrogation. The implication of such a term is needed to give effect to what must have been the mutual intention of the principal assured and the insurers, as to the risks covered by the policy.

It is submitted that Colman J explained in the most precise way why a subrogation action should not be permitted against a co-assured. While further support is seen in *Mark Rowlands* which emphasised a danger of double recovery in case subrogation against a co-assured is permitted, the recent cases on the matter adopted a different approach.

For instance, Rix LJ's view expressed in *Tyco Fire & Integrated Solutions (UK) Ltd (formerly Wormald Ansul (UK) Ltd) v Rolls Royce Motor Cars Ltd (formerly Hireus Ltd)* found some support in some cases decided recently.[116] In *Tyco*, having noted that the doctrine of circuity of action was no longer being favoured,[117] Rix LJ stated that the doctrine of an implied term in the insurance contract was replaced by a doctrine of the true construction of the underlying contract for the provision of joint names insurance.[118] The only question was whether that contract excludes the liability of B to A (the parties to the underlying contract). If it does not, then subrogation is permitted. The formulation that Rix LJ added was that the construction of the underlying contract may operate with the assistance of an implied term to the effect that co-assureds cannot sue one another for damage in respect of which they are jointly insured.[119] The true basis of the rule is to be found in the contract between the parties.[120] Rix LJ found Lord Bingham's speech in *CRS* as not representing a general applicable rule but to the facts of the contract in that case.[121] This controversial area, according to Rix LJ, preceded the latest thinking to the effect that it is all ultimately a matter of the parties' intentions as found in their contracts.

That works in a straightforward way in cases like *CRS* or *Scottish & Newcastle* where it is clear that there is to be no liability of a contractor to his employer in the area of the regime for joint names insurance.[122] What, however, is the position in a case where there is no such clarity in that direction, but on the contrary, if anything, there is, or appears to be, clarity in another direction, namely in favour of the contractor's continued liability to his employer for his negligence?[123] Rix LJ[124] said that that will have to be worked out in cases in which such problems arise and recently that was worked out by Teare J: In *Gard Marine & Energy Ltd v China National Chartering Co Ltd (formerly China National Chartering Corp) (The Ocean Victory)*,[125] the owners and charterers of a vessel were co-assureds under the policy taken out by the charterer. The vessel became a total loss with a cargo of iron ore on board. The claim amounted to millions of US dollars. The casualty was caused by the unsafeness

---

115 [1993] 2 Lloyd's Rep 582 at 613–614.
116 [2008] Lloyd's Rep IR 617.
117 [2008] Lloyd's Rep IR 617, para 75.
118 [2008] Lloyd's Rep IR 617, para 75.
119 [2008] Lloyd's Rep IR 617, para 75.
120 [2008] Lloyd's Rep IR 617, para 76.
121 [2008] Lloyd's Rep IR 617, para 80.
122 [2008] Lloyd's Rep IR 617, para 76.
123 [2008] Lloyd's Rep IR 617, para 76.
124 [2008] Lloyd's Rep IR 617, para 77.
125 [2013] EWHC 2199 (Comm).

of the port of Kashima to which the time charterers had ordered the vessel. Nomination of an unsafe port was a breach of express safe port warranty in the charterparty. At the time of the casualty the vessel was owned by OVM who demised chartered it to OLH. After the demise charter there were a series of sub-time charterparties until the last charterers in the chain chartered it under a time trip charter. This action was brought by Gard as assignee of the claims of the owner and the demise charterer. The time charterers argued that because there was no liability on the demise charterer against the shipowner, similarly insured under the same policy, the insurer cannot bring a claim against the demise charterer thus there would be no claim to be subrogated to the demise charterers' rights against the time charterers. The crucial clause was Clause 12, which provided:

> (a) During the Charter period the Vessel shall be kept insured by the Charterers at their expense against marine, war and Protection and Indemnity risks ... Such marine war and P. and I. insurances shall be arranged by the Charterers to protect the interests of both the Owners and the Charterers ... All insurance policies shall be in the joint names of the Owners and the Charterers as their interests may appear.
>
> The Charterers shall, subject to the approval of the Owners and the Underwriters, effect all insured repairs and shall undertake settlement of all costs in connection with such repairs as well as insured charges, expenses and liabilities (reimbursement to be secured by the Charterers from the Underwriters) to the extent of coverage under the insurances herein provided for.
>
> The Charterers also to remain responsible for and to effect repairs and settlement of costs and expenses incurred thereby in respect of all other repairs not covered by the insurances and/or not exceeding any possible franchise(s) or deductibles provided for in the insurances.

As the warranty was expressly stated in the charterparty, Teare J looked for another express clause which clearly exempts the charterers from liability for breach of safe port warranty. There was no express exclusion as such in the contract. Then the judge turned to clause 12 which did not expressly exclude liability for breach of the warranty but providing only that the demise charterers shall insure the vessel at their expense. It was argued before Teare J that since the insurance was at the demise charterer's expense the parties did not expressly state that there would be no right of recovery against him as commercial men would regard that conclusion as obvious, and therefore unnecessary to state. The judge, however, rejected this argument for being 'probably too simple'.[126]

Applying Tyco, Teare J found that the facts in this case were in favour of the insurer's claim: (1) there was an express safe port warranty by the demise charterers, (2) there was no code of rights and obligations in clause 12 with regard to insured losses caused by a breach of the safe port warranty, and (3) there was no express ouster of the right of subrogation in clause 12. The charterparty thus is interpreted in such a way so as to render the charterer liable to the owner for breach of the safe port warranty, notwithstanding that they were joint assured and could take the benefit of the insurance in the manner set out in clause 12. In Tyco Rix LJ said that an employer would not be entitled to be indemnified twice over, once by his insurer and once by his contractor: but as long as the recovery from the contractor returns to the insurer by way of subrogation, only the negligent contractor is out of pocket, and no one is indemnified twice.[127] Teare J adopted exactly the same approach in Gard Marine.

Gard Marine seems to be a straightforward subrogation procedure, however, it is unfortunate to disregard the parties' implied intention which becomes even stronger when the charterer pays the premium. The aim of contractual construction is to determine the parties' intention objectively and what is taken into account is what the contract would mean to a reasonable person in the parties' position who had a similar background as the contracting parties. In the commercial world,

---

126 [2013] EWHC 2199 (Comm), para 198.
127 [2013] EWHC 2199 (Comm), para 78.

as some judges have confirmed, the reasonable understanding might mean that the insurance provision is an implied waiver of contractual rights because the person who is liable first is the insurer, not the other party. If the insurer is the first liable, the insurer's payment will relive the other co-assured. It is true that an implied term cannot override an express term but will this justify on its own the disregarding of the parties' intention by taking out a composite insurance policy? A co-assured is insured to have the policy cover when the loss occurs. If the assured is negligent in principle the insurance cover is still provided. While the co-assured has been insured and paying the premium as the case may be, he will have no insurance cover if the insurer is permitted to bring a subrogation action against the co-assured for the reason that the underlying contract did not expressly exclude the co-assured's liability to the other co-assured.

It is submitted that in a case such as *Caledonia North Sea Ltd v British Telecommunications*[128] it is inevitable to look into the underlying contract to determine the insurer's subrogation rights. But it should be remembered that co-assureds are not involved in this case. In *Caledonia North Sea Ltd* an explosion occurred at the Piper Alpha oil platform in the North Sea on 6 July 1988. The initial explosion led to a series of explosions and fires with such catastrophic results that 165 people were killed and 61 were injured. At the time of the disaster the operator controlled the platform on behalf of a consortium of companies (including the operator) known as the participants. The operator acting on behalf of the participants entered into separate contracts with each contractor in relation to the particular services to be provided on the platform by that contractor. The initial explosion which led to the disaster was caused by a failure of an employee of the operator. The operators were insured against such liability and they and their underwriters settled the claims of the victims. About 37 of them were the operator's own employees. But the rest worked for contractors who had been engaged to do specialist work on the platform. After the settlement figures had been agreed with the claimants, the contractors were called upon to indemnify the operator but declined to do so. Clause 15 of the contract between the operator and the contractors contained cross-indemnities. Clause 15(1)(c) provided as follows:

> Injury to employees and damage to property of contractor
>   Injury to or death of persons employed by or damage to or loss or destruction of property of the contractor or its parent, subsidiary or affiliate corporations, or the contractor's agents, sub-contractors or suppliers, irrespective of any contributory negligence, whether active or passive, of the party to be indemnified, unless such injury, death, damage, loss or destruction was caused by the sole negligence or wilful misconduct of the party which would otherwise be indemnified.
>   and Clause 16 went on to require the contractors, at their sole cost and expense, to procure and maintain insurance to cover employers' liability and public liability. A further key provision was clause 21, which limited the indemnity in clause 16 to direct loss:
>   Consequential loss
>   Notwithstanding any other provision of this contract, in no event shall either the contractor or the company be liable to the other for any indirect or consequential losses suffered, including but not limited to, loss of use, loss of profits, loss of production or business interruption.

The essence of the arrangement was that if a contractor's employee was injured on the platform, and the operators were found to be liable to pay damages to the employee or his family, the operators were entitled to be indemnified by the contractor who had employed that employee unless the accident was wholly the fault of the operators. If the operator had paid these sums he would be entitled to repayment from the contractor. The contractor's objection related to the insurer's subrogation right. The House of Lords decided that the insurer had his subrogation right upon

---

128 [2002] 1 Lloyd's Rep 553.

payment under the insurance contract. Referring to Lord Mansfield's formulation in *Mason v Sainsbury*, the House of Lords found that it was first the contractor who was liable to indemnify the operator, not the insurer. The contract did not require the operator to have insurance; thus there was no ground on which it can be said that the contractor's indemnity is limited to indemnifying the operator if and to the extent that the operator's insurer fails to do so. Moreover, the indemnity says nothing about the contractors having to be liable to the employee. It imposes a general liability to indemnify the operator against any liability in respect of their own employees, with an exception only in a case in which the accident is attributable to the sole negligence or wilful misconduct of the operator. The existence of this exception is in itself an indication that no liability on the part of the contractors is required, because it is hard to see how such liability could ever be consistent with the accident being attributable to the sole negligence or wilful misconduct of the operator.

It therefore appears that the approach followed in *Tyco* and the cases that followed it and *Caledonia* are similar. On the other hand, whilst this approach was appropriate in *Caledonia*, it caused rather surprising and unjust results for the co-assured in the other cases mentioned.

Tyco was once again applied in *Rathbone Brothers plc v Novae Corporate Underwriting*[129] in which Burton J looked into the underlying agreement to see who was the first liable and decided that the contract did not provide that the injured party will look to the insurance as the primary source of liability and not to the contracting party. On a proper construction of the Consultancy Agreement, to which Rathbone was not a party, the insurance was not the primary source of liability.

The Court of Appeal, however, overturned Burton J's ruling. As noted above, in *Rathbone*, the policy contained an express subrogation clause, so the issue for the Court of Appeal was whether it was in principle possible to imply a term and, if so, whether there was an implied term on the present facts. Elias and Sharp LJ both accepted that it was possible to imply a term in an insurance contract excluding the right of subrogation. Elias LJ said 'I am satisfied that it could not have been the intention of the parties that the insurers should be able to enforce rights of indemnity against a co-insured where the co-insured was indemnifying the very same risk as the insurers'.[129a] Beatson J however was of the view that the exclusion of the right of subrogation was to be regarded as excluded in exceptional cases only. His Lordship noted that clear words were required to exclude the right of subrogation, and it was wrong to imply an exclusion in a contract entered into by experienced commercial parties. The Court of Appeal proceeded in *Rathbone* on the basis that the present case did not raise an issue of co-insurance at all in the strict sense that the main assured did not face liability for the claim. Therefore, the majority view in terms of being prepared to imply a term in an insurance contract precluding the insurer's subrogation right against the co-assured is not the determining ratio in the case. The ratio was that the indemnity was intended to operate only where there was no insurance in place, so that the liability of the insurers eroded the indemnity and a subrogation action could not be brought in respect of it. The position as regards co-insurance thus remains uncertain. At the time that this book is being prepared for publication *Gard Marine's* appeal is still pending and the outcome is being awaited with curiosity.

Allocation of recovery from the third party between the assured and the insurer

The assured has his right against the third party irrespective of full or partial indemnity from the insurer.[130] Therefore either the assured or the insurer may obtain recovery from the third party. As stated above the insurer has an equitable charge over recovery received by the assured up to the

---

129 [2013] EWHC 3457 (Comm).
129a [2014] EWCA Civ 1464, para 85.
130 *Commercial Union Assurance Co v Lister* (1873–74) LR 9 Ch App 483.

amount that the insurer indemnified the assured. There may be cases in which despite the insurer having paid the maximum policy amount the assured may still argue that it did not provide full recovery therefore he should keep the amount received from the third party. Allocation of recovery from the third party is rather complex and the first step should be to determine whether the policy is valued or unvalued and then whether the loss is total or partial in nature.

Valued policy

The value determined by the parties is conclusive, therefore the assured is not permitted to argue that the loss he suffered is greater than the loss indemnified by the insurer.[131] In *North of England Iron Steamship Insurance Association v Armstrong*[132] the *Hetton* was run down and sunk by the *Uhlenhorst*. The *Hetton* was insured on a lost or not lost basis valued at £6,000. The insurers paid the owner of the *Hetton* who then argued that the vessel was undervalued and the actual value was £9,000, thus the recovery from the owner of the *Uhlenhorst* should cover the shortage of the recovery from the actual value of the vessel. It was held that where the value of a thing insured is stated in the policy in a manner to be conclusive between the assured and the insurer, in respect of all rights and obligations which arise upon the policy of insurance, the parties are estopped between one another from disputing the value of the thing insured as stated in the policy. If each of the parties agrees that a certain sum shall be deemed to be the value of the thing insured, the underwriter, in the case of a total loss, is not to be at liberty to say the thing is not worth so much. The fixed amount will have to be paid irrespective of that being the proper amount or not. Likewise the assured is not at liberty to contend that it is worth more.

The decision in *North of England* was followed by *Thames and Mersey Marine Insurance Co v British and Chilian Steamship Co*[133] in which the *Helvetia* was insured for £1,800. She was valued at £45,000; the balance of the £45,000 was insured with other underwriters. The *Helvetia* sank after a collision with the *Empress of Britain* and became a total loss. Both ships were held to blame, the *Helvetia* was held liable to pay seven-twelfths of the damage, and the *Empress of Britain* five-twelfths. The underwriters of the *Helvetia* paid out for a total loss. At the time of the loss the *Helvetia* was chartered to the Dominion Coal Company. The actual value of the *Helvetia* was £65,000 and with that of the charterparty being £2,000, the parties compromised the claim for £67,000 representing the aggregate of the value of the ship and that of the charterparty. The owners of the *Empress of Britain* paid £26,900, five-twelfths of £65,000 to the owners of the *Helvetia*.

The insurers claimed to be subrogated to the rights of the defendants in that sum recovered. The assured objected to the insurer's claim for £26,900 for the reason that the insurer was entitled by way of subrogation to the proportion of five-twelfths of the amount of the policy valuation. The Court of Appeal decided in favour of the insurer. The amount recovered by the assured from the other vessel was less than the amount paid by the insurer, the insurer was entitled to recover the sum of £26,900, notwithstanding that it was based upon a value which was higher than that agreed in the policy.

The same rule applies when the loss is partial. In *Goole and Hull Steam Towing Co Ltd v Ocean Marine Insurance Co Ltd*[134] the *Goole* was valued at £4,000 and was insured for £535. The balance of the £4,000 was insured with other underwriters. The *Goole* collided with the ship the *Delphinus* and was damaged. The cost of her repair was £5,000. A collision action brought by the owner of the *Goole* against the owners of the *Delphinus* was settled upon the basis of 'both equally to blame'. The assured received £2,500 from the owners of the *Delphinus*. The cost of repair was £5,000. The question was how did

---

131 *Burnand v Rodocanachi Sons & Co* (1882) 7 App Cas 333, 335, Lord Selborne LC.
132 (1869–70) LR 5 QB 244.
133 [1916] 1 KB 30.
134 [1928] 1 KB 589.

all these figures affect the claim which the assured would otherwise have against the underwriters for £4,000? The insurers contended that as the limit of liability stated in the policy was £4,000, and £2,500 had already been recovered from the *Delphinus*, the amount due from the underwriters was £1,500, whereas the assured argued that they were £2,500 out of pocket (5,000–2,500), and that £2,500 being less than £4,000, they can claim in full from the underwriters. Mackinnon J opined that the concept of indemnity refers not to the totality of the assured's loss but rather to that part of the assured's loss which is acknowledged by the policy. Thus, when a loss has happened the question is 'what is the measure of indemnity that by the convention of the parties has been promised to the assured?' It may or may not be less than an ideal pecuniary indemnity. For instance if the assured has undervalued his ship in the valuation he has agreed upon, he may find that he has suffered pecuniary loss beyond the agreed indemnity. If the loss is partial, as is laid down in s.69, the assured is entitled in respect of such loss to the reasonable cost of repairs not exceeding the sum insured in respect of any one casualty. Although the assured's actual loss may be higher than the amount the insurer paid, the insurer subrogates into the entire amount recovered from the third party as the insurer paid the agreed indemnity for the whole of the particular average loss the assured sustained, and not merely for a part of it.

Mackinnon J found this in line with s.79(2) which provides '. . . he is thereupon subrogated to all rights and remedies of the assured . . ., in so far as the assured has been indemnified according to this Act . . .' The payment of £4,000 had not fully indemnified the assured for their expenditure of £5,000 on the repairs, but according to the bargain they have made under the policy they have been indemnified 'according to this Act' for the whole of the particular average damage which they have sustained as promised under s.69. Thus, the assured was deemed to have been fully indemnified 'according to this Act' for that particular average loss.

Mackinnon J. found that the principle applied in *Goole* and *North of England* was directly applicable in this case.

The abovementioned cases are to be distinguished if the recovery from the third party is the same or less than the amount the insurer paid the assured. In a valued policy in which the subject matter insured by underwriter A is undervalued, the assured is deemed to be his own insurer in respect of the uninsured balance.[135] In relation to the allocation of recovery from the third party, the assured is regarded as if he is another insurer that has insured the uninsured balance in the policy as co-insurer with underwriter A. In *The Commonwealth*,[136] the *Welsh Girl* was insured for £1,000 by a valued policy in which she was valued at £1,350. She sank in a collision with the *Commonwealth*. The insurers paid £1,000 to the assured and sued the *Commonwealth* in the name of the assured shipowner. An amount of £1,000 was recovered from the Commonwealth and the question was in relation to apportionment of such a sum between the insurer and the assured shipowner. The shipowner claimed 350–1,350ths of the £1,000 for himself and 1,000–1,350ths to the insurers. The insurers argued that they were entitled to take the whole of the money which has been paid into Court in respect of the loss of the ship. The court decided in favour of the shipowner. The case was found analogous to a case where the assured had effected full insurance upon the ship but with different underwriters, as if he insured his ship for £1,000 with the insurers in question and another policy for £350 on the same valuation. *North of England* was distinguished in the *Commonwealth* for the latter was partial insurance, an insurance where the amount which the insurers were liable for was less than the amount which was expressed in the policy as the value of the ship. The question was whether the underwriters were to take all that was recovered, provided it did not exceed the amount they had paid, or whether the owners and underwriters were to be treated as if there had been a proportionate division of any benefits which were recovered. The court held that the insurer subrogates into the assured's rights having regard to the risk he has taken. In other

135 MIA 1906 s 81.
136 [1907] P 216.

words when the insurer claims from the third party in the name of the assured, the remedy is sought for the underwriter to the extent to which he had insured. This is supported by the fact that in case the assured is not fully indemnified by the insurer, the assured can make a claim against the third party for the amount left uninsured. Thus, the amount recovered from the third party ought to be divided in proportion to the respective interests. The £1,000 was to be proportioned 350–1,350ths for the recovery by the assured and 1,000–1,350ths for the insurer.

Insurance in layers

In the allocation of the recovery from the third party if the insurance contract contains a deductible, that will be placed at the end of the list of recovery by the assured and the insurer. It was held that the assured is deemed to be his own insurer in relation to the deductible.[137]

In *Napier*, the House of Lords adopted the top down approach in relation to allocation of recovery in insurance in layers. Accordingly, assuming that there are two insurers insuring different layers as well as the assured's deductible, the amount recovered from the third party is allocated by starting from the insurer who stays on the very top layer and after repayment to that insurer, the remaining amount will be allocated to the next insurer from the top. In this procedure, the assured's deductible will be paid last, assuming that there will be an amount remaining after the repayment to the insurers. In *Napier*, the House of Lords illustrated this as follows: Let us assume that the loss amounts to £160,000, £130,000 has been recovered from the third party and there are three layers of insurance: (1) a policy for the payment of the first £25,000 of any loss; (2) a policy for payment of the next £100,000 of any loss; (3) a policy for payment of any loss in excess of £125,000. The third insurer is entitled to be the first to be subrogated and must be paid £35,000. The second insurer is entitled to be the second to be subrogated because he only agreed to pay if the first insurance cover proved insufficient; accordingly the second insurer must be paid £95,000. The sum of £35,000 payable by way of subrogation to the third insurer and the sum of £95,000 payable by way of subrogation to the second insurer exhausts the damages of £130,000 received from the third party. An assured is not entitled to be indemnified against a loss which he has agreed to bear; the assured acts as his own insurer for the first £25,000 loss and acts as his own insurer for any loss in excess of £125,000.

The *Commonwealth* and *Napier* can be reconciled given that, as was stated in the *Commonwealth*, the case was about partial insurance and insurance in layers was not in question. The principle articulated in *Napier* is in line with the operation of excess of loss insurance. In the *Commonwealth*, the court explained the matter as partial insurance, where different insurers insure one subject matter without necessarily having any ranking in terms of indemnifying the assured. When there is a loss the assured can make a claim representing the value insured by the policy. There is no deductible in question therefore the assured can recover his loss without having to bear some percentage of it before making a recovery from the insurer. The policy will be subject to average but the deduction made in the case of partial loss is not the same as the deductible in insurance in layers. In the latter, irrespective of the value of the policy or the amount of loss, a fixed deductible applies. Thus, in the context of excess of loss, the ranking between the assured and the insurers is set at the outset of the contract.

Napier was doubted for the reason that the stated purpose of subrogation is to prevent the assured from being paid twice, whereas the effect of disregarding the deductible is that the assured is deprived of the right to be paid in full at all before the insurer seeks reimbursement.[138] However the author is of the view that these two cases are in fact in line with each other. In the *Commonwealth*, the emphasis was that the assured was regarded as his own insurer with regard to the amount not insured when the recovery from the third party was to be allocated in a partial insurance. In an insurance in layers, however, the question is not partial insurance, the assured may or may not

137 *Napier and Ettrick v RF Kershaw Ltd* (No.1) [1993] 1 Lloyd's Rep 197, 200, Lord Templeman.
138 See Colinvaux, para 11–017; Arnould, para 31–59.

insure the entire value of the subject matter insured, rather the issue is about the ranking of the insurer's and the assured's liability. If the assured is presumed to be his own insurer with regard to the deductible he is treated as if he is another insurer in relation to the amount to be retained before making a claim against the insurer. The top down approach would be followed in the case of the assured insuring the deductible with another insurer or not insuring it but retaining it to himself as a deductible. The ranking of the first layer will not change in either case.

Costs of proceeding against the third party

Where the assured recovers from the third party and such recovery does not cover the expenses incurred in proceeding against the third party, the assured might want to deduct such expenses from the amount to which the insurer wants to exercise his right of subrogation. The assured's entitlement to recover such costs depends on the timing at which such expenses were incurred. If the insurer made the payment after the assured recovered it from the third party the insurer is not liable for such expenses, however if the insurance payment was before the expenditure was incurred, the assured is entitled to make such deduction.

If the insurers have made payment to the assured, and the assured has subsequently recovered from a third party representing both the insured and uninsured loss, the assured is entitled to recover from the insurers a proportionate share in the costs of pursuing the action against the third party.[139] The ratio in which the costs were borne should be determined by reference to the respective interests of the parties in the recoveries. For instance if the assured recovered £126,000 from third parties, against an earlier payment of £102,000 from insurers, the assured and the insurers are to bear the costs in the ratio 102:126.[140]

Subrogation and abandonment

Abandonment, as a requirement of making a claim for constructive total loss, is fully discussed in Chapter 9 of this book. Subrogation and abandonment are distinguished in several respects, the most obvious of which is that the insurer subrogates into the assured's rights against the third party irrespective of the loss amounting to partial or total loss whereas abandonment applies only to cases of total loss. The heading of section 79 of the Marine Insurance Act 1906 is 'Right of Subrogation'. However, the wording states 'Where the insurer pays for a total loss, either of the whole, or in the case of goods of any apportionable part, of the subject-matter insured, he thereupon becomes entitled to take over the interest of the assured in whatever may remain of the subject-matter so paid for.' Thus, the wording deals with a right which arises by virtue of abandonment, rather than subrogation.[141] Bowen LJ stated in *Castellain v Preston*[142] that in the case of marine insurance where there is a constructive total loss, the thing is considered as abandoned to the underwriters, and as vesting the property directly in them. The doctrine of abandonment is itself based upon the principle of indemnity. There is some overlap between s.79(1) and s.63(1) of the Marine Insurance Act 1906 which is explained in Chapter 9.

As seen in *Yorkshire Insurance Co Ltd v Nisbet Shipping Co Ltd*,[143] the insurer is entitled to recover only up to the amount the insurer paid but no more, even though the assured recovers, for example, for currency fluctuations more than the actual loss. In the case of total loss, whatever remains of

---

139 *England v Guardian Insurance Ltd* [2000] Lloyd's Rep IR 404.
140 *England v Guardian Insurance Ltd* [2000] Lloyd's Rep IR 404.
141 Arnould, 31–01.
142 (1883) 11 QBD 380.
143 [1961] 1 Lloyd's Rep 479.

the vessel in the shape of salvage, or whatever rights accrue to the owner of the thing insured and lost, pass to the underwriter the moment he is called upon to satisfy the exigency of the policy, and he does satisfy it.[144] If, moreover, her value had proved to be more than the estimated value in the policy, the underwriters would still have been entitled to the vessel so recovered.[145] If a ship had been recovered from the bottom of the sea the body of the vessel would be passed to the underwriters.[146] It is well established that upon abandonment an underwriter can recover more than 100 per cent if the abandoned property realises more than the amount paid by way of loss.[147]

Lord Blackburn referred to subrogation as a different principle to abandonment in *Simpson v Thomson*. His Lordship confirmed that the right of the assured to recover damages from a third person is not one of those rights which are incident to the property in the ship; it does pass to the underwriters in case of payment for a total loss, but on a different principle; and on this same principle it does pass to the underwriters who have satisfied a claim for a partial loss, though no property in the ship passes.

Contribution

Contribution occurs where the same assured insures the same interest with more than one insurer.[148] The aim of contribution is, similar to subrogation, to prevent the assured from recovering more than the whole loss. Therefore if the assured recovers the whole loss from one insurer which he could have recovered from the other, the insurers are permitted to contribute rateably.[149] Contribution does not apply where different persons insure in respect of different rights.[150] In *North British and Mercantile Insurance Co v London, Liverpool, and Globe Insurance Co*,[151] B and R each insured the goods separately with different insurers. The goods had been bailed to B and were lost upon a fire caused by the negligence of B. Thus B was liable to R in relation to the goods. The court held that just because R had his own insurance, B could not argue that R should claim from the insurer first. R's insurance was not a contract of indemnity to indemnify B against the claim of R, but it was a further contract that R got for his own security. If R's insurer indemnifies R then R can claim against B in R's name – that would be a typical case of subrogation but not contribution. This was not a case where the loss was to be divided, if B had not been insured at all the question would have been whether R's insurers, having paid R, would be entitled to be subrogated into his rights.

A subrogation action has to be brought in the name of the assured whereas a contribution claim should be brought by the claimant's insurers in their own name.[152] The question is whether upon the insurer's payment to the assured the party remains liable to the assured or the payment would discharge him from liability to the assured. If he is discharged from liability to the assured, the insurer may pursue a claim for contribution.[153] If the other party remains liable to the assured despite the insurer's payment the insurer may pursue a subrogation claim against the other party.[154]

---

144 *North of England Iron Steamship Insurance Association v Armstrong* (1869–70) LR 5 QB 244.
145 *North of England Iron Steamship Insurance Association v Armstrong* (1869–70) LR 5 QB 244.
146 *North of England Iron Steamship Insurance Association v Armstrong* (1869–70) LR 5 QB 244.
147 *Compania Colombiana de Seguros v Pacific Steam Navigation Co (The Colombiana)* [1963] 2 Lloyd's Rep 479, 493.
148 *North British and Mercantile Insurance Co v London, Liverpool, and Globe Insurance Co* (1877) 5 Ch D 569, 581, James LJ.
149 *North British and Mercantile Insurance Co v London, Liverpool, and Globe Insurance Co* (1877) 5 Ch D 569, at 581, James LJ.
150 *North British and Mercantile Insurance Co v London, Liverpool, and Globe Insurance Co* (1877) 5 Ch D 569, at 583, Mellish LJ.
151 (1877) 5 Ch D 569.
152 *Austin v Zurich General Accident & Liability Insurance Co Ltd* [1945] KB 250.
153 Arnould, para 31–08.
154 Arnould, para 31–08.

Increased value policy

The subject matter insured's value might increase during the currency of the policy which then might lead the assured to purchase further insurance on the subject matter insured. This is different to double insurance as highlighted by Lord Wright MR in *Boag v Standard Marine Insurance Co Ltd*.[155] In the case of double insurance, obviously, as the two sets of underwriters have to share the burden, they would be entitled to the proportionate benefit of any sums which went in reduction of the burden, and they would share both the amount of the indemnity which had to be paid, and against that they would be entitled to share the salvage in regard to which they were entitled to be subrogated in reduction of that indemnity.[156] In *Boag* however, the assured first insured the cargo at a value of £685 with Standard Marine Insurance Company. However, upon increase of the value of the cargo he purchased further insurance at Lloyds for £215. While the cargo was on board, the vessel went aground and the cargo had to be jettisoned. The insurers indemnified the assured. The general average adjustment awarded £532 in favour of the cargo owner. The increased valued policy insurer claimed £127 from the general average contribution. Standard Marine Insurance claimed that it was entitled to receive the general average contribution. The Court agreed that Standard Marine was entitled to the entire amount of the general average contribution. It was not to the knowledge of Standard Marine that an increased value policy would be taken out later. The Court explained that the wording of section 79 means that it is an integral condition of an insurance policy that the insurer has a contingent right of subrogation, which attaches and vests in them at the moment when the policy is effected. It is contingent in the sense that the state of affairs postulated may never arise, but the contingent right is there, and here the contingency has arisen, and the right vested as a contingency has become an effective right. Consequently, after Standard Marine's subrogation right arises by contract, if the assured promises with another insurer for Standard Marine's subrogation right to be shared, then that would prejudice Standard Marine's subrogation right.

It is submitted that this view is in line with the assured's obligation not to prejudice the insurer's rights after the contract is concluded. If the insurer's subrogation right does not arise until payment any action taken, or indeed any failure to take action, by the assured prior to full payment, the effect of which is to prejudice the insurer's future subrogation rights, cannot be the subject of any action against him by the insurer.[157] On the other hand, if insurer's right of subrogation arises as soon as the insurance contract is made – the right is contingent and will crystallise only on payment – the insurer does possess the contingent right against the third party prior to its making full payment under the policy.[158]

Clause 14 of ICC 2009 now provides an increased value clause. Accordingly, the agreed value of the subject matter insured shall be deemed to be increased to the total amount insured under the policy and liability under the contract of insurance shall be in such proportion as the sum insured under the contract bears to such total amount insured.

Further reading

Rose, *Marine Insurance: Law and Practice*, 2nd edn, [2012] Informa. Chapter 27.
Bennett, *The Law of Marine Insurance*, 2nd edn, [2006] Oxford University Press. Chapter 25.

---

155 [1937] 2 KB 113, 123.
156 *Boag v Standard Marine Insurance Co Ltd* [1937] 2 KB 113, 123 Lord Wright MR obiter.
157 Colinvaux, para 11–008.
158 Colinvaux, para 11–008.

Birds, 'Contribution or subrogation: orthodoxy restored', *Journal of Business Law* [2000] July, 347–350.

Birds, 'Waiver of subrogation clauses', *Journal of Business Law* [2000] July, 350–355.

Birds, 'Denying subrogation in coinsurance and similar situations', *Lloyd's Maritime and Commercial Law Quarterly* [2001] 2(May), 193–197.

Gilman et al., *Arnould: Law of Marine Insurance and Average*, 18th edn, [2013] Sweet & Maxwell. Chapter 31.

Hassan, 'Flight of the "Tabuk": the right of subrogation in salvage claims involving state responsibility', *Journal of Business Law* [2003] (January) 67–75.

Hemsworth, 'Subrogation: the problem of competing claims to recovery monies', *Journal of Business Law* [1998] March, 111–122.

Jing, 'Insurer beware – circumstances in which the insurer may lose his subrogation rights in marine insurance', *Journal of Maritime Law and Commerce* [2012] 43(1) (January), pp 129–154.

Leonard and Bramley, 'Insurers' right of subrogation against co-assureds: *National Oilwell (UK) Ltd v Davy Offshore Ltd*', *International Insurance Law Review* [1994] 2(4): 154–159.

Merkin, *Colinvaux's Law of Insurance*, 9th edn, [2010] Sweet & Maxwell, Chapter 11.

Merkin, 'Marine insurance', *British Insurance Law Association Journal* [2009] 118, 78. (Summary of Dornoch Ltd v Westminster International BV [2009] EWHC 1782 (Admlty); [2009] 2 Lloyd's Rep 420 (QBD (Admlty)).

Nicholson, 'Privity a la Canadienne', *Lloyd's Maritime and Commercial Law Quarterly* [2000] 3(August), 322–327.

Ward, 'Joint names insurance and contracts to insure: untangling the threads', *Lloyd's Maritime and Commercial Law Quarterly* [2009] 2(May), 239–261.

Chapter 14

Brokers

Chapter Contents

Introduction

Although in some cases they may act for insurers,[1] brokers are regarded as agents for the assured[2] who are authorised by the assured to effect an insurance contract between the assured and the insurers. In the London market only authorised brokers can access the Lloyd's underwriters, therefore appointing a broker is compulsory for an assured who would like to insure a marine risk in the Lloyd's market. As seen in Chapter 2 brokers play a very active role in the Open Market Placement. The broker prepares the slip and offers the risk to the underwriters and they negotiate the terms of the contract. When the risk occurs the assured again contacts the broker to make a claim against the insurers. During the currency of the policy the insurers might request the assured for instance to take reasonable precautionary steps to prevent the risk and the insurers contact the brokers to communicate such steps with the assured. It is crucially important at every stage of their relationship with the assured that the brokers know the insurance requirements of the assured and make sure that all the information is transferred between the insurers and the assured. Brokers' duties to their clients have actively been disputed before the courts in recent years and the Courts set out detailed rules explaining the scope of their duties. The legal status of brokers and their rights of remuneration are the other issues that will be discussed in this chapter. As referred to in Chapter 6 marine insurance brokers are personally liable for payment of the premium and they have a right of lien on the policy for non-payment of the premium by the assured. Brokers' liability for payment of the premium and their right of lien were discussed in Chapter 6.

Brokers: servants of the market

Brokers were defined as servants of the market partly because of the variety of clients that a broker may represent and partly because brokers may owe a duty of care not only to their clients but also to the other party to the contract. In most cases brokers are agents of the assured and the broker looks for an insurer who will be willing to insure the risk that his client, the assured, is seeking an insurance cover for. Brokers may also act for an insurer who would like to transfer the risk that he insured to reinsurers. Where there is reinsurance of an insured risk, the same broker may act on behalf of the assured in placing the insurance, and on behalf of the insurer in placing the reinsurance.[3]

The insurer, that is, the reinsured, is represented by the broker who will approach reinsurers to seek the reinsurance cover in question. In both the abovementioned cases the broker owes a duty of care in performing his contractual obligations and he owes a parallel duty of care in tort. Such duties will be fully analysed in the following paragraphs.

The broker's dual agency was recognised in *Drake Insurance plc (In Provisional Liquidation) v Provident Insurance plc*.[4] In this case the broker, as well as acting for the assured, had authority to rate each proposal and to determine the premium on the basis of the insurer's underwriting criteria.[5]

---

1 For instance where he acts as a coverholder under a binding authority.

2 *John W. Pryke & Others v Gibbs Hartley Cooper Ltd*, [1991] 1 Lloyd's Rep 602, 614; *Searle v A R Hales & Co Ltd* [1996] LRLR 68. *Anglo African Merchants v Bayley* [1969] 1 Lloyd's Rep 268; *General Accident Fire & Life Assurance Corp Ltd v Tanter (The Zephyr)* [1984] 1 Lloyd's Rep 58 Hobhouse J; The principle that a broker is the agent of the assured is now described as being axiomatic *Velos Group Ltd v Harbour Insurance Services Ltd* [1997] 2 Lloyd's Rep 461, 462.

3 *HIH Casualty & General Insurance Ltd v JLT Risk Solutions Ltd (formerly Lloyd Thompson Ltd)* [2007] 2 Lloyd's Rep 278, para 60.

4 [2004] 1 Lloyd's Rep 268, 283.

5 Similarly, in *Aneco Reinsurance Underwriting Ltd (In Liquidation) v Johnson & Higgins Ltd* [2002] Lloyd's Rep IR 91 the broker was a dual agent by acting for the insurers with regard to the reinsurance and acting for the reinsurer in relation to the retrocession arrangements.

Duties of the brokers

Modern cases have established that brokers are under the duty to exercise reasonable skill and care in performing their contractual obligations towards their clients. In parallel with his contractual duties a broker owes non-contractual duty of care to his clients.[6] In *Dunlop Haywards (DHL) Ltd v Barbon Insurance Group Ltd*,[7] Hamblen J confirmed that it is a fundamental duty of any agent to exercise reasonable skill and care in the performance of the functions which he has undertaken. The judge added that the various duties that have been held to apply to an insurance broker are no more than aspects of the general duty as it applies in the insurance broking context. The standard of care required from the broker is to observe the standards of a reasonable broker.[8] The courts will hear expert evidence from other brokers operating in the market at the same time in order to ascertain the standard of care to be expected of a professional broker.[9] It should be noted that although the general scope of brokers' duties are identified by the courts, the core duty imposed on the brokers in the context of a particular client/broker relationship depends on all the circumstances. In addition to establishing the broker's breach of his contractual-tortious duties, it will be necessary to prove that the breach caused the assured's loss. If the breach does not cause the loss, even though the broker is in breach of his duty the broker will not be liable for the loss.[10]

Since the duty exists in contract and tort, if an assured suffers loss as a result of his broker's negligence a claim may be brought against the broker either in contract or in tort. Bringing a claim in contract might have its advantages, for instance there is no requirement to prove the existence of a duty of care as is the case in tort. However, suing in tort might also have its advantages, for instance in relation to the calculation of the limitation period for a claim against a broker. The limitation period is six years both in claims in tort and contract. However, while an action in contract lapses within six years of the date on which the breach occurred (against a broker, for example, within six years of the date of his breach of duty), in tort the limitation period commences to run on the date 'at which the action accrued' (the action accrues when the claimant suffers damage). Moreover, section 14A of the Limitation Act 1980 provides for a 'discoverability test' in negligence cases in tort. This is an alternative three-year period in which to issue a claim form running from the date at which the damage, and the defendant's responsibility for it, became apparent or the date at which it should reasonably have been discovered.

As briefly mentioned above, the broker has an active relationship with his client from the pre-contractual stage until a claim is made and finalised with the parties to an insurance contract. A broker therefore owes duties at the pre-contractual and post-contractual stages.

Pre-contractual duties – duties on placement

To exercise reasonable care and skill to meet the assured's requirements

Brokers are under the duty to exercise reasonable skill and care in the fulfilment of the client's instructions and the performance of their professional obligations.[11] When presenting the risk to

---

6   Punjab National Bank v (1) N. De Boinville [1992] 1 Lloyd's Rep 7; FNCB Ltd v Barnet Devanney (Harrow) Ltd [1999] Lloyd's Rep IR 459.
7   [2010] Lloyd's Rep IR 149.
8   FNCB Ltd v Barnet Devanney (Harrow) Ltd [1999] Lloyd's Rep IR 459.
9   Arnould, para 7–06.
10 HIH Casualty & General Insurance Ltd v JLT Risk Solutions Ltd (formerly Lloyd Thompson Ltd) [2007] 2 Lloyd's Rep 278.
11 Dunlop Haywards Ltd (DHL) v Barbon Insurance Group Ltd [2010] Lloyd's Rep IR 149.

the insurer, after receiving the quotations from the insurer and at the contract drafting stage the broker is under the duty to exercise reasonable skill and care to meet the assured's requirements.[12] If the cover requested by the assured is not possible to obtain in the market the broker should inform the assured of that fact.[13] There are a number of examples illustrating the brokers' duties at this stage. In *Park v Hammond*[14] the assured was successful in his claim against the broker who took out a policy which did not meet the assured's instructions. The broker was instructed to insure the assured's goods shipped on board the *Pearl*, from Gibraltar to Dublin. The broker had effected an insurance 'on goods by the *Pearl* at and from Gibraltar to Dublin, beginning the adventure from the loading thereof on board at Gibraltar'. The goods were loaded at Malaga, the vessel then sailed for Gibraltar Bay to where she hove as to send letters on shore. The vessel did not come to an anchor at Gibraltar but the crew forwarded their letters by a boat from the shore of Algesiras. On the same day they proceeded on their homeward voyage, the vessel struck upon a rock, and the cargo was entirely lost. The insurers refused to pay for the reason that the goods were shipped at Malaga, not Gibraltar as the policy required in order to provide cover. The Court held that it was understood that the goods were to be shipped at Malaga, and the broker ought not to have effected a policy, which can only attach on goods shipped at Gibraltar.

The modern cases have been decided in the same direction as *Park v Hammond* and they explain brokers' duties to a great extent and in detail. Before moving to the modern cases it is worth mentioning *Waterkeyn v Eagle Star and British Dominions Insurance Co*[15] in which the court imposed the burden on the assured rather than the broker in terms of checking if the cover purchased by the broker met the assured's requirement. In *Waterkeyn*, the assured, a Russian businessman, instructed a broker to insure his bank in Russia against the political collapse of the bank. The then de facto government confiscated the bank but the assured's claim was rejected by the insurers. The policy wording was to cover '. . . the risk of total or partial loss arising from the bankruptcy or insolvency of all or any of the said banks as undermentioned directly due to damage or destruction of the premises and contents of the said banks through riots, civil commotion, war, civil war, revolutions, rebellions, military or usurped power . . .'. This wording clearly required physical collapse of the bank to render the insurer liable and the assured, having been left without an insurance cover, sued the broker for negligence. The court decided against the assured for the reason that the assured, being a businessman, should have read the insurance documents when they were sent to him by the broker and it was the assured's duty to take necessary steps to make sure that the broker took out the policy covering the exact risks the assured desired.

The modern cases however have gone in a different direction to *Waterkeyn*. As will be shown in the following paragraphs, a number of cases confirmed that brokers owe duty of care to their clients at the pre-contractual stage. Such a duty appears in the form of understanding the client's requirements and negotiating and drafting the insurance contracts according to the insurance that his client needs to purchase.[16] One of the examples confirming this principle is *Talbot Underwriting Ltd v Nausch Hogan & Murray Inc (The Jascon 5)*.[17] The vessel *Jascon 5*, an offshore pipelay construction barge owned by CPL, was sent to S's shipyard in Singapore for repair and refurbishment. CPL was required to arrange builders' all risk insurance which covered S as an additional co-assured and which relieved S from any subrogation proceedings by those insurers. NHM, insurance brokers, were instructed by CPL to place this policy. It was part of the instructions to NHM that S would be

---

12 *Jones v Environcom Ltd* [2010] Lloyd's Rep IR 676. The judge's ruling was not disturbed on appeal. [2012] Lloyd's Rep IR 277.
13 *Aneco Reinsurance Underwriting Ltd (In Liquidation) v Johnson & Higgins Ltd* [2002] Lloyd's Rep IR 91.
14 (1816) 6 Taunton 495.
15 (1920) 5 Ll L Rep 42.
16 *FNCB Ltd v Barnet Devanney (Harrow) Ltd* [1999] Lloyd's Rep IR 459, 468, Morritt LJ.
17 [2005] 2 CLC 868.

a co-assured. The slip policy ultimately obtained by placing brokers on behalf of NHM made no mention of S. The insurers were not informed that S was to be a co-assured. On 14 October 2003, during the currency of the policy, the vessel sustained flooding while being refloated after drydocking at S's shipyard. S incurred expense in effecting repairs to the vessel. A claim was made under the slip policy procured by CPL, but the insurers denied liability on the ground that S was not a party to the insurance. Cooke J[18] ruled on the preliminary issues that NHM's failure to obtain cover including S as co-assured was a failure to act with due care and skill in the placement of the insurance.[19]

Brokers' duties are not absolute but rather a requirement to exercise reasonable skill and care

It should be noted that the broker's duties in his relationship with his clients in the insurance and reinsurance market are not absolute but rather a duty to exercise reasonable skill and care.[20] Phillips J stated in *Youell v Bland Welch & Co Ltd (No.2)*[21] that when a Lloyd's broker accepts instructions from a client he implicitly undertakes to exercise reasonable skill and care in relation to his client's interests in accordance with the practice at Lloyd's. That general duty will normally require the broker to perform a number of different activities on behalf of the client, but the performance of those activities constitutes no more than the discharge of the duty to exercise reasonable skill and care. [22]

In *Standard Life v Oak Dedicated Ltd*,[23] Tomlinson J formulated the test to determine whether the broker is in breach of his duty. In this case the assured instructed the brokers for a professional indemnity policy against the risk of paying out compensation to the investors who trusted their money to the assured company. The risk occurred due to a cash injection, which was needed to prevent a much larger loss.[24] The assured paid compensation totalling over £100m to over 97,000 investors, the average size of each claim amounting to less than £10,000. The assured's claim was met by the insurer's policy defence that the insurance cover was subject to a per claimant deductible of £25m ('each and every claim and/or claimant'). Tomlinson J stated that the question was would a reasonably competent broker in his position reasonably have concluded that the words 'each and every claim and/or claimant' used to describe the excess in the slip and wording were sufficiently clear to meet his client's requirements without exposing the client to an unnecessary risk that insurers might argue that the cover granted was on a per claimant basis only. The judge found that no reasonable broker would have taken out such a policy in a risk as such. Tomlinson J explained the scope of the broker's duty that:

- If the cover which is needed by the client is not available, the broker should make it entirely clear to the assured what is covered and what is not covered under the policy.
- In the preparation of the policy the broker must be careful to ensure that the policy language clearly encompasses the needs of the client.
- The abovementioned duties apply on renewal of an existing policy and that at each renewal the broker must ensure that the cover arranged clearly meets the client's needs in the most appropriate manner.

---

18 The Court of Appeal dismissed the appeal. [2006] 2 Lloyd's Rep 195.
19 [2005] 2 CLC 868, para 103.
20 *Youell v Bland Welch & Co Ltd (No.2)* [1990] 2 Lloyd's Rep 431, 458 Phillips J.
21 [1990] 2 Lloyd's Rep 431.
22 *Youell v Bland Welch & Co Ltd (No.2)* [1990] 2 Lloyd's Rep 431, 458 Phillips J.
23 [2008] Lloyd's Rep IR 552.
24 See Chapter 11.

The dispute in *Youell v Bland Welch & Co Ltd* (No.2),[25] was once again related to the policy which did not meet the reinsured's requirements. In *Youell*, three liquefied gas carrying vessels were insured while under construction in the United States. The insurers then reinsured their potential liability in respect of the three insured vessels. The insulation on one of the insured vessels' tanks failed during sea trials. This was attributable to faults which were found to have infected all three vessels. They were so serious that the vessels were rendered constructive total losses when the original cover was still in force, but over 48 months after each vessel had come on risk. The insurer paid $300m in respect of its liabilities under the original policies and claimed against the reinsurers. The reinsurers denied liability on the ground that the reinsurance cover in respect of each vessel had terminated 48 months after attachment and prior to the casualty.[26] The original policy terms provided that the cover would continue until delivery. In an interim judgment Phillips J held that the claim against the reinsurers failed.[27] This judgment[28] relates to the alternative claim against the brokers who were found liable for the reinsured's loss for not being able to claim against the reinsurers. Phillips J emphasised that the reinsured wrote large lines on the original insurance because the brokers informed them that excess of loss reinsurance cover had been negotiated on terms 'as original'.[29] The brokers failed to inform them that, in contrast to the original insurance, the reinsurance was subject to the 48-month clause. Phillips J found that had the insurers been given this information they would not have accepted the reinsurance and would have written greatly reduced lines on the original insurance. They claimed as damages the payments that they had to make in consequence of being induced by the brokers' misrepresentation to write larger lines on the original insurance. Broker's failures in this transaction were:

1 Failure to inform the insurers that the reinsurance cover obtained for them was subject to the 48-month cut-off.
2 Failure to inform the insurers that the reinsurance cover available was subject to a 48-month cut-off. The brokers should have appreciated the significance of the clause and made clear to the insurers.
3 Failure to take steps to protect the insurers when the construction periods of the vessels were extended beyond 48 months.
4 Failure to draft the contractual wording with clarity. The brokers negotiated the terms of the cover on behalf of the prospective reinsured. The brokers were bound to exercise reasonable skill and care in drafting these documents so as to ensure that they gave clear expression to the terms that had been agreed.

A similar matter came before the Deputy Judge Mr Colman, QC in *Sharp v Sphere Drake Insurance* (*The Moonacre*),[30] in which the broker did not explicitly warn the assured about an exclusion clause in the policy which provided a defence for the insurers in an action by the assured against them. The assured lost his claim against the insurers but he was successful in suing his brokers for negligence. The judge adopted the analysis made in *Youell* and the duties set out by Phillips J and

---

25 [1990] 2 Lloyd's Rep 431.
26 The reinsurance contract provided:
    The reinsured shall cede to the reinsurers and the reinsurers shall accept by way of reinsurance of the reinsured their proportion of the reinsured's liability in respect of risks attaching for periods as original (up to but not exceeding 48 months) covering the interests of hull, machinery . . .
27 [1990] 2 Lloyd's Rep 423.
28 [1990] 2 Lloyd's Rep 431.
29 For the meaning of 'as original' see Chapter 15.
30 [1992] 2 Lloyd's Rep 501.

found that the broker failed to exercise the standard of care to be expected from a professional broker and was in breach of contract and of duty to the assured.[31]

Duties apply on renewal

As stated above, the broker's duty at the placement of the risk applies on the renewal of the policy and the broker owes a duty of care and how the duty is characterised depends on the facts of each case. Another list of duties of brokers is seen in *Dunlop Haywards (DHL) Ltd v Barbon Insurance Group Ltd*[32] in which case, on renewal of the policy, the cover was restricted to the assured's commercial property management activities whereas in the previous policies which expired, there had not been such a restriction in the cover. Hamblen J ruled that the broker's duty to exercise reasonable skill and care involved contractual and tortious duties to the assured and the judge listed the duties as follows:

1 to exercise reasonable care and skill in the fulfilment of the assured's instructions and the performance of its professional obligations;
2 carefully to ascertain the assured's insurance needs and to use reasonable skill and care to obtain insurance that met those needs; [33]
3 carefully to review the terms of any quotations or indications received;
4 to explain to the client the terms of the proposed insurance; and
5 to use reasonable skill and care to draw up a policy, or to ensure that a policy was drawn up, that accurately reflected the terms of the agreement with the underwriters and which was clear and unambiguous so that the client's rights under the policy were not open to doubt.

Moreover, specifically applicable to *Dunlop*, the broker owed duty to explain any changes to the terms of the assured's expiring policies necessitated by the state of the professional indemnity insurance market or the changes to the assured's structure.

A further illustration of the application of the abovementioned principles is seen in *Ground Gilbey Ltd v Jardine Lloyd Thompson UK Ltd*[34] in which case Camden Market in North London was insured against material damage, loss of profit, liability and terrorism. The policy was subject to the Survey Condition, which stated that 'cover under this Policy is conditional upon' receipt of acceptable survey reports and also 'completion to the Underwriters' satisfaction of all requested risk improvements within timescales stipulated by the Underwriters'. The clause concluded by stating that: 'Underwriters reserve the right to amend the terms of the cover (which for the avoidance of doubt includes the withdrawal of cover) if either [condition was] not satisfied.' Stallholders in the market were using liquefied petroleum gas portable heating appliances (PHAs) and the insurers required them to be

---

31 In *The Moonacre* the subject matter insured was a yacht on which the crew employed by the assured lived during the time that the yacht was laid up at Majorca in the winter. The proposal form contained a question about the yacht being used as a houseboat and the policy contained a clause excluding coverage for any period for which the vessel is used as a houseboat – unless notice be given to and an additional premium agreed by the Underwriters. The insurer refused to pay when the assured made a claim after the yacht was lost as a result of a fire – notice was never given about the yacht being used as a houseboat, no additional premium was therefore arranged. Deputy Judge Mr Colman QC held that having regard to the ordinary and natural meaning of the houseboat question in the proposal form and taking into account the expert evidence, it was the professional duty of the broker dealing with a client's proposal for yacht insurance to advise his client that the underwriters had to be told if anyone including a permanent crew was to use the vessel as living accommodation during the period of lay-up.

32 [2010] Lloyd's Rep IR 149.

33 This does not mean that a broker guarantees that every contingency will be covered: the question is whether the broker acted reasonably in ascertaining his clients' needs and would have been able to meet those needs by reference to the general availability of insurance and the practice of brokers in the market at the time. Arnould, para 7–09.

34 [2012] Lloyd's Rep IR 12.

removed immediately. The broker did not specifically draw the assured's attention to the Survey Condition. There was a major fire in the market caused by a PHA which ignited the clothes on one of the stalls. The insurers settled the claim for the amount of 70 per cent of the whole loss. The assured sued the broker for negligence and the court accepted the claim. The broker was in breach of several duties which will be mentioned below. Here it is to be noted that one of the duties that the broker was in breach of was the duty to obtain a policy which meets the assured's requirements as he failed to obtain a policy which allowed the claimants to use PHAs, as they had wished. When the insurer asked about the removal of the appliances the broker ought to have appreciated that the policy did not meet the assured's needs as the broker knew that PHAs were continuing to be used in the market.

As will be seen below with regard to the broker's post-contractual duty, at the pre-contractual stage as well the broker is not classified only as a post box that passes documents between the assured and the insurers. In *Jones v Environcom Ltd*,[35] the insurer sent various documents to the broker regarding the assured's duty of disclosure and material facts. The assured was engaged in the business of electrical goods waste recycling, operating from premises in Lincolnshire. In 2004 Environcom installed a state of the art refrigerator line which was designed to extract and destroy CFC chemicals present in the compressors within refrigerators. The work process involved the removal of compressors bolted to the bottom of the refrigerators. In most cases the bolts could be removed by spanner, screwdriver or hammer, but some had to be removed by the use of plasma guns. The evidence showed that the use of plasma guns gave rise to a risk that hot metal splatter and sparks could ignite fridges being processed. It indeed proved to be the case that the plasma guns caused ignitions in fridges. There was also a series of fires. The insurer rejected the claim on the grounds of material non-disclosure of the use of plasma guns in the process of de-manufacturing fridges and the occurrence of further fires in addition to two previous claims. The evidence showed that the broker had not specifically warned the assured of its duty of disclosure, but had sent various documents to the assured which referred to that duty. This was not however sufficient for the broker to perform his pre-contractual duty of care owed to the assured. David Steel J confirmed that 'The broker must satisfy himself that the position is in fact understood by his client and this will usually require a specific oral or written exchange on the topic, both at the time of the original placement and at renewal (particularly if a new person has become that client's representative).'[36]

Duty of disclosure and not to misrepresent material facts

As referred to in Chapter 4 under section 19 of the Marine Insurance Act it is the brokers duty to disclose to the insurer material facts or not to misrepresent them when the assured passes the relevant information to the broker at the pre-contractual stage. Moreover, under s.19(2) the broker is under an independent duty to disclose material facts which are known by him but not known by the assured. If the broker is in breach of his duty under section 19 the insurer may avoid the contract given that the broker is the assured's agent and his breach of duty of good faith is in fact the assured's breach.

The broker owes duty of care to the assured regarding performance of his pre-contractual duty of good faith. In *Jones v Environcom Ltd*[37] and *Synergy Health (UK) Ltd v CGU Insurance plc (t/a Norwich Union)*[38] it was held that a broker:

---

35   [2010] Lloyd's Rep IR 676.
36   [2010] Lloyd's Rep IR 676, para 63.
37   [2010] Lloyd's Rep IR 676.
38   [2011] Lloyd's Rep IR 500.

- must advise his client of the duty to disclose all material circumstances so that the assured is aware of and understands his duty of disclosure;
- must explain the consequences of failing to observe the duty of good faith;
- must indicate the sort of matters which ought to be disclosed as being material (or at least arguably material);
- must take reasonable care to elicit matters which ought to be disclosed but which the client might not think it necessary to mention;
- must take reasonable care to disclose any material facts of which the brokers themselves were aware and not to make material representations to insurers which it knew to be untrue.

Additionally, the broker must take reasonable care to obtain insurance that clearly meets the assured's requirements. Furthermore, a reasonable broker is required to know the difference between material and immaterial facts.[39] As already mentioned above, a broker's role is not simply passing communications between the assured and the insurer but also to exercise reasonable care and skill to ensure that the assured understands the insurer's requirements, which includes the duty of good faith.

Producing brokers and placing brokers

The broker that has been instructed by the assured might appoint a sub-broker to place the risk with the insurer. For instance in *Fisher v Smith*[40] a broker who was based outside Liverpool instructed a sub-broker who was in Liverpool and who would be able to make terms on the spot for a satisfactory premium with a Liverpool underwriter. Moreover, if the risk is desired to be insured at Lloyd's, a broker who does not have licence to insure risks at Lloyd's has to appoint a placing broker who does have the licence.[41] In *Tudor Jones v Crowley Colosso Ltd*,[42] a broker who carried on his business in the USA appointed a broker in London to insure the islands that the assured acquired in the Bahamas. Similarly, in *Dunlop Haywards (DHL) Ltd v Barbon Insurance Group Ltd*,[43] the assured's in-house brokers appointed Forbes as placing brokers as they wanted to obtain insurance from Lloyd's for renewal of the professional indemnity insurance for the assured.

It is important to distinguish the contractual relationships between the parties involved when a broker appoints a sub-agent. The assured has his contract with the producing broker who enters into a sub-agency agreement with the placing broker. Consequently, there is no privity of contract between the placing broker and the assured.[44] The placing broker's contractual claims will be made against the producing brokers and the producing broker's contractual claims will be brought against the assured. The assured may suffer loss – for instance they may not be able to claim under the insurance contract for the reason that the broker did not place the cover that the assured required – as a result of the placing broker's negligence. In such a case, in principle, the producing broker will be liable to the assured for breach of contract and he will be liable vicariously for the placing broker's negligence. As seen below, in *BP plc v Aon Ltd (No.2)*,[45] it was held that a direct action by

---

39 Arnould, para 7–10; *Maydew v Forrester* (1814) 5 Taunton 615; *Wake v Atty* (1812) 4 Taunton 493; *Campbell v Rickards* (1833) 5 Barnewall and Adolphus 840.
40 (1878) 4 App Cas 1.
41 *Velos Group Ltd v Harbour Insurance Services Ltd* [1997] 2 Lloyd's Rep 461, 463.
42 [1996] 2 Lloyd's Rep 619.
43 [2010] Lloyd's Rep IR 149.
44 *Prentis Donegan & Partners Ltd v Leeds & Leeds Co Inc* [1998] 2 Lloyd's Rep 326.
45 [2006] Lloyd's Rep IR 577.

the assured against the placing broker may be acceptable if the latter assumes responsibility to the assured. The placing broker's fee will be paid by the producing broker who then will claim his remuneration from the assured.

In this chain of relationships the producing broker owes duty of care to the assured as analysed above. In *Dunlop Haywards (DHL) Ltd v Barbon Insurance Group Ltd*,[46] Hamblen J discussed the duties that may be owed by the placing broker against the producing broker. In *Dunlop*, HPC appointed Forbes as placing broker to renew the assured's professional indemnity insurance. The assured, DHL, provided property consultancy services, including substantial commercial property valuation work for banks and building societies. DHL received a number of claims from various lenders said to arise from the provision of negligent and/or fraudulent valuation reports carried out by a director of DHL. DHL's professional indemnity insurers refused to indemnify DHL for the reasons that when the policy was renewed it was renewed by limiting the cover to DHL's 'commercial Property Management activities only'. DHL therefore sued the brokers for negligence. The producing broker was found liable to the assured but the court also discussed the relationship between HPC and Forbes. It was agreed as part of the instructions to Forbes that cover was to be no worse than the expiring cover.

The duties owed between the placing and producing brokers are akin to those owed by a producing broker to the assured, namely:

- to exercise reasonable care and skill in the fulfilment of its instructions and the performance of its professional obligations;
- to carefully review the terms of any quotations or indications received;
- to explain the terms of the proposed insurance; and
- to use reasonable skill and care to draw up a policy, or to ensure that a policy was drawn up, that accurately reflected the terms of the agreement with the underwriters and which was clear and unambiguous so that the client's rights under the policy were not open to doubt.

Moreover, in order to perform its duties to obtain quotations and place insurance, it is necessary for the placing broker to take care to ensure that the instructions are understood. A placing broker would be expected to query, clarify or confirm instructions which appear to be:

- unclear, ambiguous, or inconsistent with other information with which he is being provided;
- illogical or absurd;
- potentially disadvantageous or detrimental to the client or inappropriate to its business; or where:
- there is a disadvantage to the client arising from a change in instructions;
- there is other good reason to believe that they do not meet the client's requirements as relayed by the placing broker.
  It was also agreed by the broking experts that in general a placing broker would be expected:
- to obtain clear authority before agreeing a limitation or restriction or change in cover; and
- to draw attention to anomalies which may arise from the instructions received from the producing broker.

Applying these principles, Hamblen J held that a reasonably competent broker in Forbes' position should have appreciated that the Limiting Condition constituted a fundamental change in the basis of cover in that DHL was giving up excess cover for its riskiest activity (valuation), that there was

---

46 [2010] Lloyd's Rep IR 149.

no obvious reason for this, and that the reduction in cover would be occurring when DHL's existing policy still had three months to run. A reasonably competent broker would therefore have queried the apparent instructions, and Forbes had been negligent in failing to do so.

It should be noted that a placing broker does not owe a duty of care to the assured to ensure that the terms of the policy were drawn to the assured's attention; it is the duty of the producing broker alone.[47]

Post-contractual duties

The duty of care owed by the broker is continued at the post-contractual stage. In *Youell v Bland Welch & Co Ltd (No.2)*,[48] the facts of which are given above, the reinsurance contract was worded 'as original'. This meant that the reinsurance contract is meant to provide a back-to-back (identical) cover with the original insurance. On the other hand, while the original insurance contract did not provide such a limitation, the reinsurance cover was expressly limited to 48 months after each insured vessel has come on risk. As explained above, the broker was found negligent for drafting the reinsurance cover in a way not matching with the original insurance cover. Moreover, Phillips J held that the broker was also in breach of his post-contractual duty of care by not seeking to extend the cover after the contract was concluded and when it became clear that the construction of the vessel would take longer than 48 months. The judge noted that the insurers had wanted reinsurance 'as original' and the brokers had been unable to obtain this. Phillips J was of the view that in these circumstances it should have been clear to the brokers that, if construction of the hulls was delayed to the extent that reinsurance cover was likely to lapse, the insurers would want extension of that cover, if it could be achieved. Furthermore, the brokers should have taken into account that the insurers would rely upon them to take appropriate action if there was a risk of construction of a vessel overrunning beyond the 48-month period of cover.[49]

Youell was referred to in *HIH Casualty & General Insurance Ltd v JLT Risk Solutions Ltd (formerly Lloyd Thompson Ltd)*,[50] in which the broker was found to be in breach of his post-contractual duty of care in terms of advising the reinsured regarding the coverage issues against the reinsurers. HIH insured LDT who financed some films which would be made by Flashpoint. The number of films to be made by Flashpoint was identified in relation to three slates of films: the 7.23 slate of six films, the Rojak slate of ten films and the Award slate of five films. The insurance was to cover any shortfall on projected revenue from the making and marketing of the films. HIH reinsured the risk on a back-to-back basis. The assured did not make the number of films stated in the insurance contract and the films that were made did not generate significant revenue. As a result the investors suffered heavy losses, leading to payments by HIH in 1999 and 2000 of US$15,611,008, US$14,679,473 and US$25,092,303 to LDT in respect of the three slates of films. The reinsurers refused to pay to the reinsured in respect of the losses that the latter indemnified. In a separate action, in *HIH Casualty and General Insurance Co v New Hampshire Insurance Co*,[51] the Court of Appeal held that the statements as to the number of films to be made were warranties so that HIH had not been under any liability to make payments and the reinsurers were not under any liability to indemnify HIH for any payments which it did make. HIH then sought damages from JLT for negligence that JLT ought to have warned HIH of the breaches of warranty in respect of the reinsurance and owed a duty of care to do so.

---

47 *Pangood Ltd v Barclay Brown & Co Ltd* [1999] Lloyd's Rep IR 405.
48 [1990] 2 Lloyd's Rep 431.
49 [1990] 2 Lloyd's Rep 431, 447–448.
50 [2007] 2 Lloyd's Rep 278.
51 [2001] 2 Lloyd's Rep 161.

The Court of Appeal affirmed Langley J's judgment that the broker was in breach of his post-contractual duty of care as he did not warn the reinsured about the coverage issues in relation to the breach of warranty. A series of risk management reports of Flashpoint were distributed through JLT in late 1998 and early 1999 and they disclosed that less than the projected number in each slate of films was being produced. It was clear that each of the three slates was not successful and that each of their returns fell substantially short of the projected revenues. Nevertheless, in 1999 and in 2000 HIH made payments to LDT. The Court of Appeal held that JLT's post-contractual duties were more than to act as 'a mere post-box'. JLT had a duty of care to seek instructions or at least to ensure that HIH were sufficiently aware of the potential concern to assess what, if any, instructions to give. Lord Justice Longmore[52] said 'an insurance broker who, after placing the risk, becomes aware of information which has a material and potentially deleterious effect on the insurance cover which he has placed is under an obligation to act in his client's best interest by drawing it to the attention of his client and obtain his instructions in relation to it.'

The risk management reports, prepared and provided by Flashpoint to JLT and forwarded by JLT to HIH, had clearly indicated the film reductions and JLT had read them and had been aware of the reductions and the possible resultant coverage issue, but had not alerted HIH to it. JLT owed a duty to alert HIH to the coverage issue by drawing specific attention to the film reductions indicated in the risk management reports of which JLT was in breach. JLT was nevertheless not liable for the loss HIH suffered as JLT's breach did not cause the loss. HIH made payments either by not seeking the reinsurer's view and for some payments they paid although they knew that the reinsurers were disputing the claims.

The post-contractual duties owed by the brokers were discussed in detail in *BP plc v Aon Ltd (No.2)*[53] in which the sub-agent was in breach of his duties to the assured. BP brought a claim for damages in tort against Aon London in respect of the placement and operation by Aon London of a Global Construction All Risks Open Cover agreement. The purpose of the Open Cover was insured on an all risks basis in respect of physical loss and damage to the property of BP involved in oil and gas construction projects throughout the world. In order to obtain cover in respect of any such project, that project had to be declared to the underwriters under the Open Cover. The insurance had been placed by Aon. Aon presented the risk to London, European and US market insurers. It was determined by Aon that Aon London would handle declarations to the open cover emanating from BP's London office, whereas declarations emanating from Chicago would be handled by Aon companies in the US and transmitted to London.

Aon London declared the risks only to the leading underwriter but not to the followers. As a result BP suffered loss as the following underwriters were never under risk for the declarations were made only to the leader. In an action by BP against Aon the key question was whether Aon London's representation, judged objectively, was such as to amount to the assumption of a personal obligation as explicitly as if he were personally contractually binding himself to provide the advice, the information or the services.[54] Colman J held that an agent could incur personal liability to a client of his principal only if there was an assumption of responsibility by the agent which created a special relationship between himself and the client. Colman J's conclusion from the cases was:

[T]here has to be an express or implied representation by or on behalf of the agent by words or conduct not only that it is he who will be responsible in fact for preparing the advice or carrying out the services with proper skill and care, but that he personally will accept legal liability if

52 [2007] 2 Lloyd's Rep 278, para 116.
53 [2006] Lloyd's Rep IR 577.
54 [2006] Lloyd's Rep IR 577, para 167.

he fails to do so and if the claimant suffers economic loss by reason of his reliance on such assumption of responsibility.

Colman J was satisfied that Aon London undertook responsibility to BP to provide the services of a broker under the open cover with proper professional skill and care, and that BP relied upon that undertaking. Given that Aon's duty as brokers was to take such steps as were necessary to obtain insurance binding on each of the participating insurers for the benefit of BP and its co-assured in relation to each project properly notified, its breach of that duty occurred as and when and to the extent that it failed to declare such a project to any participant in the following market.[55] Clearly, the essence of the service which BP was entitled to expect Aon London to provide was the provision of complete cover for each notified project and not merely cover from the leading underwriters. The judge found that on each occasion when Aon London received from BP London or from BP Chicago or from Aon Illinois a notification of a project to be declared to the Open Cover, Aon London's professional duty of care was engaged. Once it received the instructions its duty attached to that project and it was obliged to take such steps as were reasonably required to procure cover by declaring the project to all the underwriters on the London and continental markets. Aon London was clearly in breach of its post-contractual duties.

Brokers' post-contractual duties were once more confirmed by Blair J in *Ground Gilbey Ltd v Jardine Lloyd Thompson UK Ltd*.[56] In 2005 the owners of Camden Market in North London insured the Market against material damage, loss of rent, liability and terrorism. Stallholders were using the liquefied petroleum gas portable heating appliances (PHAs) to keep warm in winter and removal of PHAs was a concern of the insurers throughout the years that the policy was first issued and then renewed. Before renewal of the policy in 2007 a survey was carried out and the insurers informed the broker that there had to be end-of-day checks by security, and if heaters had been used, they had to be confiscated. The renewal policy was issued on 30 March 2007, and this contained a new endorsement – the Survey Condition – which stated that 'cover under this Policy is conditional upon' receipt of acceptable survey reports and also 'completion to the Underwriters' satisfaction of all requested risk improvements within timescales stipulated by the Underwriters'. The clause concluded by stating that: 'Underwriters reserve the right to amend the terms of the cover (which for the avoidance of doubt includes the withdrawal of cover) if either [condition was] not satisfied.' It was common ground that the broker did not specifically draw the assured's attention to the Survey Condition.[57] Blair J confirmed that the broker owes his client a duty to draw to the client's attention any onerous or unusual terms or conditions, and should explain to the client their nature and effect. In this case, as the judge noted, the Survey Condition was not unusual or onerous but having considered the insurer's concern, it was potentially important and should have been drawn to the assured's attention. Furthermore, the insurers contacted the broker one more time in September 2007 and stated that 'all [PHAs] are to be removed from the premises together with any cylinders or other fuel . . . Completion: Immediate'. This email was not passed to the assured by the broker. The broker did not pass the risk improvement measures in the insurers' emails to the assured. Blair J[58] found that the insurers were concerned about the continuing use of PHAs and the risk improvement measures had 'a material and potentially deleterious effect on the insurance cover', and the brokers were under a duty to act in their clients' best interest by drawing it to their attention and obtaining their

---

55 [2006] Lloyd's Rep IR 577, para 173.
56 [2012] Lloyd's Rep IR 12.
57 On 9 February 2008 a major fire occurred at Camden Market. The cause of the fire was a PHA which ignited clothes on one of the stalls. The insurer settled the claim with the assured covering about 70 per cent of the estimated loss. The assured sued the broker for the amount that could not be recovered from the insurers.
58 [2012] Lloyd's Rep IR 12, para 78.

instructions in relation to it. The judge found that the broker was under the duty to explain to the assured that the cover might be prejudiced if nothing was done to remove the PHAs and that the parties could identify a safe PHA substitute.

Claims procedure

When a loss occurs and the assured desires to make a claim against the insurer the assured instructs the broker for that purpose. It was held that Lloyd's brokers are under the duty to collect claims when called upon to do so.[59] Moreover, where a notice of abandonment is required the broker must take care to give notice thereof in due time and in proper form.[60] The duty at this stage is to exercise all reasonable care and skill in collecting claims when asked to do so.[61] Clarke J was prepared to hold in *Johnston v Leslie & Godwin Financial Services Ltd* that the duty to take all reasonable care and skill to collect claims when asked to do so is implied into the contract between the assured and the broker by custom. Clarke J also added that (although in today's work computerisation may not require it any more) the broker is under the duty to keep the documents which later will help the assured to make a claim, for example, evidence of contract of insurance. The broker owes the duty to retain the documents so long as a claim can reasonably be regarded as possible.[62] If contributory negligence is alleged on the assured's side in terms of keeping the relevant documents it is likely that the Court would hold that the assured had his right to rely on the broker's professionalism and performing his duties under the contract.[63] Contributory negligence will be discussed in detail below.

The broker is also under the duty to collect and promptly pay over losses to his principal.[64]

Duties to underwriters

There may be circumstances where a broker is acting for the insurer. A typical example of this is where the broker is obtaining a reinsurance cover for the insurer. In such a case, as seen above, the broker owes duties to the reinsured which are akin to his duties to the assured as the reinsured is the broker's client, as the assured is.

As was explained in Chapter 2, the London Market is a subscription market and a broker may obtain more than 100 per cent subscription for the risk he has presented to the underwriters. In such a case the broker normally gives a signing indication to the insurer or reinsurers as the case may be. A signing indication is given because when more than 100 per cent subscription is obtained each line is proportionally reduced so as to ensure that the subscriptions add up to 100 per cent and no more. A slip which undergoes this process is said to be 'signed down'. When each line is automatically adjusted in this way to a particular percentage of the amount originally initialled it is said to have been signed down to that percentage. The broker gives the insurer a signing down indication when he is offering the risk. Sometimes the broker volunteers to give the information, and sometimes the insurer may ask a question about the signing down. In *General Accident Fire & Life*

---

59 *Johnston v Leslie & Godwin Financial Services Ltd* [1995] LRLR 472.
60 Arnould, para 7–16.
61 *Johnston v Leslie & Godwin Financial Services Ltd* [1995] LRLR 472, 477.
62 [1995] LRLR 472, 477, 478.
63 *Johnston v Leslie & Godwin Financial Services Ltd* [1995] LRLR 472, 483, 484.
64 Arnould, para 7–19.

Assurance Corp Ltd v Tanter (The Zephyr)[65] the Court of Appeal held that where the broker promises to sign down by his representation to the insurers, this will form a collateral contract to the primary contracts between the insurer and the assured or between the reinsured and the reinsurers as the case may be. Thus, if the line is not signed down the broker will be liable for breach of contract. In terms of the duty of care in tort, Hobhouse J[66] held that the broker owes a duty in court which is to use best endeavours to achieve the signing down which was promised. The Court of Appeal disagreed on this point. Mustill LJ[67] said a promise to use 'best endeavours' bears no resemblance to the kind of obligation to avoid doing something, or to avoid doing something badly, which is the subject matter of the English law of negligence.

Contributory negligence

In a claim between assured–reinsured and broker

In principle, contributory negligence is applicable in a claim in tort. There may be exceptional circumstances where it may apply in a claim in contract, which will be explained below. The Law Reform (Contributory Negligence) Act 1945 s.1(1) states that 'Where any person suffers damage as the result partly of his own fault and partly of the fault of any other person or persons, a claim in respect of that damage shall not be defeated by reason of the fault of the person suffering the damage, but the damages recoverable in respect thereof shall be reduced to such extent as the court thinks just and equitable having regard to the claimant's share in the responsibility for the damage.'

Accordingly, a defendant first must establish that the claimant has suffered damage partly as a result of his own fault. Second, if causative fault on the part of the claimant is established, the Court will consider the apportionment of responsibility for the loss between the parties on the basis of the relative causative potency of the claimant's conduct and the relative blameworthiness of the claimant for the relevant damage.[68]

It was stated that s.1 was adopted to override the ancient rule of the common law that if a claimant sued in tort for damages for negligence his claim would wholly fail if it were shown that he had been guilty of any degree of contributory negligence, however slight.[69] It enables the apportionment of liability so as to permit recovery of a proportion of the damage sustained.[70] Thus, section 1 has a limited application and it is concerned only with tortious liability.[71] As seen above, the broker owes duties to his clients in contract and in tort, therefore a contributory negligence defence may arise in a claim brought against a broker for breach of his duties. If the argument relied on breach of a duty in tort there is no doubt that the 1945 Act may apply. However, if the claim relies on breach of a contractual duty the question will then arise whether the application of section 1 will be extended to such a case. This was discussed in *Forsikringsaktieselskapet v Butcher*[72] in which the insurers argued that the broker was in breach of his duty to exercise reasonable skill and

---

65 [1985] 2 Lloyd's Rep 529.
66 [1984] 1 Lloyd's Rep 58, 85.
67 [1985] 2 Lloyd's Rep 529, 538.
68 *Dunlop Haywards (DHL) Ltd v Barbon Insurance Group Ltd* [2010] Lloyd's Rep IR 149.
69 Dillon LJ, *Tennant Radiant Heat Ltd v Warrington Development Corporation* [1988] 1 EG LR 41.
70 *Forsikringsaktieselskapet Vesta v Butcher* [1988] 1 Lloyd's Rep 19, 24, O'Connor LJ.
71 *Forsikringsaktieselskapet Vesta v Butcher* [1988] 1 Lloyd's Rep 19, 35, Sir R Ormrod.
72 [1988] 1 Lloyd's Rep 19. The case went to the House of Lords, since their Lordships found the reinsurers liable the broker's liability and contributory negligence were not discussed. [1989] 1 Lloyd's Rep 331.

care to obtain for the insurers satisfactory reinsurance cover.[73] The broker's defence was that the insurers had themselves been negligent in failing to ensure that the exclusion was deleted from the reinsurance cover and that this constituted contributory negligence under the 1945 Act.

Hobhouse J held at first instance that both the brokers and the insurers had been negligent, that the 1945 Act applied, and that liability should be apportioned 25/75 per cent in the brokers' favour. Hobhouse J stated that the question whether the 1945 Act applies to claims brought in contract can arise in a number of classes of case, one of which is where the defendant's liability in contract is the same as his liability in the tort of negligence independently of the existence of any contract. The majority of the Court of Appeal upheld Hobhouse J's ruling. Sir Roger Ormrod, although accepting that the Act applied in the case, followed a different route. His Lordship was unconvinced that contributory negligence, as such, at common law had any relevance in a claim in contract.[74] The Contributory Negligence Act is concerned with liability in tort only. The broker's liability for deleting the warranty from the reinsurance contract was not, but could be a breach of an implied term.[75] Sir Roger Ormrod classified the situation as one where the existence of the contract created a degree of proximity between the insurer and the brokers sufficient to give rise, on ordinary principles, to a duty of care and, therefore, to a claim in negligence.[76] Thus, the Act applied.

In *Youell v Bland Welch & Co Ltd (No.2)*,[77] Phillips J applied the rule adopted by Hobhouse J and the majority of the Court of Appeal in *Forsikringsaktieselskapet Vesta v Butcher*. The facts of *Youell* were given above. The brokers argued that the insurers were negligent in that they failed to react when the brokers gave them notice of the 48-month clause by sending them the order letters, the cover notes and the contract wording. The brokers alleged that had the insurers exercised reasonable care they would have appreciated, or at least discovered, that their reinsurance cover was subject to a 48-month cut-off and taken steps which would have resulted in their obtaining extensions of cover when the 48 month period expired. Phillips J held that the insurers owed no duty to the brokers to read the insurance wording with reasonable skill and care and to draw attention to any inadequacies in the cover. The judge was of the view that if there was such a duty a broker who has undertaken a contractual duty to exercise skill and care for his client can transfer to the client the duty of checking that such care had been exercised by the expedient sending of such a letter, with the result that if both broker and client fail to exercise care the loss falls on the client. Phillips J held that although the insurers owed no duty to the brokers to read the insurance wording with skill and care and to draw attention to any inadequacies in the cover, it does not follow from this that the insurers were not guilty of neglect of what would be prudent in respect of their own interests. An insurer who was exercising reasonable skill and care in relation to the business he was conducting would have noticed the 48-month clause and would have queried its presence and effect with the brokers.[78] The insurers were guilty of a failure to exercise reasonable care in carrying out what they accepted were customary checks on the manner in which the brokers had performed their duty. The presence of the 48-month clause should have alerted the insurers to the fact that all was not well with the services provided by the brokers and led them to take steps to ensure that whatever could reasonably be done to rectify the position was done. Phillips J stated that an essential part of the rationale underlying the bar to recovery where there has been a failure to mitigate is that the loss in question is caused by the claimant's voluntary conduct, not by the defendant's wrong. Where a claimant is unaware of the breach, the implications of his conduct fall to be determined,

---

73   The broker was negligent in terms of deleting an exclusion clause from the reinsurance contract.
74   [1988] 1 Lloyd's Rep 19, 35.
75   [1988] 1 Lloyd's Rep 19, 35.
76   [1988] 1 Lloyd's Rep 19, 35.
77   [1990] 2 Lloyd's Rep 431.
78   [1990] 2 Lloyd's Rep 431, 460.

not according to the specific doctrine of mitigation but according to the general principles of causation. If it is not reasonably foreseeable that the claimant will remain in ignorance of the breach and fail to react to it so as to avoid loss, the loss may be too remote. If the claimant negligently fails to discover the breach, so that he takes no steps to mitigate its effect, the normal consequences of negligence will follow including, where appropriate, the application of the 1945 Act. In *Youell*, Phillips J found it appropriate to deduct 20 per cent from the broker's liability and they were liable for 80 per cent of the loss that the reinsured suffered as a result of the brokers' negligence.

Two further cases which were discussed in *Youell* are worth mentioning here. Before section 1(1) of the Contributory Negligence Act 1945 was adopted, as Phillips J noted, the important test was of causation and if the claimant's fault might have caused the loss, since apportionment was not an option, the claimant would have lost his claim entirely. In *Dickson v Devitt*,[79] the broker was instructed to 'insure, marine and war risks, machinery . . . dispatched for shipment to-day per SS *Suwa Maru* and or other steamers London to Port Dickson'. The broker omitted the words 'and/or other steamers' while effecting the insurance. The terms of the insurance were sent to the assured who did not check them. The goods were shipped in the *Yasaka Maru* which was sunk by an enemy submarine and the goods were lost. The assured could not recover from the insurer as the policy provided cover for goods shipped on *Suwa Maru* only. Atkin J determined the question as whether or not the loss which the assured sustained is a reasonable and natural consequence of the broker's breach of contract. The judge stated that when a broker is employed to effect an insurance, especially when the broker employed is a person of repute and experience, the client is entitled to rely upon the broker carrying out his instructions. The assured is not bound to examine the documents drawn up in performance of those instructions and see whether his instructions have, in fact, been carried out by the broker. Atkin J took into account that in many cases the principal would not understand the matter, and would not know whether the document did in fact carry out his instructions. According to the judge, business could not be carried on if, when a person has been employed to use care and skill with regard to a matter, the employer is bound to use his own care and skill to see whether the person employed has done what he was employed to do. Similar concerns were expressed in *General Accident Fire and Life Assurance Corporation Ltd v Minet*,[80] where the broker defended the action against him by the argument that – although they did not take out the policy as he had been instructed – the terms of the reinsurance had been sent in a cover note to the reinsured who was presumed to have approved the cover in the absence of protest. Goddard LJ[81] said:

> But then it is said that the defendants delivered a cover note to the plaintiffs showing what reinsurance had been effected which they accepted without question. To succeed on this point the defendants must show that there was a ratification of their action, a ratification, that is, of their having effected a reinsurance different from that which their instructions required. The evidence entirely fails to prove this. Apart from the question whether the plaintiffs were under any duty to read the cover note, I am satisfied that the defendants have not proved that the plaintiffs understood that it did not represent the protection they desired and always desired. Mr Bunton, who was a marine underwriter, never, I think, understood the position under the original policy, and I am sure never intended to accept anything less than he had instructed Mr McRobert to obtain.

In *Youell*, Phillips J said that *Dickson v Devitt* was concerned with causation. The question in issue was whether the assured's own negligence broke the chain of causation. It was not there suggested

79 (1916) 86 LJ KB 315.
80 (1942) 74 Lloyd's Law Rep 1, 9.
81 (1942) 74 Lloyd's Law Rep 1, 9.

that the plaintiff owed the defendant a duty to inspect the insurance documents. The question was whether in failing to do so he was negligent in the conduct of his business in a respect which broke the chain of causation. The rejection of that case implied, *a fortiori*, that there was no breach of a duty owed to the defendant. In *General Accident v Minet*, Lord Justice Goddard at least implied agreement that there was no duty of any kind upon the insured to read the cover note. Phillips J did not apply either of the abovementioned two cases and awarded a proportionate remedy in line with the parties' respective fault which contributed to the loss in question. One reason for the ruling of Phillips J might be that the legal environment at the time *Dickson* and *Minet* were decided was different for the lack of availability to award a proportionate remedy and the second reason might be that in *Youell* the claimant was a reinsured who was an insurance company in the market. It is true that *Minet* was a reinsurance case as well, however, the difference was, as stated, the absence of the Contributory Negligence Act at the time. In *Youell* it is arguable that Phillips J found the reinsured 20 per cent liable as the reinsured could have understood the policy if he had read it.

Youell does not mean that the duty is transferred from the broker to the assured or reinsured if the latter signs and returns order letters which confirm the coverage obtained. Phillips J rejected the argument to this effect in *Youell* for the reason that if it is correct, a broker who has undertaken a contractual duty to exercise skill and care for his client can transfer to the client the duty of checking that such care had been exercised by the expedient sending of such a letter, with the result that if both broker and client fail to exercise care the loss falls on the client. The judge found no justification for imposing on the client a duty owed to the broker to check the suitability of the cover obtained with a degree of care similar to that which the broker is paid to employ when obtaining it.

In more recent cases it is seen that the courts emphasised that the assured is entitled to rely upon the broker carrying out his instructions, therefore the Courts are reluctant to impose a duty on the assured to check if the instructions had been carried out. Moreover, the Courts took into account that in most cases the assured will not be able to understand and interpret the terms of the policy. It is the broker's duty, due to his profession, to ensure that he obtained the cover which meets the assured's requirements and at the post-contractual stage to ensure that, if necessary, the assured is warned and understood the potential coverage issues. If the matter is about answering questions in the proposal form which were asked by the broker to the assured, having given the broker precisely the information for which he was asked, the assured is entitled to assume, when he subsequently received the proposal form and the policy, that what he had told the broker was all that was needed to bring about effective cover. It was no part of the assured's duty to second-guess his own professional adviser to impose contributory negligence.[82] In *Dunlop Haywards (DHL) Ltd v Barbon Insurance Group Ltd*,[83] the facts of which were given above, the broker argued that the assured signed the agreement without reading it, if he had read it he would have noticed the limited coverage on renewal. Hamblen J found on the facts that the assured was not at fault given that the assured asked for a summary of the cover from the brokers and also in an email to the assured the broker confirmed that the renewal had gone well. Hamblen J held that the assured had no reason to believe that his experienced brokers had failed to obtain quotes for the relevant cover on the relevant terms. In particular the judge found that the assured had no reason to believe that the broker obtained a quote for a fundamentally different and reduced cover and then failed to identify that such was the case. In all the circumstances, the assured's reliance on his professional brokers to carry out his instructions properly was reasonable, and there was no fault on his part.[84] Similarly, in *Tudor Jones v Crowley Colosso Ltd*[85] — a case in which the cover did not meet the assured's requirements, the judge

82 *Sharp v Sphere Drake Insurance (The Moonacre)* [1992] 2 Lloyd's Rep 501.
83 [2010] Lloyd's Rep IR 149.
84 In the same direction see *Ground Gilbey Ltd v Jardine Lloyd Thompson UK Ltd* [2012] Lloyd's Rep IR 12.
85 [1996] 2 Lloyd's Rep 619.

found the argument that the assured was guilty of contributory negligence in signing the certificate of practical completion for the marina without reviewing the efficacy of the cover, as 'hopeless'. Langley J held that the assured had placed the matter in the hands of experienced brokers, his instructions were clear and understood and he was assured by the brokers that he had got what he had asked for.

In a claim between placing and producing brokers

As seen above, in Youell, Phillips J decided that the reinsured should have been alerted by the 48-month limitation clause and the reinsured therefore was found to have contributed to the loss suffered mostly caused by the broker's negligence. It is arguable that in respect to contributory negligence the relationship between an insurer and an assured is different to a relationship between a reinsured and a reinsurer and between placing and producing brokers. While in the former it is not a strong argument that the assured should be alerted by the policy wording for the reason that the assured will not be able to understand the policy terms, in the latter category of relationships it is clear that the parties involved are all from the insurance market. A reinsured who also is an insurance company is expected to understand the policy wording offered by a reinsurer. Similarly, both producing and placing brokers are professionals who are subject to the duties which are akin to the duties owed by the producing broker to the assured. In a number of cases the courts discussed the contributory negligence matter between producing and placing brokers. This will not affect the assured's claim against the broker as the assured will be able to make 100 per cent of the claim from the producing broker in contract or tort, but when the producing broker turns to the placing broker in the relationship between the two agents, contributory negligence might be applicable.

In Tudor Jones v Crowley Colosso Ltd,[86] T acquired two neighbouring uninhabited islands in the Bahamas with a view to developing them as a holiday retreat. The development was to involve the construction of a marina, the necessary infrastructure works and the construction of a house, a guest house and other ancillary buildings and leisure facilities. T was a client of insurance brokers, M. M carried on their business in the USA. When T approached M to insure the developments in the Bahamas, M was not able to insure it in the USA and contacted C who carried on their business in London. C obtained cover for 'Contractors All Risk Insurance' in the London market.

The islands were struck by Hurricane Andrew during the currency of the policy. The hurricane caused substantial damage to both the marina and the works in progress. T claimed to recover for that damage under the policy. The insurers paid the claim insofar as it related to damage to the infrastructure work in progress, but refused to pay the claim for damage to the marina. A certificate of practical completion was issued for the marina works prior to Hurricane Andrew under the separate contract for those works. The marina works had been the subject of a certificate of substantial completion issued to the contractor and the policy wording contained an exclusion of indemnity for damage to any part of the works for which a certificate of completion had been issued. Exclusion clause (cl J) provided:

> The Insurer shall not be liable for loss of or damage to any part of the permanent works
> i) after such part has been taken into use by the owner . . . or
> ii) for which a certificate of completion has been issued . . .

The assured was thus unsuccessful in his claim for the part of the construction for which a certificate of completion had been issued before the hurricane. Both M and C were found liable for

---

86 [1996] 2 Lloyd's Rep 619.

their negligent act in drafting the contract in terms not meeting the assured's requirements. It was held that M, if he had acted prudently, would have known to what type of situation the exclusion would apply and if he had had any queries as to the scope of the exclusion clause, he should have raised them with C. Acting carefully and in his own client's interests, M should have read the contract carefully and appreciated the position before expressly approving the terms of the cover as they did. Moreover, C, as a prudent broker, would have drawn the exclusion expressly to M's attention. C's negligence contributed to both of the causes of loss to T. The judge found it appropriate to attribute the loss one-third to the responsibility of M and two-thirds to the responsibility of C.

Brokers' commission

The broker normally receives remuneration for placing the risk. Technically, commission is due from underwriters rather than the assured.[87] In *Power v Butcher*, Littledale J[88] said the commission is 'the amount . . . the underwriters would have allowed the broker to retain and deduct out of the premiums paid by him to them for underwriting the policies'.[89] That commission is ordinarily assessed on the premium;[90] the practice in the market is for the broker to deduct commission from the premium received before remitting it to underwriters. The broker earns the entirety of his commission when the risk is successfully placed. [91] Where under the policy payment of the premium is by instalments, commission is also payable by instalments, with brokers receiving remuneration by deductions as and when those instalments are received from the assured.[92] The broker is entitled to receive his remuneration even if the policy is cancelled. In *Velos Group Ltd v Harbour Insurance Services Ltd*,[93] Judge Hallgarten QC justified his ruling by emphasising that the premium is earned by the insurer and the broker is entitled to his remuneration on placement of the risk. Placement of the risk triggers the broker's entitlement for remuneration. A payment of premium clause merely defers payment of a liability which accrued at inception.[94] In such a case the broker is paid his commission every time premium is paid in an instalment, given that the broker deducts the premium from the payment by the assured. Judge Hallgarten QC noted that in those circumstances, as payment of commission is in practice likewise merely being deferred, there is no reason why the broker should lose his right for remuneration by reason of an agreement between underwriters and the assured cancelling the policy which ceases the premium payment. That, according to Judge Hallgarten QC, should not in any way affect or reduce the broker's rights.[95] In

87 *Great Western Insurance Co v Cunliffe* (1873–74) LR 9 Ch App 525; *Baring v Stanton* (1876) 3 Ch D 502; *HIH Casualty & General Insurance Ltd v JLT Risk Solutions Ltd (formerly Lloyd Thompson Ltd)* [2007] 2 Lloyd's Rep 278, para 60; *Velos Group Ltd v Harbour Insurance Services Ltd* [1997] 2 Lloyd's Rep 461, 463; *Wilson v Avec* [1974] 1 Lloyd's Rep 81, 82 Edmund Davies, LJ. It should be noted that in *Carvill America Incorporated v Camperdown UK Limited* [2004] EWHC 2221 (Comm) HHJ Havelock-Allan QC expressed some doubts about the existence of custom that brokerage is paid by the insurer (in this case by reinsurers) which required full trial to be determined. The Court of Appeal affirmed that this was one of the issues that require full trial to be determined. [2005] EWCA Civ 645.

88 (1829) 10 Barnewall and Cresswell 329, 344.

89 Littledale J added that the assured is supposed to have authorised the broker to take the commission from the premium paid.

90 *Johnston v Leslie & Godwin Financial Services Ltd* [1995] LR 472.

91 *Velos Group Ltd v Harbour Insurance Services Ltd* [1997] 2 Lloyd's Rep 461, 463.

92 *Velos Group Ltd v Harbour Insurance Services Ltd* [1997] 2 Lloyd's Rep 461, 463.

93 [1997] 2 Lloyd's Rep 461.

94 *Velos Group Ltd v Harbour Insurance Services Ltd* [1997] 2 Lloyd's Rep 461, 463.

95 In *Velos* the broker placed insurance covering a hull and machinery of four vessels for 12 months from 25 May 1995. The policy was in force for no longer than five of its 12 months as it was cancelled by mutual agreement between underwriters and the owners on 7 November 1995 with effect from 25 October 1995. The policy on its face referred to 'deferred' payment of premium, as per an attached clause providing for payment in four instalments, whereby in particular one-quarter of the annual premium was due and payable at inception with a further quarter due and payable two months thereafter. Both of these instalments were paid, with the consequence that as at termination the underwriters had received premium for six months.

that case the policy was subject to the Institute Time Clauses 1983, cl.22.1 of which provided for returns of premium to be made pro rata monthly net of each month should the insurance be cancelled by agreement. Judge Hallgarten QC held that this does not change but rather reinforces what he held. According to the judge, clause 22 has to be construed against the background that, prima facie, under marine policies the premium is indeed earned and payable at inception. The reference to underwriters being obliged only to make a net payment means that cancellation was intended, prima facie, to be a matter to be dealt with on a bilateral basis between underwriters and assured, without affecting or prejudicing the rights of the broker.[96] In conclusion, the broker had a vested right to their entire commission over 12 months and, absent a waiver, Judge Hallgarten QC found no reason why the cancellation agreed between the assured and underwriters should affect such entitlement.[97]

As seen in Chapter 6 under section 53 and 82 of the Marine Insurance Act 1906, despite the fact that brokers are responsible for the payment of premium, underwriters are directly accountable to the assured for any premium which may have to be returned. The question that may then arise is whether the broker is entitled to enforce their claim for commission by retaining the moneys which they received from underwriters. It may be argued that the broker is merely a conduit for repayment of the premium and thus holds such repayment in a fiduciary capacity and thus is unable to deduct commission which was due as a matter of contract. This argument was rejected in *Velos* by Judge Hallgarten QC who found no reason why the broker should not have been entitled to retain or set off by way of deduction from what was received from underwriters before being passed on to the assured insofar as there were moneys legitimately due to the broker in the form of commission.[98]

Further reading

Bennett, *The Law of Marine Insurance*, 2nd edn, [2006] Oxford University Press. Chapter 5.

Blanchard, 'Reform of the pre-contractual duty of disclosure of the agent to insure: evolution or revolution?', *Lloyd's Maritime and Commercial Law Quarterly* [2013] 3(August), 325–340.

Cole, 'A practitioner's perspective on placement duties of insurance brokers and reflections of the proposals of the law commissions', Chapter 5 in Soyer (ed.), *Reforming Marine and Commercial Insurance Law* [2008] Informa.

Gilman et al., *Arnould: Law of Marine Insurance and Average*, 18th edn, [2013] Sweet & Maxwell. Chapter 7.

Merkin, *Colinvaux's Law of Insurance*, 9th edn [2010] Sweet & Maxwell, Chapter 15.

Merkin, 'Marine insurance', *British Insurance Law Association Journal* [2009] 118, 75 (case summary on *Allianz Insurance Co Egypt v Aigaion Insurance Co SA*).

Merkin and Lowry, 'Reconstructing insurance law: the Law Commissions' consultation paper', *Modern Law Review* [2008] 71(1), 95–113.

Rose, *Marine Insurance: Law and Practice*, 2nd edn, [2012] Informa. Chapter 4.

Thomas, Sir John, 'Evolving role of insurance brokers', *British Insurance Law Association Journal* [2012] 125, 29–38.

---

96 *Velos Group Ltd v Harbour Insurance Services Ltd* [1997] 2 Lloyd's Rep 461, 464.

97 *Velos Group Ltd v Harbour Insurance Services Ltd* [1997] 2 Lloyd's Rep 461, 464.

98 *Velos Group Ltd v Harbour Insurance Services Ltd* [1997] 2 Lloyd's Rep 461, 464.

Chapter 15

Reinsurance

Chapter Contents

Definition and types of reinsurance

An insurer who has just insured a risk may want to re-insure it with another insurer. In other words, he may share the risk and the premium with other insurers. Reinsurance is therefore defined as insurance of insurance companies.[1]

An insurer may transfer the risk to another insurer proportionally or non-proportionally. Proportional and non-proportional reinsurance contracts may be in the form of facultative, obligatory or facultative obligatory. If facultative reinsurance is proportional, that contract transfers a single risk to the reinsurer. For instance, a mobile offshore drilling unit which will be carried on a barge from a port in the USA to a port in Malaysia may be insured under a voyage policy and then may be reinsured by a facultative proportional reinsurance. In this case a single risk is insured and then reinsured. In this type of contract the reinsurer and the reinsured may share the risk and the premium proportionally. For instance, if the mobile offshore drilling unit is worth £1m and if the policy is valued, upon total loss of the subject matter insured the insurer indemnifies the assured for £1m. Assuming that the reinsurer took over 50 per cent of the risk insured, the reinsured may then claim half of the loss from the reinsurer.

Reinsurance involves international transactions, for instance a Turkish insurer may insure a local risk and reinsure the risk in London. It may be the case that the insurer insures 100 per cent of the risk and then transfers the whole risk to the reinsurers in London. This arrangement is named as 'fronting' as the insurer is acting as a front for the reinsurers.

If the risk transferred is not a single risk but the insurance and the reinsurance cover a large number of risks, reinsurance appears in the form of a treaty. A treaty is a mechanism for reinsuring risks, either by class or by way of whole account.[2] A treaty is in essence a framework facility under which risks falling within its scope may be ceded to the reinsurers.[3]

Treaties may be proportional or non-proportional. In a proportional treaty the reinsured cedes to the reinsurers an agreed proportion of all risks accepted. Surplus and quota share treaties are proportional types of treaty.[4] The most common type of non-proportional treaty is an excess of loss treaty under which the reinsurers become liable when the reinsured's aggregate losses reach a stated sum.[5] If the treaty is facultative the reinsured has discretion to cede a risk and the reinsurer has discretion to accept a declaration. An obligatory treaty does not grant discretion to either the reinsured or the reinsurer. The reinsured is obliged to cede, and the reinsurer has to accept those risks covered by the treaty.[6] The risks insured are also reinsured so long as they fall within the scope of the cover. Obligatory treaty may be in the form of quota share.[7] There may be an obligation on the reinsured to keep the reinsurers informed of risks as and when they are accepted. The reinsured performs the duty by means of periodic bordereaux but unless the treaty otherwise provides a failure to declare, a risk reinsured will not prevent the risk from attaching and the only remedy open to the reinsurers is to seek damages if loss can be proved.[8] In facultative obligatory reinsurance the

---

1   *Travellers Casualty & Surety Co of Europe Ltd v Commissioners of Customs and Excise* [2006] Lloyd's Rep IR 63, para 43 and 57; Colinvaux, para 17–001.

2   Colinvaux, para 17–001.

3   Colinvaux, para 17–001.

4   Colinvaux, para 17–001.

5   In *Equitas Ltd v R&Q Reinsurance Co (UK) Ltd* [2010] Lloyd's Rep IR 600.

6   *Aneco Reinsurance Underwriting Ltd (In Liquidation) v Johnson & Higgins Ltd* [2002] 1 Lloyd's Rep 157, 165.

7   *Aneco Reinsurance Underwriting Ltd (In Liquidation) v Johnson & Higgins Ltd* [2002] 1 Lloyd's Rep 157, 165; *Glencore International AG v Ryan (The Beursgracht) (No.1)* [2002] 1 Lloyd's Rep 574, para 31.

8   *Glencore International AG v Ryan (The Beursgracht)* [2002] 1 Lloyd's Rep 574. See also *Hanwha Non-Life Insurance Co Ltd v Alba Pte Ltd* [2011] SGHC 271, where the issue was whether the treaty was wholly facultative or facultative/obligatory so that declarations were binding on the reinsurers. The latter was held to be the case in light of the fixed premium, aggregate financial limits and the requirement to make declarations a month in arrears only.

reinsured has an open option to declare risks falling within the terms of the cover, and the reinsurer is obliged to accept such declarations.[9] For instance in *Aneco Reinsurance Underwriting Ltd (In Liquidation) v Johnson & Higgins Ltd*,[10] Aneco subscribed to three units out of ten of a permanent special priority treaty which was a reinsurance of the marine excess of loss account of Syndicates 255, 258, 259 and 668 underwritten by B. The retrocession[11] was in the following terms: 'The Reassured may cede . . . and the Reinsurers shall accept . . . risks up to a maximum of $25,000 any one unit in respect of any risk as may be declared.' The facultative obligatory treaty was described as unpopular with some underwriters as the reinsured, B, could decide which risks to declare under the treaty, but the reinsurers Aneco were bound to accept them, within the treaty limits.[12]

The parties

A reinsurance contract is formed between two insurers. The insurer who covers the risk in the original insurance is called the reinsured in the reinsurance agreement, as he is the party who asks for coverage from the reinsurers. The contract between the assured and the insurer is original insurance (or underlying or direct insurance); the contract between the reinsured and the reinsurer is the reinsurance. There is no privity of contract between the assured (of the original insurance) and the reinsurer.[13] The assured's claim is to be addressed to the insurer, the assured is not entitled to claim directly against the reinsurers.[14]

Formation of reinsurance contracts

As seen in Chapter 2 the London market operates as a subscription market and the insurers take lines on insurance policies by their percentage of the risk they insure. The same applies to reinsurance in that reinsurers subscribe to a reinsurance contract. Therefore, a reinsurance broker will visit several underwriters to be able to achieve the amount of subscription which has been requested by the insurers (reinsured).

A reinsurance contract may be offered before an original insurance contract is formed. By virtue of a unilateral offer obtained from the reinsurer, a broker, while visiting the Boxes at Lloyd's, may be able to inform the insurers that in the case of subscription to the original risk, the reinsurance cover for such risk has already been obtained. This unilateral offer is called a 'standing offer' that when a broker obtains a subscription from an insurer within the conditions of the standing offer, when the risk is insured, the reinsurer is bound by the standing offer so that the risk is insured and reinsured at the same time.[15]

---

9   *Citadel Insurance Co v Atlantic Union Insurance Co SA* [1982] 2 Lloyd's Rep 543, 545, Kerr LJ.

10   [2002] 1 Lloyd's Rep 157.

11   Retrocession is re-insurance of re-insurance, that the reinsurer transfers the risk reinsured to another underwriter who will be called in this contractual relationship as retrocessionaire. In other words, retrocession is re-re-insurance.

12   *Aneco Reinsurance Underwriting Ltd (In Liquidation) v Johnson & Higgins Ltd* [2002] 1 Lloyd's Rep 157, 164. The reinsurers would not bear a proportionate part of the reinsured's account, good risks as well as bad, and they would not receive a proportionate part of the whole of the premium income. Instead, they could be discriminated against and find themselves reinsuring the poorer risks without the better ones: the process known as 'anti-selection' of risks. See page 165.

13   Hobhouse J in *Phoenix General Insurance Co of Greece SA v Halvanon Insurance Co Ltd* [1985] 2 Lloyd's Rep 599, 614; *Re Law Guarantee Trust and Accident Society* [1914] 2 Ch 617; *Versicherungs und Transport A/G. Daugava v Henderson* (1934) 49 Ll L Rep 252.

14   If the reinsurance contract contains a cut-through clause the assured may be permitted to make a direct claim against the reinsurers in case of insolvency of the reinsured.

15   *General Accident Fire & Life Assurance Corp Ltd v Tanter (The Zephyr)* [1984] 1 Lloyd's Rep 58.

Duty of good faith

The principles covered in Chapter 4 are applicable to reinsurance contracts as well as contracts of marine insurance. The reinsured is under the duty to disclose material facts to the reinsurers before the contract is concluded. For instance, in *WISE Underwriting Agency Ltd v Grupo Nacional Provincial SA*,[16] a case referred to in Chapter 4, regarding waiver of breach of the duty of good faith, the original insurance policy was in Spanish and when the reinsurance risk was presented, the Spanish word 'watch' was translated as 'clock' into English. The Rolex watches were to be carried from Miami to Cancun. The loss occurred when a quantity of goods was stolen from a container parked outside the assured's warehouse premises in Cancun. The reinsurers rejected the claim on the score of material misrepresentation of the subject matter insured, which was accepted by the court. The presentation of the subject matter insured as clocks was a material fact given that watches, and in particular brands such as Rolex, are regarded by underwriters as attractive targets for thieves, being portable, high value and easily disposable.[17]

In *Aneco Reinsurance Underwriting Ltd (In Liquidation) v Johnson & Higgins Ltd*,[18] the reinsurance agreement was in the facultative obligatory form. When obtaining the retrocession cover for the reinsurance contract the broker did not disclose the true nature of the reinsurance. This was a material fact in a retrocession contract which was in the excess of loss form.

Terms of reinsurance contracts

Reinsurance contracts may be worded as being 'subject to the same terms and conditions as original'. This wording was held to incorporate the terms of the original insurance into the reinsurance contract.[19] The way it operates in a proportional facultative reinsurance is that when the insurer is liable under the terms of the original insurance, the reinsurer will be liable. This is so because the reinsured transferred some proportionate part of the risk to the reinsurer, the reinsured and the reinsurers shared the risk and the premium, and the reinsurance contract was expressed to contain the same terms of the original insurance contract.

In *HIH Casualty & General Insurance Ltd v New Hampshire Insurance Co*,[20] the Court of Appeal explained the requirements that have to be met in analysing incorporation of terms from original insurance into reinsurance contracts. A term may be incorporated if it:

a)   is germane to the reinsurance;
b)   makes sense, subject to permissible 'manipulation', in the context of the reinsurance;
c)   is consistent with the express terms of the reinsurance; and
d)   is apposite for inclusion in the reinsurance.

---

16   [2004] 2 Lloyd's Rep 483.
17   The reinsurers nevertheless had to pay to the reinsured in this case as they were held to have waived the breach of duty of good faith.
18   [2002] 1 Lloyd's Rep 157.
19   *HIH Casualty & General Insurance Ltd v New Hampshire Insurance Co* [2001] 2 Lloyd's Rep 161.
20   [2001] 2 Lloyd's Rep 161.

Limits of incorporation

Where a reinsurance contract includes the clause 'all terms and conditions as original', the word 'all' is not to be read as comprising 'all' terms of the original policy.[21] The terms germane to reinsurance are confined to those provisions defining the period, the geographical limits and the nature of the risk undertaken by the reinsurer.[22] The incorporation clause is not to be interpreted as encompassing clauses which are inconsistent with the reinsurance agreement.[23] Even if a clause complies with other requirements, incorporation is not allowed to the extent that it contradicts the express provisions of the reinsurance.[24] It is also permissible to incorporate a term which refers to, for example, the 'insurer' by manipulating it to read 'reinsurer'.[25]

An example of a term which cannot be incorporated might be a time bar clause that requires the assured to make a claim in a 12-month period running from the date of loss. This term cannot be applied to claims made by the reinsured against the reinsurer, because the reinsured's loss cannot be assessed before the assured's loss is determined. The issue came before the Privy Council in Home Insurance Co of New York v Victoria Montreal Fire Insurance Co.[26] In this case the Western Assurance Company of Canada issued a policy for the Canadian Pacific Railway Company covering railway property situated in the United States of America, Canada and Mexico. Home Insurance reinsured the 20 per cent of the risk and the defendant Victoria–Montreal Fire Insurance Company retroceded the Home Insurance reinsurance policy. On 26 April 1900, a considerable amount of property belonging to the Canadian Pacific Railway Company was destroyed by a fire. After a lengthy inquiry, Western Assurance indemnified the assured, the reinsurer then paid their proportion of loss. The retrocessionaire then denied Home Insurance's claim against them by relying on the limitation clause contained in the original policy, and alleged by them to be incorporated with and applicable to their policy of retrocession. The Privy Council expressed their view that such a clause, namely one prescribing legal proceedings after a limited period, is a reasonable provision in a policy of insurance against direct loss to specific property where the assured is master of the situation in that he can bring his action immediately. In a case of reinsurance against liability however the reinsured cannot move until the direct loss is ascertained between parties over whom he has no control, and in proceedings in which he cannot intervene. The Court also emphasised that applying the same provision within the retrocession context might defeat an honest claim in a case where there was no default or delay on the part of the reinsured or the reinsurer as the case may be.

Jurisdiction and choice of law clauses are not incorporated by the general words of incorporation. Such clauses in direct insurance have nothing to do with defining the risk; thus they are found wholly inappropriate to disputes arising between the parties to the reinsurance contract.[27] Similarly, arbitration clauses cannot be incorporated because of their ancillary and separable nature.[28]

---

21 Pine Top Insurance Co Ltd v Unione Italiana Anglo Saxon Reinsurance Co Ltd [1987] 1 Lloyd's Rep 476; Municipal Mutual Insurance Ltd v Sea Insurance Co Ltd [1996] CLC 1515, 1527.

22 Pine Top Insurance Co Ltd v Unione Italiana Anglo Saxon Reinsurance Co Ltd [1987] 1 Lloyd's Rep 476.

23 Municipal Mutual Insurance Ltd v Sea Insurance Co Ltd [1996] CLC 1515; Home Insurance Company of New York v Victoria – Montreal Fire Insurance Company [1907] AC 59.

24 Australian Widows' Fund Life Assurance Society, Ltd v National Mutual Life Association of Australasia [1914] AC 634.

25 CNA International Reinsurance Co Ltd v Companhia de Seguros Tranquilidade SA [1999] Lloyd's Rep IR 289.

26 [1907] AC 59.

27 Excess Insurance Co Ltd & Anor v Mander [1995] CLC 838; Trygg Hansa Insurance Co Ltd v Equitas Ltd [1998] 2 Lloyd's Rep 439; Assicurazioni Generali SPA v Ege Sigorta AS [2002] Lloyd's Rep IR 480; The expression 'all terms whatsoever' does not change the position: Siboti K/S v BP France SA [2003] 2 Lloyd's Rep 364. AIG Europe (UK) Ltd v Anonymous Greek Co of General Insurances, The Ethniki [1999] Lloyd's Rep IR 221.

28 Pine Top Insurance Co v Unione Italiana Anglo Saxon Reinsurance Co [1987] 1 Lloyd's Rep 476; Excess Insurance Co Ltd & Anor v Mander [1995] CLC 838; American International Speciality Lines Insurance Co v Abbott Laboratories [2003] 1 Lloyd's Rep 267; Cigna Life Insurance Co of Europe SA-NV & Ors v Intercaser SA de Seguros y Reaseguros [2001] CLC 1356; OK Petroleum AB v Vitol Energy SA [1995] 2 Lloyd's Rep 160.

If an arbitration, jurisdiction or a choice of law clause is intended to be incorporated, the reinsurance contract should expressly state so. Incorporation of terms from the direct policy should be distinguished from incorporation of terms from other sources, such as standard market wordings. In the latter case problems may arise from inconsistency between the standard terms and the express terms of the incorporating contract, which the court will be required to resolve. For instance in *Axa v Ace Global Markets*,[28a] the reinsurance was on 'Full wording as EXEL 1.1.90.' Gloster J found it possible to reconcile the arbitration clause in standard EXEL wording with the English choice of law and jurisdiction clause in the reinsurance slip by holding that the latter related to supervision of the arbitration and challenges to any award and, accordingly held that the arbitration clause was incorporated with other standard clauses in EXEL 1.1.90.

Implied terms

In the context of proportional facultative obligatory contracts, in *Phoenix General Insurance Co of Greece SA v Halvanon Insurance Co Ltd*,[29] Hobhouse J stated, *obiter*, that a number of terms are to be implied for the protection of reinsurers. These are:

a) keeping proper records and accounts of risks accepted, premiums received and claims made or notified;
b) investigating all claims and confirm that there is liability before liability is accepted;
c) acting prudently in the acceptance of risks;
d) keeping full and accurate accounts showing sums owing and owed;
e) ensuring that all amounts owing are collected promptly, and that all amounts payable are paid promptly;
f) making all documents reasonably available to reinsurers.

The implied term 'acting prudently in acceptance of risks' was discussed in *Bonner v Cox*[30] in the context of a non-proportional reinsurance. In *Bonner v Cox*, a number of Lloyd's Syndicates subscribed to an energy risks open cover (the 77 cover). The reinsurance was in the form of an excess of loss treaty which was offered to any underwriters who subscribed to the 77 Cover. One of the declarations to that facility was an oil well in California, referred to as Elk Point. There had been a blow-out of an oil well covered by the Elk Point declaration. The reinsurers denied liability. They argued that the reinsured had engaged in 'writing against' the reinsurance. The argument was that one important risk accepted under the 77 Cover – known as the Oceaneering risk – could not have been profitable without reinsurance, and that the insurers owed an implied duty of care to the reinsurers to write the risk as if there was no reinsurance – that is, that it had to be potentially profitable in its own right. The reinsurers argued that a term implied in the reinsurance contract that the reinsured was 'to conduct the business involved in the cession prudently, reasonably carefully and in accordance with the ordinary practice of the market'. Morison J held and the Court of Appeal agreed that the *Phoenix* formulation did not apply to non-proportional reinsurance. Morrison J imposed a restrictive duty on the reinsured that (a) only to accept risks which would be written in the ordinary course of business; and (b) not to write business recklessly. The Court of Appeal rejected Morison J's suggestions. Reinsurers were protected by the duty of utmost good faith, which required disclosure of the types of business to be written, and also by their own ability to use

---

28a [2006] Lloyd's Rep IR 683.
29 [1985] 2 Lloyd's Rep 599.
30 [2006] 2 Lloyd's Rep 152.

express wordings which clearly defined the nature of the risks reinsured and which entitled the reinsurers to monitor the progress of the business. Failure to take these steps ought not to allow the reinsurers to blame the reinsured. The Court of Appeal felt that dishonesty, wilful misconduct or recklessness in the writing of a risk – as where the reinsured simply exercised no underwriting judgment – might provide a remedy, not by way of breach of implied term but on the ground that the reinsurance properly construed would not cover the risk at all. The Court of Appeal noted that in a proportional contract there is a sharing of premium and losses between reinsurer and reinsured. Its function is to allow the reinsured to write business which he would not otherwise have written by increasing his capacity. A non-proportional contract, by contrast, did not involve any such sharing and indeed the parties had their own separate commercial interests: its purpose was similarly to allow the reinsured to write business which it would not otherwise have written, not by increasing capacity but rather by affording protection for existing capacity. The Court of Appeal also noted that the authorities were against any implication of the term suggested. The Court referred to *Sphere Drake Insurance v Euro International Underwriting Ltd*[31] where even '*arbitrage*'[32] was not a breach of duty as such but was a matter for pre-contract disclosure. It was submitted that this analysis throws doubt on the other implied terms identified in *Phoenix*, and it may be thought that there is little justification for such implication given that there are various market wordings governing claims handling and that reinsurers have no right to assume that the courts will protect them if their contract is silent.[33]

Presumption of back-to-back cover

The 'as original' clause confirms the back-to-back nature of the original insurance and proportional reinsurance contracts. In proportional reinsurance the reinsured's liability forms the reinsurers' liability. The reinsurers and the reinsured share the premium and the risk. It may be the case that the reinsurers may want wider protection than the reinsured has under the original insurance. In this case the reinsurers should add expressly the clauses which they believe will provide the additional protection they desire to have. Unless the reinsurance contract contains anything which cannot be seen in the original insurance, if the reinsurance terms are written 'as original' it is presumed that the two contracts provide identical cover and when the insurer is liable, the reinsurers will be liable up to the proportional amount they agreed to cover.

In *Forsikringsaktieselskapet Vesta v Butcher*,[34] the House of Lords interpreted the warranty in the original insurance and which was incorporated into the reinsurance, in the same manner, as it was interpreted under the direct insurance. In *Vesta*, the original insurance was governed by Norwegian law which requires a chain of causation between the breach and the loss in case there is a breach of warranty. The warranty required the assured, who insured his fish farm, to provide a 24-hour watch warranty. The assured never appointed an employee to provide this, thus he was in breach of warranty. The breach however did not cause the loss since the fish farm was destroyed by a severe storm. The insurer was liable under Norwegian law. The reinsurance contract was 'as original' and it was governed by English law. If the reinsurance warranty was to be construed under English law, the reinsurers would not have been liable. However, the House of Lords held that because of

---

31 [2003] 1 Lloyd's Rep IR 525. In *Glasgow Assurance v Symondson* (1911) 16 Com Cas 109, it had been held that cover holders did not owe any duty of care to underwriters.

32 The deliberate writing of business which would inevitably produce a gross loss which would be made good by reinsurance, even though the premium received by the reinsurers was too small to cover their losses.

33 Colinvaux, para 17–28.

34 [1989] 1 Lloyd's Rep 331.

the back-to-back nature of the proportional facultative reinsurance, the reinsurance warranty was to be construed in the same way as the original insurance warranty.

The presumption was applied in *Groupama Navigation et Transports v Catatumbo CA Seguros*[35] despite the fact that the reinsurance contract contained an express warranty 'warranted class maintained'. This was the same warranty as that seen in the original insurance contract. The Court of Appeal construed the original insurance and reinsurance warranties in the same manner; the insurer was liable according to the interpretation of warranties under Venezuelan law. This interpretation was held to be binding for the reinsurers whose contract was governed by English law. In *Groupama* the warranties were identical in that the assured guaranteed maintenance of class according to the ABS (American Bureau of Shipping) Standards and Rules. Thus, the Court of Appeal held that – although the reinsurance contract contained an express warranty in addition to the 'as original' wording – the original insurance warranty was carried into the reinsurance warranty, which was to be construed in the same manner as the original insurance warranty.

The presumption of back-to-back cover did not operate in *GE Reinsurance Corp (formerly Kemper Reinsurance Co) v New Hampshire Insurance Co*,[36] in which the reinsurance contract contained a warranty which did not appear in the original insurance. The warranty in the reinsurance contract provided that a contract of employment in respect of S 'be maintained for the duration of the Policy'. The original insurance did not contain any provision relating to the employment of S. Langley J distinguished *Vesta* in which the original insurance warranty was incorporated into the reinsurance. In *GE Reinsurance*, one policy was wholly silent on the relevant words which the other contained.[37] Similarly, the presumption did not operate in *Aegis Electrical and Gas International Services Co Ltd v Continental Casualty Co*[38] where the words 'accident' and 'object' were defined both in the original insurance and reinsurance and the definitions were not identical. The definition in the reinsurance made it clear that the scope of coverage of the reinsurance was narrower than that of the direct insurance.

Non-proportional reinsurance

The presumption of back-to-back cover does not operate in non-proportional reinsurance.[39] However, it has been recently expressed that where the reinsurance is worded as original, in a non-proportional agreement, the tendency is reading the original insurance and reinsurance policy terms in the same manner, that is, as it was read under the original insurance. In *Tokio Marine Europe Insurance Ltd v Novae Corporate Underwriting Ltd*,[40] the reinsurers retroceded the loss reinsured up to £25m in excess of £53m. Under the original insurance 'Occurrence' is defined to mean 'any one Occurrence or any series of Occurrences consequent upon or attributable to one source or original cause.' A series of floods occurred in Thailand in respect of which the assured and the reinsured settled the claim and the reinsurers indemnified the reinsured. Retrocessionaire however denied liability, reasoning that occurrence within the context of retrocession is 'something which happens at a particular time, at a particular place, in a particular way'.[41] Hamblen J held that the retrocession was to cover the reinsured's exposure to losses arising from occurrences which have a defined meaning from the original insurance and which was incorporated into the Retrocession. Against that background,

---

35 [2000] 2 Lloyd's Rep 350.
36 [2004] Lloyd's Rep IR 404.
37 [2004] Lloyd's Rep IR 404, para 43.
38 [2008] Lloyd's Rep IR 17.
39 *AXA Reinsurance (UK) Ltd v Field* [1996] 2 Lloyd's Rep 233; *Tokio Marine Europe Insurance Ltd v Novae Corporate Underwriting Ltd* [2013] EWHC 3362 (Comm), para 35.
40 [2013] EWHC 3362 (Comm).
41 [2013] EWHC 3362 (Comm), para 60.

the judge held that if the parties had intended for a different type of occurrence to be covered by the Retrocession they would surely have clearly spelt out i) that that was the intention and ii) what the different meaning was to be.[42]

A similar discussion is seen in *Amlin Corporate Member Ltd v Oriental Assurance Corp*[42a] in which the reinsurers attempted to prevent the same interpretation as *Vesta* in their reinsurance contracts. In *Amlin* an insurance company, Oriental, established in the Philippines insured the owner of the Vessel, Sulpicio Lines Inc ('Sulpici'), a Philippine shipping company, in respect of its liability in the period 31 December 2007 to 31 December 2008 for loss of or damage to cargo. The cover provided under the policy of insurance contained a typhoon warranty clause in the following terms: 'Notwithstanding anything contained in the Policy or Clauses attached hereto, it is expressly warranted that the Vessel carrying subject shipment shall not sail or put out of sheltered Port when there is a typhoon or strom [sic – should be "storm"] warning at that port nor when her destination or intended route may be within the possible path of a typhoon or storm announced at port or [sic – should be "of"] sailing, port of destination or any intervening point. Violation of this warranty shall render this policy "VOID". However, should the vessel have sailed out of port prior to there being such a warning, this warranty, only in so far as the particular voyage is concerned, shall not apply but shall be immediately reinstated upon arrival at safe port.'

Oriental reinsured the risk in London. The Reinsurance Policy, which was governed by English law, contained a 'follow the settlements' condition in the following terms: 'To follow all terms, conditions and settlements of the original policy issued by the Reinsured to the Insured, for the period specified herein, in respect of sums and interests hereby insured.' The Reinsurance Policy contained a typhoon warranty which is identical to the original insurance warranty except it omitted the second paragraph (starting 'However . . .') of the original insurance warranty. One of the scheduled vessels under the original policy was the *Princess of the Stars*, a Ro-Ro vehicle and passenger ferry. The vessel left Manila on 20 June 2008 despite the warning of a typhoon. It had cargo loaded on board as well as 713 passengers and 138 crew. The vessel was lost during voyage, over 800 lives were lost and only 32 of those on board survived. In the Philippines a number of claims were brought by cargo interests against Sulpicio and Oriental. While those claims were working their way through the Philippine Courts, the reinsurers sought negative declaratory relief in England that the reinsurance warranty should be interpreted under English law but not in the same manner as the original insurance warranty.

Even in non-proportional contracts, the courts may interpret identical wording in the same manner. Thus, in *Amlin*, what the reinsurers were aiming to achieve was a situation similar to *Vesta*, that is, application of a possible interpretation of a warranty under the local law in their reinsurance contract. Such interpretation, as seen in *Vesta*, might differ from the English law interpretation of a warranty which then may render both the insurers and the reinsurers liable although the reinsurance contract is governed by English law. After lengthy proceedings[43] the reinsurers were successful in obtaining the declaratory relief sought. Lady Justice Gloster[44] was prepared to accept that the original insurance and reinsurance contract warranties should be construed identically. However, her Ladyship rejected the reinsured's argument to this effect reasoning that there was no evidence, expert or otherwise, adduced as to what would be understood in the Philippines by a typhoon warranty in the terms in which the warranty was expressed in either policy, or as to how the typhoon warranty in the Original Policy might be interpreted as a matter of Philippine law. Accordingly,

---

42 [2013] EWHC 3362 (Comm), para 61.

42a [2014] EWCA Civ 1135.

43 The Courts first discussed if the English proceedings should stay [2013] Lloyd's Rep IR 131, and then the Courts decided if the negative declaratory relief should be granted [2014] EWCA Civ 1135.

44 [2014] EWCA Civ 1135, para 35.

the clause in the reinsurance policy was to be construed in accordance with its terms and in accordance with English law.[45]

Assessing the deductibles and loss

The presumption may also operate to assess the amount that the reinsurers will be liable. In *Gard Marine and Energy Ltd v Tunnicliffe*,[46] Devon Energy Corporation (Devon), a large independent oil exploration and production company, was insured under an Energy Package Insurance. The policy was against all risks of physical loss or damage to offshore and onshore property, and business interruption. The policy was subject to a combined single limit of US$400m (for 100 per cent interest), any one accident or occurrence arising out of a Named Windstorm in the Gulf of Mexico. The policy stated:

> [the] Combined Single Limit of Liability . . . [and] the Assured's Retention . . . shall be reduced proportionately and shall apply in the same proportion as the total interest of the Assured in said well hereunder bears to 100% . . .

Gard subscribed to a 12.5 per cent share under the Original Policy. Gard then reinsured 7.5 per cent of its 12.5 per cent line with various Lloyd's syndicates including Advent whose share was 2 per cent. Glacier Re reinsured 5 per cent. The reinsurance was 'subject to all terms, clauses, and conditions as Original and to follow the Original in every respect'. The 'Sum Insured' clause in the reinsurance policy provided: 'To pay up to Original Package Policy limits/amounts/sums insured excess of USD250 million (100%) any one occurrence of losses to the original placement.'

Hurricane Rita caused Devon to suffer substantial losses. Total loss was US$912.5m, Devon's interest was about 46 per cent, that is, US$416m. The claim was settled in the sum of US$365m. Gard's share of the payment was 12.5 per cent of this amount, that is, US$45,625,000. A dispute arose in relation to the deductible. Two interpretations were suggested before the Court:

1. (100 per cent) in the sum insured clause meant that it was necessary to 'scale' the deductible to match the assured's actual interest in the insured subject matter. Thus, the deductible would be reduced from US$250m to US$114m. The amount recoverable was US$365m minus US$114m, thus US$251m. Two per cent of this amount would be US$5,020,737.

2. the deductible was not to be scaled. The full US$250m was to be deducted from the loss of US$365m: US$115m. Two per cent of US$115m = US$2.3m.

The Court accepted the first interpretation. The Court confirmed that a contract is to be construed in the way that it would have been understood by a reasonable person having all the background knowledge which would reasonably have been available to the parties in the situation in which they were at the time of the contract. The reinsurance contract was subject to the same terms and conditions as original. It was supported by expert evidence of the market for insurance of offshore energy risks that the notation '(100 per cent)' had a specialised and recognised meaning, namely, that of scaling.

---

45 [2014] EWCA Civ 1135, para 36.
46 [2012] Lloyd's Rep IR 1.

An exceptional case – *Wasa*

Although the presumption of back-to-back cover is settled law in proportional reinsurance, there might be exceptional circumstances even in a proportional reinsurance contract in which the Court might refuse to apply the presumption. This was seen in the House of Lords decision in *Wasa International Insurance Co Ltd v Lexington Insurance Co.*[47] In *Wasa* the assured purchased property insurance in the United States and reinsured the risk in London. The reinsurance was proportional, when the risk occurred, 98 per cent of the reinsurers agreed to pay but the two reinsurers refused payment for the reason that under English law the reinsurers were not liable. The original insurance contract contained a service of suit clause which entitled the assured to sue the insurer in any competent jurisdiction in the United States. The relevant Court would then apply its own conflicts of law rules to determine the law which would govern the dispute. The reinsurance contracts were subject to English law. The original insurance was from 1 July 1977 until 1 July 1980 and the reinsurance cover was for 36 months from 1 July 1977. Up to this point it seems that all was similar to *Vesta* – except the Service of Suit clause seen in *Wasa*. The assured was required to incur expenses for clean-up costs which was ordered by the Environment Agency on the sites at which the assured was active. The assured then claimed the cost from the insurer. The insurer denied liability and the assured sued the insurer in Washington. The Washington Courts applied their conflicts of law rules and decided that the law of Pennsylvania governed the insurance contract. Under the contractual construction rules in the law of Pennsylvania the court determined that 'all' within the insuring clause 'all loss of or damage to property' meant all, therefore the insurer was liable for the loss occurred not only between 1977–1980 but throughout the entire period that the loss occurred – approximately between 1946 until 1990. The insurer settled the claim. The reinsurers argued that they were not liable as the settlement amount covered expenses incurred outside the terms of the reinsurance. The House of Lords decided in favour of the reinsurers. Their Lordships distinguished *Wasa* from *Vesta* for the reason that in *Wasa* because of the Service of Suit clause the reinsurers did not know at the time they entered into the contract which law would govern the insurance agreement, therefore, they cannot be presumed to have agreed to be bound, whatever the interpretation of the original insurance contract would be. In *Vesta*, however, at the outset of the contract the reinsurers had known that the law of Norway would govern the original insurance and it was possible for them to assess the possible liability to arise in the future.

Proof of reinsured's liability in claims against reinsurers

While making a claim against the reinsurers, a reinsured will be required to establish its liability to the assured under the original insurance.[48] Moreover, the loss should fall within the reinsurance policy cover. There may be a judgment[49] given against the reinsured or there might have been an arbitration award holding the reinsured liable under the original insurance.[50] Where the reinsurance contract is written as original, normally the reinsurers will be liable upon the establishment of the reinsured's liability under the original insurance. This is so for the reason that the 'as original' wording confirms the back-to-back cover between the reinsurance and original insurance contracts.

---

47 [2009] 2 Lloyd's Rep 508.
48 *Re London County Commercial Reinsurance Office Ltd* [1922] 2 Ch 67, 80, PO Lawrence J; *Hill v Mercantile & General Reinsurance Co plc* [1996] 3 All ER 865.
49 *Lumbermans Mutual Casualty Co v Bovis Lend Lease Ltd* [2005] 1 Lloyd's Rep 494.
50 *Gan Insurance Co Ltd v Tai Ping Insurance Co Ltd (Nos 2 & 3)* [2001] 1 Lloyd's Rep IR 667, 691.

However, as seen in *GE Reinsurance v New Hampshire*, if the reinsurance contract contains a term which is not seen in the original insurance, the contracts will not be back to back in every respect and if the claim falls under the clause of the reinsurance contract the reinsurers might argue non-liability despite the 'as original' wording and establishment of the reinsured's liability to the assured.

Where the original insurance contract contains an arbitration clause, it is implicit in reinsurance contracts that the reinsurer agrees to be bound by the arbitration award even if the award is not fully consistent with strict law, subject to the reinsured having argued its case properly in the arbitration and exhausted all rights of appeal.[51] In reinsurance contracts it is mostly the case that the reinsurers and reinsured are based in different jurisdictions. The original insurance may be governed by the jurisdiction and governing law of the local law system while the reinsurance is subject to English law and jurisdiction. The controversies that may arise with regard to interpretation of the original insurance and reinsurance wording especially when the former's terms and conditions are incorporated into the latter were analysed above. Another issue to touch upon here is the binding nature of a foreign judgment which establishes the reinsured's liability under local law for the reinsurers whose contract is governed by English law. With regard to judgments Potter LJ stated, *obiter*, in *Commercial Union Assurance Co plc v NRG Victory Reinsurance Ltd*[52] that the reinsurers indemnify the reinsured pursuant to the latter's liability under the original insurance. Given that reinsurance has international character, it is within the inevitable contemplation of the parties that the reinsurance will apply to large numbers of insurance contracts made with corporations in various parts of the world and that the liability of the reinsured will be determined by courts of competent jurisdiction, or arbitrators, in many countries or states who will apply the law applicable to the original insurance. In such cases Potter LJ found it quite impracticable, productive of endless dispute, and against the presumed intention of the contract of reinsurance (absent contrary or special provision of a kind which does not exist in this case) for an English court trying a dispute concerning the reinsurers' liability to the reinsured. Thus, Potter LJ was of the view that the judgment of a foreign court is decisive and binding for the reinsurers subject to the following limits:

1 that the foreign court should in the eyes of the English court be a court of competent jurisdiction;
2 that judgment should not have been obtained in the foreign court in breach of an exclusive jurisdiction clause or other clause by which the original insured was contractually excluded from proceeding in that court;
3 that the reinsured took all proper defences;
4 that the judgment was not manifestly perverse.

However, as referred to above, in *Wasa* despite the judgment against the insurer by the Washington Supreme Court in the USA the reinsurers were held not liable in the English proceedings. Lord Mance in *Wasa*[53] found it unnecessary to decide upon the correctness or otherwise of the Court of Appeal's *obiter* observations in *Commercial Union v NRG* on the effect under reinsurance of a judgment against the insurer. The balance of dicta since the *Commercial Union* decision is in support of Lord Mance's view.[54] Most recently, it was expressly adopted by Flaux J in *AstraZeneca Insurance Company Ltd*

---

51 Butler and Merkin, *Reinsurance Law*, para C–0007. See also *CGU International Insurance v AstraZeneca Insurance Co* [2007] 1 Lloyd's Rep 142; *Commercial Union Assurance Co plc v NRG Victory Reinsurance Ltd* [1998] 2 Lloyd's Rep 600.
52 [1998] 2 Lloyd's Rep 600.
53 [2009] 2 Lloyd's Rep 508, 519.
54 *Omega Proteins Ltd v Aspen Insurance UK Ltd* [2010] EWHC 2280 (Comm); *Enterprise Oil Ltd v Strand Insurance Co Ltd* [2007] Lloyd's Rep IR 186; Contrast, however, *Redbridge LBC v Municipal Mutual Insurance Ltd* [2001] Lloyd's Rep IR 545, where the approach in *Commercial Union* was followed.

v *XL Insurance (Bermuda) Ltd.*[55] On appeal, Christopher Clarke LJ, without referring to *Commercial Union* v *NRG*, agreed with the trial judge:[56]

> In the event of dispute the existence of liability has to be established to the satisfaction of the insurer, or, failing that, by the judge or arbitrator who has jurisdiction to decide such a dispute. It is not, therefore, necessarily sufficient for the insured to show that he has been held liable to a claimant by some court or tribunal or that he has agreed to settle with him. In practice the fact that this has occurred may cause or persuade the insurer to pay, but, if it does not, the insured must prove that he was actually liable. Under English law the ultimate arbiter of whether someone is liable, if insured and insurer cannot agree, is the tribunal which has to resolve their disputes (or any relevant appeal body). It may hold that there was in fact no actual liability and that an insured who thought, or another tribunal which decided, that there was, liability was in error either on the facts or the law or both.

Where the reinsured settles the claim with the assured, in the absence of a follow the settlements clause, the reinsurers are not obliged to follow the reinsured's settlement. Thus, if the reinsurers object to the settlement, the only way for the reinsured to prove liability is either a judgment obtained by the assured against the reinsured or an arbitration award in favour of the assured. If the reinsurance contract contains a 'follow the settlements'[57] clause, however, the reinsurers may be obliged to follow the reinsured's settlement if the requirements set by *Insurance Co of Africa v Scor (UK) Reinsurance Co Ltd*[58] are met. Accordingly, where the reinsurers agreed to follow the settlements of the assured, the assured may make a claim against the insurer if (1) the risk is covered by the terms of the reinsurance contract, and (2) the settlements are bona and businesslike.

First limb: the risk falls within the reinsurance cover

Where the terms of the original insurance are incorporated into the reinsurance contract, if the risk falls within the cover provided by the former, it is then, in principle, presumed to be covered by the latter. If the reinsurance is proportional, as seen in *Vesta*, the interpretation of the original insurance under the local law is binding for the reinsurer as well irrespective of the governing law of the reinsurance contract.[59] Moreover, in non-proportional reinsurance, if the wordings of the original insurance and the reinsurance contract are identical, the interpretation of the terms in the two contracts will be in the same manner – as seen in the *Tokio Marine* case. This will then lead to the conclusion that where the reinsured proves his liability under the original insurance, this should also prove that the loss falls within the reinsurance cover. This is subject to a case in which the reinsurance contract differs from the original insurance contract as seen in *GE Reinsurance v New Hampshire* and *Aegis*. Lord Mustill's statements in *Hill v Mercantile & General Reinsurance Co*[59a] support this view. His Lordship explained that a follow the settlements clause operates in facultative reinsurance contracts where the terms of the two contracts are identical and where the parties share the risk and the premium, in order to avoid the investigation of the same issues twice. In this case the interests of

---

55 [2013] EWHC 349 (Comm).

56 [2013] EWCA 1660.

57 The early formulation of settlement clauses was 'to pay as may be paid thereon', which was not interpreted in the manner that the market had desired it to be, that is, to bind the reinsurers by a settlement entered between the assured and the reinsured. Thus, the formulation was changed to 'follow the settlements'. *Chippendale v Holt* (1895) Com Cas 197, *Marten v Steamship* (1902) Com Cas 195. See Gürses, Reinsuring Clauses, Chapter 6.

58 [1985] 1 Lloyd's Rep 312.

59 Subject the exceptional situation in *Wasa International Insurance Co Ltd v Lexington Insurance Co* [2009] 2 Lloyd's Rep 508.

59a [1996] 3 All ER 865.

the direct insurer and the reinsurers are broadly the same and it seems reasonable to hold the reinsurers to be bound by the reinsured's settlements. It should first be noted that where the reinsurers agree to 'follow the settlements' of the reinsured, so long as the reinsured's settlement is bona fide and businesslike and the risk falls within the cover of the reinsurance policy, the reinsurers are to follow the settlements although, in law, the reinsured is not liable under the original insurance.[60]

Although the above seems to be a straightforward interpretation there have been arguments before the English courts in terms of the entitlement of the reinsurers to bring the reinsurance policy defence in the circumstances stated above. In other words, the question arose whether the presumption of back-to-back cover or the incorporation clause will deprive the reinsurer of its own policy defences where the reinsured acted bona fide and businesslike in a commercial sense but was not liable as a matter of strict law. In Hiscox v Outhwaite[61] the assureds were exposed to a very large number of asbestos-related personal injury claims. Taking into consideration the potential quantum of liability in terms of both the number of parties involved and the amount claimed, in order to simplify the procedure for handling such claims, in 1984, a number of asbestos producers and their insurers – including the reinsured in this case – entered into the Wellington Agreement. From then until 1988 the Wellington Facility acted as a clearing house for all parties to the Agreement to the effect that the amounts paid in settlement of such claims to individual sufferers were shared rateably among all subscribing producers. Subsequently, the reinsured made payment to the producers irrespective of whether that producer had been named as a defendant by a claimant and irrespective of whether that producer could have been legally liable to the claimant. Therefore, the reinsured was in the position to argue that it was acting in a bona fide and businesslike manner in a commercial sense, but had made payments under the Wellington Agreement which it might not have been legally liable to make. Evans J held that the existence of the follow the settlements clause and the presumption of a back-to-back principle did not prevent the reinsurers from raising the defences provided by the reinsurance contract itself. The judge expressed the view that this was the only protection for the reinsurers if they were called upon to indemnify the reinsured for bona fide and businesslike settlements but it was shown that the reinsured was not obliged to pay as a matter of law. The view expressed by Mr Kealey QC and the Court of Appeal in Assicurazioni Generali SpA v CGU International Insurance[62] was in line with Hiscox v Outhwaite. Mr Kealey QC was convinced that the presumption of back-to-back cover together with the reinsurers' agreement to follow the reinsured's settlement did not amount to an obligation on the reinsurers to follow every single bona fide and businesslike settlement. In the Court of Appeal Tuckey LJ stated that the Scor interpretation of the 'follow the settlements' clause relieved reinsureds of the obligation to prove that the loss fell within the original cover, both as to liability and amount but such relief did not include the reinsured's obligation to prove that the loss fell within the cover created by the reinsurance. It thus remained necessary for the reinsured to prove that the claim so recognised by the reinsured fell within the risks covered by the policy of reinsurance as a matter of law. Tuckey LJ's conclusion was that the correct approach was that reinsureds 'do not have to show that the claim they have settled in fact fell within the risks covered by the reinsurance, but that the claim which they recognised did or arguably did.' Assicurazioni Generali SpA v CGU International Insurance was accepted as correct by the House of Lords in Wasa International Insurance Co Ltd v Lexington Insurance Co. Wasa[63] is a controversial case and one of the reasons for such controversy is that the application of this rule did not sit easily with the presumption of back-to-back cover.[64] It is arguable that while

---

60 Insurance Co of Africa v Scor (UK) Reinsurance Co Ltd [1985] 1 Lloyd's Rep 312.
61 [1991] 2 Lloyd's Rep 524.
62 [2003] Lloyd's Rep IR 725.
63 [2009] 2 Lloyd's Rep 508.
64 See Gürses 'The Construction of Terms of Facultative Reinsurance Contracts: Is Wasa v Lexington the Exception or the Rule?', Modern Law Review, (2010) 73(1): 119–130.

the *Assicurazioni Generali* may be regarded as a compromise approach, attempting to give independent effect to the first limb of the *Scor* test where there is a follow the settlements clause, while at the same time seeking not to undermine the effect of the follow the settlements clause, it is difficult to see how the compromise can ever work in favour of the reinsurers.

Second limb – bona fide settlements

The second limb of the *Scor* test is concerned with the proof of liability under the original insurance contract.

A reinsured may establish a bona fide nature of the settlement by proof of, upon a reasonable interpretation of the direct policy, a serious possibility that the policy covers the assured's claim and that there are no available defences to it.[65] One of the key elements in determining whether the reinsured has acted in a bona fide and businesslike fashion is whether the reinsured has appointed a competent loss adjuster and adequately supervised its conduct and questioned its findings. Reinsureds are to be identified with the conduct of their loss adjusters and any other agents they employ for the purpose of making the settlement.[66] Therefore, reinsureds will be responsible for a failure of the loss adjusters to act with good faith or in a businesslike manner.[67] It is then open to the reinsurers to establish that the reinsured's conduct was unbusinesslike. If the reinsured paid a claim which clearly falls outside the reinsurance cover but the reinsured paid it in order to maintain his relationship with the assured, the settlement will not be regarded as businesslike.[68]

If the policy covers a foreign risk, this may involve taking advice from local lawyers. However, having not sought a local lawyers' advice is not on its own sufficient to prove the unbusinesslike nature of the settlement; the Court may be convinced by other evidence that the settlement is otherwise businesslike. In *Tokio Marine Europe Insurance Ltd v Novae Corporate Underwriting Ltd*[69] the assured, Tesco, claimed against the insurers in respect of a number of premises in Thailand including six hypermarkets, seven supermarkets and 152 Tesco Express stores. The damage occurred as a result of widespread flooding of rivers and canals in Thailand in 2011. Tesco's original policy cover was limited to £100m for 'any one occurrence'. Claims were settled by the reinsured on the basis that there was only one 'occurrence' and thus only one deductible under the policy. That meant that claims adjusted somewhere between £90m and £100m were settled for £80m which, according to Field J, was undoubtedly a good settlement. The loss adjusters' report confirmed that (i) at the outset the claim was £125.3m, which after negotiation was reduced to £113.6m; (ii) the projected gross settlement was in the order of £90/100m; and (b) an opportunity to conclude an early settlement had resulted in the gross settlement figure of £82.5m which represented '*a very good and fair settlement for all Parties*'. The reinsurers argued that the reinsured did not take all proper and businesslike steps in making the settlement with Tesco. The reinsurers claimed that the reinsured failed to take legal advice from Thai lawyers as to the meaning of the underlying policy; it had failed to take scientific evidence in respect of the weather patterns; and also failed to investigate whether there were other causes of the flooding. Field J dismissed the reinsurers' defence. On the evidence the judge was satisfied that the reinsured had been entitled to conclude that there was nothing to be gained by further investigation into coverage under the original policy or by disputing the meaning and effect of the aggregating language.

---

65 Colinvaux, para 17–044.
66 *Charman v Guardian Royal Exchange Assurance* [1992] 2 Lloyd's Rep 607, 612.
67 Potter J in *Baker v Black Sea and Baltic General Insurance Co Ltd* [1995] LR 261.
68 *Charman v Guardian Royal Exchange Assurance* [1992] 2 Lloyd's Rep 607.
69 [2014] EWHC 2105 (Comm).

Qualified follow the settlements clause

'Within the Terms of Original Insurance'

Where a settlement clause expressly requires the loss to fall within the original insurance cover, a bona fide and businesslike settlement will not suffice to make a claim against the reinsurers. In *Hill v Mercantile & General Reinsurance Co plc*,[70] the clause was worded as follows: 'All loss settlements by the reassured including compromise settlements and the establishment of funds for the settlement of losses shall be binding upon the reinsurers, providing such settlements are within the terms and conditions of the original policies and/or contracts . . . and within the terms and conditions of this reinsurance.' Lord Mustill stated that this was different to the clause which was interpreted in *Scor*, thus was subject to a different interpretation than that in *Scor*. In the abovementioned clause the crucial words were 'within the terms and conditions' of the original policies and of the reinsurance. Their Lordships found that the purpose of this wording was to ensure that the reinsured's original assessment and rating of the risks assumed were not falsified by a settlement outside the terms of the cover albeit one which was reached in good faith. Lord Mustill did not agree with the argument that such a construction would decrease the effect of the use of the follow the settlements clauses. If the clause was intended to have the same effect as it had in *Scor*, the clause could have been drafted accordingly.

A similar clause was interpreted in the same manner in *Commercial Union Assurance Co plc v NRG Victory Reinsurance Ltd*.[71] The reinsurers agreed 'All loss settlements by the Re-assured including compromise settlements and the establishment of funds and the settlement of losses shall be binding upon the Re-insurers, providing such settlements are within the terms and conditions of the original policies and/or contracts . . . and within the terms and conditions of this Re-assurance . . .' The reinsured was the insurer of the *Exxon Valdez*, which ran aground in 1989. The assured incurred substantial losses, including clean-up costs, and sought to recover those costs from the reinsured under a policy which covered first and third party liability for losses caused by the cleaning up of 'debris'. The assured applied for summary judgment against the reinsured in the Texas Courts under a policy governed by English law, but then the reinsured settled the claim before trial. The reason was a local lawyer's advice that the reinsured would be unlikely to succeed. According to the lawyer, the case involved a complex construction of terms, but the judge was not experienced and the Texas jury was likely to take a pro-assured approach. Relying on this advice, the reinsured settled the claim but the reinsurer denied payment on the ground that the reinsured had a clear defence in that the policy covered only 'debris' and not oil pollution. The Court of Appeal agreed with the reinsurers that a bona fide and businesslike settlement was not sufficient on its own to prove the reinsured's liability. This was so because the follow the settlements clause was qualified to the effect requiring actual proof that the loss fell 'within the terms and conditions of the original insurance'. The reinsured should have gone ahead with the trial and if lost, then should have made a claim against the reinsurers.

Other wordings

In *Aegis Electrical and Gas International Services Co Ltd v Continental Casualty Co*,[72] the reinsurers agreed 'To follow the terms, clauses, conditions, exceptions and settlements of the original policy wording as far as applicable hereto'. The words 'as far as applicable hereto' were interpreted as a reflection of

---

70 [1996] LRLR 341.
71 [1998] 2 Lloyd's Rep 600.
72 [2008] Lloyd's Rep IR 17.

the parties intention that the reinsurance cover was not fully back-to-back with the direct cover. The effect of the qualified clause was to restrict the application of the follow the settlements obligation to settlements to which the reinsurance cover was applicable. The reinsurance provided different definitions for the crucial wordings determining the insurers' liability, thus, while the reinsured was liable under the policy, the reinsurers were not.

On the other hand, some other wordings which were added to the typical 'follow the settlement' clause were found not to have any effect on the interpretation of the clause. For instance, in *Assicurazioni Generali SpA v CGU International Insurance plc*,[73] the Court rejected the argument that 'without question' within the 'follow the settlements' clause[74] precluded the reinsurers from challenging whether the reinsured had taken all proper and businesslike steps in making the settlement. Similarly, the wordings of 'liable or not liable'[75] and 'without prejudice and ex gratia settlements'[76] were held not to alter the interpretation of the follow the settlements clause as held in *Scor*.

Claims provisions

Reinsurers' liability is formed by the reinsured's liability under the direct insurance. If reinsurance is proportional, upon the reinsured's liability to the assured, the reinsurers will be asked to meet the claim brought by the reinsured. If reinsurance is non-proportional, once the reinsured's liability reaches a certain amount, the reinsurers' liability will arise in excess of that amount. In the absence of an express provision in a reinsurance contract, the reinsured is not under any duty to notify the claim to the reinsurer or to seek the reinsurer's consent to settle the claim, and the reinsurer has no right to interfere with the manner in which the reinsured handles it.[77] Thus, although the reinsurers have no contractual relationship with the assured or no control on the claims made by the assured against the reinsured, the reinsurers will be asked to indemnify the reinsured once the reinsured is liable under the original insurance contract. Hence, the reinsurers may want to involve themselves in the claims process once the assured makes a claim against the reinsured. In order to enable to do so the reinsurers may include a clause in the reinsurance contract to this effect. There are two types of claims provisions which are seen in reinsurance contracts: Claims co-operation and claims control clauses.

Claims co-operation clauses

A claims co-operation clause requires the reinsured to co-operate with the reinsurers once there is a claim made by the assured. The co-operation may be in the form of notifying the loss to the reinsurers or not settling the claim with the assured before seeking the reinsurers' consent on the settlement.

---

73 [2004] Lloyd's Rep IR 457.

74 The clause was worded as follows:

As original: Anything herein to the contrary notwithstanding, this Reinsurance is declared and agreed to be subject to the same terms, clauses and conditions, special or otherwise, as the original policy or policies and is to pay as may be paid thereon and to follow without question the settlements of the Reassured except ex gratia and/or without prejudice settlements.

75 *Charman v Guardian Royal Exchange Assurance plc* [1992] 2 Lloyd's Rep 607.

76 *Faraday Capital Ltd v Copenhagen Reinsurance Co Ltd* [2007] 1 Lloyd's Rep IR 23.

77 *Charman v Guardian Royal Exchange Assurance plc* [1992] 2 Lloyd's Rep 607; O'Neill and Woloniecki, para 5–105; Butler and Merkin, *Reinsurance Law*, para C–0053.

Claims control clauses

Claims control clauses give more power to the reinsurers than claims co-operation clauses. The clause requires the reinsured to transfer the control of the assured's claim to the reinsurers. If there are court proceedings against the reinsured the reinsurers, if they wish, may take over defending the claim made against the reinsured.

Construction of claims provisions

Remedy for breach of a claims provision depends on the nature of the claims provision in question. A claims co-operation or a claims control clause may be drafted as a condition or a condition precedent.

Insurance conditions are mainly classified under two headings: conditions and conditions precedent. Mere conditions are interpreted in the same manner as innominate terms are interpreted in contract law that breach of a mere insurance condition entitles the innocent party to claim damages only if the breach results in only trivial consequences.[78] However, if the consequences of the breach are so serious that they go to the root of the contract, the innocent party may terminate the contract and claim damages if proved. Conditions subsequent have the same effect as mere conditions.

Conditions precedent may be (1) condition precedent to the validity of the contract, (2) condition precedent to the attachment of the risk, or (3) condition precedent to the insurer's liability. In the first category, if the condition is not met, there never is a binding valid agreement between the parties. In the second case a binding agreement may be formed but the risk does not attach unless the condition precedent is satisfied. In the third case, a binding agreement is formed and the risk attaches, however, no claim may be made against the insurer if the condition precedent is not satisfied.

Creation of condition precedent

The use of 'condition precedent'

Whether a term is classified as a condition precedent is a matter of construction. If a term expressly includes the words 'condition precedent', that normally is interpreted as an indication of the creation of a condition precedent by the parties. In *Royal & Sun Alliance Insurance plc v Dornoch Ltd*,[79] Longmore LJ stated that 'A condition precedent to the liability of the reinsurer operates as an exemption to that prima facie liability.'[80] Since it is an exemption, a party who relies on a clause exempting him from liability can only do so if the words of the clause are clear on its fair construction.[81] A clause therefore, may not be interpreted as a condition precedent if the Court is persuaded that within the contractual context the parties did not intend to create a condition precedent despite the express use of the words 'condition precedent'. In *Royal v Dornoch* the original insurance covered Directors and Officers' Liability. It should have been first necessary to establish the assured's liability to third parties which

---

78 *Friends Provident Life & Pensions Ltd v Sirius International Insurance Corp* [2005] 2 Lloyd's Rep 517.

79 [2005] Lloyd's Rep IR 544, para 19.

80 Applied by Eder J in *Beazley Underwriting Ltd v Al Ahleia Insurance Co* [2013] Lloyd's Rep IR 561.

81 *Royal & Sun Alliance Insurance plc v Dornoch Ltd* [2005] Lloyd's Rep IR 544, para 19. Longmore LJ referred to *Elderslie Steamship Co Ltd v Borthwick* [1905] AC 93, *Gordon Alison & Co v Wallsend Slipway and Engineering Co Ltd* (1927) 27 Ll L Rep 285, *Photo Production Ltd v Securicor Transport Ltd* [1980] AC 827 , 850D–851A per Lord Diplock.

then would lead to the insurer's liability. The question was whether the 72 hour notification clause of the claims or circumstances which may give rise to claim by the reinsured to the reinsurers was a condition precedent. Longmore LJ said:

> If the parties had addressed their mind to the question which clause out of a number of standard terms they would have used for the particular requirement which they had in mind, it is by no means obvious that they would have selected a form which was as draconian as the one unwisely but in fact chosen. It may very well be necessary for reinsurers to be informed within 72 hours if a fire has recently taken place or a cargo is rotting on the quayside. The sooner an adjuster or surveyor arrives, the more likely it is that he will discover the true cause of the loss. But if one is selecting a clause which will give reinsurers a degree of control over a claim for financial loss in respect of legal liability (incurred, for example, as a result of purchasing shares) the urgent need for notifying a loss within 72 hours is by no means obvious and still less is it obvious that any delay in notification should mean that the insurers' claim on their reinsurers will fail altogether.[82]

In the following examples the Courts accepted that the parties intended to create a condition precedent. In *Scor* the claims co-operation clause provided 'It is a condition precedent to liability under this Insurance that all claims be notified immediately to the Underwriters subscribing to this Policy and the Reassured hereby undertake in arriving at the settlement of any claim, that they will co-operate with the Reassured Underwriters and that no settlement shall be made without the approval of the Underwriters subscribing to this Policy.' The clause was held to fall into two parts. The first part concerned notification of claims and that was a condition precedent. The latter was concerned with co-operation with reinsurers, and not making settlements without their approval was not of that nature as the words 'condition precedent' referred to the first part of the clause only.

The clause in *Gan Insurance Co Ltd v Tai Ping Co Ltd (Nos 2 & 3)*[83] was worded and interpreted differently from that of *Scor*. The parties agreed:

> Notwithstanding anything contained in the reinsurance agreement and/or policy wording to the contrary, it is a condition precedent to any liability under this policy that
> a) The reinsured shall, upon knowledge of any circumstances which may give rise to a claim against them, advise the reinsurers immediately, and in any event not later than 30 days.
> b) The reinsured shall co-operate with reinsurers and/or their appointed representatives subscribing to this policy in the investigation and assessment of any loss and/or circumstances giving rise to a loss.
> c) No settlement and/or compromise shall be made and liability admitted without the prior approval of reinsurers. All other terms and criticisms of this policy remain unchanged.

Comparing this clause to the claims co-operation clause in *Scor*, Mance LJ found that this was more stringent and the draftsmen had separated out the three parts of the clause and had resolved to make each into a condition precedent.[84]

---

82   [2005] Lloyd's Rep IR 544, para 16.
83   [2001] 1 Lloyd's Rep IR 667.
84   [2001]1 Lloyd's Rep IR 667, 687.

Express statement of the remedy

Since defining a term as a condition precedent is a matter construction, express statement in the clause of the remedy for its breach may indicate that the parties intended to create a condition precedent by the term in question. In *Eagle Star Insurance Co Ltd v Cresswell*,[85] the reinsured agreed:

a) To notify all claims or occurrences likely to involve the underwriters within seven days from the time that such claims or occurrences become known to them.

b) The underwriters hereon shall control the negotiations and settlements of any claims under this policy. In this event the underwriters hereon will not be liable to pay any claim not controlled as set out above.

Omission however by the company to notify any claim or occurrence which at the outset did not appear to be serious but which at a later date threatened to involve the company shall not prejudice their right of recovery hereunder.

The Court of Appeal held that clear words other than 'condition precedent' may create a condition precedent. It was held that in this clause the words 'reinsurers will not be liable to pay any claim not controlled by them' were clear enough to create the equivalent remedy to a breach of a condition precedent. Moreover, the words 'will not be liable to pay any claim' were described as strong words, if not the language of condition precedent, at any rate the language of exclusion.[86]

Remedy and waiver

Breach of condition precedent discharges the insurer from liability for the claim which is tainted by the breach.[87] The difference between breach of a warranty and condition precedent is that in the former the risk terminates, therefore the assured will not be entitled to make any future claims under the policy. In the case of a breach of condition precedent however the discharge only relates to the claim which is tainted by the breach. Thus, the contract stands still and the assured might be entitled to make claims in the future until the policy terminates if the assured complies with the condition precedent before making the claim. Since the discharge occurs automatically in both warranties and conditions precedent, the two are subject to the same rules with regard to waiver, that is, it can be proved only by virtue of promissory estoppel. In *Kosmar Villa Holidays plc v Trustees of Syndicate 1243*[88] it was a condition precedent to insurers' liability that: 'The Insured shall immediately after the occurrence of any Injury or Damage give notice in writing with full particulars thereof to insurers.' The assured notified the claim more than a year after the accident occurred. There was a clear breach of condition precedent. The assured nevertheless argued that the insurers waived the breach. The assured relied on the insurer's email which said 'I have read through the file and have asked K . . . to write to you with my comments and requests for information. We have taken the view, given the possible size of this claim, not to deny liability yet and will await your reply to our various requests.' As analysed fully in Chapter 5, the first requirement of promissory estoppel is an unequivocal representation by the innocent party to the effect that he will not rely on the contractual breach. Rix LJ held – Jacob and Forbes LJJ agreed – that the insurer's representation in this email was far from unequivocal.[89] The insurer made it clear that, in order to go forward with

---

85   [2004] Lloyd's Rep IR 537.
86   [2004] Lloyd's Rep IR 537, 548. See also *Aspen Insurance UK Ltd v Pectel Ltd* [2009] Lloyd's Rep IR 440.
87   *Kosmar Villa Holidays plc v Trustees of Syndicate 1243* [2008] Lloyd's Rep IR 489.
88   [2008] Lloyd's Rep IR 489.
89   [2008] Lloyd's Rep IR 489, para 75.

this matter, it would need answers from the assured to its enquiries. Rix LJ pointed out that before the insurer could be said to be unequivocally manifesting any election to accept the claim as a matter for indemnification,[90] it was in any event entitled to a reasonable time to get to grips with this serious and lately notified occurrence. Rix LJ was persuaded that the questions which it had asked the assured and to which it had had no answer until the case was heard, showed that it was still in the stage of assimilating the circumstances of the case.[91]

Relationship between follow the settlements, and claims clauses

A controversy may arise when a reinsurance contract contains both 'follow the settlements' and 'claims' clauses. This is so for the reasons that while, by the follow the settlements clause the reinsurers agree to follow a bona fine and businesslike settlement reached by the reinsured, by virtue of a claim co-operation clause, they may require the reinsured to seek their consent before reaching a settlement with the assured. It was held in *Scor* that if a claims co-operation clause is breached by the assured, the reinsured loses its entitlement under the follow the settlements clause. It does not, however, lose its rights to make a claim regarding the loss in question. The reinsured can still claim it from the reinsurers upon proof of loss by, for example, a judgment or an arbitration award. It should be noted that in *Scor* the claims co-operation clause was not a condition precedent. With respect to the Court of Appeal's view in *Scor*, it is difficult to see any justification for the reinsured losing its right under the follow the settlements clause if the relevant claims provision, which was drafted as a mere condition, was breached. Breach of a mere condition entitles the insurer to claim damages or if the breach is so serious that it goes to the root of the contract, the insurer can terminate the contract and does not pay for the claim in question or any future claims. The position is different if the claims provision is drafted as a condition precedent. Since breach of a condition precedent discharges the insurer from liability, the reinsured loses its rights regarding that claim altogether, leaving no entitlement with regard to that claim irrespective of the proof of actual liability.

Further reading

Edelman and Burns, *The Law of Reinsurance*, 2nd edn, [2013] Oxford University Press.
Gilman et al., *Arnould: Law of Marine Insurance and Average*, 18th edn, [2013] Sweet & Maxwell. Chapter 33.
Gürses, *Reinsuring Clauses* [2010] Informa.
Gürses, 'Extra-contractual liability: an insurance overhead or a reinsurance recovery?', *Journal of Business Law* [2011] 8, 763–781.
Gürses and Merkin, 'Facultative reinsurance and the full reinsurance clause', *Lloyd's Maritime and Commercial Law Quarterly* [2008] 3(August), 366–388.
Gürses, 'The construction of terms of facultative reinsurance contracts: is Wasa v Lexington the exception or the rule?', *Modern Law Review* [2010] 73(1): 119–130.
Gürses, 'Insurance reinsurance and the Titanic', *Journal of Business Law* [2012] 4, 340–349.
Mecz and Bailey, 'Wasa International Insurance Co Ltd v Lexington Insurance Co: buyer beware', *Journal of Business Law* [2010] 1, 1–8.
Merkin, *Colinvaux's Law of Insurance*, 9th edn, [2010] Sweet & Maxwell, Chapter 17.

---

90 [2008] Lloyd's Rep IR 489, para 76.
91 [2008] Lloyd's Rep IR 489, para 79. For a similar example see *Lexington Insurance Co v Multinacional de Seguros SA* [2009] Lloyd's Rep IR 1.

Merkin, 'Reinsurance aggregations', *Law Quarterly Review* [1998] 114(July), 390–394.

Merkin, 'Incorporation of terms into reinsurance agreements', Chapter 2 in Thomas (ed.), *Modern Law of Marine Insurance* [2002] Volume 2, London: LLP.

Merkin, 'The Law Commission proposals and reinsurance', Chapter 4 in Soyer (ed.), *Reforming Marine and Commercial Insurance Law* [2008] Informa.

Merkin, '*Wasa International Insurance Co Ltd v Lexington Insurance Co*: commercial certainty in the reinsurance market', *Law Quarterly Review* [2010] 126(January), 24–30.

Schaff, '*Wasa International Insurance Co Ltd v Lexington Insurance Co*: the limits to the "back to back" presumption', *Journal of Business Law* [2010] 1, 9–23.

Weir, 'A matter of forms and substance', *Lloyd's Maritime and Commercial Law Quarterly* [2009] 2(May), 210–238.

Index

bold refers to extended discussion or term highlighted in text; n refers to footnote